Fundamentals of Demography

Fundamentals of
DEMOGRAPHY

P.K. Majumdar

RAWAT PUBLICATIONS
Jaipur | New Delhi | Bangalore | Hyderabad | Guwahati

ISBN 81-316-0371-7

Published by
Prem Rawat for **Rawat Publications**
Satyam Apts., Sector 3, Jawahar Nagar, Jaipur 302 004 (India)
Phone: 0141 265 1748 / 7006 Fax: 0141 265 1748
E-mail: info@rawatbooks.com
Website: www.rawatbooks.com

New Delhi Office
4858/24, Ansari Road, Daryaganj, New Delhi 110 002
Phone: 011 2326 3290

Also at Bangalore, Hyderabad and Guwahati

Typeset by *d'lines* DTP SERVICES, Jaipur
Printed at Chaman Enterprises, New Delhi

Contents

List of Tables

List of Figures and Boxes

Boxes

Preface

People increasingly are showing interest in issues related to population. There is a general perception that the fast growth of population has become an impediment to a faster improvement of livelihood and standard of living in many developing countries. In spite of a higher growth of economy through rapid industrialization and fast changing scenario in network communication, transportation and in many other facilities, the fruits of this advancement in the economic front, as measured by GNP or GDP, have failed to address adequately to the needs of the poor and the downtrodden. Most governments are in dire stress since they need to spend a lot more on infrastructure development – physical and social – to sustain the growth momentum. Even a 7-8 percent GDP growth rate is not good enough to cater improved facilities to populations that are still growing at around 1.5 percent a year.

The transition from traditional agricultural economy to industrial economy in today's world is in no way comparable with that experienced in the developed West some 250 years back where the transition had quite a smooth sailing. There was plenty of land for diversion to industries and infrastructure development. Even those evicted from their farm land could be absorbed either by the industries or could be rehabilitated through allocation of alternative land. Emigration too played a significant role in the adjustment process. Skill specification for those absorbed in manufacturing and other industrial activities was not a major snag for employment in the labor-intensive production system. Since World War II, there has been a sea-change in production technology, especially after the computer and IT revolution in the last 25/30 years. Today's hi tech industries' efficiency is measured not by output per capita, but by out-put per unit energy consumed. Today's sophisticated instruments and machines require the services of highly skilled persons. Even the developed countries are in short supply of technical hands of prescribed quality. It is one of the major reasons why they have opened their doors for professionals from developing countries. This has created a huge demand-supply gap in professional and skilled hands in the domestic labor market of the sending countries. The surplus labors from agriculture, which mostly are poorly educated and have no specialized skill, have no place in modern industrial and service sectors. The governments in the developing countries need to spend a larger slice of their GDP on the social sector (mostly in education and health) besides spending liberally on improving their agricultural productivity. But the fund allocated is often not adequate to maintain health and education standards even at the present level. The growth of population neutralizes the gains in GDP growth. Unequal growth of population and economy of various segments of the population calls for a decentralized planning in more critical areas.

The study of populations – their spatial distribution, composition, social and cultural inheritance, land-man relation, and changing vital events as birth, death, marriage, and migration – has become imperative in today's fast changing social scenario. A common man today has a rough idea about the size of the population (about 6,500 million) in the world, but most people probably would be surprised to learn that the world population was only 1,600 million at the beginning of twentieth century, only 900 million in 1800AD and about 200 million at the beginning of the Christian era, and that we are taking only 12/13 years today to add 1,000 million to the world population total. They will be amazed to learn that whereas females far outnumber males in the world population, India, China and a few other countries are fast approaching a situation when many eligible adult males will have to remain bachelor for want of enough eligible females; there are many countries where the state has to spend more on their senior citizens in pension and other social securities than they spend on their current employees; many industrially developed countries have reached a stage where unemployment is rising since they need to close down some of their schools and colleges, factories and other facilities since there are no takers of such services; there are quite a few countries where infant mortality is far less than the general mortality level in their populations when most developing countries are experiencing extreme difficulty in bringing down their infant and child mortality rates. These and many other parameters on which there are wide differences not only between nations but also among various segments of the population in the same country.

There are many other such issues, simple and more complex, on which populations of various countries and population segments within a defined geographic and social space differ. Differences in some such demographic parameters have roots in social, cultural, geographic and economic pursuits of different population groups. Of course this is not a one-way affair; demographic composition of population does have a tremendous impact on socio-economic development of any country at any point of time. The student and other interested readers will find that the population study is something more than academic. It would also show how population and population-related events happening far and near have profound impact on their own lives and the environment.

I have tried in this book to give a modest exposure to the reader to some of the fundamentals in population analysis. The book has been written keeping in mind the needs for the students of sociology, anthropology, political science, geography and other social sciences who are likely to be offered some course in demography at the undergraduate or postgraduate level in Indian universities. A second book, *Changing Demographic Scenario in India*, published by the present publisher, would help visualize the fat changing demographic parameters in India.

This volume has 15 chapters tracing the history of growth of world population, population theories, and sources of demographic data and the techniques of population analysis. A good amount of space has been devoted on five chapters – Fertility (Chapter 7), Mortality (Chapter 8), Human development (Chapter 12), Population and development (Chapter 13), Environmental concern (Chapter 14) and World population policy and program (Chapter 15). United Nations Development Program (UNDP) is publishing since 1990 the Human Development Report (HDR) every year. These reports publish varieties of data for almost all the countries of the world covering demographic trends, health, education, economic performances, their expenditure profile, debts and aids, energy and environment, political profile, etc. HDR has become a key document to evaluate countries' performances in demographic and socio-economic indicators. Chapter 13 gives the picture of interaction between population and the common issues concerning development – economy, technology, food and energy security and impact on natural resources. Chapter 14 deals with environmental problems and offers a quick look at some of the schools of thought on environment, the Stockholm and the Rio Earth Summit. Population programs and feasibility of a world population policy has been discussed in Chapter 15.

The statistical tables incorporated in various sections of the book mostly are from UNDP published data, Census of India and Sample Registration System. I have not hesitated to collect materials and observations, especially from Thomson & Lewis: *Population Problems, Population and Development Review* (Population Council, various issues) and some other excellent discourses on the subject as also from Human Development Reports 1999 onwards. Some web-documents have also come handy in discussions on many issues.

I am thankful to my students for many of their stimulated discussions and queries while I was teaching demography in the Department of Sociology, Kalyani University. I owe much to Dr. Debaprasad Chatterjee, Reader in Sociology, Maulana Azad College, Kolkata who took keen interest to see this manuscript through and took pains to collect various documents for the foundation of this book.

Kolkata, April 2009 **P.K. Majumdar**

1 Growth of World Population

A Historical Analysis

1.1 Introduction

There are very distinct signals that the human civilization will face a most devastating crisis in the twenty-first century and the root cause behind this will be the phenomenal rise in numbers, which already has reached a point of explosion. Vulnerability syndromes of modern-technology-based civilization are the 4 Ps – **population, poverty, pollution and proliferation** (of nuclear weapons). Population is precursor to the other three.

From a low of 1,600 million around 1900 AD, the world population was around 6,300 million at the beginning of the present century. We are taking around 12/13 years to add 1,000 million to our existing totals. If the current growth rate (1.6 percent per annum, 1975–2003) if not drastically cut, there shall be around 8,000 million people on this earth by 2025 AD. India alone could provide 1,250 million. If we continue to grow at or around the present rate, an individual will have less than 1 square meter of land space to stand upon in less than 600 years.

The unprecedented growth of population has created more problems for us than has solved them. Natural resources are vanishing fast, the support system getting weak every day, disparity between the developed and developing countries is widening, ecological balance has already been disturbed beyond repair, pollution of land, air and water have put on a serious question mark on economic growth, especially in industrial sector.

The study of population has always been associated with some social/military/economic contexts. Increasingly scientists and social planners have taken interest in population studies, not necessarily by choice, but by compulsion. Population statistics commends attention of scientists and common man alike. There is hardly any debate and discussion at national or international level on any social issue that does not directly or indirectly refers to growth or distribution of population. Any planning document refers to the population numbers – how provisions for food, housing, educational institutions, hospitals, job opportunities, infrastructure for transport and communication, etc. are to be met in view of the growing numbers.

There are others who show interest in population statistics for quite a different reason. The politicians need to know what are the opinions, attitudes and needs of the dominant/critical segment of their potential voters, who would be hard hit by tax revisions or economic liberalization, who needs relief, the areas where social services are to be strengthened, and etc.

This is not to say that population studies have no theoretical direction. Even when number was not a problem given the abundance of natural resources and space for living, philosophers and scientists seriously discussed the problems of number and quality of life along with nature's limitation to absorb the impact of growth in numbers. The science of population – its number, distribution and characteristics – became the concern of many. The cumulative knowledge about population helped in the advancement of the science. We are better equipped today for a realistic planning, we can foresee what awaits us, we can plan our campaign against poverty, illiteracy and morbidity more effectively today with improved method of measurement and analysis of population data.

The spaceship earth is fine-tuned to maintain a delicate balance between all its inhabitants. The story of its past cannot be fully recounted from what it is today. But the transformation that we have noted with anguish in the last two hundred and fifty years is an indication of what awaits us in not too distant a future; our spaceship is destined for a crash course if no course correction is applied soon.

Before we attempt for an overview of how the population with its numerous complex determinants and characteristics have evolved, we try to understand what population stands for to different inquirers.

1.2 The Concept of Population

Unlike subhuman animals, human beings are not found to settle scattered randomly all over the length and breadth of the earth. Human settlements have grown around spots that provide enough support system to allow the population to grow. Human settlements are not mere conglomeration of people; there is always a give and take amongst its members as per some unwritten but strong binding societal rules, consequential to similarities in behavior and shared value system. The society evolves. Different social groups are differentiated by their size, somewhat rigid structure and characteristics. It is also a fact that two or more social groups often would share some fundamental characteristics. It is the groups that share a common genetic pool and a common cultural background that tend to show similarities in structural and functional characteristics.

Besides genetic and cultural inheritance, there are several other things whose effects on the social group are large. However, these 'other things' often are directly or indirectly related either to genetic or cultural inheritance or both. A blend of all these factors gives credence to 'uniqueness' of a social group. It is true that cultural inheritance of a social group is closely related in some way or other to its biological inheritance. Many social scientists however believe that many cultural issues can be discussed independent of biological inheritance. Genetic pool only provides a very broad outline – a line that no human beings can touch or cross. Life in a social group revolves around a few well-defined activities. These activities are far more related to social and cultural factors than the deterministic feature of biology. Genetic scientists already have confirmed that genetically all human beings are alike to the tune of 99.1 percent. However, there are many biological scientists who believe that the genetic structure and composition, which regulate our biological inheritance, are behind the similarity and differences in the history of evolution of different population groups.

Whose influence is more pronounced in our life – biological or cultural inheritance? There is no resolution to this debate nor is it likely that the dispute would be resolved in near future. It can safely be said that many of our 'cultural inheritance' directly influences our biological bequest. For example, though marriage is primarily biological, our culture, customs and social regulations and personal preferences determine who shall marry whom and at what age. Genetic purity, if there is any, is preserved by some of our social and cultural regulatory influences – which all of us abide – willingly or by some social pressure. Conception and birth of a child are definitely physiological; but whether a child should be born before or after marriage, if one should marry not before attaining a particular age, or if there should be remarriage after divorce or death of the spouse are definitely dictated by social regulations and personal choices.

Life is a complex phenomenon, often unpredictable since it is a multifaceted constellation of so many diverse elements. The combined influences of the genetic and social ingredients make what we are, and the society cannot remain aloof to the powers of these ingredients.

How should one define a population? Generally, it has a geographic or some area reference. Usually, a population group is differentiated from another by an uninhibited land mass or by some demarcation line, imagined, real or by administrative design. Space is important in defining a population; but there could be other important parameters as well. Social scientists often would lay stress upon social similarity in identifying populations. In social research, social class – upper, middle and lower income class, industrial labor, cultivator and agricultural labor, etc. are more meaningful than many other parameters. One can think of a population that crosses the geographic or national boundaries – the labor class, the Hindus, the traders, the students and the like.

Population can be defined in very many different ways. Whether we use this or that criterion, the population (or supply or canvas) is hierarchically classified in respect to one or more characteristics. We can conceive of world population as comprised of populations of different continents; population of a continent becomes decomposable into populations of different countries of the continents; population of a country can be thought of as the sum total of individuals from all the states under it.

Although population can be defined in as many ways as there are criteria, in practice they can be grouped under five broad categories: Statistical, Demographic, Genetic, Social and Ecological.

A *Statistician* often would define a population comprised of all individuals possessing one or a few defined characteristics within a defined space – eligible voters of a constituency, PG male students of a particular university, births registered in a municipality in specified years, and the like.

Fertility, mortality and migration are the principal events, which are utilized in *Demographic analysis*. To a demographer a survey population is a collection of individuals. This collection may not be quite different from a population defined by social, biological or ecological considerations. However, a demographic population may or may not show any structural similarity between its sub-populations. Examples of demographic population are girls in their reproductive period, polio affected children, men and women with HIV positive, the refugees in the Punjab/West Bengal after partition.

Genetic or Mendelian population refers to those groups of people in whom the influence of a particular genetic line is prominent. That is, populations are differentiated by similarity-dissimilarity in genetic inheritance. When we speak of Mongoloid or Nordic or Proto-Austroloid, we actually are referring to genetic or Mendelian population. The smallest Mendelian population is the nuclear family comprised of father, mother and their children. The largest Mendelian population likewise is the entire human population on earth. In the biological kingdom there exists an unwritten universal law relating to sexual behavior. Different species evolve through this selective reproduction process. The number of genes and their structure determines the genetic specification of a species. For different species these numbers as well the structures are different. Between the two extremes (nuclear family and the world human population) we can conceive of different types and sizes of genetic or Mendelian population.

Sociology and Social Anthropology look at the population from social perspectives. Definition of population in social point of view is largely dependent upon the objectives of research and personal orientation. Social population has many parallels with Mendelian population. Like the Mendelian population, which states that a genetic population inherits similar genes, sociologists or social anthropologists view individuals in a specific population seen to display a common cultural inheritance, i.e., their social origin is almost the same. Hierarchical structure is often a consistent feature in such a population. Class, caste and occupation often stratify a population. When blood relations become the criteria in defining a population, the social group becomes a shadow of Mendelian population. Even if a population defined by social characteristics gets close to genetic population, the criteria for measuring social relations often are different from the criteria used in measuring biological relations. Dissimilarity rather than similarity is often what we observe when comparing the hierarchy in a genetic population with that in a social population.

Man and other animals not only exploit the natural or man-made environment but help consolidate or improve the eco environment as well. The science of ecology stands on this principle. The concept of *Ecological population* is concerned with the human settlements that are seen to use the natural or man-made environment almost in a similar fashion. Ecological population consists of those human groups who pursue a particular mode of living by collective use of natural or created resources in a manner decided by collective knowledge. From ecological point of view, the fishermen in India and those in Norway or Finland are part of the same fishermen population since all these people utilize the natural environment to their benefit in almost similar manner. They have different cultural background and different genetic inheritance; they have different languages, different religions and different standards of living. That is, ecological population crosses national or continental boundaries. From genetic or social points of view such a population would be regarded as congregate of a large number of independent populations.

This brief discussion makes it clear that it is impossible to get a population, which is purely genetic, social or ecological. There is no doubt whatsoever that the physical environment in which we live in has large influences in developing social relations and regulations. Similarly, our cultural inheritance determines how an adjustment is to be made between man's needs without jeopardizing the ecological balance. There exists a close relation between cultural, genetic and ecological inheritance. As such, there is considerable overlap between these population concepts. Mendelian population though is based on reproductive relations, are influenced by social and cultural background of the group (restraints relating to marriage) and also by environmental considerations as population density, distribution of population, movement of people, etc. Even the characteristics manifested by many of our social organizations have much to do with our physical environment. Cultural considerations cannot be independent of our physical surroundings.

1.3 History of Growth of World Population

Kingsley Davis has succinctly described the possible fallout of the unprecedented growth of world population. From the remotest past to the present, in this vast time-space the population growth has been like a gunpowder-coated fine thread that has been ignited long back. The sparks of the gunpowder has steadily progressed, sometimes slowly, sometimes fast, towards its target – the explosive. A time will come when the spark will reach the detonator and a tremendous blast will happen. This analogy gives a stunning picture of the stupendous impact the population explosion may have on human civilization. It also describes the huge leap in population growth from a near stationary state for most of the 1.5 million years to an explosive state in the last few centuries. The warning that Davis wanted to covey is: If the growth is not contained fast, we may have to pay a very heavy price sooner than one imagines.

Sometime in the recent past, a baby was born somewhere on the globe that pushed world population over the 6 billion threshold. It took all of human history up to 1820 to reach a global population of 1 billion; but it took just 12 years to leap from 5 billion to 6 billion. The world's population grew by only 600 million in the 19th century. It grew by 4.4 billion in the 20th century.

There are twice as many people today as there were in 1960 and the population is still growing. Even assuming a sustained decline in fertility rates, the United Nations projects a population over 9 billion in 2050. Under current trends, world population is not projected to stabilize until sometime after 2075.

The Earth is now gaining about 78 million people annually, roughly the equivalent of adding a new France, Greece and Sweden combined, or a city the size of Philadelphia every week. In 1800, London was the world's largest city with 1 million people. Today, 326 metropolitan areas have more than 1 million people and 16 cities have more than 10 million (India alone has four such metropolitan cities). By 2025, 650 cities are expected to be with populations of more than 1 million.

As a result of efforts initiated in the 1960s and 1970s to contain the growth rate, annual world population growth peaked at 86 million in 1989. Average global fertility has been halved, from a high of about 6 children per woman in the 1950s to 2.9 or less per woman today. There is not a single industrialized nation in the world with a fertility rate above replacement level [Total Fertility Rate (TFR) 2.06] per woman.

Indeed, the United States, with 2.03 children per woman, has the highest fertility rate in the developed world. The average fertility for European countries is 1.4, so is in Japan. Even in some developing nations, South Korea and Taiwan, for example, the TFRs are at or below 1.6. In the Third World countries, where 98 percent of future population growth is expected to take place, there have also been dramatic declines. The average TFR for developing countries, excluding China, was 2.9 in 2005.

We have a fair idea about the size of world population today. By the beginning of this century it was around 6,000 million, adding 2,000 million in just 25 years. World population today still grew by about 1.6 percent per annum between 1975 and 2005. It is expected to grow on an average by 1.1 percent between 2005 and 2015 [Human Development Report (HDR), 2007/08]. It is only since 1900 that we have somewhat reliable information about population for most of the countries. Prior to this, the wise guess was from some scattered incomplete information from the pages of history. Demographers have tried to reconstruct the nature of population changes from 10,000 BC, the time when, it is believed, settlements started to grow around the lakes and rivers and human population was entering into the agricultural stage. The method of backward projection was employed using assumed estimates of birth and death rates, expectation of life at birth etc. Estimates of world population since 10,000 BC are presented in Table 1.1.

It took hundreds and thousands of years to reach 1,000 million populations (1820), a little less than the current population size of India today. It then took only 110 years to add another 1,000 million (1930). The next 1,000 million took 30 years and currently we are adding 1,000 million every 12 years or so.

The balance of birth and death (natural increase) is adding about 0.2 million people everyday. How would our living spaceship appear if this growth continues unabated? A remarkable sketch of the possible fallout of this monstrous growth was noted in Davis' observation. Frank Notestein opines that nothing in this limited space can grow unstinted, not even human population. From around 2 percent in 1955, the growth rate rapidly rose to 2.4 percent in only 15 years. Since 1975, the trend had been reversed, According to United Nation's estimate the earth would have to accommodate closer to additional 1,000 million hungry mouths in 2015. Scientists and technologists of course assure us that we shall be able to develop more efficient methods to improve our productivity and discover new food chains and sources for power and thereby prevent famine becoming rampant

Table 1.1 *History of growth of world population (million)*

Year	*Estimated population*	*Time taken to double the population*	*Time taken to add 1,000 million*
10,000 BC	0.1–10		
5,000 BC	5–20		
0	200		
1300 AD	400	1300 years	
1650	500		
1700	600		
1750	700		
1800	900	475 years	
1820	1,000		Thousands of years
1850	1,200		
1900	1,600		
1920	1,830		
1927	2,000	125 years	110 years
1940	2,220		
1950	2,525		
1960	3,040	62 years	33 years
1974	4,027		14 years
1980	4,432		
1987	5,000		13 years
1990	5,320		
1999	6,000	40 years	12 years
2013	7,000		14 years
2028	8,000		15 years
2054	9,000		26 years

Source: UNDP, Davis, Carr Saunders and Wilcox, US Bureau of Census.

Figure 1.1 *Growth of world population*

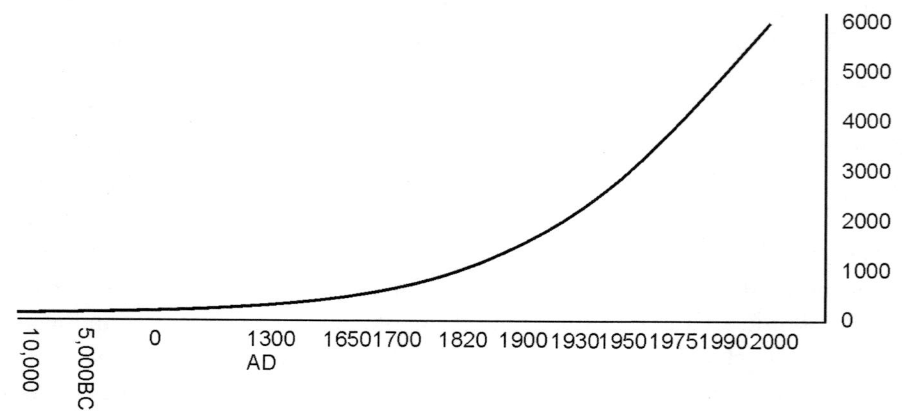

in various parts of the earth. There is not a large difference in opinion among demographers and other specialists that uncontrolled birth could become the principal cause of our misery in near future.

Figure 1.2 *World population since 1820*

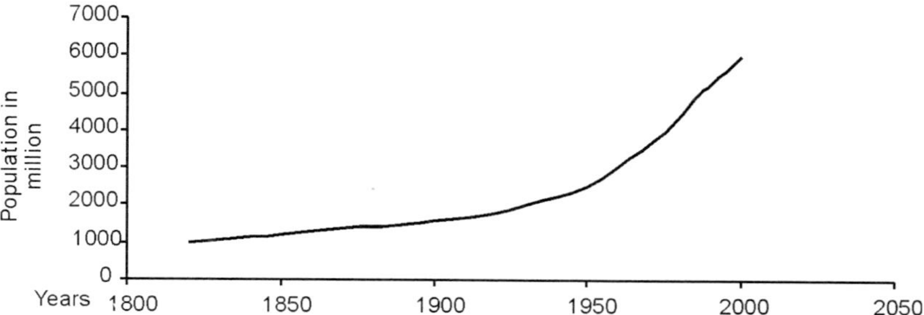

If we look back to the history of the last boarder (Homo sapiens) to our spaceship earth, it will be seen that its average growth rate has been exceedingly small, about 0.00005 percent per annum almost throughout the entire period. The growth rate in the seventies in the last century was around 0.5 million times as high as this average growth rate. Throughout the history of human civilization habitable space had been in abundance for the small human population. The hunting and fruit gathering tribes needed a very large space for supporting life system even for a small group. In Paleolithic age, a single person needed almost one square mile of land space and the population density was really trivial. Man learned agriculture and domesticating animals only some 12,000 years back. It is from then that the population density started to improve. Even then, the world population grew at a snail's space till the seventeenth century.

Learned guess from various documents available put Indian population at the time of Ashoka, some 300 years before the birth of Christ, at around 100 million, nearly half the total world population. From the scattered evidences scientists generally are of the opinion that the size of Indian population remained almost stationary between Ashoka's time and the beginning of the seventeenth century – for about 2,000 years. The birth and death rates were almost the same – a shift of, balance this or that way saw some small increase or decrease of the population. In times of peace and good harvest the population growth gained some momentum though it lasted only for a while. Within a few years drought, natural catastrophe, famine, epidemic and war created conditions not conducive to population growth. The growth curve showed sudden drops. Instead of a smooth curve, it showed irregular fluctuations. Although a consistent upward trend is noticed since the beginning of the seventeenth century, the growth line became smooth only after the first quarter of the twentieth century.

For convenience of study and analysis, a time perspective on world population growth is necessary. We can call this Cultural Revolution and population growth. The four periods that have been demarcated for such analysis are:

1. Ancient period – world population prior to 10000 BC.
2. Agricultural revolution – world population from 10000 BC to 1650 AD.
3. Middle or take-off period – world population from 1650 to 1820.
4. Industrial revolution or Modern period – world population since 1820.

World Population Prior to 10000 BC

First Cultural Revolution took place millions of years back when the primitive man learned to use fire and make weapons from stones and metals. This constitutes the longest period of human civilization; writings on the pages of this pre-historic period are very fade. It is only with imagination and wild guesses that this chapter of history can be reconstructed. Archaeological excavation discovered many relics scattered all over the canvas. From these scattered evidences historians have tried to write the cultural and social history of that period. Very high birth and death rates and very low expectation of life were the principal demographic features at that stage. Without the knowledge of how to grow food and make shelters, the primitive man's life was one of constant struggle for survival against the strong adversaries of nature. Unfriendly environment, frightful animals, and uncertainty of food – everything went against his survival. It is estimated that the fruit gatherers and hunters could use only about 20 million square miles of the earth's surface. It has been estimated that the average expectation of life at that stage could not have exceeded 10 years. Human species could have disappeared but for its very high birth rate.

World Population from 10000 BC to 1650 AD

Some 12,000 years from now, our predecessors learned to produce food grains and domesticate and rear animals for meat. This second stage of Cultural Revolution may be called **Agricultural Revolution**. Agriculture helped man to settle at a place and do away with the hitherto followed migratory life in search of food. Animal husbandry and agriculture allowed them to settle at a place; human settlements allowed villages and small towns to come up. That human civilization gained the necessary momentum from agriculture is borne by the fact that all old civilizations and cities grew around rivers and lakes. Till the time when man discovered how to grow his own food and store them for tougher times, his time and life revolved around procuring food for survival. Agriculture transformed them from biological animals to social beings; it gave them some leisure time to ponder over matters that were not directly related to biological living – he could now shift some of his attention from self to others, allocate some of his time for activities for the cause of the larger society beyond procurement of food. He started to realize that there are many other activities and occupations that one can pursue; freedom from incessant search for food allowed him to attend and try to understand the intricacies of nature and spend time on discoveries. Earlier, it was man's constant struggle for survival. To him 'today' drew all his attention and energy; he did not have the opportunity and freedom to look beyond the immediate present. With agricultural revolution, though the question of survival was still strong in his mind, the organized living and food security gave him some respite in his struggle against the adversaries. Death rate started to decline, marginally though, and the population started to grow slowly.

World Population from 1650 to 1820

Information about population of this period is also paltry. For some countries some kind of population data are available from incomplete censuses. We have better recorded history from around this time and therefore a better estimate of population for many countries. Machines started to have a significant role in the economy, and the system of agriculture also improved. Early signs of industrial revolution were looming large. Basic sciences started to take some definite shape. Communications across countries and continents started to improve. Growing crops and cultivating live-stock still continued to be the major source of economy. Introduction of new crops and vegetables increased food supply; better nutrition improved the expectation of life. Birth rate was still high, around 40–45 per thousand population and death rate started to decline slowly. Population growth rate was around 0.3 percent per annum in this period.

World Population Since 1820

The industrial revolution is the final stage of Cultural Revolution. Improved technology and growth of various types of industries not only improved productivity in the agricultural sector, the door for non-traditional industrial goods also opened up. Many scientific discoveries, revolution in transportation and communication promised a better standard of living. Improvement of personal cleanliness and the enhanced level of nutrition had obvious effects on death rates. The industrial revolution and the tremendous technological advancement during the two World Wars and thereafter have increased the efficiency in the use of the natural resources to a new height. The general standard of living improved by leaps and bounds. Medical science saw a sea change. The use of preventive medicines and broad-spectrum antibiotics eliminated many of the killer diseases like plague and small pox, and controlled tuberculosis, malaria and cholera to a great extent. Death rates started to decline sharply. Famine-like situations and epidemics could be contained easily, thanks to the vastly improved communication and transport network and global participation of international bodies like WHO, UN, UNESCO, etc. in times of crisis. Average expectation of life at birth increased by leaps and bounds. From 1,600 million in 1900 the world population crossed 6,000 million in 2,000.

The modern period can be divided into four sub-periods: 1900–1921, 1921–1950, 1951–1975, and 1975 onwards.

World Population between 1900 and 1921: The first two decades of the twentieth century saw eruption of a few dreaded diseases like plague and virulent influenza taking heavy toll of human lives in many countries. In fact, some countries registered negative growths in this period. The year 1921 is regarded as the **great demographic divide** (at least for India and many other developing countries). A secular decline in death rates was observed all over the world. Plague was totally eliminated. Diseases like malaria, cholera and tuberculosis were contained. The near stagnant growth of world population was due to the fact that many of the developed countries took to family planning methods. Birth rates therefore came down.

World population between 1921 and 1950: After the First World War, there was global recession. Things started to change at the beginning of the fourth decade. Its effect on population too was visible. Birth rates in some underdeveloped countries actually increased, often by 2–3 points. With steady declining death rates the world population started to grow fast. The population growth rate crossed 1 percent per annum mark at the beginning of the Second World War. Industrial and agricultural production climbed high to meet the increasing demands of the war. Employment opportunities increased rapidly. Common man had plenty of surplus money. *Baby boom* was observed in most countries, especially in the West. In the forties the decadal increase was around 14 percent even after deaths of millions of people in the war.

World population between 1950 and 1975: The momentum gathered in the forties continued for at least another 25 years before a brake was applied to the population growth rate. From 13.7 percent of decadal growth in the forties (a net addition of 305 million to the population in 1940), the world population jumped up by 20.3 percent in the next decade (neat addition of 532 million), 21.67 percent between 1960 and 1970 (neat addition of 658 million) and 9.8 percent in the next five years (neat addition of 362 million). That is, in a period of 25 years, there was a neat addition of 1,532 million, a 61 percent growth in 25 years over 1950 population. The average exponential growth rate in this period was about 1.92 percent.

Table 1.2 *World population (in million) by continent and development category, 1950–1985*

Region	Mid-Year population							
	1950	*1955*	*1960*	*1965*	*1970*	*1975*	*1980*	*1985*
WORLD	**2536**	**2781**	**3063**	**3357**	**3722**	**4107**	**4478**	**4889**
More developed	832	887	945	1002	1049	1095	1136	1172
Less developed	1704	1893	2118	2354	2673	3011	3343	3717
Africa	222	248	278	315	359	410	472	548
Asia	1397	1543	1713	1885	2130	2384	2618	2875
More developed	84	90	94	99	104	112	117	121
Less developed	1313	1453	1619	1786	2025	2273	2501	2754
Latin America	166	190	218	251	286	324	365	409
Northern America	166	181	199	214	226	239	264	259
Europe & CIS	572	604	640	675	703	728	749	769
Oceania	12	14	16	17	19	21	23	24
More developed	10	11	13	14	15	17	18	19
Less developed	2	3	3	3	4	4	5	6

Source: US Department of Commerce: *World Population 1983*

Estimates of populations both in the developed and developing countries in the fifties, as projected by Population Division of United Nations, failed miserably when census data for various countries around 1960 became available. The population grew much faster than what was estimated. The dangers of this unprecedented population growth were discussed in various forums as well as in the UN assembly. The pressure of population in the underdeveloped and developing countries on food supply, employment and unwise use of the natural resources were the principal aspects which were discussed in these forums. Many of the developing and underdeveloped countries were already dependent on import of food grains from other countries. The pressure rose sharply due to failure of monsoon for consecutive years in the sixties in many countries. Many foundations and the UN came forward to conduct special surveys relating to different aspects of population growth, especially in the developing and underdeveloped countries. UN accepted ‘Right to Family Planning’ as one of the Human Rights. All the countries were asked to develop their population policy. In 1974, population scientists and representatives from countries all over the world assembled in Bucharest to discuss how to combat this population growth. The Conference resolved that there was no alternative to economic and social development even in containing population growth (the slogan adopted was “Development is the best contraceptive”). Many international funding agencies and donor countries asked the recipient countries to spend a portion of the aids and short and long term loans on measures for population control.

Table 1.3 *Average annual growth rate by continent and development category, 1950–85*

Region	Period for which average growth rate is computed						
	1950–55	*1955–60*	*1960–65*	*1965–70*	*1970–75*	*1975–80*	*1980–85*
WORLD	1.8	1.9	1.8	2.1	2	1.7	1.7
More developed	1.3	1.3	1.2	0.9	0.9	0.7	0.6
Less developed	2.1	2.2	2.1	2.5	2.4	2.1	2.1
Africa	2.2	2.3	2.5	2.6	2.7	2.8	3.0
Asia	2.0	2.1	1.9	2.4	2.3	1.9	1.8
More developed	1.4	0.9	1.0	1.1	1.3	0.9	0.6
Less developed	2.0	2.2	2	2.5	2.3	1.9	1.9
Latin America	2.6	2.8	2.8	2.7	2.5	2.5	2.3
N. America	1.8	1.8	1.5	1.1	1.1	1.1	1.0
Europe & CIS	1.1	1.1	1.1	0.8	0.7	0.6	0.5
Oceania	2.3	2.2	2.1	2.1	1.9	1.3	1.4
More developed	2.3	2.2	2	1.9	1.7	1	1.1
Less developed	2.2	2.4	2.7	2.8	2.5	2.4	2.5

Source: US Department of Commerce: *World Population 1983*

Worldwide programs were undertaken to eliminate small pox, malaria, tuberculosis, etc. from the earth. Many life saving drugs were invented and benefits of these high quality researches reached the developing and underdeveloped countries soon. In spite of severe poverty and lack of education, death rates in these countries declined sharply. Birth rates however continued to be high or declining only slowly. As a result, the world population growth rate continued to increase.

World population since 1975. In the fourth quarter of the last century, 1,943 million heads were added to the 1975 total – about 48 percent increase in absolute number. The average annual exponential growth was a little less than 1.6 percent. Between 1975 and 1980, the growth declined slightly from that of the previous five years. It showed some increase in the next five years but a steady decline was observed in the remaining 15 years. The developing countries were still growing at 1.9 percent per annum. The countries in High Human Development category (UNDP classification) showed an average of 0.7 percent annual exponential growth, the countries in Medium Human Development with 1.7 percent per annum and the countries in Low Human Development category growing at an alarming 2.7 percent per annum. Average Total Fertility Rate at the end of the millennium was still as high as 2.8 (1.7 for High, 2.6 for Medium and 5.6 for Low Development countries).

Table 1.4 *Share of the continents to the total world population, 1950–2050*

Continent	*1950*	*1975*	*2003*	*2025*	*2050*
Africa	8.75	9.98	13.49	16.46	20.22
Asia	55.09	58.05	60.67	60.40	58.55
Latin America	6.55	7.89	8.62	8.75	8.61
Northern America	6.55	5.82	5.17	5.02	5.02
Europe	22.56	17.73	11.52	8.87	7.09
Oceania	0.47	0.51	0.51	0.51	0.50

Figure 1.3 *Share of the continents to world population 1950–2050*

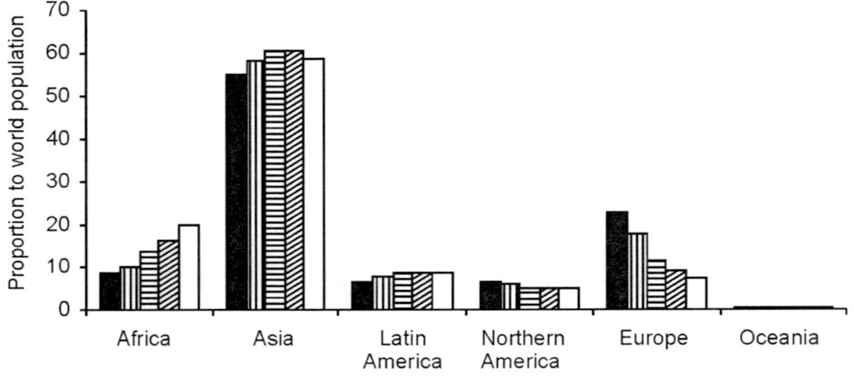

Table 1.5 *Demographic trends, world since 1975*

Country categories	*Population (million)*			*Annual pop growth rate (%)*		*Urban population*			*Total fertility rate*	
	1975	*1999*	*2015*	*1975–99*	*1999–2015*	*1975*	*1999*	*2015*	*1975–99*	*1999–2015*
Developing	2898.3	4609.8	5759.1	1.9	1.4	25.9	38.9	47.5	5.4	3.1
High HDI	891.7	1053.8	1123.0	0.7	0.4	72.6	78.3	82.1	2.3	1.7
Medium HDI	2671.4	3990.6	4707.7	1.7	1.0	29.4	41.4	49.6	4.9	2.6
Low HDI	424.4	818.2	1217.5	2.7	2.5	17.5	30.4	40.6	6.7	5.6
High income	746.1	873.2	928.4	0.7	0.4	75.0	78.7	82.2	2.1	1.7
Medium income	1843.1	2632.6	3018.6	1.5	0.9	34.8	49.5	57.6	4.6	2.2
Low income	1396.2	2356.9	3101.2	2.2	1.7	21.9	31.2	40.2	5.7	4.0
WORLD	**3987.4**	**5862.7**	**7048.2**	**1.6**	**1.2**	**37.8**	**46.5**	**53.2**	**4.5**	**2.8**

Source: Human Development Report, 2001, UNDP

Table 1.6 *World population and related statistics by region*

Country or area	*Mid-year population (thousands)*			*Density (pop/ km²)*	*% urban*	*Growth rate(%)*	*CBR*	*CDR*	*TFR*	*% of all births to women under age 20*	*Life Expecta-tion at birth*	*Mortality under age 5*	*Percent of population Under*	
													<15 yrs.	*60+ yrs.*
	2003	*2025*	*2050*	*Mid-2003*		*2000–05*							*Mid-2003*	
1	*2*	*3*	*4*	*5*	*6*	*7*	*8*	*9*	*10*	*11*	*12*	*13*	*14*	*15*
WORLD/ Regions	**6 301 463**	**7 851 455**	**8 918 724**	**46**	**48**	**1.2**	**21**	**9**	**2.7**	**11**	**65**	**81**	**29**	**10**
More developed	1 203 296	1 241 377	1 219 662	23	76	0.2	11	10	1.6	8	76	10	17	20
Less developed	5 098 167	6 610 079	7 699 061	62	42	1.5	24	9	2.9	11	63	89	32	8
Least developed	718 080	1 148 840	1 674 521	35	27	2.4	39	15	5.1	17	50	161	43	5
AFRICA	**850 558**	**1 292 085**	**1 803 298**	**28**	**39**	**2.2**	**37**	**15**	**4.9**	**16**	**49**	**148**	**42**	**5**
Eastern Africa	270 317	423 117	614 457	43	26	2.2	41	19	5.6	16	43	163	45	4
Middle Africa	100 583	172 134	266 301	15	37	2.7	47	20	6.3	23	43	207	46	5
Northern Africa	183 598	254 150	306 046	22	50	1.9	26	7	3.2	7	66	66	34	7
Southern Africa	51 678	49 576	46 602	19	56	0.6	24	18	2.8	15	46	88	34	6
Western Africa	244 381	393 108	569 891	40	41	2.6	41	15	5.6	16	50	151	45	5
ASIA	**3 823 390**	**4 742 232**	**5 222 058**	**120**	**39**	**1.3**	**21**	**8**	**2.5**	**8**	**67**	**71**	**29**	**9**
Eastern Asia	1 512 321	1 655 784	1 590 070	129	44	0.7	14	7	1.8	1	72	40	22	12
South-central Asia	1 563 173	2 097 128	2 463 916	145	31	1.7	26	9	3.2	10	63	93	34	7
South-eastern Asia	543 193	687 621	767 250	121	40	1.4	22	7	2.5	10	67	55	31	7
Western Asia	204 703	301 699	400 822	43	65	2.1	27	6	3.4	9	69	57	35	7
EUROPE	**726 338**	**696 036**	**631 938**	**32**	**74**	**–0.1**	**10**	**11**	**1.4**	**7**	**74**	**11**	**16**	**21**
Eastern Europe	300 264	267 070	221 736	16	68	–0.5	9	13	1.2	13	69	19	16	18
Northern Europe	94 816	99 134	100 072	54	83	0.2	11	10	1.6	5	78	7	18	21

1	*2*	*3*	*4*	*5*	*6*	*7*	*8*	*9*	*10*	*11*	*12*	*13*	*14*	*15*
Southern Europe	146 365	140 630	125 596	111	67	0.1	10	10	1.3	3	78	9	15	22
Western Europe	184 893	189 201	184 534	167	83	0.2	10	10	1.6	3	79	6	17	22
LATIN AMERICA & CARRIBEAN	**543 246**	**686 857**	**767 685**	**26**	**77**	**1.4**	**22**	**6**	**2.5**	**16**	**70**	**41**	**31**	**8**
Caribbean	38 692	44 586	45 814	165	64	0.9	20	9	2.4	17	67	58	28	11
Central America	142 275	186 441	211 758	57	69	1.7	24	5	2.8	16	72	38	34	7
South America	362 278	455 829	510 113	20	81	1.4	21	7	2.5	16	70	40	30	9
NORTHERN AMERICA	**325 698**	**394 312**	**447 931**	**15**	**78**	**1.0**	**14**	**8**	**2.1**	**12**	**77**	**8**	**21**	**16**
OCEANIA	**32 234**	**39 933**	**45 815**	**4**	**75**	**1.2**	**17**	**8**	**2.3**	**7**	**74**	**35**	**25**	**14**
Australia/New Zealand	23 606	27 584	30 072	3	91	0.9	13	7	1.7	5	79	7	20	17
Melanesia	7 468	10 833	13 968	14	25	2.1	30	8	3.9	10	60	72	40	4
Micronesia	526	709	863	170	44	1.7	25	5	3.4	10	72	26	35	7
Polynesia	635	807	912	75	41	1.3	24	6	3.2	8	71	26	34	7

Source: UN Population Division

But the main reason why the world population continued to grow rapidly for decades despite slowing fertility rates is something population experts call "demographic momentum". There are over 1 billion people aged 15 to 24 in the world today and nearly 2 billion under age 15 most of who are destined to become parents. In the developing world, about one-third of the population is still under age 15.

China is the world's most populous nation with 1,313 million people in 2005. But India is likely to overtake China sometime before 2050. Africa, with 13 percent of the world's population today, is projected to see 34 percent of the globe's population increase over the next 50 years. India and China together will account for another 25 percent of the increase. The current US population (299.8 million in 2005), the world's third most populous country, is projected to grow to 335 million by 2025. Most of the US population growth would be due to immigration and drop in mortality rates. Life expectancy in the US has risen from 47 years in 1900 to 77 years today. For country-wise data, see Appendix 1.

Table 1.7 *Some important world population statistics between 1975 and 2000*

Category	*Growth rate*	*TFR*		*Life expectancy at birth*		*IMR*		*Under-Five mortality rate*	
	1975–99	*1975*	*1999*	*1975*	*1999*	*1975*	*1999*	*1975*	*1999*
World	1.6	4.5	2.8	59.9	66.4	96	56	147	80
Developing	1.9	5.4	3.1	55.5	64.1	109	61	167	89
High HDI	0.7	2.3	1.7	71.3	77.0	25	7	32	8
Medium HDI	1.7	4.9	2.6	58.4	66.5	99	46	149	62
Low HDI	2.7	6.7	5.6	44.6	52.2	142	99	231	156

Source: Human Development Report, 2001, UNDP.

1.4 Human Development and Population Indicators

"Development is the best contraceptive to population growth" has been the slogan quite for some time in discussions on problems of population growth. Philosophers, economists and political leaders all agree that anything that insures human wellbeing is a part of the development process. Development no doubt implies change and describes the process of economic and social transformation within countries that insures a better and more realistic choice for all its peoples. It is a general observation that if the economy is growing sufficiently rapidly, the general socio-economic wellbeing of the whole population improves, of course not by the same degree across the population. If we have to choose a single indicator of development, there can be no two opinions as to the utility of using per capita national income or output for the same. But what is true of developed economy is not necessarily true of a developing economy. Even the developing countries that registered significant gains in GNP often show highly skewed income distribution. In many countries distributive and social justice did not accompany faster growth of economy and capital accumulation. Many economists today are arguing in line with Gunner Myrdal that economic policy of a country be directed to attack causes of poverty even if that means a temporary slowing down the economic growth.

When 'development' becomes an objective of policy, an important question must be answered – *development for what?* In earlier policy formulations, exclusive emphasis was on economic growth targets, with little or no emphasis on the beneficiaries of such a growth and to the composition of the output. The distributional consequences of economic policy could not be ignored long as also the output that is produced in a particular economic and social environment.

Of late, an integrated approach to development has been accepted which embraces the major economic and social objectives paying due emphasis on the values that societies strive for. One of the best attempts in this direction is to be found in Goulet's (1971) work. He distinguishes three basic components or core values in the wider meaning of the term 'development'. He calls them *life-sustenance, self-esteem and freedom.*

Life-sustenance refers to provision of the very basic needs such as food, housing, clothing, health and minimal education.

Self-esteem refers to self-respect and independence. On the level of nations, no country can be regarded as developed if it is exploited by others and has no power and influence to conduct relations on equal terms. The feeling of being dominated and dependence, which come from inferior economic and social status, hurt a country's pride. What is true of nations is also true of the people of a country. Economic, social and educational deprivation and dominance by other social groups and the feeling that the individual has little or no role in power-sharing and decision-making process intensify his inferiority complex.

Freedom refers to the freedom from three evils – want, ignorance and poverty and misery. People want to inculcate the feeling that he is the master of himself and he can determine his own destiny. No one is free if he cannot choose, if he is imprisoned by living on the margins of subsistence, has no education, no skills. Development is oriented to expand the range of human choice for material world and social choice, open to individuals and societies at large.

All these core components are interdependent. Low levels of life-sustenance cannot generate self-esteem and freedom. A lack of self-esteem and freedom becomes the roadblock to life-sustenance. A lack of self-esteem and economic imprisonment becomes a link in circular, self-perpetuating chain of poverty by producing a sense of fatalism and acceptance of the established order – the 'accommodation of poverty' as Galbraith has called it.

Economic growth is a necessary but not the sufficient condition of socio-economic development. A country like India can achieve high growth rate of aggregate GNP even with a half literate adult population since there are millions of literate and highly educated people around. India can particularly do well in the industrial sector, especially in hi-techs – IT and biotechnology since the country has a large surplus of highly educated and qualified persons. But that will not solve India's deep-rooted poverty and social and economic inequality. Their removal, as Prof. Amartya Sen sees it, calls for more *participatory growth* on a wider basis, which is not easy to achieve across the barriers of ill health, illiteracy, severe inequalities in social, economic and political opportunities and caustic subjugation by those in the political and social hierarchy.

Since 1990, the United Nations Development Program (UNDP), has regularly been bringing out Human Development Report (HDR). It sees human development much more than the rise and fall of national income. The root of development lies in expanding the choices people have to lead the lives that they value. UNDP has identified three fundamental capabilities for human development – long and healthy lives (more productive years), knowledge (better informed), and access to resources needed for a decent standard of living which enables him to participate with honor in the life of the community.

UNDP has developed Human Development Index (HDI) – a tool for measuring the state of development in a country. It is a composite index based on three indicators – longevity, educational attainment and standard of living measured by real GDP per capita. (Please see Chapter 12 for a fuller discussion on HDI). The index provides scores for each country ranging from 0 to 1. The countries are put into one of the three levels of human development: High Human Development (HDI score 0.80 and above), Medium Human Development (HDI score ranging from 0.50 and 0.80) and Low Human Development (HDI score below 0.50). The 2001 report shows that there were 48 countries in High Development category (57 in 2005), which included only 7 countries from Asia and none from Africa. Other countries were mostly from Europe, Northern America, some from Latin America and Australia and New Zealand. The Low Human Development group had 36 countries (32 in 2005) of which 4 were from Asia, one from Latin America and rest from Africa. That leaves 29 other countries from Africa that finds a place in the Medium Human Development category. A very large number of Latin American countries are in the Medium Development group.

Of the 6 billion people at the beginning of this millennium, the High HDI group accounts for 1,060 million, the Medium HDI countries 4,030 million and Low HDI the rest. UN projection predicts world population in excess of 7 billion by 2015 and average annual population growth at 1.1–1.2 percent. Population aged 65 and above would rise to 8.3 percent of the total population against 6.9 percent in 1999. Sub-Saharan Africa shows an alarmingly high growth rate of 2.8 percent per annum, closely followed by Arab States, 2.7 percent, South Asian countries coming next, 2.1 percent.

In the 1960s, most of the backward regions were nearly at par in growth of population, 2.5–2.8 percent per annum. Latin American countries were at the top. In the last forty years the picture has changed appreciably. There is greater diversity now in the rate of growth of population among the less developed regions. Latin America has come down to fourth spot in growth of population behind sub-Saharan Africa, Arab States and South Asia. These regions have more or less the same rankings in respect to TFR and IMR as well (Table 1.7). Many of the high HDI countries, Scandinavian countries in particular, may suffer from large-scale depopulation unless there is reversal in their fertility trend. (Appendix 1)

The difference in the average Crude Death Rate (CDR) between the developed and the less developed regions practically has vanished. As of 2000, CDR in the world population was around 10, the two regions being separated by a point or so. Western and Middle Africa still continue with high CDR, around 15.

The average Crude Birth Rate for the world total is still very high, around 26. The more developed regions have CBR around 15 against around 29 in the less developed regions. Western and Middle Africa and the Arab States continue with alarmingly high birth rates, around 45. South Asian countries still have very high CBR, around 31, compared to CBR around 18 of East Asia,.

The developed countries took about 300 years to bring down their fertility and mortality to the present levels. Most of them did not have any formal population policies. The reduction of birth and death rates is to be seen in the broader context of their social and economic development – spread of education, expanding labor market, better health management, sanitation and nutrition. A rapid decline in mortality in Asia, Africa and Latin America started from late 1930s; by late 1970s life expectancy at birth increased to more than 60 years. The rapid gains in the 20th century were propelled by medical science – antibiotics and vaccines and better health management. The reduction of poverty-induced under-nutrition in South Asia from around 40 percent to around 23 percent or less by the end of the 20th century, and the end of epidemic and famine was made possible through technological breakthroughs in plant breeding, fertilizers and pesticides, which doubled food production (India has quadrupled cereal yields since independence). This is an example of what technology can do to improve human lives on earth. It took 1,000 years for the English to quadruple wheat yields from 0.5 to 2.0 tons per hectare. A single innovation, history shows, can quickly change the course of an entire society. Mankind in general and sub-Saharan Africa in particular, is eagerly waiting for an affordable vaccine and medicine for the control of HIV/AIDS.

Of the 4.6 billion people living in developing countries, 2.4 billion are without access to basic sanitation (1998), 968 million are without access to improved water sources (1998), 34 million are living with HIV/AIDS (2000), 11 million children under age 5 die every year from preventable diseases (1998) and there are 163 million underweight children aged 5 years and less. 850 million people are illiterate (543 million are women) and 152 million boys and 183 million girls are out of schools. Around 1.2 billion people in the developing countries live on less than $1 a day and 2.8 billion on less than $2 a day.

Between 1975 and 1999 impressive changes have been observed in many indicators of human development. Data for 162 countries are available for making comparisons. In 1975, 48 percent of the population in these categories was under medium human development, 34 percent in low development category; the same in 1999 stood at 71 and 10 percent respectively. The share of rural families with access to safe water has increased by more than five-fold. IMR has declined from around 98 to 58, under-5 mortality down from 149 to 85 and TFR down from 4.1 to 2.7. Life expectancy at birth has gone up by nearly 8 years from 59 years in 1970.

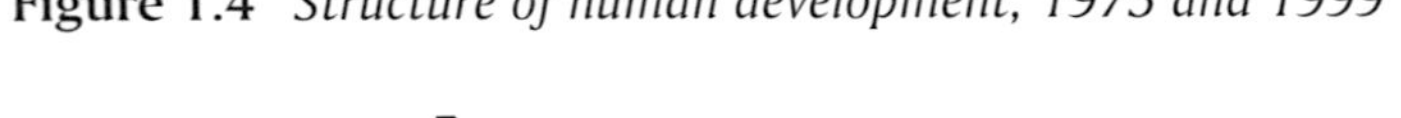

Figure 1.4 *Structure of human development, 1975 and 1999*

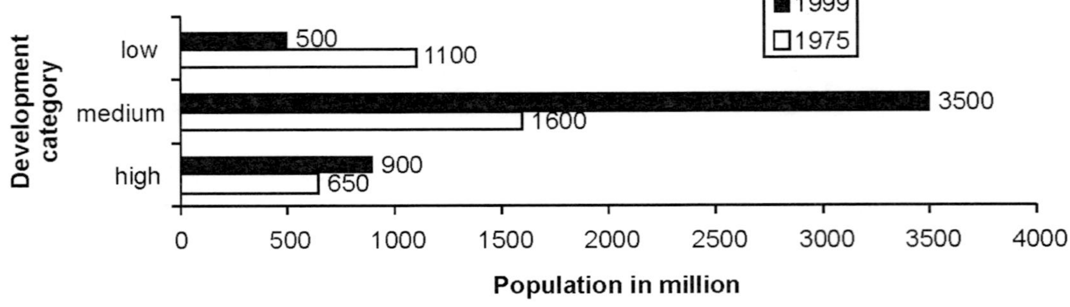

In education front, adult literacy has increased from 64 percent to a point below 80 percent. Enrolment ratio at primary level has gone up from around 83 to around 90 percent and at secondary level it is up by 42 points from 22 in 1970. More significantly, the female enrolment ratio as a percentage of male ratio is up by about 30 points both for primary, secondary and tertiary level education.

Many more people enjoy a better standard of living today; the average income in developing countries having almost doubled in real terms between 1975 and 1998, from $1,300 to $2,500 (1985 purchasing power parity PPP US $). Income poverty has declined from around 29 percent in 1990 to

24 percent in 1998 (1993 PPP US $). Economic activity rate of females (age 15+) in 1997 was 40 percent, which was 70 percent of economic activity rate of males.

'The rich are getting richer, poor poorer' is a cliché on world literature on poverty. The high profile politicians and economists often speak of 'global economy' of a 'global village'. The magnitude of the development task facing the developing countries needs to be addressed precisely. This cannot be done without a proper assessment of the 'development gap'. An intellectual exercise by A. P. Thirlwal showed that even if the per capita income in the poorer countries grow at 2 percent annually, it may take 100 years for these countries to achieve the current living levels enjoyed in the industrialized countries. The per capita income gap between the poor and the rich countries is likely to widen further. With lower growth rate in the developed countries and reasonably higher growth rate in the developing countries, the gap can certainly be reduced but cannot be eliminated altogether. The primary concern therefore is to ensure a 'tolerable' standard of living in all the countries through equitable distribution of the average level of real income.

Income levels across countries have been both diverging and converging – some regions closing the income gap and others drifting away. We find that the developing countries have to bear the burden of 77 percent of the world population and yet its share to world GDP is less than 23 percent. The very low-income countries' share to world GDP is only 6 percent when its share of world population is 60 percent. There is no evidence that the distribution of world income is narrowing. In 1960, the richest 20 percent of the world population had income 30 times greater than that of the poorest 20 percent. In 1990, the ratio was 60 times greater. The richest 20 percent of the world population consume about 84 percent of world GDP, 82 percent of energy, 90 percent of fuel oil and 85 percent of forest product. World Bank report (1992) shows that 24 top nations share about 15.5 percent of world population and 82 percent of world GDP. India, for example, accommodates over 17 percent of world population in a land area that is just 2.4 percent of the world landmass. However, 1,027 (2001 census) millions' share to world GDP is only 1.14 percent. The developed countries regulate 85 percent of world trade and commerce and investment.

The poorer countries have the potential to increase their per capita income. Relative differences will narrow as long as the per capita income growth rate of the developing countries exceeds that of the developed countries. This excess growth is absolutely necessary if the absolute difference was to be narrowed down. An average Indian, for example, lives on real GDP per capita of $3,452 compared with an average American living on $41,890 per annum (2005). Suppose the Indian's income rises by 30 percent in a specified time and the American's income registers only a 5 percent increase in the same time frame. The Indian is now better off relative to his previous income, but is not he worse off compared to an average American?

Figure.1.5 *Income gap between regions*

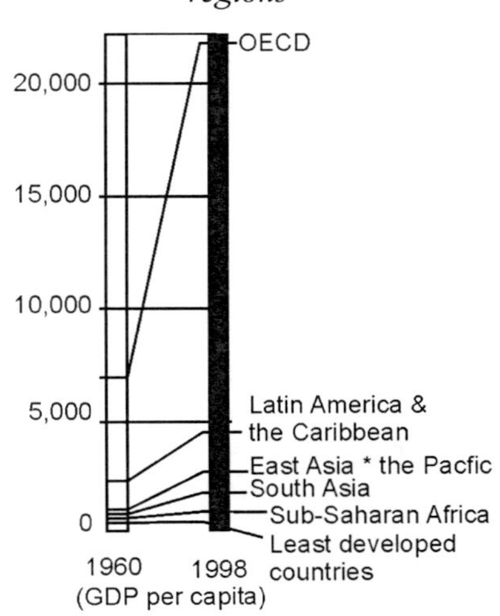

Most developing countries, either by their own realization or by pressure from IMF, World Bank and other international funding agencies, have adopted market economic policy. The open door policy though has geared up growth in spite of profound political instability, has also increased economic inequality. The growth rate in GNP in

India has been hovering around 8 percent in the last few years. It is estimated that about 1 percent growth of population in a developing country may require as much as 4 percent of GNP to maintain the standard of living just at the current level. India's population growth rate (2006) is around 1.5–1.6 percent, and it would require about 6–7 percent of GNP to create new schools, hospitals, houses, food, roads, etc. just for maintaining the present standard of living. Most of the third world countries have population growth rate around 1.9 percent. It is therefore no wonder that income inequalities in these countries are on the rise and a large segment of their population, mostly rural, has to live on subsistence level. Unless growth of population is checked and health conditions improve, these countries cannot generate sufficient surplus that can be used for improving the living condition of their people. The developed countries in spite of their lower GNP growth rate have real savings in GNP because of low population growth rate. This enables the governments of these countries to spend more on improving the quality of *human capital* by extending and improving educational facilities and health care, transportation and communication network, social security, etc.

In 1960, East Asia and the Pacific, South Asia, sub-Saharan Africa and the least developed countries had an average per capita income which was 1/9 to 1/10 of the high income OECD countries. Latin America and the Caribbean fared better had 1/3 to 1/2 of the per capita income of the OECD countries. The sub-Saharan region has worsened its position in 1998; from 1/10 in 1960 they are down to 1/18 of the OECD income in 1998. Despite reductions in the relative differences between many countries and regions, absolute gap in per capita income have increased (Figure 1.5). This is true even for the fastest growing region, East Asia and the Pacific.

The New Technologies: Today's technological transformations are electrifying and more fundamental (the power of a computer chip doubles every 18–24 months with no cost increase, genetic engineering has revolutionalized agriculture) and are driving down costs (the cost of one megabit storage fell from $5,257 in 1970 to $0.17 in 1999). Some of the fruits of this technological revolution are

- Genetically modified seeds offer the hopes of multiplying crop yields with pest- and drought-resistant properties without the need for increase in farm inputs.
- Biotechnological research produced a vaccine for Hepatitis B in 1989. Concerted researches are on to develop vaccines for HIV/AIDS and other diseases endemic in some developing countries.
- Internet, mobile telephones and other information and communication technologies enable people to communicate and obtain information in ways never before possible. Doctors can help and conduct operations on critical patients from the lab in a different continent; traders and businessmen can know exactly the price situation of a commodity all over the world – e-commerce has broken barriers of distance and market information. E-governance has become the *mantra* in modern corporate governance.
- IT industries have enormously increased the potential for service sector. The multinational giants, banks, hospitals, insurance companies and many others have resorted to outsourcing from the low and medium developed countries utilizing their indigenous brain power at a considerably lower remuneration to keep down the cost of their products and stay in cut-throat global competitive market. India's information technology is a glaring example of how the Indian brainpower in developing the most sophisticated software can open up a new avenue for

employment generation and earn foreign currencies for the country. The revenues earned by Indian IT sector jumped from a meager $150 million in 1990 to $4 billion in 1999.

- There is considerable skill shortage in Europe, USA and Japan. The opening up of the global labor market for skilled and technology professionals have helped these and other countries to hire professionals and skilled persons from developing countries like India. USA in 2000 approved 195,000 work visas each year for skilled professionals. Of the 81,000 visas approved between October 1999 and February 2000, 40 percent were for individuals from India and more than half of these were for IT-related occupations. The skyrocketing demand for IT personnel has made top scientists and technologists globally mobile. A secondary effect has surfaced: a new kind of business or 'brain diaspora'. A strong link is built between Silicon Valley and Bangalore on the Indian diaspora in economic network as they invest at home, but facilitating contacts for market access as well.
- IT revolution has given a very low-cost access to information almost about everything one may wish to know. Internet is breaking the barriers of space and geography, making the age-old communication process redundant, making markets more efficient and creating opportunities for creation of altogether a different type of employment. The quantity of information that could be sent over the entire Internet in a month can now be sent over a single cable in a second.

However, the diffusion of technology innovation has been very uneven. About 80 percent of the Internet users are located in the OECD countries. A third of the world population does not have access to electricity though power generation and grid delivery was initiated as early as 1831. The scale of disparity can be seen from Figure 1.6. Technology is also unevenly distributed within countries. India, the home to a world-class technology center in Bangalore, ranks at the lower end of Technology Achievement Index, TAI (0.201 against Finland's 0.744, Korean Republic's 0.666, Singapore's 0.585 and China's 0.299).

Figure.1.6 *Digital divide between regions for electricity consumption and telephone mainlines (adapted from HDR 2001)*

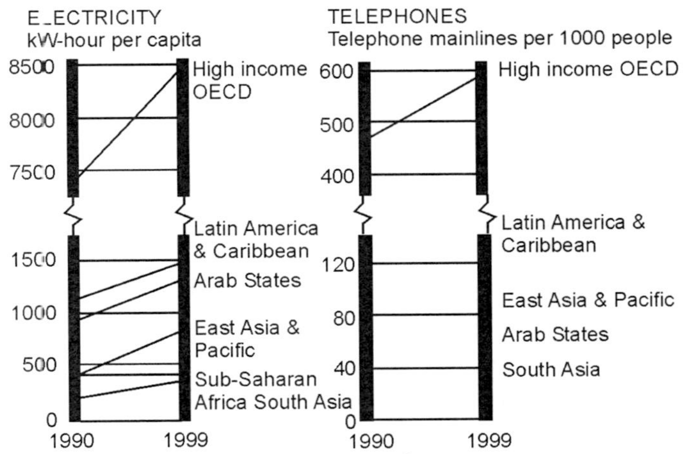

29 OECD countries spent about $520 billion only on R&D in 1998, more than the combined economic output of the world's 30 poorest countries. OECD countries had a share of 91 percent of the 347,000 new patents issued in the year. Although a large sum was invested globally in health research in 1998 ($70 billion), only a meager $300 million was spent for developing vaccines and medicines for HIV/AIDS and another $100 million on malaria research.

Currently, a serious debate is going on in Europe and USA over the use of chemical fertilizers and pesticides and genetically modified (GM) crops. "Go Bio" has been the slogan in the industrially developed countries for some time. Even the cereal and vegetable traders would indicate that bio-fertilizers and bio-pesticides have been used for the items in the display rack along with price stag. The Western consumers do have the luxury of becoming health conscious since they have a comfortable pay packet and do not face food shortages or nutritional deficiencies. Yet the multinational giants are only too keen to widen their market for pesticides and chemical fertilizers in the developing countries. The developed countries would not hesitate to cancel huge consignment of tea (or some other agricultural product) from India or from some developing country because pesticide residue in the product violated the EU norm. The beverage giants who take every possible care for conforming to the strict EU norms in Europe and USA, takes a lackadaisical attitude when selling the same product in the developing countries (the Cola conflict in India).

As regards the intensity of consumption of chemical fertilizers, the advanced countries were far ahead of the developing countries some three decades back. The initiative for modern farming in the developing countries started in the 1960s. People were still hesitant to break away from their traditions. In that initial stage, the farmers had to depend almost entirely on imported seeds, fertilizers and equipments. It did not take the farmers and planners long to realize that to feed teeming millions some alternative to traditional method of cultivation was necessary. Indigenous production of fertilizers, pesticides, tractors etc. are indispensable to cope with the situation. Expansion of irrigation facilities, extensive campaign and extension work, rotation of crops, multiple crop from the same land, establishment of outlets for fertilizers and seeds throughout the country, bank loans on easy terms and indigenous R&D with local wild varieties of crop helped achieve Green Revolution in many developing countries.

Table 1.8 *Diffusion of technology in agriculture, 1970 and 1998*

Region/ Development Category	*Fertilizer consumption (kg per hectare of arable and permanently cropped land)*			*Tractors in use (per hectare of arable and permanently cropped land)*		
	1970	*1998*	*% change*	*1970*	*1998*	*% change*
Developing countries	19.2	100.7	424.5	1.9	7.7	305.3
Least developed	3.4	18.1	432.4	0.6	0.7	16.7
Arab States	16.6	44.9	170.5	2.4	7.4	208.3
East Asia & the Pacific	33.9	193.3	470.2	1.0	5.9	490.0
Latin America & the Caribbean	21.8	71.3	227.1	5.1	9.7	90.2
South Asia	13.6	98.6	625.0	0.7	9.5	1257.1
Sub-Saharan Africa	7.4	13.8	86.49	1.8	1.5	–16.7
OECD	99.8	118.3	18.5	31.4	40.6	29.3
High human development	97.1	114.6	18.0	28.7	40.2	40.7
Medium human development	24.4	118.1	384.0	2.2	8.7	295.5
Low human development	4.5	28.8	540.0	0.5	2.6	420.0

Source: HDR 2001, UNDP

In the last thirty years, use of chemical fertilizers and pesticides has increased many folds in all the developing regions. The advanced countries seem to have reached a saturation point in terms of fertilizer use. East Asia & the Pacific region is far ahead of all other regions in the use of fertilizers, South Asia is catching them fast. In fact, countries in high and medium human development categories are at par in the use of chemical fertilizers and pesticides at the beginning of this millennium. However, the cultivation in developing countries still remains labor intensive, presumably due to huge problem of unemployment. Human and animal energy still dominate agriculture partly because of surplus labor and mostly because the poor cultivators cannot afford to make huge investment in procuring agricultural equipments like tractors. Fragmented and small land holding also are important factors for lesser use of tractors and other modern gadgets in cultivation in the poorer countries.

The developing countries are sure to gain high rewards from new technologies, but they also face greater challenge in managing the risks. The farming community in the developing countries is keen to increase higher yields per hectare land and greater nutritional value from their produces. They are also keen to use less pesticides and chemical fertilizers but for a different reason – costs. The genetically modified crops are welcome for the fact that the GM crops are drought-prone and less susceptible to become pray to insects and pests and for reasons of higher production. They are concerned about their soil and the environment, but increase in production is often their primary concern. At the initiative of the developed countries, a global ban on manufacture of DDT is afoot, but this ban does not take into consideration the fact that this pesticide has a tremendous beneficial effect in malaria control in tropical countries.

Technologies offer particular advantages to developing countries, but they pose greater risks as well. A pragmatic assessment about the potential costs and benefits of the new technology is required. Biotechnological research if not carried out with all the safeguards and monitored by national/international regulatory bodies, it can be turned into weapons if governments or terrorist organizations choose that path. Information and communication technology is already facing a tremendous problem – invasion to privacy and in money laundering and in trade and arms.

Some technologies pose a potential threat to human health. Power plants and automobiles' use of fossil fuels (coal and petroleum) increase suspended particulate matters, sulphur dioxide and other oxides of nitrogen and carbon which may lead to respiratory problems. Nuclear reactors remain the potential source of radiation hazard. Disposal of used-up nuclear fuel remains the headache in all countries.

Some genetically modified foods may introduce new allergens into foods causing problems in some people. Many vaccines and medicines could have some unexpected side effects. Radiation from mobile phones is thought to affect tissues causing cancer. Yet, the mobile telephone service both in developed and developing countries has expanded by leaps and bounds only in over a decade. Its decided advantage over fixed landlines far outweighs the health hazards for which conclusive data are still lacking.

Gene flow from genetically modified corn is more likely in environment where there are many corn-related wild species than in one without such indigenous species. GM organisms could destabilize ecosystems and reduce biodiversity. There is already a hue and cry in India over the use of BT cotton. Use of technologies demands good national policies. The developing countries often lack the type of regulatory measures necessary for use of such technologies often from want of vision and more frequently from lack of fund to maintain such regulatory bodies keeping a close look at things on the ground. USA for example, has three regulatory bodies – Department of Agriculture, Food and Drug Administration, and Environmental Protection Agency – all well funded to act as watchdogs regulating genetically modified organisms. The poor management of the regulators, mostly in the developing countries, led to use of HIV-infected blood transfusions in the 1980s, which is one of the major reasons of spread of HIV. Looking at the prospect, many developing countries are offering better budgetary support for biotechnology research without strengthening the regulatory bodies. Cyber crime has already become a global phenomenon. Portals are being used for display of pornographic materials. The cyber laws often are inadequate to deal with these crimes the nature of which is changing every hour. Even the most advanced countries have no full proof mechanism to deal with such crimes and aberrations.

We are at a point of transition – from the age of steam engine and electricity, which were at the back of the industrial revolution, to network and biotechnology, which are enhancing brain-power. Industrial age was structured around vertically integrated organizations. Digital technology is structured both along vertical and horizontal networks resulting in a very tough competition among all sections of organizations. Foreign Direct Investment (FDI) can give the buoyancy and growth that the developing countries need so urgently, yet this may be a source of major concern for agony lest a similar market slump that happened in Latin American countries and in East Asia in 1997 devastate the economy of the developing countries. The East Asian and the Latin American markets collapsed due to massive inflow of short term capital, followed by sudden reversals. Between 1990 and 1996, the capital inflows exceeded 5 percent of GDP (in some countries it reached between 13 and 20 percent of GDP). The results of such economic crisis are multifaceted – bankruptcies, rocketing interests, rising poverty, surge of unemployment, cut in budgetary provisions in social sector etc.

From a near zero reserve in 1991, the foreign exchange reserve in India increased to over $300 billion in early 2008. It is to be noted that a large chunk of it is due to short-term inflow of capital (FII). Indian industries generated $7.7 billion in 1999, 15 times the level of 1990, and exports from a meager $150 million in 1990 to about $4 billion in 1999. An estimate shows that India's exports could rise to $50 billion by 2008, 30 percent of which will come through IT industries, which would be about 7.5 percent of the GDP. Employment in IT industry is likely to rise from 180,000 in 1998 to about 2.2 million. That would be 8 percent of India's formal employment. This shows how the adoption of new technology can create a radical change in income generation and employment to skilled persons. India needs huge sums for investment in infrastructure sector to make India a destination for FDI. The economists and the government are in dilemma if the foreign exchange reserve should be used for infrastructure development and for debt repayment.

Here is a godsend chance to the developing countries to take advantage of the space created by the developed and industrialized countries to stamp their presence in the global map. The emerging global business model of intermediation, business outsourcing and value chain integration make the developing countries their destination for the reason that at a fractional cost they can buy the services of highly skilled and motivated professionals from these countries. The countries need to concentrate on developing the necessary infrastructure and give the entrepreneurs and the brains of the country a chance to participate in the social and economic transformation of the country. Massive investment is needed in infrastructure – education, health and road and network communications to help them participate in the global economy. They also need to enlarge their domestic demand so that national economy can be sustained event if the export suffers because of global recession for some reason or other.

The donor countries, the IMF and the World Bank often would impose harsh conditions to the recipient countries for utilization of the loans advanced. They often would interfere, indirectly though, in chalking out policies and economic programs of the recipient countries. The accumulated external debt for different regions is shown in Table 1.9. The debt service ratio was as high as 40 percent of the GNP for the developing countries in 1985. It declined by about 4 percentage point in 1997. To repay the loan amount and the interest thereon, many poor countries had to ask for additional loan from these agencies. The debt service ratio as percentage of GDP is on the rise in many countries. Arab countries have successfully scaled it down to 3.5 percent in 1999 from 5.5 in 1990. The position is really alarming in the Latin American & the Caribbean countries, a two-fold rise in debt service ratio to GDP just in 10 years.

Table 1.9 *External debts for countries in different developing regions1985 and 1997*

	*Total (US $ millions)**		*As % of GNP*		*% of exports of goods and services*		*As % of GDP #*	
Region/Dev. Categories	*1985*	*1997*	*1985*	*1997*	*1985*	*1997*	*1990*	*1999*
1	*2*	*3*	*4*	*5*	*6*	*7*	*8*	*9*
All developing countries	**915,690.60**	**2,001,755.00**	**39.9**	**36.0**	**28.7**	**18.4**	**4.0**	**5.8**
Least dev. countries	71,411.00	134,713.20	62.4	92.3	20.5	12.4	2.7	2.8
Sub-Saharan Africa	95,328.20	198,224.20	74.0	66.3	25.2	13.7	3.9	4.6
Arab States	138,570.00	201,196.90	41.6	45.7			5.5	3.5
East Asia	71,281.30	290,787.40	18.0	22.0	18.5	8.6	3.8	5.2
East Asia (excluding China)	54,585.30	144,090.40	59.9	32.9	27.8	8.6		
South-East Asia & the Pacific	107,596.70	356,228.20	56.2	61.3	30.5	14.7		
South Asia	68,024.10	161,295.80	15.8	25.7	15.8	19.9	2.6	2.8
South Asia (excluding India)	27,073.40	66,891.00	12.8	26.8	10.9	20.5		
Latin America & Caribbean	408,877.70	702,817.10	58.3	33.9	38	35.6	4.0	8.1
China	16,596.00	146,697.00	5.5	16.6	8.3	8.6	2.0	2.1
India	40,.950.70	94,404.20	19.2	24.9	22.7	19.6	2.6	2.3

* *HDR 1999*, # 2001, UNDP

To begin with, a poor country has but only a few options to participate in the global IT market. Skill matters more than ever in this changing scenario. The developing countries just cannot import knowledge, technologies and equipments at their will. If they do they will have to pay heavy price for it as per the tighter *intellectual property right* (Trade-related Aspects of Intellectual Property Rights, TRIPS). They have to identify such technologies that have potential benefit for their countries. These again need to be continuously upgraded to remain competitive in the global market.

The less developed countries took only about 50 years to bring down their mortality level close to the level observed in developed regions. They have taken the advantage of medical research and discoveries of broad-spectrum antibiotics and life-saving drugs developed in the first world countries to bring down their CDR. They have used the 'late comer's advantage' to bring down mortality drastically. But controlling fertility has something to do with education, social awareness, life style, prejudices and superstitions, value system and nature of occupation. The model followed in the West in controlling fertility cannot be applied in the less developed countries. International pressure on these countries to develop a low birth regime population program has been the major factor behind drop in their fertility level. Improvement in IMR, child and mother health care, better health infrastructure and spread of education can only accelerate the process in democratic set up.

WHO, UN and other international bodies dealing with public health can take the credit of controlling many of the dreaded diseases that took heavy tolls on human lives earlier. But now a more dreaded disease HIV/AIDS may have a devastating effect on all our efforts to improve the expectation of life at all ages. Every 40 people out 100,000 world population have contracted HIV/AIDS infection. The worst affected region is sub-Saharan Africa. The Human Development Report 1999 shows 111 out of every 100,000 people in the region have contracted AIDS. The industrialized countries are not far behind them (99/100,000). Sixteen countries, mostly from sub-Saharan Africa, have experienced reversal in human development due to HIV/AIDS pandemic. Quite a few countries experienced decline in expectation of life at birth between 1970 and 1997 (Uganda, Zambia, Zimbabwe, Bulgaria, Latvia, Russian Federation, for example). While advances in health care and technology have increased life spans in the last century on an average by 20 years worldwide, the AIDS epidemic has caused life expectancy in some African countries to plummet in recent years. In Botswana, life expectancy has fallen from 62 years in 1990 to 44 years in 1998. In Zimbabwe it has fallen from 61 years in 1993 to 49 years in 2000. HIV/AIDS infection is presumed to be the principle reason behind this decline in expectation of life. Some of the sub-Saharan African and South Asian countries are also experiencing rise in tuberculosis (121/100,000 and 98/100,000 respectively). South Asian countries have large proportion of infants with low birth weight (32 percent). Infant mortality is still alarmingly high in sub-Saharan Africa (IMR 107) and South Asia (IMR 69).

1.5 Causes of Population Explosion – Increasing Birth Rate or Decreasing Death Rate?

It is often argued that the unprecedented growth of population in the twentieth century has been due to high birth rate. We do not have any evidence that could suggest that reproductive capacity of man has increased. On the contrary, evidences are plentiful that birth rate has been declining, slowly though. Migration could be a fact behind growth of population in a particular region, but it has nothing to do with the world population growth. So to understand the cause of population growth, we have to analyze one of the key demographic variables – *mortality*. It is the firm conviction of the population scientists that the answer to population growth lays in downward movement of death rate.

Declining death rate in the twentieth century was principally due to incredible improvement in medical sciences and spread out of public health services. The decline in death rate in the earlier centuries was due to a completely different set of reasons. The advancement in agricultural and industrial production and vast improvement in the public distribution system and environmental sanitation played a major role in upgrading our living standard. Due to vastly expanded transportation network, food and other consumer goods could reach the end users fast. Over and above this, there are a few epoch making discoveries in medical sciences that radically changed the concept of health management. Combined together these prevented untimely deaths, gave enough weapons to fight against most diseases, and better public health awareness.

Through most of the period of human civilization, man had to fight constantly against climatic adversity, the deadly animals, hunger and diseases. Most people died early, long before reaching the reproductive age. In this uneven struggle those who survived suffered from malnutrition and contracted to many types of diseases making them half dead. In the given circumstances there was only one motto before them – survival – multiply as fast as one could to make up the losses due to death. If the birth rate was not maintained at the biological limit, the human species could have disappeared from the earth long back.

The role of medical science is still debated in controlling death rate. Prior to nineteenth century, medicines and health practices seem to have little effect in arresting high death rate. Death rates definitely started to decline steadily long before the medical sciences developed. It was improvement in the supply line and distribution system, improvement in agricultural and industrial productivity, better transport facilities, cheap power and better housing facilities that were at the root of decline in death rate.

Decreasing birth rate has been associated with modernization of our social system and economy. Initially, decreasing death rate had practically no influence on birth rate. While death rate continued to dip low, birth rate remained almost unchanged. Only when there were visible signs of improvement in expectation of life at birth that death rate started to have an impact on birth rate. While death rate has declined generally very fast all over the world, birth rate has declined only very slowly.

In the remote past it was a historical necessity to have very high birth rate to supply manpower to fight against all kinds of adversaries. Our traditional institutions (religion), the social systems and values encouraged high reproduction. In the Hindu Puranic literature the mother of a large number of children earned commendation from all (even a few decades back the elderly people used to bless the newly wed bride by saying 'have a long life and God bless you with hundred children'). The Bible also clearly said "Be fruitful and multiply". Birth limitation was against the social order. If the social tradition encourages more children in a family, birth rate cannot but be high. In such social systems, whenever death rate falls, the population growth shows an upward trend. The same thing has happened in Europe, is still happening in many of the developing countries.

Max Weber, founding father of modern sociology, had analyzed the close relationship between religious doctrines and economic institutions and had shown how the religious values have helped propagate Capitalism. In his widely read and discussed book *The Protestant Ethic and the Spirit of Capitalism*, Weber had shown that the values preached in modern Capitalism owe much to Protestant ethics. Hard labor, self-employment, discipline, savings, faculty of judgment, unrestricted competition and personal initiative are key to progress of Capitalism. These qualities are highly praised in Protestant doctrines. The wide spread acceptance of this religious doctrine created a favorable ground for acceptance of a social and economic order that are rooted in private enterprise and individual ownership and non-stop production process. There is a saying that grass will grow even if the farmer sleeps; but the wheel of the machine would soon stop if it were not attended by a skilled labor. Capitalists have used this dictum in their favor by propagating the message that God's blessings would be showered on them who look after them well.

The change in economic condition asked man to review the necessity of numbers in the production process. In this competitive individual ownership structure of industries, a large family was inept to the growing demands of the economy. This realization led people to gradually adopt a small family norm. In the changed economic order children were not considered as 'production durable'. In traditional agriculture-based economy, wealth flow was from child to parents since traditional occupations did not require any specialized training. As a result, children at the age of 10–12 years are found actively participating in cultivation and other traditional jobs along with the elderly members of the family. Direct or indirect employment began early in their childhood.

Modern industries demand the services of educated and skilled workers. To meet this demand, parents have to bear the cost of education and training for a long period. After completion of education and training, these children often would find their workplace far away from their ancestral homes. There was not much of a time gap between entry into gainful occupation and marriage. As a result, the child has very little to contribute to his root family after meeting the obligations to his own family. Parents today spend a lot of money and labor on rearing and education of their children and that too over a considerable period. In return, parents receive a very small or no financial return from their children in this changed economic scenario. In industrial economy, wealth flows from parents to children. That is, social structure and order and economic production systems are organically related. This dependent relation prescribes adoption of small family norm – resulting in curtailment of birth rate.

1.6 Old and New Balance between Birth and Death Rates

Population scientists have attempted to analyze historical demographic data of the European countries, and countries peopled by persons of European origin, keeping an eye on their education, economy and technological advancement. The picture of the growth of population in these countries is quite transparent. In the remote past, the population grew very slowly, that is, birth and death rates were closely similar. This balance or equilibrium in the two rates has come back again in these developed countries. The early equilibrium state lasted for hundreds and thousands of years. Between these two states of equilibrium, in the perspective of the age of human civilization, which is trivially small, the population has expanded very fast. If this very short duration of the intermediate stage is eliminated from the picture, we find that the natural increases due to excess of birth over death in these two stages are almost similar. The state of balance observed in the two extreme ends of the history of human population on earth has been referred to as **old balance** and **new balance** respectively. In the former situation, high birth and death rates compensated the effect of either, resulting in a near *zero growth situation*. The same zero growth situations are again observed in the *new balance situation*, but this time low birth rate compensating the effect of low death rate. Figure 1.7 shows how the developed countries passed from a stage of 'old balance' (A) to the stage of 'new balance' (C) through the period of 'transition' (B). In stage B, death rates declined fast, birth rate only slowly. The shaded portion of the graph indicates how the population has grown between the two stages of equilibrium.

Figure.1.7 *From 'old balance' to 'new balance'*

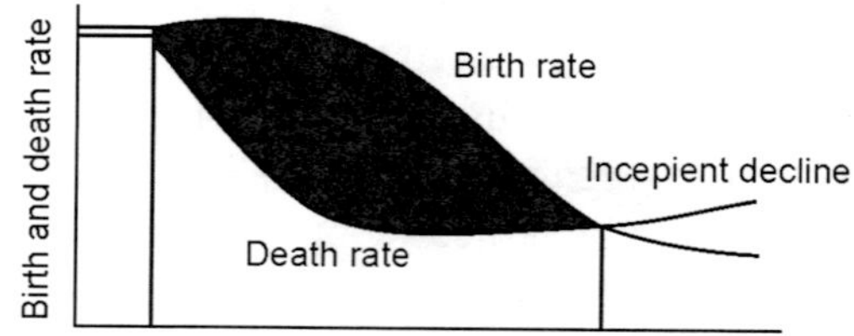

The 'old balance' overwhelmingly dominated the history of human population. The inhospitable natural environment did not support life system.

Death rate was so high and life span so small that survival of the species was seriously at stake. The mothers in 'old balance' had to bear child almost every year since most children would not survive beyond a few days or weeks. Only a very few of those who survived would reach adulthood and be able to reproduce. The mothers remained too busy to carry and rear children, fighting lost battles against dreaded diseases and eternal mourning. Malnutrition, hunger and struggle for a handful of food were the fateful reality of these early men and women. For any venture for starting an industry requires a lot of planning, discipline and steady supply of skilful workers. When no body knew if he or she would survive the next day or the next week, the question of taking programs for imparting education and specialized training, a must condition for running a machine, did not arise. The wheels cannot run without expert attendance. There was no guarantee that the person attending the machine would be present the next day in good health. Starting educational institutions for the common man was also unpragmatic since most of the children enrolled would die before they could complete their school education. To incur huge expenditure to see a boy or girl completes a course was totally unrealistic. The government and the family today invest large sums for getting a doctor or engineer or even a clerk. In the 'old balance' stage, this investment would have been several thousand times the present level of expenditure.

In the 'new balance' stage, these considerations have no role at all. Health of individuals has become a dependable asset in most countries. Human resource is plentiful in the 'new balance' stage. There is no dearth of skill, no uncertainty about the presence of persons linked to a machine. Today one can plan, 50 or 100 years ahead, for complex social, economic and technological changes.

In the 'old balance' stage, the social and economic thoughts revolved round a handful of people. Making provisions even for this handful of people were difficult. We definitely are worried about the size of human population of today, more specifically of tomorrow. We are worried for fast running down of natural resources; yet we are confident that human mind will definitely apply to find a solution to the problems that might emerge.

Death rates have declined, probably to nearly a level of biological limit in many countries. Most dreaded diseases have either been eliminated or preventive measures discovered to contain them. Birth rate too is falling progressively. We have no doubt whatsoever that the current and the future healthy adults would take charge of the fast changing social, economic and technological set-up. Agricultural and industrial productions have increased by leaps and bounds. Unless the total system breaks down due to some natural or man-made disaster, the wheels of the machine will not stop. The proportion of children and persons suffering from malnutrition and ill health in the total population is coming down gradually. The trend probably is irreversible.

The stage of 'new balance' appeared in the West sometime after the Industrial Revolution. Demographers believe that without modernization of agricultural and industrial sectors no country can ensure a reasonably good lifestyle for its people. They also believe that the more we take the benefits of sc-tech innovations to shape our personal social life, the faster we will advance towards this stage of 'new balance'. The more the people move up from the poverty line, the more they would adapt to the benefits of sc-tech changes. Essentials for modest living would be within their reach.

Death rate compared to birth rate declined much faster. In the intervening stage, the population expanded slowly at the beginning and then rapidly. The impact of this growth was different for different countries. The expanded population was a blessing for countries that were rich in natural resources and space but deficient in numbers to utilize their resources. Expansion of population boosted agricultural and industrial production; the surpluses were exported to earn foreign exchanges and better technology; the increased defense and striking power of the country earned a sense of awe and admiration from others. The stable and healthy economy encouraged more investment in R&D, development of new industries and upgrading technological know-how.

Traditional social values received a heavy jolt as industrialization took a steady hold in our economy. The emergence of nuclear families shook many of our traditional ideas and beliefs. Agricultural lands have been fragmented; pressure on land has been mounting. Rural employment is getting smaller and smaller. The social and economic environment was just the right type that encouraged heavy out migration (rural to urban).

1.7 Demographic Transition Theory

In the late twenties of the last century, Warren Thompson described a theory that relates the growth of population to the health of economy the population was passing through. This in the course of time came to be known as Demographic Transition Theory. Though based on historical data, the simplicity of its structure enables a pragmatic and sensible analysis of changes in birth and death rates in a population. Thomson spoke about it in 1929; C.P. Blacker discussed it in greater detail in 1947. However, neither Thomson nor Blacker is given the credit of founding the theory since none of them tried to explain why birth rates change. Frank Notestein in 1945 tried to explain why change in birth rates differs from one country to another. He drew our attention how religious preaching, moral codes, social laws and regulations, education, customs, structure of family etc. in the underdeveloped countries encourage high birth rate. To avert decline in population as a result of high death rate, high birth rate was necessary under the prevailing social systems. The religious and social strictures started loosing relevance as death rates started to fall. The strictures against birth control were either lifted or became dysfunctional as certainty about better health and long life gradually became a reality. Birth rates started to fall even in orthodox societies.

If negative factors were responsible for pulling down birth rates in the developing countries, a cluster of positive factors brought down birth rates in the industrially developed countries. Notestein drew attention to such issues as fast enlargement of urban areas, the increasing and ever changing character of urban polity, evolution of an urban-centric culture in which the joint/extended family system lost much of its relevance. High personal aspiration was at the heart of this urban-centric culture. Large families are not only expensive, they act as obstacle to go beyond the limits of traditional beliefs and sentiments. Notestein wrote another article in 1953 where he asserted that the urban-centric industrial culture was at the root of declining birth rate. The increased use of technology-driven economy provided opportunity for a better standard of living and made life extremely fast and competitive. Notestein argued that high birth rate in underdeveloped countries were due to three fundamental reasons – *high death rate, lack of enough opportunity to accomplish one's aspirations and the economic value of children.* With modernization and lowered death rate, these determinants for continuation of high birth rate gradually lost relevance.

There is a persistent trend in demographic transition theory writings which claims that *rationality* comes only with industrial, urban society, and a related strain that regards traditional agrarian societies as essentially brutish and superstitious. The assumption of pre-transitional irrationality in the theory enters through references to cultural lags in making fertility adjustments to the emerging new urban and industrial conditions. Notestein in 1945 argued that the supports for high fertility "change only gradually and in response to the strongest stimulation" and described "a population increasingly freed from older taboos and increasingly willing to solve problems rather than accept them". The belief that increasing rationality with modernization still is an integral part of the transition theory has also been demonstrated in the United Nations Population Studies. We quote from the publication:

> The past record in the more developed countries demonstrates ... [a] deliberate regulation of fertility [which] defies age-old custom.... A high frequency of childbirth ... was necessary for the continuation and security of families and this found emphatically strong support in the prevailing values and customs. In many cultures ... children provided a much needed insurance against destitution in old age. Associated with such cultural norms has been the regard for women in their seemingly principal function as bearers and rearers of children, limiting thereby their participation in economic and social roles held to be mainly the prerogative of men.

Summing up, the transition theory states: Industrialization brings down death rates first in all countries, birth rates decline much later through prevention of death and adoption of technology for birth control. There is always a time gap between drops in death and birth rates. Because of this time lag, the population expands. Before the transition begins, the population remains almost stationary due to very high birth and death rates. Some essential similarities in social and economic setting are observed in all developing countries – pressure of population, low productivity, excessive dependence on agriculture, low level and backdated technology, poor communication and transportation network, ambivalence to public health and sanitation, poor health infrastructure, dearth of preventive medicine, and high birth and death rates. Nutritional deficiency and inadequate food supply not only are causes of high death rate and morbidity, often are responsible for fluctuation in population growth rates. In most non-industrialized countries the social fabric is generally conducive to high birth rate. These countries have a huge surplus labor. Due to lack of industrial growth these labors swarm around agriculture. Agricultural production though increases, a large segment of the labor force are denied full-time employment. Even though price of commodities escalate, price of labor often sinks. A large proportion of the masses therefore have to live below the poverty line.

Thomson and Notestein have observed four stages of transition: A. High birth and death rates, B. High birth rate but declining death rate, C. Declining birth and death rates, D. Very low death rate but larger than birth rate.

Death Rate	Birth rate	
	High	Low
High	+ + (A)	+ – (D)
Low	– + (B)	– – (C)

Stage D is a very temporary phase since it creates a condition conducive to depopulation. The problem that emerges from this is avoided often by allowing immigration. The production process is maintained at the level before depopulation started with the help of these immigrants. The government encourages birth, often providing incentives for every additional child to couples. The birth rate is restored to such a level as would help counter the chances of depopulation. Many European countries faced this problem in the thirties of the last century. In the nineties some Scandinavian countries faced this problem. Many countries would be in stage D in near future.

The first three stages (A, B and C) actually constitute the demographic transition – *high potential growth, transitional growth and incipient decline.* This three-tier classification can be looked from a different perspective:

1. Description of historical growth of population in a time perspective;
2. Classification of population growth profile for countries all over the world;
3. The attempted explanation for the changes in the growth of population;
4. Prediction of the types of changes likely to happen in the underdeveloped and developing countries in the coming years, the order in which they will approach the stage C.

High Potential Growth: The first stage depicted in the transition theory is similar to 'Old balance' we discussed earlier. The countries, which in the recent past were in this stage, were mostly dominated by tribal population, still adhering to old traditions and culture. Nearly totally dependent on agriculture, these countries had very high birth and death rates. Malnutrition and lack of health awareness created conditions favorable for high death rate, especially infant and child mortality. They lacked the skill and know-how needed to tackle epidemic, famine, war and natural calamity. When things were favorable – good harvest, no epidemic, no war and no natural disaster – the population grew. The possibility of a high growth is embedded in the 'Old balance' itself.

Many of the Asian and African countries were in this stage even a few decades back. Presently, death rates have declined considerably in these countries and the population is growing fast. Of course a few countries even now have space for growth of population since population density is still low in spite of their high growth rates. The picture is quite gloomy in most other countries. Currently, most of these countries have moved to the next stage.

Transitional Growth: The enormous potential energy embedded in 'Old balance' stage once freed, the population reaches the second stage – 'Transitional growth'. The countries where the death rates started to decline but birth rates continued at the same level or declining only slowly compared to the decline in death rate, such countries already have entered the second stage of transition. The changes leading to this stage in Europe were initiated in the Agricultural Revolution of the 18th century. The increased availability of food, improvement in transportation facilities and public distribution system, health awareness and supply of safe drinking water are some of the key factors responsible for the check in death rates, especially children, in these countries. Continuation of high birth rate (or slow decline) was often due to inertia and faith in traditional values. The decline of death rate is basically a physical phenomenon, while birth, though a physical phenomenon, is socially and culturally determined. The *cultural lag* induces considerable gap between death and birth rate. In the transition period, the yearly natural increase could be 2–3 percent or even higher. For reasons of fast growth of population, this period is often called the stage of **population explosion.**

Before the end of the twentieth century, most countries were in this stage. The countries where death rates could be contained very effectively but not much progress was made in curtailing birth rate, their populations really exploded. This was observed in many of the Latin American, South European, East and South Asian countries and Africa. This explosive growth may be seen as a prelude to industrialization and urbanization.

Most European countries entered stage B long before others. Europe passed through stage two before the medical advances of the mid-20th century. Reduction of mortality in Europe were mostly through improvements in water supply, sewerage, food handling, and general personal hygiene following the lead from growing scientific knowledge of the causes of diseases and the improved education and social status of mothers.

In fact, most of the countries in Europe, North America, Oceania and Japan are already in the third stage or leaving it. The populations in these countries are growing at 0.5 percent per annum or even less. Some countries in the second stage are either still growing fast or already have reached a growth level from where a steady fall is expected. Although the Northern and Western European countries are pioneers in controlling these vital rates, the countries in the developing countries are taking far less time to pass through the stages of population transition compared to that in the developed regions. The medical science, transport and communication network and technology were still embryonic when the developed countries put on their thought on population control.

Incipient Decline: The stages of population transition can be compared with the behavior of a winded spring. The first stage of population growth (A) is like a spring fully winded. The parallel to the second stage of population growth is the behavior of the spiral spring when the brake is suddenly released. The spring expands violently. When the pressure is fully released, the spring occupies a very large space. This state can be compared with the third stage of transition. The spring fully compressed has enormous *potential energy*. By releasing the pressure, the potential energy is converted into kinetic energy, expanding the size of the spring. The spring generally expands to a level a little more than it is due. As a result, the expansion is followed by a small compression and this expansion-contraction continues for some time till all the potential energy is fully expended.

The developed countries already have achieved a balance between birth and death rate (New balance). In the 'Old balance' stage, the population was small and was stationary but with a high potential for expansion. In the third stage the population again is stationary, but the size is very large and all the potential energy expended. Both birth and death rates are nearly at their biological minimum. The population in the third stage is due to the expansion it experienced during the second stage. In some of the countries birth rates went below death rates resulting in negative growth. But this is only a temporary phase, comparable to the oscillating compression-expansion phase of a spring. That will be of a very short duration. Sooner or later the population will come back to the third stage. Theoretically, the fourth stage (D) is possible. It is possible to bring fertility down to zero, but the same cannot happen to mortality.

Causes of rapid decline in mortality are almost the same in all developing countries (control of communicable and parasitic diseases). But the same cannot be said about decline in birth rate. Different countries adopt different means to control birth. Generalization in this regard is not feasible.

The countries that are already in the third stage show certain common characteristics – full literacy, high productivity and stable economy, very high standard of living, and immigrant population is fast increasing since Total Fertility Rates (TFR) in these countries are already under replacement level. Degenerative and non-communicable diseases had been the major taker-of-life. Parasitic and infectious diseases and diseases related to malnutrition and childbirth still dominate in many developing countries.

Some theorists consider that a *fifth stage* is needed to represent countries that have undergone the economic transition from manufacturing based industries into service and information based industries called *deindustrialization*. Countries such as Germany, Italy, Spain, Portugal, Greece, UK and most notably Japan, whose populations are now reproducing well below replacement levels – are not producing enough children to replace their parents' generation. China, South Korea,

Hong Kong, Singapore, Thailand and Cuba also show TFR below replacement level, but they are not showing a fall in population yet since their populations are relatively young due to strong growth in the recent past.

However, many countries that now have *sub-replacement fertility*[1] did not reach this stage gradually but rather suddenly as a result of economic crisis brought about by the post-communist transition in the late 1980s and the 1990s. Examples include Russia, Ukraine, and the Baltic states. The population in these countries is falling due to fertility decline, emigration and, particularly in Russia, increased male mortality. The death rates are increasing due to *diseases of wealth* such as obesity, causing a gradual fall in population in addition to ageing.

Donald Bogue has used a slightly different nomenclature for the stages of demographic transition. He calls stage 1 as *Pre-transitional stage*, stage 2 *Transitional* and stage 3 as *Post-transitional*. Bogue, however, has suggested a finer sub-division of stage 2.

2a. *Early transitional*. Death rate is falling; birth rate continues to be high. Since health of mothers shows signs of improvement, birth rate may increase marginally. The population starts to grow slowly.

2b. *Mid-transitional*. Both birth and death rates are declining but the former is way behind the latter. Population growth accelerates.

2c. *Late transitional*. Both birth and death rates have declined considerably though birth rate is still higher than death rate. Decline in death rate has been slowed down. A large proportion of the population has adopted birth control practices. Population growth rate has been slowed down and the population is likely to reach a zero growth rate soon.

Bogue has analyzed the growth of world population and suggested some indexes associated with the two extreme ends of transition. In one extreme were the countries that experienced CBR and CDR nearly at their biological limits (55 per thousand), General Fertility Rate (GFR) at around 235 and TFR at 7500 per 1,000 women in reproductive age. In the other extreme are countries where birth rate is down to around 15 or even less, death rate around 10, GFR 60 and TFR around 2200. The position in respect to demographic transition of a country can be understood with reference to these two sets of indexes. A graphic picture of the nature of change experienced between 1980 and 2000 by the developed and developing countries are shown in Figure 1.8.

Van Nort after historical analysis of demographic transition came to certain conclusions, which are stated under:

> From a high fertility to low fertility regime can be looked as a transformation from *biological model of fertility* to *economic model of fertility*. The biological model of fertility epitomizes a socio-economic scenario where fertility is determined primarily by biological factors, the social and psychological attributes of a country play only a nominal role. The economic model of fertility espouses a socio-economic fabric in which the fertility responds to a market that is committed to a pragmatic distribution of amassed resources, primarily economic. The complex psychological and social state, symbolic of a typical city-centric industrial culture, influence all issues related to fertility. It is hypothesized that changeover from a biological model to economic model of fertility brings down the fertility level of a nation slowly from its biological limits. The more a person's personal thoughts and his occupation solicit

1 Sub-replacement fertility is a TFR that is not high enough to replace an area's population. In developed countries sub-replacement fertility is below 2.1 children per woman's life time, but it could be as high as 3.3 in some developing countries because of higher mortality rates. Taken globally, the TFR at replacement is 2.33 children per woman, which includes two children to replace the parents, with a third of a child extra to make up for the different sex ratio at birth and early mortality prior to the end of their fertile life.

Figure.1.8 *Change in birth and death rates in developed and developing countries*

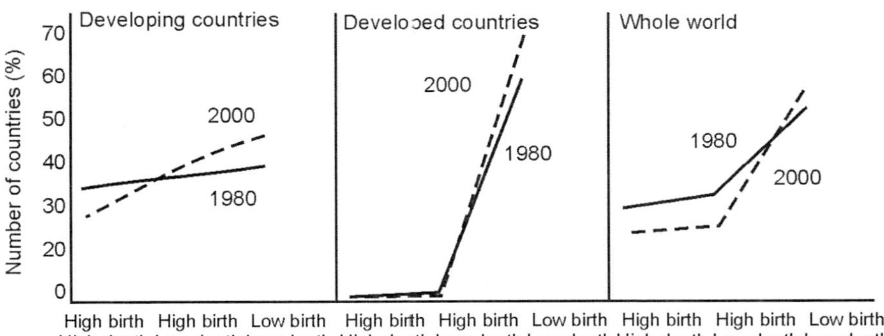

social approval, the more it is likely that many of his personal decisions (giving birth to a baby is primarily a personal decision) would be taken against a broader perspective.

This theorization dealing with changeover from a high-fertility-high-mortality regime to a low-fertility-low-mortality regime would point to operation of geographical and social and economic developmental forces.

Birth and death rates differentiated by geographical regions: Most of the European countries, North America, Australia and New Zealand, Japan and Russia are either have completed the transition or are close to the new balance stage. Birth rates in these countries are 15 or lower, very high life expectancy at birth (over 77 years) and annual growth rate less than 0.5 percent. Many of these countries' growth rates are almost zero (some even negative) or a low stationary growth rate. Even some Latin American countries like Uruguay, Argentina and Chile, experiencing moderate climatic condition, have low fertility. In tropical America (Middle and South America), birth rates still are high, death rates low to medium high.

Both in East and Southeast Asia birth rates are pretty high (CBR around 28). African nations showed very high fertility even in the eighties of the last century (around 43), which continues to be high in the beginning of this century, around 38–39; annual growth rate around 2.7 percent. Arab countries have birth rates around 34 with death rates at 10 or less.

Social and economic development: Apart from geographical differentiation, the few other factors that have a large say in death and fertility issues are:

1. All industrially developed countries have very low mortality. Further decline from the level already achieved may not be possible.
2. The vaccines and other preventive medicines against small pox, plague, tuberculosis, malaria etc. and worldwide campaign against these killer diseases have paid rich dividends. Asian, African and Latin American countries have greatly benefitted by this health campaign and the preventive medicines developed in the West.
3. Mortality will decline further, but only slowly. The pace of decline will be dependent upon the state of social and economic development in the country. The deterrent to faster decline in death rate in South Asia and Africa lies in shortage in food, poverty, superstition and lack of education.
4. There appears to exist an inverse relation between industrialization and fertility. All industrialized countries have low mortality. But that cannot be said about fertility as well.

Industrialization, urbanization, modernization or spread of education cannot singly or jointly fully explain fertility situation in a country. One can quite confidently point out to direct and indirect causes of mortality decline. More or less the same methods are used to contain diseases and curtail mortality all over the world. But time, space, geography and culture often have a say on controlling birth rate. Not all the methods are equally good for birth control for all populations. The results of abortion and sterilization are far surer than oral contraceptives or other methods of control of birth.

There is no doubt that birth control measures are far more effective in the developed countries than in the developing countries. The developed countries have responded to the slogan: "Small family is a happy family". Why is the response from the developing countries not that encouraging? The population scientists have discussed the problem time and again, but have failed to come to a definite answer. The problem of population explosion could have been tackled more effectively had one or few reasons for ambivalence to birth control were established. But one thing is very clear: key to birth control lies in child and infant mortality.

Coale has attempted to uncover the reasons behind adoption of "small family norm" in the developed countries.

- The sharp decline in general death rate and infant and child mortality in particular has assured a long life for everyone. This has assured people that not many births are really needed to achieve a desired family size.
- The modern industrial economy vis-à-vis agricultural economy does not regard children as economic assets to a family. International Labor Organization (ILO) and World Trade Organization (WTO) have proclaimed that child labor (14 years or below) must be stopped in all countries. Most countries have adopted policies to make education for all children below 14 year compulsory.
- With modernization of social and economic environment the social status of women has improved. They are getting education and accepting occupational career. This has changed status of women – their education and economic freedom go against unrestricted reproduction.
- In a predominantly agricultural economy, the necessity of formal education is less direct. In this family background the traditional ideas and customs continue to give direction to our thought process. In the industrialized urban culture the traditional social and religious values are fast loosing their significance. A more pragmatic attitude, irrespective of cultural traditions and practices, dominates the city-centric man.

Second Demographic Transition

The end point of the "classical" or first demographic transition (FDT) was supposed to be a stationary and stable population corresponding with replacement fertility, zero population growth, and life expectancies higher than 70 years. As there would be an ultimate balance between deaths and births, there would be no "demographic" need for sustained immigration. Moreover, households in all parts of the world would converge toward the nuclear and conjugal types, composed of couples and their offspring.

Since the middle of the last century, developed countries have been going through further demographic changes. The degree of commonality of these changes has led some demographers to think these countries having been going through what they term the *Second Demographic*

Transition (SDT). SDT sees no such equilibrium as the end-point. New developments bring sustained sub-replacement fertility, a multitude of living arrangements other than marriage, postponement of marriage and parenthood, disconnection between marriage and procreation, and no stationary population. The adoption of modern contraception, especially the pill, has played a catalytic role, giving individuals the possibility to almost completely control their reproduction. In consequence, the populations would face declining sizes if not complemented by new migrants (i.e. replacement migration), and they will also be much older than envisaged by the FDT as a result of lower fertility and additional gains in longevity. Migration streams will not be capable of stopping aging, but only stabilize population sizes. Nonetheless, the outcome is still the further growth of 'multicultural societies'. On the whole, the SDT brings new social challenges, including those associated with further aging, integration of immigrants and other cultures, less stability of households, and high levels of poverty or exclusion among certain household types (single member family, lone mothers).

The idea of this distinct phase stems directly from Philippe Ariès's analysis of the history of childhood (1962) and his subsequent article, "Two Successive Motivations for Low Fertility" (1980). In his view, during the FDT, the decline in fertility was "unleashed by an enormous sentimental and financial investment in the child." Ariès refers to this as the "Child-king era," and the fertility transition was carried by an altruistic investment in child quality. This motivation is no longer the dominant one. Within the SDT, the motivation for parenthood is adult self-realization, and the choice for just one particular lifestyle in competition with several others. The altruistic element focusing on offspring has weakened and the adult dyadic relationship has gained prominence instead.

The second element that sparked the SDT-theory was the conviction that the *cyclical fertility theory* as formulated by Richard Easterlin would no longer hold and that sub-replacement fertility was to become a structural, long term feature in Western populations. In Easterlin's hypothesis, small cohorts would have better employment opportunities and hence earlier marriage and higher fertility, whereas large cohorts would have worse economic life chances and display the opposite demographic responses. The cyclical reinforcement then stems from large cohorts of parents giving birth to small cohorts of children and vice versa. The SDT does not expect cyclical effects that would be strong enough to determine the fertility trend. Rather, it advances that other effects, both economic and cultural, have an overriding capacity in conditioning these trends.

The third element that conditioned the SDT theory is the major role given to the ideational factor and to the dynamics of cultural shift. The SDT theory fully recognizes the effects of macro-level structural changes and of micro-level economic calculus. As such it is not at odds with the core arguments of neo-classic economic reasoning. The SDT view does not consider these explanations as "sufficient" but merely as "non-redundant". By the same token, the cultural factors involved are "non redundant" elements and not "sufficient ones". The SDT is therefore an "overarching" theory that spans both economic and sociological reasoning. And it does not do so by taking value orientations as endogenous or by considering culture as a form of addiction, but by treating ideational changes as exogenous influences that add stability to trends over and beyond economic fluctuations. The SDT furthermore links cultural shifts to dynamic processes of cohort succession, and to a recursive model of value-based selection and individual values reorientation as a function of paths followed during the life course.

Finally, a major stepping stone of the SDT theory has been Maslow's theory of changing needs (1954). As populations become wealthier and more educated, the attention shifts away from needs associated with survival, security and solidarity. Instead greater weight is attached to individual self-realization, recognition, grassroots democracy and expressive work and education values. The SDT theory is therefore closely related to Ron Inglehart's concept of "post-materialism" and its growing importance in political development. The direct consequence of this is also that the SDT predicts that the typical demographic outcomes (sustained sub-replacement fertility, growth of alternative living arrangements) are likely to emerge also in non-western societies that equally develop in the direction of capitalist economies, with multi-level democratic institutions, and greater accentuation of Maslowian "higher order needs".

Third Demographic Transition

David Coleman (2006) after analyzing the past fertility, mortality and behavioral changes in some of the industrialized countries is of the opinion that these countries are now experiencing a set of population processes that amount to a *Third Demographic Transition* (TDT). The key features of these countries are persistent low fertility and high immigration. He writes,

> The processes...resulting from low fertility combined with high immigration, are significant because they are changing the composition of national populations and thereby the culture, physical appearance, social experiences, and self-perceived identity of the inhabitants of European nations.

Coleman remarks, if these processes persist, it would bring some permanent changes in these countries, and this whole set of transformation may lead to a *Third Demographic Transition*. According to this theory, any population with below replacement level fertility where, through net immigration, the size of the population is either maintained at a constant level or increases, will eventually be transformed until that population is predominantly and eventually entirely of immigrant origin. The original population has been displaced. Furthermore, even if the fertility of immigrant populations, initially high, falls to the level of the host population, this will not ultimately prevent this replacement. Coleman also notes that future immigration from poor countries will be supported by chain migration, and by the rights of immigrants currently accepted by host countries, notably post-World War Two human rights conventions. Immigration, he writes, is facilitated by

> ...[T]he transformation of the host societies' institutions, culture, language, and politics into forms more conducive to continued migration, so that in some respects they come to resemble more closely those of the sending countries.

From projections of ethnic/racial composition of populations from some of the countries, he showed that proportion of people of 'foreign origin' in many of these countries could go up above 20 percent before 2050. Further change will continue beyond 2050. Coleman believes that there would be a massive transformation of ethnic or racial composition for Europe and elsewhere.

Population statistics supports what Coleman has said about quantum of immigration in the developed regions. Sine 1975, the number of international migrants worldwide has more than doubled. At the start of the 21st century, one out of every 35 persons worldwide was an international migrant. In 2002, almost one in every 10 persons living in the more developed regions of the world was a migrant.

Criticism of Demographic Transition Theory

Demographic transition theory, strictly speaking, cannot be claimed as a population theory. At best it is a model (Demographic Transition Model, DTM), developed from the historical evidences from Europe and other western countries. It is a transcription of the historical changes in population of the world, the facts being drawn from hazy records of events scattered over space and time. Though the stages of transition are applicable to all the countries of the world, on many minute details the dissimilarities between countries are often more glaring than similarities. The rates of decline in birth and death, the relation of the change in one to the other, the time perspective in these changes often are very different for different countries. The quantum of natural increase in two countries may be the same even though the two countries have different birth and death rates. Industrialization is not a prerequisite for mortality decline although all industrialized countries have low death rates. Even some of the less industrially developed countries have less mortality than the more industrially developed countries (Kuwait, Malaysia, Mauritius for example have CDRs below 7, while Hungary, Austria, USA, Germany have CDR around 10). Even two countries from the same geographical region and experiencing similar industrial development may display considerable differences in birth and death rates (Peru and Uruguay, Romania and Bulgaria, for example).

In the European countries' mortality decline, industrial development, urbanization and spread of education all started almost simultaneously. The decline of population growth was noticed quite sometime after this. Had the developing countries followed the same model, by the time they could achieve a balance between birth and death, the population would have expanded so much so that their sheer size of the population would have stood an unassailable barrier to any development. Social engineering in the third world countries led to faster decline in birth and death rates resulting in decline of growth rate.

The governments of the European countries had little or no direct role in the countries' fertility decline, nor did they set any target by which the birth rates were to be brought down to a desired level. In a sense, they did not have any specific population policy. In the last half of the previous century, family planning was not only included in national planning, it was accorded priority status in all developing countries. The socialist countries too were not far behind. There was a time when it was thought that 'development was the best contraceptive to population growth', but the perception of the menace of unchecked population growth was soon realized. The mood of those at the helm of national politics is clearly reflected in the Fifth Five-Year Plan of India, 1974 where it was stated, "education and development can wait, but not population".

The summary of the selected part of the speech delivered by Hua Kuo-Feng, China's Prime Minister, in the National People's Congress shows how China looked at the problem of population growth.

> Family planning is a very important issue before the country. The controlled growth of population will play a very significant role in the country's economic development and in child and mother's health care. This control will bring desired changes in many other areas. The annual population growth rate has to be brought down to less than 1% within three years from now. The government will take every possible measure to realize this goal.

The limitations of the demographic transition theory stand out clearly when population changes in the developing and developed countries are compared.

- The theory does not explain why the fall started though late in some countries made quick recovery in the end.
- The theory also fails to explain the variability in the relationship between the timing and speed of mortality decline and those of the fall in fertility.
- The social-class pattern of fertility decline is not explained by the theory. What explains the fertility decline among the rich is not necessarily applicable for the poor, and vice versa.
- There was no international pressure for fertility control when transitions started in the developed West. Though the transition theory proclaimed that a balance between birth and death would be reached in all countries, it did not anticipate the role the state would have to play on their own realization of the problem or at the behest of mounting international pressure to take steps to hasten population decline.
- Many countries still are almost at the same stage of demographic transition. We cannot say that they would experience the same pattern of change in future. Natural resource, geographical location, biological and cultural inheritance and population density besides the nature of economic progress would decide the course a country would adopt for population stabilization.
- Much of the argument for transition theory rests on the concept "rational". The term "economically rational" frequently is substituted for "socially rational" for the simple reason that in the latter certain mode of behavior would be considered rational from some religious and community considerations. Even so, the criteria employed are highly ethnocentric, highly laden with Western values. It is rational for a man to maximize expenditure on individuals in his nuclear family. But in many non-Western societies, people spend with pleasure on members outside their nuclear family – brothers, sisters and old parents. So, the fundamental operating force is social, and one's economic behavior is rational only in so far as it is rational within the framework established in a particular social fabric. The demographic transition theory has a Western bias – rationality is judged by maximization of satisfactions given the Western social ends.

The brief discussion on the history of world population change points to a few important deductions:

1. Fast mortality decline is behind population explosion in most countries.
2. There is epidemiological change in the causes of mortality and morbidity as the countries pass from the 'Old balance' to the 'New balance' stage.
3. Mortality decline and industrialization go hand in hand. Public health measures and preventive medicines are more readily accepted across countries. The same cannot be said about birth control measures. People take interest in birth control long after industrialization has taken a firm root and mortality significantly declined.
4. The technologies for birth and death control are accepted by the upper class first. It trickles down to the lower strata slowly. This trickle down effect is secular, although religious faiths and socio-economic environment might hasten or deter the trickle down process.
5. Fertility declines first in urban areas. That is why, at a point of time, the birth rates could be very different in urban and rural areas. The near equality situation in death rate in rural and urban areas is generally achieved faster than equality in birth rates.
6. The geographical and class differences in mortality are decreasing fast due to enormous progress in controlling infective and parasitic diseases.

7. Even though the developing countries are way behind in spread of industries, level of technology, spread of education etc., they have caught up with the developed countries in arresting general mortality level.
8. No method of controlling birth can be said good or bad. Different countries have achieved their birth control targets using different methods.

1.8 A Few Other Demographic Transition Models

Like Thomson and Notestein others too have tried to relate population transition to social, cultural and economic history of the nation. We briefly discuss some of them.

1.8.1 C. P. Blacker's Five Stages of Population Growth

(I) *High Stationary Population*: This stage is similar to Thomson and Notestein's High Potential Growth. In a very underdeveloped economy and traditional social system, the difference in the two rates is negligible and therefore the population is almost stationary or growing very slowly with irregular fluctuations. Famine and epidemic regularly take heavy tolls on life. His analysis shows that 22 percent of world population was at this stage till 1930.

(II) *Early Expansion Stage*: Improvements in the food supply brought about by higher yields in agriculture and better transportation prevent death due to starvation. Frequent famine and epidemic are under some control; medical facilities are extended to the common man; preventive medicines put some check on infectious diseases; death rate starts to fall slowly. Birth rate however continues to stay almost at the biological limit. As a result, the population starts to grow. Blacker estimated that 40 percent of world population was at this stage in 1930.

(III) *Late Expanding Stage*: Birth rate starts declining quite sometime after death rate has dropped appreciably. As death rate started to decline fast; population started to grow fast as well. People started to realize that higher number of births in a family is no longer required. As childhood death continues to fall and incomes rise, parents become increasingly confident that fewer children will suffice to help in family business and care for them in old age. The cost of children to parents rises by the introduction of legislation for compulsory education. The public opinion and propaganda by the state are in favor of adoption of a small family norm. By 1930, 22 percent of the world population was believed to have been at this stage. The stages II and III of Blacker combined are comparable to Thomson and Notestein's Transitional Growth stage.

(IV) Low *Stationary Population*: Both birth and death rates are very low. Like stage I, the population almost is stationary with a very large base. Increasing female literacy and employment lower the uncritical acceptance of childbearing and motherhood. Working women have less time to raise children; this is particularly an issue where fathers traditionally make little or no contribution to child-raising, as in southern Europe or Japan. Birth control measures are universally accepted. Standard of living is very high. The resulting changes in the age structure of the population include a reduction in the youth dependency ratio and eventually population aging. By 1930, 14 percent of the world population was in this stage.

(V) *Declining Population*: The countries, which are highly developed industrially and have very high per capita income, are at this stage of transition. Whenever death rate exceeds the nearly stable birth rate, the country faces depopulation. Such a situation was observed in stage I and could be replicated after Stage IV. The population in these countries generally have adopted "one-child" norm. This negative growth rate is a temporary phenomenon and continuation of the situation may encourage immigration to support the production processes.

1.8.2 Karl Sax's Four Stage Transition

Sax identified four stages in demographic transition that has historically accompanied economic progress and industrial development.

(I) *High Stationary Stage*: This stage portrays a high fluctuating stationary population with high mortality and birth rates. The prevalent economy is characterized by low productivity, low standard of living, total dependence on agriculture, primitive production process, poor communication and transport, widespread illiteracy, universality of marriage, early marriage, deep rooted beliefs in traditions, customs about the family size etc. The economic advantages of a large family in primitive society are well documented. The prevalent high death rates necessitated people to multiply in sufficient numbers so that necessary security for old age of the parents can be bought. Most developed countries passed through this stage much before industrial revolution.

(II) *Early Explosive Increase*: Death has started to decline but birth rate continues at a level experienced in stage I. That is, there is considerable time lag between the declines of the two vital rates. High potential of growth of population in the first stage is actually realized in stage II. The countries in this stage experienced considerable improvement in agriculture; supply of food became regular causing mortality to decline. Income levels rise; medical facilities also improve. These tend to increase birth rate and reduce death rate. The net rate of growth pushes the population growth to an explosive stage. This is the most critical period for a developing economy. Most of the developed countries took more than 100 years to come out of this stage. The population in the countries recently going through this stage of transition has increased by 2–3 percent per annum. India was passing through this stage between 1960 and early eighties.

(III) *Late Explosive Stage*: Fertility has declined steadily and is well under 30; mortality has reached as low as 11–12; further decline in mortality will be a very slow process; rural urban differences in mortality rates is diminishing; rural fertility is considerably higher than urban fertility. Natural increase rates range between 10 and 20 per thousand. Advanced agriculture and modern industry are taking care of the economic health of the country. The population movement from rural to urban and commercial centers is growing fast.

(IV) *Low Stationary Stage*: The birth rates, between 10 and 20 per thousand, are almost balanced by low mortality rates (around 10 per thousand). The rate of natural increase is 0–0.6 per annum. Most of Europe, North America, Australia and New Zealand, and Japan are already in this stage. High industrial productivity, use of advanced technology, mechanized agriculture, high proportion of urban population, very high standard of living, very high standards of health and communication and transport infrastructure, hundred percent literacy and very high expectation of life at birth etc. characterize

Figure.1.9 *Karl Sax's four stages of transition*

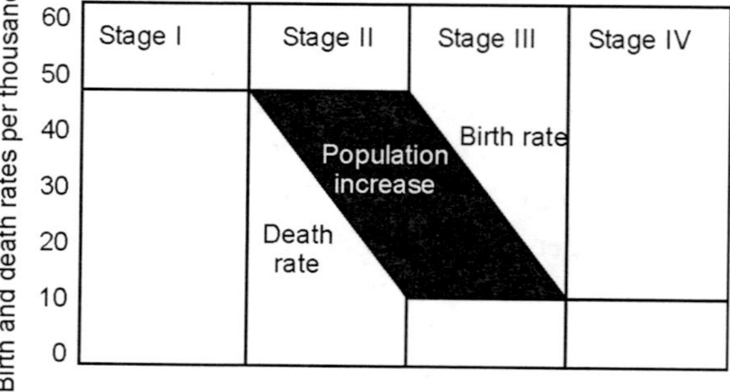

the countries at this final stage of transition. Economic disadvantages of a large family are universally recognized. Economic roles for women outside home are accepted. Internal migration (especially long distance) for economic reasons increases. Traditional joint families crumble.

These four stages describe the transformation of a primitive society into a modern industrial-urban society, from a high vital rates regime to a low vital rates regime, from a poor agro-based low productive economy to a hi-tech industry and technology-based efficient and productive economy.

1.9 Population Growth in the Major Regions After the Second World War

From mid-seventies the average world population growth rate started to decline from a high of 2.1 percent in 1965–70 to about 1.6 percent in 2000. However, even with population growth rate curtailed, the absolute increase every year is still higher than that in the previous year. It is mostly because of the expanding population base. Since 1950 we have added around 2,000 million and we still are adding around 75–80 million every year. UNDP estimates that the average annual growth rate between 2003 and 2015 would be around 1.1 percent. Even if this growth is achieved, we shall be adding about 700 million by 2010 and another 400 million in the next 5 years. In 1950, about 32 percent of the world population was from the more developed regions, in 1995 this came down to about 27 percent and in 2000 their share was down to about 23 percent and then to only 18 percent in 2008. By 2050, the developed country's share is likely to be only 14 percent. Between 1950 and 2000, the population in the developed regions grew by 50 percent while the developing regions grew by 170 percent. Africa's population, currently growing faster than any other major region, is projected to account for 21 percent of world population by 2050, up from just 9 percent in 1950. India and China, with a billion-plus each in 2008, make up about 37 percent of the world total. Growth rate by developed and developing countries appear in Figure 1.10.

It is prudent to project population for a decade or two. Even for population groups whose intrinsic rate of increase is zero may, consequent upon its age composition, continue to increase in size for several decades before the stability is reached. The population division of UN predicted that world fertility would be reduced to net replacement level sometime after 2050 although most of the developed countries would have attained this by 2010. By then the average expectation of life at birth would have reached 75 years. The currently developed regions' share of the world population will drop to less than 11–12 percent around 2050. South Asia alone would be the home of half of the world population. World Population reached

- 1 billion in 1804
- 2 billion in 1927 (123 years later)
- 3 billion in 1960 (33 years later)
- 4 billion in 1974 (14 years later)
- 5 billion in 1987 (13 years later)
- 6 billion in 1999 (12 years later)

World Population may reach:

- 7 billion in 2013 (14 years later)
- 8 billion in 2028 (15 years later)
- 9 billion in 2054 (26 years later)

Source: United Nations Population Division: *World Population Prospects*, 1998

Figure 11.10 *Population growth rate, 1950–2000*

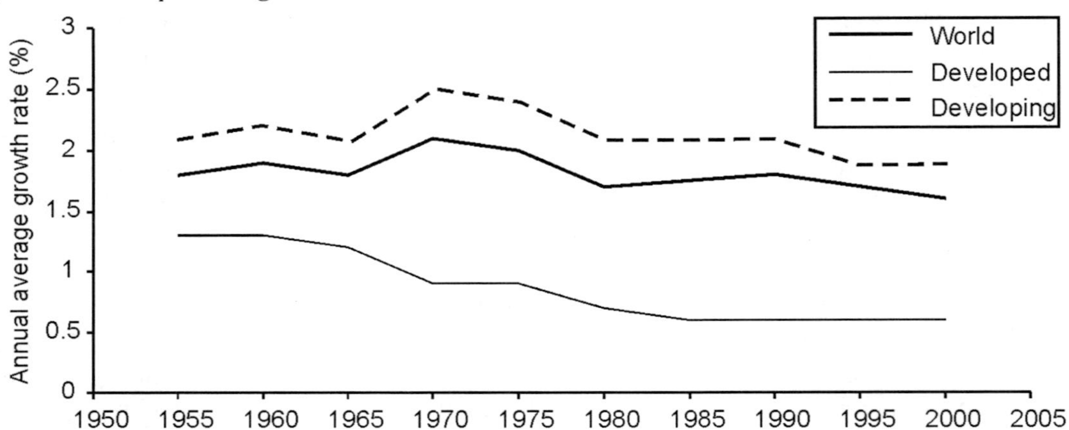

The shares of world population in Africa, Asia and Latin America have been rising steadily. More than half of the world population lives in four countries – China, India, USA and Russia. More than 80 percent of the world population lives in 30 countries.

Figure 1.11 *Population of 30 largest countries in the world, 1975 and 1999*

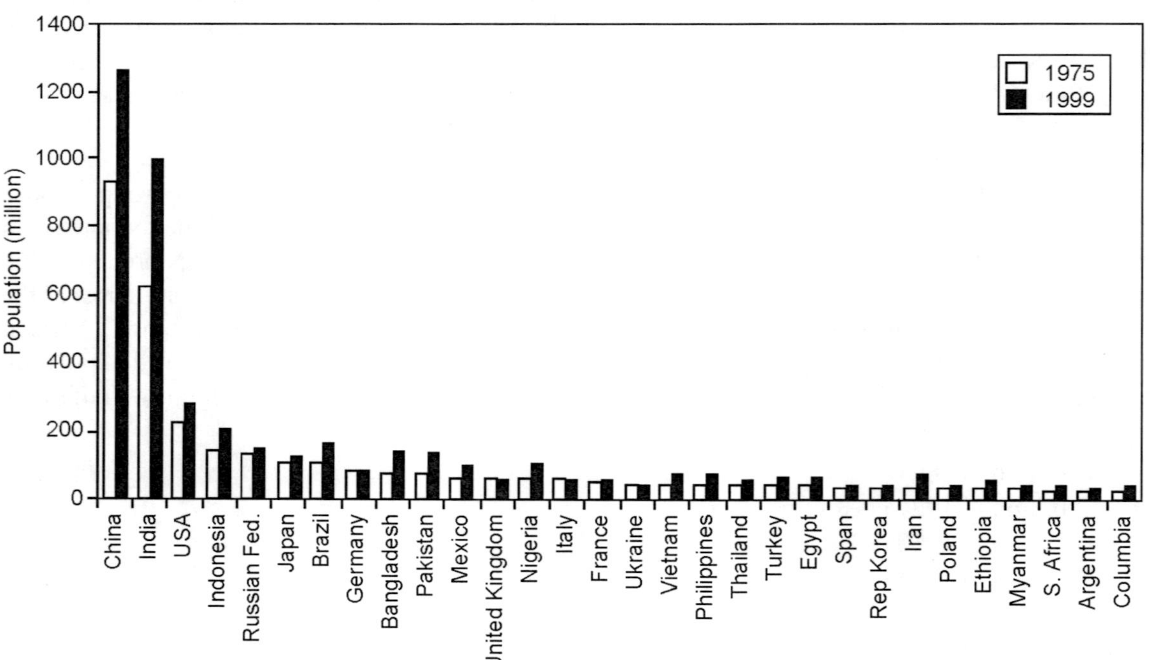

There is considerable variation in birth, death and growth rates between different continents. Of late the differences have declined but are unlikely to vanish in the next six or seven decades. We give a brief account of population growth in different continents.

Table 1.10 *Population (in million) in world's 30 largest countries 1975 and 1999*

Countries	*1975*	*%*	*1999*	*%*	*Growth rate 1975–99*	*Total fertility rate 1975*	*Total fertility rate 1999*
1	*2*	*3*	*4*	*5*	*6*	*7*	*8*
China	928	23.276	1265	21.576	1.3	4.9	1.8
India	621	15.576	993	16.937	2.0	5.4	3.3
USA	220	5.5179	280	4.7757	1.0	2.0	2.0
Indonesia	135	3.386	209	3.5647	1.8	5.2	2.6
Russian Federation	134	3.3609	146	2.4902	0.4	2.0	1.2
Japan	112	2.8091	127	2.1661	0.5	2.1	1.4
Brazil	108	2.7088	168	2.8654	1.8	4.7	2.3
Germany	79	1.9814	82	1.3986	0.2	1.6	1.3
Bangladesh	76	1.9062	135	2.3026	2.4	6.4	3.8
Pakistan	70	1.7557	138	2.3537	2.8	6.3	5.5
Mexico	59	1.4798	97	1.6544	2.1	6.5	2.8
UK	56	1.4046	59	1.0063	0.2	2.0	1.7
Nigeria	55	1.3795	111	1.8932	2.9	6.9	5.9
Italy	55	1.3795	58	0.9893	0.2	2.3	1.2
France	53	1.3293	59	1.0063	0.5	2.3	1.7
Ukraine	49	1.229	50	0.8528	0.1	2.2	1.3
Vietnam	48	1.2039	77	1.3133	2.0	6.7	2.5
Philippines	42	1.0534	74	1.2622	2.4	6.0	3.6
Thailand	41	1.0283	62	1.0575	1.7	5.0	2.1
Turkey	40	1.0033	66	1.1257	2.1	5.2	2.7
Egypt	39	0.9782	67	1.1428	2.3	5.5	3.4
Spain	36	0.9029	40	0.6822	0.5	2.9	1.2
Rep. Korea	35	0.8779	46	0.7846	1.1	4.3	1.5
Iran	34	0.8528	69	1.1769	3.0	6.4	3.2
Poland	34	0.8528	39	0.6652	0.5	2.2	1.5
Ethiopia	33	0.8277	61	1.0404	2.6	6.8	6.8
Myanmar	30	0.7524	47	0.8016	1.9	5.8	3.3
South Africa	26	0.6521	43	0.7334	2.1	5.4	3.1
Argentina	26	0.6521	37	0.6311	1.4	3.1	2.6
Columbia	25	0.627	41	0.6993	2.0	5.0	2.8
Combined	**3299**	**82.744**	**4746**	**80.948**			
World	**3987**	**100.0**	**5863**	**100.0**	**1.6**	**4.5**	**2.8**

Source: Human Development Report, 2001 (UNDP)

Figure 1.12 *Change in TFR for 30 most populous countries, 1975 and 1999*

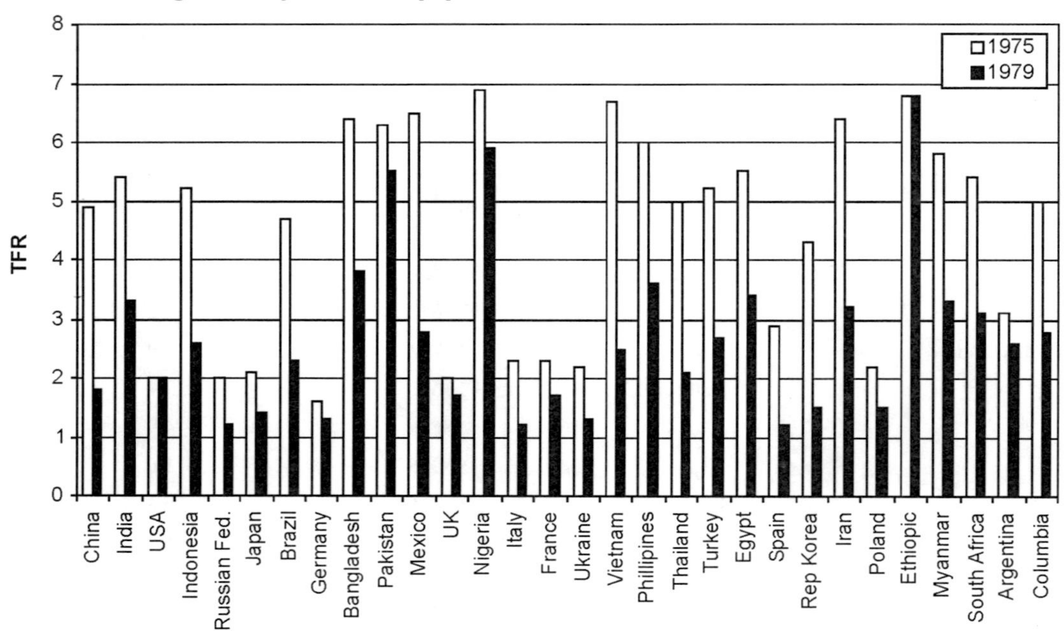

Africa

Africa has 60 states divided into 5 regions (Appendix 1). The population estimate in the continent is 850,558,000 as of 2000–05. Africa still continues to be the least developed continent with highest CBR (37) and CDR (15) in the world. Except Northern and Southern Africa, the other three regions – Eastern, Middle and Western Africa still have birth rates between 41 and 47. Southern Africa has the smallest birth rate in the continent (CBR 23); it has a death rate (17) not really compatible with the type of birth rate it has. *World Population Prospects* 1950–2050 (UN) have listed 45 highly HIV/AIDS affected countries. Of these 35 are from Africa. South Africa ranks highest in HIV/AIDS infection. Sub-Saharan Africa has HIV/AIDS of 8.7 percent of all persons in the age group 15–49 as against 1.1 percent in the 15–49 world population. All the countries in Southern Africa (5) are in the 'high infected' list. In fact, the whole of Africa except the Northern region has very high degree of HIV/AIDS infection. In effect, between 1970 and 1997, 14 countries from different parts of the world registered decline in expectation of life at birth of which 8 are from Africa; Botswana, Zambia and Zimbabwe losing by 2-digit points in the last three decades. Death rates in almost all the countries have increased, presumably due to HIV/AIDS epidemic. Growth rates in most of the countries have declined due to some fall in birth rates. It would be no wonder if birth rates in many of these countries pick up to compensate the tremendous loss of lives likely to continue for years due to HIV/AIDS infection. Africa has the highest proportion of < 15 years age group (42 percent) in the total population. It has the highest Young Age Dependency Ratio, about 80 percent. Under age-five mortality (148 per 1,000) is nearly twice as much as the average in the world population. IMR in most African countries still continues to be alarmingly high. Sub-Saharan Africa also has the highest tuberculosis infection (121 against 61 per 100,000 in the world population).

Table 1.11 *CDR, CBR and other statistics for seven countries in Africa experiencing decline in life expectancy*

Countries	CDR		CBR		Growth rate		Life expectancy		Infant mortality	
	1983	2003	1983	2003	1983	2003	1970	2003	1970	1999
1	2	3	4	5	6	7	8	9	10	11
Botswana	11	21	43–47	31	3.2–3.6	0.9	52	40	99	46
Burundi	17–18	21	45–50	44	2.7–3.3	3.1	44	41	135	106
Malwai	22–25	24	48–54	45	2.3–3.2	2.0	40	38	189	132
Rwanda	17–18	22	48–51	44	3.0–3.4	2.2	44	39	124	110
Uganda	15–18	17	46–50	51	3.0–3.5	3.2	46	46	110	83
Zambia	15–16	28	47–49	44	3.1–3.4	1.2	46	32	109	112
Zimbabwe	15–16	27	47–50	32	3.0–3.5	0.5	50	33	86	60
S. Africa	10–11	17	32–35	23	2.3–2.6	0.5	53	48	80	54
AFRICA	15–17	15	43–47	37	2.8–3.2	2.2		49		

Source: *World Population 1983* (US Department of Commerce), HDR 2001 (UNDP), *UN World Population* 2002

The estimated current growth rate in Africa is 2.2; Middle and Western Africa have growth rates higher than 2.6, Southern Africa has the least, 0.6 – a substantial part of this must be due to HIV/AIDS epidemic. From 2.2 percent annual growth rate in 1950–55 it reached 3 percent level in early eighties. In the last decade and a half, the growth rate has considerably been arrested. Whereas the share of population of Africa to the total world population was less than 9 percent in 1950, it rose to about 11 percent in early eighties. Currently this has gone up to 13.5 percent. It was the third largest populated continent till 1975. In 2003 it has dethrone Europe from the second spot. UN projection shows that the continent's share to world population by 2025 would be about 16.45 percent and by 2050 it is likely to have 21 percent share of world population. In a little over 50 years since 1950 it nearly has quadrupled its absolute population size. All sub-regions except Northern Africa (none of the countries in this part of Africa have alarming HIV/AIDS infection) have death rates over 15.

Southern Africa, the smallest sub-region in the continent with a population around 52 million (2000–2005), a net addition of 17 million in the last 20 years, has consistently maintained lowest crude birth rates in the continent (24 in 2000–05), which is at par with the average birth rate in the less developed regions (vide Table 1.7); but the average crude death rate is twice that of CDR in the less developed region. Some twenty years back CDR in Southern Africa was about the same as the average of all the less developed countries. The average annual growth rate in the region was 2.3 percent in 1950–55. It rose to an all-time high of 2.6 percent during 1960–70. It has steadily declined since then because of fertility reduction. However, the sharp fall in growth rate in the last decade or so has been due to rise in CDR (11 in 1983 to 18 between 2000–05), obviously due to HIV/AIDS epidemic. The trends for this sub-region (in CBR, CDR and growth rate) reflect primarily the population dynamics of South Africa, which constitutes 88 percent of the sub-region's population. UN projection shows that the total population in this sub-region will go down to around 49.6 million in 2025 and to 46.6 million by 2050.

Northern Africa added 63 million in 20 years over its total population of 120.6 million in 1983 (23.4 percent of the population of the continent). By 2000–05 its share to continent's population is 21.6 percent. By 2025 its share is likely to go down further to 19.6 percent and by 2050 it would be about 16.9 percent. Northern region's annual population growth rate rose from 2.4 percent in 1950–55 to 3.0 percent in 1983. The current growth rate is about 1.7 percent. It has brought down CDR from 12 in 1983 to only 7 in 2000–05. The birth rate has come down from around 41 in 1983 to 26 in 2000–05. Egypt is the most populous country in the region; it's share being 39 percent of Northern Africa's population. Current growth rate is 2 percent with CBR 27 and CDR 6. Tunisia, a small country though (only 5 percent of the region's population), has the slowest growth rate (1.1 percent) in the region with CBR 17 and CDR 5. None of the countries in this region is in the special list of countries with high HIV/AIDS infection

The Eastern and Western Africa together share over 60 percent of Africa's population. Of the 18 countries in East Africa, 12 are in the high-alert list of HIV/AIDS infection. 28 percent of Africa's population lived in this region in 1983. In 20 years its share has gone up to 31.8 percent. By 2050 every third African would be from this sub-region. Ethiopia is the largest country in this sub-region with 26 percent of Eastern Africa's population. Kenya had an estimated growth rate of 8.1 percent in 1977, had the highest fertility level (CBR 54, TFR 8.1) for any country in the world. Population growth rate of Kenya was brought down to around 4 percent in 1983 – product of high decline both in fertility and mortality. Currently, its annual growth rate is 1.5 percent with CBR 33 and CDR 17.

Western Africa has 16 countries of which 11 are in the critical list of HIV/AIDS infection. Its share to Africa's population in 1950 was the same as that of East Africa. The current estimate shows its share as 28.7 percent as against 31.8 percent of East Africa. It had population growth rate, CBR and CDR similar to that in East Africa in 1983. This sub-region has the highest population growth rate, 2.6 percent with CBR as high as 41 and CDR 15. Nigeria has the largest population share, 50.7 percent with annual growth rate of 2.5 percent and CBR 39 and CDR 14. Nigeria is also the most populous country in Africa with about 14.6 percent of Africa's population. The growth rate of this

Figure 1.13 *Radar plot of crude death rate in the continents, 2000–05*

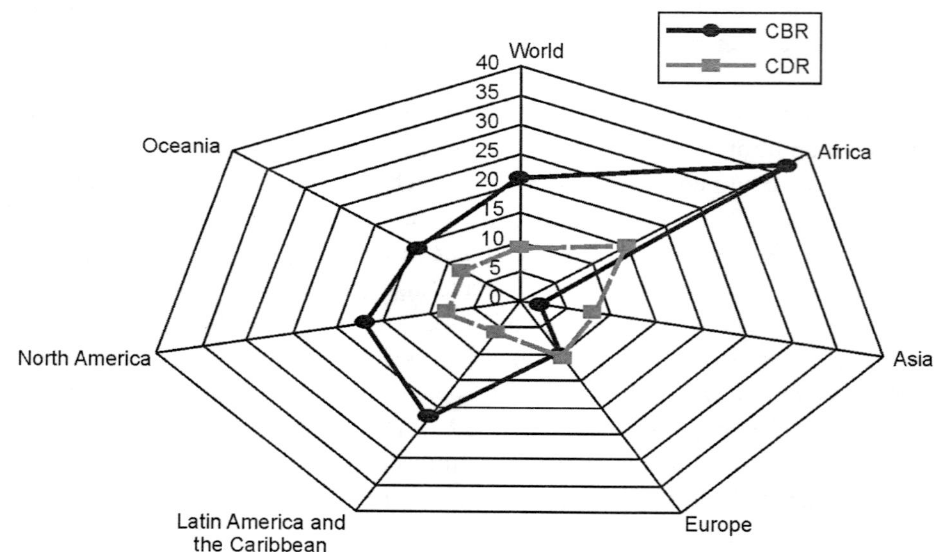

country in the eighties had something to do with exodus of some 0.4 – 2 million immigrants from Ghana and other places.

Middle Africa's current population share is about 12 percent of total population of Africa. It has a very high annual growth rate, 2.7 percent, very high birth and death rates, 47 and 20 respectively. UN projection estimates that the population share of the sub-region may go beyond 14.8 percent by 2050. Of the 9 countries in this sub-region, 7 are in high HIV/AIDS risk list. Democratic Republic of the Congo is the largest country in this sub-region with about 52 percent share of Middle Africa's population. It has very high annual growth rate, 2.9 percent and near biological limit in fertility, 50, and CDR 21.

Africa's economy is predominantly agricultural. Because of political violence and military coups every now and then, development has been held hostage in many countries. Many countries have to depend on international aids and borrowing. Density of population in Africa is still very low, 28 per sq km. Literacy rates in most countries are low. In sub-Saharan region about 80 percent people still live in villages. Arab countries have much higher urban population, more than 54 percent.

The 2001 HDR report shows that the Low Human Development group has 36 countries, 4 are from Asia and one from Latin America and rest from Africa. 29 countries from Africa find a place in the Medium Human Development category.

ASIA

60.67 percent of the world population lived in Asia in 2003. Asia is the house of 75 percent of those living in less developed regions. Asia's share to the world population is likely to come down to 58.5 percent in 2050. Six out of 10 most populous countries are in Asia (China, 1,304 million, India, 1,065 million, Indonesia, 220 million, Pakistan, 154 million, Bangladesh, 146 million and Japan, 128 million).

Annual growth rate of population in the continent was 2.0 percent in 1950–55, reaching a high of 2.4 percent in 1965–70, gradually declining thereafter. The estimated growth rate in 2000–05 is 1.3 percent. Average CDR in Asia has reached 9 per thousand populations. Except Afghanistan (CDR 21), death rates in all other countries are below 14. Kuwait and UAE have attained CDR 2, probably lowest anywhere in the world. Afghanistan has the highest CBR (47) in the continent. Yemen (45) and few other countries still have exceedingly high birth rate with the result that these countries are still growing at an alarming rate, beyond 3 percent. Both CDR and CBR vary considerably between sub-regions and between countries in the same sub-region. Death rates in most countries have stabilized at a much lower level (most developing countries have reduced CDR by between 0.35–0.50 point per annum in the last 25 years) than it was 25 years back.

Asia has the second highest current growth rate, only after Africa. Much of the decline in population growth rate in Asia is attributable to drastic reduction of fertility in China. From an annual growth rate around 1.8 percent in China, the same in 2000–05 is estimated to have come down to only 0.7. There has been a birth rate reduction by 8–10 points after 1980. Between 1965–70 and 1980–85 the aggressive birth reduction policy in China brought down the annual growth rate from 2.9 to 1.5 percent, nearly a 50 percent reduction just in 20 years. Current growth rate in China is likely to be around 0.5 percent per annum.

Fertility has declined substantially in most of the major Asian countries from seventies in the last century and more countries have joined them since the eighties. Average birth rate has fallen from 28–31 in the eighties to about 21 in 2000–05. Crude death rates in the eighties were already in 10–11 brackets. It has dropped by another 3–4 points in the last 20 years. However, mortality under age 5 and IMR are still quite high. By the mid-eighties the life expectancy in many countries reached 60 years. The current life expectancy on average is estimated at 67 years. Japan has the highest expectation of life, 82 years.

Both Young Age Dependency and Old Age Dependency in Asia are very close to world averages. Population density is highest in the Asian continent (120/km^2). Except Western Asia, the picture is almost the same in all sub-regions in this regard. The range of urbanization varies widely. All the countries in Eastern Asia except China have very high urban population, between 57 and 100 percent (Hong Kong). Generally, the proportion of urban population is considerably low in Asia. South Central Asia (which includes India, Pakistan, and Bangladesh) has an average of 31 percent of the population living in urban areas. Bhutan is the only country in the region which has single digit proportion of urban population. Iran, the oil-giant, has 66 percent of its population living in urban areas. Agriculture still is the occupation of the majority except in Western Asia where most countries are petroleum majors that regulate the supply of this 'liquid gold' to most countries of the World. In most West Asian countries urban population is very high. Bahrain, Israel, Kuwait, Lebanon and Qatar have 90 percent or more people living in urban areas.

Europe

Whereas the developing countries started to apply a brake on the growth of population mostly in 1970s and 1980s, the developed countries, which already had slower growth rate compared to the developing countries nearly at all points of time, exercised a further moratorium on their population growth rates in the 1950s. The populations in these countries were growing by around 1 percent though considerable variation was observed between the regions from a low of around 0.4 percent in Northern Europe to a high of 1.7 percent in Soviet Union in early 1950s. Within a span of 30 years, the average growth rate in Europe came down to a little over 0.4 percent, Northern and Western Europe hovering between 0.1– 0.2 percent. The estimated average annual population growth rate in 2003 is (–) 0.1. Eastern Europe, which had more than the average annual growth rate in Europe between 1950 and 1985, showed a dramatic decline in growth rate since then. Incidentally, this coincides with the disintegration of Soviet Union in early 1990s. TFRs in most European countries either are at or below the replacement level. Currently, Eastern Europe is experiencing fastest decline in annual population growth, (–)0.5. It is estimated that if this pattern of fall in growth rate continues, Eastern Europe shall have 33 million fewer people than 300 million of the present. It may loose more than 80 million by 2050. Both Russian Federation and Ukraine have large negative growth rates, (–)0.6 and (–)0.8 respectively. All other regions in Europe have annual growth rates very close to zero. Eastern Europe is the largest block in Europe, accommodating over 41 percent of Europe's total population. Nearly half the population of Eastern Europe and about 20 percent of total population of Europe lives in Russian Federation. Russian Federation is the fifth most populous country; the four countries ahead of it are China, India, USA and Indonesia. Soviet Union was the third most populous country prior to split of the Union.

In 1950, the share of Europe to total world population was about 22.6 percent. It lost 5 percent to others by 1975; currently its share to world population has dropped to 11.5 percent (vide Table 1.7). If we take a close look at the graph (Figure 1.3), it will appear that Europe lost its share to world population to Africa. Growth of Africa is a mirror image of that of Europe. Europe has already lost 2 million populations between 1975 and 2003. This trend is likely to continue for some more years. However, depopulation cannot continue over a long period of time. Sooner or later some readjustment in growth rate (by improving death rate probably) is likely to happen. Presently only one point differentiates average CDR from average CBR for European countries. Most of the European countries have CBR hovering between 8 and 10. TFR has fallen from 2.5 to 1.5 indicating fertility has fallen below replacement level. In the final quarter of the last century Northern and Western Europe had lowest fertility. But the differences between regions have now largely been wiped out. Life expectancies at birth have remained among the highest in the last few decades. Population under age 15 has been falling in Europe and in all other developed countries. It is likely to go down to 15–16 percent by 2015; the proportion in 65+ age group may fall short of the young age group by no more than 3–4 percentage points. Currently, net migration rate hovers around zero.

Adult literacy (15 years and above) in Europe is close to 100 percent. Mean years of schooling (intensity of education) among 15+ years is close to 10 years. The European countries like those among other industrially developed countries have a large contingent of scientists and engineers engaged in R&D. They have around 3,000 research scientists per 100,000 people in their countries. They spend more than 2 percent of GNP in R&D. Their hi-tech exports have doubled in 20 years; currently the hi-tech export is between 20–21 percent of total goods exports.

Contrasted to world average of 48 percent, 74 percent people in Europe live in urban areas. Northern and Western Europe have as many as 83 percent people living in urban areas. There are quite a few countries, which are totally urban.

Latin America and The Caribbean

There are 46 large and small states in this continent; the Caribbean Islands have as many as 24 states. Together they constitute a little over 7 percent of the continent's population, down from 8 percent in 1980's. This sub-region has more diverse demographic characteristics than the other sub-regions. Growth rates vary from (–) 0.3 (Grenada and Saint Kits) to as high as 3.5 in Turks and Calicos Islands. Birth rates vary from 12 to 30 and CDR from 6 to 15. Some countries have negligible rural population and many countries have far less than 40 percent urban population. Proportion of persons in the young age group varies from around 19 (Barbados) to around 38 (Haiti). Population density in this sub-region is very high, 165 per km^2 as against only 26 in the continent. Barbados has the highest population density, 629 per km^2.

This continent's share in the world population in 1950 was 7 percent. Currently, its share has increased to 8.6 percent. Between 1950 and 1970, the population growth in the continent was faster (2.6–2.8 percent) than that in any other region. Since 1970, Africa has overtaken it in growth rate. From 2.3 percent per annum in 1985, it has quickly brought down its growth rate to 1.4 percent in 2003. Growth rate in the Caribbean and the Central America is below 1 percent. South America, the largest region with 66.67 percent of the population of the continent, has 1.4 percent annual growth rate. A large variation is observed in growth rates between the countries in the region, from 0.2 (Guyana) to 2.5 percent (French Guyana). Brazil is the seventh most populated country (178 million) in the world and the largest in Latin America and the Caribbean.

Central America has remained the most disturbed region for continuing civil strife. Large segments of populations of El Salvador, Nicaragua and Guatemala have emigrated or become international refugees. Of the 8 countries in Central America, 6 have annual growth rates around 2 percent. Mexico is the largest populated country in this sub-region having about 73 percent of the

Central America's population. The population parameters of Central America are mostly determined by Mexico's population parameters. Although most of the countries in this sub-region have high growth rates, the average growth rate (1.7 percent) is largely influenced by Mexico's annual growth rate (1.5 percent).

The trend in population growth in Latin America and the Caribbean is set by the trend prevailing in the Tropical South America. Birth rate in the continent was between 30 and 32 in 1985. It came down to 22, 1 point higher than the world average in 2003. There is considerable variation in CBR among the countries in the continent – from 12 in Bahamas and Cuba to 32 in Nicaragua and 34 in Guatemala. Temperate South America is demographically as well as climatically distinct. The vital rates in Argentina, Chile and Uruguay have consistently remained lower than the rates observed in most other countries in the continent. Incidentally, this sub-region is highly urbanized compared to the rest of Latin America. Since 1970, Argentina has experienced net immigration, especially from Bolivia, Brazil, Chile, Paraguay and Uruguay for political and economic reasons. On the other hand, Chile and Uruguay has lost population through emigration. CDR in the continent (6) is considerably lower than the world average. Most countries have very low birth rates, only Haiti has a double digit CBR (15). Mortality under age 5 is 41 as against the world average of 81 per 1,000. Life expectancy at birth is 70 years, which is 5 years above the world average. Persons in below 15 year age are 31 percent, which is 2 points above the world average. It is in the Central America where the young age segment is considerably high (34 percent). Level of literacy in Latin America is around 95 percent. Non-agricultural low population growth areas have better literacy rates.

North America

North America accounts for only 6.3 percent of the world population. 90.86 percent of the population in the continent lives in USA and another 9.1 percent in Canada. Three other very small countries in the continent are Bermuda, Greenland and Saint-Pierre-et-Miquelon. The population parameters of USA almost wholly determine the same of the entire continent. Compared to Europe this continent has a very high growth rate (1.0). In 1950 the annual growth rate in the continent was 1.8 percent. It came down to 1.0 around 1985. CBR is as high as 14 and CDR 8. It has a TFR at replacement level. IMR has come down from around 20 in 1970 to around 7 in 1999. Under-five mortality is also down from 26 to about 8. Maternal mortality is about 8 per 100,000. Level of HIV/AIDS infection is considerably high, 0.61 percent in 15–49 age-group. Expectation of life at birth is 77 years; Canada has a higher life expectancy, 79 years. Per capita expenditure on health in USA is highest in the world, \$4180. Public expenditure on health is about 5.8 percent of the GDP. GDP per capita in USA (\$31,872) is second highest in the world, next only to Luxemburg. USA spends huge sums on military, though down from 5 percent in 1990 to 3 percent of GDP in 1999. It must have gone much higher since 9/11 terrorist attack in 2001. USA spends 5.4 percent of GDP on education. Adult literacy is 100 percent with combined enrolment ratio (primary, secondary and tertiary) at 95 percent. Although the total dependency ratios in Europe and North America are the same, the Young Age Dependency in North America is 33 percent as against 25 percent in Europe. The position of the two continents gets reversed with respect to Old Age Dependency. 16 percent of the North American population is in age group 65+. North America is a big continent but sparsely populated, (15 per km^2). 78 percent of the population lives in towns and cities. USA has huge immigrant population, people coming from all over the world. Contribution of agriculture to GDP of

USA is only 2 percent and that from industry is 27 percent; the service sector alone contributes 71 percent to the GDP. Average annual unemployment rate (percentage of labor force) in 1990–98 in USA was 5.9. Female economic activity rate as of 1999 is 58.4 percent, which is about 80 percent of the male economic activity rate. 85 percent of women are in the service sector, only 13 percent in industry. 65 percent of male workers in USA are in service sector and 34 percent in industry.

Oceania

Oceania has maintained a very small share to world population, around 0.5 percent, since 1950. The annual population growth rate in this region has declined from 2.3 percent in 1950–55 to about 1.2 percent in 2003 with CBR 17 and CDR 8. Both Australia and New Zealand have growth rates around 1.0 and birth and death rates hovering around 13 and 7 respectively. These two together share 73 percent of the continent's population. The rest of Oceania's population is dispersed among thousands of islands that constitute the less developed regions: Melanesia, Micronesia and Polynesia. CBRs in these regions are still very high; a few countries have CBR in excess of 30. Expectation of life at birth varies between 60 and 79 years, with an average of 74 years. Both Australia and New Zealand have high Old Age Dependency Ratio. The rest of the countries mostly have high total and Young Age Dependency Ratio. Australia-New Zealand region is very thinly populated, about 3 per km^2. Micronesia has high population density, 170 per km^2. New Zealand experienced high emigration between 1977 and 1980; it has slowed down since.

Except for Australia (92 percent), New Zealand (86 percent) and Nauru (100 percent), the proportion of urban population in Oceania is low. Many of these island countries even do not have much labor in agriculture for the simple reason that the soil, climate and other characteristics necessary to pursue agriculture are lacking in these island countries. These island countries have to import a sizeable portion of food products. Literacy is generally high for the countries for which adequate information are available.

2 Demographic Analysis

Some Fundamentals

2.1 Demography: Its Evolution

There are hundred and one reasons for studying population. The most obvious reason of course is advancement of the science – develop hypotheses and theories about changes in population characteristics, test them and predict the course of events related to population (composition, distribution and movement), given the changes taking place in science, technology and in social, economic and environmental domains. Population statistics is a fundamental necessity for any sort of planning for a country – food, housing, road and transport, schools, hospitals, employments and other necessities. Demographic data are utilized by politicians to associate themselves with views expressed by various population groups on important topical issues, their aspirations and commitments, for election to democratic bodies, collection of taxes, allocation of funds for health, education and other social services. The number and its distribution are equally important in planning and its execution – in schools, hospitals, industries and in all public and private initiatives.

The French scientist Achille Guillard first used the term Demography in 1855 in his book *Elements de Statistique Humaine on Demographic Comparee.* The term Demography is derived from two Greek words, *Demos*, meaning people, and *Graphein*, to draw or write. Presently, demography stands for measurements by statistical methods of various characteristics of human population. Its principal concern, however, is with size, distribution and growth of population of a region or nation or the world. The constituents of growth or change are births, deaths and migrations. Therefore, a demographer's primary concern is with fertility, mortality and population transfer from one region to another. They take keen interest in studying interaction between social, economic and political activities and demography related processes as size, distribution, composition and change in numbers determined by fertility, mortality and migration.

We have seen how demographers tried to reconstruct the history of population from educated guesses and scattered and scanty data obtained from historical, archaeological and anthropological sources. Simultaneously, they analyzed contemporary demographic, social, cultural, political and economic events to develop theories and models, construct hypotheses, subject them to rigorous testing and come out with conclusions that have far reaching effect on population policy and management. The demographers are seen to shed valuable link between population and such other aspects as natural resources, labor supply, production and consumption, investment in infrastructure and social welfare.

The demographers study populations with all their characteristics both at a single point (cross-sectional) and at different points of time (longitudinal). Whereas the former provides valuable information for comparing various population groups spread over space (age and sex composition, vital rates, generic composition), the latter provides an opportunity to study relation between two populations in an area at two points of time, that is those aged x at a time t are survivors of those aged $x - n$ at the time $t - n$, subject to mortality and migration. This helps projection of population and its likely composition, changes in birth and death rates, and also changes in expectation of life at different ages.

Demography did not achieve its current status so easily. In the developed countries, especially in Europe and USA, demography is taught as an independent discipline. Population statistics are extensively used in researches by international agencies like UN, FAO, WHO, World Bank etc. Though demography or population study often is an integral part of such disciplines as economics, sociology, anthropology, geography and statistics of many universities, there is hardly any commonality in their use of methodology and analytical plan for using demographic data. Only a few of Indian universities and research institutes offer full-fledged courses on demography.

Guillard used the term to denote 'mathematical knowledge of the social, intellectual, physical and ethical aspects' of a population. Long before Guillard, Aristotle and Plato in their writings discussed various problems relating to population. The English mathematician William Petty did some important work on population. He was inclined to regard this discipline as Political Arithmetic. His friend and research associate John Graunt is given the honor of 'founding father' of modern demography.

If Graunt was to be credited with founding of experimental demography, Petty must be given the credit for founding applied demography. Graunt's book *Natural and Political Observations – Made upon the Bills of Mortality* was the first-ever book on experimental and theoretical demography. From the records preserved in churches and cemeteries in London and around, Graunt studied in great details the information recorded for each married and deceased person and analyzed the collected information and tried to estimate, birth, death, marriage, migration rates and their interdependence. He noted that the sex ratio at birth favored male babies. He also noted mortality changes with age. He also observed variations in mortality and causes of mortality with time and space. Based even on utterly inadequate information, Graunt prepared a table for age-specific death rate. This can be regarded as the true ancestor of modern Life Table. Graunt also sketched the nature of population changes taking place in London city.

William Petty went a step further and tried to relate various population statistics to social, political and economic backdrop. Even with improved techniques of analysis and computational aids, the modern demographers often find it too mind-boggling to analyze and interpret many population issues. Petty did try to find answer to some such complex issues even though there was no apt technology to support his analysis and research. He tried population projections; he tried to show how urbanization was related to economic and social structure; he tried to understand population structure and distribution in relation to 'active age group' in the population; he gave considerable thought to problems of unemployment and partial employment and other social problems; he tried to estimate gross national productivity.

The paths shown by Graunt and Petty about how to make use of even incomplete and limited information in scientific analysis encouraged the later scientists to take up similar such exercises but on a larger scale in England and Western Europe. For example, Halley in England in 1693 prepared a complete Life Table. The upper limit of this Life Table was 84 years. The Life Table gave a very clear picture about the Stationary Life Table Population. Two years later, George King provided a comprehensive description of the size of the populations, their structures and distributions for England and Welsh. Sebastian Vauban repeated the same in France in 1707. He recommended annual population count and also suggested the nature of organizational set up needed for such a regular enumeration. Between 1741 and 1765, Johann Sussmilch, a Lutherian clergyman with

Germanic thoroughness, wrote a sequence of articles based on demographic data from parishes in Germany, in which he discussed a range of issues relating to population. It was a mix of stupendous effort and creative imagination on his part to prepare reliable documents for world population of his time. Sussmilch presented a variety of ratios on issues relating to population – marriage and population size, birth and death, birth and marriage, age-specific fertility and mortality, death rate in the population, etc. He made causal analysis of death. He constructed Life Tables separately for rural and urban Germany. He also dealt with the impact the different factors have on fertility – age at marriage, diseases, untimely death, problems in conjugal life, breast feeding for a long period of time, fear of pregnancy and such other factors. Swedish scientist H. Nicander computed age-specific fertility based on census data for the period 1780–95.

The periodic census slowly became a regular feature in many countries even before the end of the eighteenth century. USA, France and England started registration of birth and death and regular census at the beginning of nineteenth century. Before the end of the nineteenth century regular census became a permanent feature in nearly all European countries and the countries where the Europeans had settled or had established colonial rules. Since World War II, the United Nations took initiative for periodic census in all countries of the world. Certain procedural changes in census improved the quality of census data. Simultaneously with census, large-scale sample surveys helped collect reliable data on issues that cannot usually be covered in regular censuses. Demographers now have more reliable complete population data for countries and the entire world canvas.

During the whole of the nineteenth century and the first quarter of the twentieth century, demographers' primary attention was on death and death related statistics. Death rates all over the world, especially in the third world countries, were still alarming. Famine and epidemic were regular features. Although the population showed positive signs of growth in spite of prevalence of high death rate in almost all the underdeveloped countries, the growth rate never appeared alarming. This is not to say that other population questions did not receive attention of the population scientists. Frank Lorimer in his essay "Development of Demography" informed that on the very first year of compulsory registration of birth and death, age of the mother, age at marriage, birth order etc. were designed for recording. The program however fell through the very next year. Based on data collected in 1855, J. Mathews in 1866 tried to find relation between age at marriage, conjugal period, birth order etc. and fertility.

The beginning of the nineteenth century saw a sea change in attention and debate among the intellectuals all over the world over the issue of future of population in the context of foreseeable change in economic and social order. The eighteenth century may rightly be termed as the beginning of 'age of reason'. The primary concern of the intellectual class in Europe and elsewhere was to study closely the social order and develop strategic plans to improve the lot of the poor. Godwin and Condorcet believed that advances in science would lead to great abundance, while man's reason would keep the numbers within limits. A second group of thinkers were skeptic about how much science could deliver to check poverty from going up or how the lot of people could be improved. A new era in demography began to emerge with the publication of a small booklet by Thomas Robert Malthus (1766–1834) in 1798. The impact that his population theory had on the intelligentsia was profound. The word 'Malthusian' has passed into the language having become synonymous with pressures leading to poverty or increased mortality resulting from uncontrolled growth of population.

His first publication lacked support of any statistical evidence. This was soon rectified. In the later editions of his book Malthus cited statistics from different countries in support of his arguments. According to Malthus, the power of population is indefinitely greater than the power in the earth to produce subsistence for man since the law of diminishing return operates in agriculture. The industrial revolution changed the agricultural production so much so that people started to believe that science and technology have the power to frustrate the effect of population growth. But towards the end of the twentieth century when population grew at its fastest pace and when even shadows of famine and epidemic could be seen in many underdeveloped countries, there was a revival of interest in Malthusian doctrine. The world opinion was against the unrestricted growth of population. Various international bodies unequivocally proclaimed that poverty was the greatest 'pollutant' and that this cannot be removed without applying an effective check on the growth of population.

By and large, the eighteenth century demographers were partly successful in analyzing demographic data, which by all counts were not quite ideal. Eventually, the requisite quality of data began to materialize and the nineteenth century demographers could sharpen their measuring tools. Precision and accuracy marked the analytical results.

Dr. William Farr (1807–83) was a pioneering figure in experimental demography. It was under his direct guidance and supervision that *compulsory registration of birth and death* began in England in 1839. The schedules he prepared for census and registration of birth and death are still largely followed world over with some modifications and additions here and there. He was credited with the publication of the official Life Table for the first time in England. He received ample support and advice from John Finlaison, the first President of the Institute of Actuaries, in inauguration of vital registration and accurately forecasting births, deaths and marriages from the recorded data. While analyzing mortality data, Dr. Farr drew attention to problems of public health and sanitation and to many social and economic issues. He tried also to relate death rates to seasonal variation, housing condition, population density, age, sex, and occupation.

Primary data for demographic analysis became easily available in most of the developed countries. Along side, statisticians too came forward with improved tools and techniques for analysis of such data. The importance of age and sex-specific death rates were gaining considerable importance in differential mortality analysis. For comparing death rates in two or more populations, such techniques as *standardized death rates* and *expected death rates* were developed.

Two very important factors lay behind the vastly improved analysis of death rates at the close of the nineteenth century. First and the foremost is the rapid progress of life insurance business. The success in insurance business depends upon precise and accurate determination of age specific death rates (probability of dying of a person aged x before attaining age $x + s$). The value of a premium is calculated on the probability that a person of aged x would die before he attains the age $x + s$. The second reason is the increasingly greater role shouldered by the state to matters relating public health, especially in urban areas. The pace of industrial growth and development is closely related to the health of the workforce.

The fast progress in medical science, especially discovery of a number of life-saving drugs and spread of vaccination against many of the dreaded diseases, public health awareness, expansion of health infrastructure and improved communication and transport network brought down death rates in all ages; expectation of life increased through all the age spectrum; famines and epidemics came under close control. The population started to show a steady upward growth.

Birth rates did not receive due attention so long death rates continued to be high. Once death rates were under some control, attention of the demographers shifted to birth rates, more so after World War II. The population growth rate showed signs of alarm in the forties and fifties of the twentieth century. The demographers shifted their attention to birth rates, social class differentials of fertility, fertility related to lifestyle and social customs, population composition, population movement, active population, and such other issues which have some bearing on fertility. In the national planning program, population size, its distribution and its quality started to receive increased attention.

The attention of demographers to birth rates was actually drawn in the middle of the nineteenth century. Their attention was drawn to two events:

1. The total recorded number of deaths in France exceeded the total number of recorded births in 1854; and
2. France received a decisive defeat at the hand of Prussia in 1870.

These two events made many to believe that France became weak through lack of population growth. The fact of the observation also suggested that the decline in fertility might have started much earlier and that the fertility decline could be more in the upper strata than in the lower.

By the time the demographers shifted their attention to fertility, methodology and tools for analysis of mortality data had advanced remarkably. The accepted measures of differential mortality were tried for fertility differentials as well. But soon it was realized that fertility measures were much more complex than the measures of mortality. The population scientists have moved away from their early approach to analyze fertility data. The *quality of life* obtains greater significance than birth rate in relation to population size. Differential analysis obtains greater significance in all fertility analysis. Our attention has been drawn to such important determinants as geographic location, economic and social class, psychology, racial difference and migration. Fertility analysis has become the major domain for demographic analysis especially after 'birth control and planned family' movement obtained serious attention in most of the developing countries since 1960. The research papers and reports that come out today show absolute dominance of issues related to fertility.

The intrinsic relation that exists between birth, death and population structure led to development of *analytical theory of population*. The concept of *stable population*, which is at the center of the analytical theory, gave rise to *pure or theoretical demography*. As early as 1760, the celebrated Swedish mathematician Leonard Euler showed that if a population experienced the same birth and death rate and if the population was totally closed to in- and out-migration, then the population would show a constancy both in terms of age-sex composition and the sex ratio at all ages. Following the leads suggested in Euler's prototype, R. Bockh in 1879 estimated the Net Reproduction Rate, (NRR), for Berlin. This lead was followed by many other demographers. The most important contribution in this came from R. R. Kuczynski. The two volumes of the book *Balance of Births and Deaths* is considered as the Bible of modern theoretical demography. He used reproduction related data from almost all countries in this document.

The most important studies on population came from Alfred J. Lotka. Between 1907 and 1925 he extensively wrote how the utility of the concept of stable population can be derived from experimental demography and also how analytical demography could be used profitably in exploratory studies. He computed a few interesting indexes that could help compare two or more populations at different points of time or populations scattered over space. Commenting on the contribution of Lotka to modern demography, Frank Lorimer wrote:

> Lotka now developed a complete general theory of the interrelations of the primary biological processes, including the age and sex structures and other functions of the stable populations and the relations of generational to instantaneous changes in closed mammalian population under constant conditions.

2.2 Definition of Demography

This brief overview of evolution of demography makes it clear what demography is all about and how its scope has enlarged from simple description of population changes over time and space to a complex analytical process revolving around growth and distribution of population with due attention to such determinants as geographic location, economic and social class, psychology, racial difference and migration. The need for studying distribution, structure and changes in population had never been so intensely felt as has been in the past few decades. Yet, a formal definition of demography is necessary not only to give the discipline a base of its own but also to differentiate it from other disciplines that have human beings as their principal area of influence.

To define demography we need to start with what we mean by 'population'. We have discussed it at length in the previous chapter. The influence of statistics is immense in demography. As such, 'population' to a demographer refers to an aggregate of people possessing some specified characteristics within a precisely defined area. We can use either geographic or social space or both to demarcate one population from another. Presently, we try to understand what precisely demography is.

The credit of adding the word to our vocabulary goes to Guillard. The term has variously been used in economics, geography, sociology, anthropology and other social sciences. They have defined the term from their own viewpoints to suit their conveniences. Therefore some definitions are too narrow; others are too broad to include a wide variety of things.

Thomson and Lewis have emphasized on the *study of the size, composition and the distribution of population* when they said

> The population student is interested in a population's size, composition and distribution and in changes in these aspects through time and the causes of these changes. ... (He) is interested in these changes because they are related to human welfare.

Von Mayor provides a more measurement-oriented definition:

> Demography is the numerical analysis of the state and movement of human population inclusive of census enumerations and registration of vital processes and of whatever qualitative analysis can be made of the state and the movement of population on the basis of fundamental census and registration data.

This definition shows its close link with statistics and acknowledges its historical origin. It is a kind of continuous inventory, a kind of biological bookkeeping, and analysis of the human population and its vital processes. Both qualitative and quantitative aspects of the population have been emphasized.

Donald J. Bogue defines demography as

> ...[T]he mathematical and statistical study of the size, composition, and spatial distribution of the population...through the operation of five processes of fertility, mortality, marriage, migration and social mobility... its long run goal is to develop theories to explain the events that it charts and compares.

Hauser and Duncan offer a more or less similar definition:

> Demography is the study of size, territorial distribution and composition of the population, changes therein, and the components of such changes, which may be identified as natality, mortality, territorial movement (migration) and social mobility (change of status).

The Multilingual Demographic Dictionary defines demography as the

> Scientific study of human populations, primarily with respect their size, their structure and their development.

W.G. Barckley stressed on the aggregative nature of demography. He wrote

> Demography does not deal with the behavior of individuals but only with the aggregates of people or even part thereof. The numerical portrayal of human population is known as demography.

The Multilingual Demographic Dictionary differentiates between various aspects of demography – demographic statistics, economic demography and social demography. The latter two addresses to the "study of relations between demographic phenomenon on the one hand and economic and social phenomena on the other".

One can decipher certain core features of 'demography' to which most of these definitions address:

- Like statistics, its emphasis is on the problems of the aggregate – the mankind, and is less concerned with individual problems;
- It draws heavily from mathematics and statistics in selecting and developing tools to sort out problems confronting human population;
- It emphasizes on relative measures of size, composition and distribution in the context of time and space;
- The genetic, social, economic and geographic components together determine the quality of the population.

In demographic analysis two different viewpoints seem to work simultaneously – stationary and changing population. In the first instance, the size of a population, its structure and distribution at a point of time are discussed. Two or more populations are compared for these characteristics in the same time frame. Such analysis throws light on differentials for the demographic events as also how these characteristics change over time. The second set of analyses and discussions usually revolves around the determinants that hasten or deter changes in the structure and distribution of the population. The population scientists often would develop models to show how and why the population and its structural and distributional features change and also the likely effect these changes have on growth, welfare and health of the population. In this comparative analysis, one can use different populations or different segments of the same population.

Demography is a unique social science discipline that has attracted attention of scientists from almost all disciplines. Like statistics, it has been immensely benefitted from inter-disciplinary interactions and its potential users. Yet, demography has not lost sight of its objectives and its distinguishing character. The primary objective of demography has remained the exposition of the changes in population structure and its distribution and its relation with the changing economic, political and social scenario in national and global perspective. The demographic research has its own compulsions. Yet, feedbacks from others are welcome, and, in fact, such feedbacks often has enriched and given some new direction to their enquiry and analysis.

2.3 Macro- and Micro-Demography

The difference between 'macro' and 'micro' study lies in the size of the 'unit' used in data collection and analysis. Macro-demography studies the whole population of a region or country or an aggregate of people known to share a common culture or genetic origin or some other common social, economic or other characteristics. Usually the units for macro-demographic studies are the continents, nations or the states or larger administrative units within a country – the state of West Bengal or the metropolitan city Mumbai, or even a district, say, Darjeeling. The studies of slow or rapid growth of population, birth rate, death rate, sex ratio, dependency ratio, migration, public health system etc. are examples of macro-demographic studies. Many other issues as literacy, employment, income distribution, production-consumption, living standards, relation between population and economic development and environment are all part of macro-demography.

The 'units' of micro-demography are not only small they are included in the larger macro-units. That is, they constitute the internal or primary elements of macro analysis. Of course this 'unit' is totally dependent on the 'basic and autonomous units' of macro-demography. Micro-demography studies the nature of changes in some of the demographic characteristics of a population group that influence the structure and distribution of the population or help bring some readjustment in population groups. The micro-demography uses individual, family, small community or village as the unit for understanding causal connections to some of the changes observed in the population groups.

Generally, macro-demography dominates in demographic research. For population and economic planning we need demographic data on a macro-level. We need to identify which are dependent and which are independent variables and the relations between the variables. In macro-level analysis the contributions of the intermediate or intervening variables are not readily understood. At the national level we observe that as the income of an average person increases, birth rate falls. The relationship between income and birth rate is low negative. But macro-level data fails to explain why birth rate declines as per capita income increases. To get to the answer we need to study what changes and adjustments are observed in the family as a result in increase in household income and how these changes relate themselves to reproductive behavior. That is, what leads a common man to accept a small family norm and how an increase in income can facilitate this change of heart, can be understood only from the interrogation of the couples and other members in the family. This calls for a micro-level study.

Since we concentrate our attention on smaller units in micro-analysis, we possibly can have a better idea about how one's education, aspiration, social customs and regulations, and others jointly help determine population growth or changes in some of its characteristics. Macro- and micro-demography are complementary to each other. *The basic unit in demography is always the individual.* Examples of macro and micro-demography:

Macro-mortality studies: Role of vaccination in elimination of small pox/polio; regional differences in infant mortality; causes of mortality in the country.

Micro-mortality studies: Why some communities have reservation against polio vaccination? Role of education in public health awareness; do parents discriminate sons and daughters in matters relating to their health and education?

Macro-fertility studies: The relation between birth rate and economic development, urbanization and industrialization; the differences in birth rate between rural and urban population; religion and birth control etc. often are objectives of macro-fertility studies.

Micro-fertility studies: What is an ideal family size? Cost of rearing a child, family planning awareness and interest in birth control, need for education and aspiration for children – are examples of micro-fertility study.

Macro-migration studies: Net migration rate by regions; type of migration in India; migration and industrial development; sex difference in migration.

Micro-migration studies: Individual and family decisions behind migration; impact of immigration from Bangladesh on West Bengal's economy; why is migration rate high with educated people? How has rural economy been affected by rural-urban migration?

2.4 Is Demography a Science?

A science is a systematic body of knowledge about nature – physical, social or biological. It endeavors to discover the laws of nature that help to understand the cause and effect relations in a given phenomenon. The subject matter or the contents of different sciences differ. "The unity of science consists alone in its method, not in its nature" (Karl Pearson). "It is the approach rather than the content that is test of Science" (G. Besianz and M. Besianz).

All scientific studies follow an established path:

1. *Premises*: Statement of the hypotheses and objectives to be attained by the research.
2. *Observation*: The subject matter of the study is to be precisely and accurately observed with the help of some standard tools.
3. *Recording*: Make a careful record of all that have been observed in pursuance of the objectives of the research.
4. *Classification*: After the necessary information are collected and recorded, the next most important task is to organize and classify them into categories and arrange them in a sequence that is in commensurate with the research objectives. As Karl Pearson stated, "The classification of facts, the recognition of their sequence and relative significance is the function of science".
5. *Conclusion and generalization*: How does the analysis of classified data endorse or negate the hypotheses framed? What common rules appear to ensue from the analysis of the classified data? Can a general principle be derived from the observations made? Can a logical thread be established between the premises and conclusions? How efficient are predictions from the cause-effect relationship established in the study?
6. *Verification*: No scientific research is complete without verification of the conclusion and generalization. The research is to be repeated with a second or third sample and see if the conclusions tally.

Demography generally follows the benchmarks made out for science and scientific method. Demography collects facts through observation. Those facts only are retained for analyses that are believed to be related to the premises with which the study was started. Demographic data are factual and most often collected through census – a method used for door to door enumeration of people. The observations are classified consistent with the objectives of the study. The rules of demography are true; no matter if they are applied to this or that country, so long the countries are in the same stage of transition. The micro-level demography can establish cause and effect relationship and from macro demography the relations between variables can be studied precisely and predictions made. Over the years there has been an all round improvement in tools of measurement in demography and in analytical models. The population scientists can predict with a small margin of error how the demographic and related social events are going to take shape in near future. The fact of the matter today is that we have no ground to question Irene Taeuber's remark, "With improved data, new techniques and the precise measurement of the demographic transition that is occurring, demography has become a science rather than literature".

Population studies and demography has almost become synonymous. Population studies emphasize on the analytical interpretation of the population dynamics. It studies population composition from all possible perspectives, its growth and its interface with economic, social, cultural, geographical and ethnic issues. Demography although is primarily concerned with variables such as birth, death and migration as they affect the population size, its composition and growth, it has expanded its horizon to include many other issues that directly or indirectly influence the quality and quantity of human numbers, not necessarily restricted to a particular region or time span. Increasingly, demography has come closer to population studies and there is hardly any distinction between the analytical methods employed by either, borrowing heavily from mathematics and statistics.

2.5 Demography and Other Sciences

Very few social science disciplines can boast of having such wide application in every sphere of our collective life – national planning process, politics, economic development and what not. It has penetrated and permeated into other disciplines – actuarial science, agronomy, economics, social policy, economic geography, human biology, science of environment and ecology, history, sociology and anthropology.

Unfortunately, demography is still not given an independent status. Even only a few of the universities all over the world have faculties completely dedicated to teaching and carrying out research exclusively in demography. Demography is most extensively taught in four faculties – statistics, economics, sociology and geography. Even in the dictionary of occupational titles in USA, demographers are listed and described under the title sociologists.

Demography and Sociology: Demography and sociology both regard man as a social animal and that as a unit of society human beings have to perform a series of activities both as an individual as also as a partner of a larger group. A sociologist uses demography both as a tool and provider of social space for understanding social relations, social issues, social interactions, social reactions and the evolution and continuation of social processes. The study of population would be largely incomplete and could be misleading too if social and cultural issues do not receive the attention it deserves. Demography is not simply a study of population composition, sex ratio in the population, prevailing or changing birth rate, death rate, migration rate or marriage rate. They are meaningful only in the context of social, cultural and economic background of the human aggregate under scrutiny.

Demography, when viewed as an applied science, has closest relation with sociology since study of composition and distribution of a population cannot be understood without reference to the social environment that nurtures them. Even when structures and compositions are to be understood about a population, the frequently used criterion is social.

Both fertility and migration have a strong social base; often they are treated as part of a social phenomenon. Even change in death rates, especially age-sex specific death rates, and marriage rates are intimately related to social customs and cultural determinants.

The population policy, which basically is a demographic issue, is discussed and debated in social, cultural and economic context. The measures recommended and practiced for controlling birth rate differ from one country to another primarily because of the social and cultural circumstances prevailing in those countries.

A typical reciprocal relation appears to exist between social status on the one hand and fertility and mortality on the other. Class position has proven ascendancy over others in explaining fertility, expectation of life and even some of the principal causes of mortality and morbidity in a population.

Demography and Anthropology: Both disciplines share human populations as their research subject, though they focus on complementary aspects. Demography's primary concern is with the dynamic forces defining population size and structure and their variation across time and space; social and cultural anthropology focuses on the social organization shaping people's production and reproduction. Given these different focuses, the methodological approaches too are quite different: demography's stress is on quantification, statistical modeling, and hypothesis testing; anthropology is mostly qualitative, based on case studies, and inductive. Anthropological demography, an emerging branch, uses anthropological theory and methods to investigate demographic phenomena. The main theoretical concepts in anthropological demography are culture, gender, institutions, and political economy; its empirical research approach includes a mix of quantitative and qualitative methodologies applied to case studies. Ethnographic fieldwork and participant observation are often central to this approach, as is interpretative reading of primary data and historical material.

Anthropologists tend to be skeptical about demographers' emphasis on statistical representativeness and on the comparable nature of data collected through standardized surveys; they claim that the demographers pay little attention to the validity of the data, to the analytical models and their interpretation. Despite such divergences, scholars in both disciplines have occasionally come together, working in multidisciplinary research teams, and created complex research models to build on mutual strengths and reduce disciplinary limitations, thus launching the field of anthropological demography. Anthropological demography within demography is still evolving.

Demography and Economics: Most significant contribution to demography, both in theory and application, has come from economists. Population studies are integral part of course-contents in graduate studies in economics. Population size, its distribution and skill quality are key factors in the total production and consumption process. Labor supply and labor productivity are dependent upon the size and skill composition of the population supply. Resource management, employment generation and distortion in income distribution are key issues that confront today's economists more than what they did hundred years back. There can be no uncertainty that raising the level of living of people is very closely related to the population growth.

Population explosion in the developing countries has derailed some of their economic programs. Investment priorities, economic and development planning have often been derailed by the population explosion. For every 1 percent growth of population in a developing country like India it is estimated that about 4 percent of GDP are to be spent on infrastructure development alone – on additional schools, health centers, roads and transports. Globalization and cheap labor in the developing countries have become contentious issues in WTO. Economic issues have effects, direct or indirect, on fertility, mortality, emigration and immigration, population density, urban-ward migration, and many other things.

Demography and Human Ecology: Human ecology is concerned with birth, which gives the population base. Ecology also deals with environment and its relationship with every form of life on this earth. Ecology sees human population in terms of the extent to which people share in exploiting and developing the same environmental resources.

Sometimes human ecology is referred to as bio-demography. Human ecologists use demographic data as economists or sociologists or social planners or other social scientists do. As Otis Duncan said, "Human ecology provides a general perspective, heuristic principles and concepts and specific hypothesis of first rate significance to the demographer". Ecologists often would use demographic variables as independent variables in many of their causal models. For example, a small dispersed population cannot have social organizations of the type of a large population that is concentrated in a defined space.

Demography and Geography: Distributional perspective of population brings geography and demography close to each other. Population settlements seem to develop in places according to the climatic, temperature and rain fall experiences of the place. Population growth and its dispersion have close relationship with geography. Even in modern geography birth, death and migration are widely discussed.

Demography and Statistics: Both statistics and mathematics have contributed much in precise measurement of trends of demographic events. Special analytical tools and models have been developed by statisticians to analyze complex population data. The concepts of stable and life table stationary population, net reproduction rate (NRR) and population projection are a much sought after information in population and developmental planning. Both demography and statistics use aggregative data in their analyses.

2.6 Three Fundamental Variables in Demography

For any country or region of a country the population size is dependent on three factors only – birth, death and migration. Nothing else is required to explain population changes in a place. The population change in a place is explained by:

- Birth of a few babies;
- Death of a few persons;
- Some people come in from some other place and settle (in-migration);
- Some people leave the place and settle elsewhere (out-migration).

Any one of the four reasons stated above can singly or conjointly change the size and composition of population of a place. In population analysis therefore we need precise and accurate information on these four factors. From the first two, we get a composite variable – *natural increase* (birth–death) of the population. Besides these three principal variables, the demographers use biological (sex, age, religion) and social (marriage, education, occupation, income, social class) variables in population analysis.

2.7 Some Basic Concepts in Demographic Analysis

Observation: Experimental or fully controlled enquiries are out of question in demography. The demographer has to rely on his observation or the information parted with him from time to time, open as they are to the conflicting influences of psycho-social factors operating concurrently. The study can take an experimental tinge when the demographer studies the same population at different time points or when he studies different populations at the same point of time. For a causal inference the researcher needs to focus on micro units, possibly to individual or family.

Cohort and Secular Analysis: A *cohort* consists of a group of people sharing a common temporal demographic experience over a defined period of time. This could be the number of people who were born in the same year and the same day, or number of women all married at a particular age, or number of persons who started their educational or occupational career together. Cohort study is important in demography since the occurrence rate of an event is strongly influenced by the length of time elapsed since the occurrence of another event. For example, the event of birth can be studied in relation to mortality, the event of marriage in relation to fertility.

Not necessarily all demographic analyses are cohort analysis. We may concentrate on a period of time and study vital rates for the period. Such analyses may be described as S*ecular Analysis.* Sample Registration Data or National Sample Survey data are of this type. Cohort and secular analysis may be simultaneously employed to supplement one another, and two taken together may throw considerable light on an event than either used in isolation.

Differentials: Whenever analyzing population data we have to classify it into meaningful groups and subgroups. The experiences of each such group in respect to demographic event are measured separately and the results compared to provide additional information how the event operates and their concomitant factors in various strata. The study of 'differential mortality' and 'differential fertility' is encouraged in population studies. Some of the often-used differentials as geographical location or region; religion, race, climate, occupation, education, industry, residence etc. may be significantly related to this regional or locational divide. Occupation acts as an important differential both in fertility, mortality and migration. Whatever the divisions and subdivisions are, the strata so formed must be as homogeneous as possible. Other differentials could be the nature of job (mining workers, hazardous industry, blue/white color job, etc.), income, housing accommodation, education, and the like.

3 Nature and Sources of Demographic Data

3.1 Introduction

The information a demographer collects are classified into two categories:

1. Information about personal characteristics as age, sex, education, occupation etc.; and
2. Information about rates of birth and death – the vital events. Migration, marriage, divorce, etc. are also included under vital events.

Two principal methods are employed for collection of demographic data – by enumeration at a point of time and by recording events as they occur over a period. Census and sample surveys are examples of the first method, and provide 'stock' data. Birth, death, migration, marriage, divorce, etc. constitute 'flow' data, obtained from the records of the respective registers maintained by authorized state agencies, are examples of the second category.

There are four sources for demographic data: Civil Registration System, Continuing Register, Census and Sample Surveys.

3.2 Civil Registration System

Every country has some system in place for recording the principal life events such as birth, death, marriage, divorce, etc. The advanced countries have over the years developed a nearly foolproof system of registration of these life events after long persuasion and rigid enforcement of law. The developing countries still have a long way to go in enforcement of their laws in this respect. Some success has been achieved in birth and death registration but not in respect to marriage and divorce.

Usually, the Municipalities, Corporations and Panchayats or local bodies are given the responsibility of maintaining registers for births and deaths. The hospitals, health centers, nursing homes send periodic reports of birth and death to their respective municipalities. When births and deaths occur outside institutional care, certificates from the attending doctors are submitted to municipality for registration in a given format. The registration offices issue certificate of registration. As all these documents are pooled together, one can work out the total number of incidences of birth and death in a region or country in a given period of time.

Registration system is an age-old practice though reasons for registration had often been different from that in today's registration. Its first reference was found in Japan as back as 720 BC. In the Christian countries, the ecclesiastical authorities maintained records of burials, baptism and wedding long before the modern system of registration was introduced. Its reference is found in France as early as 1308. 'Bills of mortality' were registration statement issued by parish clerks, especially in times of plague epidemic, showing the number of deaths registered with causes thereof. Civil registration in England and Welsh was formally introduced in 1839 under the dynamic leadership of Dr. William Farr. Prior to this the registration system was not quite scientific, realistic and reliable. Dr. Farr worked hard for long 40 years and developed methods for recording the vital events of a population. With some minor modifications, the inventory developed by Dr. Farr is used in almost all the countries.

Maintaining a civil register for the vital events received considerable resistance from many quarters. The Church, politicians and military were often against it. Earlier, information related to population were kept secret primarily for reasons of defense of the country. Even today, some countries still have reservations to share the population statistics with other countries. In fact, in some of the socialist countries (China, for example) even their own men often are denied the exact information.

The 1989 United Nations' Convention of the Rights of Child (CRC) declared:

> The child shall be registered immediately after birth and shall have the right from birth to a name, the right to acquire a nationality as far as possible the right to know and be cared by his or her parents.

The Convention also laid down a broad outline of the format of the registration. Registration should include child's name, sex, date and place of birth, and the name, address and nationality of both parents.

Civil registration in India. Although registration of birth and death dates back to the time of Maurya Chadragupta, the first documentary evidence of registration was found in Goa. The Portuguese occupied and settled in Goa in 1510. It is in Goa where the oldest records of birth, death and marriage are found. In British occupied India, birth registration was started in 1670, death in 1720 and marriage much earlier, in 1604. But formal civil registration in India was introduced in the later part of the nineteenth century under British rule. Birth and death registration in India was started in 1860 primarily for evolving preventive measures against colossal loss of human lives due to frequent famines and epidemics throughout the length and breadth of the country. In 1886, the then rulers passed an Act for registration of birth, death and marriage throughout the country. The registration however was not made mandatory. As such, the promulgation of the Act did not produce the desired result. The need for a more scientific documentation of these vital events has from time to time been discussed and Commissions appointed (Health Survey and Development Committee, 1946, Vital Statistics Committee, 1949, for example). Even as early as the publication of the third Census Report, the Registrar General and Census Commissioner G. F. Hardy wrote:

> It would appear hopeless for many years to come to expect anything like complete registration of births and deaths in India, and I would suggest that it would be well to concentrate efforts in this direction upon certain small but representative areas in various parts of India.

It took more than 60 years to implement Hardy's recommendations. Some serious talks began in the sixties of the last century when it was realized that the population projections in early fifties were miles behind the actual 1961 census figures. The assumptions made about parameters like birth rate, death rate, expectation of life etc. had little semblance with what was happening in the real world. The national planners realized that strict implementation of Civil Registration Act throughout the country is a must but that would take quite sometime before the registration data could be trusted upon for analysis of demographic events and population projection. National Sample Survey Organization (NSSO) was entrusted with collection of various types of data through large-scale sample surveys. A new entity came into being in the form of Sample Registration Scheme (SRS) under Registrar General of India for continuous registration of birth and death throughout the year in selected sample blocks in the line suggested by Hardy.

Since the promulgation of Birth and Death Registration Act, 1969, registration of birth and death, especially in cities and urban areas has improved considerably. Earlier, registration was voluntary. Since a sizeable number of births now take place in hospitals, health centers and nursing homes, birth registration has improved both in rural and urban areas. The records of birth in these institutions are sent to the local registration authority routine. In urban areas, the cremation grounds and graveyards are under the direct control of the local municipality. Death certificates have been made mandatory in inheritance of property or putting up claims for insurance and bank deposits. This aspect is still neglected in villages where the local administration is sloppy and less than efficient. Civil Registration centers under the control of the Office of the Registrar General of India are spread all over the country. The state health departments depute especially trained health workers to assist the municipalities in recording these vital events. The Working Group on Birth and Death Registration reported that at the national level, approximately 55 percent of births and 45 percent of deaths were registered in India in 2001.

3.3 Continuing Register

There are many other public agencies that maintain registers for their specific requirements. In the developed countries permanent population register (social security number is given to every person) is maintained for administrative and legal purposes. The correctness of population census can be verified from this. Social Security Department, intelligence agencies, forensic, police, motor-vehicles and income tax department, telephone companies, electric offices, life insurance corporations, election commission, municipalities, ration offices and many others maintain various types of information about some cross-section of the population of their interest. Information collected from these agencies may come handy in demographic analysis of selected segments of the population.

3.4 Census

If the civil registration of vital events is looked upon as photographs taken in a movie camera, census may be thought of as providing a portrait of the major events in a population taken by a still camera. The picture frame gives a vivid description of the constituent elements and their spatial distribution at a particular point of time. Census generally refers to periodic counting of every people within the geographic confines of a region or country. Usually census is taken every 10 years. In unusual circumstance the date for census may be changed.

Modern census is not restricted to counting of human heads alone; the counting may include agricultural land and agricultural production, houses, industries and industrial production, domestic animals, even wild animals in conservatories (tiger census, for example). There is a good many differences between the modern census and the census of the earlier days – in terms of objective, purpose, methods and use of the census data. It has not been easy to convince people and those in charge of the defense of the country about the need for a regular counting of all people. Census data have become indispensable for such purposes as national planning, defining the assembly segments, distribution of national resources to various states, and in science and technology.

The word Census is derived from the Latin – *Censere*, meaning *to value or count*. The population count in earlier times was never for the purpose of demographic analysis. Census was conducted to work out the defense strength of the country. In Rome, population was counted to estimate the strength of the healthy adult males. Obviously, the counting helped the ruler to engage these people for the defense of the country. In China, census was carried out primarily to identify people from whom tax could be collected. Americans used census to determine people's representatives from the Federal States. This has remained one of the major intents of census in all countries in addition to using it for other purposes. India uses census head count to determine the size of representatives both in parliament and assembly, and local bodies from a particular state as also to decide on the share of revenue and assistance from the central budget for different states and for other purposes.

In ancient times, only some special groups were brought under census – to take a stock of man power for the defense of the country, to identify tax payers, landlords, cultivators, business men etc. The ideal of this primitive type of census was 'count those that count'. In modern census, count everyone in the interest of the nation. The modern census is the total process of collecting, compiling and publishing demographic, economic and social data pertaining, to a specified time or times, to all persons of a defined territory.

Early Census: Unlike civil registration, census has a very long history. There are historical documents that even some 5,000 years back population count was a regular feature in Sumerian civilization. In Egypt counting of people in different occupations was in vogue. During Chou dynasty in China (1050 BC – 247 BC), the rulers conducted population counts for administrative reasons. Population count invariably meant that those counted would either be asked to join the army or pay tax. The counting therefore always contained some amount of bias and error. The population count was never secular irrespective of age and sex of those counted.

In Rome, census was used both for the defense and administration of the state. Servious Tullious (578 BC – 534 BC) carried out the first ever census in Rome. A remarkably simple and ingenious method was followed in the population count. On a particular day of a religious festival every year, every citizen had to show his or her respect for the ruler by personally depositing a coin of particular denomination to the treasury. The value of the coin was determined by age and sex of the person. The collected coins were counted separately by their denomination. The size of the population and its age-sex distribution could readily be ascertained from these forced deposits. It is needless to say that the treasury became richer by this souvenir from the citizens.

Historical documents show that first-ever complete census was conducted in Nuremberg in 1449. Every citizen, irrespective of age and sex, was counted. This was done at a time when enemy from all directions seized Nuremberg. Since Nuremberg was cut off from the outside world, it was necessary to take a stock of the food situation relative to the size of the population and also for developing a distribution mechanism for optimum use of the limited resources. The population count of course was never made public. In 1662, Norway conducted population count on everyone, 12 years and above, for making the defense of the country strong. Louis XIV carried out census in various parts of France. However, the results of the count were never made public in his lifetime. Canada started regular periodic census in 1664 and the same continued uninterrupted till 1750. The first census report, a 152-page document, was published in 1666. The document dealt with such issues as total population, distribution of the population by age and sex, number of married persons, persons in different occupations, etc. This was accomplished 350 years past in the history – a remarkable achievement by all counts. There are historical documents to show that population was counted in selected regions in India at the time of Ashoka (270 BC – 230 BC).

Modern Census: The modern regular periodic census began midway in the 18th century (Sweden, 1749, Norway and Denmark, 1769). Although the first census was conducted in Virginia (USA) in 1624, the periodic census became an integral part of American Constitutions in 1787.

Dates of initiation of modern periodic census in selected few countries including India are as follows:

England	1891	Belgium	1829
France	1835	Japan	1873
India	1881	Egypt	1897
Russia	1897	China	1951

By the middle of the nineteenth century most countries in Europe had instituted periodic census in their countries. Currently, over 95 percent of the world population is covered by regular census.

Census Techniques – De facto and De jure. Two techniques are followed for census operations. *De facto* census technique records a person at the place he happens to be on the census night no matter if it was his residence or only a transit point. This was largely followed in England and in India as well but was discontinued later. The counting had to be completed in a single day all over the country in *de facto* technique. A huge army of enumerators was to be engaged in the process. To prevent normal movement of people, a national holiday was to be declared and the public transports were to be stopped from plying. There was no provision for 'post enumeration check' (PEC). Once the enumeration was over by this technique, one could proceed directly to tabulation and analysis of the data. The problem really arises with a big country like India where completing the enumeration in a single day is really a tough job. Once we allow the enumeration to be completed within, say seven or ten days, we cannot expect that people would remain stationed in their normal place of residence. This situation would invite a person being counted at more than one place or even some may not be counted at all because of mismatch between his stay at a particular place and the date of counting at that place. The tourists, salesman and vagabonds, that is, the 'floating population' would create serious problems in this type of enumeration.

In *De jure* technique the people are counted where they are on the census day and then regrouped into their usual place of residence. Thus, a Mumbaikar who was in Delhi when the enumeration was carried out would be recorded in Delhi but relocated to Mumbai later. The *de jure* technique finally counts an individual at his 'usual place of residence'. It is a bit cumbrous and time-consuming process since all documents relating to the person, who was counted at a place other than his normal residence, will have to be sent to proper census authority of the destination area. The problem really arises when a person has two or more houses at different places and he spends some part of the year in all these houses. The problems with the 'floating population' can largely be overcome by this technique. However, it may so happen that the timing of movement of a person is such that he is not counted at any of the places he had visited while the enumeration work was on.

The *de facto* census is consistent with the freeze picture of a population defined by a 'snap shot'. With a small population not quite dispersed over space, *de facto* technique could be the best option. Because of time constraint, the census schedule has to confine to a few basic questions only. There are many sources through which errors could creep in because of the vast nature of the exercise in a very limited time span.

De jure census allows one to use a schedule seeking more information from each person. Inaccuracies in recording and chances of skipping persons from enumeration are less with this technique. The census operation can be conducted with a smaller fleet of enumerators than are needed in the other technique. The real difficulty arises in the definition of 'usual place of residence'. Since the enumeration is staggered, there shall be new incidences of birth, death and migration, the account of which may not be fully covered in 'post-enumeration check' (now called 'post-enumeration survey' PES in India). The problem is really serious with those who really have no fixed place of residence. The tabulation work cannot proceed till the controversial data are relocated to their actual place of origin. This would delay the publication of the result making the data less useful to their users. The *de jure* method could be successfully used in vital registration since people from distant places come to a hospital and the incidences of births and deaths can be relocated to the normal places of their origin.

Of the two methods, the enumeration on *de-jure* basis is more difficult to achieve without the risks of omission or multiple count. Enumeration of *de-facto* population appears simple but will be difficult to put into operation unless the movement of population is restricted on the census day and the entire enumeration is got through on a single night which is operationally difficult specifically when large population of 1,000 millions has to be covered by *canvasser method*. In practice, therefore, enumeration on a 100 per cent *de-facto* or *de-jure* basis is impossible. Often a judicious mix of the two is resorted to.

Canvasser and householder methods are the two recognized methods of census enumeration. Under 'canvasser' method the enumerator approaches every household and records answers on the schedules after ascertaining the particulars from the head of the household or other knowledgeable adult persons in the household. Under the 'householder' method the enumerator distributes the census schedules to each household in his census block and the head of the household is requested to fill the answer for all members of his/her household and the enumerator later collects back the answered schedules soon after the census day is over. A country like India where questionnaire literacy is very low, the 'canvasser' method is the only practical method for enumeration. Additional information for graduate persons is usually collected by householder method.

3.5 Sample Surveys

A demographer wishes to get answers to many complex questions, which cannot be collected through a census schedule. Even a young adult can reply to the schedules that are canvassed in a census. The enumerators usually have no special training in demography. It is also for this reason that more complex questions relating to social and economic issues are left out of normal census schedules. Asking land related questions, questions on agro-practices, income and expenditure, birth control etc. require special skill on the part of the interrogator.

Sample surveys are a vital source of demographic data, second only to Periodic Complete Census. However, from user perspective Sample Surveys are sometimes more important and reliable than even the complete census. The survey data are much fine-tuned since the data are collected under direct supervision of professional persons by specially trained field staff. No measurement is error free; census enumeration is not exception to that. It is only through sample surveys that we can determine the character and the nature of error in census data. Sample surveys (NSS, SRS in India, for example) for getting vital population data have gained momentum in the recent past for various reasons. This technique produces not only the same kinds of information about population as the other two techniques – vital registration system and the periodic census, it gives much detailed and fine tuned observations since the survey sample plans are designed to optimize the variability inherent in the population, and checks and cross-checks for every bit of information is assured since the size of the sample is small and that the surveys are carried out by a trained army of investigators. The sampling technique employed gives a good account of the range of errors likely to be committed and make necessary adjustments to compensate for the error.

Sample surveys become obvious source of data on many intricate issues. Sample surveys are still not substitutes for complete enumeration, but days are not far away when large sample surveys would become the obvious choice for values of some parameters that play critical roles in most direct and indirect estimation in analytical demography. The sample surveys currently are conducted for three broad reasons:

1. It is used to supplement the current census on issues that cannot be covered through census enumeration. It also provides a check on the accuracy of the census count. Simultaneously with census, sample survey under the aegis of Census Commissioner is conducted on more complex social and economic issues with the help of trained investigators. Such surveys are conducted on 1–20 percent of the population.
2. It can be used for updating the results of a complete census taken sometime before.
3. Sample surveys are conducted independent of the census leading to independent estimate of demographic events at any point of time. In India, many independent bodies as the Registrar General of India, Indian Statistical Institute (ISI), Central Statistical Organization (CSO), Indian Population Council, National Sample Survey Organization (NSSO), Sample Registration Scheme (SRS) etc. conduct such surveys.

The manner in which the sample is chosen is very pertinent to the inferences made from the sample studies. Efficient sampling requires stratification and this can be achieved if a reference framework is worked out on the basis of the recent complete count. Region-specific census blocks could be our unit from which the samples are drawn. This is done in Sample Registration Scheme, SRS in India since 1964.

Sample surveys are integral part of a census operation in that some sort of sample survey is employed in every phase of the work of the Census Commissioner – at the planning stages, in enumeration itself, in the course of processing and tabulating data, and as part of subsequent evaluations of the quality of statistics collected.

3.6 Accuracy and Errors in Demographic Data

Demography collects information about human beings. No one expects that the information so collected would be completely free from error. A population scientist has the conviction that with better planning and improved methodology, the errors could be brought down to a minimum. For achieving this, we first need to look at the sources through which such errors often would enter into. Three major sources have been identified.

1. *Error of Coverage:* This generally is a problem related to census. The information must be collected from each and every independent unit of the universe. It must be assured that every information are collected from all the targeted units of the population and that no unit is counted twice or more on the same event. With a vast population, as in India, which is scattered all over the canvas, there always remains the doubt if all the units of the universe have really

been covered. Such errors in coverage can be reduced only if the enumerators are aware that this coverage error could put a serious question mark on the efficacy of the whole exercise. No one can for sure say that India had 1,027,015,247 persons on March 1, 2001. How can we be sure that the population was not 5 or 10 million more or less? An idea about under or over estimation can be had only from subsequent sample surveys. PEC survey could provide an estimate of such coverage error.

When the population is very large and population density at some places is very thin, especially in the remote hilly areas or other inaccessible areas, some gap between the actual population and the target population is probable. In spite of all the measures taken some of the very remote and inaccessible areas might remain uncovered.

2. *Error of Response:* The enumerator records information as are supplied by the respondent. He has no time to verify if the information supplied are true or not. The respondent too often does not know the exact answer to some of the questions asked. Even the respondent may not have understood the question properly. For example, a large segment of our rural people would not know their date of birth what to speak of date of birth of their parents or the daughter-in-law. As such, reporting of ages would be very approximate. This is one kind of error, which we can do nothing about. But there would be instances where there would be a deliberate attempt to misguide the interviewer. On questions of land holding, income, production etc. some respondents deliberately give a distorted figure. This is in spite of the assurances given by the enumerator that the information collected from them would be used for demographic analysis only and that any information collected by the census authority could not be used against the person in any court of law. But that would not always convince them. On the question of type of family many respondents would say that they have a traditional family although their children or brothers have separate family units living under the same roof. This they often would do as a cover up for their land holding in excess of permissible limits under the law. Often we are aware that the story is fabricated, but the enumerator has no option but to record what the respondent has said.
3. *Errors in Recording and Tabulation.* This type of error happens when the enumerator or the tabulator is unmindful to his job. Some errors happen when answers are recorded by symbols. Errors often would be committed while entering data in the computer and arranging the same in some particular order.

If errors are not rectified at the early stage, nothing can be done to set them right at a later stage. When anomaly is found while collecting data, it must be attended to at the same instance. In PEC phase some extra care need be taken to rectify incongruity detected in the normal census enumeration. To minimize errors while collecting data and to detect if the data contained any error, the following guidelines may be followed.

1. The events or characteristics on which information are to be collected must be defined properly. For example, there was a sharp decline in female employment between 1961 and 1971 Census in India. The definition of an 'employed female' adopted in 1971 Census was quite different from the definition of 'work' followed in earlier enumerations. In fact, the definition of 'work' has undergone considerable modifications over the years.
2. Ensure that an individual is counted once and only once. Multiple counting of the same individual can be eliminated if we are a little careful in post-enumeration check (PEC) phase.

3. The respondents are to be motivated to give true answers to the questions posed. They are to be assured that the information collected in the census will be used for population analysis of the country. That there is a legal protection against using the census data for purposes other than research must also be stressed.
4. A proper classification of the probable responses to any question insures proper recording of responses.
5. Errors may enter into the data at various stages of copying, tabulation and transfer of data to the disc.

It is admitted that the macro-level data in demographic studies errors cannot be eliminated altogether. However, seriousness of these errors and omissions can be checked quite easily.

1. The *internal consistency* in a particular document can be checked. For example, anomalies in recorded ages can easily be checked if we compare the recorded ages of mother and her children. Various information collected on the same individual or family can be checked for their consistency.
2. Some sort of continuity and consistency are observed in some of the major variables through consecutive censuses. Distribution of the population by age and sex, birth, death and infant mortality rate, sex ratio, etc. does not generally change drastically over night. So are the causes of mortality, migration and occupational distribution. This is what the demographers would like to call "serial consistency". There is a vast drop in sex ratio (F/M) in 0–4 age group in 2001 census in India. Such and many other observations put a question mark on the quality of census data in India.
3. Sample surveys on selected regions or groups are conducted either simultaneously or sometime after the census. The sample results for those segments of the population can be compared with that of the census to give an index of accuracy of either. Since sample survey results are more accurate and dependable, the errors if any in the census data can be determined. Such anomalies often are observed in cause of death analysis as well.
4. Information obtained on selected issues from various sources – census, registration and sample survey must be comparable. For example, we know from the census data about how many children of either sex are currently in schools and colleges. The same data can be directly obtained from the school and college rosters. The vital registers provide enough information for babies born, their age distribution, the incidences of their death, etc. The same are obtained from the census data as well. The aggregate picture obtained from these sources should generally agree.
5. Those who were aged x in 2001 would be $x + 10$ in 2011. How many of those aged x in 2001 are likely to survive till 2011 can be estimated from age-specific mortality rates. The absolute size of the population in $x + 10$ year age group sometimes is significantly larger than the size of the population in x age group 10 years back. By no stretch of imagination can this increase be explained by in-migration, especially in those age groups where the anomalies are mostly concentrated. The observed size in 2011 and the expected size on the expectation of survival from 2001 can be compared to estimate the strength of error for various age groups. The actual size estimated from the reported population share by age groups for all the age groups in successive Indian censuses since 1901 has been calculated (vide Table 4.2 in Chapter 4, *Changing Demographic Scenario in India*). The anomaly is found consistently in 10–14 and

25–29 year age groups both for the male and female populations as we compare their absolute numbers in these groups with those in 0–4 and 15–19 age groups respectively observed in the previous census enumerations. The same anomaly is observed in other age groups, though to a lesser extent. This really raises the question how reliable our enumerations are. Similarly, the sex ratio in any age group cannot change dramatically in successive censuses if there was no visible reason to justify such drastic changes. Such anomalies are also observed in the Indian Census data. Even though the census data over the years show some kind of serial consistency, these observations raise serious questions about the reliability of the basic data from which we try to have an idea about the serial consistency.

The quality of demographic data all over the world has improved in the last two decades or so. Age specific fertility and mortality measures are fairly accurate and reliable. The population scientists make fairly accurate projection of the size of population for not too a distant future date based on expected average growth. Even by applying compound interest formula, we can estimate the likely size of the population quite easily. There is always the scope for further improvement of demographic data. This aspect need to be sincerely addressed both by demographers and those in administration.

4 Theories of Population

4.1 Pre-Malthusian Population Thoughts

There has been a lot of noise in all international forums about the impact the massive population increase is having on our natural resources, forest, ecology and bio-diversity, environment, supply of food and other essential commodities and fund crunch for social sector and activities relating to improvement of infrastructure. The more organized expression of concern for uncontrolled growth of population in the last 50 years does not imply that population related issues have drawn attention of the intelligentsia, politicians and planners only in the recent past. There is ample evidence in recorded history that concern for population was expressed time and again by the then rulers and their advisors and the wise men of their times.

Population count was popular even some 5,000 years back among the Sumerians. It was that long back they realized that the social, economic, political and defense of a country were intricately related to the size and growth of population. With little or no progress in science and technology, a nation had to depend entirely on the 'active part' of the population for its economic progress. A nation's military capability depended upon the size of the army it had since modern warfare equipments were unknown in that period. Natural calamity, epidemic and frequent war took heavy toll of human lives. For these and other reasons the strength of population was considered an asset for a country. Religious preaching and ethical prescriptions supplied the needed support for an increase in population for the economic wellbeing, defense and material prosperity of a nation.

Progress in science and technology and industrial revolution brought in a silent revolution in our community life. This in turn slowly changed the complexion of the social, economic and political fabric of nations. Scientific and technological advancement improved the quality of life; with declining death rate the population started to rise. Through improvement in agricultural and industrial output, there was a change in production-related thoughts as well. The capital-intensive production gradually took over from labor-intensive production. Re-assessment began as to how effectively the existing natural resources and the energy options can be used. The economic and military strength and the state of human development of a country are judged by the standard of living of the common man, their education, skill and the extent to which the country's economic and social administration and the defense are organized by the state-of-the-art management. The sheer size of the population is no longer considered an asset or potential strength of a nation. The population thoughts cannot remain aloof to these contrasting social and economic realizations. Population growth signify development and military strength of a country in one system, the same is regarded as abhorrent to growth and prosperity of a nation in the other school.

The Chinese philosopher Confucius stressed on the need for a balanced growth of population. Unless agricultural production improved, the state cannot earn sufficient revenue to manage its affairs effectively. With fewer people, agricultural production would suffer and the revenue collection would sink. Too many people would create unwelcome pressure on land, as also on state's economy. "Optimum Population" dominated the discourses by most of the Chinese philosophers. As and when a severe depopulation at a place due to natural calamity or some epidemic arose, the surplus people from other locations could be diverted to that place and a population balance between different regions could be restored. Though Confucius spoke of optimum population, he generally supported the growth of population.

The Greek philosopher Plato expressed his opinion on the size of population while analyzing the characteristics of a city-state. The minimum size of the population necessary to bring the full potential of a man and the state to fruition is what he called 'the most desirable size of the population'. Plato also said that the population should be large enough for defense of the country and to sustain its economic activities; at the same time, he said that the population must not be so large as to create problems for smooth administration. He supported eugenics and therefore was not averse to infanticide if that would eliminate mentally and physically crippled children. When the population size exceeds a limit, the larger families must be asked to adopt birth control measures. He recommended establishment of colonies to deal with the problems of surplus population. When the population experienced a sudden decline, the state must declare incentives for higher fertility. Immigration could be encouraged in extreme cases.

At about the same time as Plato, India saw the rise of a great political scientist and philosopher, Kautilya. In his *Arthashastra*, he discussed what would be the most favorable size of the population in view of the political, economic and defense requirements of a nation. The ideal size of the population in a village, he thought, should be between 100 and 500 agricultural families for every 1–2 sq mile of land area. The number should not fall below this level in any circumstances. He calculated this most desirable number with reference to availability of agricultural land and mining potential of the place.

In Roman literature there are ample evidences which suggest that the Romans not only supported higher growth of population, they provided incentives for higher fertility as well. The unmarried persons and those who had no children were asked to pay additional taxes. The Roman Empire seemed to have remained busy in war all the time and therefore they needed a huge contingent force comprised of healthy adults for their army.

Between fifteenth and eighteenth century and thereafter the world saw a sea change in standard of living, especially in Europe. The discovery of America and the naval route to India and many new discoveries in science, especially in areas of explosives and printing machines, ushered in a technological and industrial revolution. Death rates declined, population started to grow. The growing international trade, expansion of industries and opening out new colonies took care of the growth of population. Capitalism became deeply rooted in European countries, especially in England, France, Portugal and Spain. These developments favored growth of population. Attitude towards growth of population is reflected in the contemporary writings: "The King's glory is in the multitude of people" (Gullalime Bude), "There is no wealth or strength but in men" (Jean Bodin).

Mercantilist School

In the pre-Malthusian modern era the Mercantilist School of Political Economy had to offer a population theory of some consequence. This school regarded a large population as profitable for social and economic advancement of a country. The adherent to this school advocated adoption of such social schemes that would promote growth of population – encourage marriage, support large families, ensure better public health, discourage emigration and encourage immigration. Growth of population would guarantee the proper use of internal resources; accessibility to cheap labor would also be assured in the process. Lower labor rate would bring down the cost of production giving a competitive platform in international trade. Internal demand for the products would also increase, which in turn would help increase the labor demand. In Mercantilist economy, gross domestic product and state of health of national economy received greater attention than per capita increase in income. The population in Mercantilist economy obtains significance because of political and economic implication of a large labor force at cheaper rates and military strength of the country.

The two fundamental aspects of Mercantilist economy are: (a) production has to be increased to make the nation wealthy, and (b) strategies have to be worked out for export promotion of various commodities. Without the growth of the labor force, production cannot be increased. There would be fierce competition in international trading and to become a major player in the export market the product must be kept cheap without compromising on quality. This competition in international trading often would lead to serious confrontation between nations and demand military intervention. To meet these exigencies, the population must grow and grow fast. This competition and growth of population would inevitably lead to inflation and labor exploitation. Such countries are found to promulgate many restrictions on the common man – unmarried people are taxed in many different ways, marriage and high fertility are encouraged, soft attitude for relations outside marriage, emigration is strictly discouraged and immigration encouraged.

Classical School of Economics

Adam Smith, the founder of Classical School of Economics, unlike the Mercantilist school, was more analytical in his approach to different aspects of population. He tried to analyze the impact the increased population would have on various segments of a population. Adam Smith too favored the growth of population. He felt that the population growth would expand the demand for commodities and at the same time the increased labor supply would encourage *division of labor* for a more efficient production system. The supply market being large, labor component in production would be cheap. Increase in demand for a commodity results from the fall in the price, quality remaining the same. Assured of a high profitable return from investment, more entrepreneurs would put in money on a variety of products. With industrial climate becoming more favorable, the labor market would expand and the family income would rise. Although labors are paid less, their share of contribution to GDP increases. Adam Smith was optimistic about the possible impact the increased population supply would have on the economy of a country. Growth of population would expand both the labor market and consumers. With division of labor and diversification of products, the demand for labor would remain high and chances of becoming unemployed would also lessen.

A semblance of the views expressed by Malthus on population could be seen in the writings of Machiavelli, Botero and Cantillon. Machiavelli and Botero were of the view that the surplus part of a population would automatically be eliminated through poverty, hunger and diseases. Botero also said that the population continues to grow fast up to a certain span of time. Thereafter, the rate of growth would decline; the growth rate even may turn negative bringing down the absolute size of the population. He was of the opinion that resources necessary for sustaining life on earth are limited. This resource limitation would not allow the population to grow beyond a point. He also spoke that decrease in soil fertility, natural calamity and epidemics and poor health condition are natural deterrent to population growth. Even after admitting that food production cannot be increased beyond a point and that food is necessary for survival, the population of a nation, he said, is an indicator of the wealth, prosperity and its authority.

Cantillon discussed the relation between the size of a population and the standard of living of its people. His two main arguments were that (1) the population of a country grows at a rate appropriate to its state of economy, and (2) the growth rate of population diminishes as the standard of living of the common man improves. In population analysis, he stressed on cumulative wealth and on fairness in distribution of the national income among the masses rather than on the absolute size of the population.

By the middle of the eighteenth century, Robert Wallace among others expressed opinion against state's sympathetic and welfare role in improving the standard of living of the poor labor class. He was against the "Poor Law" and said that the dole from the state or the Church offered to this poor would not help improve their life style; the nation as a whole would suffer in consequence. The provision of charity, which is the other name of begging, only would encourage higher birth rate among these poor. Babies born in these families would have a better chance to reach their adulthood. The pressure of the population on earth would mount; a more prosperous human civilization would remain only a dream. For this reason Wallace opposed the liberal attitude of the state towards these downtrodden. Because of high birth rate in these families, the population of a country would reach a staggering high, which would bring all developmental activities to a halt. To combat this man-made disaster, the state may have to strictly enforce sterilization, restriction on marriage, soften its attitude towards infanticide and even may have to take measures to get rid of the senior citizens. But such drastic measures will not be accepted in civilized society. Therefore anarchy and civil war would let loose to solve the problem of population.

Towards the end of the eighteenth century, what Hung Liang-Chi, nicknamed as Chinese Malthus, told about population closely resembles what Malthus had said in 1798. Like Malthus, he drew attention to the fact that there was an imbalance between population growth and supply of basic necessities for sustenance of life. The growth of the latter can never match the growth of the former. The population may grow by 5 to 25 times in 100 years, but production of essential commodities can grow only by 3 to 5 times in the same time span. That is, hunger, poverty and ill health would be constant companions of the poor.

The groundwork so nicely done by John Graunt and William Petty and scientists from various discipline made the task of Malthus that much easier. Census and other socio-economic data from many countries provided a realistic picture of population change in different parts of the world. The fundamentals of population, especially differential mortality, were already under close scrutiny of the population scientists. In spite of noteworthy improvement in production of consumer goods due to progress in science and technology, the difference in the rates of growth in consumer goods production and in population growth did not weaken. It was a general agreement that rate of growth of population far exceeded the rate of food production growth and that large population was a serious obstacle to the social and economic progress of a nation. This paradigm shift in population thought is visibly noticed in Malthusian doctrine.

4.2 Primary and Secondary Theories of Population

Growth of population has attracted attention of scientists from various disciplines – philosophers, economists, bio-scientists, sociologists, anthropologists, political scientists, environmentalists and geographers. Naturally, they looked at the growth and distribution of population from their points of view. Several theories have been proposed to explain the changes in population. Population had remained at the center stage in many such theories (*Primary Theories*). In many other instances, however, the scientists tried to understand and explain population change through the eyes of some of their established theories (*Secondary Theories*). At the center of primary theory of population are the various aspects of the population – *how* does the population change, *why* such changes occur and *what* of the population changes as a result. In secondary theories the scientists examine some economic premises, social classes, values, industrialization and modernization of lifestyle etc. in relation to changes in some population characteristics. These really do not constitute the basic domains of demography. The scientists, however, often find that without making much alteration these tenets can well be adapted to explain many features of a population. It is not difficult to identify the theories of the first kind since they primarily address to the structure, distribution, movement and growth of population. It is with the second type we often have some dilemma. Some of their issues are so closely related to population that they are likely to be confused as primary theories of population.

4.3 Natural and Social Theories of Population

Population theories, from ancient times to the present, can broadly be classified as *Natural* (biological and mechanistic) and *Social*. The analysis of population in *natural theories* rests on the principle that 'biological' behavior (hunger for food and procreation) is universal. This is the natural principle of survival for all animals including humans. The proponents of such theories are hesitant to admit that man has the intellect and capacity to rise above these biological cravings. Since basic facts of life, determined by nature, are the same for all biological animals, man, being a part of this system, cannot be exception to this universal rule. The tenets of biological inheritance helps pacify our agony over what mayhem the growth of world population can play in denying quality of life on this earth, but it helps very little in evolving solutions to problems created by the facts of inheritance.

Social theories, on the other hand, try to explain population growth in terms of factors or events that are basically man-made and therefore man-changeable. It does not deny the basic facts of nature, but believes that much of it are correlated with the social and economic environment and therefore steps in the right direction can be taken, that is, creating an environment that would motivate people to adopt means and devices to lessen or neutralize the conditions that favor or trigger uncontrolled growth of population. No wonder that modern demographic analyses took up social and environmental issues in an aggressive manner to understand population growth and also to device strategies to contain the growth of population. Their principal argument is that the biological inheritance only defines a limit, a limit that cannot be reached even remotely by any individual. Take birth rate for instance. The recorded history does not show a single example when women could produce as many babies as her reproductive cycle would permit. Although the baby-producing machine is delimited by the 40-week period of pregnancy, the actual reproduction level that can be attained by a woman is very finely tuned to many social conventions, traditions and folklore. A physiologist would precisely lay down the years between which a girl is expected to remain fertile. But the fact of the matter is that certain of our customs and obligations would determine when the sex relationship was to begin – before the start of puberty or well after that, before marriage or after marriage. Most societies have some unwritten but established rules, which are part of their cultural traditions. Even today, most societies advocate sex relations only after marriage. There are communities where a girl has to prove her *fecundity* even before marriage. The concepts of an ideal family and model family size have roots in our value system. In some societies a large family is still valued and there are many others that would even go to take some punitive action to dissuade people from having large families. Value of children is largely social, economic and psychological.

The process of evolution must have caused to change some of the physical characteristics of man. But such changes have taken place so slowly that it cannot possibly be held responsible for lowered death rates today. The differences in mortality between one nation and another and even between different regions within the same country are often so manifest that our genetic bequest is incapable of explaining this variation. We were nomadic for reasons of survival at some point of time. We settled down once we discovered ways and means to support our life system. But vastly superior communication and transportation and industrialization have made us mobile again. The increased incidences of internal and transnational migration have a bridging effect on the differences between cultures and regions.

Theories are in abundance pertaining to growth of population and changes in some of its dominant characteristics. We discuss only a few of them here.

4.4 Malthusian Doctrine

No one has ever sparked of so much debate and divide among intellectuals from all disciplines and politicians as did Rev. Thomas Robert Malthus (1766–1834) when he published a thin book but with a long title in 1798.

> An Essay on the Principle of Population, as it Affects the Future Improvement of Society with Remarks on the Speculations of Mr. Godwin, M. Condorcet and Other Writers

The sixth edition of the book was published in 1826 with a modified title and healthier in volume.

> An Essay on the Principles of Population, or a View of its Past and Present Effect on Human Happiness, with an Enquiry into our Prospects Respecting the Future Removal or Mitigation of the Evils which it Occasions

The moralist tinge expected of a man attached to the Church is noticeable even in the choice of words for the title of his book. This highly learned clergyman became the Professor of History and Political Science in East India College, London in 1805. Though he never visited India, he was well conversed with social, political and economic life of the people of India through the military academy which taught the would-be military and civil administrators of East India Company in India. The debate and the highly charged exchanges that emerged with the publication of the booklet have not subsided even after two hundred years of its publication. That relevance of Malthusian doctrine in understanding population dynamics is far from over is demonstrated when the demographers divide evolution of demography into three distinct stages – pre-Malthusian, Malthusian and post-Malthusian.

Though Malthus is acknowledged as the Father of Modern Demography, a lot has been talked about his assertions on the fall-out of population growth on social, economic, political, moral and ethical issues facing humanity. The great philosophers Plato and Aristotle had discussed population and suggested how the problems originating from population growth were to be dealt with. What Tertullian said in the second century AD about the possible imbalances between demand and supply of life-supporting resources due to population growth, Malthus has restated it in a more organized manner and with a holistic approach to the problems of population growth. We take a look at what Godwin and Condorcet had said, which in part prompted Malthus to write about what he thought about the consequences of uncontrolled growth of population. His conviction about the unhappy consequences of unchecked population growth is established when he writes,

> The happiness of a country does not depend, absolutely, upon its poverty or its riches, upon its youth or its age, upon its being thinly or fully inhabited, but upon the rapidity with which it is increasing, upon the degree in which the yearly increase of food approaches to the yearly increase of an unrestricted population.

Marquis de Condorcet, a French philosopher and mathematician, strongly attacked the Church and the imperialist tradition. He urged to raise voices against the exploitation and anti-people administration by the King and the Church. Only by eliminating the imperialist rule, he said, can we remove the differences between classes, between nations and between men. His assertions were that men would become rational, hatred would disappear, sickness and diseases would be under control, and productivity would improve. He believed that the average people would enjoy a long life, people would take proper care for their children, and chances of population explosion would disappear. Condorcet's principal argument was that people fail to bring the best out of them because of the oppressive and unkindly social systems gifted by imperialist tradition and the overpowering influences of the Church.

William Godwin almost echoed what Condorcet had said. He attributed the root of all human misery and unhappiness to poor administrative machinery: corrupt rulers, bad laws, greedy employers and so forth. Man-made social institutions cannot shake off their responsibility for man's despair and unhappiness. He believed that if some of these institutions were abolished and others reformed, people's sufferings would disappear. He also believed that an ideal social system can be developed that would usher in an era of social justice; war between nations would be eliminated, there would be no unhealthy competition between people and nations, and there would be no need for a government. Man would be employed only in collecting the necessaries of life, and consequently, each man's share of labor would be light, and his spare time ample.

Both Condorcet and Godwin had attacked the Church and the imperialist tradition for the gloom of mankind. It was hard for Malthus to accept the blame squarely put on the Church. A true Christian, he believed that man alone was responsible for all his distresses. A large part of Malthus's essay on population therefore was devoted in refuting the arguments mostly of Condorcet and Godwin. That population cannot grow beyond a level largely determined by the levels of means of subsistence, is not disputed by any. Godwin himself said, "There is a principle in human society, by which population is perpetually kept down to the level of the means of subsistence." The sole question is: What is this principle? Is it some obscure and occult cause?

Among his contemporaries, Malthus got inspiration from Mathew Haley, David Hume, Sir Walter Railey and Robert Wallace all of who pronounced that birth rate tends to surpass death rate. If unchecked, population growth may spell disaster to mankind. Railey said that the population increase will exceed the ideal number; disease, hunger and war would become operative to contain this surplus number. The GP and AP contrast suggested by Malthus to show how the power to reproduce far exceeded the power to produce subsistence was borrowed from Haley's observations.

To appreciate contribution of Malthus, it is necessary that we take a glimpse at the intellectual, political, economic and social tradition of his time. We look at the economic scenario of his time. The British economy was passing through the worst form of crisis – widespread famine, disease, poverty and unemployment were rampant. Agriculture was passing through a period of crisis in the later half of the eighteenth century. Upsurge of industrial revolution was there, but it was also observed that the industries prospered at the expense of agriculture. Economic inequality, widespread unemployment, poverty and hunger, exploitation of labor, and acute imbalance between population and food supply nearly broke the social order.

Malthus took up his pen, at least partly, to challenge the views expressed by Godwin and Condorcet and some others. They were so bitter against 'every present establishment' that they were convinced that once they were eliminated, a happier state of society would evolve and 'progress of man towards perfection' would become a reality. Malthus, unlike his many contemporaries, appears quite pessimistic, when he said:

> I have read some of the speculations on the perfectibility of man and of society with great pleasure. I have been warmed and delighted with the enchanting picture which they hold forth. I ardently wish for such happy improvements. But I see great... unconquerable difficulties in the way to them. ...[N]othing would give me greater pleasure than to see them completely removed.

Malthus made two postulates:

> First, *That food is necessary to the existence of man.*
>
> Second, *That the passion between the sexes is necessary and will remain nearly in its present state.*

These two laws appear to be *fixed laws of our nature*. He believed that they will ever cease to be what they now are. Malthus made oblique remarks to Godwin when he said "...[Some] writer has supposed that on this earth man will ultimately be able to live without food and ...the passion between the sexes may in time be extinguished". He further said,

> ...(P)ower of population is indefinitely greater than the power in the earth to produce subsistence for man... This natural inequality of the two powers of population and of production in the earth, and that great law of our nature which must constantly keep their effects equal, form the great difficulty that to me appears insurmountable in the way to the perfectibility of society.

Malthus drew our attention also to the fundamental similarity observed among all animals and plants in the biological world – the tendency to reproduce more than that can be sustained by the bounties of nature:

> The race of plants and the race of animals shrink under this great restrictive law. And the race of man cannot, by any efforts of reason, escape from it. Among plants and animals its effects are waste of seed, sickness, and premature death; among mankind, misery and vice.

But the tussle between man's propensity to 'be fruitful' and the dearth of space and supplies for his survival is much more complex than is found with sub-human animals and plants. Man's superior intellect has given him power to device ways and means to develop a harmony between his numbers and the limited resources. Reason interrupts his reproductive career and asks him whether he may not bring beings into the world for which he cannot provide the means of subsistence. The warning if not heeded, the population would grow fast and push a large proportion of the population to live much below the subsistence level.

The labor force in the market would be in much excess of the demand, the price of labor consequently would be cheap, and the price of provisions would at the same time tend to rise. The laborer must therefore work harder to earn the same as he did before. Shortage of food and space for living would increase mortality rates; growth of population would be arrested. The cheap labor would encourage farmers to use more labor on their land, bring more land under cultivation, new industries would come up and the means of subsistence would come to a level from where it was set out. In the recorded history, Malthaus observed this oscillatory movement often goes unnoticed since the *histories of mankind are histories only of the upper classes.*

Work is good, he said, so is marriage; it compels man to get involved in work. He did not foresee any basic change in our thinking and attitude resulting from social progress. Malthus felt that laws of nature are infallible. For this reason the want of the poor would never disappear. He believed that neither there would be any basic structural change in our society nor there would be changes in some of its more fundamental characteristics.

What would become of the growth rate of a population if the prevailing birth rate were allowed unabated? How about the production of food and other necessities if all our natural resources were maximally utilized? To the first question Malthus said that there had never been a complete freedom in our reproductive behavior, nor there would be in times to come. It is hard to find any civilized society where no restriction has ever been imposed on child or early marriage. Ignorance, illiteracy, unhealthy environment, harmful occupations and strenuous labor would cause untimely death to many and therefore the full reproductive potential would never become operative.

In answer to the second question, Malthus drew attention to USA, where the means of subsistence have been more ample and consequently the checks to early marriages fewer than in any of the modern states of Europe, *the population has been found to double itself in 25 years.* This happened even when many of their cities and urban areas registered higher death rates than birth rates. As an explanation as to why death rates were high in cities, he argued that the birth rates in those cities were higher than the usual and therefore the death rates were pushed up by nature's dictate.

Malthus also had drawn our attention to the fact that where agriculture is the only source of living – no unhealthy and harmful occupations – the social rules and regulations and life style tend to be simple. There was no social pressure against early marriage. The population in such areas was found to be doubling every 15 years. Malthus thought that even such a high growth rate was considerably less than what was possible under ideal conditions. He cited extensive research works of Petty and Euler and came to the conclusion that population could get doubled in 10–12 years. In fact, in some regions such high growth rates were observed though only for a short period. The longest period required for doubling the population was 25 years. That is, the population grows in GP every twenty-five years. Although accurate estimate for production of food and other supplies was not easily available, Malthus expressed strong doubt if growth rate of food production could match the population growth rate. He agreed that food production can be improved by acquiring more cultivable land and by application of better technology; space for housing, road etc. can also be looked into through clearing of forests and making use of non-arable land. But pressure on land and other natural resources would mount as population grows. Fertility of the land would also diminish because of it's over use. Population growth would continue unabated if provisions for food and other necessities were made available all the time. The reproductive behavior of one generation would positively influence the same in the next generation.

> Population, when unchecked, increases in a geometrical ratio. Subsistence increases only in an arithmetical ratio.

That is what made Malthus to state, "... the power of population is indefinitely greater than the power in the earth to produce subsistence for man".

Malthus examined the production processes of many countries in Africa, Asia and China and Japan in particular. These countries would take many years to double their food production; in consequence famine would be rampant there. He believed that neither improved technology nor increase in the area of cultivation would be able to manage the seemingly unmanageable situation. Even if it is assumed that population of the world would double in 25 years, and natural resources would not be exhausted fully, the situation could be frightening even in a period of two centuries and a quarter. Taking the population of the world at any number, the human species would increase in the ratio of – 1– 2– 4– 8– 16– 32– 64– 128– 256– 512– ... and so on and subsistence as – 1– 2– 3– 4– 5– 6– 7– 8– 9– 10– ... He wrote:

> ...(T)he power of population being a power of a superior order, the increase of the human species can only be kept commensurate to the increase of the means of subsistence by the constant operation of the strong law of necessity acting as a check upon the greater power.

On the consequences of the disparity between these two "powers", he wrote:

> By that law of our nature which makes food necessary to the life of a man, the effects of these two unequal powers must be kept equal. This implies a strong and constantly operating check on population from the difficulty of subsistence. This difficulty must fall somewhere; and must necessarily be felt by a large portion of mankind.

A large-scale emigration to settlements in untried foreign soil could provide only a partial solution. Malthus believed that emigration policy of a country to reduce poverty by lessening pressure on subsistence would be short lived since there would be reduction in death rate, increase in early marriages and a greater number of births per marriage. A great emigration necessarily implies unhappiness of some kind or other in the country that is deserted and also to the country of destination. A problem of a different kind for the emigrants would arise as a result. Leaving their families, connections, friends, and native land, the migrants now will have to make extraordinary efforts for adjustment with people, climate and resources at the place of their destination. The population redistribution both within the country and outside can ease the pressure of population for a particular country or region for some time. But a day will come soon when the receiving countries will enact laws against immigration.

Checks on Population Growth: Malthus believed that two of man's characteristics, essential to the sustenance of the life system were *immutable,* are the two *natural laws* that oppose each other: (1) the "need for food", and (2) the "passion between the sexes". Malthus had no doubt whatsoever in his mind that the great deficit in food supply ultimately would control the growth of population. This *ultimate check* becomes operative at the time of famine and epidemics. To show that population rise was closely related to the levels of means of subsistence, he cited the instances of the new colonies settled in healthy countries, where there was plenty of room and food, population had increased with astonishing rapidity. There are other *immediate checks*, usually man-initiated, that operate to keep the population under check. The shortage of food supply would lead to introduction of various restrictions; the poorer segment of the population would be under severe strain due to malnutrition and diseases. Besides, certain natural disasters invariably would affect the poor and the downtrodden most.

Malthus spoke of two kinds of checks – *preventive and positive checks*. In the first edition of his book, he did not talk about the former; he made amends to his original formulations in the second edition.

Preventive or prudential check: especially if it was voluntary, relates only to human population. These checks are applied to bring down birth rate. In Malthus's words, "Preventive checks include late marriage, chastity, and other similar measures aimed at checking population growth deliberately".

Superior intellect of man has given him the faculty of reasoning. His education and social status would prompt him to weigh if uncontrolled fertility would lower his social status. He would try to explore all possible avenues to improve the standard of living for his family. He would reflect on if large number of children in the family would be an advantage or an obstacle to achieving the life style he was aspiring. Malthus advocated universal education as a means to countering 'population principle'.

Malthus spoke of two kinds of preventive checks – *Moral Restraints* and *Artificial Restraints*. He was not against control of birth. Being a Catholic, he however could not support artificial control of birth though he was aware that this could become an important tool for controlling birth in near future. He campaigned for the sanctity of marriage bed. Being an atheist, Malthus could not approve 'free sex' although he admitted that free sex would reduce marriage rate. An unshackled intercourse could be a powerful incitement to early attachments. He felt celibacy was the only route to escape the wrath of positive checks. He advised women to remain unmarried till the age of 28. He regarded artificial birth controls as *vice* or *sin*.

Positive Checks: In the first edition of his essay, Malthus emphasized only on positive checks. All the factors that operated as principal determinants of death rates, i.e., as destroyers of "life already begun", are all positive checks. It is through these checks, however unwelcome, that the nature ultimately brings balance between population growth and the means of subsistence. These checks include famine, diseases, pestilence, natural calamities, vicious customs, great cities, unwholesome habitat, occupational hazards in mines and industries, war, etc. Malthus writes, "The table of nature is laid for limited number of guests and those who come uninvited must starve". He believed that positive checks become inevitable whenever there is a pressure of population on means of subsistence. It operates periodically in all states, in all economies.

Malthus has been severely criticized for his opposition to *Poor Laws*. He admits that Pitt's Poor Bill in England (a clause in the bill was "a shilling a week to every laborer for each child he has above three") was undoubtedly instituted for the most benevolent purpose, but he believed that they did not succeeded in their intention. He wrote:

> They certainly mitigate some cases of very severe distress which might otherwise occur, yet the state of the poor who are supported by parishes… is very far from being free from misery.

The Poor Laws of England, Malthus observed, tend to depress the general condition of the poor in two ways. Their first tendency is to increase population without insuring supply of adequate provisions for their support. A poor man may marry with little or no prospect of being able to support a family without some outside help. Poor Laws were to be held responsible, at least partly, therefore to create the poor, whom they maintain. Those who are not supported by parish assistance would purchase a smaller quantity of provisions and consequently more of them must be driven to ask for support.

Second, the more diligent and contributing members of society would have to grudgingly accept a cut in their wages to help perpetuate the disgraceful 'dependent poverty'. Malthus had no doubt whatever that the parish laws of England had contributed to raise the price of provisions and to lower the real price of labor. He advocated "the total abolition of all parish-laws".

On the issue of profit generated from manufacture of articles and agriculture, Malthus was of the view that the industrialist must be allowed to use the profit for starting new industries or in expanding the existing ones, of course with a profit motive. That will expand the employment market. If the profit was to be given away by way of increase in labor wage, job markets will not enlarge. He was against liberal increase in labor wages. High wages, he argued, ruin the workmen. Without apportioning an amount for future necessity, they would spend it in drunkenness and dissipation since they got accustomed to rely on parish assistance for support in misfortune. Higher wages to labor had not been welcome by Malthus for another completely different reason. More money would give the labor a feel-good experience, prompting him to spend more time on leisure than on work. Their attendance in the industry would become irregular and productions suffer.

He compared labor in England with the post-revolution labor in France. Birth rates among labors declined fast in France. In consequence they enjoyed better share in national income. The revolution had given them a sense of self-esteem and self-sufficiency. They were found to be committed to their work, eager to save for days of uncertainty, and showed restraint in marriage and procreation. A good government always works for the betterment of its people. But if in the name of good governance, the state offers dole to the poor and not encourage them to become self-sufficient and improve their skill and productivity and promote savings habit, Malthus felt, the general condition of the people would not change much. There could be hundreds and thousands unemployed even in the best-administered governance. Instead of 'dole', the state could offer other assistance, such as land and similar other facilities to make them stand on their own feet, but not the charity that puts them in a position of dishonor and disgrace.

He advocated the building up a social and economic order that would "raise the relative proportion between the price of labor and the price of provisions." Consumer base in the country needed expansion to give a boost to production. Increase in production would expand the employment market, but the job seekers would far exceed the job opportunities created. He drew our attention to a fable that described a race between rabbit and the turtle. Under normal circumstances, the turtle (production) cannot overtake a rabbit (birth rate) in a race. The turtle can overtake the rabbit only if the latter goes to sleep for a considerable time. The law of nature cannot bring production of basic necessities at par with population growth rate. Only by restricting the size of the labor force and keeping the labor market competitive, i.e., a relatively surplus job market could increase the labor wage and improve the living standard of the poor. Malthus favored a relatively small surplus population in the interest of production and economy of the country. But he was against its *unchecked growth.*

Malthus appears critical about industries and trade "which cause the labors of agriculture to be worse paid than the labors of trade and manufactures. … [A] country can never produce its proper quantity of food while these distinctions remain in favor of artisans."

One of Malthus's principal contentions was that the growth of means of subsistence could not match the growth rate of population and therefore the operation of preventive and positive checks invariably trimmed the size of the population. His major attention was on agricultural output since no one could live without food. When the art of agriculture did not change, the total output increase would show a diminishing return even if the successive increases in capital and labor were by equal amounts. That is, the marginal returns to successive doses of capital and labor would be declining.

Gide and Rist's observation appears significant: "It means as if the law of diminishing returns were the real basis of the Malthusian laws, although Malthus himself makes no express mention of it."

From the analysis of his two postulates, taking cue from historical and contemporary experiences, he came to three deductions which constitute the *principal theme* of his population theory. They are:

1. That population cannot increase without the means of subsistence;
2. That population does invariably increase where there are the means of subsistence unless prevented by some powerful checks; and
3. Those checks which keep population on a level with means of subsistence are all resolvable into moral restraints, vice and misery

4.5 Criticism of Malthusian Doctrine

Malthus is hooked as a pessimist, plagiarist, and torchbearer of capitalism. The mention of Malthus evokes a compounding reaction in any discussion, bringing religion, politics, economics, science and technology at the same breath.

Although Malthusian doctrine is a natural theory of population, the probability of improvement of the poor and backward lot of the population remains at the focal point of this multifaceted analysis. Two of the greatest philosophers of the eighteenth century, Rousseau and Condorcet expressed their unflinching faith that progress of science and technology and wisdom of man would usher in an era of opulence and in the process a society would emerge that would eliminate differences between the poor and the rich; peace and happiness would prevail. Malthus questioned the feasibility of ever attaining such an ecstatic ideal state of humanity and tried to show from historical and contemporary evidences that such dreams could not be translated into reality. He could never make himself believe that a classless society, a dogma dear to the heart of the communists, is ever possible.

Two hundred years of more accurately recorded history of change in population and other attendant events since the publication of the Malthusian doctrine allows us to take a more objective look at what Malthus had said about population growth, rigidity of social order and improvement in the means of subsistence. In the last two centuries industrial revolution, the mesmerizing development in science, technology and medicine, the incredible improvement in food production and other necessities of life, fast increase of the employment market, the two World Wars, the vastly improved global communication and transportation network, man's invasion into space and so forth have changed the face of the spaceship earth and its occupants totally. Many are hasty to pronounce the verdict that Malthusian doctrine be rejected outright. But there are others who maintain that the time is not ripe as yet to announce the final verdict on Malthus's theory.

It is true that many of Malthus's prediction did not come true. He said that when unchecked, the population would grow in GP and the means of subsistence in AP. That really did not happen. The industrial revolution, constant up-gradation of technology, more land under cultivation and the use of extensive irrigation and bio-chemical fertilizer have increased by many times the average food production per unit land. This has helped till today maintain a balance between the size of numbers and the supply of food grains. In fact, per capita availability of food grains has increased substantially. However, the scientists have warned that if birth rate is not brought down quickly, food, power and housing problems may become a serious issue in no distant future. Malthus did admit that by bringing more land under cultivation and by improved art of agriculture food production can be improved though not commensurate with the growth of mouths to be fed. He could not foresee the developments, discoveries and inventions in the years ahead of him, especially in genetic engineering and bio-technology. The preventive, curative medicines and surgery have brought down death rates to near a biological limit. His 'moral restraint' has taken the form of 'social and cultural restraints' in modern times.

Even some of the most popular theories in physics have been subjected to modifications or complete replacement. The complex ingredients of any problem unravel only gradually and theory related to this needs to be adapted and amended to make it a better explanatory principle. Any particle attaining the speed close to that of light will not follow the Newtonian Laws of Motion. That does not nullify the Newtonian Laws. Newtonian laws still are applicable to objects that move with low to moderate speed.

Malthusian doctrine does not seem to have much relevance to the European or more developed countries. The populations in these countries are either stationary or are growing very slowly. But it must not be forgotten that the high standard of living in these countries and near full employment to their citizens have become possible since their production surplus finds easy market in the Third World countries. In most Third World countries the birth rates still are high, population is still growing fast, and a very large segment of the population is lying below the poverty line. The shadow of famine appears every now and then. A very large proportion of people in the active age group is either unemployed or has no stable source of income. National income in many underdeveloped countries is almost totally dependent on agriculture even today.

The disparity in growth between means of subsistence and population, as was postulated by Malthus, also did not come true. That the population has grown from around 900 million in 1800 to around 6050 million in 2005 clearly indicates that growth of food production had at least been proportional to the growth of population. The time taken for doubling the population has progressively decreased from 105 years since 1800 to only 40 years since 1960. If the present decline in growth rate continues unchecked, the next doubling of population may take place around 125 years from now.

In the literal sense, there could be no doubt that power to grow in numbers is always greater than the power to produce food and other necessities of life. The question is: Has the human population used its power of reproduction fully? The answer is 'No'. There have always been some constraints for unchecked growth of population. That means of subsistence still bothers the scientists, technologists and politicians is amply clear in discussions and debates in national and international forums. If natural resources are so plentiful, why should we then bother about population growth rate? Is not it a fact that many third world countries still have to import huge quantity of food grains and other necessities from the developed countries? Don't this production of surplus food grains and other commodities in the developed countries help keep their unemployment rate to the minimum? Isn't the affluences observed in the developed countries dependent on the poor state of affairs in the developing countries? The population scientists are bewildered to observe that birth rates in the backward segment of the population in the developing countries are increasing with improvement in their financial condition. A new dimension has been added to Malthus's forewarning in the food front – the preservation of the natural ecosystem and biodiversity and ever increasing problems of environmental pollution. This is receiving far greater attention since the sixties of the last century. That is a different issue which will be discussed at an appropriate place.

Newton's theories today are taken as the starting point for studying movement of all heavenly bodies. Likewise Malthus' doctrine can be taken up as a working relation between population growth and production of basic necessities for life. Politicians, demographers, and other scientists are of one opinion that something ought to be done to check the growth of population in view of the fast depletion of natural resources, forest cover and increase in environmental pollution. They are worried that many countries are falling behind in attaining the Millennium Development Goals (MDG) in most social and demographic indicators. We are fast approaching an explosive stage, which is unlikely to spare the developed countries as well.

We bring out some of the major deficiencies in Malthus's population theory.

1. Malthus seemed to have stressed a great deal on limited scope for bringing more land under cultivation and improvement of agricultural technology. He could not even dream of harvesting two or three crops from the same piece of land and that with better agricultural management it would become possible to increase production by several times. His prediction about agricultural production did not come true because of revolution in agricultural practices observed since the middle of the nineteenth century. Use of bio and chemical fertilizers, hybrid seeds and tractor, advanced agricultural and food preservation technology, innovative sources for varieties of consumer goods etc. have increased production of basic necessities beyond his imagination. Malthus's notion on food supply was based on a static economic law of diminishing return. He could not foresee that this can be postponed for a foreseeable future through miracles of technological progress and agricultural management.
2. He did not realize that fast growth of industrial production, expanded communication network, and improved distribution can improve the living standard of the common man.
3. Malthus did not realize that some epoch making discoveries could altogether change our traditional views about many issues. Vast progress in medical science, especially the vaccines, antibiotics and surgery, has enhanced survival rate at all ages. Since a greater proportion of babies born today are entering into their reproductive ages, the need for frequent pregnancy of mothers has now become unnecessary. The fear of losing lineage is over.
4. Malthus did not foresee that immensely improved communication would ease movement between and within countries. The European countries could establish colonies in other continents to ease the pressure of their population. Even the resources from these colonial settlements could be used to make up the short fall in some of the resources in their own country. Keeping an eye on the export market these countries could enhance their production, which gave a boost to employment.
5. Because of improvement in the transportation network, food and other supplies could be sent fast to areas where famine-like situation, epidemic or natural calamity arose. Famine and epidemic have largely been contained. India in the sixties of the last century experienced drought, flood and other calamities, which depressed the food production so much so that a famine-like situation arose. But such a grave situation was averted by importing food grains from USA and other countries. International aids and loans rescued India from this adverse situation.
6. Malthus failed to appreciate the role the modern contraceptives could play in controlling birth because of his theological stubbornness. He kept a blind eye to this most potential check to uncontrolled population growth. He believed that suffering and fear of more suffering would motivate people to limit their size of family. We now believe that behind moral restraint as well

as producing babies lies the fear of insecurity. Birth control has succeeded in countries that are economically well off and educationally advanced. Proper motivation for birth control is still lacking in many of the third world countries.

Malthus puts his readers in dilemma when he says, "growth rate of population is higher than that of means of subsistence." Was he telling us that population was actually growing faster than the means of subsistence? Or, was he trying to send the signal that unless population growth rate was checked, the level of means of subsistence attainable would be inadequate to support the population? Kingsley Davis rightly said that the fact that the population was growing was indicative of the fact that the means of subsistence was also growing. Otherwise, death rate instead of falling would have increased. Without a proportionate increase in production of food and other necessities, the population of the world could not have reached the present size. The fact of the matter is that population growth was never a problem with many countries since it was accompanied by increased national income and productivity.

7. Malthus probably was right when he said, "...(T)he passion between the sexes is necessary and will remain nearly in its present state." But child bearing and sexual instinct are not necessarily related. One can be sexually attached to a person without wishing a baby by the union. Even this instinctive behavior is modified or restrained by education, other sources of entertainment and social regulations.
8. Population and shortage of resources could be accepted as one of the important causes of war in earlier stages of civilization. The other positive checks, which Malthus referred, operate in all countries, thickly or thinly populated. Natural calamities are not peculiar to over-populated countries. They visit even the developed countries with low population growth rate. But their effects are not horrendous in the developed countries as are in the underdeveloped ones which have poor infrastructure and calamity management programs.
9. Population can grow both by rising birth rate as also by declining death rate. Malthus stressed on the first only. That could have been the case in high stationary growth stage. Population of the world in the last few centuries has grown due to faster decline in death rate due to tremendous advancement in medical science in arresting mortality from many fatal diseases as also better distribution of food grains and other necessities.
10. Malthus unduly emphasized on food. Growth of population of a country is related not to level of food production but to its *total wealth*. A really wealthy country can easily procure foodstuffs from other countries by way of a direct purchase or in exchange of their produces or technologies. Britain is a typical example that imports most of its food requirements from other countries in exchange for its industrial products and machinery. When Malthus spoke of shortage of food, he appears to highlight the plight of those who are purely vegetarian. But in today's world, a very large segment of the population is non-vegetarian who make a good mix of grains and vegetables with animal protein in their meals. The share of cereals in common man's dish has come down in many countries, especially the developed and high developing countries.

British Prime Minister William Pitt the Younger (in office: 1783–1801 and 1804–1806), after reading the work of Malthus promptly withdrew a bill he had introduced that called for the extension of Poor Relief. Malthus's writings strongly influenced Whig reforms which overturned Tory paternalism and brought in the Poor Law Amendment Act of 1834. Concerns about Malthus's theory helped promote the idea of a national population census (1801) in the UK. Today world organizations such as the United Nations Population Fund acknowledge that the debate over how many people the Earth can support effectively started with Malthus. Other examples of applied Malthusianism include the 1972 book *The Limits to Growth* published by the Club of Rome, and the Global 2000 report to Jimmy Carter, the then President of USA. Malthus continues to inspire and influence futuristic visions. K. Eric Drexler in his *Engines of Creation* (1986) wrote, "In a sense, opening space will burst our limits to growth, since we know of no end to the universe. Nevertheless, Malthus was essentially right."

Malthusian doctrine directly or indirectly influenced many other disciplines. Economics and biological sciences appear to have been in the receiving end most. David Ricardo, a close friend of Malthus, took the doctrine a step ahead when he formulated his famous theory "Iron Law of Wages". He said that price of labor increases whenever there is shortage of labor in the market. Increase in income leads a surge in population, which brings more people in the labor market and the labor price drops. A balance in the price-level is maintained by the fluctuation in labor flow. It is for this reason that the poor labors cannot change their social and economic status. Alfred Marshall went on to say that the Malthusian doctrine provided the foundation of modern economics. He considered the doctrine as a hallmark in the application of inductive method in social sciences. Edward East in his book *Mankind at the Cross-roads* remarked that if the present population trend continues, the total arable land available for agriculture would be insufficient to provide food to the teeming millions in spite of faster technological up-gradation.

Charles Darwin expressed his indebtedness to Malthus for his Theory of Evolution. He acknowledged that only after he had read Malthus that the principle of "natural selection" in the biological kingdom became clear to him. Malthus's observation that population in excess of what can be sustained by the natural resources must wither away tells the story of incessant "struggle for existence" in the biological world. Not all are able to adjust in this highly competitive environment. They must die sooner or later if unable to adjust to their surroundings. Even those who survive this ordeal must undergo modifications in some of their characteristics. That is how the new species are evolved. Darwin, a life-long admirer of Malthus, referred to Malthus as *that great philosopher*. The modern ecological biologists have accepted much of Malthusian doctrine. The Social Darwinists notice that the "struggle for existence" is true of human populations as well, and the 'seeds of evolution' is embedded in human society. Therefore, that segment of the population, which would fail to adjust to this unkind competitive world, must fade away slowly. In support of their claim they have cited the instances of those tribes that already are in the process of extinction.

The first Director-General of UNESCO, evolutionist and humanist Julian Huxley, wrote of "The Crowded World" in his *Evolutionary Humanism* (1964), calling for a "World Population Policy". Huxley openly criticized Communist and Roman Catholic attitudes to birth control, population control and overpopulation.

Interest in Malthus's doctrine dropped on his death in 1834. Industrial revolution brought in considerable change in social and economic order in most of the European countries. The vast improvement in food production made us forget Malthus's premonitions. Rapid industrial growth absorbed hundreds and thousands of labor and industrial production changed the economy of a country decisively. Some 19th-century economists believed that improvements in the division and specialization of labor, increased capital investment, and other factors had rendered some of Malthus's warnings implausible. Pressure of population on food was again felt around the end of the nineteenth century. Interest in Malthus's doctrine was revived as a result. When the nation prospers, we think of Malthus no more. But whenever uncertainty appears over supply of food and other basic necessities, we fall back on Malthus and initiate measures to curb the growth of population. Many 20th-century economists, such as J. L. Simon, have criticized Malthus's conclusions. They note that despite the predictions of Malthus and the Neo-Malthusians, massive geometric population growth in the 20th century has not resulted in a Malthusian catastrophe, largely due to the influence of technological advances and the expansion of the market economy, division of labor, and stock of capital goods. Simon even went on to say that "people are becoming scarcer, even though there are more of us". There are many who are skeptical of the view that population growth directly causes poverty and underdevelopment. *Redistributionists* often interpret high fertility as not so much the cause but the effect of poverty. They argue that poverty, lack of economic security, the high mortality rates of children, the low status of women and other factors force people to have large families. They also believe that population is a problem since it helps intensify the impoverishment of the masses. For some redistributionists, the solution to the problem lies in changing the status of poor people, particularly of women, through education and reform. Repetto (1979) and the World Bank (1984) provide a clear statement of this approach.

Commentators today generally regard Malthus's theory as an *approximate* natural law of population dynamics for all species: this is because scientists have evidences that nothing can sustain exponential growth at a constant rate indefinitely. Malthusian doctrine may not have much relevance in the developed countries today, but they must thank Malthus for his warning note on the consequential effect of over-population. They took up measures to check it.

Resurgence of Malthusian doctrine from time to time has been due to three fundamental reasons – fast growth of population, people's general awareness to implications of fast growth of population and scarcity or erosion of some of our natural resources. Malthus's theory, in spite of many inherent limitations, would remain relevant, at least to the third world countries, since there is hardly any difference in opinion that we must consciously and drastically cut population growth rate. Scientists from various disciplines are in complete agreement that many of our natural resources are non-renewable, especially in food and energy sector and there would be scarcity of space for housing, shortage of potable water, forest area squeezed so much that the Green House Gases in atmosphere would rise appreciably and the average temperature would shoot up and there would be unpredictable climatic changes. Malthusian theory has once more gained an audience in the population debate in the last thirty years. The oil crisis of the 1970s and then at the beginning of this century and the famine in parts of Africa in the 1980s all seemed to vindicate Malthus. It seemed that he had been right, that human numbers had outstripped the ability to sustain them, not only with regard to food, but also with regard to resources such as oil, minerals, land, and water. The world community today is asking for a *sustainable development*.

In a sense Malthus could be called the father of modern family planning campaign as well. Although he did not support artificial control of birth, he visualized its possible role in controlling birth rate. He was opposed to free sex on the ground that it would break the family ties, instances of divorce would increase and the children born from the promiscuous relations would be at a psychological disadvantage for their identity crisis. He strongly advocated adoption of preventive checks. He opposed marriage of mentally handicapped and severely physically challenged persons. He recommended curtailing the reproductive period by increasing the age at marriage of girls. Most of the developing countries are trying to increase the age at marriage by promulgating legislative measures. Malthus's opposition to Poor Laws can be seen as a measure to persuade the government to institute penalty measures against those who did not put a check on birth. The surer way to check the population growth, he observed, was to bring down death rate, especially infant and child mortality, spread of education and awareness of the evils of unchecked growth and disbanding unwholesome habitat.

4.6 Neo-Malthusians on Population

Ironically, given Malthus's own opposition to contraception, his work exercised a strong influence on Francis Place (1771–1854), whose neo-Malthusian movement became the first to advocate contraception. Place published his *Illustrations and Proofs of the Principles of Population* in 1822. neo-Malthusians are economists and population scientists who have unflinching faith in the basic tenets of Malthusian doctrine. One can call neo-Malthusianists a cult and neo-Malthusianism a movement propagating the views of Malthus. The Malthusian society was formed in 1877 and gave the needed momentum to spread in England and USA.

The neo-Malthusians, unlike Malthus, stood for artificial control of birth by using modern family planning techniques. To them no price was greater if it could check birth rates. Like Malthus, they believed that sexuality is universal but they distinguished between sensuality and the desire for having a baby. Neo-Malthusians admit that most societies are fairly more open today; the social, economic, religious and cultural attitudes do undergo changes and adapts to the 'dominant world view' about the need to keep the size of family limited. Neo-Malthusians do not treat women merely as baby producing machines. They want women to have a greater say on the question of giving birth to a baby. Some suggest that because of their exclusion from power and from access to safe reproductive technology, many women have more children than they otherwise would wish. The importance of gender equality for the stabilization of population is not only supported by feminist contributors but by significant sections of the population movement. Neo-Malthusians admit that

- Women may like to escape the pangs of birth;
- Marriage, child bearing and rearing may be looked upon as serious hindrance to their aspirations and personal freedom; and
- Educated and employed women, especially those in white-collar jobs have a point when they say that conception and birth to babies bring some physical deformation and make them unattractive.

Neo-Malthusians have departed from Malthus when they say that the growing individualism in the modern cut-throat competitive society has given rise to a concept of 'happiness' that is not in conformity with the traditional regimentation and family life. In the more developed countries people do not worry of their old age because of the state sponsored security measures. In more orthodox societies, the want for children as old age security still continues since the state cannot as yet provide such security. That seems to be the reason why the proportion of 'never married persons' in these societies is increasing. Another factor the neo-Malthusians recognize is that religion has lost much of its charm and influence on people in today's scientific world.

Birth control measures are presently adopted in all developed economies. In the developing economies, the practice is still confined mostly to those who can be regarded as the creamy layer. The poor and the illiterates still multiply at an alarmingly high rate. Even a great social thinker like Bertrand Russel could not but express his dismay at the shift of balance in the population distribution. He said, "What is regrettable at present is not the decline of birth rate in itself, but the fact that the decline is the greatest in the best elements of the population."

The neo-Malthusians went a step further to argue that the users of the common resource (land, air and water) will inevitably destroy the resource upon which existence of human and all other life forms depend. In 1968, two influential 'neo-Malthusian' works were published, reintroducing the language of limits into the population debate. Ever since publication of Paul Ehrlich's *Population Bomb* (1968) and Garrett Hardin's "Tragedy of the Commons" (1968), warnings about the limits of sustenance, of resources, food, energy, land, the environment, have flown fast and furious. This population-resource debate has found plenty of support from politicians and government and non-government agencies, especially in the developing countries. Many scientists however countered this claim by pointing out that methods can be and are being developed that will allow for sustainable use of common resources. In years past, the main concern coming from the neo-Malthists was fear of total mineral resource depletion. In recent years, the neo-Malthusian argument, especially with regard to petroleum, has shifted from concern over resource depletion to effects of mining and mineral usage on the environment. Fears over land degradation due to mining, air pollution due to burning of petroleum and coal, water pollution due to oil spills and industry waste, among others are now the main thrust of the neo-Malthusian argument with regard to minerals resources, petroleum in particular.

The neo-Malthusians have gone ahead further to declare that food would become the principal deterrent to population growth in foreseeable future. Prices of food, especially cereals, in the world market have gone up by more than 30 percent in recent years. Because of diversion of a large proportion of farm land for cultivation of corn, sugarcane and others in USA, Europe and other countries for production of "bio-fuel" as also due to frequent drought in most wheat and rice producing countries, price of food grains and most other food stuff have gone up sharply. Already "food riots" have been witnessed in many developing countries. The scientists fear that with the global climate change, a fallout of intense atmospheric pollution, there will be more frequent droughts, more damaged crops and famines, more epidemics, more dying forests and more international conflicts.

A neo-Malthist, William Catton, provides a modern theory to explain the world's current population explosion. Catton's main premise is that the earth has a limited capacity to provide resources for its population. If the population exceeds this carrying capacity then environmental damage will occur, ultimately reducing the carrying capacity itself. He said, we are living beyond our means and using up future reserves of resources. Eventually, our economic systems will collapse resulting in a rapid decline or die-off of population. Catton contends that population will return to level that can be supported but due to the environmental damage already done, it will not be as great as it was before the die-off occurred.

4.7 Karl Marx on Population

Much opposition to Malthus's ideas came in the middle of the nineteenth century with the writings of Karl Marx (*Capital*, 1867) and Friedrich Engels (*Outlines of a Critique of Political Economy*, 1844), who argued that what Malthus saw as the problem of the *pressure of population on the means of production* actually represented the *pressure of* the *means of production on population.* They viewed it in terms of their concept of the reserve army of labor. In other words, the seeming excess of population that Malthus attributed to the seemingly innate disposition of the poor to reproduce beyond their means actually emerged as a product of the very dynamics of capitalist economy. Engels called Malthus's hypothesis "...the crudest, most barbarous theory that ever existed, a system of despair which struck down all those beautiful phrases about love thy neighbor and world citizenship."

If Malthus's doctrine on population is looked upon as the finest example of 'natural theory', Marx is to be regarded as the chief advocate of 'social theory' of population. The two theories originate from two distinctly different social and economic governances that were followed in many countries before the fall of communism in the East European countries and the Soviet Union and 'economic liberalization or globalization' took the world by storm a few years back.

Many eminent economists and social and political thinkers of the nineteenth century were opposed to the views of the Classical School of Economics founded by Adam Smith. Adam Smith believed in individuality, individual rights to property, self-interest and in unbounded competition. Many of those who were opposed to Adam Smith's formulations, took up Malthus, whose writings were influenced by Adam Smith's economic thoughts, as their target for violent criticism even without making a proper analysis of what Malthus wrote about population. It is no wonder that Marx, one of the greatest social thinkers and the pioneer of scientific socialist movement, would inflict scathing attack on what Malthus had said whom he looked upon as an agent of the capitalist outfit. But what is not clear is why he used abusive languages and took the issue to a personal level with Malthus. Did he realize that he did not have sufficient data and sound reasoning to contradict what Malthus had said? The following quote shows how popularity of Malthus, who ardently supported Adam Smith's economic formulations, led agitated Marx to hold his pen against him:

> I should like to remind him that this work, in its first form, was nothing more than a school boyish, superficial and parsonic declamatory plagiarism from Defoe, Sir James Stuart, Townsend, Franklin, Wallace and others, and did not contain a single sentence thought out by Malthus himself.

Although in his monumental work *Das Capital* he did not specifically state what his population theory was, Marx's theory can be christened as a "Theory of Surplus Population" – an extension of the principal premise in his crusade against capitalism. His view on population is clearly explained in the following quote:

> It is the working population which, while effecting the accumulation of capital also produces the means whereby it is itself rendered relatively superfluous, is turned into a relatively surplus population, and it does so in an ever increasing extent. This is a law of population peculiar to the capitalist method; and in fact every method of production that rises in the course of history has its own peculiar, historical valid law of population. It is only for plants and animals that there is a law of population in the abstract; and that only in so far as man does not interfere with them.

The quote clearly points poverty as the fall-out of unemployment or underemployment (surplus labor) resulting from capitalistic system of production. If we are to believe what Marx said about the theory of population (a theory of population is related to the mode of production), one would like to ask what the law of population under a socialist regime really is. Since Marx believed that socialism was opposed to capitalism, then the Marxist view on population must be opposite to what Malthus propounded. What Marx probably wanted to convey was that under socialist rule there would be no dearth of job. Every healthy individual would have an appropriate job and would enjoy a reasonably good standard of living. Creation of job opportunities would have nothing to do with the pressure of population. That is, in communism population would never become a problem. In socialist literature, 'population problem' or 'population pressure' is absent. For increasing production on national level new job situations are created, and the population is required to man the created vacancies.

In the erstwhile communist countries birth control measures have often been adopted vigorously. But even while adopting such measures they claimed that such measures did not contradict Marxian doctrine. It has been stated in Great Soviet Encyclopedia that there can be no surplus population even when the population grows fast in true socialist tradition. But that there was need to curtail birth at times was not disputed even in the communist countries. The reasons cited for planned family were child and mother health care and unrestrained labor force.

Marx's views on population, rather his objection to Malthusian doctrine, can be summarized as under:

- Surplus population is the consequence of capitalistic system of production that profit from the abject poverty of the masses;
- The wealth of the country is concentrated at the hand of a few individuals. The demand for labor fails to keep up with the increasing number of job-seekers, creating a huge reserve army of unemployed. The price of labor is kept at a minimum because of bargaining power of the fund managers and their profit motives;
- For more profit, the capitalist introduces labor saving machines and technology; labor is rendered surplus. With spread of unemployment, wages decline, poverty increases and capitalists make more profits;
- It is rubbish an argument that the population increase is due to improvidence and biological factors;
- Inequality in land distribution, mediaeval land tenure, uneconomic land holding and uncertainty in land tenure etc. are responsible for low agricultural productivity;
- It is the proletariats that keep the wheel of production move and provide profit to the capitalist while they are subjected to exploitation. The capitalists are vampires that live on the blood of the poor labor. They get richer and fatter the more they suck blood;
- No universal population theory is possible. The production process undergoes changes with time and therefore the theory of population is to be attuned to the demands of the production system. The principle of surplus population operates under capitalism;
- Unemployment is a characteristic feature of capitalism. With decay in capitalism, the conditions would ease for evolving a collective method of production that would ensure employment to everyone and good living for every able-bodied worker, no matter how fast the numbers increased. It would bring down death rates considerably.

In pre-revolution Russia, Lenin opposed "birth strike". But he supported and encouraged abortion and use of contraceptives purely on "humanitarian grounds". Young age dependency in Russia declined considerably in the early twenties, which helped communist Russia immensely in its take-off stage. It is estimated that Russia had 100 million less babies and young children at the start of the Second World War. That is, Russia would have been 100 million people more strong in the early forties had it maintained through the thirties the pre-1920 birth policy. The leadership withdrew regulations for birth control. Russia suffered heavy loss of life in the two wars. Death rate in that period exceeded birth rate. To get back at the replacement level, there was need for reversing the birth control policy.

A more aggressive policy of birth control was observed in China. In 1955–56 the leadership realized that the plan for production both in agricultural and industrial sector could not be realized if some control was not exercised on population growth. They however did not make it public that the birth control policy they advocated had any thing to do with reducing the population growth rate. The impression given was that the adopted steps were intended to improve public health and welfare of the people.

What the Chinese Prime Minister Hua-kuo-Feng said about population while presenting the details of national planning program is summarized below:

- Family planning is a very important concern.
- Planned and controlled population growth is essential in the interest of planned national economy and health of mother and the child.
- This planned and controlled population growth would be extremely helpful in production, job market and education.
- Within the next three years the population growth rate would be brought down to one percent per annum.
- To arrive at this target a strict resolve from everyone is needed.

Prime Minister Hua in his address to the national assembly set targets only in five areas – industrial production, agricultural production, cereal production, steel production and population growth rate. The details of do's and don'ts appeared in state-owned newspapers: In planned population growth the emphasis is on "planned". Besides birth control it includes delaying marriage and giving fewer births. The rural males and females were asked not to marry before the age 25 and 23 years respectively. In urban areas the respective ages were 27 and 25 years. All couples were discouraged to have more than two children. They were also advised to see that there was considerable gap between the two children. China was formulating procedures to push for adoption of a one-child norm.

In China abortion was legalized as early as 1957. In 1972 the government announced that the cost of abortion was to be borne by the state. The new Criminal Code (1979), had no reference to abortion. With the inauguration of China's one-child campaign in 1979, induced abortion became an important component of national effort to reduce population growth rate. Abortion was one of the four "planned birth operations", the other three being vasectomy, tubectomy and insertion of intra-uterine device.

The picture of urgency to arrest population growth becomes more transparent in P. C. Chen's article "Evolution of China's Birth Planning Policy" published in *World Population and Fertility Planning Technologies* (1982). He writes:

> The State Council Birth Planning Staff Office sets yearly targets for natural increase rates in the various provinces… Each province, upon receiving the target that the central government has established for it, … allocates a birth quota for each of the prefectures under its jurisdiction. The process is repeated downward until it reaches the production team… The production team must work out its birth plan … assigning permission to have children to those couples who have observed the three reproductive norms. Childless couples and couples intending to marry soon who have observed the late marriage norm have first priority, followed by couples who have one child aged three or older. If the eligible number of couples is larger than the quota allowed, some eligible couples must wait until the following year… Each production team, having worked out its team plan, submits it to the brigade, which in turn works out a brigade plan. The brigades send their plans up to the commune….
>
> Once a commune birth plan is approved, the members of the commune are expected to implement it. Couples who have been given permission to have a child are issued a 'planned birth card' and may forgo

> contraception; others are expected to practice contraception or to undergo abortion in the event of contraceptive failure… Because every unplanned birth in defiance of the community decision means that an eligible couple must give up a birth permission they deserve and have earned, there is a collective interest in seeing that the community plan of births is carried out… In the process, community and/or peer pressure ensures its successful implementation.

The unchecked population growth is still the major headache of all national leaders, no matter if they belong to communist or capitalist block. Even those who proclaim, "Communism is the cure for all diseases", do not hesitate to apply stringent measures to control population growth. They would strongly canvas, even going to the extent of coercion, the need for adoption of a small family norm among their own people, but would not admit "uncontrolled births give rise to poverty". They would overtly defend Marxian doctrine on population, but covertly admit that the population growth in excess of production of essential commodities is an 'index of weakness of the social and economic system'. To show their solidarity with Marxian views, the communist countries would refrain from voting in the United Nations on motions concerning population control. They would declare that in the interest of mother and child health care and for a more prosperous future they were not averse to birth control, but that act would have nothing to do with Malthusian pronouncement.

Criticisms of Marx's Views on Population

- Marx was obsessed against capitalism. Apparently that was why he took up his pen to spit venom against Malthus who he considered a stooge of capitalism. He was not sure if Malthusian doctrine could be refuted by facts and reasons. He would have done better to espouse his theory of population, if any, than to resort to personal ridicule and vilification. There is reason to believe that Marx gave only a cursory glance to the first edition of Malthus' book and did not go through later editions where Malthus modified some of his earlier views, made extensive reference to contemporary data on population and related factors from different countries in support of his theory.
- In most communist countries birth control has seriously been followed, often to a level of coercion. Russia and China have advocated planned parenthood, of course citing reasons not always in line with what Malthus had said in favor of birth control.
- Marx held capitalistic system responsible for surplus population. Most developed countries in the world today do not have a socialistic set up. Yet the proportion of poor and unemployed by their national standard is far less than what were observed in the erstwhile communist countries.
- Marx said communism was the cure-all of all ills of society. Wherever communists took hold of power of the state, the voices of the people were not allowed to surface. Newspapers, TV and radio became state organs. Even a decade or two back the outside world had to scoop out information from China about the state of affairs with the common man. The international bodies like UN did not know for certain the exact population figures of China. The veil gradually has lifted only since the final quarter of the last century. The welcome entry of multinational companies (MNCs) and foreign direct investment (FDI) in China has thrashed away the age-old state monopoly over all economic and social issues. The more realistic Chinese leadership invited private capitals with the assurance that the government would impose no restriction on the limits of their profits or on what the investors would do with their profits. Abundance of skilled labor and low labor cost has effected a dramatic change in Chinese

economy. Advanced capital-intensive technology is gradually replacing labor-intensive production and creating a surplus population, which the state intends to control through persuasive and even coercive measures. The fall of communism in East European countries and the compromised position in China, the last bastion of communism, seem to suggest that there was a gap between scientific socialism as prophesied by Marx and what has been practiced in the last three-quarter of a century. That is, implementation of Marxian philosophy has gone away from the path of realism.

4.8 Esther Boserup, Ronald Lee and Others on Malthusian Doctrine

Malthus's account was a fairly accurate portrayal of the demographic cycles of boom and bust that characterized much of pre-modern Europe and many other agrarian societies. But there are many who do not believe that population growth constitute a problem. Some even believe that the growth of population has the potential to stimulate economic growth and innovation. Esther Boserup, a Danish demographer and agricultural scientist, and Julian Simon, an American economist, turned Malthus upside down. They contended that population growth is not necessarily bad and may well be beneficial. Boserup's thesis contended that densely settled populations provide the motivation and resources necessary for technological breakthroughs. She pointed that in poor agricultural countries' population growth led to technical improvements in agriculture, raising productivity and providing more food per person than before.

4.8.1 Boserup's thesis on "Agricultural Intensification"

Esther Boserup is distinguished by two intellectual achievements: a seminal theory of population to rival Malthus in importance, and the pioneering work on the role of women in human development. Her most notable work is *The Conditions of Agricultural Growth: The Economics of Agrarian Change under Population Pressure* (1965). The book presented an in-depth analysis of the agricultural practices right from the primitive period. She contradicted Malthusian view that there is a declining rate of return for each additional unit of labor in an agricultural economy with constant technology and that agricultural methods determine *population* (via food supply). Instead, she contended that *population determines agricultural methods.* Agricultural production can be improved through technological breakthroughs and intensification of efforts. A major point of her book is that "necessity is the mother of invention".

She argued that when population density is low enough to allow it, land tends to be used intermittently, with heavy reliance on fire to clear fields and fallowing to restore fertility. Numerous studies have shown such methods to be favorable in total workload and also efficiency (output versus input). In Boserup's theory, it is only when rising population density curtails the use of fallowing, that lands are moved towards annual cultivation. The less fertile plots require intensive fertilizing, field preparation, weed control, and irrigation. These induce agricultural innovation but increase marginal labor cost to the farmer as well: the higher the rural population density, the more hours the farmer must work for the same amount of produce. Therefore workloads tend to rise while efficiency drops. This process of raising production at the cost of more work at lower efficiency is what Boserup describes as "agricultural intensification".

Boserup did not deny the fact that population reached the turning point, time and again, when the food supply was reaching exhaustion. Whereas Malthus said that the extra people (the poor and the unskilled) must be sacrificed, Boserup said that at such turning points man thought out plans for upgrading the productivity of the food supply. Under pressure of numbers, people put more labor and intense effort into feeding themselves, and find ways to get more food grains out of the land. They cultivate the land more intensively: add extra manure, extra fertilizer and extra water and improve their crop strains. They always *invent* their way out of the Malthusian crisis. Indeed, the Malthusian trap may even drive the development of technology. By analogy, one can say that the Malthusian trap drove 18th century Europeans to industrialize.

Boserup was not averse to a large population. She, in fact, emphasized the positive aspects of a large population. In simple terms, Boserup suggested that the more people there are, the more hands are available for work (echoing Mao: "Each mouth comes with a pair of hands"). She asserts that before the Industrial Revolution, the main advantage of a dense population was "the better possibilities to create infrastructure". She argued that the irrigation technology for agriculture, the building and maintenance of roads, the canalization of a river, and the laying of the railroad system became possible only with the support of a large population. Boserup argued that population growth is the prime cause of changes in agricultural practices. As population increases, more pressure is built on the existing system, which stimulates invention. The changes in technology allow for improved crop strains and increased yields.

Boserup sees population pressure as a major cause of change in land use (less time permitted for fallowing), agricultural technology, land tenure systems, and settlement form. She maintains that population growth is the cause rather than the result of agricultural change and that the principal change is the *intensification of land use*.

Some believe that in the final analysis, the market mechanism can help establish a dynamic equilibrium between population growth and resources. The fact of the matter is that growth of population, fast decline in mortality and consequent increase in life expectancy are enough indications of a faster increase in agricultural production and other necessities of life. Although the per capita cereal consumption has declined over the years, consumption of fruits, vegetables, dairy products and animal protein are on the rise. The 1999 Human Development Report, points out that "despite rapid population growth, food production per capita increased by nearly 25 percent during 1990–1997. The per capita daily supply of calories rose from less than 2,500 to 2,750 and that of protein from 71 grams to 76."

Global food production has enjoyed tremendous increase over the last 20–25 years save the last 2–3 years. Most of these gains are due to the technological advances made through 'Green Revolution'. Recently, there has been concern in many quarters that the green revolution has 'lost its edge' and is no longer able to ensure that production levels keep pace with population growth. However, this view does not take into account that current yields are not at 'best practice' levels. While many farmers in developed and developing nations alike have taken advantage of green revolution methods, many are not maximizing these methods and other farming techniques to increase production and reach potential yields. Many scientists are optimistic that a new green revolution can be achieved through better techniques and through bioengineering. Even the official projections from the World Bank, FAO, and IFPRI agree that agricultural researchers can repeat the Green Revolution.

Boserup's work has had a varied response from readers; many economists have been less than enthusiastic. Her central argument that intensification reduces labor productivity remains unproven. There are few who would buy the argument that an increase in the frequency of cropping is the only possible response to population pressure; the extensive margin can be extended, higher yielding crops adopted, and methods that increase yields introduced independently of increases in the frequency of cropping. There are many who argue that Boserup's *intensification model* cannot work indefinitely if the population growth is not contained. At some point, the population may get so huge that they cannot be fed no matter how inventive their scientists are. Indeed to feed more mouths, people have to dig deeper into the environment, divert more biological productivity for themselves, demand more from the soil, and use more water, more fertilizer, more pesticides etc. Can the environment really sustain this kind of pressure torture in the long run?

Boserup's thesis is a dynamic interpretation of agrarian change. Yet, it is difficult to accept the proposition that population pressure is the only cause for agrarian change or that the increased frequency and technology up-gradation of farming is the only response to population pressure. Boserup developed her ideas in connection with traditional farming systems in South East Asia, but her ideas are being applied to global agricultural patterns. If Boserup is right, then the most advanced agricultural technology should be found in places that are closest to a Malthusian crisis. High-tech agriculture should have been found in places with large dense populations of near-starving people. Unfortunately, the places with the food shortages tend to have low-tech agriculture, and the high-tech parts of the world tend to have high living standards and plenty of surplus food. Further, growth and expansion did not necessarily mean better lives for the people in such societies. Boserup herself and other researchers have noted that peasants and workers in more developed agrarian societies probably worked longer hours, consumed fewer calories, were exposed to more infectious diseases, and suffered from more despotic rulers than people in less developed societies that practiced swidden (temporary agricultural plot) agriculture and even hunting and fruit gathering populations.

World market for agricultural produces is regulated by a few industrialized countries – USA and EU in particular. Both USA and EU spend over $250 billion each to subsidize the farmers. It is for this huge subsidy that their farmers can market their produces at a very liberal rate and the world can be fed with necessary supplies. If subsidies are withdrawn, even partially, the world food prices would escalate to a height causing serious problems for countries that depend considerably on import of food grains (Africa in particular). Farmers of the Third World countries may get better price for their produces and that may even encourage them to increase productivity, but the consumers, especially the rural poor, would be hard hit by price hikes. If the farmers in the food-surplus countries downgrade their production to maintain the price of food grains at a higher level, there is every possibility of famine invading many countries. The craze for bio-fuel also will see a substantial diversion of normal agricultural land.

Although there is intellectual merit in both the Malthusian (especially neo) and the Boserupian arguments, there is relatively little evidence offered by advocates on either side. The general style of argument is one of illustrative examples and extrapolation. There is, however, a small group of researchers, mostly economists and economic demographers, who have made serious efforts to measure or simulate the impact of demographic factors on economic development. These results have been mixed, and there is not a consensus of views among experts or policy makers.

4.8.2 Synthesis of Malthus and Boserupian thesis by Ronald Lee

Malthus and Boserup point to opposite predictions of the impact of population on the economy of agrarian societies. However, both have expressed worry over uncontrolled growth of population. Whereas Malthus had talked about the potential for a population to face environmental limits,

Boserup spoke about how those limits could be overcome through culture and high-intensity technology. Both of them probably are right in their own way. The question is who was right in his/her prediction? Ronald Lee sees merit in both. He has offered a phase diagram analytic device to present a formal synthesis of Malthusian and Boserupian theory, offering a flexible framework within which to view historical change (*Malthus and Boserup: A Dynamic Synthesis*, 1986). An important question addressed by the analysis is whether a Malthus-Boserup system would be expected to move onward and upward forever. Two key (and controversial) assumptions were made: (i) that eventually diminishing returns would set in as both labor and technology increased while resources remained fixed; and (ii) that there is a cost associated with maintaining any technological level, due to the need for the maintenance of human and physical capital stocks without which the technology could not be implemented and sustained. With these assumptions, the system, after first accelerating and then decelerating, comes to rest at a high technology-high population stable equilibrium, beyond which neither increases in population nor technology can be sustained. The Boserup space, within which technological progress automatically occurs, may occupy only a limited portion of the phase space, but that Malthusian forces will steer population and technology into that region. In addition, the analysis illustrates how a preventive check that is too weak may lead to a stable equilibrium at a medium level of technology rather than at the high level that would have been attained with a stronger preventive check, possibly at a higher population density. Similarly, the effects of too strong a preventive check, too high exogenous mortality, or too strong extractive institutions might lead to medium technology equilibrium where a higher one might otherwise have been realized. It is also shown how progress to the highest technologies might occur by transition through a sequence of intermediate stable equilibria, at each of which the system might be indefinitely delayed. Lee acknowledged the role of division of labor in the Boserupian transition – "the larger the population engaged in non-food producing activities, the greater the possible division of labor and the greater the possibilities of technological advance."

Lee's observation seems quite impressive. There were probably many traditional societies that suffered from overpopulation and a few that were able to "move to the next level" as a result of population pressure. The few historical societies that did move to higher levels of agricultural productivity were the ones that were able to expand their populations and dominion, primarily through *conquest*.

The empirical implications of the theory and the possibilities of testing its main predictions have not been explored as yet.

4.8.3 Julian Simon's Thesis of population as "The Ultimate Resource"

There are a small number of scholars and policy advocates who assume, following Boserup's arguments, that large populations will stimulate technological change and productivity. The most ardent advocate of this position is Julian Simon, whose book *The Ultimate Resource* (1981) argued that each person was a potential source of ingenuity and creativity. Societies with larger populations would be more likely to develop because of their larger number of potential scientists, inventors, and creative minds. Simon argued that a growing human population is "the ultimate resource". The collective potential of a country is intricately related to its size of population. He rejected the Malthusian conclusion that poverty was the inevitable result of population growth. Instead he argued that if a society had a certain level of freedom (especially free markets), then more people meant more talents and more ideas. In a free market these new talents can be utilized. Productivity will go up for the society as a whole, and everyone would benefit. From this perspective, more people mean more problem solvers, since human creativity has the potential to overcome the limits of nature.

Julian Simon emphatically said that population has never increased geometrically. Population increases at all kinds of different rates historically, but however fast it increases, food increases at least as fast, if not faster. In other words, whatever the rate of population growth, the food supply increases at an even faster rate. Simon said the scare that farmlands are blowing and washing away is a fraud upon the public. The aggregate data on the condition of farmland and the rate of erosion do not support the concern about soil erosion. The data suggest that the condition of cropland has been improving rather than deteriorating.

Just about every important long-run measure of human material welfare shows improvement over the decades and centuries, Julian contends. In spite the fact that the developed countries use power more intensely and abundantly, the air in these countries is irrefutably safer to breathe than the so-called low-polluting countries. Water cleanliness has improved. The environment is increasingly becoming healthy, with every prospect that this trend will continue.

4.8.4 Coale and Hoover "dependency ratio" Model

The model focuses on the relationship between population and economic growth and the impact of age structure on savings. This was explicitly elaborated in the book *Population Growth and Economic Development in Low Income Countries* by Ansley Coale and Edgar Hoover (1958). High levels of fertility, it is argued, create a very youthful age structure with a high ratio of children to working age adults. Coale and Hoover coined the term "dependency ratio" to characterize this aspect of the age structure. If fertility were to be reduced, they said, the change in the dependency ratio would allow for a substantial diversion of economic resources from the care and maintenance of children to productive economic investment (*demographic dividend*). The greater economic savings would occur at the household level as families with fewer children could afford to invest more in their education and health; at the societal level with more state revenues becoming available for investment in productive capital. The empirical evidence in support of the model were mostly simulations that made assumptions about how different scenarios for declining fertility in India and Mexico lead to greater savings and higher economic growth. The thrust of the model is that declining fertility would lead to rapid economic growth consequent upon the lowering of dependency ratio and enlargement of the working population.

The major flaw in the thesis is the assumption that the proportional reduction in consumption with fewer children will be invested productively. It is quite possible that parents with three children instead of six will simply change their consumption patterns rather than save and invest the funds that were not spent on the additional children. The distinction between consumption and investment is unclear at the household level since many poorly educated parents may consider additional children to be an investment. At the societal level, any reduction in aggregate expenditures necessary to maintain a youthful population could simply be diverted to the military budget or extravagant state expenditures rather than making investments in reproductive health and child care, higher quality education, housing, roads, irrigation facilities etc. The dependency ratio thesis also failed to gather adequate support from researches conducted in the 1970s and 1980s that examined the relationship between family size and household savings and between national fertility levels and national savings rates.

4.9 Some Other Biological/Natural Theories of Population

4.9.1 Sadler's Theory of Density

Michael Thomas Sadler (1780–1835) opposed Malthusian doctrine in his book "The Law of Population". His theory can be summed up as: *The fecundity of human beings varies in inverse ratio to the density of population.* This fecundity, in contradiction to the theory of Malthus, is affected not by wretchedness and misery but by happiness and prosperity of the species. Some of his conclusions are:

- With increasing density of population, fertility would diminish and the population would stabilize at a point where people would enjoy greatest happiness.
- There was a direct link of proportionality between population growth and food supply. If the population grew the masses would produce what they require. He repudiated the geometric growth postulate of Malthus.
- High death rate would lead to increase in birth rate and *vice versa*.

Sadler kept the reader in doubt by the use of the word "fecundity". In today's scientific vocabulary the word "fecundity" is used to refer to *the physiological capacity to conceive and bear living children.* Did he really mean that with increasing density of population the physiological capacity to conceive and bear children would diminish or did he mean that "fertility" or birth rate would diminish? It is obvious that fertility cannot be high without fecundity being high as well. But fertility of a girl depends not upon fecundity alone; there are a host other factors that determine the actual number of births to be given by a woman in her reproductive years. Sadler did not explain how population density, which is defined by physical space, is related to a physiological event.

4.9.2 Pearl and Reed's Theory of Logistic Curve

Queteled in 1835 told that with increasing density of population, the growth rate of population tends to slow down. Verhulst expressed this with the help of a mathematical curve, which he called *logistic curve*. The logistic theory was not used in population until in 1920 when Pearl and Reed rediscovered it in connection with experiments with yeast, fruit flies and chickens. The conditions of the experiments were:

1. The starting population was small compared to space provided for it;
2. Food was supplied in ample quantity and from external source;
3. The space limit and the environment were held constant.

Under the stated set up, Pearl observed the species tended to multiply fast initially, tended to maintain the growth rate until a very high density was reached. The multiplication rate decelerated and ultimately the growth ceased. Pearl concluded: Population

Figure 4.1 *Logistic curve of population growth*

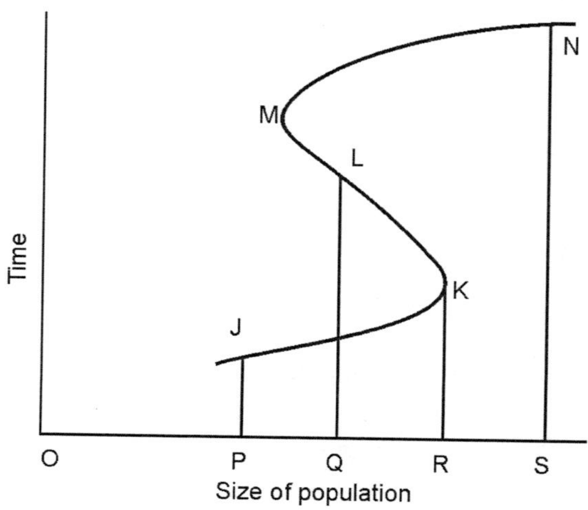

wanes and waxes, rises and falls and increases rapidly and slowly and on the whole it is ever increasing.

The theory states that the population does not follow any geometric progression path. When the growth rate is plotted, it shows an irregular path – growing fast at times and retarding afterwards. The cycle repeats itself. The population growth is restricted by the availability of space.

The logistic is drawn with time in the y-axis and population in x-axis. The curve takes the shape of a big S. Population growth rate from OP (Figure 4.1) is steady till it reaches OR. From the point K it starts declining until it reaches M wherefrom it starts increasing again. Even when it falls, the population stays at a higher plateau.

The experiment cannot be conducted on human population for obvious reasons. What is true of fruit flies, no one expects would be applicable for human population as well. Other individual characteristics and those in the environment dictate human fertility behavior. Even where the logistic described the past population growth better than any other curve, there is doubt that population would continue to follow the curve in future.

4.9.3 Herbert Spencer on Individuation

Herbert Spencer (1820–1903), the English philosopher, was of the view that all social and biological changes occur due to operation of natural forces. Like Sadler he too absolved man from any responsibility from the control of his increase in numbers. The growth of population weakens man's interest in reproduction. Man would reroute his time and effort for personal, scientific and economic advancement. He saw an antagonism between individuation and genesis. The reproductive desire would be weakened the more the individual has to exert for achieving cherished result in the specialized field of work. Spencer visualized a natural reduction in the reproductive capacity, more specifically among women, as more time and energy is spent on personal development and excellence.

Spencer believed that social evolution encouraged individuation, which in turn would bring down man's reproductive capacity. The more complex the life becomes, the less interested a man would be to give birth to babies. It is only in a simple society that the fertility rate would be high. Spencer also tried to link between the size of the man and the fertility rate. He commented, "The minutest organisms multiply asexually in their millions."

With high birth rate, death rate would also be high because of lower chances in individuation, Spencer contended. Decline in death rate would increase expectation of life, which in turn would bring down birth rate. To quote him, "When population growth tends to become excessive and thereby extinction of species, individuation steps in and resolves all differences".

He was not against population growth. He believed that population would create more manpower for exploitation of natural resources. This he believed would foster social, economic and cultural advancement.

Spencer's theory appears to have some relevance in western countries. They have reached a very high level progress in education, science, technology, and economy, all of which are necessary ingredients for individuation. However, there is no evidence that fecundity of women in these countries has declined.

4.10 Some Other Social Theories of Population

4.10.1 Henry George's Theory of Social Maladjustment

Henry George (1839–1897), an economist, said that excessive growth in sub-human species have a disastrous effect on means of subsistence since they cannot produce their own food. It is a different proposition with man. With the growth of population there is simultaneous growth in food production.

He agreed with Spencer that improvement in intellect would see a decline in fecundity resulting in a fall in birth rate. Although he said that population would not press on the means of subsistence, he admitted that food production could suffer if farm land remained concentrated at the hands of a few. He talked of land reforms and advocated a single tax on land. He believed that the cultivator was not needed to pay any other tax other than the rent for tilling the land. However, he believed private ownership detrimental to production. He admitted that the suggested tax reform could become a reality only if reduction in birth rate was achieved. When George was writing this essay in 1879, the need for conscious control of birth was already in the air in the West. He was confident that birth control would play a decisive role in checking population growth rate.

4.10.2 Dumont's Social Capillarity Theory

Arsene Dumont (1849–1902) studied the population growth of France in the later part of the nineteenth century and came to the conclusion that human beings go up the social ladder by improving his life style by a process closely similar to the physical capillarity action. He called this *social capillarity*. As he moves up by the surface tension action, he draws himself out of the social milieu and away from the family and becomes less interested to reproduce himself. Dumont said, "... what gravity is to the physical world, capillarity is to the social order" provided social stratification was not a roadblock to upward mobility. He further said, "The development of numbers in a nation is in inverse ratio to the development of the individual." The movement from a lower class to a higher one is the *raisonne de etre* of decline in birth rate.

In rigid social stratification, as in India, influence of social capillarity is very small to be effective to bring down population growth rate. Social capillarity operates optimally in societies where democracy has taken a deep root in all spheres of social activity. In most of the Western countries democratic governance is well tested and there is practically no obstruction in moving from one class to another. People remain so engrossed with achieving the desired life style that they have little opportunity of getting too much involved in family life.

There is considerable convergence between Spencer and Dumont on antagonism between desire for achieving social excellence and desire for reproduction. Spencer's theory is basically biological. The antagonism between individuation and genesis is attributed to force of nature. Dumont ascribed the antagonism to the motive to go up in the social ladder. There is considerable depth in Dumont's theory and has the potential for application in real life situation. An individual in an occupation where there is little opportunity to develop will not be easily drawn into capillary movement and therefore he is likely to remain attached to family and produce more babies.

The time and energy of the poor, who incidentally have low education and meager skill, are burned up in producing children and in procuring food and other necessities for the family. Only if they can reroute their resources including time, effort and money to production of wealth, can they pass through social capillarity. Dumont showed that city dwellers are more eager to rise in social ladder than their counterparts in villages. Life is fast and competitive in cities; the individual has to be innovative if he was to survive in this fierce struggle. Therefore, he is compelled to curtail birth rate since the cost of bringing up children in cities is exceedingly high. There is less competition in villages, caste structure is rigid, less opportunity for vertical mobility and ignorance and superstition survive. Orthodoxy, ignorance and lack of vigor contribute to poverty; high birth rate prevails.

Dumont has given an intelligent explanation of the phenomenon of differential population growth in various segments of the same society and also between societies. Thompson and Lewis have nicely summed up the contribution of Dumont's social capillarity theory:

> On the whole this statement of relation between individuation and genesis seems a decided improvement over Spencer's. It has the merit of directing more attention to the actual conditions under which people live as important factors in developing preventive checks to population growth, checks which could render the subsistence check less operative. Malthus hoped for this result although he did not approve of contraception as Dumont clearly did.

4.11 Economic Theories of Population

4.11.1 Economists in Population Analysis

Scientists from many disciplines have contributed generously on issues relating population growth and the wellbeing of people, resource management, industrial development, pollution control, and etc. The economists as a class stand out clearly by the volume they have written on population and clearly have established how modernization, industrial development and above all the quality of life are intimately related to birth rate and population growth in a society.

Whether we want it or not, the world for a long time is divided between two clusters of nations – in one cluster are the nations that have achieved a very commendable control over birth rate thereby bringing the population growth rate to a near stationary condition and the countries in the other cluster still continue with high population growth rate. The first group countries are industrially and economically well ahead of others. They use the most sophisticated technology both in industrial and agricultural production and have a decent standard of living. The countries in the second cluster are not only economically far behind the nations in the first group, their economy is still largely dependent on traditional agriculture and their standard of living is well behind in comparison with the developed countries. Demographic forecasts are that fluctuations will be a dominant feature than a secular trend in future fertility scenario in modern industrially developed populations. In less industrially developed populations, the fertility decline will show a secular trend. It is therefore no wonder that the economists dominate in the debate and discussion on population.

4.11.2 Optimum Theory of Population

Most population theories grew out of reaction to the Malthusian theory of population. Optimum theory of population takes the entire economic aspects of the population and attempts to develop desirable norms regarding population. To Prof. Edwin Cannan goes the credit for introducing the term "optimum" in the field of population.

The relation between population numbers and food supply was the basic theme in Malthusian doctrine. In optimum theory, population numbers are studied in relation to wealth produced. Every society needs a minimum size of the population to run and maintain its essential services. Maximum size is to be judged in relation to the robustness of the economy, separately for every section of society. It is the "working force" that remains at the focus of optimum theory of population. In primitive society, when both birth and death rates were very high, population did grow without a proportionate increase in the working population. With decline both in birth and death rate, the equation has changed – there are more people in the "active age group" (15–59) today than there were a few decades back. The question is: Can this active age group increase its size without affecting a diminution in its quality? The contention of optimum theory is that from national point of view, population must address to the potential labor component, and every increase in the labor force affords an opportunity to exploit the material and intellectual resources of the country.

Different authors have defined the term "optimum" in a different way:

- The population at which the standard of life is a maximum is optimum population (Boulding).
- Optimum population is that which gives maximum income per head (Dalton).
- Optimum population is that which makes the maximum returns possible (Robbins).
- Optimum population is that which produces maximum economic welfare. Maximum economic welfare is not necessarily the same as maximum real income per head but for all practical purposes they may be taken as equivalent (Carr-Saunders).
- Quantitatively, it implies a set of economic and social conditions which will allow each citizen an opportunity to satisfy his fundamental needs according to certain minimum standards. Qualitatively, it means a population program which, while guaranteeing the continued maintenance of a people, takes into account the eugenic as well as ethnic improvement of the population. Obviously, a fixed optimum is an impossibility (Ferenezi).

The core aspect in all these definitions is "maximization of economic welfare for every citizen". Dalton's definition "maximization of income per head" is quite straightforward and simple and is easily used for measurement purposes. Robbins views optimum population from national income point. An increase in population is desirable, Robbins contends, as long as it helps increase in production. Carr-Saunders definition is more inclusive since perception of 'welfare' is value judgments concerning income distribution and composition of output.

Economists look at population as provider of 'manpower' required for exploitation of natural resources and promotion of economic growth. As long as the 'optimum' point is not reached, much of the natural resources would remain unexplored. When the population crosses this point, the nation would fail to maximize return since the burden on resources would become heavy and become disproportionate. In the ideal combination of different factors related to production, population therefore has a major role. Specialization and division of labor, the key in the modern production processes, will not be attended with work force far short of the number required or when the supply far exceeds the desired level. The point at which the external economies are fully utilized and diseconomies are averted is the optimum size of the population. The national gross production and income per capita at this point become highest. It is not a static population with fixed composition. The optimum point would shift with time as more resources are used and more items are included in the production list. The technology, capital and labor component in the production process jointly put premium on this optimum number.

Figure 4.2 *Optimum population*

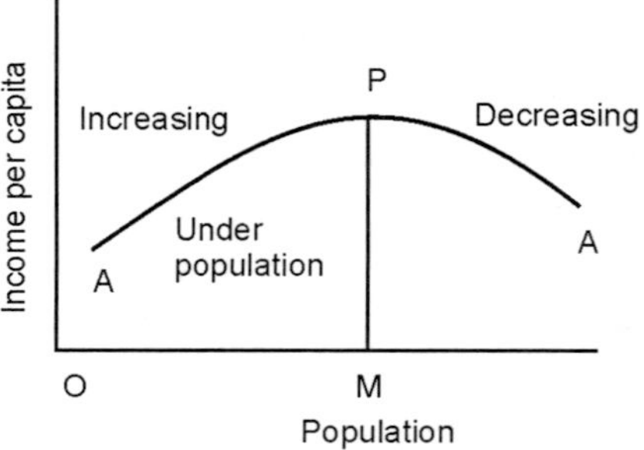

The optimum population theory asserts that the function *y(P)* increases over a range of low value of P, reaches a maximum point and decreases as P increases. The optimum population function is

$$Y = y(P) \qquad \ldots(4.1)$$

where $y\ (P)$ is the per capita real income and P is the size of the population. The function could be represented by a simple curve concave to x-axis with a single hump.

The population growing up to the point P (Figure 4.2) is accompanied by an increase in per capita income. Beyond OM further increase in size of the population is harmful to per capita income. To begin with, the law of increasing returns operates. As the population increases, marginal and average productivity too increases. At the point P the law of constant return takes over and beyond P the law of diminishing returns overtakes the economy. Dalton has offered a simple formula for measurement of maladjustment between actual and optimum population.

$$M = \frac{A - O}{O} \qquad \ldots(4.2)$$

where M is maladjustment in the population, A, the actual population and O, the optimum population. $M = 0$ is indicative of ideal or optimum state prevailing. If the actual population is 1,000 million and optimum population is 900 million, then maladjustment in the population is (1,000–900)/900 or 0.11. The optimum point is not a static point. With change of production technology, output per capita is likely to increase, thus shifting the optimum point. Exploitation of additional natural resources is likely to push up the point higher in near future

Carr-Saunders in his book *The Population Problem: A Study in Evolution*, published in 1922, made references to two fundamental issues related to population – the quantity and the quality. Most population theories concentrate on either of the two, often making only passing reference to the other. Carr-Saunders felt that it was necessary to take a more pragmatic look at population of any country. The structure, distribution and volume of the population are constantly adjusted to the demands of the environmental issues. These changes can be brought about by two distinct means – modification of genetically determined factors and changes in social 'traditions'. Of the two, the latter is more important. There has always been a conscious effort in all societies and in all times to work out a harmonious balance between population and its given environment.

Carr-Saunders maintained that man has always striven to attain an optimum number, a number most befitting to the economy of the day. This optimum is not fixed for all time, "…it is constantly varying as the condition referred to vary and as skill has tended to increase throughout history so has the number economically desirable tended to increase." Carr-Saunders believed that man controlled his numbers for the welfare of his people, and for this he looked to the social institutions and his social and physical environment for useful clues. While opposing Malthus, Carr-Saunders admitted that adopting preventive checks alone can ease the population pressure. He paid no credence to Malthus-cited positive checks.

Demographers today are concerned with numbers but more so with their quality, a concern which stimulated Carr-Saunders to develop his optimum population theory. The major thrust of his theory was on welfare of the masses. The present day economic and social progress and knowledge-based technology accentuate participation of specialized and skilled labor in the production process. The trend in today's demographic analysis – differentials of fertility, mortality and migration by education, occupation, economic and social status, rural-urban origin etc. owe its origin, at least partly, to Carr-Saunders' work.

If the technique of production undergoes change and if production output per capita improves, there would be an upward shift of the optimum population. The tapping of additional resources and improvement in technology would make the optimum point a volatile one. The increasing proportionate returns with increase in labor up to a point and a diminishing proportionate return beyond that point is depicted in the graph (Figure 4.3).

Figure 4.3 *Optimum population with varying average labor product*

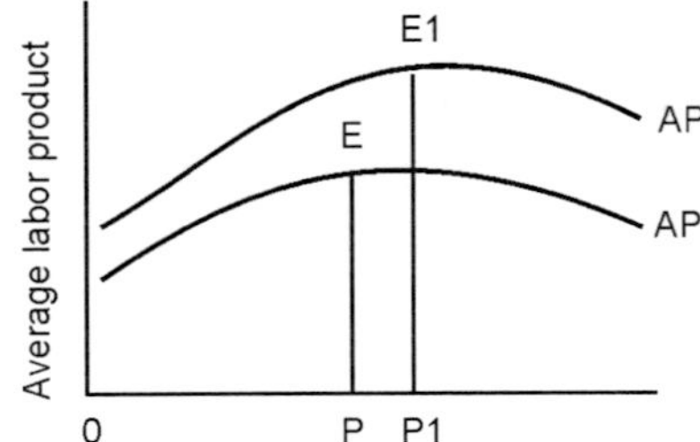

The optimum population theory has been criticized mainly on the difficulty of ascertaining a unique value of the optimum at any point of time. Moreover the per capita income growth or per capita GDP growth cannot capture the economic reality of a country. Increase in wealth often leads to concentration of income in a few hands. Income inequality, that is, the distributional aspect often is ignored in per capita income. Optimum theory of population ignores this aspect. The social and institutional conditions in a country often have a decisive say in the level of population. This aspect is also ignored in optimum population theory. Its certain commanding features need mention.

- It advocates to device ways and means to control population growth. In other words, it supports the family planning program.
- It tries to establish the connection between population and economic welfare. Optimum population, therefore, is a dynamic concept.
- It regards population an agent of production and therefore without improving the life style and skill of the labor, production cannot be improved. Production will suffer both from under-population as also from over-population.
- The optimum population is discussed in relation to per capita income, which can reasonably accurately be measured from the national income.
- The theory accommodates preventive checks to see that the population does not go beyond the desired number at a point of time. When population goes beyond the optimum number, the theory recommends exploration of new resources, new products and increase in the efficiency of workers. So long the natural resources are not exhausted and production efficiency is maintained (skill and technology are not wanting), increase in population does not pose any threat to a nation.
- The theory lends support to welfare economics. Some theorists, Carr-Saunders for example, ask for welfare considerations of the people be given due considerations while working out this optimum number.

Many non-economists find it difficult to accept the idea that fertility decisions could be "explained" using economic models – but economists have long accepted that such models are appropriate, and have devoted considerable effort to their development. While they generally agree on the relevance of such an approach, there is considerable disagreement about the form the model should take.

4.11.3 Becker's Model (Price of Time Model)

For a long time economists were somewhat bemused about the apparent contradiction between income and birth rate. Since restricted income is an impediment to child-care, the well-off families should have no problem with higher birth rates. Yet, it is a historical truth that there is a secular decline in fertility as per capita income increases; cross-sectional studies often show small families are associated with high income couples or no relation between income and fertility. The secular decline in fertility as income rises apparently implies that children are "inferior" consumer durables in an economic sense. Many non-economists object to this approach pointing to the fact that one can trade in a car or a refrigerator if its performance is unsatisfactory; the same is not true of children.

The issue has received increasing attention since 1960 when Richard Easterlin and others spoke of "taste" as an important variable in the relationship between economic factors and fertility. The economists attending to analysis of population changes are broadly divided into two schools. Garry Becker and Richard Easterlin headed these two blocs. Both are based on the common assumption of an underlying positive relationship between income and fertility, and both attempt to put forward explanations for the negative relationship, which has often been observed in modern experience. We select Harvey Libenstein and John Caldwell as those who generally do not side with either of the two schools. Hoffman & Hoffman's "Value of Children" approach is also included in this write-up to give an idea about social and psychological approach to understand how the intermediate variable also help in understanding fertility behavior of couples.

Economists have tried to examine and explain population growths on the same basic principle of demand-supply of a consumer commodity. A child has been compared with a consumer durable. As the price of a commodity fluctuates with demand and supply, so does the price of a child. In all economic theories of population, it is implicit that a dynamic equilibrium exists between the demand and supply of children. This equilibrium seems to operate both at individual, national and cross-national levels.

Garry Becker published an article in 1960 claiming that the same economic framework that economists use in the analysis of demand for durable goods could explain variations in completed fertility. His arguments rested on two fundamental postulates:

1. The representative household behaves rationally on the basis of *unchanging tastes*, and
2. The prices of commodities desired by the representative household are unaffected by that *household's consumption decisions*.[1]

Becker argued that the nature of use of a commodity or the leisure time activities in a family often could not capture their utility in a household. Becker school uses a microeconomic model of 'home production' to explain parental decisions about the family size, which is a balancing act between various exogenous and endogenous forces. A household creates a few basic "commodities" with the contribution of all its members, by the cost of time input and the cost for the services and commodities it acquires. Couples seek to maximize the total satisfaction derived from such basic non-marketable commodities as good health, education, and satisfaction from children and enjoyment from leisure time activities, each of which is produced in the household. Becker contended that a family does not receive utility directly from its consumption of market goods and

---

1 These two postulates in the more familiar language of economists are: (1) the existence of a stable and well-behaved utility function for the representative household, and (2) a budget constraint for that household which is linear in the arguments of the utility function.

leisure. The family produces within the household the more basic commodities (health and satisfaction from children) with the help of time supplied by its members and the goods and services purchased from the market. Becker thinks in terms of a family utility function. He goes on to say further that satisfaction from the children is dependent on the number of the children as also their 'quality'. The Becker school admits that 'quality' cannot be improved without necessary inputs, both material and time spent by the members in childcare.

Economists have long been aware that there are two effects when income rises: an "income effect" that causes us to purchase more of all "normal" goods, and a "price effect" as rising hourly wages raise the "opportunity cost" of any activities requiring an expenditure of our time. The opportunity cost of any activity is the value to us of the "next best" thing we might have done with our time. Thus, the opportunity cost of time spent on children might be thought of as the wage that is foregone by not working outside the home. Becker and his colleague Jacob Mincer applied these concepts in the context of "production" within the home, pointing out that households produce utility for their members using inputs from the market and the time spent by the household members. Becker in his analysis had shown that two opposing forces are embedded in any income – "income effect" and "cost effect" (or "price effect"). An increase in the number of children does not necessarily follow from increased income. The relation between fertility and the two opposing forces of income acts in reverse direction – a positive relation with 'income effect' and a negative relation with 'price effect'. Becker and Mincer pointed out that children are "more time intensive" than other goods, that is, the "opportunity cost" of children represents a higher proportion of their total cost than does the opportunity cost of most other goods. As a result, as our incomes rise the cost of children rises more rapidly than the cost of other goods and services. The "price of time model" assumes that since childcare has traditionally been a woman's responsibility, men's earnings should have almost exclusively a positive "income effect" on fertility, while women's earnings mostly should have a "price", or negative effect. This effect could be significant both during the fertility transition in the early stages of economic development, as also during baby booms and busts in industrialized nations. In poorer economies, women's status and level of education generally increase with development (both in absolute as well as relative terms to men), causing the "opportunity cost" of children to rise as well. This increase in cost might outdo the rate of growth of income, leading fertility to decline even as income rises in developing countries. To Becker and his followers (Becker School is often referred to as Chicago School), birth rate declines only when "cost effect" exceeds "income effect".

In the context of a given income, there exists a relationship of substitution between the number and "quality of children". This school believes that with the rise in income the *aspiration* the parents have for their children also rises. With this rising levels of aspiration, cost for childcare increases. Thus, even though the income increases, the demand for additional child decreases. Parents are assumed by the Becker camp to desire three things:

- Commodities for their own consumption,
- Children, and
- Commodities for consumption for their children (goods and services).

That is, as income increases, parents want to spend more both on themselves as also on each of their children. This positive relation between desired expenditure per child and parental income causes the children to be more expensive to wealthier parents than the poorer ones. Becker has used the phrase "child quality" to refer to expenditure per child. Equating "child quality" to "expenditure on child" appears confusing. Not all expenditures on a child *per se* are related to the notion of quality (parent's expenditure on terminally ill children, for example). Becker realized this and made amends to the definition of "quality". In 1976, Becker and Nigel Tomes gave a broader definition: "Child endowments and the quantity and quality of children". That is, child quality depends upon the level of expenditure per child plus a host of *other influences* over which parents have little or no direct control. This set of influences referred to as "endowment", includes inheritance of physical and psychological characteristics as also the social environment in which the child is reared. The inclusion of "endowment" in the model makes comparison of fertility between generations possible.

Another controversial aspect "taste" is somewhat a key in Becker's model. Becker is of the view that increased income does not necessarily change taste of parents; only the income and cost effects are changed. These two have opposite consequences on the desire for a child. Generally, the cost effect dominates over income effect.

Becker and Lewis hold that the "shadow price of children" with respect to their number (i.e., the cost of an additional child holding the quality constant) is greater the superior their quality is; also; the "shadow price of children" with respect to their quality (i.e., the cost of a unit increase in quality with number of children constant) increases with the number of children. That is, when the number of children is large, any improvement in their quality is expensive since the improvement has to apply to a large number. Similarly, an increase in number is expensive when the children are of high quality since high quality children cost more. Since the 'shadow price of quantity' depends on quality and "shadow price of quality" depends upon quantity, quality and quantity are said to be closely related. About income elasticity with respect to number and quality, Becker and Lewis argue that the direct effect of an increase in money income is to increase both the number and quality of children. They however believe that true income elasticity with respect to quality is considerably greater than that with respect to quantity. The societies that emphasize on the quality of children, their birth rates do not go up as the per capita income increases. Therefore, parents who insist on a better quality for their children remain satisfied with fewer children. If their income rises, they can think for an additional child only if that does not ask for a compromise on the quality of children. Those who are indifferent to quality may not have any motivation to limit their family size irrespective of their income.

Becker also argued that the improved contraceptive knowledge has eliminated the link between "joy of marriage" and family size, and changes in economic structure has eliminated the income motive for procreation in Western societies; under the circumstances, children should be treated primarily as consumer goods.

Theodre W. Schultz is one among those economists and demographers who strongly supports the Chicago School. Like Becker he also believes that care and upbringing of children obtains primacy to all other considerations. To parents no sacrifice and satisfaction are any greater than to see their children healthy, educated and well placed in their life. Schultz has drawn our attention to four fundamental thoughts in modern economics relevant in the economic analysis of fertility.

1. The concept of "human capital",
2. The theory concerning the allocation of human time,
3. The household production function, and
4. A view of the family that contains both consumer choice and household production decisions including the bearing and rearing of children.

Expenditure on children may be considered as investment in human capital that provides services in return over future periods. Children in poor families often can supplement family income and remain potential sources of security to parents in their old age. To paraphrase Schultz, children, in a very important sense, are the *poor man's capital.*

The allocative decisions with respect to market and non-market goods are a high priority in modern economic thoughts. Most mothers (marketable good) do not directly earn money. But bearing and caring a child (non-marketable good) are highly labor-intensive activities of mothers and are no less important than the services of a skilled labor.

The "household production function" has become a very useful analytical tool in microeconomics. A child is looked upon as a special kind of commodity not comparable to the other commodities available in the market. The production of a child requires special kind of inputs, both in terms of time, services and goods purchased.

The family is a decision-making unit; it maximizes its utility in consumption and also determines the allocation of human time and of goods in the production activities of the household.

4.11.4 Easterlin Hypothesis (Relative Income Hypothesis)

In 1966, Richard Easterlin challenged the Becker formulation by showing that the movements in the age-specific fertility rates of young women over time tended to be positively related to the movements in an index of *intergenerational relative income,* calculated as the ratio of the current income of young married couples to the level of income they had experienced as kids and adolescents in their parental family.[2] The explanation offered by Easterlin for this covariance rejected the notion held by many (Becker and his followers) that taste was not a variable in the relation between income and fertility. Esterlin contended that taste was not immutable and he showed how the upbringing, i.e., experience in the parental household in the adolescent years can systematically change one's taste. The craving for having a child would diminish if desire for non-child goods among parents increases. Contrasted to Becker, Easterlin group contends that the force, which offsets the underlying positive income effect, is related to parents' aspirations for their own "material standard of living". Most economists today accept the idea that the gap between aspirations and resources available to satisfy them can significantly affect economic behavior. The tension between income and aspirations (or tastes) may therefore affect fertility, since couples finding income insufficient to satisfy their tastes for consumption goods can make their available resources stretch further by limiting family size.

The introduction of the concept of socialization by Easterlin in model building is a vast departure from traditional economic analysis of fertility. Easterlin however did accept the traditional assumption that price of commodities desired by the representative household are unaffected by household's consumption decisions. That is, he rejected Becker's first postulate and accepted the second.

Easterlin brought into notice of two fundamental principles in examining the economic issues related to population growth. Both of them can be related to "inter-generational echo effect".

- The fertility decision of one generation (and the circumstantial factors that have a role in such decisions) influence the supply of labor in the labor market in the next generation;

2 Inter-generational relative income is defined as the ratio of the mean money income of families with head 14–24 years old to the mean money income of families with head 35–44 years old five years earlier.

- The environment created for upbringing young adolescents in one generation shapes taste for children and consumer goods in the next generation.

Easterlin is the foremost exponent of the importance of "relative income" in the economic analysis of fertility. The relative income actually refers to the income achieved in relation to the desired standard of living. Consumption aspirations of young people are formed during adolescence in their parents' households. Therefore, the parental households in their adolescent years provide the base for the "desired standard of living". Current market experience and the life style experiences of the peer group determine one's perceived income status. That is, their assessment of lifetime earnings is based in part on their current economic and employment situations. Thus, the balance between expected earnings and desired standard of living standards of young adults – their relative income – is measured by comparing employment experience of the young husbands with that of their fathers several years previously. Ratios of both income and employment rates are used as measures of comparative employment experience.

The basic tenet of Easterlin hypothesis is that *the changing balance between the earning possibilities of young adults and their desired living levels influences fertility*. In Easterlin's words:

> The basic idea is that if young men – the potential breadwinners of the households – find it easy to make enough money to establish homes in the style desired by them and their actual or prospective brides, then marriage and childbearing will be encouraged. On the other hand, if it is hard to earn enough to support the desired style of life, then the resulting economic stress will lead to deferment of marriage and, for those already married, to the use of contraceptive techniques to avoid childbearing, and perhaps also to the entry of wives into the labor market.

In support of his hypothesis, Easterlin showed that a rise in the relative income status of young persons between 1930s and 1950s in USA was associated with a rise in fertility rate and a subsequent decline in relative income status during the late 1950s and the 1960s, when fertility also declined. After World War I an economic depression was observed all over the world. Easterlin hypothesized that the young adults in the 1950s, who were born and raised in the depression and war years, set a lower threshold on average than young adults in the 1960s and 1970s, who were raised in the affluent postwar years. Compounding this effect of changing tastes, young adults in the 1950s were members of a very small 'birth cohort' (product of the 1930s baby bust) relative to the size of the rest of the labor force, so that their wages were driven up relative to those of older workers in their parents' generation. The result was higher wages relative to their own (already low) material aspirations, that is, even after achieving a desired level of living they were left with sufficient economic resources for raising a large family. The war-casualties of hundreds and thousands of men and women resulted in a serious disturbance in age distribution in the population and temporary decline in population growth rate. For these two reasons, birth rates in the population went up at the end of the war, making children appear very affordable. Thus, young couples in the 1950s entered enthusiastically into marriage and family formation, causing the postwar *baby boom*. The bust, according to the relative income model, occurred when those baby boomers flooded the labor market some twenty years later, depressing their own wages relative to those of their parents – and thus relative to their own expectations.

In addition to its application to the baby boom and bust, the relative income model sheds light on the problem of out-of-wedlock fertility among teens and young adults. When a pressured generation chooses to delay/forego marriage, more young women will be at risk of non-marital pregnancy. As the War ended the production level in industries and elsewhere fell considerably resulting in a slump in the labor market. Simultaneously, a huge number of young adults, born in the forties, had thronged into the labor market, which by then already had shrunk. These young adults spent their childhood and adolescent years in affluence. Lack of adequate number of suitable jobs in the market on the one hand and higher standard of living and taste on the other, put the new generation of young adults in considerable dilemma whether to marry or postpone marriages. Those already married started using contraceptives to avoid childbearing.

Easterlin was of the opinion that there is a *cyclical change* in rises or falls in fertility, supply of labor in the market, and rises or status quo in aspirations and tastes. He cited three applications of his hypothesis. He presented recent US data on the relative affluence of young adults and relative cohort size that conform to his earlier findings and predicted an upturn in fertility in the 1980s. He also showed that relative income status might explain long term secular trends in fertility in the nineteenth century US farm families. He also suggested that the relative income concept may have implications beyond fertility behavior in that it may explain the absence of positive relationship between economic growth and perceived levels of welfare since rising aspirations may have negated the satisfaction anticipated from increases in income.

In the historical context young men's earnings have been viewed by young couples as the primary component of their own total income, the basic determinant of their own standard of living. Easterlin focuses primarily on *male* relative income, defined as young *men's* earnings relative to the material aspirations of young adults. Male relative income in the United States experienced a sharp decline from 1970 to 1985, with some improvement occurring again after 1995. During this period white young men in US experienced, on average, a forty percent decline in their relative income; young African Americans experienced a 60 *percent decline*.

Even though he admitted that some social and psychological factors may have some say in fertility decisions, Easterlin maintained that tastes for consumer goods and aspirations are key determinants of fertility. Use of pills or other contraceptives may hinder the sex life. Mother of many babies may put working wives in considerable stress. Easterlin, however, emphatically said that even though the "psychic and opportunity cost" may have some role in birth planning, they cannot fully and adequately explain the rise or decline of fertility in the population.

Easterlin's model focuses on "relative birth cohort size": the size of a given cohort relative to that of its parents' cohort. Although relative cohort size may have significant effects at many points in the life cycle, the focus in Easterlin's hypothesis is at the point of labor market entry, when members of a given cohort are in their late teens or early twenties, just emerging from high school or college. In the United States relative cohort size at this point of labor market entry was halved during the 1950s, then doubled in the 1970s, and then halved again in the 1990s. Currently, the relative cohort size is about 1:2. Relative cohort size is a direct function of fertility rates at any given time: high (low) fertility produces large (small) relative cohort size.

Studies have demonstrated that the primary effect of *relative birth cohort* size is on male relative income, acting through changes in the ratio of young men's earnings relative to their fathers' earnings. This effect occurs largely since young, less experienced workers are not perfect substitutes in the labor market for older, more experienced workers, and the "production function" is sensitive to the balance of these two types of workers. If there is an oversupply of one type of worker relative to the other, the wages of the oversupplied group will tend to go down relative to the wages of the undersupplied group. This will occur even in a period of strong economic growth: in that case the wages of both groups might rise, but the wages of the oversupplied group generally will not rise as rapidly as those of the undersupplied group. The age group in greater relative supply will experience increased levels of unemployment and under-employment.

Easterlin in 1975 modified his hypothesis and admitted that *supply determinants* do have a role in birth control. He accepted instability in demand-supply equilibrium in his hypothesis. He admitted that desire for a child (supply) depends both upon some of the personal characteristics of parents as also upon the regulations and cultural traditions of the society of their origin. That is, some personal and social factors operate both for demand and supply of children. The two sets of causes for demand and supply are unrelated. With time, the characteristic features of these factors may change totally independently.

Easterlin's relative income model predicted fertility to increase after 1980. That did not happen. Some suggest his model errs by ignoring effects of the female wage. Women's wages did not increase as assumed in "price of time" model, after controlling for changing levels of education and experience. Fertility rates in US at that time simply stabilized, and have not changed greatly until very recently. Recent studies bring together the "price of time" and "relative income models", testing for effects of both relative income and women's wages on young women's age-specific fertility rates – particularly that of women in their twenties since the relative income theory is expected to be most relevant at younger ages. In theory, the female wage is expected to exert both a positive (income) and a negative (price of time) effect on fertility. In reality, however, proponents of the price of time model expect that any positive effect would be greatly outweighed by its negative effect (Diane Macunovich 1995). The combined "relative income and price of time" model explains the observed pattern of fertility in the second half of the twentieth century in US, and estimates a strongly positive effect of male relative income and a strong underlying negative price effect of the female wage. The study reveals that interaction terms in the model show that the price effect of the female wage has been declining over time, while its income effect has been increasing with declining male relative income.

4.11.5 The Tussle Between Becker and Easterlin Schools of Thought

We have said at the beginning of our discussion that economists interested in the analysis of fertility are broadly divided into three rival camps, Gary Becker and Richard Easterlin led the two major factions, while those distanced with either side formed the third group. The present discussion is on the status of current conflict between the two major camps.

There was a period when researchers from any of these two camps were either totally ambivalent to the developments in the other or made only passing references. For example, a conference volume edited by T.W. Schultz, a staunch supporter of Chicago School, on the deliberations of National Bureau of Economic Research, 1974 made very scanty reference to research papers by Easterlin group. The conflict has gone beyond the confines of fertility analysis – the members of the Easterlin group attacked on the economic foundations of the works of Becker group. The basic differences between the two schools are discussed hereunder.

1. Becker considers 'taste' basically is unchangeable. Easterlin while opposing this went on to say that personal tastes (aspirations for consumer goods and better standard of living) increase with income rise.
2. Becker school maintained that the relative price of children and relative price of goods consumed per child are not independent of household decisions. Easterlin, on the other hand

believes that the price tag associated with commodities that are procured for child rearing is not flexible. The price level for these commodities is unrelated to the general consumption pattern in the household. That is, they maintained the assumption of constant prices for desired commodities. Whereas the Becker group in the course of debate and discussion discarded postulate 2 but held to postulate 1 of 1960 formulations, Easterlin contingent discarded postulate 1 and accepted postulate 2.

3. The dependence of prices on household decisions in the Becker model is the result of specifications that may be appropriate for the analysis of fertility decisions, but many doubt its applicability as an economic model to the demand for consumer durables. The specification in question is the assumption that the family cares about its average level of expenditure per child, but not on the expenditures on each child separately. Easterlin hypothesis is an alloy of economic theory with psychology and sociology.
4. Parents in Becker model are assumed to desire three things: children, commodities for their own consumption, and commodities for their children's consumption. More wealthy parents allocate more money for child rearing. With rise in their income, they allocate more funds for each child – a reason why children in well-to-do families are costlier than those in the poorer families. Easterlin does not agree that with rise in income child rearing cost also increases. The parents spend a sizeable share of the increased income on consumer durables appropriate for their taste. Tastes go high as income rises and after meeting the demands of this rising taste and aspiration very little is left for other expenditures. That is, relative income does not rise even though the income rises.
5. Easterlin has used relative income in place of absolute income as the most important variable. Easterlin hypothesis therefore enables one to compare the income experience of two generations. In the earlier formulation in Becker's model this aspect of comparison between generations was not properly dealt with. Becker and Tomes in 1976 redefined "child quality", which includes level of expenditure per child and a host other influences upon which the parents have little or no direct control. This shift in paradigm from 'expenditure per child' to 'expenditure per child and a host other influences' (which they called *child endowment*) makes comparison possible in an inter-generation context. The claim that Becker's model was based on pure economic theory was no longer tenable after the enlargement of the definition of "child quality". The authors came out with a remarkable statement that also constitutes their first direct reference to Easterlin's work:

   > Our conclusions about the effects of economic growth on the number of children are similar to those reached by Richard Easterlin... Both Easterlin's and our own analysis are based on changes in the economic position of children relative to their parents.

6. The major question on the nature of the offsetting force in the relation between number of children and parent's income was not resolved in both the theories. A further narrowing of the differences between the rival camps was possible. Easterlin explained the decline in fertility of rural women in US in the nineteenth century by use of a model in which farm families desired to leave as a bequest to each child as much wealth in real terms as their own parents gave them. This desired level of bequest per child brings Easterlin camp formulation very close to the desired level of expenditure per child in the Becker model. The two specifications now differ only in what constitutes the 'other thing' in the phrase 'holding other things constant'. The

Becker group holds that the *desired level of expenditure per child* to be 'related to parental income', while the Easterlin group expects *bequests* (and expenditure) per child to be independent of parental income. Both agreed that this 'other thing' really is responsible for the relation between income and fertility. To Becker, it is "parents' aspirations for their children's material standard of living", to Easterlin, it is "changing level of aspiration for their own standard of living and tastes for consumer goods".

The differences between the two camps have considerably been narrowed down. The major difference now relates to "what" really has the "offsetting effect" in the underlying positive income effect on desire for a child. The area of agreement between the two sides now exceeds the area of disagreement.

Economists believe that there is room for compromise between the two contending schools. An idea of such conciliation could be found in J. A. Bank's writing: *Prosperity and Parenthood*, written in 1954 or even in the writings of John S. Billings as early as 1893. Banks wrote,

> … (I)t cannot be denied that the attitude toward the material comforts of modern existence and the growing expensiveness of children and adolescents contributed their share to the acceleration in the fall of family size.

Both the principal arguments of Easterlin (attitude toward the material comforts of modern existence) and Becker (the growing expensiveness of children and adolescents) are blended in Bank's arguments. The two notions can easily be regarded as aspects of a single explanation. Taking singly, they cover only a part of the phenomenon – fertility change. Billings' writing on the same theme is more instructive:

> [One] cause [of the fertility decline] is in the great use of things which were formerly considered as luxurious, but which now have become almost necessities. The greater temptation to expenditure for the purpose of securing or maintaining social position, and the correspondingly greater cost of family life … lead to the desire to have fewer children in order that they may be each better provided for.

Warren C. Sanderson's comment on the present status of conflict between the two camps is instructive.

> Today, a student of economic demography has at his disposal a number of closely related economic models. The choice between them should depend on the details of the particular study. Choosing between the Easterlin and Becker frameworks on any general grounds, however, is almost guaranteed to be counterproductive. It would be like removing one blade from a scissors or deleting either the concepts of demand or supply from the economist's tool kit. The initial Becker model was an attempt to break with the past and to emphasize the unique contributions of traditional economic theory. In more recent work, the situation has been reversed. The discipline of attempting to use economic theory to analyze fertility decisions has led to new developments in economic models that have made them more consistent with the views by demographers and sociologists.

4.11.6 Harvey Libenstein's Selective Rationality Theory

Libenstein's Selective Rationality theory, also popularly known as Cost-Benefit or Utility Analysis among economic demographers, is a true blend of economics, psychology and sociology.

Two basic decision-making entities in microeconomic theory are *households* and *farms*. Households are presumed to operate "rationally", i.e., maximize utility, or satisfaction; and farms are also presumed to operate "rationally" in the sense that they endeavor to maximize profits and minimize costs. Microeconomic theories have developed in such a way as to be completely independent of socio-political considerations. But the actual behavior of the household or the farm often does not conform to this maximization and rationality principles. People join voluntary organizations and work for it though there is no remuneration for undertaking assignments given to them by the organization. Many poor couples do not adopt birth control when it is in their economic interest to do so. Explanation of such issues, Libenstein felt, requires induction of psychological and social considerations beyond the scope of traditional economic theory.

In this physical world, every consumer good is associated with two diametrically opposing forces – cost and benefit or utility. The cost of a consumer good does not depend upon the consumer, but benefit does. The price of a car does not depend on who purchases it. But the benefit of having a car by a practicing physician or a top executive is much more than with a common man. For a doctor or an executive the price of the time he can save having a car is much more than the cost of the car. That is, utility of a thing is user-specific and the rationality for having it or not having it is also individual specific.

In economic analysis, a child is a marketable consumer durable. According to Libenstein, if the parents find that social, psychological and economic utility of having a child are far greater than the cost of bearing and rearing the child, they might give a serious thought to having an additional child. That is, parents expect some thing in excess of the cost of child rearing – happiness, social and psychological satisfaction and possibly security at old age, which encourage them to have a child. The parents have their own rationale for wanting an additional child. Libenstein spoke of three major types of utility of a child from the viewpoint of their parents:

1. *Income utility* – utility of the child as a productive agent, child as a source of supplementary family income.
2. *Security* – the utility of the prospective child as a personal source of security, especially at old age or in times of some crisis in the family.
3. *Consumption utility* – utility of the child as a source of personal pleasure and happiness.

Libenstein spoke of two types of costs for a prospective child – direct and indirect. Direct cost includes conventional expenses of bearing and rearing the child (health, education, general maintenance, etc.) till the child becomes self-supporting. The indirect costs refer to the *opportunity costs* (freedom of movement, sacrificing many personal wants, anxiety and etc.) that the parents have to forego because of the childcare.

Changes concomitant to economic development alters the cost and utilities of an additional child. With economic development per capita income rises, chances of survival improve, and the employment market expands and newer jobs are created. All these combined tend to influence the motivation for having an additional child or not. With increase in per capita income, there is less need to use children to supplement the family income. Increase in per capita income implies more time must be spent on the education and training of children. The children will enter the employment market late and would stay there for a comparatively short period. That is, utility of children as productive agents would diminish with rise in per capita income.

As the income rises, parents would be better equipped to make provisions for their own future (personal savings, insurances, etc.). With national income improving, the government would be in a position to institute various welfare measures (social security such as pension, unemployment allowance, medical insurance, etc.). Therefore the utility of prospective child – as productive agent and security in old age – would diminish with the increase in national and per capita income.

With rise in income the life style changes, so changes one's social position. This improved status and better standard of living ask for higher expenditure on every child. With better economic environment, the competitions are stiff and parents have less time to attend to many of the standard duties in the family including that of the children. One often would hire hands even for sundry jobs. Life becomes complex and fast. The working mothers under such pressing conditions would not desire for an additional child.

Level of nutrition improves as income rises. Expectation of life increases as a result. Improved life expectancy means more eventful years ahead and better chances for enjoyment and happiness. When the child is expected to live long, the parents are likely to receive psychological and material support from their children for a longer period. That is, their old age security is assured even if they did not have much in saving and security.

With better health care facilities (an attendant fact of growth of national economy) infant and child mortality would decline, a fact that will discourage utility of an additional child in nuclear families and for individuals in modern hi tech occupations. In such nuclear families, the utility of an additional child is far less because once they become adult and self sufficient, their responsibilities might be shifted elsewhere. It is very likely that they would not be able to stay in their parent's family. A separate establishment for his own family often would prevent him from paying as much attention to his aging parents as he would have liked. However, every child becomes an asset in families engaged in traditional occupation.

Libenstein has drawn our attention to another important aspect. Cost factor associated with a child of a given quality is not the same for all birth orders. Resources acquired for rearing the first child can be reused for the second or subsequent child, in which case the cost of rearing second and subsequent child becomes less without making any compromise on quality. Similarly, altogether different types of resources might be required for subsequent children because of availability of more modern, expensive or inexpensive, resources in the market. A first timer father or mother, especially in a nuclear family, may look for resources, which ultimately may prove to be redundant or superfluous. The parents can cut down many costs from their experiences with the first child (often called the experimental child) without compromising on the quality of the facilities offered to the child.

Utility of a child for personal joy and happiness often poses a ticklish question. Even a few decades back, children were born in large numbers and died in large numbers too. That is, only a fine line distinguished a birth from a death. Under such circumstances, development of a close tie with children whose fate still remained unknown was difficult. A child is a poor man's only asset. Because of his low economic status, often social status too, it is hard for him to develop extra-familial interest. That is why the parents may feel deeply attached to the surviving children. For the middle and lower-middle class families the situation is somewhat different. These families have high expectations but limited resources. They are obliged to follow a small family norm.

Libenstein is of the opinion that all parents behave rationally. Parents, no matter from what strata they come from, want to maximally utilize their limited resources for gratifying their aspirations. The aspirations include both children and consumer goods. They believe that the desired level of satisfaction cannot be had from market goods alone; at the same time their importance in one's personal life cannot be ignored. Children alone cannot fill in the void created by their absence in the household inventory. The demand for a child therefore would depend, among other things, upon parents' income, value of a child compared to other consumer goods, and the order of preference between a child and consumer durables. The relation the demand of a child has with these three are:

- Parents' income – *positive*,
- Value of child relative to other consumer goods – *negative*, and
- Preference between a child and consumer good – *positive*.

In traditional economic theory, 'households' and 'farms' are the basic decision making units. Libenstein argues that the relation of workers to households is not well developed. With the contractual relation between workers and farms, it is presumed that the objectives of farms are identical with the objectives of individuals who are a part of the farm. Implicit in such assumption is that groups behave as if they were individuals. Libenstein disputes the aptness of this assumption since it cannot analyze intra-household and intra-farm differences and the ways these differences relate to economic decisions of the household and the farm. The selective rationality, Libenstein contends, permits such analysis since the basic decision-making units are "individuals". The 'unit' of analysis of fertility behavior both in Becker and Easterlin model is the "household". Much of selective rationality is based on some fundamental psychological assumptions *that people work out a compromise between the way they would like to see they behave and the way they wish to behave in absence of constraints of any sort.*

The behavior of an individual (reproduction is a behavior), Libenstein observes, depends upon:

1. Individual's primitive urge, which psychologists identify as ***id***, that is, the manner in which an individual would like to behave had there been no social constraints;
2. What behavior others expect of him, that is, the sense of morality, ***super-ego***, that is generated in him by social constraints;
3. The individual has to encounter many social and environmental restrictions – ***the constraints,*** to reach his desired goals.

Libenstein believes that everyone has to face variety of pressure situations while pursuing a higher-level goal. He therefore often will need to modify or compromise his behavior and action to avoid the discordant note between the goal and the constraints from his social environment. His ideal would be to maximize both the demands of *id* and *super-ego*. This compromised decision does not cause any disaster to his mental peace. This in nutshell is Libenstein's selective rationality.

Libenstein's views on income effect on birth and death rate and on population increase run as follows:

1. Fall in per capita income increases death rate. This will tend to increase the three types of utilities of children to parents. A scaling down of cost of upbringing would result from high death rate. This would act as an incentive to produce more babies.
2. With increasing per capita income, death rate falls quickly but birth rate takes time to shrink. That is, there is a lag between increase in per capita income and fertility decline. As and when the per capita income shows a significant rise and the death rate sinks, economic utility of children falls since the parents are economically well off to make adequate provisions for their old age. The cost of upbringing the children increase. This cost factor far outweighs the anticipated utility from children; birth rate declines. Libenstein believed that decline in birth rate is a concomitant effect of economic development. With abject economic poverty come illiteracy

and ignorance and the rationality demanded for birth control would remain a far cry. Therefore attention must concentrate primarily on economic development and its distributive justice. Measures to control birth rate can become effective in a democratic set up only when the constraints to economic wellbeing are removed.

However thought provoking this cost-benefit analysis of fertility behavior may appear, it is not easily applied in a reality situation. Before the theory can be applied, one needs to identify all those elements that determine the cost and benefit of having a child, and also to decide upon a plan on how to measure them. This is a complex issue often evoking conflicting opinions on identification of the factors and measuring their cost/utility. One possibly can reasonably well measure the economic cost of upbringing a child; but the sacrifices and loss of freedom by parents, the anxiety and tension relating to child's health and education or the happiness they derive from a child cannot be evaluated on a monetary scale. Moreover, the opportunity cost of parents in cities cannot be compared with that of parents living in villages.

The economic theories on fertility grew out of nature of population growth observed in the developed countries in the West. The social and economic fabric of these highly industrialized and developed countries with a high per capita income and consumption are not comparable by any stretch of imagination with those in the developing countries. These models relating to fertility are a good approximation of the situations prevailing in the developed countries. They have not been found to work well in the developing countries. Giving birth to a child may not have anything to do with parents' 'desire for a child', especially among the illiterate rural masses engaged in traditional occupations or having no fixed occupation at all in most developing countries.

4.11.7 John Caldwell's Intergenerational Wealth Flows

John Caldwell's wealth flows theory proposes a direct link between family structure and fertility. As per this theory, there are only two major forms of family structure, differing chiefly in the direction of wealth flows among generations. In 'primitive' and 'traditional' societies, net wealth flows are primarily upward from younger to older generations (bottom-up) and individual interests are subjugated to shared interests. In developed nations, family structure is organized in terms of downward wealth flows (top-down) – parents provide facilities for education and skill development for children's economic wellbeing.

The theory proposes that fertility decisions in all societies are economically rational responses to familial wealth flows. In societies with net upward wealth flows, the economically rational decision is to have as many surviving children as possible, since each additional child adds positively to a parent's wealth, security in old age, and social and political wellbeing. In the net downward wealth flows societies, the economically rational decision is to have no children or a minimum number allowed by a social-psychological disposition that derives pleasure from children and parenting. The worldwide transition from high to low fertility regime is the result of a change in family structures from upward to downward wealth flows – from child-to-parents to parents-to-child.

These new values, derived from the educated, middle-class in the west, are now being exported to the developing world through mass formal education. Implicit in the educational materials and expectations of schools is the individualistic value system that produces downward wealth flows. Labor markets make the adoption of these individualistic values, which are adversative to the family or group production characteristic of pre-transition societies, economically feasible. The transition from 'traditional' to 'modern' family structure occurs when a critical mass of individuals adopt the new values, and respond with low fertility. The attainment of mass education in a country should therefore precipitate and predict the fertility transition.

The most serious challenge to the wealth flows theory has come from evolutionary biologists. The argument that prior to modernization, upward wealth flows characterized human family structures is inherently adversative to theory in evolutionary biology. Biologists expect net wealth flows to be downward in all organisms, including humans. The researches generated by the evolutionary biological critique of wealth flows theory have stimulated the development of a new theoretical framework for understanding human demographic patterns.

4.11.8 Hoffman & Hoffman: Value of Children

Value of children appears directly or indirectly in most fertility analysis. Libenstein's *selective rationality theory* or Caldwell's *wealth flows theory* explicitly admit that perception of income, security as well as psychological utility for having one or more children has a lot to do with fertility behavior of persons. Hoffman and Hoffman developed a social psychological theory in which 'Value of Children' (VOC) as an intermediate variable occupies the central spot. The model thus developed takes into account both objective and subjective aspects of fertility decisions. The authors of course admit that this 'central intervening variable' is dependent upon socio-demographic and socio-economic determinants. In order to identify the content of VOC, Hoffman & Hoffman (1973) utilized various inductively collected empirical findings and divided them into nine categories:

(i) adult status and social identity,
(ii) expansion of self, ties to a bigger entity, and 'immortality',
(iii) morality: religion, altruism, good for the group, norms regarding sexuality, action on impulse, and virtue,
(iv) primary group ties and affection,
(v) stimulation, novelty, and fun,
(vi) achievement, competence, and creativity,
(vii) power, influence, and effectiveness,
(viii) social comparison, and competition, and
(ix) economic utility.

These categories are integral part of the VOC model. It also takes several other influential factors into account: *alternative sources* of the value of children (public social-security system may make up the economic value of children), *costs* of children (direct financial cost and time spent on rearing, indirect opportunity cost (abstaining from other goods and activities in favor of children), *barriers* against the attainment of value of children (financial despondency and less than ideal housing condition, or maternal illness) and *incentives* that make it easier to reach the desired value for having children.

The central assumption in VOC is that the value of children varies by societies, and has various far-reaching consequences for generative decisions and the type of parent-child relation. The VOC essentially offers an interdisciplinary, integrative explanatory concept that mingles essence of different approaches from various disciplines. The VOC list is inductively drawn from the existing empirical researches and not deductively drawn from any theory. The theoretical status of VOC remains unclear since the list of value system may have to be changed or enlarged when we move away from intra-cultural studies to studies across widely varying cultures.

5 Population Composition and its Distribution

5.1 Introduction

Population generally refers to human aggregates within a defined space. Not all aggregates attract the attention of a demographer or a population scientist. We can talk of population of elected members to assemblies or parliaments, population of viewers or listeners to some TV or radio program or industrial population. These populations are more readily a result of political, ideological, cultural and economic influences rather than of demographic influences. These and other such aggregates could be the population for many social surveys depending upon the purpose and objectives of such surveys. A demographer however would be interested to study a human aggregate as a product of mortality, fertility, and migration.

The aggregates studied by demographers often are not "groups" in the sense a sociologist or a social psychologist would like to address. The aggregates studied as groups have certain common features – there is observable direct or indirect communications, which are socially structured, and which presumably have some distinctiveness. A demographic population may not meet any of the qualifications that would illustrate them as sociological groups. A demographer often may deal with some hypothetical populations. These are hypothetical aggregates that are assumed to have been born on a particular day and are assumed to follow age-specific birth and death rate. These are Life-table populations.

We have discussed earlier the paramount importance of information of the size and structure of population with its variegated characteristics, both for short and long term national and regional planning. Growth of population does not necessarily mean that all the segments of the population are growing in a similar fashion. With no restriction on birth, the children and the young age group grows much faster than the other parts. When birth control measures are strictly implemented, the proportion of the child and young age population drops rapidly. Decision on expansion of basic facilities as schools and colleges, health centers and resolve to make more investment for improving the quality of these provisions can be taken only when the government knows what changes are noticeable in the growth of population and its structure. A drop in the proportion of the young age group invariably would be attended by a growth in the size of the 'active population'. A comparison of birth and death rates tells us how fast the population is growing and how the proportion of the 'active population' in the total population is changing. This enables a government to plan its strategy to create new employment situations and organize training and education programs to accommodate the new entrants to the job market. The contemporary picture of the distribution of the population and the accompanying changes in its different segments are exceedingly important in social and economic planning.

5.2 Sex Composition

Sex ratio in the population, which indicates the nature of balance of the sexes in a population and in its various segments, is a fundamental demographic measurement. It is the number of one sex per hundred persons of the other sex. In most countries sex ratio is the number of males per hundred females. Dividing the total number of males in the population (or a segment) by total number of females in the same population (or the same segment of the population) and multiplying the result by 100 or by a constant K obtains the sex ratio. Some countries (India, for example) define sex ratio as the number of females per 100 men.

$$\text{Sex ratio} = \frac{\text{Number of females}}{\text{Number of males}} \cdot K \qquad \ldots(5.1)$$

$$\text{or,} \quad = \frac{\text{Number of males}}{\text{Number of females}} .K \qquad \ldots(5.2)$$

It can also be defined as ratio of females (or males) in the stated population.

$$\text{Sex ratio} = \frac{\text{Number of females}}{\text{Number of males} + \text{Number of females}} .K \qquad \ldots(5.3)$$

$$\text{or,} \quad = \frac{\text{Number of males}}{\text{Number of males} + \text{Number of females}} .K \qquad \ldots(5.4)$$

In Indian census, equation (5.1) is employed in computation of sex ratio. This formula is also used in Life Tables. Equation (5.3) is used for computation of various measures of growth (GRR and NRR, for example). The value of K is usually taken as 100 or 1,000. A perfectly balanced population has a sex ratio 100 (Eqs. 5.1 and 5.2). With sex ratio more than 100 (equation 5.1) (as in the state Kerala and UT Pondicherry), there is a surplus of women in the population; with less than 100, the number of females is short of number of males (in all other states in India). Whenever referring to sex ratio, one therefore must specify which definition of it has been followed.

Customarily, four types of sex ratios are reported – live birth sex ratio or sex ratio at birth, still born birth ratio, sex ratio at fertilization, and sex ratio in the population. The first ratio is often called the primary sex ratio, the second one the secondary ratio, and the third one, the tertiary sex ratio. In all countries for which reliable demographic data are available there are more male than female births. In most of the developed countries where prenatal losses are low, the sex ratio at birth (M/F) is generally around 105. In countries where prenatal losses are high, the sex ratio is around 102 in spite the fact that female babies are more likely to be unregistered than male babies. Sex ratio in the total population is generally reported in census and sample survey reports.

Demographers long back realized that the number of babies born per 1,000 populations, which in scientific terminology is called Crude Birth Rate, CBR, does not portray the potential for reproduction. CBR fails to foretell either the time-specific population distribution or the changes in birth rate with time. Since only the girls can conceive, it is more important to know how many 'future mothers' are born than how many babies. Even if there was no change in the age-specific distribution, the population growth may show upward or declining trend over the years if there was any change in the sex ratio at birth. Other things remaining the same, a change in the sex ratio at birth will have a major effect on population growth for generations. Demographers for this reason have developed more precise growth rates: Gross Reproductive Rate, GRR, and Net Reproductive Rate, NRR. Both utilize sex ratio at birth in growth estimation.

We have said earlier that sex ratios at birth in all countries for which reliable information are available is slightly in favor of male babies. It is also a fact that male mortality in most ages is higher than that of females presumably because of their greater involvement with the outside world. They therefore are prone to various types of diseases and accidents than females in the population. Besides, they have to face the occupational hazards far in greater degree than females. Giving birth to a baby is a defining moment in a girl's career; yet this is the time when they are most vulnerable to certain types of diseases and the risk factor is generally high in their reproductive period, especially between 15 and 30. In the underdeveloped countries the health of a girl deteriorates fast due to frequent childbirth. In India, even today more than 400 mothers would die at the time of delivery for every hundred thousand babies born. Once they cross the reproductive period (15–49 years), their survival rates in each of the remaining years are higher than their male counterparts.

5.3 Age Composition

If sex composition of a population speaks about any distortion in the population, the age composition of a population is probably the most important component of population from planner's point of view. However, unlike sex composition, computation of age composition of a population is much more complicated for various reasons. The first problem arises from the fact that a population can be classified in a variety of ways – from single age classification to a grouping as young age group (< 15 years), active age group (15–59 years) and old age group or senior citizens (60 + or 65+ age group). The second hurdle is a proper definition of age. Do we define it as age on the last birthday (*lbd*), which usually is the practice in demographic analysis, or do we refer it to completed years, months and days? Even if we agree on a definition, it may prove difficult for accurate recording of ages and describing the population on such definition. This is especially true in countries where births often take place outside institutional care and formal recording of birth (by statutory bodies) still remains inadequate and inefficient. The rural populations in these countries are either largely illiterate or have very low level of education. Even today, a researcher often has to make a guess about the probable age of a person from such signatures or anchor points as "born in the year when Bangladesh became independent", "the year when the cyclone devastated the entire area", "the year when Godhra massacre took place" etc. There can be many other sources through which errors may creep in. Often there would be deliberate under or over reporting of age.

Two types of questions are usually asked for getting age data. We may ask: "How old were you on your last birth day?" or "What is your date of birth?" The former will give age only in completed years and the latter will furnish age in years, months and days. In Indian census, a variant of the two is used: "How old were you on January 1 (of the census year)?" The answer to either of the questions posed will depend on if the person interviewed knew his actual date of birth. The enumerators are specifically instructed not to ask: "How old are you?" It has been observed that the reported ages tend to cluster around numbers that are multiples of 5 when such a question is put to. The single-age classification from such data is likely to distort the age distribution much more than when a five-year period as 0–4, 5–9, … is used for age classification. By increasing the interval length (less than 15 years, 15 – 30 years, … 60 + years) the errors would be less serious but would severely reduce it's utility and precision.

Population under age 15 in the world today is 30 percent of the total population (Table 5.1); the same in India is about 34 percent. In high-income countries the young age group's share to total population is only about 19 percent, which is likely to come down to around 16 percent by 2015. The proportion of aged people (65 + years) in the world population is about 7 percent as against about 5 percent in India. The high-income countries in the world are highly burdened with their senior citizens; their number is likely to cross 18 percent by 2015 from the current level of below 15 percent of the total population. The total dependency ratio in the world is likely to fall to around 52 percent in 2015 from about 59 percent observed in 1999.

Table 5.1 *Young and old age population – world and India, 1999*

Regions	< 15 1999	< 15 2015	65+ 1999	65+ 2015	Dependency ratio 1999			Dependency ratio 2015		
					Young	Old	Total	Young	Old	Total
WORLD	30.2	25.8	6.9	8.3	48	11	59	39	13	52
High income countries	18.6	15.8	14.5	18.3	28	22	49	24	28	52
Middle income countries	27.8	22.2	6.5	8.5	42	10	52	32	12	44
Low income countries	37.2	32.3	4.4	5.2	64	6	70	52	8	60
Least developed countries	43.2	40.4	3.1	3.4	80	6	86	72	6	78
INDIA	33.9	26.9	4.9	6.4	55	8	63	40	10	50

Source: Human Development Report 2001, UNDP

The division of the world population between high- and low-income countries displays a considerable divergence in the population composition by age. The later group is burdened with young age people, necessitating substantial investment in social infrastructure (health, education, food supply, job opportunities, etc.); the high-income countries are beset with problems related to making adequate provisions for old-age security to a large proportion of the population. The average expectation of life in some of these countries is already close to the highest average (85 years) achievable. With state-sponsored security provisions, the increasing size of the senior citizens is probably not an immediate threat to most of these countries. But in many low-income countries the average expectation of life is also fast increasing resulting in a fast increase in the size of the old-age population. The UNDP forecasts that by 2015 the young-age population in the low-income countries will drop from the current level of 37.2 percent to around 32.3 percent (a 14 percent reduction) and the proportion of old-age group would rise from 4 percent to 5.2 percent, a 30 percent increase over the present level. There shall be a sizeable increase of job seekers in the low-income countries (where unemployment is already a critical issue) in the next 15 years. The high-income countries would experience a rise in the dependency level – the senior citizen segment would over compensate the reduction in the size of young age category.

Median age: The age distribution of a population is always skewed (+ve Sk) and therefore arithmetic mean is a poor indicator of the average age of the population. For an asymmetric distribution, median is more meaningful than mean. Because of relatively greater concentration of people in the higher age groups (due to low birth and death rates), the developed countries have high median ages. In fact, the population growth rate and the level of socio-economic development of a country can be gauged from the median age of its population. The countries where the median age of the population is low, (countries where children and adolescents constitute a very sizeable segment of the population) tend to have very high birth rates. As the median age increases, the proportions of people in the active age group and old age group increase.

Table 5.2 *Median age of different categories of countries, 1999 and 2015*

Countries	*1999*	*2015*
WORLD	25.75	33.36
High income countries	38.47	40.95
Middle income countries	31.89	35.06
Low income countries	25.96	29.16
Least developed countries	21.33	23.54
INDIA	28.15	32.32

The median age in Table 5.2 has been calculated by taking active age group consisted of persons in 15–64 age group instead of 15–59 which normally is taken as the active age population. Had the computation been done on 15–59, the median age of the world population in 1999 would have been about 2 years higher, around 27.5 years. The world population is very much adult today than it was 15–20 years back because of declining birth rate. The median age is likely to go up appreciably by 2015 due to a sharp drop in young age dependency ratio, from 48 in 1999 to 39 in 2015. The least developed countries would improve the median age of their population by a small margin, so are with the high income countries. Whereas most countries would cut down their total dependency ratios by a large margin because of considerable cut in young age dependency ratio, the high income group could experience an increase in total dependency because the cut in the percentage of population in <15 years is likely to be more than compensated by the increase in the old age population. India would increase median age but its relative position would remain unaltered compared to both low and medium income countries.

Dependency ratio: In a family (a nation can be viewed as a large family) all are consumers, only a few are producers. There are two distinct segments of a population that are directly or indirectly dependent upon the economic activities pursued by another segment. Through International Labor Organization ILO promulgations, children under 15 years cannot be employed in any gainful activity. In fact, under the aegis of World Trade Organization (WTO) many countries have put embargo on import of products, especially from developing countries, if the manufacturing units were found to have employed children aged below 15 years. It is argued that these are the formative years and everyone should have access to basic education and other amenities that would help develop one's personality to its full potential. This segment is referred to as *Young Age Population* by demographers. Every country has its legislative compulsion to ask its people to retire from active services in the organized sector. The retirement age varies from country to country and also for different types of jobs. Usually, 60 years of age is reckoned as the age of retirement. The 60+ age segment (65+ in developed countries) is regarded as the *Old Age Population* of a country.

The age at which a boy or a girl should enter into gainful occupation depends upon certain cultural considerations and largely upon the economic compulsions of the family and the country. The more the country is dependent on agriculture/traditional occupations, that is, the occupations requiring very little or no specialized training, the more easily the young children are drafted into family economic activities as cultivation, weaving, rearing and tending of domestic animals, etc. In the more industrialized countries, the young children start their economic career relatively late since their job-market demands a minimum level of education and specialized training for jobs. The organized sector in all countries follows an age-norm in respect to recruitment to and retirement from the services. The ages 15 and 59 are most generally taken as the respective age limits for recruitment and retirement. There is some variation between countries and between types of job. Demographers regard this age group as the *Active Age Group* and the entire population between 15 and 59 years is regarded as the *Active Part of the Population*. All the three segments of the population share the income generated by this active part. Demographers have constructed three types of *dependency ratios* to ascertain the buoyancy of an economy as also the age-trend of a population.

(A) Young Age or Youth Dependency Ratio

$$\frac{\text{Size of the population (male \& female) in the age group 0–14 years at a particular point of time}}{\text{Size of the population (male \& female) in the age group 15–59 years at the same point of time}} \times 100 \quad \ldots(5.5)$$

$$= \frac{{}_{14}P_0}{{}_{59}P_{15}} \times 100$$

(B) Old Age or Aged Dependency Ratio

$$\frac{\text{Size of the population (male \& female) in the age group 60+ years at a particular point of time}}{\text{Size of the population (male \& female) in the age group 15–59 years at the same point of time}} \times 100 \quad \ldots(5.6)$$

$$= \frac{{}_{\infty}P_{60}}{{}_{59}P_{15}} \times 100$$

(C) Total Dependency Ratio

$$= \text{Young Age Dependency Ratio} + \text{Old Age Dependency Ratio}$$

$$= \frac{{}_{14}P_0}{{}_{59}P_{15}} \times 100 + \frac{{}_{\infty}P_{60}}{{}_{59}P_{15}} \times 100 \quad \ldots(5.7)$$

UNDP worldview has been presented in Table 5.1.

There has been some modification in the definition of old age dependency ratio, especially with reference to developed countries where an average person lives well above 75 years and the job market demands the services of professionals, educated and skilled workers. The working-age population in the more developed countries consists of people aged 15–64. The Human Development Report published by United Nations Development Program regards population aged 65 and above as the old-age group.

With this modification, the developed countries have a total dependency ratio around 50 percent and the developing countries often have the same above 65 percent (85 percent in the least developed countries). The countries with high population growth rates tend to have high young age and total dependency ratio as well. A silent revolution has occurred in the last 100 years – unseen, unheard, and yet so close. The biggest achievement of the century is longevity. All over the world life expectancy has risen, leading to a sharp rise in the number of older persons. The high-income countries had on an average 78 years of expectation of life at birth as against only 59 years in the low-income countries at the beginning of the present millennium. Because of high expectation of life, the population in the developed countries in the age group 65+ is often as high as 14.5 percent. Their old age dependency as a result could go up to 22 percent or around, very close to or even larger than their young age dependencies. The developing countries on the other hand often suffer from acute shortage of employment opportunities and most countries are forced to adopt plans for retirement below the age 60 years in the organized sector. In India life expectancy has gone up from 20 years in the beginning of the 20th century to over 63 years today. Better medical care and low fertility have made the elderly the fastest growing segment of society.

In France, it took 120 years for the gray population to double from 7 to 14 percent of the total population. But the gray population in India has doubled in 25 years since 1951!

Table 5.3 *Estimates of old age population in India*

Year	*No of older persons*
1901	12 million
1951	20 million
2001	73 million
2025	a whopping 175 million!

While the number of senior citizens has gone up, quality of their life has deteriorated, especially in the developing countries. Industrialization, migration, urbanization and westernization have severely affected value systems. With disintegration of traditional joint and extended families, the natural support system for the seniors has crumbled. The fast-changing pace of life has added to the woes of the older person. In India

- 90 percent of older persons are from the unorganized sector, with no social security at the age of 60.
- 30 percent of older persons live below the poverty line and another 33 percent just marginally over it.
- 80 percent live in rural areas.
- 73 percent are illiterate, and can only be engaged in physical labor.
- 55 percent of women over 60 are widows, many of them with no support whatsoever.

There are nearly 200,000 centenarians in India. The above observations are likely to be more or less valid in most other developing countries.

The proportion of the young age group in the population in the developing countries started to rise after 1921. But the real change occurred after the World War II when death rates in all ages in most countries started to decline fast. Between 1950 and 1980 population growth rates in all the developing countries reached a new high. The young age population rapidly rose; old age population also rose but only marginally. Since 1980 the growth rates in most countries showed clear signs of decline due to fall in birth rates as a result of worldwide campaign for adoption of small family norm and the UN and other world bodies' massive participation in family planning program in the high growth countries.

Indian story is no different from that of most other developing countries, especially those in the low-income category. Population in India started to grow rapidly immediately after independence. The proportion of the population in the active age group remained around 55–56 percent till the eighth periodical census. Thereafter this ratio has declined significantly, showing signs of reversal of the trend after 1981. The losses in the ratio of active age population are mostly due to gains in the young age segment, especially in the age groups 0–9. There appears a quantum jump in dependency ratios since the 1961 census, more so for young age group. This was the period when the decadal growth rate in the country was around 24 percent and there was a sharp decline in death rates in all ages. With improved mortality situation the population base increased significantly and <15 years age group constituted over 40 percent of the population. The proportion of persons in the 65+ years for both sexes also showed significant rise as a result of increase in the expectation of life.

The changes in the age composition have far reaching effect on the economic wellbeing and social security of a country. A large young age segment would demand a large share of the GDP investment in education, health and childcare, generation of employment and other infrastructure facilities. A gain in the proportion of aged in the population requires making provisions for old age security – provident fund, gratuity, pension, medical care, etc. It is to remind the reader that whatever investment we augment for the young age group is a productive one since the country and the family would continue to earn through them for many years. But there is no expectation of a return from whatever amount we spend on our senior citizens. This we spend to express our gratitude for the services they rendered to the country and the family for a very long period.

In the developed countries the social security provisions in their governance covers everyone who are out of job, temporarily or permanently. Health problems are taken care of by medical insurances. In the developing countries, the situation is far from rosy. In India, it is only in the organized sector that there is some provision for provident fund, gratuity, employees' state insurance (ESI) and pension in some instances. Certain types of insurances (against accidents, fire, crop failure, medical expense cover, etc.) have recently been introduced. Insurance giants of the first world countries are looking at this vast market with glee. But such insurance covers remain out of bound for the majority of the rural and urban poor. The Manmohan Singh Government have brought out legislation to assure 100 days' employment in a year or unemployment allowance for one member from each family in the long run.

Actual dependency (totals of young age and old age group) ÷ (number actually in employment in 15–59 or revised 15–64 age group) is much higher in all societies since only a fraction in the active age group are directly engaged in gainful occupation (in more developed countries hi tech industrial and service sectors, which are the principal providers of job, require highly skilled persons and therefore many cannot enter into employment market before the age of 20–25 years). UNDP data show that even in USA and UK the unemployment rates in 1999 were above 5 percent. Unemployment rate

Figure 5.1 *Population pyramid, India 2001*

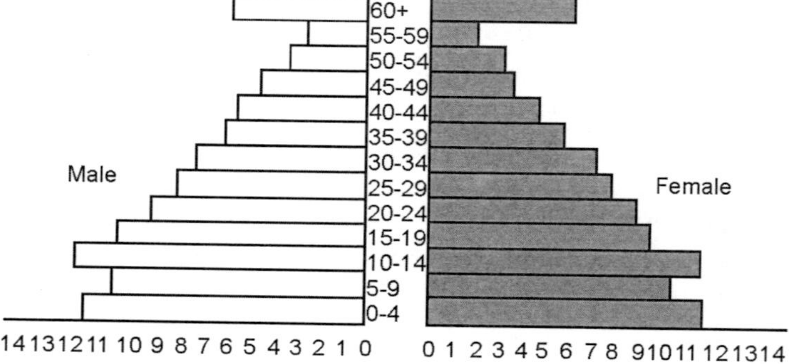

among females (as percentage of male unemployment rate) in some of these countries was around 150–200 percent (in USA it was 107 and in UK 75 percent). One can easily imagine the enormity of the problem in the low-income countries.

Population Pyramid: A population pyramid generally presents age and sex distribution of a population. Age is presented in the Y-axis, percentage (or absolute number) of male and female population in the X-axis. Distribution of male population is shown on the left of Y-axis (by histogram or bar diagram) and that for female on the right. A few examples of population pyramid are presented in Figures 5.1 and 5.2.

Figure 5.2 *Different types of population pyramid*

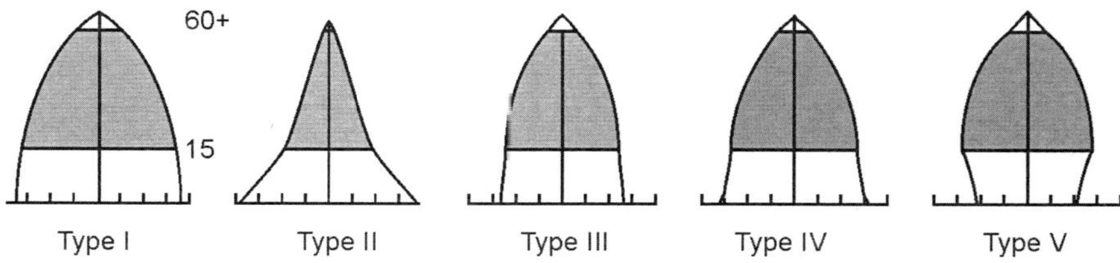

Drawing population pyramid is not a part of the analytical procedure in demography. But it has a special appeal for the reason that it captures the differences in the male-female population composition and the nature of changes observed over the years in a single shot. One can compare the composition and distribution of population in different regions or countries or the same country at different points of time.

Demographers have examined population pyramids of different countries at different points of time. They have observed some essential similarities between them and also have noted some divergences. From the analysis of these pyramids, demographers have come to the conclusion that the pyramids throw considerable light on (a) the socio-economic situations prevailing at a particular point of time, (b) birth and age specific death rates and (c) the stages of demographic transition the countries are in. Demographers have classified these pyramids into five categories (Figure 5.2) after intensive study of a large number of such pyramids.

Type I: In this the base is quite large; the slope of the bounding lines slowly increases till they meet the nodal points on the Y-axis. The two lines drawn parallel to the X-axis indicate the ages 15 and 60+ years, which give us a fair idea about the nature of dependency ratio in the population. The countries represented by such a pyramid have high young age dependency ratio. When birth and death rates are really high before they start declining, such a pyramid is usual. The median age of the population groups represented by such a pyramid is low and the total dependency ratio is very high. India a few decades back displayed this type of population pyramid.

Type II: It has a larger base compared to type I pyramid. The two sidelines meet the vertex taking the shape of a bow. This type of pyramid is observed in countries where high birth rates still continue, but child mortality is declining fast leading to a fast growth of the population. Young age and total dependency ratio are both very high and the median age is falling. Sri Lanka, Mexico, Brazil were in this stage a few decades back.

Type III: It has the shape of a beehive. Both birth and death rates are low and the base is not quite large. The two bounding lines move almost parallel but they take a sharp turn as they approach the apex. The countries in the Western Europe display this type of age distribution. Median ages for these countries are very high, so is their average expectation of life. Although the young age and total dependency ratios in these countries are low, the old age dependency ratio in this type of pyramid is comparatively high. India's current population is approaching Type III.

Type IV: This bell-shaped pyramid is observed in countries where the birth rate has shown signs of increase after both birth and death rates remained low for a long period. Canada and USA displayed such type of change a few decades back. This really has resulted from Type III pyramid with sudden increase in the base population because of increase in birth rate, death rates still remaining low. This is only a transient phase. The population distribution will soon go back to Type III. Even a few decades back the median age in these countries was among the highest. Both young and total dependency ratios are increasing in these countries.

Type V: This too has resulted from Type III and therefore is only a temporary phase for a population. Unlike in Type IV, the birth rate in countries displaying such a pyramid is even smaller than the death rate. Because of a shrink in the base as a result of marked and rapid decline in fertility and a very low and stable death rate, the population has started to show a negative growth rate. If this negative imbalance continues for a prolonged period, many of the schools, colleges and industries will have to be closed and unemployment would follow. Many of the Scandinavian countries, Japan and others displayed this type of distribution most of who however recovered quite quickly. According to UNDP estimate (2001), Hungary and Estonia showed negative annual population growth between 1975 and 1999. UNDP predicts that as many as 13 countries with high human development index (HDI) would go through negative growth rate between 1999 and 2015, Estonia showing as low as (–) 1.1 percent annual growth rate. Five more countries in the high HDI category would be in zero growth rate stage. It is projected that as many as 9 of the medium HDI category countries could also show a negative annual growth rate between 1999 and 2015 (Belarus, Bulgaria, Ukraine, Georgia, for example). Even in thirties in the last century many of the European countries faced a similar situation. Like type IV, Type V pyramid too has a short life and the countries in this stage would soon go back to the most stable stage III.

5.4 Population Density

Normally, the geographical area of a country does not change. Therefore, with increase in population, population density of the country would also increase. By mid-2003, population density of the world was around 46 per km^2, with least developed countries having the density at 35, the less developed countries at 62 and the more developed countries at 23. Asia has the highest population density (120) and Oceania, the least (4).

We can apply two different definitions to population density: (a) Number of people living in per square kilometer (or mile) at a particular point of time, and (b) Proportion of the total population of the country living in a defined region, no matter what geographical area it occupies.

5.5 Urban-Rural Divide

One of the most discussed topics in population studies is how fast the urban areas are growing. Emergence of cities is comparatively a recent phenomenon considering the length of the period when the first seed of human civilization was sown on this earth. Though there is considerable difference between demographers and also among social planners on the definition of cities, there is considerable agreement that 'cities' appeared between 3000 BC and 5000 BC.

A city is a very large village, yet it is something more than that. A new kind of social organization is observed centering on non-traditional economic activity and political power distribution among rulers, officials, traders and merchants and the religious leaders. Traditional oral communication is largely replaced by more formal communiqué, usually through some written documents.

The rise of a city depended upon among other things the presence of villages that produced (agricultural) more than the village population needed for their own consumption. That was the reason why the first cities appeared in the rich valleys of the major river systems of the world (Ganges in India, Nile in Egypt and Yellow River in China). The city population generally specializes in production activities other than agriculture. Local resources are important, but more important are their connectivity with villages and other cities.

The complexion of cities changed considerably in the eighteenth century as man learned to use coal and petroleum, the high-energy fuels, in almost every area of production. The beauty of these new sources of energy is that they release energy in far excess to that spent for producing them. This latest induction in the economic activity further brought in a sea-change in demographic, social, economic and political events. An altogether new society arose as a result – the industrial society with its distinctive urban culture. The surplus energy from the energy revolution gave the necessary feedback to produce more from the same unit area of agricultural land. Not only that, there was a large surplus of food stock, a large proportion of those engaged in agricultural production could be transferred to industries. Industries needed more than a labor-man-power; it needed skilled and specially trained people to run machines and other complex industrial operations. Spread of education and diversification of the education system became an urgent necessity. Spread of international trade made surplus food and consumer products from the industries play a critical role in making a nation's economy strong and stable. As the industrial society grew in its stature, the urban-rural divide, especially in developing countries, became more and more pronounced even though it is admitted that industrialization also changed the lifestyle of the rural people.

There was a time when it was thought that number of persons engaged in occupations other than agriculture was to be proportional to the surplus in agricultural production (Malthus). But increased trans-boundary trades between countries due to improved communication routes and liberalized international trade policies (lower customs duty, lifting quantitative restriction, outsourcing, etc.) created conditions conducive to diversification of consumer products keeping an eye beyond the domestic market. Everyday newer consumer products create opportunities for fresh employment or facilitating relocation of employment. However, the hypothesis of surplus agricultural produces in long-term perspective still could play an important role in the growth of urban centers.

The growth of economy and enlargement of employment potential consequent upon it are not sustainable if the domestic market does not provide the necessary support. A country cannot rely upon import of food and fiber for meeting its domestic requirement perpetually for the simple reason that import routes often are vulnerable in the face of changing world conditions. Great Britain is a typical example of urban-rural imbalance and the country faced the problem of over population when it lost its colonial possessions (India in particular), which had supplied it with food, fiber and other natural resources abundantly at a cheaper rate.

The expansion, development and nurturing of urban areas, especially in the developing countries, are often at the cost of agricultural land. Total cultivable land has over the years shrunk so much so that a large segment of the rural population had to migrate to urban areas in search of job since the land available per capita for cultivation has become uneconomic by all counts. With the adoption of modern agricultural technology, the importance of collective human labor has largely been eroded. The displaced labor from agriculture is moving out to urban areas to make some kind of a living. Urban population is growing in the developing countries far in excess of its level of industrialization.

The technological changes attendant upon the extensive use of electricity has also provided a base for redistribution of population and restructuring of many of our economic activities. The space and distance factor are no longer impediment to industrial growth. Thousands of commuters from distant localities man these industrial establishments, mercantile offices and the business and trade centers. This has created another kind of urban area – the suburban. The suburban movement has greatly been accelerated by improved road and rail links and provision of such characteristically urban utilities – electricity, sewage disposal, shopping center, bank, telephone, schools and colleges, health centers, etc. There is a clear distinction between these urban agglomerates and the larger densely populated cities organized around industries, trade and business centers.

There is considerable variation in the definition of 'urban' between countries, even in the same country at different time points. However there are some broad parameters, which most countries try to go by while delineating urban from rural areas. Population size, population density, proportion of non-agricultural workers, presence of municipalities or similar such local self-government, all seasons road, potable water supply, sewerage, transportation network, administrative units and trade centers, industrial area, etc. are some of the important factors that are taken into account while declaring a geographic or administrative unit as urban area. By administrative notification some notified area are also declared as an urban area although they may not meet the accepted criteria for declaring them as urban. In smaller countries where human settlements are few, administrative notification is widely used for the purpose.

According to UNDP estimate, about 38 percent of the world population lived in urban areas in 1975. In 25 years the percentage climbed to almost 47 percent and by 2015 more than half of the world population was likely to be living in urban areas. In the developing countries, the urban population has risen from 26 percent in 1975 to around 39 percent in 1999. By 2015 this can further go up by about 9 percentage points. UN population data (2003) reveals that 78 percent of North American population lived in urban areas; second in the rank list were Latin America and the Caribbean (77 percent), followed by Oceania (75 percent) and Europe (74 percent). Both Asia and Africa are tied up at 39 percent. Australia and New Zealand segment of Oceania has the highest urban population (91 percent).

5.6 Population Composition by Level of Education

Education is regarded the single most important instrument through which an individual can bring into fruition the potential endowments he has, lift his capability levels and inculcate an attitude to overcome the constraints. Since periodic census has become a general feature with most countries, we have a fairly reliable statistics about the literacy rates in all these countries. The census authority also collects information on how many boys and girls are enrolled into schools, colleges and in higher education and also the drop out levels at various stages. However, most countries fail to provide reliable data on the distribution of the population by their level of education. However limited such information are, it is a fact that not only literacy rates are high in urban areas vis-à-vis rural areas, urban people are far ahead in their average level of education than their rural counterparts.

The developed countries nearly have 100 percent literacy. They have close to 10 years of formal schooling (intensity of education) on the average. The difference between the sexes is also being wiped out. Literacy rates in the developing countries are often discouraging. There is a good deal of variation between countries. Whereas the Latin American countries are almost at par with the developed countries in literacy, most African countries still have poor literacy rates, often not exceeding 50 percent point. Women in the developing countries lag far behind male literacy rates. Literacy rates in the Asian countries is somewhere between that of the Latin American and African countries. The central and south Asian countries have a poor record in spread of education among the masses.

One of the best indicators of spread of education is adult literacy rates (15+ years), more so for the females. Table 5.4 gives some idea about the spread of education among different categories of countries in female literacy.

Table 5.4 *Female adult literacy and enrolment at primary and secondary level, 1997 (UNDP)*

	Female adult literacy			*Female net enrolment ratio*					
	Rate	*Index 1985=100*	*As % of male rate*	*Primary*	*Index 1985 = 100*	*As % of male rate*	*Secondary*	*Index 1985 = 100*	*As % of male rate*
1	*2*	*3*	*4*	*5*	*6*	*7*	*8*	*9*	*10*
All developing	62.9	122	79	82.9	108	94	54.8	128	83
Least developed	38.1	141	65	54.8	116	83	24.6	119	66
Sub-Saharan Africa	49.6	144	75	51.8	101	85	35.8	111	76
Arab States	46.4	150	66	82.1	113	91	56.8	130	85
East Asia	94.0	105	96	98.3	99	101	94.5	111	102
South-East Asia	84.4	113	91	97.5	106	99	56.9	126	95
South Asia	38.6	137	59	72.1	116	86	46.0	135	70
Latin America	86.2	108	98	92.4	108	98	65.8	116	101
Industrialized				99.9	102	100	96.3	106	100
World				85.2	107	95	60.8	119	87
INDIA	39.4	134	59	71.0	111	86	48.0	133	68

It is a documented fact that levels of urbanization and industrialization are closely related to spread of education in the population. The countries having low levels of literacy have agriculture as the principal occupation of the majority. In the industrialized countries, urban population constitutes nearly 75 percent of the total population; the same in the developing countries is about 39 percent and only 25 percent in the least developed countries. Education is also closely related to many other demographic parameters. Both birth and death rates have come down fast among the educated people in all countries. The countries that have registered high average expectation of life and low infant and child mortality have higher levels of literacy as well. The causes of death in the developing countries still remain closely related to health awareness, public health and hygiene issues. The following table gives an idea about how literacy and spread of education are related to some of these fundamental issues.

Table 5.5 *Some demographic and social characteristics of the world population closely related to education (UNDP, 2001)*

Category of countries	*Life expectancy at birth*		*Infant mortality*		*Growth rate*	*Urban population*		*Total fertility rate*	
	1970–75	*1995–2000*	*1970*	*1999*	*1975–99*	*1975*	*1999*	*1970–75*	*1995–2000*
1	*2*	*3*	*4*	*5*	*6*	*7*	*8*	*9*	*10*
All developing	55.5	64.1	109	61	1.9	25.9	38.9	5.4	3.1
Least developed	44.2	51.3	149	100	2.6	14.3	25.4	6.6	5.4
High HDI	71.3	77.0	25	7	0.7	72.6	78.3	2.3	1.7
Medium HDI	58.4	66.5	99	46	1.7	29.4	41.4	4.9	2.6
Low HDI	44.6	52.2	142	99	2.7	17.5	30.4	6.7	5.6
High income	72.0	77.8	21	6	0.7	75.0	78.7	2.1	1.7
Middle income	62.6	69.2	85	32	1.5	34.8	49.5	4.6	2.2
Low income	49.6	59.0	126	80	2.2	21.9	31.2	5.7	4.0
World	59.9	66.4	96	56	1.6	37.8	46.5	4.5	2.8
INDIA	50.3	62.3	127	70	2.0	21.3	28.1	5.4	3.3

It is well documented in the history of social and economic development that public investments in education yield high return to nation as a whole. Even after taking lessons from history, the dilemma still remains: where should the country direct its investments? Have today's fast changing world of technology made investments in secondary and tertiary education as important as those to primary education – or even higher? Most developing countries still find it hard to increase public spending on education. Even the highly advanced countries in the West find it tough to spend more than 5 percent of their GNP (10 to 15 percent of total government expenditure) on education; many developing countries cannot go beyond 4 percent (government spending almost at the same level or even higher as those in the developed countries). The governments in the developed countries spend one-third or more in primary education, around 40–45 percent in secondary education and close to 25 percent in tertiary education. The developing countries spend close to 50 percent at primary level, 25–30 percent at secondary and below 20 percent at the tertiary level. A better picture of public spending is obtained from per pupil expenditure. We reproduce in the Table 5.6 the estimate of public spending per capita for different regions. Though the data refers to that in 1997, it gives us an idea of the spending mode of governments for different levels of education per capita.

In absolute terms, the advanced countries' per capita spending at any level of education is much more than the per capita income in most developing countries. Whereas most of the developing countries share about two-third of the per pupil expenditure at the tertiary level, the developed countries leave a very high proportion of per pupil expenditure at the tertiary level to individual initiative. While primary and secondary education is highly subsidized in the advanced countries, tertiary level education is not. Except in Latin America and a few others in the transition mode, all developing countries have to bear most of the financial burden of education at all stages.

Table 5.6 *Average public education spending per pupil by region, 1997 (estimated)*

Region	Average		Primary and secondary		Tertiary	
	US $	% of GNP per capita	US $	% of GNP per capita	US $	% of GNP per capita
WORLD	1,224	22	999	18	3,655	66
Advanced countries	5,360	21	4,992	20	6,437	25
Developing countries	194	16	150	12	852	68
Sub-Saharan Africa	252	11	190	8	1,611	68
Middle East	584	22	494	19	1,726	66
Latin America	465	14	392	12	1,169	35
East Asia	182	14	136	11	817	64
South Asia	64	15	44	11	305	73
Transition countries	544	26	397	19	603	33

Source: HDR 2001

The social benefits of primary education has extensively documented in reduction of level of fertility and improved health care of mother and the child. Universal primary education has been accepted as the worldwide goal. But in today's world, intensity of education (average number of years of schooling) is gaining importance for the simple reason that development of skill quality has become a necessary appendage to the kind of jobs that are created today. Therefore, state financing in secondary education is absolutely necessary. More attention to tertiary education has become all the more crucial since the technological revolution demands a very high skill quality and training for jobs that are created at domestic and international arena. Tertiary education is very expensive, especially in science, engineering, management and medicine. Governments in the developing countries are in real dilemma if tertiary education should be left largely to private funding. Increasingly it is being felt that the government alone cannot finance in this skill development exercise; a suitable mix of public financing, private initiative and the direct contribution of individuals need to be worked out. The courses that generate guaranteed high private returns (management, technology and medicine), the state must follow a recovery mechanism for the huge sum spent by it on their education.

A rethink on public investment in courses that generate very high private returns has become all the more necessary since most of the rich countries have opened their doors to these professionals from the developing countries. These professionals are lured by the salary and other perks they are offered as also because of the opportunities they could get to improve their skill quality under a very competitive and healthy work environment. Some 100,000 Indian professionals land in USA alone every year. The receiving country did not have to incur any expenses on these professionals for their education and on-job-training at any stage (which is prohibitively very high in their own country). This "brain drain" from the developing countries like India makes it very difficult to retain these very people for domestic technology development. It is time that the countries like India, which is the principal supplier of software engineers to Silicon Valley and many IT companies elsewhere, seriously address taxing on these lost talents. A very modest estimate puts the operating costs per such students run to anywhere between US $ 8,000–10,000 for a four year program. If the capital and replacement costs are added to this, the cost of training each student would amount to US $15,000–20,000. That is, for every 100,000 professionals leaving India every year, the resource loss is worth around US $2 billion. India spends about 0.7 percent of her GDP in tertiary education (it amounted to about US $3 billion in 2000). The government needs to decide if it must follow a suitable recovery mechanism for the huge sums that are spent for their specialized training.

5.7 Working Population

Difficult though, we must try to address to such issues as: How many people of our society are engaged in producing goods and services the society needs? How many are non-producers by choice and how many through circumstances? Does the ratio between producers and non-producers change over time? What is the composition of the labor force by sex, age, educational attainments, rural-urban origin and so forth? Is there a shift in occupational distribution as a result of changes in the technological level attained and the economic policies followed by the state? These and many other issues relating to labor force of a country need to be addressed to plan all its developmental activities.

The proportion of population in productive years can only compare the potential of human resource of various countries. The less developed countries have this proportion less than that in the more developed countries since they still have a very large proportion of population in below 15 years category (Table 5.1). In the more populous countries like China, India, Indonesia and Brazil, the absolute size of the productive segment in the population is huge. This could be a boon for a country if it has the technology and the capital to produce diverse products and services much in excess of the domestic demands. For a developed economy as in USA or UK, the size of its economically active population is not so much of a problem as is the case with developing economies. The state of economic development of a country determines the characteristics and composition of its working population; similarly, the socio-cultural characteristics of the population determine, at least in some measure, the pace and level of economic activity. Population is both a dynamic agent of production and the beneficiary of the production process. As an agent of production, man contributes his labor and skill as the most important input in the production system, and the system gives back the goods and services for satisfying man's various needs. The three components of production are capital, technology and labor. Technological revolution has changed the equation between the three considerably. From a labor-intensive production mechanics to a capital-intensive system, the importance of traditional labor is largely over. The technology-capital marriage, though have marginalized the traditional labor, has introduced a large variety of products and services that can absorb the surplus labor from the traditional economy provided they orient themselves to adapt to the requirements of energy-intensive production requirements.

The high population growth rate in low-income countries puts a heavy premium on their economic resources. For upgrading the technology and for diversification of products and services and at the same time remain competitive in today's global market (free trade with quantitative restrictions largely removed), a country needs huge capital, which the low-income countries cannot muster. The investment outlay of the highly populated countries get diverted for providing the necessary social inputs like education, health, food and shelter, and such other items to ever increasing numbers. It has been estimated that for one percent rise in population per annum in a developing economy, the state needs to invest four percent of its GDP just to maintain the living standard at the level already achieved. With current 1.6 percent (1975–99) average annual growth rate, about 6.5 percent of world GDP would be needed just to render social and educational facilities and provide employment of the same average kind as it exists now. That is, the developing economies would fail to generate enough capital to create new jobs to accommodate the multiplying job seekers. A survey on a sample of less developed countries (reported in HDR) shows that over 65 percent of their total investments were in social sectors just to maintaining per capita income at a constant level. The same in the developed countries was less than 26 percent.

To assess the impact the population growth has on national income, we need to measure the addition resulting in output through this additional population and deduct therefrom the amount used up by this increased population. Their net contribution to the national economy would depend upon the technology, type of equipment used, the qualitative composition of the labor force and also its size. Low income countries suffer both from availability of capital equipment and advanced technology, and the major reason for their low skills is low level of education and overwhelming size of the job seekers. The population itself is a stumbling block for a faster growth of capital formation.

Without infusion of new technology and massive capital, sustainable employment cannot be generated. Since the state has to spend a big chunk of its gross receipts from taxes on the social sector and in development of infrastructure, the capital has to come from the indigenous private players, FIIs and FDIs. To lure them to invest more on industries, especially in manufacturing sector, the socio-political climate and education-skill-base of the labor force need to be improved. This only can generate a high level of economic activity and create new employment situations. Since the backlog of unemployment and rapid rise in job seekers, the rate of investment has to be really huge to overtake the rate of population growth. This is a Herculean task for all low-income countries, especially those where the industrial culture has yet to be fully established.

Agriculture still remains the major source of employment in the developing countries. But the rise in population has upset the land-man ratio. The supply of land is inelastic. In fact, both forest and cultivable land had to be sacrificed to build roads, towns, industries, dams and for other purposes. As the family size increases, the sub-division of family-owned land leaves each member with a smaller, often uneconomic holding. Farmers become agricultural laborers even in their own land. As the number of dependents increase, per capita productivity falls. The family has more consumers than producers. The estimated per capita arable and permanent cropland in 1983 was around 0.31 hectare acre (ha); in the less developed regions it was 0.23 ha and in Asia it was as low as 0.19 ha per capita (FAO, 1985). This must have gone down further in the last 20 years.

There has been a steady decline in the share of agriculture to GDP in all countries. UN Statistical Year Book, 1985 showed that agriculture contributed approximately 20 percent to GDP of the developing countries in the early eighties; in North America and Europe it was about 9 and 6 percent respectively. The UNDP report 1999 shows agricultural income contributed only 13 percent to GDP in the developing countries compared to only 2 percent in the industrialized countries. The share of industries to GDP in the industrialized countries has gone up by around 6 percentage points. In the same period, industry's share to GDP in the developing countries too improved by 8–9 percentage points. The service sector presently contributes about 51 percent to national economy in the developing countries and 64 percent in the industrialized countries. The developed countries, however, are already facing some serious problem: the fast aging population has created shortage in skilled and professional hands. They are opening their doors for skilled hands and professionals from the developing countries. Even the European Union is presently planning to grant "blue card" to attract highly qualified migrants, along the line of "green cards" allotted in the US.

Besides the industrialized countries, East Asian countries excluding China and the South American countries displayed a less dominant role of agriculture in their national economy. However, that cannot be said about other developing countries where agriculture still is the principal occupation of the masses, somewhere between 40 and 45 percent of the total working force. Even today 55 percent of Indian working population has agriculture as their principal occupation. At the same time it must also be admitted that fragmentation of land holding and increased use of tractors and other mechanical devices in farming is displacing labor from agriculture. There is reason to believe that this surplus labor from agriculture is mostly educated youth. A majority of them have not been absorbed by industries though some of them may have found some sort of an employment in the service sector.

Table 5.7 *Macroeconomic structure for different regions, 1997 (as percentage of GDP)*

Regions	*Service sector*			*Consumption*		*Gross domestic*		
	Agriculture	*Industry*	*Service*	*Private*	*Government*	*Investment*	*Savings*	*Tax revenue*
1	*2*	*3*	*4*	*5*	*6*	*7*	*8*	*9*
All developing countries	13	36	51	61	12	27	27	
Least developed countries	33	25	42	79	11	20	11	
Sub-Saharan Africa	20	34	46	66	17	18	17	
Arab States				55	21	21	24	
East Asia	13	44	43	50	11	37	39	10
East Asia (excluding China)	4	36	60	56	11	35	33	19
South-East Asia & Pacific	13	40	47	56	10	34	34	16
South Asia	25	29	46	72	10	23	18	11
South Asia (excluding India)	25	26	49	78	9	19	13	13
Latin America & the Caribbean	8	32	60	67	12	22	21	
Eastern Europe & CIS	11	36	53	64	15	23	22	
Industrialized countries	2	34	64	63	16	21	21	26
China	19	49	32	46	12	30	43	5
INDIA	25	30	45	70	10	24	20	11

Source: Human Development Report 1999, UNDP

Although the age segment 15–59 (alternatively 15–64) is regarded as the active part of a population, there is no guarantee that all of them are economically active. In fact, in no country we find that hundred percent of the active part is economically active as well. There shall be 'non-workers' but not necessarily they are to be regarded as unemployed. There shall be people who are non-workers by 'choice'. Those pursuing education or those who have decided to retire premature or retire after reaching a certain age, or who are physically or mentally disadvantaged to take up or continue with their occupational career are all non-workers, not necessarily unemployed. A large proportion of the female population in all countries remains confined, either by choice or by circumstances, to looking after domestic affairs for which there is no direct economic return.

However, often no clear distinction can be made between 'non-workers' and 'unemployed'. Often one is used to mean the other as well. In the developed countries, especially in temperate and cold climatic regions, people remain physically sound and active for a longer period. The demand for some of the professional and highly skilled persons continues even after they had attained statutory age of retirement. The self-employed persons (doctors, engineers, lawyers, businessmen and other professionals) remain active as long as their health would permit. It is only in the organized sector that there is an upper and lower age limit for an employee. The private sector often would allow high level executives and highly skilled professionals to stay with their organization even beyond the prescribed upper age limit. In the unorganized sector as in agriculture, tea plantation, construction work, and others the age restriction for employment is hardly recognized. In the developed countries there is a continuous modernization and up-gradation in the industrial sector. Most of the moderate to highly remunerated positions is reserved for better educated and trained persons. Their entry age in gainful occupation often is 25 years or even more. In schools, colleges, universities and other technical institutions the entry age often is as high as 25 years and they remain in service for a shorter period as well.

The story is somewhat different in the developing countries. There is always a cutthroat competition for every single vacancy. Hundreds and thousands are unemployed. To keep the expenses down, many in the unorganized sector do not hesitate to employ child labor. In the developing countries a 10/12 year old child often would take part in cattle tending, agriculture and in many other economic activities. There are some small-scale and household industries, where young children are preferred to adults for some kind of operations (silk and carpet industry, for example). The ILO's stricture that children below 15 years cannot be employed and that the products of the industries employing child labor are to be boycotted, have affected export business of these cottage and household industries in the developing countries. Being a member of WTO, India and other developing countries have forced to phase out child labor. Even then, a significant proportion of children aged 5–14 still are in our workforce. It has declined by about 30 percent between 1981 and 1991.

Table 5.8 *Working children in the age group 5–14, India 1981 and 1991*

Residence	*1981*			*1991*		
	Boys	*Girls*	*Children*	*Boys*	*Girls*	*Children*
Rural	10.0	7.8	8.9	6.6	6.3	6.4
Urban	3.7	1.6	2.7	2.8	1.2	2.0
Combined	8.6	6.4	7.6	5.7	5.1	5.4

Source: National Human Development Report, 2001

6 Techniques of Population Analysis

6.1 Basic Concepts in Population Analysis

Demographers, social planners and administrators have to use a variety of information relating to population, past and present, for planning in their respective field of operations. We have discussed how some of these population related information are collected. The principal objective of the study of population characteristics is to understand how the changes in many of our social and economic institutions with time are also reflected in changes in the population parameters. A clear message is that the success of policy implementation largely depends upon how the population attributes respond to the engineered changes in the larger social setting. The population data collected through census or surveys or from some other sources need to be analyzed keeping the user perspectives in mind. Some techniques of analysis of population data are as old as the population study itself. But the population scientists are always in search of more efficient and sensitive methods and techniques of analysis of population data. We discuss in this chapter some of the most commonly used techniques of population analysis.

A beginner needs to be acquainted with the most commonly used terms and concepts used in all demographic analysis. A common man often uses these terms as well. But often a demographer or a population scientist uses these terms in a more specific and restricted manner. The information collected through census, registration system, continuing registers and sample surveys give us some idea about the size of human population in a defined locality, its age and sex composition, educational attainments, persons married, the labor and its composition, how many people of different ages and sexes have died in a particular time period, number of babies born, size of in- and out-migrating population and etc. Most often the absolute measure of such events will serve our purpose. However, a relative number rather than the absolute number would be more meaningful if we were to compare two or more aggregates at a time point or comparing the current situations in a locality or a region with that of some previous period or if we were to use the observed trends from such comparisons to predict changes at a future date. We cannot stake a claim that education has spread appreciably from the information that 100 boys and girls are found to go to schools in a village. But when we say that 100 children from among 150 in the village in 7–14 years age group go to school, we definitely are better equipped to comment on the spread or popularity of education in the village.

For these and other reasons we need to take recourse to such relative numbers as ratios and rates. These relative numbers help us understand the true nature of the situation prevailing in a village or in some aggregate and also compare the same with some other village or aggregate or even compare the events of the same village with those obtained some 10 or 20 years earlier. These ratios and rates are meaningful if they are computed from a relatively large sample. The relative numbers computed from small samples often will not give us a trustworthy picture of the situation in the population. When reporting statistic from a small sample, we need to report the absolute number simultaneously with proportions calculated for different categories. When we refer to a big population like that of India or one or more of its states, it is more than sufficient to state that about 15 percent of the population of India are in the age group 7–14 years in a population of about 1027 million in 2001.

6.2 Ratios

Ratio is a quantity that expresses the relative values of two numbers. If a and b are two numbers associated with two independent events, then the ratio of the two numbers can be a/b or b/a. The first expression tells us what part of b is a, and the latter expresses a reverse relationship, that is, what part of a is b. It can also be stated as what part of (or multiple of) the value of the second number is the first number, or what the value of the first number is for a unit value of the second number. This ratio is not dependent on the value of a specific number. The ratio of 2 is to 4 or the ratio of 100 to 200 or 0.000045 to 0.00009 are the same, ½ or 0.5.

The Human Development Report, 2001 (UNDP) shows that of the 162 countries for which Human Development Index, HDI, have been calculated, 48 are in the High Human Development category (HDI = 0.80), 78 are in Medium Development category (HDI = 0.50–0.799) and 36 countries are in Low Human Development category (HDI < 0.50). The 1999 report deals with 174 countries of which 45 are in High Development, 94 in Medium Development and 35 in Low Development category. We cannot directly compare the two sets of observations since number of countries in the two analyses is different. Ratios computed separately for the two reports can help do this. Ratio, a relative number, is helpful in evaluating differences in the two distributions.

Table 6.1 *Proportion of countries in different human development categories, 1999 and 2001*

Categories	*1999*		*2001*	
	N	*Proportion*	*N*	*Proportion*
High Development	45	0.259	48	0.296
Medium Development	94	0.540	78	0.481
Low Development	35	0.201	36	0.222
All countries	174	1.000	162	1.000

Source: Human Development Report, 1999 & 2001, UNDP

Once they are converted into proportions, it becomes easier to say that a substantial reduction has occurred in the Medium Human Development category mostly because of upward movement of a few countries. It is very likely that some of the countries in Medium category in 1999 have improved their HDI in 2001 and some, only some, may have gone down on the scale so much so that they have been pushed down to Low category in HDI in 2001. Or, it may have something to do with HDI values of those countries whose names do not appear in one of the lists. The values appearing in third and fifth column of Table 6.1 are ratios.

Proportion is also a ratio. Whereas in ratio any of the two events can be put in the denominator, in proportion only the larger of the two values is put in the denominator. If a person spends $600 for house rent out of his monthly income of $6,000, then one-tenth of his salary is spent on house rent. That is, for every unit income he spends 1/10 of it on paying house rent. Out of estimated 6301 million-population size of the world in 2003, 3283 million people lived in Asia. So the share of Asia's population to world population or the proportion of the world population living in Asian countries is 3283/6301 or 0.521. That is, for every unit population of the world, Asian countries' share is 0.521. To be precise, we can say that more than half of the world population lives in Asia.

Percentage is also a ratio, rather a proportion. If we multiply the above proportion by 100, i.e., 100×(3283/6301), we no longer are expressing the numerator by a quantity, which is ≤ 1. That is, in the extreme case the numerator could be equal to the denominator. The proportion multiplied by 100 gives a number which expresses 'for every 100 people of the world there are 52.1 Asians'. That is, 52.1 percent of the world population live in Asian countries. Instead of 100, we could have multiplied the proportion by 1,000 or 10,000 or 1,000,000 and the resultant value would be expressed as … per thousand or … per 10,000 or … per million. In mathematical expressions, the simple ratio *a/b* is generally used.

Different types of ratios are used in demographic and other analyses:

(a) *Ratios involving the same universe.* Let us assume that there are 20 girls and 30 boys in a PG class. Then for every boy there are 20/30 = 0.67 girls. Here, both boys and girls belong to the same class, that is, they are from the same population or sample. When both numerator and the denominator are drawn from the same population we are referring to (a) ratio $\left(\frac{a}{b} \text{ or } \frac{a}{b}\times 100 \text{ or } \frac{a}{b}\times k \text{ or } \frac{b}{a}\times k\right)$.

(b) *Proportion.* Here too both *a* and *b* in the proportion belong to the same population or sample. In (a) we compared one part with another part. The ratio of *a/b* or *b/a* could be less than 1, greater than 1 or equal to 1 depending upon if the absolute value of the numerator was smaller than, greater than or equal to the absolute value of the denominator ($a < b$, $a > b$ or $a = b$). In a proportion, on the other hand, the numerical value of the denominator can at best be equal to the numerical value of the numerator, in which case the ratio is equal to 1. That is, a proportion is always ≤ 1. If a population or sample is divided into two or more parts, and since no part can be larger than the population or sample of which it is a constituent part, the ratio of any part to the whole shall be less than or equal to 1 depending upon if the entire population is comprised of elements from different parts or one part alone. Thus, in a class of 30 boys and 20 girls there are altogether (30+20) students and the proportion of boys in the class is 30/(30 + 20) = 0.60. If *a, b, c*… are the component parts of a population (or sample), then proportion of *a* in the population is *a*/(*a*+*b*+*c*...). When a part comprises the whole population (only boys/girls in a class), then the proportion of that part to the total population is 1 [*a*/(*a*+0+0..)]. When 100 multiply this proportion, the resulting value will be referred to as percentage in the population (or per thousand if the multiplying factor is 1,000).

(c) There could be instances when two numbers to be compared are obtained from different universes or when the two numbers are obtained from two different sources. The ratio between such two numbers will belong to a different class (c). In demographic analysis, many statistics refer to measurements the data for which are obtained from different sources. We can measure population density in two different manners:

1. Population of a state is expressed as its population share to the national population (as when we expressed that Asian countries' share to world population is 52.1 percent). If P_T is the total population such that $P_T = P_1 + P_2 + P_3 + \ldots$, then the measurement P_i/P_T belongs

to (b) class of proportions where the numerator and the denominator come from the same universe and the numerator is included in the denominator.

2. When geographical area divides the population size of a state or region, we have the most common measure of population density, expressed as population per sq km or per sq mile. Population density of the world in 2003 was 46 per km^2 and that for Asian Continent was 120 per km^2. If P_i is the population of a region and A_i is its geographical area in km^2, then P_i/A_i gives the population density of that region. The data for numerator and denominator come from different sources. This ratio belongs to (c) category. The examples of two types of population density are explained in the following table.

Table 6.2 *Two types of population density for selected few states in India*

States	*Population 2001*	*Area in sq km*	*Density/sq km*	*Density as proportion to India total*
1	*2*	*3*	*4*	*5*
INDIA	1,027,015,247	3,287,263	324	1
Delhi	13,782,976	1,483	9,294	0.01342
Chandigarh	900,914	114	7,902	0.000877
Kerala	31,838,619	38,863	819	0.031001
Bihar	82,878,796	173,877	880	0.080699
West Bengal	80,221,171	88,752	904	0.078111
Madhya Pradesh	81,181,074	443,446	183	0.07904

We can collect data on number of boys and girls in age group 7–14 years reading in schools from the school registers of a region. But the number of boys and girls in that age group in the region can be had from some different source, probably from the regional census office. Thus, 'enrolment ratio' in schools belongs to (c) category of ratios. Space and time frame must be the same for computing this type of ratio. Number of school-going children is obtained in 2005 and the total number of children is obtained from 2001 census. The two cannot be related since the time frame for them is different.

Types of ratio described in (a) and (b) produce pure numbers since units both in the numerator and denominator are the same. The third category ratios may be free from units as in 'enrolment ratio' or 'voting percentages' or may not be free from units as in computation of population density with reference to geographical area (population/km^2).

Some Extensively Used Ratios In Demographic Measurements

1. *Sex ratio:* In demographic analysis sex ratio in the population is a very important variable. Generally, quite reliable count of males and females in the population or among babies born in a particular space and time frame can be obtained. Sex ratios at birth, in the total population or in various age groups are vital in most demographic analyses. The sex ratio in a population or sample is variously calculated: (M/F)×100 or (F/M)×100 or [M/(F+M)]×100 or [F/(F+M)]×100. (M/F)×100 is usually used in computing sex ratio at birth. (F/M)×100 is generally used in ascertaining sex ratio in the total population in India. F/M is used in some measures as Net Reproductive Rate (NRR).

2. *Child-Woman Ratio (CWR):* Most fertility measures require painstaking collection of reliable information on exact number of birth and the number of women giving birth to these babies and some of their personal and social characteristics as current age, religion, education, birth order and the like. When such indexes of fertility cannot be calculated easily, child-woman ratio can give us a very useful indication about the current fertility level in the population. We need to know the size of the population in the age group 0–4 years and the size of the female population in 15–49 age group. Usually the source of both is census data or figures projected from the census data. CWR gives us (a) type ratio.

$$\text{CWR} = \frac{{}_4P_0}{{}^{f}_{49}P_{15}} \times 1{,}000 \qquad \ldots(6.1)$$

where ${}_4P_0$ refers to children in a population who have not celebrated their fifth birthday as yet and ${}^{f}_{49}P_{15}$ refers to female population in the age group 15–49 in the same population in the same time frame.

CWR is especially useful in countries where birth and death registration are incomplete or faulty. CWR is only an approximation since a sizeable proportion of babies born would die every year. That is, the number in 0–4 age group really represents the number of surviving children and not a sum total of babies born in the last five years. In 1961, CWR in India was 659, which dropped to 547 in 1981 and then to 468 in 2001.

Table 6.3 *Child-woman ratio, CWR, India 1901–2001*

Census year	***1901***	***1911***	***1921***	***1931***	***1941***	***1951***
0–4 (M+F)	29907587	34261314	31006428	36783703	43139313	48716986
15–19 (F)	59390538	62596259	60896394	68295870	75627936	86375337
CWR	503.57	547.34	509.17	538.59	570.42	564.02
Census year	***1961***	***1971***	***1981***	***1991***	***2001***	
0–4 (M+F)	66271044	79687443	86262438	108082520	120231861	
15–49 (F)	100508421	121754883	157785307	200362768	256792371	
CWR	659.36	654.49	546.71	539.43	468.21	

Figure 6.1 *Child-woman ratio, India 1901–2001*

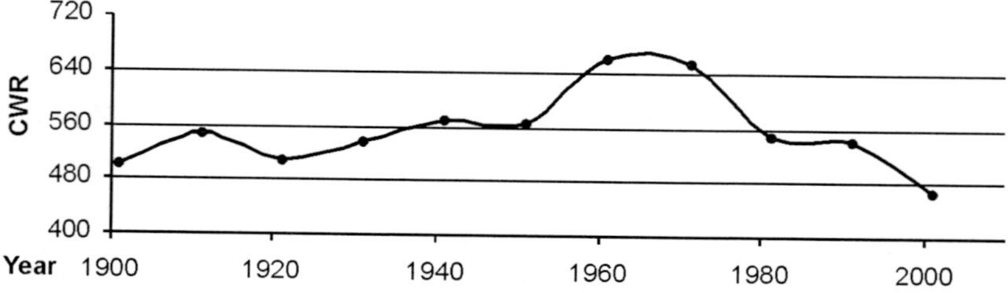

3. *Dependency ratio:* All members in a family are consumers, but only a few are producers or earning members. People in the age group 15–59 years are regarded as economically active. Other members in a family are dependent on their income. Persons in the age group 0–14 years

(<15 years) is the Young Age segment of the population and those in 60 years and above is the Old Age segment of the population (65+ years in more developed countries). A rough idea of productivity of the economy of a country can be had from the Dependency Ratio in the population. Three types of dependency ratios are calculated:

Young age dependency ratio:

$$\frac{\text{Number of persons in the age group } 0-14 \text{ years}}{\text{Number of persons in the age group } 15-59 \text{ years}} \times 100 \qquad \text{...(6.2)}$$

Old age dependency ratio:

$$\frac{\text{Number of persons in the age group } 60+\text{years}}{\text{Number of person in the age group } 15-59 \text{ years}} \times 100 \qquad \text{...(6.3)}$$

By combining (6.2) and (6.3), we get the total dependency ratio.

Total dependency ratio:

$$\frac{\text{Number of persons in the age groups } (0-14) \text{ and } 60+ \text{ years}}{\text{Number of persons in the age groups } 15-59 \text{ years}} \times 100 \qquad \text{...(6.4)}$$

The young age, old age and total dependency ratio in India in 1999 were 55, 8 and 63 percent respectively.

6.3 Rates

With time vital events as birth, death, migration, marriage, work participation, and other events undergo changes. The quantum of such change in the population is measured by their respective *rates.* The changes in the intensity of these events play a critical role in observed social change in a country. To understand the impact of changes in these and other events, we need data at intervals of time: 5, 10 or more years or even 1-year interval. On most occasions we compute *vital rates* taking full calendar year as the unit. Most widely used yearly vital rates are birth and death rate, infant mortality rate and work participation rate.

There is no fundamental difference in the calculation of *ratios* and *rates.* Most often the ratios that we calculate are of (c) category described in Sec. 6.2. Birth, death, migration, marriage and many other events bring in some change in the population distribution and its other characteristics. To understand the nature and strength of these changes, we need to compare events at two different time points. The census data is ideal for this purpose for those events that change only slowly. A large time gap gives an opportunity to assess if the changes are real and substantial. Data on number of births or deaths are usually obtained from registration offices. (In most countries data on these vital events are obtained from special sample registration schemes. SRS in India is doing this since 1964.) The obtained size of births or deaths is entered into the numerator; the figures for the denominator come from the census data. 'Interest rate', 'rate of increase in pay', 'growth rate' are all linked to time. So are birth rate, death rate, marriage rate, maternal mortality rate and many others.

Suppose 50 children are born in a village having a population of 1,000. The ratio of birth to population is (50/1,000) or (50/1,000)×100 or 5 percent. That is, for every 100 people there are 5 live births. But from this statement it is not clear if 5 babies were born per 100 people every year or in a period of 10 years. If 50 babies were born every year, the birth rate in the village would be interpreted as close to biological limit of reproduction. However, if 50 babies refer to live births in the past 10 years, and if we presume that the total population in the village had remained stationary at 1,000 (this can happen only if number of births and number of deaths in a year are the same and there is no in- or out-migration), we would readily admit that the birth rate is 5 per thousand every year (as also deaths), a figure that is at the other side of the biological limit indicating that depopulation may start in the village anytime.

When we express a ratio with a fixed time frame, that is the events recorded in numerator and in the denominator are in the same time frame, the ratio is referred to as *rate.* For example,

$$\text{Birth rate} = \frac{\text{Number of live births in a region in a specified time period}}{\text{Total number of persons in the region in the same time period}} \times K \qquad \ldots(6.5)$$

$$= \frac{B}{N} K$$

Most vital rates are expressed in "per thousand population". That is, K = 1,000. For example, India registered 25.8 live births per thousand population in 2000 and 8.5 deaths per thousand population in the same year. That is, birth rate and death rate in India were 25.8 and 8.5 per thousand respectively in the year 2000.

Rates are most frequently used in measurement of most vital events. Generally, to express changes or in measurements involving vital events the term 'rate' is used. Since it is a most often-used measurement concept, it is sometimes misused too. Various survey reports often would report "literacy rate", "vaccination rate", etc. when they really are ratios. Since these terms are in use for a long time, we do not change them from rate to ratios. However, it must be remembered that all rates are ratios, but some ratios are rates.

6.4 Natural Increase

Natural increase or growth means surplus (or deficit) of birth and death, that is, B–D. When B–D is positive, population grows; when negative, population declines. The change in the size of population due to birth and death is called natural increase (or decrease) in population. If P_{t1} is the size of the population at a time point t_1 and P_{t2} is the population at a time point t_2, then the population change in the time period $t_2 - t_1$ due to birth and death alone is:

$$P_{t_2} - P_{t_1} = \sum_{t_1}^{t_2} (B - D) \qquad \ldots(6.6)$$

or, $$P_{t_2} = P_{t_1} + \sum_{t_1}^{t_2} (B - D) \qquad \ldots(6.7)$$

This relation indicates that the population change between time points t_1 and t_2 can be had from the difference between total number of births and total number of deaths (equation 6.6). In this expression it is presumed that *net migration* is nil. $P_{t_2} - P_{t_1}$ therefore measures the absolute growth of population between time point's t_2 and t_1. The absolute growth does not give us any signal about the intensity of growth. Relative growth provides the answer we are seeking. We have to calculate the population at point of time t_2 relative to population at the time point t_1. Two alternatives suggested are:

Ratio of population increase $=P_{t_2}/P_{t_1}$ ...(6.8)

or, $$\frac{P_{t_2}-P_{t_1}}{P_{t_1}}=\frac{P_{t_2}}{P_{t_1}}-1$$ ...(6.9)

Population of India between 1971 and 2001 is presented below. The table clearly shows that the population has progressively increased from one census to the next and that the absolute increases in numbers have gone up in every decade. The last column however shows that though more numbers have been added in consecutive decades, the decadal growth rate actually has declined progressively.

Once the growth rates of populations are known, comparison of growths in various states and regions becomes possible. Of course, the growth rates of various segments become comparable only if all of them refer to the same time points.

Table 6.4 *Population of India, absolute and relative growth, 1971–2001*

Census year	*Population*	*Absolute growth*	*Relative growth*
1971	548159652		
1981	685184692	137025040	24.99728674
1991	843930861	158746169	23.16837648
2001	1027015247	183084386	21.69423995

Very precise description of absolute natural growth of a population of the size as that of India is never possible. Birth and death related statistics obtained through SRS is very good for estimation at national level, but some conflicting observations appear when applied to states or regions, the populations of which are highly heterogeneous on most social and economic variables. Problems encountered in studying growth rate are not so much due to inaccuracy in estimation of birth and death rate as often are due to movement of people. There is no guarantee that people will continue to stay in their ancestral homes generation after generation, especially in this age of globalization and hi tech economy. A certain proportion of people always would move for various reasons – personal, social, economic, political as well as due to natural catastrophe. But some moves often change the distributive character of the population in a locality. The effect would be more pronounced if the observations are taken after a large time gap.

When we are talking about world population, the growth of population is due to natural increase alone. But when we speak about the population of a country or a region, migration does affect the tally. Population of large and international cities grows much faster than all other places. They grow fast not because of natural increase but because of in-migration from various parts of the country as also from other countries. Therefore, the change in the size of population at a place over a time period is the result of these four factors:

1. total number of live births (B),
2. total number of deaths (D),
3. size of out-migration (O), and
4. size of in-migration (I).

We can think of a general equation, which takes into account all of these four factors simultaneously.

$$P_{t_2}-P_{t_1}=(B-D)_{t_2-t_1}+(I-O)_{t_2-t_1}$$ ...(6.10)

Equation (6.6) is a special case of the Equation (6.10), where the last term on the RHS, i.e., $(I-O)_{t_2-t_1}=0$.

6.5 Vital Statistics Method

By vital statistics we refer both to such demographic fundamentals as birth, death, migration, marriage, etc. as also the methods and techniques used for analysis of these vital events. The information that are collected through registration system, census, sample surveys, etc. are classified to obtain a frequency distribution. These absolute numbers may have some utility to administration and other consumers of the data, but the demographers would hesitate to use the data as they are for they would like to unravel something more from such innocent looking figures to understand the problems of the population in their interlocked relations. They would try to work out the rate of the vital events than taking their absolute values *per se*. The definition of the rate of a vital event is:

$$\frac{\text{Number of times the vital event has occurred in a locality within a specified time frame}}{\text{Number of persons exposed to the same risk of the vital event in the locality in the said time frame}} \times 1{,}000 \qquad \ldots(6.11)$$

For computing the rate of a vital event we have to address simultaneously to the following three issues:

(a) a particular vital event (birth, death, migration, etc.);
(b) counting the number of times the event has occurred within a defined geographical area (or a social group); and
(c) the time period (1, 5, 10 years, etc.) for which the count of the event is made.

All those persons who are exposed to the risk of the vital event in the defined space and time constitute the population. Since the size of population of a country or a region is changing every moment, the arithmetic mean of the size of the population between the time limits t_1 and t_2 represents the size of the population (entry in the denominator). When the time period refers to a whole year, mid-year population (as on 1st July) is taken as the average size of the population. From integral calculus, this value is obtained by $\frac{1}{t_2 - t_1}\int_{t_1}^{t_2} P_t\,dt$. A very close approximation to this quantity can be obtained by taking the average of the numbers at the start and at the end of the period, The inclusion of the clause "exposed to the risk of the vital event" in the denominator allows us to make a probabilistic statement as well: *the probability of occurrence of that vital event in the given time frame to any individual who are exposed to the same risk of the vital event.* Crude death rate 10 per thousand in a year means the probability of dying of a person included in the population in the said year is 0.01.

Some of the common vital rates computed for a population are: Crude rate of natural increase, Crude rate of birth, Crude rate of death, Infant mortality rate, Maternal mortality rate, Marriage rate, Divorce rate, General fertility rate, Total fertility rate, Marital fertility rate, Net reproduction rate, Survival rate and Growth rate.

6.6 Measures of Mortality

There are several measures of mortality; some are very simple, others quite complex; some are direct measures, some indirect. Also the errors committed in using this or that measure vary. These measures have different areas of application.

6.6.1 Crude Death Rate, CDR

This is the most frequently used and most easily calculated index of mortality in a population. CDR gives a general picture of mortality situation prevailing in the entire population. CDR in a population or its segments often finds mention in all formal and informal reports dealing with population. CDR, sometimes represented by m, is calculated by the formula:

$$\text{CDR or } m = \frac{\text{Number of deaths during the year}}{\text{Mid-year population in that year}} = \frac{D}{P} \times 1{,}000 \qquad \ldots(6.12)$$

D refers to the total number of deaths occurring to all segments of the population and from all causes within a geographical (or social) boundary and in the same time frame, usually a calendar year.

CDR not only gives us a broad picture of the mortality situation prevailing in a population, it also gives us a probabilistic statement of dying of an individual within the time period. Though very handy, CDR has several limitations. If we will refer to the definition of the rate of a vital event (6.11), we come across the phrase "exposed to the same risk of the vital event". CDR therefore assumes that the *risk of dying* for every individual in P is the same. This is an untenable assumption since the newly born babies, very young children and aged people die in larger numbers than those in the middle age groups. A mining labor has greater risk of life than a teacher or an office clerk. Women are more vulnerable in certain ages than men. There are considerable differences in death rates between regions and between communities, and even among the educated and illiterate people. For this reason it is not desirable to compare death rates of two countries or two states or regions of the same country by CDR. CDR for India in 2000 was 8.5, a figure very similar to those in many developed countries. Yet, India has an average expectancy of life of 63 years only when most developed countries have expectation of life at birth well over 75 years. Whereas the developed countries have 20 or less infant mortality (IMR), India still had 68 IMR in 2000. That is, share of infants and young children in the deaths registered in a year is very high in India. In the developed countries the old age group contributes most significantly in the total number of deaths registered.

CDR can reasonably well compare death rates at two not very distant points of time of the same region for the reason that age and sex composition of a population generally do not change over night. When the population is relatively large, and there is fair amount of stability in economic, social and political front, the general composition of the population remains more or less at a stationary level. When CDRs for several consecutive years are known, a general index for those years can be obtained by taking simple arithmetic mean of CDRs of those years.

$$\begin{aligned}\bar{m} &= \frac{D_1 + D_2 + \ldots + D_n}{P_1 + P_2 + \ldots + P_n} \times 1{,}000 \\ &= \frac{m_1 P_1 + m_2 P_2 + \ldots + m_n P_n}{P_1 + P_2 + \ldots P_n} \times 1{,}000 \qquad \ldots(6.13) \\ &= \frac{\sum_1^k m_i P_i}{\sum_1^k P_1} \times 1{,}000\end{aligned}$$

If D_1 (6.13) refers to the number of those babies who die before attaining their first birth day and P_1 total number of babies who have not yet celebrated their first birth day, D_2 number of babies die out of P_2 number of babies who are between their first and second birth day, and so forth and so on, then m_1, m_2...are the death rates for the ages 1, 2... (6.13) in that case is CDR calculated from the death rates at different ages in a population.

6.6.2 Specific Death Rates, SDR

CDR speaks of the average mortality rate in the general population. But mortality rates vary between ages, between male and female, between urban and rural people, between various occupational groups, and etc. CDR gives the mortality picture in a population at a glance but does not say if persons in some specific group in the population have the same probability of dying as in the total population. Specific death rate, SDR provides answers to this question. Generally, the population is classified into different segments by age, sex, residence, religion, occupation and other social and economic characteristics. We can compute mortality rate for all these segments separately. SDR is a ratio of the number of deaths in a specified segment in a specified space and time frame to the mid-year size of this segment in the said space and time frame multiplied by 1,000. SDR therefore is a CDR of a specific segment of the population.

The most widely used specific death rates are sex and age-specific death rates. Let ${}_nD_x$ is the number of deaths recorded for persons in the ages x and $x+n-1$ last birthday. The mid-year population size for this age group is ${}_nP_x$. Then Age-Specific Death Rate ASDR (${}_nm_x$) is defined as

$$\text{ASDR or } {}_nm_x = \frac{{}_nD_x}{{}_nP_x} \times 1{,}000 \qquad \text{...(6.14)}$$

When $n = 1$, i.e., the last birth day (lbd) is x (a person dies within x and $x + 1$ years), the ASDR becomes annual age-specific death rate, and is given by

$$m_x = \frac{D_x}{P_x} \times 1{,}000 \qquad \text{...(6.15)}$$

When calculating ASDR for females, D_x in the numerator would refer to number of female deaths and P_x in the numerator would be for females in that particular age. For non-annual ASDR the symbolic relation would be as in (6.13).

When both age and sex-specific death rates are calculated, the following symbols are used.

$${}_n^F m_x = \frac{{}_n^F D_x}{{}_n^F P_x} \times 1{,}000 \qquad \text{...(6.16)}$$

Superscript F (or f) is to be replaced by M (or m) when age-specific death rate for males is to be estimated. If we wish to calculate age-specific death rate of urban females, the symbolic presentation of ASDR would be

$${}_n^F m_x^U = \frac{{}_n^F D_x^U}{{}_n^F P_x^U} \times 1{,}000 \qquad \text{...(6.17)}$$

With specific death rates, comparison between two population groups becomes more meaningful. Crude death rate for males in India was 8.9 against 8.1 of females in 2000. For getting an answer to the question why there was such a large difference, we may look for clues in sex-specific ASDR. SRS data show that IMRs for male and female babies are almost the same, around 71. But between age 1 and 3, the death rate among female babies is 1.5 times as large as that of male babies. Female death rates continue to be higher till about the age 24. Thereafter, male death rates overtake female death rates. By the time age 50 is reached, male death rate is 1.64 times higher than that of female death rate. That is, from 25 years onward the probability of a woman dying is much smaller than that of a man. And this continues till the end of either's career. But even with lower death rates after the 25th year, the losses of life experienced in the early years, especially in the age group 1–3 years, could not be compensated by higher survival rates at higher ages. That is why, sex ratio in the population in India continues against women.

We can compute *cause specific death rate* as other specific death rates are calculated. We have to classify deaths according to causes of death. The subscript x in D_x in equation 6.15 would refer to 'cause of death' rather than age at death though both can be combined to give age-specific death rate for a particular cause. The denominator (P_x) remains the same and refers to the population group for which causes of mortality were to be indexed An illustration for calculation of ASDR appears in Table 6.5.

Estimation of age-specific death rate is really difficult. Unless we know accurately the age of the deceased (we have to rely on the age reported by the doctor in his death certificate), errors are bound to creep in measures of ASDR. We do not have such a problem with CDR. Life Tables cannot be constructed without the accurate knowledge of age and sex-specific death rates.

Although age and sex-specific death rates are the most wanted death statistics, ASDRs are not without limitations. Though ASDRs are more scientific and practical and they can successfully be used for year-by-year comparison of two or more populations of different types, no unified picture about the mortality in a population can be had from ASDR. For this, we have to fall back on CDR or some such other measure.

6.6.3 Standardized Death Rate, STDR

We have seen that ASDR do not tell us if population A has larger or smaller mortality rate compared to that of population B. One can compare two populations for their mortality level only if we could calculate some sort of an average taking into consideration the variability in different segments of the populations. The simplest such measure is CDR. CDR, in fact, is the combined average of the age-specific death rates in a population. If m_1, m_2, ... m_k are the average mortality for different age groups, the composite mean from these means is given by

$$\bar{m} = \frac{m_1 P_1 + m_2 P_2 + \ldots + m_k P_k}{P} \times 1{,}000$$

$$= \frac{D_1 + D_2 + \ldots + D_k}{P} \times 1{,}000 \qquad \ldots(6.18)$$

$$= \frac{D}{P} \times 1{,}000$$

where $P = \sum P_i$ and $D = \sum D_i$. Let m^a and m^b represent the CDR for the populations A and B. By equation (6.18), we can write

$$m^a = \frac{\sum m_x^a P_x^a}{\sum P_x^a} \quad \text{and} \quad m^b = \frac{\sum m_x^b P_x^b}{\sum P_x^b}$$

Table 6.5 *Computation of ASDR, given total estimated 1999 population of India*

Age-group	*% to total population*	*Estimated population, P_x*	*% of deaths*	*Deaths in age-group, D_x*	*Age-specific death rate*
Col.1	*Col.2*	*Col.3 = col.2 × 984928511*	*Col.4*	*Col.5 = col.4 × col.3*	*Col.6 = (col.5/col.3) ×1,000*
0–4	11.7	115236636	26.8	2243667	19.47
5–9	10.7	105387351	2.2	184182	1.75
10–14	11.9	117206493	1.8	150694	1.29
15–19	10.3	101447637	2.3	192554	1.90
20–24	9.2	90613423	2.6	217669	2.40
25–29	8	78794281	2.6	217669	2.76
30–34	7.6	74854567	2.7	226041	3.02
35–39	6.4	63035425	2.8	234413	3.72
40–44	5.7	56140925	3	251157	4.47
45–49	4.5	44321783	3.6	301388	6.80
50–54	3.8	37427283	4.4	368363	9.84
55–59	3	29547855	5.6	468826	15.87
60–64	2.4	23638284	6.5	544173	23.02
65–69	2.1	20683499	9.1	761842	36.83
70–74	1.3	12804071	7.7	644636	50.35
75–79	0.8	7879428	7.7	644636	81.81
80–84	0.3	2954786	4	334876	113.33
85 +	0.2	1969857	4.5	376735	191.25
	100	983943583	99.9	8363521	

Note: The 1999 population has been estimated using compound interest law taking 1991 population as the base year population. The average annual growth was taken as 1.95 percent. Percentage of age group population to total populations (col.2) is that for the year 2000 (SRS). It is assumed that age distribution for the year 2000 is also valid for the year 1999. Col.4 is the SRS estimated percentage of death in each age group. CDR for 1999 is assumed to be the same as that for year 2000, i.e., 8.5. 8.5 multiplied by 984928511 (estimated 1999 population) gives the total number of deaths (8371892) likely to be recorded in 1999–2000. This is ∞Dx, ... the sum total of deaths in the population. This multiplied by the proportion of deaths in age-group (col.4/100) gives estimated number of deaths in each age-group. ASDR then is calculated by the usual formula. The column totals for estimated values do not agree with the numbers we had started with. The minor difference can be attributed to the approximate values for various proportions. The estimated ASDRs closely agree with SRS data for 2000 except in the last two age-groups.

Even if the two CDRs have the same value, we cannot say that age-specific death rates of the two populations are similar. Implicit in this statement is the fact that the relation of similarity will hold only if $\sum m_x^a P_x^a = \sum m_x^b P_x^b$ and $\sum P_x^a = \sum P_x^b$. It is also a fact that equal specific death rates of all age groups in the two populations do not lead to the conclusion that m^a and m^b are the same. m^a and m^b would be identical only if the variable weights assigned to ASDRs of both the populations are the same, that is, the ratios $P_x^a / \sum P_x^a$ and $P_x^b / \sum P_x^b$ are similar. This can happen only if the age distribution of two populations is identical. Our experience is that no two countries or two segments of a population display identical age distribution in the population.

The solution to comparability of general mortality rate in two or more populations is obtained if we could use identical weights for ascertaining ASDRs for the populations we are trying to compare. Since the weight assigned to mortality rate of a specific age group in a population is different from that in the other population $\left(P_x^a/\sum P_x^a \neq P_x^b/\sum P_x^b\right)$, we can use the weights observed in a third population $\left(P_x^S/\sum P_x^S\right)$ to both the populations A and B. This third population is called the ideal or *standard population* S. With this standardization, new average death rates can be worked out.

$$m^a = \frac{\sum m_x^a . P_x^S}{\sum P_x^S} \quad \text{and} \quad m^b = \frac{\sum m_x^b P_x^S}{\sum P_x^S} \qquad \ldots(6.19)$$

This age-adjusted new crude death rate is referred to as Standardized Death Rate, STDR.

The selection of the standard population in calculation of STDR is vital. STDR will be heavily dependent upon the age composition in the standard population. Two different standard populations would invariably produce different results. When we intend to compare death rates for different regions or states, the age distribution of the whole country would be an ideal one to substitute the observed age distribution of the states or regions. However, one must insure that the substituted distribution is not radically different from the distributions which it substitutes. Ideally, Life Table Stationary Population distribution of the standard population is best in computing STDR.

The method we have discussed just now is a *direct method* for estimation of STDR. For each of the populations including the standard one, the age-specific death rate (m_x) and number of persons in each age (P_x) group (or their proportions in the total) must be known. There would be many instances where CDR and age distribution are known but not the ASDR. The method followed for estimation of STDR in such a situation is referred to as *indirect method*.

In indirect method estimation however, ASDR for the standard population must be known. Suppose m_x^S is the ASDR in the standard population and also suppose the ASDR, m_x^a in population A is also known. We can compute 4 different types of average death rate:

(a) $\sum m_x^a . \frac{P_x^a}{\sum P_x^a}$ (CDR of population *A*)

(b) $\sum m_x^a . \frac{P_x^S}{\sum P_x^S}$ (STDR of population *A*)

(c) $\sum m_x^S . \frac{P_x^a}{\sum P_x^a}$ (STDR of standard population *S* taking population *A* as the standard)

(d) $\sum m_x^S . \frac{P_x^S}{\sum P_x^S}$ (CDR of standard population *S*)

If we closely look at the four computed average death rates, an approximate relation could be established between these four: (b) × (c) = (a) × (d). We can find out a close approximate value of STDR for population A from this:

$$(b) = \frac{(a) \times (d)}{(c)}$$

$$\text{That is STDR of } A = \text{CDR of } A \times \left[\frac{\sum m_x^S \cdot (P_x^S / \sum P_x^S)}{\sum m_x^S \cdot (P_x^a / \sum P_x^a)} \right] \quad \ldots(6.20)$$

$$= \frac{\text{CDR of } A \times \text{CDR of } S}{\text{STDR of } S}$$

The ratios within parentheses in (6.20) are the adjustment factors. We show in the following table the computation procedure both by direct and indirect method. SRS data for 2000 has been used to compare general mortality rates in West Bengal and Tamil Nadu, the standard population being India 2000.

Table 6.6 *Steps in the calculation of standardized death rate*

							Total number of deaths			*STDR (direct method)*		*STDR (indirect method)*	
	West Bengal		*Tamil Nadu*		*India*		*WB*	*TN*	*India*	*WB*	*TN*	*WB*	*TN*
Age group	*Proportion to total*	m_x^{WB}	*Proportion to total*	m_x^{TN}	*Proportion to total*	m_x^{IND}	*Col.2× Col.3*	*Col.4× Col.5*	*Col.6× Col.7*	*Col.3× Col.6*	*Col.5× Col.6*	*Col.2× Col.7*	*Col.4× Col.7*
1	*2*	*3*	*4*	*5*	*6*	*7*	*8*	*9*	*10*	*11*	*12*	*13*	*14*
0–4	10.1	13.2	9.2	12	11.7	19.5	133.32	110.4	228.15	154.44	140.4	196.95	179.4
5–9	9.1	1.3	8.7	0.7	10.7	1.7	11.83	6.09	18.19	13.91	7.49	15.47	14.79
10–14	12	0.9	9.2	0.9	11.9	1.3	10.8	8.28	15.47	10.71	10.71	15.6	11.96
15–19	10.3	1.3	9.6	2	10.3	1.9	13.39	19.2	19.57	13.39	20.6	19.57	18.24
10–24	9.3	1.7	9.6	2.4	9.2	2.4	15.81	23.04	22.08	15.64	22.08	22.32	23.04
25–29	8.2	2.1	9	2.5	8	2.8	17.22	22.5	22.4	16.8	20	22.96	25.2
30–34	8.8	2.2	8.4	3	7.6	3.1	19.36	25.2	23.56	16.72	22.8	27.28	26.04
35–39	7.2	2.9	7.2	3.5	6.4	3.7	20.88	25.2	23.68	18.56	22.4	26.64	26.64
40–44	6.5	3.3	6.5	4.9	5.7	4.5	21.45	31.85	25.65	18.81	27.93	29.25	29.25
45–49	4.8	6	5.4	6	4.5	6.8	28.8	32.4	30.6	27	27	32.64	36.72
50–54	3.9	7.9	5	9.3	3.8	9.9	30.81	46.5	37.62	30.02	35.34	38.61	49.5
55–59	3	16.3	3.8	17.7	3	16.3	48.9	67.26	48.9	48.9	53.1	48.9	61.94
60–64	2.4	23.7	3.2	21.8	2.4	23.1	56.88	69.76	55.44	56.88	52.32	55.44	73.92
65–69	2	40.7	2.4	36.7	2.1	38	81.4	88.08	79.8	85.47	77.07	76	91.2
70–74	1.2	47.9	1.5	50.8	1.3	50.2	57.48	76.2	65.26	62.27	66.04	60.24	75.3
75–79	0.7	86.1	0.8	88.5	0.8	82.8	60.27	70.8	66.24	68.88	70.8	57.96	66.24
80–84	0.3	109.3	0.3	112	0.3	101.4	32.79	33.6	30.42	32.79	33.6	30.42	30.42
85+	0.2	180.5	0.2	168.6	0.2	164.7	36.1	33.72	32.94	36.1	33.72	32.94	32.94
	100		100		100		697.49	790.08	845.97	727.29	743.4	809.19	872.74
			CDR				6.97	7.9	8.5				
			STDR (direct method)							7.27	7.43		
					STDR (indirect method)							7.32	7.69

Converted into STDR, the difference in the general mortality rates in West Bengal and Tamil Nadu get reduced considerably, from about 1 point prior to standardization to only 0.16 after standardization by direct method and 0.37 when standardization is done by indirect method.

6.7 Measures of Fertility

Almost similar methods are followed in the measurement of birth rate or fertility in a population. Birth rate in a population is the ratio between the number of live births in a specified time and space to the mid-year population (in some indexes, women or married women population) in the same time and space multiplied by 1,000. Risk of dying may differ from one segment of population to another, but the risk always remains. The same is not true for births. Only women in a specific age group can be exposed to the risk of giving birth to a baby. There is no ground to assume that chances of giving birth to a baby are the same for all segments of the female population. Although the risk of dying remains in all ages and in all segments of a population so long a person is alive, the actual death ends all speculations about it. But giving birth to babies can be repeated as long a woman remains in her reproductive period.

1. Birth of a baby by a virgin mother is not quite a serious issue in most developed countries. But birth outside marriage relation is still despised in orthodox countries like India. Even though two women are in their reproductive ages (15–49), the chances of giving birth to a baby could be distinctly different had one of them been married, the other not. Had both of them been married approximately at the same age, there could be a somewhat similar chance for each giving birth to a baby.
2. One can reasonably well anticipate the arrival of the first baby after a girl is married. But prediction of birth for higher order is not easy for many reasons. The first order birth in India accounts for more than one-third of all births in a year. Usually, the first birth is recorded within a year or two of the marriage. But the subsequent births cannot be predicted. The arrival of the second and subsequent child depends on health of mother, duration of breast-feeding, the sex of the first child, health of the child and a host other factors. The arrival of the next child often would be delayed if the couple already has two or more children. We cannot say that probability of giving birth to a baby by a girl married at 15 years and another girl married at 30 years the same.
3. Even when two women are of the same age and both married, we cannot say that they have the same probability of giving birth to a baby for the reason that one may be sick or suffering from malnutrition or has some gross abnormality in menstruation cycle or has developed some serious complications during the last pregnancy. In fertility prediction, we talk of 'risk of exposure' often making no mention about the risk of getting divorced or separated, becoming widow, occupational hazards and the risk of death. These other events can directly or indirectly affect a woman's achieved fertility.
4. The rural poor and the illiterates still marry at young age. By the time they reach 25, they often are mother of three or more children. Women marry late in urban area because of their education and level of exposure to mass media. Therefore, there would be considerable difference in the risk of exposure among educated and illiterates and rural/urban origin.
5. The conception probability of a woman is seriously affected by divorce or death of husband. The current age of the woman is important, but more important is the length of conjugal life already she had.

6. A large gap between the age of the husband and that of the wife does affect sexual relations. We relate fertility to a woman's age, husband's age is not taken into cognizance at all.
7. Not all women in a population can produce babies. Women cannot give birth to a baby before the 'cycle' begins; she becomes infertile after the 'cycle' stops. And there is considerable variation among women as to when their 'cycle' would begin, when end.
8. Scientists have not succeeded in devising a method by which they can state how many of our women are fecund. It is believed that fecundity varies with age. Though scientists agree that this physiological capacity to conceive is not uniform throughout the reproductive period, they do not have a clear idea as to how this physiological capacity changes with age.
9. Some women give birth to twin babies. Should this be taken as an instance of single birth or two births? What should be the unit of fertility analysis – number of live births or number of times a woman gave birth to babies?
10. Whether one desires or not, death is inevitable. But that is not true about birth. Yearning for a child by the couple or otherwise has a large role in the birth of a baby. The couple may accept a small family norm; the spacing of birth may be influenced by many considerations including pressure of other members of the family and even some outside pressure.

From this discussion it becomes clear that unlike death birth is a complex issue. There is considerable pressure from various sources and agencies that have vital roles in the couple's decision to give or withheld birth. Added are the facts that birth registration is still very incomplete and faulty.

Since most countries have contained death rate appreciably, the attention in the last few decades have been on birth and birth related issues since birth reduction alone can restrict population growth. Several measures of birth rates have been devised. Though these have been devised to measure birth rates, they also throw light on the phenomenon of birth. We discuss below some of the commonly used measures of fertility.

6.7.1 Crude Birth Rate, CBR

The same procedure as CDR is employed in computing CBR. Sometimes CBR is symbolically written as i'. In computation of CBR and other birth rates only live births are taken into consideration.

$$\text{CBR or } i' = \frac{B}{P} \times 1{,}000 \qquad \ldots(6.21)$$

where B refers to the total number of births registered in a defined geographical area (or a social group) within a time frame (usually a complete year), P is the mid-year population in the defined space and time. The criticisms raised against CDR are equally applicable to CBR as well. Two other major faults in this measurement are that one part of the population (males, about half the size of a population) is not 'exposed to the risk' of giving birth to babies. Regarding the other half, it is only a restricted segment of the women population (15–49) who could be exposed to the risk,

6.7.2 General Fertility Rate, GFR

The two major objections to the use of CBR can largely be overcome by this index, which uses only the women in the reproductive age group in the denominator. In place of P, the quantity $\sum_{x=15}^{x=49} {}^{f}P_x$, i.e., the mid-year population of women in the age group 15–49 is used in the denominator. This is an impressive improvement over CBR and its formula reads

$$\text{GFR, } i = \frac{B}{\sum_{x=15}^{x=49} {}^{f}P_x} \times 1{,}000 \qquad \ldots(6.22)$$

Ages 15 and 49 are the two limits of the 'child bearing age'. Before we can use this formula a decision has to be taken about what should be regarded as limits of the 'child bearing age'. The age of puberty is not the same for girls coming from cold, temperate and hot climatic regions. In tropical region puberty starts early. In the cold and dry climatic region, women remain fertile a bit longer. In computation, this difference of a few years in the denominator may change the size of the effective population considerably giving a smaller or larger GFR. The limits of this 'child bearing age' differ from country to country or between regions. The demographers however for making comparable observations, generally use (15–49) as the reproductive period for women of all countries and regions. There is a strong argument in favor of bringing the upper limit down to 44 years since very few births are recorded all over the world for women beyond 44 years.

GFR actually informs us the extent to which women in their reproductive period contributes to increase the size of the population. This index uses both sex composition and partially the age distribution of one segment of the population in estimation of birth rate in the population. The greatest fault in this index is that it regards women between 15 and 49 years are equally fecund and are exposed to the same risk of giving birth to a baby. If it is assumed that the probability of giving birth to a baby is much stronger for a girl just married than others in the higher age groups, then it must also be admitted that proportion of girls actually married around the lower end of the reproductive age group would be much smaller than those near the other end. Similarly, proportion of widows and divorcees would be much smaller at the lower end than those near the upper end. Time and space may have some role in such variability as well. For this reason, comparison of fertility levels between two countries or regions by GFR is not quite dependable.

Table 6.7 shows that of the 45.5 percent Indian women (all ages) are registered unmarried (current status) in 2000, 33.8 percent belong to less than 14 years, and another 7.8 percent in 15–19 year age group. Only about 0.3 percent of Indian women remain unmarried in ages beyond 30 years. Of the 46.5 percent currently married women more than 30.6 percent are in 30+ age group, 15–19 age group contributes only 2.3 to the total of 46.5 percent. Only about 8 percent of Indian women are widows/divorcees/separated, and none of them comes from below 20 years age. 5.9 percent of women in this category are those aged 50 years and above. That is, only about 2.1 percent women in their child bearing ages are widows/divorcees/separated. So, widowhood, divorce and separation have some impact, small though, on birth rate in India. GFR in India has come down from 127 in 1988–90 to 104 in 1998–2000 (Table 7.23). GFR in 1998–2000 in urban and rural areas were 76.5 and 112.7 respectively.

A major correction for GFR is achieved by calculating the ratio from among those who actually are married at any point of time. Ever-married women in the age group 15–49 years replace the denominator of the equation (6.22). The resulting fertility index is known as General Marital Fertility Rate, GMFR. GMFR in 2000, according to SRS, was 139.2 for the entire Indian population and 111.1 and 148.8 for urban and rural populations respectively.

Table 6.7 *Percent distribution of female population in India by their marital status and age group, 2000*

Age group	*Never married*	*Married*	*W/D/S*	*Total*
< 10 yrs	22.1	0	0	22.1
10–14	11.7	0	0	11.7
Below 14	**33.8**	**0**	**0**	**33.8**
15–19	7.8	2.2	0	10.0
20–24	2.8	6.4	0.1	9.3
25.29	0.7	7.3	0.2	8.1
Between 15–29	**11.3**	**15.9**	**0.3**	**27.4**
30–34	0.2	7.3	0.3	7.8
35–39	0.1	5.1	0.4	6.6
40–44	0	5.1	0.5	5.6
45–49	0	3.8	0.6	4.4
50–54	0	3.0	0.8	3.8
55–59	0	2.0	0.9	2.9
60+	0	3.2	4.2	7.7
All ages	**45.5**	**46.5**	**8.0**	**100.0**

Source: SRS Statistical Report 2000

6.7.3 Child-Woman Ratio, CWR

We have talked about CWR earlier in this chapter. This index is useful when there is scarcity of reliable data on birth. Equation (6.1) is the formula we use for computing CWR. CWR in India has come down from 227 in 1991 to 200 in 2000.

$$\frac{\text{CWR (2000)} - \text{CWR (1991)}}{\text{CWR (1991)}} \times 100 = -11.89 \text{ per cent}$$

6.7.4 Age-Specific Fertility Rate, ASFR

The concept of ASFR is similar to that of ASDR. This is a more refined and most important measure of fertility in a population. A few other indexes of fertility and growth rate are computed using ASFR. It is usually calculated for every single year, 15 to 49 or for some broad groups as 15–19, 20–24, ... ASFR often is represented by i_x.

$$\text{ASFR, } i_x = \frac{B_x}{{}^f P_x} \times 1{,}000 \qquad \ldots(6.23)$$

where i_x is the age-specific fertility of women of age x, B_x is the number of live births given by women in age x but less than x+1 in a defined space and time and ${}^f P_x$ is the average size of the women population in age x but less than $x+1$. We can compute ASFR between any two age limits by making necessary modifications in numerator and denominator.

$$\text{ASFR}, \; {}_n i_x = \frac{{}_n B_x}{{}^f_n P_x} \times 1{,}000 \qquad \ldots(6.24)$$

${}^f_n P_x$ actually refers to the size of women population between ages x and $x+n-1$ complete years.

Utility of ASFR is similar to that of ASDR. In all countries, ASFRs in early ages remain small; the index rapidly increases till around 30 years and then declines until it comes down to near zero around 49 years. Like ASDR, ASFR too cannot be used to compare the overall fertility situations of two countries or regions. ASFR is less precise than ASDR. Not all of ${}^f_n P_x$ are equally exposed to the risk of giving birth to a baby. It is those who are married in this age group give birth to babies. A more precise specific fertility index ASMFR along the line of GMFR is calculated wherever the proportion of currently married women in the age group is known. The formula of ASFR is suitably modified to include only the married population in making the estimate.

$$\text{ASMFR}, \; {}_n i_x^m = \frac{{}_n B_x}{{}^f_n P_x^m} \times 1{,}000 \qquad \ldots(6.25)$$

where ${}^f_n P_x^m$ refers to currently married women population in the age group x and $x+n-1$ age group. Obviously, the value of ASFR would be smaller compared to ASMFR. ASFRs for various age groups for India have been presented in Table 7.11. ASMFR separately for rural and urban India, 2000 is presented in Figure 7.6.

6.7.5 Total Fertility Rate, TFR

Standardized death rate was specially developed with a view to obtain an index of general mortality rate in a population so that mortality situation prevailing in a population could be compared with that in another population. It was a hypothetical estimate since weights assigned to ASDRs to obtain a composite mean was derived from a standard population. TFR, which provides a general index of fertility in a population, is more direct than STDR but with two major assumptions (1) that every woman who enters the child bearing age gives live births as per the age-specific fertility rates for each age, and (2) that no woman shall die before she leaves the reproductive period. With these two assumptions, TFR is the number of babies expected to be born to every woman had they exactly followed ASFRs for every single age in the reproductive period. In a sense, TFR is simply the summation of ASFRs.

$$\text{TFR} = \sum i_x = \sum_{x=15}^{x=49} \frac{B_x}{{}^f_{49} P_{15}} \qquad \ldots(6.26)$$

This expression tells us that if 1,000 women enter the child bearing age together, then TFR is the number of children to be born by these 1,000 women at the time when they leave the reproductive period. If the multiplier 1,000 is dropped (which generally is), TFR simply will mean the average number of babies to be born to mothers at the end of their reproductive career. When ASFRs are calculated for broad age groups (15–19, 20–24, ...), TFR is computed as

$$\text{TFR} = \frac{5 \times \sum_{15}^{49} \text{ASFR}}{1{,}000} \qquad \ldots(6.27)$$

Not every woman shall start her reproductive career at the age 15. Even some may not marry at all. A more precise index, Total Marital Fertility Rate, TMFR, therefore shall be the one that is based on married women in 15–49 age group. TMFR is calculated from ASMFR.

$$\text{TMFR} = \frac{5 \times \sum_{15}^{49} \text{ASMFR}}{1,000} \qquad \ldots(6.28)$$

TFR is the most frequently used index of birth rate in a country. According to UNDP Human Development Report 2001, TFR for the world population has dropped from 4.5 in 1975 to 2.8 in 1995–2000. High human development countries had TFR 1.7 in 1995–2000 compared 2.6 and 5.6 respectively for the medium and low human development countries in 1995–2000. TFR and TMFR for the national population, India, were 3.2 and 4.8 respectively in 2000.

Calculation of ASFR and other indexes based on it is shown in the following table. The data are from 1981 Indian census.

Table 6.8 *Computation of ASFR and related statistics from 1981 data, India*

x	${}_5^fP_x$ *(million)*	*Prop. Married*	B_x *(million)*	${}_5i_x$ = *Col.4/Col.2*	${}_5^fP_x^m$ = *Col.2×Col.3*	${}_5i_x^m$ = *Col.4/Col.6*
1	2	3	4	5	6	7
15–19	31.03	0.441	1.707	0.055	13.68	0.125
20–24	29.18	0.849	5.457	0.187	24.77	0.220
25–29	25.74	0.944	4.788	0.186	24.30	0.197
30–34	21.47	0.948	2.941	0.137	20.35	0.145
35–39	19.52	0.932	1.718	0.088	18.19	0.094
40–44	16.64	0.878	0.765	0.046	14.61	0.052
45–49	14.22	0.868	0.300	0.021	12.34	0.024
$\sum_{15}^{49}$	**157.80**		**17.676**	**0.720**	**128.24**	**0.857**

Multiplying column 5 and column 7 by 1,000, we get ASFR and ASMFR respectively. Computed values for other indexes are shown below.

$$\text{GFR} = \frac{\text{Sum of col. 4}}{\text{Sum of col. 2}} \times 1,000 = \frac{17.676}{157.80} \times 1,000 = 112$$

$$\text{GMFR} = \frac{\text{Sum of col. 4}}{\text{Sum of col. 6}} \times 1,000 = \frac{17.676}{128.24} \times 1,000 = 138$$

$$\text{CBR} = \frac{\text{Total number of births}}{\text{Total population (685.2 mill. in 1981)}} \times 1,000 = \frac{17.676}{685.2} \times 1,000 = 26$$

$\text{TFR} = 5 \times \text{col.}5 \times 1,000 = 3,600$ or 3.6 births per married woman

$\text{TMFR} = 5 \times \text{col.}7 \times 1,000 = 4,285$ or 4.285 births per married woman

6.8 Measures of Migration

Like birth and death, migration is one of the fundamental variables in demographic analysis. Change in population in a country or region has a component in migration. We have seen that increase or decrease in the size of population is dependent on natural increase (birth-death) and the net of in- and out-migration (I – O) in a specified time period. It is relatively easy to collect reasonably accurate data on birth and death in a country or a region, but for information on migration there is hardly any reliable administrative machinery in any country. International migration can to some extent be counted through visas issued by various countries. But the international boundaries often are so porous that illegal immigration/emigration cannot be stopped. Some of the eastern states in India have porous boundaries with Bangladesh. Illegal immigration has been a serious concern for these states.

There is no mechanism in India and elsewhere to keep a watch on the movement of people from one state to another and also within the state. We have to wait for the census (or some specially conducted sample survey) to get relevant information about migration – streams of migration, causes of migration, etc. The transit statistics, if there is any, provide us with information separately for those in-migrating and those out-migrating. Population movements between two places A and B have two components. Movements from A $\rightarrow$ B and from B $\rightarrow$ A in a particular period of time together constitute *gross or total migration* of either place if the exchange of population for either is only between these two places. In most population analysis gross migration receives no particular attention. Either in-migration or out-migration or net of in- and out-migration are most frequently used for such analysis.

Migration is not as simple as the exchange of population between two places. Invariably A receives population from various places B, C, D,... and send out people to different places as well. The intensity of migration may be strong for some places, weak in others.

Gross migration rate is calculated for a region and not for a single place. Gross migration rate is defined as

$$\frac{\text{Number of persons moving out from their residence for settling in another place in a region in the same year}}{\text{Mid-year population of the region in the same year}} \times 1{,}000 \qquad \ldots(6.29)$$

$$\text{Out-migration} = \frac{\text{Number of persons leaving the region in a year}}{\text{Mid-year population of the region in the same year}} \times 1{,}000 \qquad \ldots(6.30)$$

$$\text{In-migration} = \frac{\text{Number of persons received from outside by the region in a year}}{\text{Mid-year population of the region in the same year}} \times 1{,}000 \qquad \ldots(6.31)$$

$$\text{Net migration} = \frac{\text{In-migration} - \text{Out-mirgration}}{\text{Mid-year population}} \times 1{,}000 \qquad \ldots(6.32)$$

Another frequently used concept in migration is *effectiveness of migration.* This is computed for two places or regions A and B. It is the ratio of net migration in A (or B) for reasons of movement between A and B to the total exchange of population between A and B.

$$\text{Effectiveness of migration} = \left|\frac{\text{Net migration in } A}{\text{Total exchange of population between } A \text{ and } B}\right|$$

$$= \left|\frac{\text{Net migration in } B}{\text{Total exchange of population between } A \text{ and } B}\right| \quad \ldots(6.33)$$

Effectiveness of migration is expressed in absolute value, though the numerator may be negative or positive in either A or B. If x number of persons move from A to B and y number from B to A, then $(x+y)$ is the size of the population exchanged between A and B. $(x-y)$ is the net migration in A and $(y-x)$ is the net migration in B. That is effectiveness of migration between A and B is

$$\left|\frac{x-y}{x+y}\right| \text{ for } A \quad \text{and} \quad \left|\frac{y-x}{x+y}\right| \text{ for } B$$

Usually $(x-y)$ or $(y-x)$ is $\neq$ zero. In extreme case, A sends people to B but does not receive any or vice versa. In that case the values of numerator and denominator become the same and effectiveness of migration is 1. In the other extreme case A may send out as many people to A as it receives from B, i.e. $x = y$ giving the value of ratio of either as zero.

Since the principal source for migration information is decennial census, some of those who had migrated in this ten-year period may have died before the next census is taken. After partition of India in 1947 there was a huge population exchange between India and Pakistan. In 1971, the Bangladesh war of liberation pushed huge number of people to north-eastern states of India. That is, there was a sudden surge in the population in these states due to increased migration from Bangladesh. After the war, some went back to their native places, but a good number of them decided to settle in India. The increase in population in India between 1971 and 1981 has two components: the natural growth and the immigrants mainly from Bangladesh. A sizable number of those who were counted as migrants in 1981were also among the migrants listed in 1971 or even earlier. The surviving migrants from 1971 census and the new migrants between 1971 and 1981 together constitute the migrated population in 1981. Let the net migrants in 1971 population is M_{1971} and their survival ratio between ages x and $x+10$ is ${}_9P_x$, and let M_{1981} stand for net migrants in 1981 head count. Then, the size of net migrants between 1971 and 1981 is $M_{1981} - M_{1971} \times {}_9P_x$.

Those who were aged 10 or more years in 1981 must have been alive 10 years back as well. That is, the proportion of individuals surviving in 1981 from 1971 census must be equal to the number of person-migrants recorded in 10 years and older age group. Therefore,

$$\text{Survival ratio} = \frac{\text{Sum of the population aged 10 years and above in 1981}}{\text{Enumerated population in 1971}} \quad \ldots(6.34)$$

If we further assume that the risk of dying of the migrants is the same as that in the local population, we can calculate the net migrants in 1971 surviving to 1981. Deducting this number from that of net migrants in 1981, we get the size of net migrants between 1971 and 1981.

Table 6.9 *Out-, in-, and net-migration in selected few states in India 1971 and 1981*

State	*Pop. (mill)*	*In-migration (000)*			*Out-migration (000)*			*Net migration (000)*		
		Male	*Female*	*Total*	*Male*	*Female*	*Total*	*Male*	*Female*	*Total*
1	*2*	*3*	*4*	*5*	*6*	*7*	*8*	*9*	*10*	*11*
					(a) 1971					
Andhra Pradesh	45.5	330	414.4	774.3	508.7	552.6	1061.3	–178.7	–138.2	–287
Bihar	56.4	448	724	1172	1356.3	845.1	2201.4	–908.3	–121.1	–1029.4
Kerala	21.4	137.3	126	263.3	586.3	356.3	942.6	–449	–230.3	–679.3
Maharashtra	50.4	2091.8	1507.9	3599.8	494.9	644.9	1139.8	1596.9	863	2460
Punjab	13.6	875.1	783.7	1659.9	627.5	565.7	1193.3	247.6	218	466.6
Uttar Pradesh	88.3	667.5	998.7	1666.1	2030	1431.2	3460.9	–1362.5	–432.5	–1794.8
West Bengal	44.3	3162	2130.6	5292.6	336.6	443.4	780	2825.4	1687.2	4512.6
					(b) 1981					
State	12	13	14	15	16	17	16	19	20	21
Andhra Pradesh	53.6	358.9	510.8	869.8	596.1	726.2	1322.3	–237.2	–215.4	–452.5
Bihar	6.99	461.2	886.6	1347.8	1437.2	1099.6	2536.9	–976	–213	–1189.1
Kerala	25.4	176.2	179.5	355.7	631.7	480.1	1111.7	–455.5	–300.6	–756
Maharashtra	62.8	2586.2	2046.4	4632.7	609.2	880.5	1489.7	1977	1165.9	3143
Punjab	16.8	903.6	853	1756.6	627	669.1	1296.2	276.6	183.9	460.4
Uttar Pradesh	110.9	672.3	1308	1980.2	2725.6	2130.5	4856.1	–2053.3	–822.5	–2875.9
West Bengal	54.6	3220.8	2471.2	5692	399.7	581.7	981.4	2821.1	1889.5	4710.6

(c) Surviving migrants

State		*Migrants surviving from 1971 (000)*		*Net migrants during 1971–81 (000)*	
	Survival ratio	*Male*	*Female*	*Male*	*Female*
	22	*23*	*24*	*25*	*26*
Andhra Pradesh	0.90860	–162.4	–125.6	–74.8	–89.8
Bihar	0.89278	–810.9	–108.1	–165.1	–104.9
Kerala	0.91149	–409.3	–209.9	–46.2	–90.7
Maharashtra	0.92829	1482.4	801.1	494.6	364.8
Punjab	0.93545	231.6	203.9	45.0	–20.3
Uttar Pradesh	0.89366	–1217.6	–386.5	–835.7	–436.0
West Bengal	0.92516	2613.9	1560.9	207.2	328.6

6.9 Measures of Population Growth Rate

By population growth we mean any change in the size of a population, rise or decline. We have seen that there are only three sources through which population change can take place – birth, death and migration. Measurement of population growth, absolute or relative, is essential for economic and social planning. Both in short and long term planning the actual size of the population at a particular point of time, the current average annual growth rate and the projected growth rate and estimated size of the population 15 or 20 years or beyond are critically important.

Growth of population is generally measured in two different ways: (1) by absolute or relative natural increase, and (2) by the process of replacement, that is, how one generation replaces the previous generation. We can also think of another measurement of growth – how certain segments of the population (child, agricultural labor, industrial labor, urban population, persons in the reproductive/active/old age group, etc.) are changing in size with time. Since growth of any segment of a population is intrinsically related to the growth of the general population of which they are constituent parts, our discussion on growth will remain confined to the general population. In national and other planning, information on segmental growth of population becomes vital. The methods of growth analysis start with the assumption that the current birth, death and migration rate would not change abruptly.

6.9.1 Absolute or Relative Change in Number

This is the simplest method of growth analysis of a population. It is just a comparison of the size of population in a defined geographical space between two time points.

Absolute increase of a population is related to births, deaths and in- and out-migration.

$$\text{Absolute increase} = P_{t_2} - P_{t_1} \qquad \ldots(6.35)$$

$$= (B-D)_{t_2-t_1} + (I-O)_{t_2-t_1}$$

where P_{t_1} is the size of the population in time t_1 and P_{t_2} is that for time $t_2 \cdot B-D$ refers to surplus of birth over death (or the reverse) in the time period t_1 and t_2, I and O refers to in- and out-migration in the same time period. We often need a relative index of growth than an absolute increase in numbers.

$$\text{Growth rate} = \frac{P_{t_2} - P_{t_1}}{P_{t_1}} \times K \qquad \ldots(6.36)$$

or, $$\frac{P_{t_2}}{P_{t_1}} \times K \qquad \ldots(6.37)$$

The problems encountered in such measures arise from lack of precise information on in- and out-migration. Relative strength of the three variables birth, death and migration in population growth cannot be measured with good degree of accuracy. Such measures have tolerable reliability when they are used with census data.

Crude rate of natural increase. The volume of international migration has come down radically in the last few decades. Incidences of emigration and immigration therefore do not have significant impact on population numbers for most countries. However, internal migration is on the rise in most countries because of improved connectivity and growth of industries and the service sector. Population of some states and some of their population parameters are changing due to internal migration more than that in others.

Since birth and death data can be obtained more reliably than data on migration and also since these two variables have the most significant effect on growth in numbers (some urban areas defy this assumption), they are the natural selection for measuring the growth rate of a population.

$$\text{Crude rate of natural increase} = P_{t_2} - P_{t_1} = (B-D)_{t_2-t_1} \qquad \ldots(6.38)$$

We can compute this crude rate of natural increase from CBR and CDR as well.

Crude rate of natural increase = CBR – CDR (6.39)

Compound population growth rate. The absolute or the relative measures of growth discussed above though are useful for comparing growth rates of different regions of a country, their limitations are often far greater than their usefulness. When comparing growth rates of two countries, the data for comparison must refer to the same period. This rarely happens in reality. The frequent anchor points for such comparisons are the census years. Census years of different countries often would not be the same. When such is the case, the decadal growth needs to be converted into average annual growth rate. Population in India in 1991 was 843,930,861 and that in 2001 was 1,027,015,247. By applying equation (6.36) we get the decadal growth rate.

$$\text{Decadal Growth Rate} = \frac{1,027,015,247 - 843,930,861}{843,930,861} \times 100 = 21.69$$

That is, annual average growth rate (simple) is 2.169 percent. This average annual growth rate is in respect to the population in 1991. Even if we presume that average annual growth rate for all the years between 1991 and 2001 was identical, it does not mean that the absolute growth in numbers for every year were the same. That is, 183.048500 million people were added to 1991 total and at the beginning of 1992 the population size was around 862,235,711. A 2.169 percent growth in 1992–93 would mean that 18.701893 million people would be added to population total at the beginning of 1992–93. That is, about 0.4 million more people were added in the year 1992–93 over and above the year's addition in 1991–92. It is to be remembered that growth of population is continuous; every second some people die and some babies are born. Like the compound interest addition on a fixed bank deposit, the population also grows according to the same compound interest principle except when some natural catastrophe destabilizes the usual growth. If we assume that annual growth rate (r) remains the same for the entire period, then population in the t_2th year by the compound interest law would be

$$P_{t_n} = P_{t_1}(1+r)^n \qquad \ldots(6.40)$$

or, $$\frac{P_{t_n}}{P_{t_1}} = (1+r)^n$$

or, $$\log\left(\frac{P_{t_n}}{P_{t_1}}\right) = n\log(1+r)$$

where P_{t_1} is the base year population and P_{t_n} is the population in the nth year.

$$\log\left(\frac{1,027,015,247}{843,930,861}\right) = 10\log(1+r)$$

or, $9.01158 - 8.926301 = 10\log(1+r)$

or, $0.0085273 = \log(1+r)$

or, $1 + r = 1.01983$

or, $r = 0.01983$

or, $r = 1.983\ \%$ per annum

The estimate of the average annual growth rate of population obtained from equation (6.39) assumes that the growth has taken place only once in a year (as yearly/half-yearly interest on deposit in bank account). Since population grows every moment, we need to use exponential equation to estimate the average annual growth rate.

$$\frac{P_{t_2}}{P_{t_1}} = e^{nr} \qquad \text{...(6.41)}$$

where e is the natural base of logarithm.

$$\frac{1{,}027{,}015{,}247}{843{,}930{,}861} = 1.21694 = e^{nr}$$

or, $10\,r = 0.1958$

or, $r = 0.01958$

or, $r = 1.958$ % per annum

Equation (6.40) gives a precise estimate of average annual growth rate of population in the decade 1991–2001. But the index does not tell us the cause of growth of population – natural increase (CBR – CDR) alone or a combination of natural increase and international population movements.

6.9.2 Replacement of Population

People die, but before dyeing they leave behind successors. If parents leave behind one son and one daughter, then these two are *exact replacement* of the previous generation. Birth and death are natural phenomena; a new group, not necessarily of the same size as the departed one, fills up the void created by death of a group of persons. If the replacement group has the same sex composition as the replaced one, then the size of the population does not change though there may be some qualitative change in population characteristics. When the replacement level is greater or less than the size of the population being replaced, the size of the resulting population may change as also some qualitative aspect of the population. The replacement level deals with birth and death alone and indicates if the birth rate is different from the death rate in the population.

Birth and death statistics can be had from the corresponding registers (or SRS where civil registers are inadequate or faulty). In all countries there shall be some immigrants, however small their size may be compared to the size of the total population. Birth and death rates of immigrants often are different from that of indigenous people. However, this effect may not be substantial if the immigrants constitute only a very small fraction of the population. In that case we would be committing hardly any error if it were assumed that birth and death rates of immigrants were not different from those of the local population. The rate of natural increase and rate of population growth are not identical although they could be if there were no international migrations. We now discuss the methods of measuring replacement level in a population.

Vital Index: This is the simplest measurement of replacement level in a population. This is the ratio between the total number of births and total number of deaths in a population in a specified period of time.

$$\text{Vital Index} = \frac{B}{D} \times 1{,}000 \qquad \text{...(6.42)}$$

Though a good picture is obtained about the replacement level in the total population, no clear indication can be obtained from this index about the nature of change the population is likely to experience in future. Growth of population of a country depends upon the female population, especially those in their reproductive age group. How many *female babies* are born is more important than how many babies are born. Similarly, female deaths (especially those in the reproductive age group) among all deaths registered are the information that really matters in computation of replacement index. All these issues are not addressed by the vital index.

Gross Reproduction Rate, GRR: How many female births a woman gives is more important than the total number of births given by the woman. Age-specific-female birth rate rather than age-specific birth rate is of prime importance in making a realistic estimation of the population growth. The same formula as that for estimation of age-specific birth rate is used for computation of age-specific-female birth rate except that both numerator and denominator in the equation address to females.

$$\text{Age-Sex-Specific Birth Rate, } {}^{f}i_x = \frac{{}^{f}B_x}{{}^{f}P_x} \times 1{,}000 \qquad \ldots(6.43)$$

where ${}^{f}B_x$ refers to number of female births by mothers of age x, ${}^{f}P_x$ is the number of females of age x but less than $x + 1$. The sum total of the age-specific-female birth rates for ages $15 < x < 49$ is the Gross Reproduction Rate of the population. Like TFR, GRR is a hypothetical number. As in TFR, it is assumed that women who are 15 years today will remain alive till they are 49 years old and each of them would experience the same age-specific-female birth rate in the population.

$$\text{GRR} = \sum_{15}^{49}\left(\frac{{}^{f}B_x}{{}^{f}P_x}\right) = \sum_{15}^{49} {}^{f}i_x \qquad \ldots(6.44)$$

Unlike TFR, GRR is expressed as the *number of live female births* given by a woman in her entire reproductive period. Like TFR, GRR is generally calculated for 5-year period instead of every year for a woman.

$$\text{GRR} = 5 \times \sum_{15}^{49}\left(\frac{{}^{f}_{5}B_x}{{}^{f}P_x}\right) = 5 \times \sum_{15}^{49} {}^{f}_{5}i_x \qquad \ldots(6.45)$$

How do we know the number of live female births in some specific age group? This can be calculated in two ways: (1) divide births in each age group of mothers into sons and daughters, that is, while doing the tabulation of birth for each age group, we can record the male and female births separately; or (2) we make an age-specific birth tabulation and multiply each row data under 'Birth' by the sex-ratio at birth or sex-ratio in the population. Though sex-ratio in the population as a multiplying factor is more dependable, the sex-ratio at birth as the multiplying factor is more logical. We multiply the number of children born in each group of mothers by F/(F+M) to estimate the number of female live births in each age group of mothers. Of course, in doing so we make another assumption that sex ratio at birth at every age of mothers is the same (${}^{f}B_x / B_x = k$). Then

$$k = \frac{\sum_{15}^{49} {}^{f}B_x}{\sum_{15}^{49} B_x} = \frac{{}^{f}B}{B} \text{ (say)}$$

In that event,

$$^{f}B_x/B_x = {}^{f}B/B \qquad \ldots(6.46)$$

or, $$^{f}B_x = B_x \times \frac{^{f}B}{B}$$

or, $$\frac{^{f}B_x}{^{f}P_x} = \frac{B_x}{^{f}P_x} \times \frac{^{f}B}{B}$$

or, $$^{f}i_x = i_x \times \frac{^{f}B}{B}$$

Therefore, $$\text{GRR} = \frac{^{f}B}{B} \times \sum_{15}^{49} i_x = \frac{^{f}B}{B} \times \text{TFR} \qquad \ldots(6.47)$$

The following tabular set up may be followed for estimating the number of male and female births by age of mothers. Table 6.11 shows computation of GRR and some other birth statistics from 1981 census and SRS 2000 data. In computation of GRR, sex ratio is taken as 100/205.

Table 6.10 *Number of male and female children born by mothers' age*

Age of Mother, x	*Number of Mothers, $^{f}P_x$*	*Number of Male babies, $^{m}B_x$*	*Number of Female babies, $^{f}B_x$*	*Total number of babies born, $^{m}B_x + {}^{f}B_x$*
1	*2*	*3*	*4*	*5*
15	$^{f}P_{15}$	$^{m}P_{15}$	$^{f}P_{15}$	$^{m}P_{15} + {}^{f}P_{15}$
16	$^{f}P_{16}$	$^{m}P_{16}$	$^{f}P_{16}$	$^{m}P_{16} + {}^{f}P_{16}$
17	$^{f}P_{17}$	$^{m}P_{17}$	$^{f}P_{17}$	$^{m}P_{17} + {}^{f}P_{17}$
..	..	..	..	..
..	..	..	..	..
48	$^{f}P_{48}$	$^{m}P_{48}$	$^{f}P_{48}$	$^{m}P_{48} + {}^{f}P_{48}$
49	$^{f}P_{49}$	$^{m}P_{49}$	$^{f}P_{49}$	$^{m}P_{49} + {}^{f}P_{49}$

Net Reproduction Rate, NRR. In GRR we assumed that women shall not die or become widow at any age between 15 and 49 years and that they would give birth to female babies according to the current age-specific fertility rates in the population. That is, if ^{f}N number of women start their reproductive life together (at age 15 years) and the same number of women end their reproductive career together (at age 49 years) and each of them produce female babies according to specific rates at each age group, then the average number of female births per woman is the GRR of the group. Any number of women can start their reproductive life together, but all of them would survive till the end of the reproductive period (zero mortality in ages 15–49 years) is too fanciful an assumption.

Growth of a population is related both to birth and death rates. This fact of the matter receives due attention in Net Reproduction Rate, NRR. Like GRR, NRR is also a hypothetical index. It estimates the average number of female babies born to mothers at the close of their reproductive career who start their reproductive life together and all of them strictly follow the current

Table 6.11 *Computation of GRR and other statistics from information on proportion of women in reproductive age group and age-specific fertility, 1981 and 2000 data*

	2000				1981			
Age of mothers	**Proportion to total female population**	**Size of female Population (million) N_i**	$_5i_x$	**Live births (million)**	**Proportion to total female population**	**Size of female population (million) N_i**	$_5i_x$	**Live births (million)**
15–19	10	49.574	0.0511	2.533	9.38	31.028	0.055	1.707
20–24	9.3	46.104	0.2187	10.083	8.82	29.175	0.187	5.458
25–29	8.1	40.155	0.1845	7.409	7.78	25.735	0.186	4.787
30–34	7.8	38.668	0.1008	3.898	6.49	21.468	0.137	2.941
35–39	6.6	32.719	0.0531	1.737	5.90	19.516	0.088	1.717
40–44	5.6	27.761	0.0217	0.602	5.03	16.639	0.046	0.765
45–49	4.4	21.812	0.0077	0.168	4.30	14.224	0.021	0.299
Sum	51.8	256.792	0.6376	25.430	47.70	157.785	0.72	17.672
Female population		495.74				330.79		
Total population		1027.02				685.19		
CBR		25.73				25.79		
GFR		102.92				112.00		
TFR		3188				3600		
GRR		1.56				1.76		

Source: Census data, 1981; SRS Statistical Report, 2000

age-specific birth and mortality rates. To compute NRR we need to construct a Life Table (construction of Life Table is discussed in Chapter 10) on the basis of age-specific mortality rates ($^f m_x$). $^f L_x$ column of the Life Table indicates the average size of the cohort ($^f l_0$) in the complete year between age x and $x + 1$. If $^f i_x$ is the age-specific female birth rate, then $^f i_x \times ^f L_x$ is the number of female babies born to mothers of age x. During the entire reproductive period (15–49) the total number female babies born would be $\sum_{15}^{49}(^f i_x \times ^f L_x)$. That is, $^f l_0$ number of women in their life span would give birth to average number of female babies

$$\frac{1}{^f l_0}\sum_{15}^{49}(^f i_x \times ^f L_x) \qquad \text{...(6.48)}$$

This measurement of population growth is referred to as Net Reproduction Rate, NRR. In computation of NRR, generally $^f l_x$ instead of $^f L_x$ is used.

$$\text{NRR} = \frac{1}{^f l_0}\sum_{15}^{49}(^f i_x \times ^f l_x) \qquad \text{...(6.49)}$$

$$=\sum_{15}^{49}({}^f i_x \times {}^f_x p_0) \quad \text{since}\left(\frac{{}^f l_x}{{}^f l_0}={}^f_x p_0\right)$$

${}^f_x p_0$ is called the *survivorship ratio* or *survival ratio* or *survivorship values* for females. When 5–year instead of 1–year age-specific fertility and mortality data are used, NRR is computed by the following formula:

$$\frac{1}{{}^f l_0}\sum_{15}^{49}({}^f_5 i_x \times {}^f_5 L_x) \quad ({}^f_5 L_x = {}^f L_x + {}^f L_{x+1} + {}^f L_{x+2} + {}^f L_{x+3} + {}^f L_{x+4}) \qquad \ldots (6.50)$$

If we compare the two equations (6.46) (GRR) and (6.48) (NRR), it would become evident that GRR is a special case of NRR where none in the cohort ${}^f l_0$ dies before completion of the reproductive period (${}^f l_x$ and ${}^f L_x = {}^f l_0$). In that case, ${}^f l_x / {}^f l_0 = {}^f L_x / {}^f l_0 = 1$ and the values of NRR and GRR become the same (NRR = GRR).

Table 6.12 *Computation of GRR and NRR (given ${}^f l_0$ = 10,000, F/(F+M) = (100/205)*

Age x	${}_5 i_x$	${}^f_5 L_x$	*Col.2×Col.3*	*Survival factor* ${}^f_5 L_x / {}^f_5 l_0$	*Col.2×Col.5*
(1)	*(2)*	*(3)*	*(4)*	*(5)*	*(6)*
15–19	0.0283	46857	1326.053	0.93714	0.02652
20–24	0.1251	46321	5794.757	0.92642	0.11590
25–29	0.1624	45926	7458.382	0.91852	0.14917
30–34	0.1213	45417	5509.082	0.90834	0.11018
35–39	0.0826	45013	3718.074	0.90026	0.07436
40–44	0.0411	44429	1286.032	0.88858	0.03652
45–49	0.0073	43975	321.018	0.87950	0.00642
Total	0.5681		25413.398		0.51907

$$\text{GRR} = 5\sum_{15}^{49} {}_5 i_x \times \frac{F}{F+M} = \frac{5 \times 0.5681 \times 100}{205} = 1.3866 \ (\textit{from col.}2)$$

$$\text{NRR} = \frac{1}{{}^f l_0}\sum({}_5 i_x \times {}^f_5 L_x) \times \frac{F}{F+M} = \frac{25{,}413.398 \times 100}{10{,}000 \times 205} = 1.2397 \ (\textit{from col.}4)$$

An alternative formula for computing NRR using col.6 information can also be used. There shall be some discrepancy, small though, between the two values of NRR.

$$\text{NRR} = \frac{5}{{}^f l_0}\sum_{15}^{49} {}_5 i_x \times {}^f l_{x+5} \times \frac{F}{F+M} = 5\sum_{15}^{49}({}_5 i_x \times {}^f_{x+5} p_0) \times \frac{F}{F+M}$$

$$= 5\sum({}_5 i_x \times \text{Survival factor}) \times \frac{F}{F+M} = \frac{5 \times 0.51907 \times 100}{205}$$

$$= 1.26602$$

When the value of NRR is 1, birth and death rates in the population has reached a stage where the new generation (female population) makes exact replacement of the previous generation. That is, a woman gives birth to only one female child on average before she dies. The population size under the circumstance does not change. NRR > 1 indicates that the population is growing, and NRR < 1 points to depopulation. Most of the countries are trying to attain NRR = 1 (TFR equivalent of 2.06 or 2.1) as quickly as possible. Migrants are excluded both from GRR and NRR (both deal exclusively with the cohort who started their life together). If there were reason to believe that there is substantial emigration or immigration, it would be wise not to use GRR and NRR for computing growth of a population. In fact, with high emigration or immigration or both, computation of population growth index becomes difficult.

Replacement index: In computation of NRR we need information about age-specific birth and death rates of the female population or their survival ratio, stationary population, etc. Often such information are not easily obtained. When such is the case, *replacement index* can be used as a fair substitute for NRR. Suppose, distribution of the population by age and sex is known but we have no information about the age-specific fertility in the population. We can compute Child Woman Ratio, CWR (6.1) either from the census data or data obtained from a large sample survey. Let this CWR is represented by R_a ('a' stands for actual population). We compute CWR from L_x column of Life Table ${}_4L_0 / {}_{49}^{f}L_{15}$ and call it R_s ('s' stands for Life Table stationary population). Both R_a and R_s must refer to the same time period. When the second one divides the first ratio, we get *Replacement Index.*

$$\text{Replacement Index} = \frac{R_a}{R_s} \qquad \text{...(6.51)}$$

This ratio can be equal to, greater than or less than 1 indicating the population is stationary, growing or declining. Population in a Life Table is stationary since every year the same number of babies is born and the same age-specific death rate is maintained over the years. The total number of deaths from all ages is the same as the number of babies born every year. CBR and CDR remain exactly balanced. When the data do not permit computation of NRR, Replacement Index can be used to obtain an approximate measure of replacement level in a population.

Table 6.13 *Computation of replacement index, India 1981 census data*

Women in 15–49 years age group (million)	157.8
Women population of all ages (million)	330.79
Proportion of female babies in 0–4 years age group	12.87 %
Number of female babies in 0–4 age years group (million)	37.78
$R_a = {}_4^fP_0 / {}_{49}^{f}P_{15}$	0.2394
$R_a = {}_4^fL_0 / {}_{49}^{f}L_{15}$	0.1692
Replacement Index R_a / R_s	1.4149

7 Fertility

Social and Economic Determinants

7.1 Introduction

Conceiving and giving birth to a baby are definitely very closely related to the biological demands and the physiological changes in the organism throughout the reproductive period. But when a girl would start her reproductive career and how many live births she was likely to give in her reproductive period is a matter that remains a couple's choice, most clearly dictated by social and economic demands, and not so much by the biological determinants. Malthus of course emphasized the importance of supply of food in controlling birth rate in a population. If the food production is plenty, the population would continue to increase fast provided there was no powerful check operating against such growth of population. Malthus admitted that uncontrolled birth rate cannot continue for long. The lack of balance between growth of population and growth of food production would result in many adversities and would bring down birth rate consistent with the level of food production. Malthus admitted that although food, shelter and supply of other basic necessities have significant roles in birth rates, there are other social, cultural, political and economic considerations that often would play important role in determining growth rate in a population.

The biological causes – general health of girls, various diseases, especially sex related, lack of reproductive power, infecundity, quality of food intake – definitely have something to do with childbearing; but the desire to have a child or not points to an uncertain relation with these physical factors. Even the presence or absence of some of these biological antecedents is often closely related to many social and environmental constraints. Population scientists today are unanimous that improved social and physical environment, state's greater attention to social and health sector – better education for all, improved health care, lower infant, child and maternal mortality – are some of the reasons behind check in growth rate of population. Better nutrition and health care of girls have significantly improved the childbearing potential of girls in modern era. But with improved living standards and great increase in expectation of life and declining infant mortality rate, the birth rate in the general population has been falling steadily. Social and cultural factors have a decisive role in arresting population growth rate throughout the world. We first take up the biology of fertility and then see how the social and other factors influence fertility.

7.2 Fecundity and Fertility

The extent of fecundity, which is the biological potential and the physiological capacity to participate in reproduction, in a population is rarely known. The absence of this potential is infecundity or sterility. A girl in the reproductive age, on the other hand, exhibits fertility – the actual ability to give birth to a baby. A fertile woman is one who has ever given a live birth. No significant study has been carried out to ascertain fecundity of the girl population in various age groups. Fecundity of a girl is established beyond doubt only when she produces a baby. But that does not mean that a girl who does not produce a baby is infecund. A girl's fecundity varies according to the monthly cycle.

Women are fertile only about seven days in each *menstrual cycle*. Ovulation occurs at about the fourteenth day of their menstrual cycle, this obviously being the most fertile time for females. The exact point of ovulation varies however. If the egg is not fertilized by the male's sperm, the egg will break down within 1–2 days into its components and be reabsorbed by the body. However, sperm can survive for a longer period, five days. So, a successful conception can result during seven days of the female cycle; five days before and two days after ovulation.

The study of this cycle is important when one is trying to prevent conception by 'rhythm' method. The 'cycle' is temporarily stopped immediately following a birth. In this 'post-partum' period it is not possible for a girl to conceive. The length of post-partum infecundity is related to the extent of breast feeding or 'lactation'. Some social and religious taboos in most society prevent intercourse following birth of a baby. There is a large gap between the actual fertility level attained by a girl and her actual physiological capacity to produce babies. This is true in all societies, even among primitive peoples, in all times. In the more economically and educationally advanced people, the difference is much wider since they invariably adopt some birth control measure. However, producing babies is related to the sex health of either of the couple. A girl may be fecund, but the partner could be partially or fully infertile. The proportion of couples by whom children cannot be born is however very small in the population.

7.3 Infertility and Miscarriages

With a rise in postponement/termination of pregnancy (by using fertility preventive drugs or by some other means), can create an infertility problem. Miscarriage risks are more with elderly women, about 30 percent between 35 and 39 years and above 50 percent beyond 42 years. Birth defects, especially those involving chromosome number and arrangement, also increase with the age of the mother. According to the March of Dimes (March of Dimes is the name of a United States health charity), at age 25, a woman has about a 1-in-1,250 chance of having a baby with Down syndrome (abnormal condition of a child); at age 30, a 1-in-1,000 chance; at age 35, a 1-in-400 chance; at age 40, a 1-in-100 chance; and at 45, a 1-in-30 chance.

A couple is said to be infertile if the couple has not conceived after 12 months of contraceptive-free intercourse if the female is under the age of 34 or the couple has not conceived after 6 months of contraceptive-free intercourse if the female is over the age of 35 or the female is incapable of carrying a pregnancy to term. Couples with *primary infertility* are those who never have been able to conceive. There are incidences of *secondary infertility* that have difficulty in conceiving after already having conceived and carried a normal pregnancy. Technically, secondary infertility cannot be ascribed if there has been a change of partners. Some women are infertile since their ovaries do not mature and release eggs.

Generally speaking, it is estimated that one in every seven couples has problems in conceiving. This is more or less true in most countries independent of the level of the country's development. Women become less fertile as they get older, especially beyond age 35. The effect of age on men's fertility career is less clear.

In about 15 percent of cases the infertility investigations show no abnormalities. Abnormalities are likely to be present but not detected by current methods. Possible problems could be that the egg is not released at the optimum time for fertilization, that it may not enter the fallopian tube, sperm may not be able to reach the egg, fertilization may fail to occur, etc. It is increasingly recognized that egg quality is of critical importance and women of advanced maternal age have eggs of reduced capacity for normal and successful fertilization.

7.4 Fertility Related Problems in Ageing Population

Women's fertility peaks around the age of 23–24, and often declines after 30. With a rise in women postponing pregnancy, this can create an infertility problem. It has been observed that 75 percent of woman at age 30 would become pregnant within a year even if no fertility drug is used. The same drops to 66 percent when the woman is 35 and only 40 percent when she is 40. The miscarriage rates increase with ageing population.

Erectile dysfunction increases with age, but fertility does not decline in men as sharply as it does in women. There are examples of males being fertile even beyond 90 years. The fertility decline in men is mainly due to decline in sperm count with age. This does not correlate directly with any absolute decline in fertility, since there are still enough sperm cells left for fertilization. Sperm count declines with age, with men aged 50–80 years producing sperm at an average rate of 75 percent compared with men aged 20–50 years. Aging sperm can be a significant and even the sole cause of severe health and developmental hazards in offspring, including autism, schizophrenia, and cancer. The older the father, the higher is the risk of problems.

7.5 Indirect Social Factors Regulating Fertility

It must be understood that every means of fertility control has to be seen in the backdrop of the social and cultural heritage of a particular society. Even two societies may follow the same method of birth control, but their origins as also the purposes could be very different. In a more orthodox society as in India, the increase in the age at marriage of girls would curtail the effective reproductive period and bring down the average fertility level of girls for the simple reason that premarital sex relation is a taboo in such society. The increase in age at marriage in the West may not have the same effect on fertility as their counterparts in more orthodox countries. Free sex and sex experience before marriage is gradually becoming a part of their life style.

Taking individually, we shall find some correlation between fertility and most of our social and economic practices. But prediction on the basis of such relations may fall far short of the actual. One can easily predict what the volume of a gaseous substance would be since we know that there are only two predictor variables – pressure and temperature. But behind any social event (birth, for all purposes, is to be regarded as more a social event than merely biologically determined), there are a host of variables which make any prediction from a combination of only a few very difficult. In social and demographic analysis, a researcher selects only a few important variables, either from his personal experience or from studies by other researchers in similar areas, eliminating many others that are not considered important enough or for which sufficiently reliable data are lacking. In fertility studies we can keep aside premarital and extra-marital relations from our study design. But this factor often will have some substantial role in discussions relating to fertility in other societies. Moreover, identification of variables and measurements thereof in social sciences and demography are still lacking the fineness and strength that we associate with other sciences. Therefore, we must remember these formidable hurdles while we direct our attention to some of the more indirect and direct social and economic factors thought to be important in any discussion on fertility. We shall discuss how the *intermediate variables* (suggested by Davis and Blake and modified/simplified by others) play critical role in causal analysis of change in fertility in a population. We discuss some of the formidable constructs that are discussed in most fertility analysis across populations from most countries.

Marriage rate: Childbirth though is not necessarily related to formal marriage, most societies despise childbirth outside marriage relations. Marriage still is regarded as one of the most sacred institutions in all societies. Sex relations violating the sanctity of the marriage bed nevertheless is deplored in all old cultures. Marriage is that solemn institution which hold the human civilization together, assures children resulting from the wedlock to receive proper attention and care from their biological parents in their formative years.

Though marriage is universal, most countries have certain regulations about who ought not to marry, at what minimum age they should marry and how the problems arising out of an unsuccessful marriage could be resolved. The proportion of people remaining unmarried is rising, most possibly due to fast pace of life and increasing complexity in our entire socio-economic endeavor.

Marriage rate should not be looked upon as a current experience of a society. All current marriages have roots in the varying marriage experiences of the past generations. The proportion married in a particular age at a given time is constituted of the survivals of married individuals from earlier years plus those married at that age in the study year. Marriage rate refers to the proportion of persons in a particular age group married in the current year. Marriage rates therefore are subjected to wider fluctuations than *proportions married.* There is a good degree of constancy in the proportion of married people in most age groups. Thus, proportion married in age group 50–60 tend to be constant in time though there could be no new marriages taking place in that age group. At advanced ages, proportions married are affected mostly by mortality experiences. On the other hand, proportion married in a lower age group may suddenly drop (because of strict implementation of marriage laws) and in some other age segment the proportion may go high since all those who could not be given to marriage earlier because of legal implications becomes eligible to marry once crossing that age limit. Sometimes the analysis is carried out on 'ever-married' persons; this sum is obtained by combining married, widowed and divorced, and is not appreciably influenced by mortality at the older ages.

Marriage rates can be used to compare influence of social changes on marriage experience in a particular age group with the experiences of the same age group in previous or subsequent years. Hence, marriage rates are better pointer to immediate future, whereas the proportions married in an age group refer to long term trends in the population.

If we take a look at what is happening in India in this regard, it would appear that current marriage rate has declined in spite the fact that population is still growing fast. As of 1991, of the 192,602,000 married women in India (145,401,000 from rural areas), 30,356,000 (22,446,000 from rural areas) girls got married during 1981–86 and 28,247,000 (21,193,000 in rural area) during 1986–91. Whereas 49.3 percent of those who got married during 1981–86 were below 18 years of age, the same marginally dropped to 45.4 in 1986–91. Even though there was 7 percent drop in incidences of marriages below 18 years in urban area from 1981–86 figure, still 29.7 percent of girls got married earlier than the stipulated minimum age at marriage of girls in 1986–91. A major shift has however been noticed in the proportion of married girls in the two age groups 15–19 and 20–24. From 69.57 percent of married girls in 15–19 age group in 1961, the percentage dropped to 35.28 in 1991. A significant drop was also noted in the next age group. These observations are indicators that India is on the right course of population growth correction.

Among the married girls in 1961 about 15 percent were in the age group 15–19 years. This proportion came down to 9 percent in 1991. Of the 54.5 percent ever married females in 2000, only 4 percent belonged to age group 15–19 years. In urban area it was only 2.3 percent.

Table 7.1 *Percentage of currently married females to all females in India for different age-groups over the years*

Year	*Age group*						
	15–19	*20–24*	*25–29*	*30–34*	*35–44*	*45–49*	*15–49*
1961	69.57	91.76	94.17	91.43	82.56	69.73	84.42
1971	55.41	88.83	94.95	94.00	88.07	78.03	83.40
1981[a]	43.44	84.46	94.35	94.86	90.76	83.15	80.74
1991[b]	35.28	81.81	93.97	95.14	92.75	87.56	80.18

Source: Office of the Registrar General, India
(a) Excludes Assam
(b) Excludes Jammu & Kashmir

Whereas the proportion of married couples in 15–19 (age of wife) has progressively come down, both in rural and urban areas, a little more in the latter, no such trend is noticed with other age groups except in 40–44 where the proportion has marginally improved. Marriage rates expectedly are highest in the 20–24 age group. Marriage rates in other higher age groups are also more than what are observed in 15–19 age group.

Decline in death rates: Since the middle of the twentieth century death rates all over the world have declined rapidly. In the last 50/60 years food production, transport and communication network have improved greatly both in developed and developing countries. Even some of the developing countries have lowered their death rates so much so that they are almost at par with the achievements in death control in the developed countries. Because of faster control over death rates, people in the developed countries willingly accepted a small family norm and adopted suitable means to control birth. Lower infant mortality rate (IMR) and high standard of living have seen a huge increase in the expectation of life in the developed countries. The enormous improvement in life expectancy has given them the option of having a small family as well. General decline in mortality, more specifically the rapid reduction of infant and child mortality, probably has the most significant role in triggering fertility transition. Analysis of fertility and mortality decline in most developing countries in the period 1950 to 2000 suggests that the fertility transition begins if relative cohort size begins to increase among young labor market entrants. The popular image of developing countries tends to be one of ever-increasing relative cohort size, given high fertility rates. High mortality rates among children and young people imply relative cohort size does not begin to increase until well after the start of decline in infant mortality. Once it begins to increase, in country after country the fertility transition has also begun.

In the developing countries the death rates have declined much faster than what had been observed in the developed countries. What the developed countries could achieve in a period extending over 300 years, the developing countries could achieve the same in less than 60 years. But that has not happened with birth rates. The developed countries too faced the similar problem when their death rates started to decline but with a difference. The population base for these countries was very small in those days, and therefore the absolute increase in the size of population was not too much of a problem for them. But the same kind of transition in the developing countries has been associated with a very large population base. For example, if India could achieve the type of death and birth rate she has today some 50/60 years ago, the annual absolute increase in numbers would have been 4 million or so as against current absolute increase of about 16 million per annum. It is for this reason that the developing countries must bring down their birth rates as quickly as possible, most surely by the next 15–20 years.

Age at marriage: Malthus though was in favor of a small excess in population to ensure competitiveness in the labor market and urged people to keep up the sanctity of marriage, he advocated women to marry as late as possible, preferably not before 28 years. Even today most countries discourage any birth violating the marriage norms. Generally, the reproductive period of a girl is 15–49 years. That is why many countries are trying to increase the age at marriage thereby curtailing the effective reproductive period. In some countries the minimum age at marriage of girls has already been raised to very high (25 years in China, for example). In some others, along with the increase in age at marriage restriction has been imposed on childbirth per couple (again China, for example). In fact, India and China were approximately at the same level of population growth in late 1970s. Whereas India was growing at around an average of 2.0 percent per annum, China was growing at 1.3 percent during 1975–99. The projected average annual population growth in China between 1999 and 2015 is 0.7 percent vis-à-vis 1.3 percent in India. The more important parameters behind population growth rate are life expectancy at birth and IMR. China has outshone India on both counts. Table 7.2 shows the achievement of the two countries in a period of about 30 years on these important parameters.

Table 7.2 *Some comparative statistics for China and India*

	Expectation of life at birth		*Infant mortality rate*		*Under five mortality rate*	
	1970–1975	*1995–2000*	*1970*	*1999*	*1970*	*1999*
China	63.2	69.8	85	33	120	41
India	50.3	62.3	127	70	202	98
World	59.9	66.4	96	56	147	80

Source: Human Development Report 2001, UNDP

Although India was the first country to officially adopt family planning as early as 1951, the political compulsions of parliamentary democracy prevented it from employing any stern measure to implement its policy prescriptions. India, after long deliberations, increased the minimum age at marriage of girls to 18 years in 1976 although the population experts have urged that this should be raised to at least 21 years. Even though the minimum age at marriage Act for men and women has been passed long back, there is hardly any official mechanism to ensure that the Act is not violated by anyone. Unless registration of all marriages is made mandatory (the Apex Court in India has asked the governments to develop mechanisms for strict implementation of the Marriage Act), people would continue to violate the age norms for marriage. China could implement once a decision was taken at the highest political level; India could only ask people to realize the potential benefit they could derive when they adopted a small family norm. The choice to adopt or not to adopt small family norm was left to the wisdom of individual couples.

In the West, people generally marry late. There is some indication that childlessness is more among those that marry late. In fact, the number of childless couples is on the rise in Western countries. Although infecundity in the general population often is well below 5 percent, some studies have shown that infecundity is more among those who marry late (25 years or more). It has also been observed in these studies that sterile couples (either or both) are more in urban population than in rural population. Urban people because of their better educational background not only marry late, they use contraceptives and abortions quite frequently to prevent unwanted births. Some scientists believe that use of oral contraceptives for a prolonged period and frequent abortions could lead to sterility among women. It has also been observed that chances of miscarriage are more with very young and aged mothers. The Mysore Population Study as also various rounds of NSS and other sample surveys in India show that the average number of children born to women decline with the increase in their age at marriage.

In the Vedic period Aryan boys and girls were initiated (given sacred thread) at the age of 8 years. With time the Aryans started marrying non-Aryan girls who did not know Sanskrit and therefore were denied sacred initiation and religious rites. Slowly, the age of sacred initiation became the age of their marriage. Although this virgin marriage has generally been discarded in modern India, girls in villages even today get married quite early. Lack of education, early marriage, superstition and ambivalence towards family welfare and birth control are key reasons behind the high birth rate among women, especially in rural India.

Polygamy: Not very long ago polygamy was a common practice among males in India and many other countries. Most countries today have strong laws against marrying a second girl if the man already had a wife by an earlier marriage. Polyandry, unlike polygamy, had remained confined to a few tribal groups (Toda and Janusari, for example). What relation polygamy (or polyandry) has on birth rate is not clear. Even if there is any, their impact on population growth in a country could be only very marginal. In India, polygamy was fairly common among higher caste socially and economically influential persons even a century back. Giving a girl in marriage in such families (regarded as "kulin") often was considered a status symbol. There are plenty of examples of the practice of polygamy (and even polyandry) in our epics. Polygamy in the Muslim community was prevalent even in the recent past. The rulers of India and native states often had large number of wives.

Polygamous marriage, however, has to be seen in the context of the effects such marriages have on procreation. This has to be seen in the context of age of the male person and the possible frequency of intercourse with his wives. To earn the "kulin" status, the male person had to work hard for achieving financial and social power. In most instances, the age gap between husband and some of his wives was 50/60 years. Often the aged husband may have become impotent because of his age. Polygamous marriage also prevented frequent union with all the wives. Although the males could have many children from their different marriages, the average number of children born per wife was bound to be fairly small.

Separation and divorce: Separation and divorce are common phenomena in the West. Separation can happen shortly after marriage or even after a long conjugal life. Separation and divorce had never been an important issue in our traditional family culture. Although legislative measures have been adopted to ease the end of unhappy marriages, it is only among the educated upper middle class people that the issue has gained some acceptance in recent times. Whereas the incidences of separation and divorce in the Western world can be taken up as an index of marriage failure, the lower incidences of separation and divorce in the East cannot be regarded as the success of marriage systems in these countries. Tradition and culture play very important role in mitigating many disharmonies that often would develop among the couples.

The nature of impact separation and divorce could have on the birth rate of a country or a segment of the population would depend upon:

1. the rate of incidences of divorce and separation (in India, it may not constitute more than 1 percent of all marriages);
2. the age of the husband and wife at the time of separation;
3. years of conjugal life before the separation takes place;
4. the rate of remarriage after the separation (very few among women remarry in India); and
5. the years after separation/divorce such remarriage takes place.

Some surveys have been conducted in different countries on the impact of separation on birth rates. Predictably, it has a negative impact on birth rate. Of course this largely would depend upon if the separated couples would lead a celibate life in the time interval between separation and remarriage.

Widowhood: The resistance against widow remarriage has eased considerably in most countries. Widow remarriage is legally protected in India. In spite of legislative support the incidences of widow remarriage in India and other orthodox countries is not quite popular yet. Widow marriage is comparatively more popular among tribal, lower caste groups and in some religious communities.

While trying to relate widow marriage to birth rate, the following issues must be carefully looked into:

1. the ratio of the widow and currently married persons in the population;
2. the age at which the girl becomes widow;
3. the number of live births given before the girl became widow;
4. the number of years elapsed before the widow remarriage takes place; and
5. the rate of widow remarriage.

Social perception of widow remarriage differs greatly between countries and between ethnic groups of the same country. There was a time in India when widows did not have the right to live what to speak of their remarriage. They were forcibly burnt on the pyre of their late husband. The Act to abolish *satee* was passed in 1829. As against the practice of *satee*, an altogether different system was also in vogue where the widow was asked to marry the brother of her deceased husband (levirate system). In the matriarchal family, widow marriage rate is comparatively high. In spite of the Hindu Marriage Act, 1955 we seldom see the remarriage of widows. According to 1951 census report there were 123 widows per thousand females. The rate must have come down in the last 60 years. Still there are more than three times as many widows as there are widowers in the Indian population. Lowered death rates and increased expectation of life all over the world has brought down the proportion of widows (also the widowers) in the female population.

In the beginning of the twentieth century, about 18 percent of all women in India were widows. After 100 years this ratio has come down to less than 8 percent. Widows in the reproductive age group (15–49 years) today constitute only 2.1 percent of the female population of all ages (1.9

percent in urban area). The percentage of widowed/divorced/separated females of aged 10+ in 2000 was 10.3 (3.1 for males). The maximum percentage of widowed/divorce separated females among the larger states are in Tamil Nadu (14.2) followed by Andhra Pradesh (13.8), Karnataka (13.5) and Kerala (12.6) – all from the Southern region. The minimum of such incidences are observed in Haryana (7.4) and Bihar (7.6). Among the females aged 15+ such percentages are 12.3 for rural and 11.6 for urban population. The percentage of widows or divorced or separated in age 15+ was in the range of 14.0 to 16.1 in the southern states and least in Haryana (8.7), Bihar (9.3), Uttar Pradesh (9.3) and Rajasthan (9.4).

Post-partum abstinence: Sex relation during the period when the child is breast fed is a taboo in most societies. This period sometimes extend to 2 years or more. The more the period is prolonged, the more is its impact on fertility. In orthodox families the mother and the child remain under direct care and supervision of the mother-in-law or some elderly lady of the house. With the disintegration of the joint/extended family system, this physical separation of the nursing mother from the husband is no longer possible. Breast-feeding delays the restart of the menstruation cycle. The greater the delay in the restart of the cycle, the larger would be its impact on birth rate. Breast-feeding today often has become a forgotten chapter in child rearing in many educated families. Bottle feeding is replacing breast-feeding although the child specialists all over the world advocate that "there is no substitute to breast milk".

Menstruation and abstinence: Sexual relation with a menstruating girl is banned in every society. But the abstinence often is recommended for different reasons. Some look at intercourse in this time 'a dirty affair'; others look at the menstruating girl as impure. In orthodox Hindu families women at this state of physical condition are not allowed to perform any religious rites; they even are not allowed to go to the kitchen and are debarred from many other such things. The period is too small to have any significant impact on birth rate. Even under normal circumstances, people do not enjoy intercourse everyday.

Celibacy: Some people in all countries do not marry throughout their life. However, they constitute only a small minority in the total eligible population. Every society encourages people to marry and lead a normal family life. Only the physically and mentally handicapped and those suffering from some serious diseases (AIDS, epilepsy, for example) are not encouraged to marry. Although celibacy is generally discouraged in all societies, in some religion (Buddhism, for example) people are asked to honor celibacy up to certain age. In Vedic Age, celibacy was urged while boys and girls were going through education and training at the house of their Master (Guru). This increased the age at marriage both for boys and girls and had some effect on their reproductive performance.

The proportion of unmarried people in the population in most countries is rising. It is around 10 percent of all eligible persons. The pressure of economy and increased complexity in social relations is thought of as possible explanations for the rise in proportion of unmarried persons. The Buddhist and Catholic priests do not marry. Even among Hindu monks (*sadhus*), marriage is not frequent except in certain sects. People may not marry for some personal reasons. But that does not mean that they do not have any sexual relation. In the present day society, many men and women live together without going through any contractual agreement for marriage. The number of unmarried fathers and mothers is on the rise in the West.

Frequency of coitus: Sexual intercourse does not happen every day. Health condition, mental disturbance, excessive physical activity, family quarrel, etc. often would dictate sex behavior of a person. Sex is so personal and sensitive an issue that no major fact finding survey on frequency of sexual intercourse can be undertaken. The frequency of sexual intercourse is likely to be more in open society as in the West than in an orthodox society as in India. Even if we accept that West is ahead of East in this respect, it cannot be said that the probability of conception per coitus is more in the West simply because of the fact that contraceptives are more frequently used by males and females in Western society than in a traditional orthodox society.

Education: In the modern world scenario, the developed countries have displayed remarkable change both in their economic pursuits and in social relations. This has happened because of wide spread education base in these countries. The attitudinal change that started with industrial revolution has further been reinforced by spread of education and professional training. That we can control many aspects of nature and that nature can be made to work for the wellbeing of mankind is no longer a philosophic concern. It has been proved as a certainty without any reservation. If the uncertainty of nature can be won over, why not a radical change in our primitive ideas about birth and death and many other aspects of social relations? Education has largely freed us from the shackles of primitive ideas and some of the age-old conventions.

As we look into the demographic history of the world population, we see that the countries having persistently encouraged education and expansion of knowledge horizon amongst their masses are the ones that have succeeded in scientific and technological innovations, industrialization and high standard of living among its people. Birth control has been most successful in these countries even without much campaign for it; average annual population growth rate is one of the lowest in these countries. Education has remained the kingpin in smooth demographic transition. The statistical relations that are found to exist between many dependent and independent variables often are largely due to the presence of education as moderator or intermediate variable. In the world spectrum we see that the countries having high standard of living also have higher educational attainments. The more the country is developed educationally and economically, the less is the average birth rate of its couples. Better economic health leads to acquisition of better education; the better the level of education the better is the freedom to select appropriate job. Higher and better education gives a man freedom of thought. It enables a man to look at things from wider perspectives – the fallout of uncontrolled population growth on the limited resources on which we have to sustain life for a greater length of time.

How education helps us directly and indirectly to control birth rate can be summed up as under:

1. Education delays marriage, especially of girls;
2. Education delays entry into employment market;
3. Delay of entry into employment market delays marriage;
4. Education changes one's tastes, generates higher aspirations;
5. Education helps one to appreciate the social changes;
6. Education helps inculcate a faith in one's abilities and potentials;
7. Education brings in an attitudinal change, gives him/her the necessary flexibility to fast adapt to changing circumstances and innovations;
8. It helps develop a mental set to look beyond self;
9. Education encourages more migration and prepares the person to become a global citizen.

Many studies have found a significant effect of rising women's status, especially the price effect of their rising wages. Through an increased ability to work outside the home and contribute to household income, they definitely stand a better chance to contribute to family's planning decisions, especially in family planning decisions – and perhaps even more importantly they no longer have to rely on their reproductive capacity to justify their own existence. Education is key to this changing status of women.

Many surveys have found a U-shaped effect of education on fertility: both low and high levels of education produce relatively high fertility, while middle levels result in the lowest levels of fertility. Often the explanation given for this observation is that the first few years of education contribute to women's basic knowledge of nutrition, the causes of disease, and the functioning of their own bodies, and as a result produce a healthier population in which mortality and morbidity levels are reduced. Middle levels of education then provide the "price effect" as women's potential earnings rise – and also enable women to understand and accept a wider array of contraceptive methods. And at the highest levels of education it is possible that the "income effect" of women's

Table 7.3 *ASFR by level of education of women, India 2000*

Age group	*Education level of women*								
	Illiterate	*No formal education*	*Below primary*	*Primary*	*Middle*	*Class X*	*Class XII*	*Graduate & above*	*Total literate*
1	*2*	*3*	*4*	*5*	*6*	*7*	*8*	*9*	*10*
					Total				
15–19	96.1	94.5	67.6	34.4	23.4	18.7	14.3	22.5	35.0
20–24	289.4	284.5	298.1	194.6	187.5	143.5	87.4	94.5	191.5
25–29	229.8	195.5	212.2	149.7	144.9	143.9	124.3	126.8	159.8
30–34	134.9	109.7	90.1	60.5	55.7	61.3	62.4	63.2	70.9
35–39	78.4	52.5	32.9	17.9	20.7	17.7	22.1	24.8	25.9
40–44	32.6	17.1	9.7	6.1	7.2	3.7	3.0	4.5	7.8
45–49	11.4	6.4	2.7	1.3	2.4	1.0	0.5	0.0	2.3
					Rural				
15–19	98.5	94.3	71.5	35.0	25.1	21.2	18.3	16.7	39.3
20–24	288.2	268.2	300.0	191.6	183.5	142.5	96.7	87.6	202.0
25–29	230.6	184.1	211.4	145.3	146.7	132.0	125.1	123.9	161.9
30–34	134.6	107.8	89.1	59.6	58.2	55.4	56.0	67.0	72.4
35–39	81.6	54.5	35.7	21.0	23.0	21.0	25.3	33.7	30.2
40–44	33.7	18.6	11.0	7.2	6.0	3.5	6.0	11.2	9.5
45–49	12.3	6.4	3.0	2.0	1.0	1.8	0.6	0.0	2.7
					Urban				
15–19	75.4	96.9	49.1	32.4	19.5	15.2	11.2	30.5	24.4
20–24	299.6	383.9	291.3	203.3	196.6	145.0	79.4	97.6	170.6
25–29	223.9	257.8	214.4	159.7	141.4	158.8	123.6	127.9	156.1
30–34	137.8	119.7	93.3	62.3	51.5	67.7	67.5	62.0	68.2
35–39	58.3	44.6	26.0	12.1	17.5	14.9	20.2	22.8	19.7
40–44	25.0	10.7	6.4	4.1	8.8	3.8	1.8	3.2	5.5
45–49	6.3	6.3	2.2	0.3	4.0	0.5	0.4	0.0	1.8

Source: Sample Registration System Statistical Report 2000

wages – which enables them to purchase low-cost replacements for their own time with children – might become more significant.

The following age-specific fertility rate by level of education of women and residence in India, 2000 clearly shows how education and urbanization can change our age-old beliefs in traditions.

Occupation: Traditional occupations vis-à-vis modern technology based jobs have some differential role on births. Modern industrial occupations demand higher level of general education and special professional training. The industries attract people from all social strata, varying in social background, mentality and taste. A new culture – industrial culture – develops due to close interaction between peoples from various backgrounds in the industrial environment. The organized sector has developed and expanded with the modern occupations – in the manufacturing sector, trade and commerce, IT and telecom and other service sectors. The nature of these occupations is such that people are asked to move constantly, within the country or abroad. These occupations have given man a type of space totally different from the one in which he was reared and nurtured. Life has become fast – he/she has to move thousands of kilometers with a short notice. The joint and extended families have been replaced by nuclear families. With this, all the responsibility for rearing children has fallen squarely on the shoulders of their biological parents. These developments have lead to 'singles culture'. The motto of this new culture is: think fast, move fast and leave all those habits and possessions that detract you from adapting to the demands of the fast changing economy.

Education and dedicated training had little or no role in traditional occupations. People could learn the trade merely by observing and imitating what the elders in the family or the villagers do. These vocations descended smoothly from one generation to another and became a family occupation. People in traditional occupations lived at the same place for generations denying the experiences of the changing world. They continue to live in isolation like that in a remote island. Although the joint family system is disintegrating fast, the shadow of the ideals of the joint family looms still large on them.

Agriculture related occupations still value children as assets for the family – often they are the poor man's only asset. The environment created through generations demand that the child of a farmer becomes a farmer, a weaver a weaver. Such an environment demands that the children start their apprenticeship even before they had crossed their childhood. These children become a part of the production system early and start contributing to family income directly or indirectly. The mentality that is associated with traditional occupation is not conducive to adopt innovations and new initiatives. Modern agricultural practices along with impact of radio, TV and other mass media have changed some of the traditional ideas and values. Science and technology and specially extension of health care facilities in rural areas have changed the way of life quite a bit. But because of poor education base of the rural population, the developing countries are yet to get a real break-through in birth control. Children still remain the 'gift of God' to them.

Income: We have seen that Easterlin's model focuses on "birth cohorts": individuals who were born in the same year or period and who will thus experience all of the various stages of the life cycle at about the same time. A crucial aspect is the size of a given cohort relative to that of its parents' – the "relative cohort size". Relative cohort size is a direct function of fertility rates at any given time: high (low) fertility leads to large (small) relative cohort size. Studies have demonstrated that the primary effect of relative birth cohort size is on male relative income: the ratio of young men's earnings relative to their fathers' earnings. The less experienced young workers are not perfect substitutes in the labor market for older, more experienced workers, and the "production function" is sensitive to the balance of these two types of workers. The wages of oversupplied group goes down relative to the undersupplied group. Even during strong economic growth, wages of both groups might rise, but the average wages of the oversupplied group will not rise as rapidly as those of the undersupplied group.

It is a common presumption that individuals are ultimately concerned with *per capita disposable income*, relative to their desired standard of living (Easterlin). In the attempt to close the gap between income and aspirations, members of relatively large cohorts will be inclined to make a number of adjustments: increased female labor force participation, delayed/reduced marriage, if already married couples would prefer to have fewer children in order to spread their income over fewer heads. When a pressurized generation chooses to delay/forego marriage, more young women will be at risk of non-marital pregnancy. This factor, together with delayed or reduced fertility within marriage, also a function of relative income, means that an increased proportion of all births will be outside of marriage. This perhaps explains to an extent the rush of out-of-wedlock fertility that happened in the US since the 1970s, as well as its marked decline in the 1990s. An individual evaluates his/her earning potential as dictated by the market. Given this level of personal earnings, an individual then decides how many people can be supported on that income: self only? self plus spouse? self and spouse with children? Per capita disposable income is what is available to the individual and his/her dependents after making these demographic choices.

A 1995 Gallup Poll indicated a surprising tenacity among Americans, in terms of traditional gender roles: it reported that "nearly half of the Americans surveyed said the ideal family structure was one in which only the father earned the living and the mother stayed home with the children" (T. Lewin 1994). Some other studies (Diane Macunovich 1995) confirm that only the male partner's economic resources affect the transition [from cohabitation] to marriage, with positive economic situations accelerating marriage and deterring separation. Several surveys of college students between 1990 and 1995 suggest that nearly 90 percent of students (not much sex difference) aged 18 to 21 expected to have at least two children. On average the young women *do not* expect to delay childbearing until after they are settled in a career. A surprising 85 percent expect to have their first baby by age 30, 96 percent by age 33. The study reported that the young women on average would work about 43 hours a week before having children, but then cut back the average to about 22 hours per week when children were under three years old. Young men generally shared these expectations for their wives, although a high proportion of them would like their wives to drop out of the labor force altogether, or work 20 hours per week or less while children were young. Respondents were asked to rank the following possible career arrangements for parents in the presence of young children:

(a) both parents work full time outside the home
(b) both parents work part time
(c) wife full time and husband part time
(d) husband full time and wife part time
(e) husband full time and wife at home
(f) wife full time and husband at home

Men ranked (d) and (e) highest and (a) lowest, while women ranked (b) highest, (d) second highest and (a) lowest.

The two most popular models (*price of time* and *relative income*) dealt mainly with income potential of male members. But many researches show a good relationship between fertility and female labor force participation. It is often claimed that low birth rates have resulted from women's increased labor force participation; but there are others who direct our attention to the other way around: *fertility declined, and therefore women were "freed up" to enter the labor force*. Often people assume that changes in the female wage were the causal factor: women's wages rose, attracting women into the labor forcing them to reduce their fertility through mechanisms discussed in the "price of time" model. This is rather a simplistic argument for the relationship between female labor wages and reduced fertility. However, one must remember that changes in wage often are exogenous – increases in wage are caused by women themselves: their level of education and experience in the labor market. Wage earning by women definitely has a negative impact on fertility.

The relationship between income and fertility is really very complex. The type of relationship (often negative) found between income and fertility at the macro level does not reflect the pattern of relationships that are observed for segments pegged at different ranges of absolute per capita income. When the disposable income is very high, the couple may decide to go in for a larger family by buying goods and services from the market. When children are considered as economic assets, couples may decide to produce more babies knowing that they would not have to spend much on children's education and upbringing.

Urban-rural differential: Birth rate among urban people is significantly less than that among rural people. This is true both of developed and developing countries. Some of the key differentials between the two groups of people are: level of education, modern occupation, dependence on monthly salary, health facility, residential accommodation, standard of living, facilities for education of children, fast pace of life, stiff competition, recreational facilities, exposure to mass media, etc. – all in favor of urban people. Urban people are confronted with a composite culture since people from different regions and various social strata, religions and languages concentrate in urban areas. A large majority of urban population are migrants. They adopt many of the customs of the indigenous people including the language. The indigenous population too absorbs some of the customs of the in-migrants. The urban people have a better opportunity to know the cultural diversity of the country.

In urban-centric civilization, culture and life style are not only complex, the life is very fast too. There are vast complexes of opportunities, which an educated and intelligent person can utilize to earn more, obtain recognition from others and improve upon one's social status. Village life is still simple, easy paced and without much competition. Urban way of life is a constant struggle for existence and survival. Only the fittest can survive and prosper there. A person needs a different kind of mind-set to flourish and strengthen his position in urban society. It is a journey through a difficult terrain – one needs to travel light under the given situation.

Religious faith: Historically, fertility declines show how important cultural and ethnic factors are in determining the responsiveness of fertility levels to socioeconomic changes. There seems to be better communication about fertility matters within than between ethnic groups. Major world's religions vary in their emphasis on the value of children and their prescriptions regarding contraception and family size. Likewise, ethnic groups differ for historical and cultural reasons in their receptiveness to Western values concerning work, achievement, and economic advancement, all of which are intricately related to fertility behavior. For this reason, any comparison between countries must take into consideration the ethnicity, religion and culture more generally. The pioneers of family planning movement all over the world have remained the targets for aggression and denunciation by the more orthodox religious institutions. Except for past few centuries, the history of human population has been a story of constant struggle for survival. 'To live and let live' has been the motto of all human races in their fight against nature that has at times been unduly harsh on mankind. Religion, which gives solace in despair and direction and meaning to life, cannot remain silent on issues relating to survival. To bring in discipline, harmony and order in society, to inculcate a relation of friendship and trust among all peoples and to look for something beyond what this physical world can offer, man invented religion. All these religions articulate some truth that crosses the boundaries of time and space; they address to many other aspects that are aimed at teaching a common man how to discharge his duties and responsibilities to his family, neighbors and all that make our existence on this earth so attractive and meaningful.

With the passage of time, some of these preaching's were amended, some abandoned altogether. Religion must keep pace with changing nature of the world – its peoples and its physical and social environment. Interpretation of religion must have a close link with reality. It cannot be an obstacle to attaining higher and superior goals of life. Despite strong resistance from the Church, birth control in the West has received the support of the common man. Though the religious leaders were in no mood to support the birth control movement, we could not leave everything to "wishes of God" for God also asks us to provide every opportunity to make our children healthy in body and soul. Many religious institutions had to revise their stand on birth planning.

People all over the world were united when survival of human civilization was at stake. High birth and death rate were not confined to any particular region or a particular group in the long past. We can find some sermon in every religion that favored high fertility. The more the people are uneducated, the less they appreciate the science of physiology behind every birth. It is these uneducated and superstitious people that find the hand of some supreme power behind every birth. Today, even in the most conservative families the ice has started melting; they slowly have started to realize the need for birth control and planning.

Of the four major religions, only Buddhism (and Islam to an extent) has discouraged high birth rate. Buddhism has strongly said against the race for accomplishing earthly desires. It preaches that individual happiness be sacrificed for the family, family for the village, village for the country, and even country for the sake of mankind to make it free from ignorance.

In Hinduism, no clear indication is available if it really supports higher birth or not. Hinduism, in fact, accommodates people of various sects and faiths; many a folkways have been incorporated into it. Men and women all over India worship Shiblinga (depicting phallus). One therefore may be tempted to believe that Hinduism encourages high fertility. Hindus believe in rebirth. It is also their conviction that unless their sons perform the last rites, the departed soul remains unsatiated. Hindus, by nature are non-violent and therefore may appear against birth control. On the other hand, the hermits referred to in Hindu religious and *puranic* literature, who left all worldly desires and led a rather solitary life away from the glares of civil society in search of a supreme goal for life, still are the idols for Hindus. The Hindu religion stresses more on spirituality than on morality in its concern for human fertility.

Islam, strictly speaking, is not a religion; it is a socio-political movement to provide a space for women to regain their lost prestige in society. In the Arab countries, polygamy was a rule than exception. The Muslim Saint Muhammad asked his disciples and followers not to have more than four wives. It was really a gallant step to restore the dignity and honor of women. Nothing has been clearly stated about the number of children one should have. Koran has, however, some direction in this regard. It has been said there that Allah (God almighty) wants your happiness and peace; He does not want any misfortune befall on you. The same Koran also asks men to marry those girls only who are very fertile.

In the context of Hindu population in India many highly placed religious leaders (Sankaracharyya of Puridham, for example) have asked Hindus to pay no heed to the propaganda on family planning and birth control. Of late, this has also become a highly contentious political issue between secular forces and Hindu fundamentalists. These fundamentalists argue that by taking the advantage of Muslim Personal Law, the Muslims in India would numerically dominate Indian population in not too distant a future. That the Muslim dominated countries are also very anxious about the result of unchecked growth of population could be clearly seen when the then Food and Agriculture Minister in Pakistan in mid-1960s gave a public statement that the country must seriously give a thought to the unwelcome competition between growth of food production and growth in numbers in the population.

Both the Catholic and Protestant Churches still are against artificial control of birth. The Orthodox Church still believes that to produce babies is the principal motive behind all marriages. In 1930, the Cardinals assembled at Lambeth voted in favor of birth control. Just 10 years before this, a similar assembly expressed a somewhat different view. They agreed that giving birth is the principal objective of any marriage. However, if the couple decided against a birth, they ought to practice abstinence than use artificial means to control birth. Artificial control of birth was still regarded immoral in most religions. Even late Pope Paul II, the most respected and influential Head of the Vatican was known for his anti-birth planning stand. Even the election of Benedict XVI as the new Pope already has raised the fear that the stand of the Church on birth control, homosexuality and gay marriage would be more rigid. There are about 1.1 billion Catholics, spread over all the continents and a huge number of them are from developing countries most of them are still illiterate or poorly educated. But birth limitation process is already on the move all over the world in spite of conflicting stands taken against it by various religious groups; the course is irreversible and therefore it cannot anymore be put into the back gear.

In the last few decades the social, religious and other resistances to birth control movement have weakened considerably. Even the religious and political leaders have come to realize the inevitable consequences of unrestricted population growth. Caste and religious divide and the associated politics in India's parliamentary democracy have retarded its development in many spheres. We, in India, could not bring all our people under one uniform civil code (which is one of the major demands of Bharatiya Janata Party, BJP); we could not implement the Minimum Age at Marriage Act, 1976 especially among backward classes, ethnic groups and illiterates for fear of loosing the vote bank; the two-child norm could not be implemented for lack of support from political parties; we could not use the two-child norm as a tool for preventing people not responding to our National Population Policy (NPP) from contesting elections or occupying government positions; we could not even draft laws to prevent criminals from becoming law makers. Even most of the states and political parties are reluctant to listen to Supreme Court's judgment that the states must develop mechanisms to register every marriage. The momentum generated in the 1960s and 1970s by using the propaganda machinery and sterilization camps (including compulsory sterilization during mid-1970s) has kept the ball rolling – the birth rates have been declining indicating that a sizeable number of our people have understood the necessity of birth control. If we could rise above the short-term gains or losses in politics and if we could take a concerted drive to remove illiteracy from our population, the population growth could have declined much faster.

Muslims in India are the fastest growing population segment. They increased their share to total population from about 9 percent at the time of partition in 1947 to 13.4 percent in 2001 (their share was 11.2 percent in 1991). They have the largest share of their population in the age group 0–6 years, 18.7 percent against the national average of 15.9 percent (Hindus 15.6, Christians 13.5 and Jains 10.6). Literacy among Muslims is only 59.7 percent against the national average of 65.38 (Jains have the highest literacy, 97.4 percent, followed by Christians at 80.2 percent). The decadal growth rate for Muslims is about 29 percent as against 21.34 percent in the total population in India during 1991–2001. Even in fertility, they are ahead of all other religious communities.

7.6 Direct Social Factors

Fertility is directly related to abortion, infanticide, use of contraceptives, etc. Whether one shall adopt this or that method of birth control is a personal choice; it also depends upon the general practices in the community to which he/she belongs. We have seen how the social environment plays a critical role in the relation between fertility and indirect social factors. The social influence is much more on adoption of direct social factors for curtailing fertility. There are considerable variations in the use of these methods in countries that have successfully brought down their birth rate. One does not hesitate to adopt the means developed in other countries to prevent death. But fertility is a different matter, more personal and social than deaths in a family. When to have a baby, their number, how many of them are boys and how many girls are not only dictated by personal preferences, the cultural, religious and other social correlates also have a significant say in these matters. However, their exact impact on birth rate has not been evaluated precisely in any society or any culture.

In orthodox families, sex is still a forbidden topic of discussion, even among husbands and wives. Curiosity in the young minds about sex and reproduction is a normal thing. Family and educational institutions jointly have to take up the responsibility of educating young boys and girls about the science of reproduction of all living organisms. Once they realize the science behind reproductive process as also why it is necessary to keep birth rates down, they shall be able to discuss matters related to sex more freely among themselves as also with adults. The more the inhibition, the more inquisitive they would become. That sex education must be a part of the curriculum, at least in the higher classes in schools, has strongly been recommended by educationists and social activists

Oral pills and other contraceptive devices: Many tribal societies have been found to use certain herbal and medicinal plants – their roots and leaves, for temporary sterilization of both men and women. However, their effectiveness and dependability in birth control have not been studied scientifically. Often the tribal people would not make public the plants and herbs they use for such purposes. The most common birth control method, extensively used for ages in every society, is coitus interruptus. That is, at the peak of excitement, phallus is withdrawn so that ejaculation takes place outside the vagina. Glass from his survey has shown that before the advent of chemical and other contraceptives, even the developed countries in the West did bring down birth rates by *coitus interruptus*. With the discovery of pills, jelly and rubber condoms, birth protection have become more scientific and fail-safe.

Since the 1980s, Acquired Immuno-Deficiency Syndrome, AIDS has become the most dreaded disease all over the world, especially in South Africa, India and many other developing countries, more so in sub-Saharan Africa. Sexual intercourse is the principal source through which AIDS spread fast. Transmission of HIV through contaminated blood, use of the same injection needle with different persons, certain drugs made from blood serum, and even HIV infected mothers as carrier of AIDS to babies in the womb are some other important sources through which AIDS spread. The slogan all over the world is "use condoms to prevent AIDS infection and spread of the same to others". As a result, the consumption of condoms has gone up. Condoms are likely to play a major role both in prevention of pregnancy and spread of HIV infection.

Abortion: Premature termination of pregnancy has been there and would continue to play a major role as long as the pregnancy is unwelcome for some reason or other. Abortion has been practiced even in more orthodox societies, sometimes without the knowledge and consent of the husband. Abortion did not have an easy taking even in some of the most developed countries a few decades back. But perceptions started changing as the world population started to grow fast. Most countries have passed laws to make abortion legal. Some countries have extended facilities for abortion at state expenses. Japan did bring down birth rate very fast after World War II by making abortion as one of the major tools for preventing births. In 1970s abortion rate in Russia was about 41 for every thousand women in reproductive age group.

Once the family planning movement gained momentum, India needed to have a law to make abortion legal. In 1971, India passed Medical Termination of Pregnancy Act (MTP), similar to the British Abortion Act, 1967. As per the Act, MTP is permitted if continuation of pregnancy

1. poses life threat or some physical damage to the mother;
2. leads to so much stress that possibility of some mental disorder cannot be avoided;
3. leads to a birth who is likely to be deformed or crippled or mentally retarded; and
4. is unwelcome because it was caused by rape or against the will of the woman.

These conditions require that a doctor must certify that abortion is in the best interest of the pregnant woman giving specific reasons for his advice. Abortion is discouraged beyond 12 weeks of pregnancy.

The legislation has eased abortion and also its misuse. Abortion in India, for example, has extensively been used in some states and among certain segments of the population to avoid female births (also male births among the prostitutes). The problem has aggravated so much so in a few states that female population in the population and more specifically in 0–6 year age group has fallen alarmingly. As a result, the government has been forced to prohibit pre-determination of sex. But it is doubtful if the general public and the clinics would pay heed to this government stipulation. The sex ratio (F/M) in the age group 0–4 was as low as 901 in India in 2001.

The rate of abortion is more frequent in women below 20 and above 35 years. Abortion beyond the recommended pregnancy period (12 weeks) is not safe for the mother. Both giving birth and abortion for women aged over 35 years are associated with greater risk of life. However, no systematic study on proportion of death of mothers due to abortion is available. Abortion still remains a secret episode in most families, especially in orthodox society. Medical studies have shown that frequent abortion is harmful for the health of a girl and may even lead to sterility.

Temporary and permanent sterilization: In the initial years of family planning campaign in India, the government stressed on temporary sterilization of women and therefore promoted the use of Intra-Uterine Contraceptive Device (IUCD, popularly called "loop"). Till 1976, over 6.4 million women were brought under this program. Since then, 'loop' lost favor with its users for several reasons:

1. heavy bleeding after the loop was inserted;
2. physical discomfort and many other symptoms;
3. repeal of the 'loop' long before its intended period;
4. mismatch between the size of the 'loop' and the sex organ of the woman;
5. lack of expertise and experience of the doctors in 'loop' insertion;
6. incidences of pregnancy even after insertion of 'loop'; and
7. the 'loop' users were not informed about a few problems like nausea, excessive bleeding, headache, etc. which are likely to follow the 'loop' insertion and that there was nothing to worry about them.

Indian government opened up various camps (in addition to improving the facilities in hospital and clinics) in different parts of the country. But the initial enthusiasm for 'loop' faded away. In all the underdeveloped countries, especially among the backward classes, permanent sterilization has been accepted as a better option than 'loop', pills or condoms. Since the later part of 1960s vasectomy (male sterilization) and tubectomy (female sterilization) started gaining popularity in India. By 1984–85 about 130 million couples were brought under family planning program of which 49 million opted for permanent sterilization. Currently, around 4.5 million couples undergo sterilization every year of which males' share is only about 2 percent.

Although most of the developing countries have adopted permanent sterilization for their birth control program, the impact of sterilization on birth rate has not been very clear. Men and women in India who undergo sterilization had an average age well over 35 years and most of them already had given birth to more than 4 children. It is argued that had they not undergone the operations, they would not have added much to the size of the population since they were already on the wrong side of their reproductive career.

Infanticide: Infanticide has remained a common curse in all societies through ages. Though the incidence of infanticide has been checked considerably, it has not been stopped altogether. Both religious and economic reasons operate behind infanticide. In some societies twin babies bring bad omen for the family. That is why one of the two babies is killed. The child is often killed if he/she is born with teeth; the mother dies at the time of birth; the child has some gross abnormality or if the child is born on an inauspicious day. Religion may have some small role in killing of babies immediately after their birth, but it is the economic reasons that haunt them to die. In Indian society birth of a male child brings joy to the family for the fact that religious rites can be performed only by a male child; with the birth of male child the family can hope for continuation of a family lineage. It is for this and other reasons baby girls are the natural victims of infanticide practices.

Eskimos kill the babies just born by freezing them in ice. The practice is still so common that the girl population in the Arctic region is going down fast. Infanticide was quite a common practice in China and India. People in China like that in India considered girls a burden on the family. Dowry system in marriage had been the principal reason for the killing of a girl child, especially in economically disadvantaged families. In patriarch families, it is the male child who only carries the family name.

Even when a girl child is not killed immediately after birth, she remains a complete neglect in a family that has to toil really hard to make the two ends meet. Under such pressing condition, girls are the sacrificing goats to keep their brothers assured of necessary food and other life-sustaining supplies. Malnutrition makes the girls easy pray to diseases; they lack the necessary strength to survive against any adversity. They therefore have a much higher death rate in their childhood days. This remains one of the major reasons for the falling sex ratio in India.

For an overwhelming greater length of time man had to fight against high death rate and to compensate these inevitable deaths the supply of babies had to be kept at a very high level. Higher birth rates had to be encouraged to keep enough numbers to take over the batons from their predecessors. It is therefore not easy to break away from the tradition of so many thousand years and switch over to adopting a small family norm. Infant and child mortality in developing countries definitely have declined in the last 50–60 years. But the mortality rates in these groups continue to be still high by all standards. The poorer and illiterate families cannot take the risk of loosing family name if they had only one or two children. In the developed countries control of death rate, improvement in literacy level, switching over from agriculture to industrial economy, improvement in standard of living and birth control have happened almost simultaneously. There was not much time gap between the joint operation of the antecedents and the consequents. In the developing countries death rates have declined much faster without an attendant improvement in social and economic sectors, which are more relevant as far as a change in attitude to birth is concerned. The population there has grown fast because of a good check on death rate alone. It is the social and economic factors that can narrow the gap between the birth and death rates. Even in many developing countries the urban population has quickly taken the limited advantages they are offered in social and economic sectors, and their current average fertility rate is quite comparable to that in some of the more developed countries. The problem still is very acute in the developing countries for the simple reason that they do not have any surplus to invest in social sector (health and education, in particular) and modernize their economy. For every 1 percent rise in population, the country needs to allocate more than 4 percent of its GDP to provide the basic necessities even at their current level. Can the developing countries wait for the social and employment sectors to improve and create an environment for a change in attitude of the common man before birth rates fall? In the seventies and eighties, the rhetoric had been "development is the best contraceptive". How long do we wait for the development to make a substantial change in attitude towards birth planning? The grass would grow even when unattended. So, something ought to be done, and quickly, lest the population size overwhelm all our concerted effort to improve the standard of living of our people.

7.7 Fertility Program Evaluation

Many fertility evaluations neglect to account for the intervening variables other than those inherent in the program. Most programs emphasize on contraception and as such many evaluations presume that it is sufficient to study program acceptance and use of contraceptives to determine the program impact. If such other variables as abortion, abstinence, age of entering into sexual union, divorce and separation, etc. are not taken into consideration, the program evaluation is likely to be faulty. If these rival variables are not given due attention, it is easy to overestimate the importance of contraception, thus, the role of the program. The linkage between development and fertility decline is very complex. Development programs clearly are aimed at improving the existing socio-economic parameters in the developing countries. The emphasis in such programs is intended to raise productivity, increase income, and promote education, health and wellbeing. The underlying assumption is that if fertility is determined by these socioeconomic factors, then such programs are bound to have a significant impact on fertility. This mutually interacting relationship, that is, fertility affects development, and development affects fertility, is becoming an acceptable notion.

The effect of high fertility and rapid population growth on development goals has been the focus of many investigations, at least since the time of Coale and Hoover's effort in 1958. But the notion that development programs, other than family planning programs, may affect fertility is a somewhat newer and more novel idea. Yet, the search for the precise linkage, the nature and strength of the relationship between development and fertility, has proven to be quite illusive. Berelson suggested "thresholds" or levels of various indexes of socio-economic development at which fertility could be expected to decline based on the experience of countries already well into the transition. Kingsley Davis and Judith Blake in 1956 proposed how such complex social, economic, psychological and physiological factors interacting at the household level but affected also by societal, natural and even chance elements should be studied while evaluating any fertility program, no matter where the program is undertaken.

Davis and Blake (1956) proposed that any cultural or structural factor affects fertility through 11 *intermediate variables* centering around intercourse, conception and parturition, and said, "In analyzing cultural influences on fertility, one may well start with the factors directly connected with these three processes. Such factors would be those through which, and only through which, cultural conditions can affect fertility". The 11 variables are

Intercourse

1. Female age at marriage and proportion marrying
2. Taboos in intercourse, frequent separation of couples, etc.
3. Sanctions on sexual activity outside marriage
4. Excess male mortality and consequent early widowhood

Conception

5. Contraception (all methods)
6. Sterility
7. Fetal wastage and still births
8. Voluntary sterilization

Gestation and Parturition

9. Age at menarche and menopause
10. Lactation
11. Abortion

Davis-Blake framework unfolded how fertility programs initiated by various agencies can be evaluated. Davis-Blake model of fertility analysis has been used extensively and in the course many have condensed these 11 variables/added some more and reclassified such fundamental variables. A very ambitious effort to understand relations between fertility and development was carried out by United Nations, Department of International Economic and Social Affairs, Population Division (*The Work of the Task Force on Inter-Relationships Between Population and Development,* 1981). The report suggested a very comprehensive matrix framework for analyzing 10 population variables, including fertility; 15 development indicator variables; 14 economic variables, 15 socio-cultural and exogenous variables (group structure etc.); and seven instrument variables (family planning programs etc.). Several volumes of case studies also are reported, but they generally have not generated or led to a methodology which makes possible the "monitoring" of the interaction between fertility and development programs. They were mostly retrospective studies of past events and are of limited usefulness in predicting future relationships or consequences.

The key characteristics of intermediate variables are that they are necessary for fertility change, and that the direction of change in fertility resulting from a change in an intermediate variable is unmistakable. Thus any background, cultural, or other factor must operate through one or more of these variables (or some extension), and it must have an effect on fertility whose direction (if not size) through that variable is unambiguous.

Bongaarts developed a simple version of this "intermediate variables framework", which could actually be used for empirical estimation and that the relative strength of the variables could also be determined through structural equations. He recorded the 11 intermediate variables into the "proximate" determinants: namely, marriage, contraception, lactation and abortion, which account for most of the controls exercised in practice over fertility; finally, he added the notion of a "natural fertility" level towards which fertility inevitably tends in the absence of any constraint by the "proximate" determinants. Whatever effect development programs have on fertility must proceed through one or more of these proximate variables. Thus, raising the level of education, health, or income does not change fertility directly; raising the level of one of them does (or may) affect, however, one of the intermediate variables which do in turn affect fertility. Bongaarts (1977, 1982) simplified the Davis-Blake framework into four intermediate variables associated with the vast majority of the variation of fertility between and within populations:

1. proportions currently married at each age weighted by marital fertility at that age;
2. proportions using contraception of varying levels of effectiveness;
3. postpartum infecundity associated with breast-feeding or postpartum abstinence; and
4. the extent of induced abortion.

Bongaarts (1982) demonstrated that the remaining factors either do not have a large effect on fertility (e.g., spontaneous intrauterine sterility) or do not vary much between populations (e.g., permanent sterility).

The search for direct linkages between development programs and fertility can proceed through this framework. However, the proximate variables of Bongaarts are "macro" in nature, whereas fertility occurs at the "micro" level. This is to be remembered while impact of the intermediate variables of fertility is assessed.

While Davis-Blake frameworks remain the guiding principle for unraveling the linkages between fertility or population growth and many other socio-economic developments, population displacement, rural-urban differentiation, women autonomy and reproductive behavior, fertility transition, etc., there are numerous instances where Davis-Blake list of 11 intermediate variables have been modified. W. C. Robinson and J.F. Kantner, for example, modified them into five sets of intermediate variables:

(A) Proportion of women 15–49 years of age currently married which includes Davis-Blake variables 1 and 4

(B) Proportion of currently married women 15–49 years of age seeking to avoid pregnancy or live birth. (D–B variables 5, 8 and 11)

(C) Proportion of currently married women 15–49 years of age in lactational amenorrhea (D–B variable 10)

(D) Proportion of currently married women 15–49 years of age suffering nutrition-connected or other impairments to fecundity (D–B variables 6, 7 and 9)

(E) Social structural factors affecting fertility apart from all other factors (D–B variables 2 and 3).

Robinson and Kantner suggested that all development programs can be categorized according to their likely effect on fertility – directly and indirectly.

Direct effects which aim at:

— increasing the availability of contraception, voluntary sterilization and/or menstrual regulation;
— increasing the use of contraception, voluntary sterilization and/or menstrual regulation; and
— decreasing exposure to pregnancy by promoting increased breast-feeding, and increasing the age at marriage for women.

Indirect effects which aim at:

— improving the health, nutrition and wellbeing of the people;
— increasing the income, productivity and technological base of the society; and
— effecting social change such as income redistribution, land reform or other fundamental structural changes.

7.8 Current Fertility Situation in the World

In this section we shall see that though the world populations are greatly scattered spatially, the world aggregate is gradually assuming the profile of a global village in respect to some of the mortality indicators. CDR, the most common indicator to describe about the health of a population for different countries are converging very rapidly. CDR for the worst segment of this global village Africa in 2002 was 15 per 1,000 (the same CDR also for the least developed countries); CDR for the most advanced segment, Latin America, was 6 per 1,000 population. In some other indicators, however, the observations are not that encouraging. For example, life expectancy at birth in Africa was only 49 years compared to 77 years in Europe, mortality under age 5 years was 161 per 1,000 populations in the least developed region compared to only 8 per 1,000 in North America. IMR in least human development category came down from 142 to 99 between 1975 and 1999, the same in high human development countries dropped from 25 to 6 in the same period.

Such a degree of convergence between countries and regions, however, was not observed in the correction of birth trends and in population growth rates. There is 27 points gap in CBR and 3.7 points gap in TFR between least developed regions and Europe. Whereas the population in the least developed regions is still growing at an alarming rate of 2.4 percent every year, the population of Europe is declining at an appreciable rate. Because of massive spread of HIV/AIDS in sub-Saharan African countries, the average death rate in Africa

Table 7.4 *Birth and growth statistics for different continents and regions*

Region	*CBR*	*TFR*	*Growth rate*
WORLD	21	2.7	1.2
Most developed regions	11	1.6	0.2
Less developed regions	24	2.9	1.5
Least developed regions	39	5.1	2.4
Africa	37	4.9	2.2
Asia	21	2.5	1.3
Europe	10	1.4	–0.1
Latin America	22	2.5	1.4
North America	14	2.1	1.0
Oceania	17	2.3	1.2

Source: UN World Population data, 2002

Figure 7.1 *UN projection of total fertility (children/woman), 1950–2300*

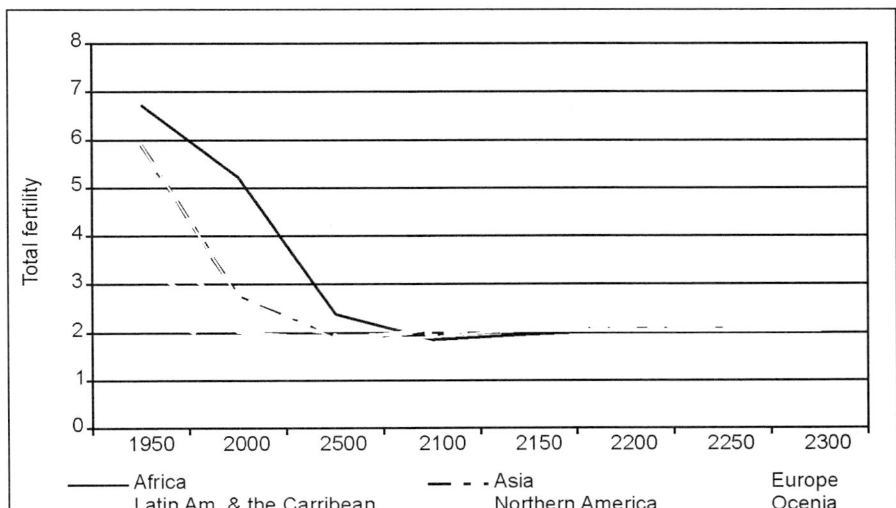

is likely to go up and a sharp drop in life expectancy in many of these countries could push up birth rate as well. The death rates in the developed countries are likely to go up because of a sharp increase in the size of population in 65+ ages and a large reduction of young age group in the population. Unless birth rates in these countries rise, the population growth rate is likely to dip further. If such a situation arises, which is more likely to happen at least for a brief period, these industrially advanced countries may have to make amends to their immigration policy lest they are forced to shut down some of their schools, colleges and production units.

Traditionally, long-term projections have assumed that fertility in all countries, developed and developing, would eventually stabilize at replacement level, leading to a stationary population. There are two general arguments in favor of this assumption. First, replacement level fertility may be seen not as the most likely outcome, but as a mathematically convenient benchmark which prevents population from steadily growing or declining (UN 1999). Second, it has been supported on the basis of a systems view which holds that demographic rates of a population are not just the sum of individual behavior; they reflect the tendency of the demographic system to maintain itself (Vishnevsky). This view sees the falling mortality rates that mark the onset of the demographic transition as a disturbance of a system in homeostasis; birth rates fall as the system inevitably re-establishes balance between the two rates, and fertility seeks replacement level in order to preserve the system. Advocates of the second argument cites examples from recent history that fertility could be stimulated to rise to replacement level in currently low-fertility countries by a wide range of factors, including pronatalist government policies, increased nationalism, a renewed emphasis on traditional roles for women, or a shift away from materialist values.

TFR has been below replacement level in 20 European countries between 1980 and 2000, and currently close to 60 countries have sub-replacement level TFR (HDR 2007/08). In large parts of several European countries total fertility has been at or below 1.0. At least 10 developing countries have reached sub-replacement level fertility as well (e.g., China, Thailand, and North and South Korea). UN long-term projection to 2300 made some critical assumptions regarding the trend in total fertility (children per woman) for various regions. In the medium version of projection it is assumed that decline would be from 2.8 children per woman in 1995–2000 to about 2 children in 2045–2050. Over the long run, total fertility is projected (medium version) to settle at around 1.85 children per woman in each country – somewhere between the current rate for Northern America (which is just below replacement level) and the rate for Europe (which is currently well below). For the developing countries, decline from the higher fertility levels would be somewhat slower and once these countries' fertility reach a range of 4–5, a faster decline (as much as 0.12 point a year) would ensue. Some countries may have to wait a bit longer beyond 2050 to reach the projected level. Fertility in developed countries, which already is close to the long-range levels, is likely to reach them by 2045–2050, proceeding along a smooth path. This allows for some cases where fertility initially moves away from these levels (e.g., dropping even further below) for five or ten years.

There are arguments supporting the assumption of fertility declines below replacement level. These can be grouped together under the term "individuation" (Bumpass 1990), of which there appears to be no end in sight: the weakening of family ties both in terms of declining marriage rates and high divorce rates, the increasing independence and career orientation of women, and the value change towards materialism and consumerism. Individuation, together with increasing demands and personal expectations for attention, time and also money to be given to children, is likely to result in fewer couples that have more than one or two children and an increasing number of childless women.

Although fertility typically continues to fall even after reaching replacement level, there is no clear pattern to subsequent fertility trends. In some countries, fertility falls quickly to very low levels, in others the fall is gradual, in some others as in the US and Sweden the fertility had risen to replacement level after it declined well below that level (Sweden has recently seen another rapid decline).

One argument against the assumptions that TFR will remain very low in these countries is that since TFR is a period measure, it is affected by changes in the timing of births even if the actual number of births women experience over their lifetime does not change. Since the mean age of childbearing has been increasing in many industrialized countries (even in less industrialized ones) over the past several decades, part of the decline in TFR has been due to this timing effect and not to a change in the completed fertility of women. Bongaarts and Feeney argued that TFR was likely to increase in foreseeable future once the mean age of childbearing stops rising, as had happened in the 1980s in USA when fertility rose to its current value just below replacement level. An additional argument against continued very low fertility is that surveys on European women indicate that they want to have about 2 children (Bongaarts 1999). Of course, there are many reasons why they may fail to meet this desired fertility level – competing and tempting career plans, divorce, infertility; but this observation definitely suggests that fertility is unlikely to remain very low, especially if societies made it easier for women to combine careers and childbearing.

Demographic Dividend

A fresh reason for attending to fertility dynamics has emerged – the *demographic dividend*. As fertility rates fall late in the demographic transition, a special window may open up for a faster economic growth and human development. As fertility falls, the young age dependency rate declines effecting a change in the age distribution – relatively more people in the adult age groups that comprise the productive labor force. This improvement in the ratio of productive workers to child dependents in the population makes faster economic growth and fewer burdens on families. As the demographic window of opportunities open, per capita output improves lessening burdens on families and society.

Demographic dividend played a significant role in the "economic miracles" of the East Asian Tigers – South Korea, Hong Kong, Singapore, and Taiwan. As their birth rates fell in the mid-1960s, elementary school enrolments declined and a part of the funds previously allocated for elementary education could be moved to improve the quality of education at the secondary and at higher levels. This helped rapid industrialization between the early 1960s and 1990s and enabled the countries to follow an export-driven model of economic development with the exportation of goods to highly industrialized nations. Domestic consumption was discouraged through government policies such as high tariffs. The Four Asian Tigers singled out education as a means of improving productivity; they focused on improving the education system at all levels; heavy emphasis was placed on ensuring that all children attended compulsory elementary and high school education. Money was made available on improving the college and university system. Economic boons in Ireland (the Celtic Tiger) in the 1990s are believed to be consequent to legalization of contraception in 1979 and subsequent decline in the fertility rate. The ratio of workers to dependents in Ireland of course improved due to lower fertility but was enhanced further by increased female labor market participation and a reversal from outward migration of working age population to a net inflow. In contrast, a country's high fertility and youth dependency rates (most African countries) contribute to their economic stagnation.

The demographic dividend, however, does not last forever. This window of opportunity has a limited life. With time, the age distribution changes again – as the large working age population moves into the older, less-productive age band and is followed by the smaller cohorts born during the lower fertility regime. When this occurs, the dependency ratio rises again, this time involving the need to care for the elderly, rather than the need to take care of the young.

However the fall in demographic pressure due to fast decline in birth rate does not necessarily mean that the country would capitalize upon the released resources for effective improvement of quality of life of the common man. In a democratic set up the chances are that the released resources would be utilized for creation of developing long lasting capitals, both human and physical (health, education, other social and physical infrastructure).

The demographic dividend is delivered through several mechanisms:

- Provisions can be made for intensification of education and development of skill;
- Having fewer children enhances the health of women;
- With fewer children women can take up jobs outside home since they are likely to be better educated and more productive in the labor force than the older cohorts;
- The shift away from a very young age distribution favors greater personal and national savings;
- Parents are under less strain to make provisions for children.

The magnitude of the demographic dividend appears dependent on the ability of the economy to absorb and productively employ the extra workers, rather than a pure demographic gift. When the window of opportunity closes (it will happen sooner or later), those that do not make full use of the demographic dividend will face more intense pressures in a position that is weaker than ever.

8 Mortality

Levels, Differentials and Causes of Death

8.1 Introduction

There are two fundamental differences between fertility and mortality situations prevailing in any country or society. Even in the remote past when life depended on the whims of nature, death rate compared to birth rate was small. Since birth rate was nearly at its biological limit to keep the population growing, death rate needed to be curtailed; this was not easy against the uncertainty in supply of food and nutrition. Other factors that could keep the death rate down – such as proper shelter, technological know-how and medicine needed to fight diseases and natural adversities were at their rudimentary stage. Population in the past, it is believed, did not show any sign of steady growth for thousands of years. That the population in modern times is still growing in most countries is a proof that death rates in the population are still decreasing. In the middle stages, death rates fluctuated in all countries because of epidemic, famine or war. Secondly, fluctuation of death rate had generally remained small compared to birth rate. The mortality situation has steadily improved as the age of human civilization advanced. When the climate was good for agriculture, there was no shortage of food, no epidemic outburst and no war, death rates declined. No more do we need to depend totally on nature for our food; there has been a radical transformation in medical science and other technologies; death due to frequent wars between countries have come down; transport and communication network has improved remarkably to send medicines and other supplies to any ailing part of the world; there is some shelter for most people, which helps reduce exposure to natural calamities. There is no question of death rate shooting up suddenly. It is for this reason that we can fairly accurately predict the death rate for a population in the next five or ten years. But prediction of birth rate for a distant future has often failed. Death rate, unlike birth rate, responds quickly to prevailing social and economic standards in the country. That is, secular declining trend in mortality is more universal than decline in fertility trend. That is why fertility rate as a single base is less reliable and effective than mortality in population projection. Figure 8.1 shows how death

Figure 8.1 *Birth and death rate in India, 1901–2001*

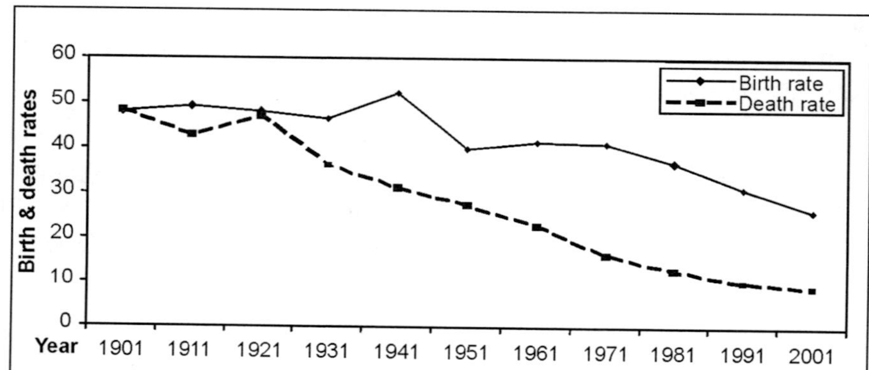

Table 8.1 *IMR of top and bottom 10 countries along with statistics for few other related variables*

Country	*Life expectancy at birth (years)*		*Infant mortality rate (per 1,000 live births)*		*Under-five mortality rate (per 1,000 live births)*		*Probability at birth of surviving to age 65 (% of cohort)*		*Maternal mortality ratio (per 100,000 live births)*	
1	*2*	*3*	*4*	*5*	*6*	*7*	*8*	*9*	*10*	*11*
	1970–1975	*2000–2005*	*1970*	*2005*	*1970*	*2005*	*Female 2000–05*	*Male 2000–05*	*Female 1990–05*	*Male 2005*
					Bottom 10 IMR countries					
Iceland	74.3	81.0	13	2	14	3	92.4	88.7	..	4
Sweden	74.7	80.1	11	3	15	4	92.3	87.0	5	3
Japan	73.3	81.9	14	3	21	4	93.8	86.1	8	6
Finland	70.7	78.4	13	3	16	4	91.8	81.0	6	7
Singapore	69.5	78.8	22	3	27	3	90.8	84.4	6	14
Slovenia	69.8	76.8	25	3	29	4	90.1	77.6	17	6
Czech Republic	70.1	75.4	21	3	24	4	89.0	75.3	4	4
Switzerland	73.8	80.7	15	4	18	5	92.6	86.1	5	5
Netherlands	74.0	78.7	13	4	15	5	90.4	84.4	7	6
France	72.4	79.6	18	4	24	5	92.2	82.1	10	8
					Top 10 high IMR countries					
Sierra Leone	35.4	41.0	206	165	363	282	37.6	30.4	1,800	2,100
Angola	37.9	41.0	154	180	300	260	33.9	27.5	..	1,400
Niger	40.5	54.5	197	150	256	330	54.4	56.8	590	1,800
Equatorial Guinea	40.5	49.3		123	..	205	44.7	39.7	..	680
Congo	46.0	45.0	148	129	245	205	38.8	33.3	1,300	1,100
Chad	45.6	50.5	154	124	261	208	50.5	43.7	1,100	1,500
Guinea-Bissau	36.5	45.5	..	124	..	200	40.9	34.2	910	1,100
Mali	40.0	51.8	225	120	400	218	54.1	44.3	580	970
Rwanda	44.6	43.4	124	118	209	203	34.5	28.3	1,100	1,300
Côte d'Ivoire	49.8	46.8	158	118	239	195	40.7	34.9	600	810

Source: UNDP: Human Development Report 1007/2008 (data for 2005)

rates have steadily declined in the last 100 years in India. The declines in death rate in most other countries (save the countries having high HIV infection) also follow a similar secular trend.

8.2 Differences in Mortality Levels Among the Countries

Till about the middle of the last century, a very large disparity was observed both in birth and death rates as also in expectation of life at birth between different countries, or more generally between different regions. The differences have narrowed down considerably in the last 50 years. North-western Europe, America, Canada, Australia, New Zealand, Japan and many others have death rates so low that no further tangible improvement in death rate is possible. Infant mortality in many of these countries even has gone below the countries' general mortality level. In fact, as many as 19 countries recorded their IMRs in the range 4 or less in 2005 (HDR, 2007/08) when as many as 18 countries still had IMRs 100 and above. It is the old-age segment of the population that contributes most to a country's general mortality level in the developed countries. In the low developed countries, where the age distribution is still highly positively skewed (35 percent or more of the population in below 15 years age group), it is the mortality among infants and children that really control the attained general mortality level and expectation of life at birth and other ages. In early 1970s, 72 percent of African countries had CDRs 15 per thousand or more. 59 percent of the Asian countries were in this high death rate category. In the last 30–35 years, a remarkable change in death rate has happened even in the least developed countries (Table 8.2).

Table 8.2 *CDR and other statistics by continents and regions under development scanner, UN world population data, 2002*

Region	*CBR*	*CDR*	*TFR*	*Mortality under age 5 years*	*Life expectancy at birth*	*% of population in <15 yrs*	*Growth rate*
WORLD	21	9	2.7	81	65	29	1.2
Most developed regions	11	10	1.6	10	76	17	0.2
Less developed regions	24	9	2.9	89	63	32	1.5
Least developed regions	39	15	5.1	161	50	43	2.4
Africa	37	15	4.9	148	49	42	2.2
Asia	21	8	2.5	71	67	29	1.3
Europe	10	11	1.4	11	74	16	–0.1
Latin America	22	6	2.5	41	70	31	1.4
North America	14	8	2.1	8	77	21	1.0
Oceania	17	8	2.3	35	74	25	1.2

Of late, there has been an increase in death rate accompanied by severe fall in expectation of life in some of the countries in Africa and elsewhere. The rapid spread of HIV/AIDS in these countries has reversed the trend in death rate. On average, there has been 7–8 points rise in CDR in these countries between 1983 and 2003. CDR has nearly doubled in Botswana, Zambia and Zimbabwe. Life expectancy in these three countries has dropped by 12 to 17 years. Sub-Saharan Africa has HIV/AIDS to 8.7 percent of all persons in the age group 15–49 as against 1.1 percent in the 15–49 world population.

In the early eighties of the last century, 66 percent of the developing countries brought down CDR to 14 or below (32 per cent in Africa, 82 percent in Asia and 95 percent in Latin America). 99 percent of the developed countries had CDR below 14. In the eighties 47 percent of the developing countries and 60 percent of the developed countries had CDR 9 or even below. Death rates in most countries have stabilized at a much lower level (most of the developing countries have reduced CDR by 0.35 – 0.50 point per annum in the last 25 years) than it was 25 years back. As a result, growth rates in most countries have been arrested or are declining. Table 8.2 shows estimated position of regions in respect to CDR and other related statistics.

It is interesting to note that 8 of the 10 top ranked countries with incredible low IMR are all from Europe (Table 8.1). The remaining 2, Japan and Singapore are from East Asia. None of the European countries find their names in the top 10 countries having least CDR (Table 8.3). The West Asian countries have the lead role in bringing down CDR almost to the biological limit.

Table 8.3 *Countries at the highest and lowest level of general mortality (CDR)*

Rank	*Country*	*CDR*	*Rank*	*Country*	*CDR*
	Highest CDR countries			***Lowest CDR countries***	
1	Sierra Leone	22.1	10	French Guiana	3.7
2	Swaziland	21.2	9	Palestinian territories	3.7
3	Angola	20.5	8	Saudi Arabia	3.7
4	Afghanistan	19.9	7	Syria	3.4
5	Mozambique	19.8	6	Bahrain	3.2
6	Lesotho	19.2	5	Brunei	2.8
7	Zambia	18.8	4	Oman	2.7
8	Guinea-Bissau	18.4	3	Qatar	2.4
9	Liberia	18.3	2	Kuwait	1.9
10	Central African Republic	18.1	1	United Arab Emirates	1.4

The more developed countries are very close to zero growth rates; quite a few are losing their populations. The countries in this category have a slightly higher death rate compared to world average and even many of the less developed countries. This we already have said is due to a very high expectancy of life – the old age group contributes most to the death rate in these countries vis-à-vis the less developed ones where infant and child mortality are still very high and the young age in the population dominate the population distribution. Crude death rate applied to a whole population of people can give a misleading impression. The number of deaths per 1,000 people can be higher for developed nations than in less-developed countries, despite standards of health being far superior in the developed countries. This is because developed countries have relatively high proportion of older people who are more likely to die in a given year, so that the overall mortality rate can be higher even if the mortality rate at any given age is lower. A more complete picture of mortality is given by a Life Table which summarizes mortality separately at each age. A life table is necessary to give a good estimate of life expectancy.

The most glaring differences between developed and developing countries are in child mortality rates and proportion of persons below 15 years in the population distribution. Under 5 mortality in the world population is still very high, 81 per thousand, which in the developed countries are only 10 as against 161 in the least developed countries (HDR 2001). Under 5 mortality is very high, 148, in Africa, most in Central Africa, 207, and Eastern Africa, 163 and least in Northern America, 8 per thousand. In South-Central Asia, it is 93 per thousand children. Western Europe has very low child mortality, 6 per thousand children under age 5. CBRs are still very high in the developing countries but that will come down fast if child and infant mortality could be put under check. IMR in the world population came down from 96 in 1970 to 56 in 1999. In this period, the high human development countries brought IMR down from 25 to 7, often below their general mortality level. The developing countries' achievement in IMR in the same period has been a reduction from 109 to 61. In the least developed countries IMR has dropped from around 149 to 100 in the same time span. The low income countries still have IMR as high as 80. In the high human development countries, probability at birth of surviving to age 65 years is 88 percent, vis-à-vis only 47 percent in the low human development countries.

There are many developing countries that have almost similar or even lower level of CDR than some of the developed countries (Table 8.2). Yet, they have much higher rates in some other indicators of mortality. Sweden and Myanmar have identical CDR (11), but how different they are in IMR (Sweden 3 and Myanmar 79) and mortality under age 5 (Sweden 4, Myanmar 112). Kuwait has one of the lowest CDR (1.9 per 1,000) among all the countries in the world, yet it still has room for further improvement in infant (11 per 1,000) and child mortality (13 per 1,000). The country's CBR is 20 (TFR 2.9) and it is one of the fastest growing countries (2.5 percent) in the world.

Table 8.4 *CDR and a few other mortality indicators of selected few countries*

Country	*CDR**	*IMR**	*Mortality under age 5 years #*	*Life expectancy*
Comoros	8	64	92	58.8
Egypt	6	41	48	66.3
Korea, Republic	6	5	58	74.3
Argentina	8	19	23	72.9
Brazil	7	34	46	67.2
Ireland	8	6	7	76.1
Sweden	11	3	4	79.3
China	7	33	43	69.8
Kuwait	2	11	13	75.9
Myanmar	11	79	112	55.8
India	8	70	84	62.3

:* UN World Population, 2002, # Human Development Report, 2001, UNDP

The gap between the developed and developing countries has been bridged fast in CDR, but in other key indicators of health of the population the developing countries are far behind the developed countries. There is 26 years gap in life expectancy between the most developed countries and the least developed countries; between the less developed and developed countries the gap is still 13 years on an average (Table 8.1). Life expectancy at birth is 65 years for the world population.

Middle Africa has as low as 43 years life expectancy. Zambia has the lowest life expectancy (32 years) and Japan the highest (82 years).

The developing countries today are not far behind the developed countries as far as their CDRs are concerned. Since infant and child mortality in the developing countries are still very high, there is a possibility that CDRs in these countries could go even beyond the level already attained by the developed countries as their infant and child mortality come down once they have some surplus in their GDP to invest in health and other social sectors. Because of very low birth rate and unrelenting rise in the proportion of people in 65+ years age group (65+ years population is likely to be around 16–18 percent in 10–15 years time), CDR in developed countries would further rise and create a situation favorable for depopulation unless they increase their birth rates. A very large share of national GDP of these countries will have to be spent on social security for the senior citizens. The developing countries too will improve upon their expectation of life as infant and child mortality rates come down.

Infant and child mortality rates are then the key factors that separate a developed country from an underdeveloped one. The picture becomes clearer when we compare the average expectation of life age by age. At higher ages, the difference in average expectation of life between a developed and an underdeveloped country fast diminishes. Once the cohort crosses the childhood stage, uncertainty of life fast diminishes. That is, the difference in average expectation of life is largely due to differences in infant and child mortality.

Table 8.5 *Proportion of death to total deaths by age and sex, India 2000 (SRS data)*

Age-group	*Total*	*Male*	*Female*
< 1	20.5	19.9	21.3
1–4	6.3	5	7.8
0–4	26.8	25.9	29.1
5–9	2.2	1.8	2.6
10–14	1.8	1.7	1.8
15–19	2.3	1.9	2.7
20–24	2.6	2.2	3.1
25–29	2.6	2.6	2.7
30–34	2.7	2.7	2.7
35–39	2.8	3.1	2.4
40–44	3	3.6	2.3
45–49	3.6	4.2	2.9
50–54	4.4	5.2	3.4
55–59	5.6	6.4	4.8
60–64	6.5	6.9	6.2
65–69	9.1	9.6	8.6
70–74	7.7	7.8	7.7
75–79	7.7	7.5	7.8
80–84	4	3.7	4.3
85+	4.5	4.2	4.8

8.3 Mortality Differentials

8.3.1 Mortality Differences by Age and Sex

Age and sex are the two major components in all demographic analyses. Pregnancy until the birth of at least a *male baby* is on the list of natural selection in most developing countries. In all societies and countries sex ratio at birth is in favor of male babies. Reliable statistics on sex ratio of the stillborn babies or babies whose birth was prevented by abortion is not available. Even then the specialists are of the opinion that in embryonic stage the sex ratio is in favor of males. It has also been observed that among the spoiled fetus the sex ratio is also in favor of males. This is a secular trend, observed in all societies and in all times for which some data are available. Although male babies are in small excess at the time of birth, their death rate is also high in the days and months following the birth. Before the end of the

Figure 8.2 *Proportion of death to total deaths by age and sex, India (SRS 2000)*

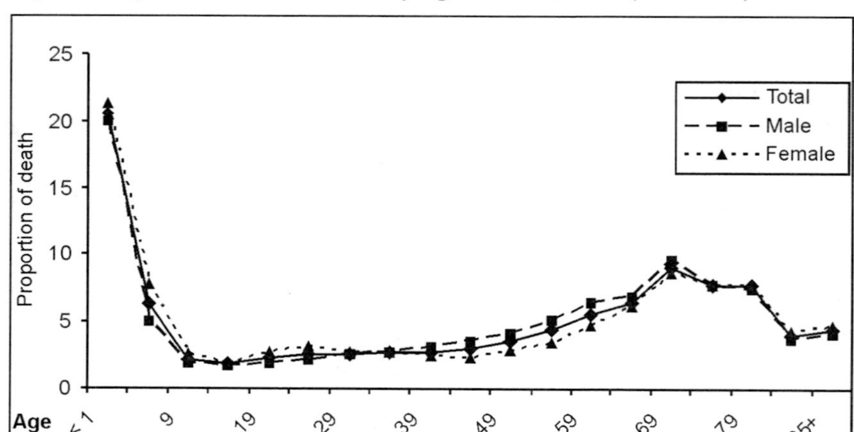

fourth birthday the number breaks even between boys and girls. Girls continue to have an edge over boys almost in all ages except for a brief period during their pregnancy. Proportion of deaths by age and sex to all deaths in India 2002 is presented in Table 8.5.

Males generally have to shoulder the major economic responsibility for the family in most societies. Though they are given some preferential treatment in their formative years, they remain susceptible to diseases, ailments, accidents and many other vagaries of life because of their greater exposure to external surroundings and frequent contact with people from various walks of life than females. Even a few decades back a woman's time was spent mostly in kitchen, in rearing children, attending to the needs of the other members of the household, i.e., she was out and out a house-keeper. Economic participation of women among socially and economically backward classes had been a common thing. However, such labor requires neither special skill nor education. Of late, women too are equipping themselves with necessary skills and are entering into labor market wherever opportunity exists.

Women have a somewhat greater risk of life, mostly at the initial years when they start giving birth to babies. Once they are out of the early childbearing age, their

Table 8.6 *CDRs of 16 larger states by sex, India 2000 (SRS data)*

States	*Persons*	*Males*	*Females*	*Males/Females*
Kerala	6.4	7.4	5.5	1.9
Tamil Nadu	7.9	8.6	7.2	1.4
West Bengal	7.0	7.4	6.6	0.8
Maharashtra	7.5	8.2	6.8	1.4
Andhra Pradesh	8.2	8.9	7.5	1.4
Punjab	7.4	7.7	7.0	0.7
Karnataka	7.8	9.1	6.4	2.7
Himachal Pradesh	7.2	8.2	6.2	2.0
Orissa	10.5	10.8	10.3	0.5
Gujarat	7.5	8.1	7.0	1.1
Assam	9.6	9.9	9.2	0.7
Haryana	7.5	7.9	7.1	0.8
Rajasthan	8.5	8.4	8.6	–0.2
Madhya Pradesh	10.3	10.3	10.3	0.0
Bihar	8.8	8.6	9.0	–0.4
Uttar Pradesh	10.3	10.1	10.4	–0.3
INDIA	8.5	8.9	8.1	0.8

life risk remains at a lower level compared to their male counterparts. In most countries, especially in the developed ones, women numerically dominate in the total population of the country (F/M > 1.00). In fact, they have higher expectation of life in almost all ages. In India, as also in some other countries, males are dominant partner in the population although they are more vulnerable to various types of old age diseases vis-à-vis females once they cross 40 years or so. In India, females' effective reproductive period is much shorter than those in most other countries in the developed world. Most women in India have their last babies born before they are 35 years. In reality, they have a greater risk factor only between 15 and 30 years.

Both at the beginning and towards the end of the career, risk of dying is much higher in all populations. After the initial years, age specific death rate starts to decline and it continues at about the same level until about 45 (Figure 8.2). Age-specific death rates clearly show that risk of dying is different at different phases of life. That is why age- and sex-specific death rates are used most frequently in population projections.

Even within the same country there could be considerable variation in death rates, and more generally in most socio-demographic indicators between states, sexes and urban-rural residence (Tables 8.5–8.8). Percentage distribution of deaths by broad age group for 16 larger states in India is presented in Table 8.7. Kerala's achievement in containing death at all ages is amazing. Half the numbers of states are already in the low regime of infant and child mortality. But the BIMARU (Bihar, Madhya Pradesh, Rajasthan and Uttar Pradesh) and four other states (Orissa, Gujarat, Assam and Haryana) distort the all-India picture altogether.

Table 8.7 *Percent distribution of deaths by broad age groups, India and 16 larger states, SRS 2000*

	Broad age group					
States	***<1***	***1–4***	***0–4***	***5–14***	***15–59***	***60 +***
Kerala	3.9	1.0	4.9	1.0	24.9	69.1
Tamil Nadu	12.4	1.5	14.0	1.8	36.8	47.5
West Bengal	14.9	4.0	18.9	3.2	31.0	46.9
Maharashtra	13.4	2.2	15.6	2.7	31.7	50.0
Andhra Pradesh	16.9	2.1	19.0	3.2	34.1	43.8
Punjab	15.3	3.1	18.4	2.0	30.8	48.7
Karnataka	16.0	3.5	19.5	2.3	37.4	40.8
Himachal Pradesh	15.7	3.1	18.8	1.3	25.6	54.4
Orissa	22.0	4.8	26.9	4.2	29.5	39.5
Gujarat	20.9	5.8	26.7	3.1	30.4	39.9
Assam	21.0	6.4	27.4	5.3	36.1	31.2
Haryana	23.8	5.5	29.4	3.1	29.3	38.2
Rajasthan	29.2	10.2	39.4	3.9	23.8	32.8
Madhya Pradesh	26.5	7.5	34.0	4.9	28.2	32.8
Bihar	22.3	9.2	31.5	5.4	26.1	36.9
Uttar Pradesh	26.6	10.1	36.7	4.4	25.2	33.7
INDIA	20.5	6.3	26.8	3.9	29.6	39.6

Table 8.8 *Age-specific death rate by residence and sex, India 1981 and 2000*

Age-group	*1981*	*2000*								
		Total			*Rural*			*Urban*		
		Total	*Male*	*Female*	*Total*	*Male*	*Female*	*Total*	*Male*	*Female*
1	*2*	*3*	*4*	*5*	*6*	*7*	*8*	*9*	*10*	*11*
< 1		71.1	70.5	71.6	77.3	76.2	785.	46.1	48.0	44.1
1–4		5.8	4.7	7.0	6.6	5.4	7.9	2.9	2.1	3.7
0–4	41.2	19.5	18.6	20.6	21.7	20.6	23.0	11.5	11.3	11.7
5–9	4.4	1.7	1.5	2.0	2.0	1.8	2.2	0.9	0.7	1.2
10–14	1.7	1.3	1.2	1.3	1.4	1.4	1.4	0.7	0.6	0.8
15–19	2.4	1.9	1.6	2.2	2.1	1.8	2.5	1.3	1.2	1.4
20–24	3.1	2.4	2.2	2.7	2.7	2.3	3.1	1.8	1.9	1.6
25–29	3.2	2.8	2.9	2.7	3.1	3.2	3.0	2.0	2.3	1.7
30–34	4.0	3.1	3.3	2.8	3.2	3.2	3.2	2.6	3.5	1.7
35–39	4.4	3.7	4.4	3.0	4.1	4.8	3.4	2.8	3.5	2.0
40–44	5.8	4.5	5.5	3.3	4.9	5.9	3.8	3.3	4.4	2.2
45–49	8.5	6.8	8.1	5.3	7.5	8.9	6.0	5.0	6.2	3.6
50–54	13.2	9.9	12.2	7.4	10.0	12.2	7.7	9.6	12.3	6.5
55–59	20.6	16.3	19.1	13.4	16.7	20.2	13.1	15.3	16.3	14.2
60–64	33.0	23.1	26.6	19.7	23.7	27.7	19.9	21.0	23.1	18.9
65–69	46.4	38.0	44.2	32.3	38.8	44.6	33.3	35.6	42.8	28.8
70–74	97.4	50.2	56.6	44.4	52.4	59.0	46.3	42.4	47.9	37.5
75–79		82.8	90.0	76.0	83.4	91.6	75.6	80.6	84.4	77.3
80–84		101.4	104.8	98.3	99.5	101.8	97.3	108.2	115.8	101.5
85+		164.7	178.6	152.4	168.1	183.2	154.2	153.1	161.6	146.7
CDR	12.4	8.5	8.9	8.1	9.3	9.6	8.9	6.3	6.8	5.9

For ready comparison, ASDRs for 1981 has also been presented in the same Table 8.8 (col.2). It is clear that ASDRs have substantially declined in all ages except at higher ages. The decline has been most significant both in 0–4 and 5–9 ages. The patterns however are similar. Proportion of deaths in higher age groups has increased fast in the last 20 years.

This pattern is observed in all countries and at all times. The curve (Figure 8.3) runs almost parallel to the X-axis beyond 9 years till it takes an upward turn somewhere around mid-forties. This U-shaped curve shows that mortality risk is high both at lower and higher ages. The up-turn for the male population happens a little earlier than that for women. At the lower end of the scale females have a slightly greater risk of life, but after age 30, risk of dying of males far exceeds that of females.

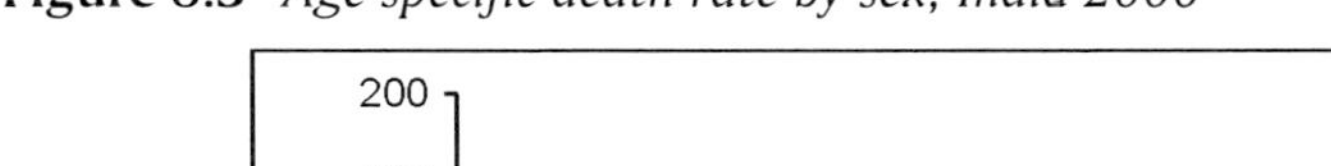

Figure 8.3 *Age-specific death rate by sex, India 2000*

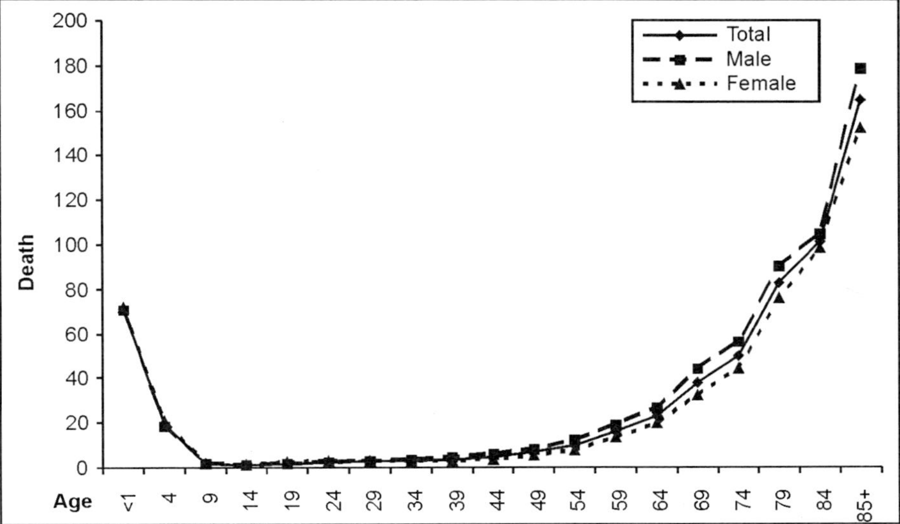

8.3.2 Mortality Differences by Residence

Because of very high population density, rising environmental pollution level due to presence of unwholesome manufacturing industries and lack of free space and fresh air, cities and towns earned the bad repute as destroyer of human lives. The almost complete lack of sanitation until about the beginning of the twentieth century, crowding the city dwellers in houses with little or no ventilation, sewage and drinking water running down the same open gutters, water-logging for breeding mosquitoes, made them perfect platforms for contagious parasitic and infectious diseases. It is no wonder that plague, cholera, tuberculosis, small pox and malaria, which were regular features in underdeveloped countries even at the beginning of the twentieth century, appeared as epidemics mostly in towns and great cities. Slum-dwellers still constitute a large proportion of population (about one-third) in most cities in India even at the beginning of the new millennium. The health of a city and quality of the civic services offered by it depends in considerable degree upon the size of these slum-dwellers.

Before modern vital statistics made it possible to compute actual differentials in deaths between rural and urban communities, the early comparisons showed that death rates in rural communities generally were lower than that in urban communities. Such comparisons were made with CDRs. The age composition of population in cities differed considerably from that in rural population. It is the younger people with better health and education that migrated to urban areas as industrialization advanced. Occupational hazards too complicated the computation of general death rates. Age and occupational adjustments in computation today made comparison of death rates more realistic.

The fruits of research in medical sciences – discovery of antibiotics, vaccination against various diseases and modern health care reached the urban people first. Most advanced clinics and specialized hospitals are all located in big cities in most of the developing countries. Although the governments have endeavored to extend health facilities even to remote rural areas, the health centers cater only very limited services to the needy poor. Whereas 72 percent of Indian population lives in villages, about 75 percent of state allotment on health goes to urban hospitals and clinics.

There is a real dearth of qualified doctors, pathologists and other health workers in villages. The improved health care in cities and towns as also because of affordability of an average urbanite to avail of the opportunities created by continuous up-gradation of health facilities, death rates in urban area came down faster than in rural area. In the early 1980s CDR in India was 12.7; urban CDR was 7.9 against CDR of 13.9 in rural area. In the last twenty years CDR in the total population has come down to 8.5, that in urban population to 6.3 and to 9.3 in rural area. The gap now has narrowed down considerably. The age-sex-specific death rates too show that urban people are better placed than the rural people in all broad age groups.

Table 8.9 *Estimated death rates for some broad age groups by sex and residence, India 2000 (SRS Statistical Report 2003)*

Age group	Total			Rural			Urban		
	P	*M*	*F*	*P*	*M*	*F*	*P*	*M*	*F*
0–4	19.5	18.6	20.6	21.7	20.6	23.0	11.5	11.3	11.7
5–14	1.5	1.4	1.6	1.7	1.6	1.8	0.8	0.6	1.0
15–59	4.3	4.9	3.8	4.6	5.1	4.1	3.5	4.2	2.8
60 +	47.3	52.6	42.3	48.3	54.1	42.9	43.6	47.5	39.9

Table 8.9a *Percentage distribution of death by type of medical attention received before death, India 2000 (SRS Statistical Report 2003)*

Institutional			Medical attention other than institutional			No medical attention		
Total	Rural	Urban	Total	Rural	Urban	Total	Rural	Urban
20.9	17.4	35.9	65.9	67.5	58.9	12.7	14.6	4.6

The true difference between rural and urban death rates is difficult to measure since many villagers seek admission with terminal illness in city hospitals and die there as well. The data in Tables 8.8 and 8.9a does not give the true picture of the type of health care that is available in rural India. Only 14.6 percent of rural deaths are not actually attended by qualified doctors.

More pragmatic computation should be based on rural farm and non-farm communities as also for different sexes. Urban death rates should also be computed separately for slum-dwellers and for blue and white-collar occupations. Deaths recorded in hospitals, no matter if the patient admitted was from the same city or from outside, often are counted against the administrative jurisdiction in which the hospital/nursing home is situated. Institutional records, both for birth and death, often would show names of persons who were not residents of the locality. Therefore, death (and birth) rates in urban area get somewhat inflated.

It has been observed in many studies that rural death rates (age- and sex-specific), though are different from those in city populations, are almost similar to death rates in smaller towns. So, both rural and urban death rates need to be calculated for farm and non-farm populations, for different grades of towns and cities as also by major occupations of the deceased.

8.3.3 Mortality Differences by Occupation or Profession

Occupational and professional hazards must be regarded as one of the principal reasons why a middle-aged man is more vulnerable to health problems than a middle-aged woman. This aspect of differential mortality has not been studied extensively. NSSO has in their various rounds tried to study this aspect of mortality in India, but those were based on rather small samples. Even then it can with some confidence be said that those working in coal and other mines, foundries, paint and chemical plants, cement factories or where explosives are manufactured anywhere on this earth have greater risk of life than those engaged in white-collar jobs. Risk of life is greater in industrial occupations than in traditional occupations. Besides the risk factor associated with the occupation, the non-skilled workers have greater risk of life than the skilled workers. With improved technology and capital-intensive production, industrial accidents have come down considerably.

Risk of tuberculosis is common among miners. Tuberculosis, silicosis and respiratory diseases in general are common in quarries and cement factories. Accidents are frequent in coal mines, in construction and transport. Occupational differences in mortality have narrowed down in Western countries because of strict implementation of occupational norms and enormous improvement in the work environment, especially those in hazardous category. Mortalities associated with diverse occupations, it is often argued, is not so much due to the nature of occupation as such as are due to the standards of living which the different occupations can give effect to. Occupations largely determine the family income, which in turn decides the physical environment of the worker and of his family at home.

8.3.4 Mortality Differences by Geographical Factors

The hot humid atmosphere in Africa, Asia and Latin America had a decisive role on mortality and morbidity of people living in these continents even a few decades back. Mortality differentials on such climatic grounds are not rated high today. But physical factors do contribute to death rate. A vast country like India has enormous diversity in physical environment and climate. In some places, the day temperature in mid-summer often would reach 50°C or more; there are places where the temperature at the same period would be in the pleasant twenties. There are some hilly areas as in Jammu & Kashmir, Uttaranchal, Himachal Pradesh and Arunachal Pradesh where there would be snow cover for days and people would experience sub-zero day temperature. Typhoons and tornados often devastate many costal regions all over the earth. The coastal areas of Orissa, Andhra Pradesh and Tamil Nadu often are hit by cyclones. Coastal regions of Orissa and Andhra Pradesh were ravaged by a high-intensity cyclone a few years back, causing deaths to thousands of people. The Tsunami devastation of 26th December, 2004 is still fresh in our mind. More that 200,000 people lost their lives in Indonesia, Sri Lanka and Andaman and Nicobar Islands and Tamil Nadu in India. Gujarat had a high intensity earthquake, destroying almost all houses in some high-density places and killing hundreds of people and domestic animals. Large areas in Assam, West Bengal and Bihar are flooded every year taking very heavy toll on life and property. Pakistan occupied Kashmir experienced serious devastation of life and property from high intensity earthquake a few years back.

Climatic change due to global warming has increased tornados and typhoons in North America, Japan, China and in many other regions causing great losses of lives and properties. USA and Europe experienced heat waves unprecedented in the last 60 years. A state of emergency was declared in New York since weather experts forecast that mercury level may reach 43°C in high summer in 2006. In a recent press release, NASA confirmed that 14 percent of the Arctic Ice, of the size of Pakistan/Turkey has disappeared between 2004 and 2006 as a result of global warming. Coastal areas of many countries and many islands may go under water soon. Vector diseases are likely to be intensified in Asia and Africa.

8.3.5 Mortality Differences by Religion

There appears some difference in mortality among various religious groups in India. These religious groups are not necessarily uniformly distributed throughout the length and breadth of the country. Often they are settled in some pockets. Sikhs, for example, are mostly located in Punjab. Parsees are found mostly in urban areas of Maharashtra. Christians comprise a large segment of population of Kerala and Goa. The Muslims are found in all states, but they concentrate mostly in Jammu & Kashmir, Bihar, West Bengal, Uttar Pradesh and Andhra Pradesh. Hindus of course are to be found everywhere in large proportions. So, when we try to compare mortality among various religious groups, we have to keep in mind the special features that accompany those pockets or regions. There is not much of a difference in mortality of the two major religious communities in rural areas. Death rate among the Sikhs and Christians are similar. Both Hindus and Muslims have higher death rates compared to most other religious communities in India.

8.3.6 Mortality Differences in Peace and War Conditions

There are mortality differences between peace and war conditions. Malthus said that war along with epidemics and famine are positive checks against population growth. That is, uncontrolled growth of population creates a condition in which the standard of living of the masses falls; severe shortage of food and other commodities poses serious problems to mankind. Human rationality becomes a victim to biological demands. In early periods of human civilization, frequent wars between countries and population groups had often been for procuring wealth, food and other necessities. Destruction of life brought down the population to a reasonable size. Population growth in those periods showed frequent fluctuations, from very fast growth to even decline. When the condition of scarcity was not felt and when there existed some peace, population grew fast due to lowered death rate. Drought, flood, famine, epidemic and war came back in cycles preventing uncontrolled growth of population.

In modern times purposes of war have changed as also the mode of war. War today does not remain confined between two countries – World War I and II are good examples. The war effect, direct and indirect, was felt in all countries. In earlier days war usually was fought at places far away from human habitations – in vast open space or in mountains and other places away from populous cities and villages. It was rather a one-to-one combat and death rate was high among the military personnel. The civic population and the economy were largely spared except when the winners entered the city to take possession of it, which often was accompanied by looting of private wealth. But modern war has changed completely. These days war is fought mostly for economic and political gains (war in Iraq and Afghanistan, for example). The targets of aggression often are factories, power generation units, bridges, large dams, airports and other key installations. War is now fought with technology and the principal target often is dense cities, economic zones and key defense installations. High explosive rockets, missiles and airdropping of bombs at strategic places, have largely replaced conventional weapons. The war is regulated from within the confines of a control room; everything is computerized. The end of World War II came when Hiroshima and

Nagasaki were blown off by atom bombs. The extraordinary devastation power of these two small bombs has put a brake on its use any further. Today's nuclear bombs are thousand times more powerful than those experimental bombs used in 1945. About 40 million people died in World War II, more than 20 million in Soviet Russia alone. The economic fallout of war India had with China and Pakistan is still not over.

8.3.7 Other Mortality Differentials

Demographers have drawn our attention to a few other mortality differentials. The death rate among married persons generally is lower than that among unmarried persons. It is argued that those who are not mentally and physically quite steady prefer to remain single. Marriage makes a man/woman more responsible and organized and asks him/her to be in command over family affairs. The discipline and norms of married life help increase the expectation of life. But it is also a fact that women live much longer than men and a high proportion of the aged women are widow, especially in orthodox countries like India. Hindu widows in India would often change their food habit after the death of their husbands. Most of them would become vegetarian, would go without cooked food and even water periodically on religious grounds. In spite of these self-imposed restraints on physical comfort, they have relatively fewer health problems than men.

The most dominant denominator in most mortality still is income poverty. The affluent can choose his physical environment and healthy dwellings, has no problem for nutrition and can pay due attention to health for all the members of his family. Poor are in perpetual poverty; even these toiling masses cannot help the two ends meet. Excessive labor, malnutrition, poor physical surroundings, dwellings and neighborhood make them easy pray to diseases. No wonder that mortality rate is high among the poor.

8.4 Infant and Child Mortality

Discussion on mortality would remain incomplete if mortality of infants and children are not discussed in some detail. We have noted in our discussion on CDR and ASDR that the mortality situation prevailing in a population is generally dictated by deaths in two major age-groups – 0–4 and 60+ (or 65+) years. Life expectancy at birth, which also is an indirect estimation of mortality level in a population, largely depends upon the survival of infants and children. The state of health of a country is easily judged by death rates in 0–4 age-group, especially between birth and the first birthday (age < 1 year). The fact that the average length of life in the developed countries is above 76 years and the average infant mortality rate IMR in these countries is in a single digit, often less than their average CDR, is not a mere coincidence. Whereas the general mortality level in the population of a developing country is largely dependent upon infant and under-five mortality rates, the same in the developed countries depends upon the survival progress of their old-age group. Table 8.10 shows how infant and child mortality has changed between 1970 and 1999 along with percentage of people not expected to survive beyond 40 years and probability at birth of surviving to age 65. The high income countries are well ahead of the developing ones in all these parameters. The tabled data also suggest that the developing countries would be able to bring down their general mortality as IMR and child mortality rates improve in these countries. There is hardly similar such scope for the developed countries since both IMR and under-five mortalities has already reached the achievable lowest. Unless they further bring down mortality rates for ages 5 to 59, CDR in their populations are likely to rise or hover around 9-10 if their birth rates continue at the current range. Still today, there is no better single indicator of living and general health conditions in any population group than IMR. But the tremendous improvement in health services in general and infant and childcare in particular will soon relegate IMR to a less important position. It has already happened in high income, high human development countries. India in the decade ending 1991 reduced the percentage of people not expected to survive to age 40 by 5 percent, females and rural people improved the survivorship more than males and urban people (Table 8.11).

Table 8.10 *IMR, child mortality and some other statistics for some categories of countries*

Countries	*IMR*		*Under five mortality*		*% of people not expected to survive to age 40*	*Probability at birth of surviving to age 65 (1995–2000)*		*% of population (1999)*	
	1970	*1999*	*1970*	*1999*	*1997*	*Female*	*Male*	*under age 15*	*65 and above*
1	*2*	*3*	*4*	*5*	*6*	*7*	*8*	*9*	*10*
Developing	109	61	167	89	14.6	68.3	61.2	33.1	5.0
Least developed	149	100	243	159	30.8	46.0	41.7	43.2	3.1
High income	21	6	26	6		88.8	80.0	18.6	14.5
Middle income	85	32	121	39		78.2	67.1	27.8	8.5
Low income	126	80	202	120		59.0	53.6	37.2	5.2

Source: UNDP: Human Development Report 1999, 2001

Table 8.11 *Persons not expected to survive beyond age 40 by sex and residence, India 1981 & 1991 (percentage)*

Residence	*1981*			*1991*		
	Males	*Females*	*Persons*	*Males*	*Females*	*Persons*
Rural	23.4	27.1	25.2	18.3	21	19.6
Urban	13.6	14.7	14.1	11.5	11.3	11.4
Combined	21.5	24.5	23	16.9	19.1	18

Source: National Human Development Report 2001, Planning Commission, Government of India

Infant mortality measures the deaths of children under age 1 year (< 1 year). IMR is defined as

$$IMR = \frac{{}_1D_0}{{}_1P_0} \times 1{,}000 \qquad \ldots(8.1)$$

John Graunt, working on parish registers in London, estimated that in 1662 only about 640 children out of 1,000 born survived to age 6. At the end of the eighteenth century, about 800 babies out of 1,000 born survived till their first birthday in Sweden. The following compilation will give an idea about how life expectancy and IMR have gone hand in hand in the history.

Table 8.12 *Life expectancy and IMR – glimpses of history*

	Life expectancy at birth			*IMR*		
		1970–75	*1995–2000*		*1970*	*1999*
Prehistoric	20–35			200–300		
Sweden, 1750s	37	74.7	79.3	210	11	3
India, 1880	25	50.3	62.3	230	127	70
Sri Lanka		65.1	71.6		65	17
U.S., 1900	48	71.5	76.5	133	20	7
France, 1950	66	72.4	78.1	52	18	5
Japan		73.3	80.5		14	4
Sierra Leon		35	37.3		206	182

The first year of life is most important to many for various reasons. To parents, birth of a baby brings joy in the family together with anxiety – many sleepless nights are spent at the bedside of the baby in attending, caring and in silent prayer to God for the health and wellbeing of the child. This anxiety continues till the baby reaches adolescence stage. The first year of a baby is critical mostly because of health related reasons. The baby is yet to develop resistances to fight diseases.

Demographers look at the first year of a child's life with keen interest. These infants symbolize the true future of a population. A clear picture of the composition of the population, the ratio between its various segments, birth and survival rates, etc. become traceable from the number celebrating the first birthday. The mortality rate of infants in most countries still remain a critical index of health awareness, health infrastructure and planning, economic progress, education of mothers, availability of life-saving drugs, primary vaccination cover, etc. We have seen earlier that a faster rate of decline in CDR does not necessarily mean a faster rate of decline in IMR. CDR is a composite index derived from age-specific death rates in the population. Infant mortality remains a very important component in CDR in developing countries. But it is the old age mortality that will ultimately dominate the CDR level of a population. Risk of dying is largest at both ends of life. By curtailing or minimizing this risk at the beginning, we prolong the life span and push the high risk period further up. In most developed countries, the probability of dying in the very year of birth is almost the same as that at age 60. Probability of dying in the very first month after the birth is almost the same as that at age 70. 'Reproductive wastage' is an important topic in all demographic deliberations. 'Reproductive wastage' actually refers to all deaths between the start of pregnancy and the fifth year of the child. The time period of reproductive wastage is divided as

(a) pre-natal mortality,
(b) infant mortality, and
(c) childhood mortality.

8.4.1 Pre-natal Mortality

This refers to all fetal wastages. Though no reliable statistics can be obtained for pre-natal mortality, such wastages, it is presumed, account for about 25 percent of all reproductive wastages. With space and time, such wastages often would vary. Scientists believe that maximum fetal wastage is immediately after pregnancy. Such wastages decline with the age of the fetus. They also believe that sex ratio of the wasted fetus is against male babies. Natural and planned abortion is mostly responsible for fetus wastage. Stillbirth, the other component of fetal wastage, has largely been contained by improved health care of expecting mothers and close monitoring of the health and growth of the baby in the womb. Scientists also have observed that stillbirth is minimum when the age of the expecting mother is about 25 years and when there is a gap of 3 years between the last birth and the present pregnancy.

8.4.2 Infant Mortality

Death of a baby born alive but not surviving till his/her first birthday is reckoned as infant mortality. Infant mortality in the developed countries has come down rapidly, thanks to the decline in fertility. Every baby born is an asset to parents and to the state as well, especially in the developed countries, because of nearly zero-order growth rate there. Every possible care for the expecting mother and highly specialized institutional support for the mother and the baby have succeeded in great reduction of infant mortality in the developed countries.

We have stated earlier that the developing countries made good use of inventions and discoveries in medical sciences, carried out mostly in developed countries, to bring down the general mortality levels in their populations very fast. Unlike mortality in the general population across the globe, which is as low as 9 per 1,000 population (10 in the most developed countries and 15 in the least developed countries), under-five mortality in the world population is still very high, 81, (varying from 10 in developed countries to 161 in the developing countries) and IMR 56 (8 in the developed countries) even though the developing countries brought it down from 109 in 1970 to 61 in 1999. At 56, the world's infant mortality rate has never been lower; however, differences across the world are substantial. Africa's rate (88) is ten times higher than the average rate (8) for the developed countries. In Africa the highest levels of infant mortality in the world are observed, with rates as high as 165 in Sierra Leone. On average the rate for Asia (56) is somewhat lower than that in Africa, but some Asian countries such as Afghanistan have rates (150) as high as anywhere in the world. On the other hand, Hong Kong's rate (3.2) is very low, illustrating that the most variation in IMR occurs in Asia. Both Europe and North America have low levels of infant mortality, with average rates well under 10. However, European variation is not inconsequential; rates in at least some parts of Eastern Europe are nearly 10 times higher than that in northern European countries such as Iceland and Sweden.

The gap in the life expectancy between the highest and the lowest (Japan 82.3 years, Sierra Leon 41.8 years) is a whooping 42 years (HDR, 2007/08) in spite the fact that general mortality situation round the world has improved greatly. We may get answer to most of these vital issues from the causes of mortality among infants and children below age 5 years.

Causes of Infant Mortality

Bourgeois-Pichat (1952) classified infant mortality into two causal categories – endogenous and exogenous mortality. The first category comprises "those cases in which the child bears within itself, from birth, the cause resulting in its death, whether that cause was inherited from its parents at its conception, or acquired from its mother during gestation or delivery". Exogenous causes refer to "those cases in which the infant picks up the factors which causes its death in the environment in which it lives". McNamara (1982) referred endogenous deaths to those deaths that are caused by "factors such as the congenital malformations, the circumstances of prenatal life, and the birth process". Exogenous infant death is "caused by infection, parasitic and respiratory diseases, accidents and other environmental and external causes". Endogenous causes, which usually are the causes of neonatal death, may extend beyond the period of infancy to cause such degenerative diseases of later life as heart disease, cancer, diabetes and even AIDS. It is the exogenous causes that is avertable through preventive medicines, technology, education, medical know-how and better nutrition. Scientists are confident that deaths from intrinsic factors can also be controlled in the near future (by genetherapy for example).

In the more developed countries *neonatal mortality* (death within the first 4 weeks) has the largest share in their IMRs. Causes of neo-natal mortality are primarily organic along with deficiency in nutrition during pregnancy or some injury at the time of birth. Exogenous factors are primarily responsible for *post-neonatal mortality* (age of one month to the first birthday). Nearly two-thirds of infant mortality in India and other developing countries happens within the first month of the child's birth. Whereas IMR in the world still hovers around 56, it is about 100 in the least developed and only 7–8 in the developed countries.

Table 8.12 shows how IMR has changed in India between 1911 and 2000. About 50 percent reduction in IMR has been possible between 1976 and 2000. A 21 percent reduction happened between 1988–90 and 1998–2000; the drop varied from 33 percent in Kerala to about 14 percent in Rajasthan. As of 2000 record, there is a wide divergence in IMR among the states in India, from a low of 14 in Kerala to as high as 95 in Orissa. Kerala is the only state where IMR in rural area is smaller than that in urban area.

Table 8.13 *Infant mortality rates in India, 1911–2000*

Year	*IMR (five year average)*	*Year*	*IMR (five year average)*		
1911–15	204	1971	129		
1916–20	219	1976	129		
1921–25	174	1981	110		
1926–30	178	1985	96		
1931–35	174	1991	80		
1936–40	161	1995	72		
1941–45	161	2000	*Total*	*Male*	*Female*
1946–50	161	Total/Combined	68	67	69
1946–50	134	Rural	74	72	76
1951–61	146	Urban	44	45	42

Source: 1911–50:Based on annual reports of the Public Health Commissioners
1951–61: From the Census Actuary
1971–2000: Sample Registration System

Infant mortality is usually divided into two categories: (1) Neonatal mortality (death before 29 days of birth) and (2) Post-neonatal mortality (death between 29 days to less than one year). Neonatal mortality rate (NMR) is defined as

$$\text{NMR} = \frac{{}_{29days}D_0}{{}_1P_0} \times 1{,}000 \qquad \ldots(8.2)$$

and post-neonatal death rate, PNMR, is

$$\text{PNMR} = \frac{{}_{1\,year}D_{29\,days}}{{}_1P_0} \times 1{,}000 \qquad \ldots(8.3)$$

The distinction between neonatal (and perinatal) and postneonatal mortality is important since the risk of death is higher close to the delivery date, and the causes of death near the time of birth are quite different from those later in infancy. Therefore, effective interventions to reduce infant mortality need to take into account the distribution of ages at death of infants.

Neonatal mortality is further subdivided into *early neonatal mortality* (0 to < than 7 days) and *late neonatal mortality* (7 to < than 29 days after birth). Birth weight is a critical factor in mortality within the first 4 weeks of birth. The underweight may be due to delivery of the baby before the full term or due to poor health of the mother. UNDP's Human Development Report, 1999 states that 18 percent of infants in the developing countries have low birth weight. In South Asian countries this is as high as 32 percent. Even in the industrialized countries 6 percent of infants have low birth weight. In India, every third child born has low birth weight. In economically backward families, the expecting mothers do not get enough nutrition during their pregnancy. Protein and vitamin content in an expecting mother's diet is far from what is required for her during pregnancy. A poor man's wife has to perform all the household responsibilities and therefore she does not get the necessary rest that she needs at advanced stage of her pregnancy. The problem gets further aggravated if she already has a baby who still needs direct care of mother. Under-weight of the baby is noticed both with very young and old-aged mothers. Since adoption of National Population Policy 2000, a number of steps have been taken by the Central government to address to the health of mother and her child in India. Every pregnant mother who registers her pregnancy in the health center is given a registration card which entitles her of receiving free tetanus vaccine, iron tablets and free medical check up and advice. The government takes the financial responsibility for the surgical delivery of the baby when necessary. The pregnant woman receives Rs.500 in cash and also compensation for traveling to health centers for check up.

A very significant cause of mortality in the very first few days of the birth is birth injury. Infection at the time of delivery (99 percent of births in developed countries receive intensive medical attention, that in the developing countries is only 38 percent), especially when umbilical cord is severed, breathing trouble, pneumonia and tetanus are the major reasons for death at this period. Measles, diarrhea, respiratory trouble and poor sanitary conditions mostly contribute to mortality in late neonatal and post-neonatal stages. 95 percent of babies in the developed countries receive primary vaccines as against only 61 percent in the developing countries. Exogenous factors contribute most to mortality in the very first month of birth. Endogenous factors contribute most to post-neonatal mortality. This could be due to some hereditary factor or some macrobiotic infections. Added to these could be severe malnutrition (when the mother fails to breast-feed the baby) or infection through breast milk. Waterborne diseases most often are behind infant mortality in the underdeveloped countries. Lack of sanitation and safe drinking water in villages and slums is a common problem in most underdeveloped countries. In the hot summer months when there is scarcity of water everywhere, infants and children become easy prey to gastro-enteric diseases. The cyclical variation of infant and child mortality is symptomatic of poor economic development of a country. Early-neonatal and late-neonatal mortality in India contribute 47 percent and 17 percent respectively to all infant deaths. The share of post-neonatal mortality to total infant mortality is about 34 percent. Still births and infants dying within 7 days of birth together constitute a separate index – peri-natal mortality rate (PMR). The risk of death is higher close to the delivery date, and the causes of death near the time of delivery are quite different from those later in infancy. Therefore, for planning effective interventions to reduce infant mortality we need to take into account the age distribution of infant deaths. Child and infant mortality indicators of India are presented in Table 8.14.

Table 8.14 *Child and infant mortality indicators, India 2000*

Indicators	*Total*	*Rural*	*Urban*
Child (below 5 years) mortality rate	20	22	12
Infant mortality rate	68	74	44
Neonatal mortality rate (NMR)	44	49	27
Early neonatal mortality rate	32	35	19
Late neonatal mortality rate	12	13	8
Post-neonatal mortality rate (PNMR)	23	25	16
Still birth	8	9	7
Peri-natal mortality rate (PMR)	40	44	26

Source: SRS Statistical Report, 2003

An important factor in reducing post-neonatal mortality is adequate nutrition, particularly breast milk, which provides babies with both the nourishment and the antibodies to fight infectious diseases. However, adequate breast milk depends upon how well mothers were nourished during the period of pregnancy as well as when breast-feeding. Also important is the proper use of breast milk substitutes and supplements – mixing formula with unclean water and/or diluting formula for cost-savings reasons, both known to occur in developing countries, have negative effects on the health of infants. The promotion by multinational corporations of breast milk substitutes to women in poorer countries has been one of the travesties of our times. It is estimated that 1.5 million deaths a year could be prevented by breast-feeding alone.

The issue of HIV-infected mothers' breast-feeding has become controversial. Based on some evidence of mother-to-child transmission of HIV through breast-feeding, some countries have instituted policies that recommend that mothers with HIV should not breast-feed. In contrast are policies that promote breast-feeding even in areas with high HIV prevalence. Since breast-feeding protects against infectious diseases that take lives of millions of infants every year, there is a policy debate about the best course of action. Researchers do not know if the protection against infectious diseases afforded by breast-feeding outweighs the risks of HIV transmission to children. However, the World Health Organization (WHO) Collaborative Study Team on the "Role of Breast-feeding on the Prevention of Infant Mortality" observed that the breast-fed babies of mothers with HIV had six times the protection against deaths from diarrhea in the first few months of life than babies not breast-fed. In the second half-year of life, protection against both diarrhea and acute respiratory infections was about double that for non-breast-fed babies. Protection declined with age of child, and was greatest for the children of the least educated women. It appears the benefits may outweigh the risks for breast-feeding (HIV transmission) at least for a limited period and for poorer women, who are unable to afford safe substitute milk. However, another issue to consider is that breast-feeding may negatively affect the health of mothers with HIV/AIDS.

Another cause of infant mortality is violence. Beating of wife, closely linked with patriarchal social structures, may lead to both pregnancy loss and infant mortality. Other violence, such as infanticide, is extremely difficult to document, but it seems likely that some portion of the "missing girls" in India and China were the victims of infanticide. When infanticide is practiced, it is most likely a response to difficult economic circumstances (and coercive population policy, as in the case of China) in conjunction with male-child preference.

Violence against babies is not limited to developing countries. Violence to infants in the form of head trauma, including *shaken baby syndrome* (SBS), has been observed in USA too. In 2000, Suzanne Starling and James Holden found that in both a western and southern US sample men are more likely to be perpetrators of violence, with biological fathers (not necessarily married to the mother or living with the child) the most likely to cause fatal or nonfatal head trauma to infants, followed by boyfriends. The victims are more likely to be boys, with an average age of six months.

Excluding violence, neonatal mortality (in contrast to post-neonatal mortality) is less likely to be the direct result of social, economic, and environmental conditions. Major causes of neonatal mortality include low birth weight, premature birth, congenital malformations, and sudden infant death syndrome (SIDS). In developed countries most infant mortality is concentrated in the early neonatal period.

Overall, income and education, both at the societal and individual levels, are closely associated with infant mortality. While the link between infant mortality and level of socioeconomic development is not perfect, the infant mortality rate is commonly used more than any other index as a general indicator of socioeconomic wellbeing and medical and public health.

The countries facing population explosion obviously have very large young age population and still have alarming infant and child mortality. IMRs in these countries rise and fall with the change in the climatic conditions. S. Chandrasekhar has tried to relate this seasonal and cyclical variation in IMR and child mortality to economic prosperity of a country. He classified all the countries of the world into four groups according to the level of IMR prevalent in these countries.

Table 8.15 *Change of IMR and life expectancy at birth, 1985–1999*

Region	*IMR*		*Life expectancy*	
	1985	*1999*	*1985*	*1999*
World	78	56	60	66.4
Developed regions	16	6	73	77.8
Developing regions	88	61	57	64.1
Africa	112		49	49
Sub-Saharan Africa		107	43	48.8
Asia	83		59	67
East Asia & The Pacific		34		68.8
South Asia		69		61.9
Arab States		44		65.9
North America	11		74	77.0
Latin America	62	32	64	69.3
Europe	15	6	73	77.8

(a) Very high IMR (125 or more),
(b) High IMR (between 75 and 125),
(c) Controlled IMR (between 35 and 75), and
(d) Low IMR (< than 35)

In 2005, there were as many as 18 countries, mostly from sub-Saharan Africa, that still had IMR in excess of 100 of which 8 countries had IMR exceeding 120. IMRs in Sierra Leon and Angola were 165 and 154 respectively. In India, there are only two bigger states, Kerala and Maharashtra, that have IMR below 50. All other states have IMRs above 50 and five of these states have IMR 75 or more. Except in Kerala, all the other larger states have rural IMR well above 50.

It has been observed that infant mortality is significantly high with the first order births. Mothers of these babies are mostly below 20 years. Most of these mothers did not have any previous experience of pregnancy. They definitely lack the experience and necessary guidance from others in childcare. Infant mortality has been observed to be least with the second child. IMR increases progressively with third and higher order births. The smaller the time gap between the current and previous birth, the higher is the probability of infant death. Death rate among twin babies is more than that with single births. Twin babies have smaller birth weights, a fact that necessitates extra care in respect to nutrition and handling, which most poor families cannot afford.

Beyond the first year of life, it is mostly the exogenous factors that clearly play a major role in the health of a child. Most common childhood diseases, some are deadly fatal, are polio, chicken pox, measles, mumps, diphtheria, pertusis or whooping cough, and tetanus.

8.4.3 Child Mortality

Death of infants and children under age of five is referred to as *child mortality*. *Under-five or child mortality rate* is the number of children who die by the age of five, per thousand live births. In 2007, the world average was 68. About 25,000 young children die every day, mainly from preventable causes. Child death in the world in 1990 was 12.7 million. It dropped to 9.2 million in 2007. About half of child deaths occur in Africa. One in six children in sub-Saharan Africa dies before their fifth birthday. Sierra Leone has the world's highest child mortality rate (262 in 2007). There were 41 countries where at least 10 percent of children under five died in 2006. All but three were in Africa. Ten of the 41 countries recorded higher child mortality rates compared to that in 1990. The largest improvement between 1990 and 2006 happened in Latin America and the Caribbean. They cut their child mortality rates by 50 percent. World's child mortality rate has dropped by over 60 percent since 1960. According to an estimate by UNICEF, one million child deaths could be prevented annually at a cost of US $ 1 billion per year. Reduction of child mortality is the fourth Millennium Development Goals (MDG) of the United Nations. Of the 189 countries pledging the MDGs, only 60 countries would meet the millennium goal of reduction of child mortality by two-thirds in 2015 (India not included in the list). Cross-country data show that fall in child mortality among the poorest 20 percent is only half the average rate of decline. It clearly indicates that the gap in child mortality between poor and the rich is widening.

According to UNICEF, most child deaths (70 percent in developing countries) result from one of the following five causes or a combination thereof: acute respiratory infections, diarrhea, measles, malaria, and malnutrition. About two-thirds of child death is preventable. Malnutrition and lack of safe water and sanitation contribute to half of all these children's deaths.

8.5 Maternal Mortality[1]

United Nations estimated global maternal mortality in 2000 at 529,000, of which less than 1 percent occurred in the developed countries. Most of these deaths have been medically preventable for decades, since treatments to shun such deaths have been well known since the 1950s. According to Women's International Network News figures, worldwide maternal mortality ratio (MMR, the number of maternal deaths per 100,000 live births) is 430, with a sharp division between developing countries, where MMR is estimated to be 480. In the developed countries the ratio is only 27. If this is translated into women's lifetime risk of dying from pregnancy/pregnancy-related reasons: 1 chance in 48 in the third world countries contrasted to 1 in 1,800 in developed countries. In sub-Saharan Africa the lifetime risk of maternal death is 1 in 16, for highly developed nations only 1 in 2,800. Highest maternal mortality is observed in Sierra Leon, 2100, and least in Ireland, 1. Lowest maternal mortality is observed in Northern Europe. High rates of maternal deaths occur in countries that have high rates of infant and child mortality reflecting prevalence of poor nutrition and medical care.

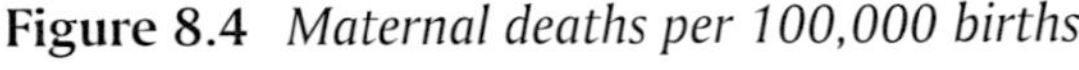

Figure 8.4 *Maternal deaths per 100,000 births*

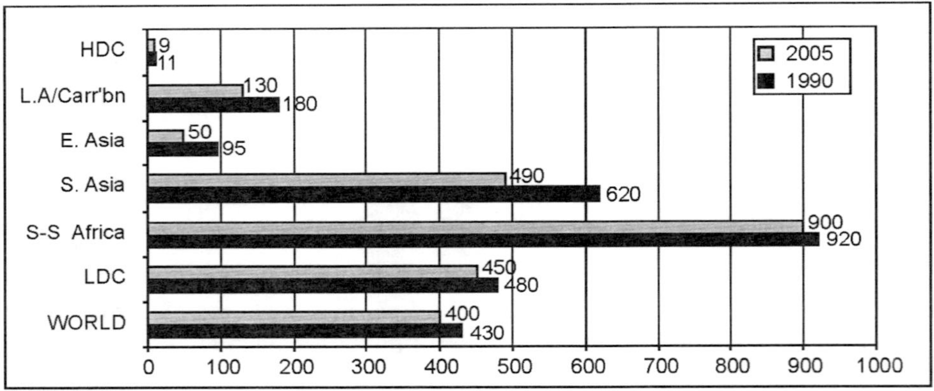

The most common direct causes of maternal death are severe bleeding (25 percent), infection (15 percent), unsafe abortion (13 percent), eclampsia (pregnancy-induced hypertension, often accompanied by seizures, 12 percent), and obstructed labor (8 percent). Obviously, many of these complications get aggravated if proper medical attention is not provided to the laboring mother.

Many argue that roots of maternal mortality lie in social, economic, health and political factors. They view that maternal mortality risk is associated with the risks that a girl or woman has to face (malnutrition, poor health, female genital mutilation, early marriage and pregnancy, lack of family planning mechanisms especially for child spacing) in her day to day life. To them, it is a social justice issue. Others however argue that maternal mortality is a public health problem since institutional medical intervention can and does check the type of mortality and therefore the way to reduce maternal mortality is through the provision of emergency obstetrical care.

Even admitting that medical and social factors play important roles in maternal mortality, we must say that medical interventions are extremely important, more so in complicated cases, in

1 A maternal death is defined as the death of a woman while pregnant or within 42 days of termination of pregnancy, irrespective of the duration and site of the pregnancy, from any cause related to or aggravated by the pregnancy or its management but not from accidental or incidental causes (WHO).

reducing maternal mortality, as long as such interventions are carried out by trained health personnel. Especially important is competent emergency obstetrical care. Family care is important for the health of mother and the baby in the womb, but it is the health care guidance and institutional emergency care that really can reduce the incidences of maternal mortality. Regular check-up during the entire period of pregnancy, nutritional (milk and protein rich) diets, vitamin and iron capsule supplements, vaccination against tetanus, sufficient rest, etc. are a must for the expecting mothers. In the developing countries, family planning services, which operate to advice couples to opt for a limited number of births as also spacing of births, can help reduce not only birth rates but prevent maternal mortality as well.

Maternal mortality is generally low in societies that value women's education and higher social status. Educated women will marry late, thus avoiding early pregnancy and complications thereof. Abortion now-a-days has become an important tool to prevent unwanted pregnancy. Most countries provide legal support to abortions. Access to legal abortion can largely prevent maternal death or some serious injury. Legal abortion is carried out in a clean and healthy environment with necessary support system to deal with complications, if there be any. It is estimated that as high as one-half of illegal abortions lead to maternal mortality in Indonesia, where abortion is denied legally. This would translate to 1 million maternal deaths in a year in Indonesia. However, orthodox societies do not generally approve abortion, no matter if the state has enacted laws to legalize it.

It is estimated that about 26 million babies are born every year in India of which 1.7 million die at or around the time of birth. Within the first four weeks another 1.1 million babies die. 4–5 mothers for every 1,000 babies die at the time of birth of their babies. Such loss of life aggregates to about 0.13 million every year. Death of mothers at the time of delivery and death of infants in absolute terms are one of the highest in India. The Government of India fixed a target to bring down the maternal mortality to about 2 per thousand by 2007 and 1 per thousand by 2012. Attempt will be made to bring down infant mortality rate to 45 by 2007 and 28 in 2012 from the observed 68 in 2000.

The Health Ministry of Government of India has identified some of the major reasons for maternal and infant mortality:

- Lack of trained mid-wives in remote rural areas;
- Traditional delivery method under untrained 'dai' (mid-wives) is still followed in backward regions;
- Neither a doctor nor a trained mid-wife is available to attend to the complexities that may arise at the time of delivery;
- The physical infrastructure is so poor in remote areas that a pregnant woman often cannot be taken even to the nearest primary health center;
- Life-saving drugs and blood often are not available in the rural, even in district hospitals;
- Operation theatres, if there is any, are in a dilapidated condition to undertake even a simple surgery.

For this and many other reasons pregnant mothers in remote areas have to leave everything to chances. Abject poverty is one of the principal reasons why a pregnant woman is not sent to the nearest health center or a hospital. Even after the child is born, health care remains a far cry both for the mother and the child. Such observations generally are true in most of the underdeveloped countries.

The Indian government has introduced an insurance program so that mother and the child do not suffer because of fund crunch. It is contemplated under this scheme that medical insurances would cover all medical expenses both for the mother and the child from the start of pregnancy to six months after the birth of the baby. All those who are under 'below the poverty line' (BPL) category are entitled to register their names with the district health directorate. Though the details of the project have not been finalized yet, Rs.1,200 would be given ad hoc to the mother at the time of delivery. The government would also bear all medical expenses incurred at the time of delivery. Both public and private clinics and hospitals where the pregnant woman is admitted would be covered under this scheme. The medical insurance would reimburse all expenses even when it exceeds the prescribed limit. A sum of Rs.150,000 million per annum would be allocated for this. In return, the pregnant mother would have to pay only Rs.5 per month for the insurance cover.

In India, 45 percent of the children born belong to these BPL families. From about an average of 6 children per married woman in 1970, the number has come down to an average of 3 children per woman currently. Although the government has been advocating every married couple to adopt a 2-child norm to check the population growth, the government would continue with the policy of leaving the choice of the number to the respective couples. The birth statistics in India shows that one-third of all babies born are under weight. Physical growth of 45 percent of these babies is retarded because of lack of proper nutrition. Vigorous health and family welfare campaign together with this medical insurance program would, it is hoped, bring down infant, child and maternal mortality and encourage people to adopt small family norm.

8.6 Estimation of ASDR

The most important death statistics is ASDR. The proportion of deaths in age groups to total deaths adjusted for 1,000 deaths give us ASDR. We can reconstruct the life table assuming that the CDR and CBR for males, females and total for India in the year, say, 1999 will not be materially different from those for 2000. With this assumption we estimate the total number of births and deaths, sex-wise and their likely distribution in various age groups. For that, we need to have an estimate of the total population of India in 1999 assuming that the average growth rate (1.95 percent p.a.) between 1991 and 2000 is applicable for 1999–2000 as well. We further assume that the break up of 1999 population into male and female follows the same male-female ratio obtained for 2001 data. Instead of computing population size for 2000 by compound interest law taking 1991 as the base year, we calculate the likely number of births and deaths for each sex, age-wise for the year 1999–2000. Assuming further that the migration does not materially alter the population totals, the natural increase when added to the estimated 1999 population total would roughly yield population total for 2000. Of course, we calculate 2000 population total independently from 1991 population total as well. The difference between these two estimates would indicate the nature of error we are likely to commit through such manipulation.

Using compound interest law, 1999 and 2000 estimated populations are:

$$\text{1999 total population} = P_{1991}(1+i)^n = 843{,}930{,}861\ (1+0.0195)^8 = 984{,}928{,}511$$

$$\text{2000 total population} = P_{1991}(1+i)^n = 843{,}930{,}861\ (1+0.0195)^9 = 1{,}004{,}134{,}617$$

The same method is used for estimation of the size of male and female populations in 1999 taking 1991 male (437,597,929) and female (406,332,932) populations as base year populations. The respective figures are calculated as 510,708,515 and 474,219,996 for males and females.

Addition of number of males, females and total to the estimated 1999 totals, obtained by the net of (birth-death) addition between 1999 and 2000, gives a second set of estimates for respective totals for the year 2000. CBR and CDR are expressed as simple proportions (cells 1 and 2 of Table 8.16). Total births are divided proportionately between males and females (cell 12 = cell 4 × cell 11; cell 20 = cell 4 × cell 19). Number of deaths for male, female and total is estimated directly by multiplying the 1999 estimated totals by the respective CDRs. Net of (birth-death) is added to respective 1999 estimates to give the estimates of the populations for 2000. Compound interest law also does a separate estimate for 2000 populations. The error in percent is shown in the last row of the Table 8.16.

Table 8.16 *Estimation of population of 2000 from CBR and CDR*

	Total	*Male*	*Female*
1991 (base year)	843930861	437597929	406332932
1999	984928511 (1)	510708515 (9)	474219996 (17)
CBR/1000	0.0258 (2)		
CDR/1000	0.0085 (3)	0.0089 (10)	0.0081 (18)
Proportion of M & F		0.517302 (11)	0.482698 (19)
Total birth (1)×(2)	25411155.6 (4)	13145243 (12)	12265913 (20)
Total death (1)×(3)	8371892.35 (5)	4545305.8 (13)	3841182 (21)
Birth-Death			
(net addition to 1999 total)	17039263 (6)	8599936.7 (14)	8424731.1 (22)
Estimated 2000 population	1001967775 (7)	519308452 (15)	482644727 (23)
Estimated 2000 population			
by compound interest law	1004134617 (8)	520667331 (16)	483467286 (24)
Percent difference between			
two estimates	0.216	0.261	0.170

Actually, this exercise is needed to make an estimate of the instances of death in the country between 1999 and 2000. Computation of ASDR requires that persons registered as dead in each age group is known. This is computed by the simple arithmetic $p_x \times_\infty D_0$, where p_x is the proportion of deaths in the age group x to the total population of deaths. It is assumed that proportion of persons in any age group to total population will be close to the proportion of deaths in the same population. For example, estimated number of deaths in age <1 in Total column (col.5, Table 8.17) is

$$ {}_1^T D_0 = \frac{{}_1^T p_0 \times_\infty^T D_0}{} = \frac{20.5 \times 8{,}363{,}520}{100} = 1{,}716{,}238 $$

Similarly, estimated number of female deaths in 25–29 is

$$ {}_{29}^F D_{25} = \frac{{}_\infty^F p_{25} \times_\infty^F D_0}{100} = \frac{2.7 \times 3{,}837{,}341}{100} = 103{,}712 $$

Once age-specific deaths are obtained, ASDR is obtained by the formula

$$ {}_5 m_x = \frac{{}_5 D_x}{{}_\infty D_0} \times 1{,}000 $$

The male age-specific death rate in 5–9 ages is:

$$ {}^{M}_{9}m_5 = \frac{{}^{M}_{9}D_5}{{}^{M}_{\infty}D_0} \times 1{,}000 = \frac{81{,}816}{4{,}545{,}306} \times 1000 = 18 $$

Table 8.17 *Computation of ASDR*

Age-group	*Proportion of deaths by age and sex*			*Absolute number of death by age and sex*			*Age-specific death rate*		
	Total	*Male*	*Female*	*Total*	*Male*	*Female*	*Total*	*Male*	*Female*
1	*2*	*3*	*4*	*5*	*6*	*7*	*8*	*9*	*10*
< 1	20.5	19.9	21.3	1716238	904516	818172	205	199	213
1–4	6.3	5	7.8	527429	227265	299612	63	50	78
5–9	2.2	1.8	2.6	184182	81816	99871	22	18	26
10–14	1.8	1.7	1.8	150694	77270	69141	18	17	18
15–19	2.3	1.9	2.7	192553	86361	103711	23	19	27
20–24	2.6	2.2	3.1	217669	99997	119077	26	22	31
25–29	2.6	2.6	2.7	217669	118178	103712	26	26	27
30–34	2.7	2.7	2.7	226041	122723	103712	27	27	27
35–39	2.8	3.1	2.4	234413	140904	92188	28	31	24
40–44	3	3.6	2.3	251157	163631	88347	30	36	23
45–49	3.6	4.2	2.9	301388	190903	111394	36	42	29
50–54	4.4	5.2	3.4	368363	236356	130600	44	52	34
55–59	5.6	6.4	4.8	468826	290900	184377	56	64	48
60–64	6.5	6.9	6.2	544173	313626	238153	65	69	62
65–69	9.1	9.6	8.6	761842	436349	330342	91	96	86
70–74	7.7	7.8	7.7	644636	354534	295771	77	78	77
75–79	7.7	7.5	7.8	644636	340898	299612	77	75	78
80–84	4	3.7	4.3	334876	168176	165170	40	37	43
85+	4.5	4.2	4.8	376735	190903	184377	45	42	48
				8363520	4545306	3837341	1000	1000	1000

8.7 Causes of Death

Even in early twentieth century plague, tuberculosis, small pox, malaria, cholera, influenza, and a host other diseases appeared as epidemics taking heavy tolls on human lives. With the medical discoveries since World War I, especially the antibiotics and vaccines and the extended public health care system, improved sanitation and supply of potable drinking water, most of these diseases came under considerable control or have almost been eliminated. Death rates started to slide down steadily across the globe.

Though death rates across the globe has been contained in large measure because of availability of advanced curative and preventive medicines and improved health infrastructure and improvement of average nutrition level, *morbidity levels* in most of these countries continue to be high because of deficiency in immunization programs in the less developed countries, especially in south-east Asia and the African countries (particularly in East Africa) along with nutritional deficiency and the environmental and sanitation hazards.

In medicine, epidemiology and actuarial science, *morbidity* refers to:

- the state of poor health,
- the degree or severity of a health condition,
- the prevalence of a poor health condition: the *total* number of cases in a particular population at a particular point in time,
- the incidence of a disease: the number of *new* cases in a particular population during a particular time interval.
- disability irrespective of cause.

The term *morbidity rate* can refer either to the incidence rate or to the prevalence rate of a disease. Whereas mortality rate (for different causes) can be measured quite easily and precisely, morbidity rate in a population, least to speak of cause-wise documentation, often remains only an intelligent guess from circumstantial evidences.

The Global Burden of Disease Study (sponsored by WHO and the World Bank) calculated 'disability-adjusted life-years' (DALY) caused by a wide range of diseases and conditions and estimated the percentage that could be attributed to various risk factors, including childhood and maternal malnutrition. The latest Burden of Disease report ranks *being underweight* as the single most significant risk factor for both death and DALYs in "high mortality developing countries" – a group that includes almost 70 countries with a combined population of more than 2.3 billion people. Disability-adjusted-life-years for India are presented in Table 8.18.

Six of the ten leading risk factors for DALYs in the high-mortality countries are related to hunger and malnutrition, including underweight, deficiencies in zinc, iron, vitamin A, and unsafe water, sanitation and hygiene, which contribute to malnutrition by causing infections that prevent digestion and absorption of nutrients. Underweight and micronutrient deficiencies rank lower as risk factors for death and disability in more advanced developing countries with lower mortality rates. Even then the nutrition-related conditions still dominate the list of risk factors. Among low-mortality developing countries – which includes China, and several other countries in Asia and most of South America – underweight and iron deficiency remain among the top ten risk factors. They are joined on the list by overweight and a number of other diet-related risks that contribute to non-communicable chronic diseases such as ischemic heart disease, high blood pressure, cancer and diabetes.

Disease burden estimations based on sound epidemiological research provide the foundation for public policy. Which diseases and what interventions does public policy needs to focus upon are normally derived from such evidences. Well researched longitudinal data can enable judicious targeting and help decide what needs to be done where, for whom, and when. Conversely, the absence of such good quality empirical data can affect program designing and consequently outcomes. India has ample evidence of such impacts, often due to the mismatch between disease burden and its causal factors, and the interventions adopted and priorities in resource allocation.

8.7.1 International Classification of Death (ICD)

For formulation of any health policy we need to clearly identify the causes of death and morbidity in the country. Causes of death are often categorized as *proximate* and *non-proximate.* Proximate (or immediate) causes of death are those that finally lead to death; e.g., heart disease or cancer.

Table 8.18 *Health conditions and "disability-adjusted life-years" (DALYs) lost in India, 1998*

Disease/health condition	*DALYs lost x 1,000*	*Share of the total burden of disease (%)*
Communicable diseases, maternal and perinatal conditions		
Tuberculosis	7,577	2.8
HIV/AIDS	5,611	2.1
Diarrhoeal diseases	22,005	8.2
Malaria and other vector-borne conditions	4,200	1.6
Leprosy	208	0.1
Childhood diseases	14,463	5.4
Otitis media	475	0.1
Maternal and perinatal conditions	31,207	11.6
Others	49,517	18.4
Non-communicable conditions		
Cancers	8,992	3.4
Diabetes	1,981	0.7
Mental illness	22,944	8.5
Blindness	3,699	1.4
Cardiovascular diseases	26,932	10.0
COPD* and asthma	4,061	1.5
Oral diseases	1,247	0.5
Others	18,801	7.0
Injuries	45,032	16.
All listed conditions	200,634	74.6
Others	68,319	25.4

*COPD: chronic obstructive pulmonary disease

Source: Peters D., A. Yazbeck, G. Ramana, R. Sharma, L. Pritchett, A. Wagstaff: *Raising the Sights: Better Health Systems for India's Poor*. The World Bank; 2001

Non-proximate causes of death are the factors that increase the likelihood of experiencing one of the proximate causes. For example, tobacco smoking is a non-proximate cause of death due to its link to lung cancer (a proximate cause). Non-proximate causes are the risk factors for dying from a particular proximate cause. The proximate causes of death are themselves further broadly categorized as: *communicable diseases*: infectious and parasitic diseases (deaths of infants and maternal mortality are usually included in this category) and *non-communicable diseases*: chronic and degenerative diseases; and deaths due to injury (accidents, homicide, and suicide).

Deaths are classified using a standard coding system called the ICD (International Classification of Deaths). World Health Organization has been organizing and publishing ICD since 1946. ICD is revised periodically to reflect changes in medical and epidemiological knowledge and in the light of diseases that are either new or of growing importance as taker-of-life, such as HIV/AIDS and the cognitive dementias such as Alzheimer's disease. The details of the tenth revision of ICD, which came out in 1999, are presented in the Appendix 2. The broad categories of ICD-10 are similar to the ninth revision.

Within each category are a number of exclusive classes that are further divided into specific diseases. For example, *circulatory diseases* are broken down into ischemic (coronary) heart disease and cerebrovascular diseases, among others, which are further divided into more detailed causes.

Infection and parasitic diseases are further classified into respiratory infection, tuberculosis, malaria, HIV/AIDS, etc. Respiratory infection is sub-divided into lower tract and upper respiratory infection. It is in the specificity of these subcategories that the ninth and tenth revisions differ most. While the ninth revision contains about 4,000 codes, the tenth revision contains nearly twice as many. ICD has become a very useful tool in the analysis of trends and differentials in causes of death, longitudinal and cross-sectional comparisons and in the assessment of the progress in overcoming life-threatening diseases and conditions. The ICD, however, has a number of limitations.

Table 8.19 *International statistical classification of diseases and related health problems 10th revision (version for 2007)*

Chapter	*Blocks*	*Title*
I	A00–B99	Certain infectious and parasitic diseases
II	C00–D48	Neoplasms
III	D50–D89	Diseases of the blood and blood-forming organs and certain disorders involving the immune mechanism
IV	E00–E90	Endocrine, nutritional and metabolic diseases
V	F00–F99	Mental and behavioral disorders
VI	G00–G99	Diseases of the nervous system
VII	H00–H59	Diseases of the eye and adnexa
VIII	H60–H95	Diseases of the ear and mastoid process
IX	I00–I99	Diseases of the circulatory system
X	J00–J99	Diseases of the respiratory system
XI	K00–K93	Diseases of the digestive system
XII	L00–L99	Diseases of the skin and subcutaneous tissue
XIII	M00–M99	Diseases of the musculoskeletal system and connective tissue
XIV	N00–N99	Diseases of the genitourinary system
XV	O00–O99	Pregnancy, childbirth and the puerperium
XVI	P00–P96	Certain conditions originating in the perinatal period
XVII	Q00–Q99	Congenital malformations, deformations and chromosomal abnormalities
XVIII	R00–R99	Symptoms, signs and abnormal clinical and laboratory findings, not elsewhere classified
XIX	S00–T98	Injury, poisoning and certain other consequences of external causes
XX	V01–Y98	External causes of morbidity and mortality
XXI	Z00–Z99	Factors influencing health status and contact with health services
XXII	U00–U99	Codes for special purposes

First, cross-national comparisons are affected by variations in data quality. These variations result from differences in the diagnostic skill and type of training of the certifying medical attendant, in the accuracy of the diagnosis recorded on the death certificate, and in the accurate coding of the information. At an even more fundamental level, the ICD is based on a number of assumptions: medical personnel are present at the time of a death and the cause of death is recorded by medical personnel; Registrar of Death has the necessary skill to correctly assign a code to the cause of death. These assumptions do not necessarily hold in the less developed countries and/or in times of social and political turmoil, such as war. Thus, while ICD data are often accurate for Western countries, they are not that accurate for less developed countries.

Second, the ICD requires a single cause statement of death. Death at old age (and even at early age) may have resulted from multiple causes. Classification based on a single cause may distort the picture of mortality causation. A person may have died from TB or pneumonia which might have resulted/aggravated from lower immunity level due to HIV/AIDS.

Third, since ICD categories may change over time, trend analysis will be affected.

Fourth, when a new cause of death emerges (AIDS/HIV emerged in 1980s and the ninth revision of ICD became operational in 1979), it remained uncategorized till the next revision of ICD in 1999.

8.7.2 Variation in Causes of Death between Developing and Developed Countries

There is wide variation in causes of death between developed and developing nations. Hence a global summary of causes of death is not useful. The distribution of causes of death is noticeably different in the two different conglomerations of countries of the world. *Diseases of the circulatory system* and *cancer* (both associated with aging) are the chief taker-of-life in the developed countries, accounting for approximately two-thirds of all deaths. In contrast, these diseases account for only one-third of deaths in the less developed world. *Infectious and parasitic diseases*, which often attack young people, are the major killers in the third world countries, making up 43 percent of all deaths. Another important contrast lies in *deaths associated with childbirth* (deaths both to infants and to mothers), which make up 10 percent of deaths in less developed countries but only 1 percent or less in more developed countries.

Table 8.20 *Comparison of leading causes of death for developing and developed countries, 2001*

Causes of death in developing countries	*Number of deaths*	*Causes of death in developed countries*	*Number of deaths*
HIV-AIDS	2,678,000	Ischaemic heart disease	3,512,000
Lower respiratory infections	2,643,000	Cardiovascular disease (Stroke)	3,346,000
Ischaemic heart disease	2,484,000	Chronic obstructive pulmonary disease	1,829,000
Diarrhea	1,793,000	Lower respiratory infections	1,180,000
Cerebrovascular disease	1,381,000	Lung cancer	938,000
Childhood diseases	1,217,000	Car accident	669,000
Malaria	1,103,000	Stomach cancer	657,000
Tuberculosis	1,021,000	High blood pressure	635,000
Chronic obstructive pulmonary disease	748,000	Tuberculosis	571,000
Measles	674,000	Suicide	499,000

Source: WHO World Health Report 2002. Countries grouped by WHO Mortality Stratum, with Developing Countries representing regions with High and Very High Mortality, and Developed Countries representing regions with Low and Very Low Mortality

Assuming that the 'best estimates' of causes of death is not much different from the actual, the global data informs that the *chronic and degenerative diseases* predominate in the West; the infectious and parasitic diseases (along with nutrition and childbirth-related deaths) prevail in the less developed countries.

Figure 8.5 *Ten leading causes of death in developed and developing countries*

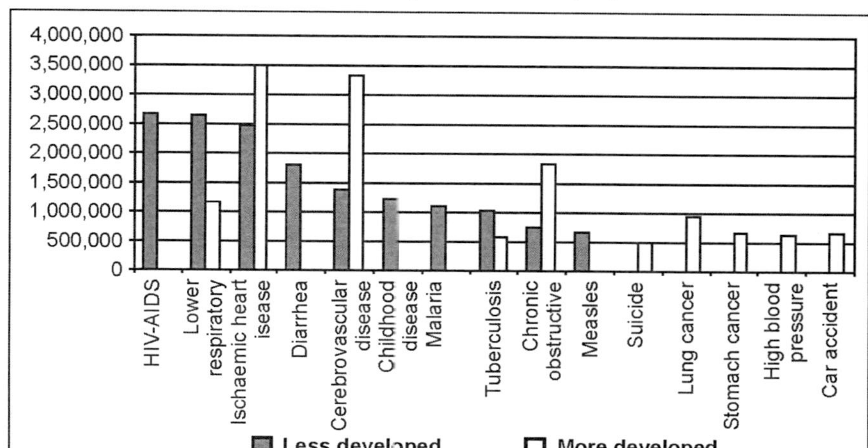

Top 10 causes of death separately for developing and developed countries are presented worldwide in Table 8.20.

According to the WHO the ten leading causes of death are given under by sex in 2002:

Table 8.21 *Ten leading causes of death worldwide*

Group	*Cause*	*Percent of deaths*	*Deaths per 1,000 per year*		
			All	*Male*	*Female*
	All causes	*100*	*1000*	*1000*	*1000*
A	**Cardiovascular diseases**	**29.34**	**268.8**	**259.3**	**278.4**
	Ischemic heart disease	12.64	115.8	121.4	110.1
	Cerebrovascular disease (Stroke)	9.66	88.5	81.4	95.6
	Hypertensive heart disease	1.60	14.6	13.4	15.9
	Inflammatory heart disease	0.71	6.5	6.7	
	Rheumatic heart disease	0.57	5.3	4.4	6.1
B	**Infectious and parasitic diseases**	**19.12**	**175.2**	**185.1**	**165.1**
	Respiratory infections	6.95	63.7	63.5	63.8
	Lower respiratory tract infections	6.81	62.4	62.2	62.6
	Upper respiratory infections	0.13	1.2	1.2	1.2
	HIV/AIDS	4.87	44.6	46.2	43.0
	Diarrheal diseases	3.15	28.9	30.0	27.8
	Tuberculosis	2.75	25.2	32.9	17.3
	Malaria	2.23	20.4	19.4	21.5
	Childhood diseases	1.97	18.1	18.0	18.2
	Measles	1.07	9.8	9.8	9.9
	Pertussis	0.52	4.7	4.7	4.8

Cont'd...

Cont'd...

	Tetanus	0.38	3.4	3.4	3.5
	Sexually transmitted diseases excluding HIV	0.32	2.9	2.9	2.9
	Syphilis	0.28	2.5	2.7	2.3
	Neoplasms other than malignant	0.26	2.4	2.4	2.4
	Meningitis	0.30	2.8	2.9	2.7
	Tropical diseases	0.23	2.1	2.5	1.6
	Leishmaniasis	0.09	0.8	1.0	0.7
	Trypanosomiasis	0.08	0.8	1.0	0.5
	Hepatitis B	0.18	1.7	2.3	1.0
	Hepatitis C	0.09	0.9	1.1	0.6
C	**Malignant neoplasms (cancers)**	**12.49**	**114.4**	**126.9**	**101.7**
	Lung cancers	2.18	20.0	28.4	11.4
	Stomach cancer	1.49	13.7	16.7	10.5
	Colorectal cancer	1.09	10.0	10.3	9.7
	Liver cancer	1.08	9.9	13.6	6.2
	Breast cancer	0.84	7.7	0.1	15.3
	Esophageal cancer	0.78	7.2	9.1	5.2
	Lymphomas, multiple myeloma	0.59	5.4	5.4	5.4
	Oral cancers and oropharynx cancers	0.56	5.1	7.1	3.1
	Prostate cancer	0.47	4.3	8.6	0.0
	Leukemia	0.46	4.2	4.7	3.8
	Cervical cancer	0.42	3.8	0.0	7.7
	Pancreatic cancer	0.41	3.7	3.9	3.5
	Bladder cancer	0.31	2.9	4.0	1.7
	Ovarian cancer	0.24	2.2	0.0	4.4
	Uterine cancer	0.12	1.1	0.0	2.3
	Skin diseases	0.12	1.1	0.8	1.4
	Melanoma and other skin cancers	0.12	1.1	1.1	1.0
D	**Respiratory diseases**	**6.49**	**59.5**	**61.1**	**57.9**
	Chronic obstructive pulmonary disease	4.82	44.1	45.1	43.1
	Perinatal conditions	4.32	39.6	43.7	35.4
	Asthma	0.42	3.9	3.9	3.8
E	**Unintentional injuries**	**6.23**	**57.0**	**73.7**	**40.2**
	Road traffic accidents	2.09	19.1	27.8	10.4
	Falls	0.69	6.3	7.5	5.0
	Drowning	0.67	6.1	8.4	3.9
	Poisoning	0.61	5.6	7.2	4.0
	Fires	0.55	5.0	3.8	6.2

Cont'd...

Cont'd...

F	**Digestive diseases**	**3.45**	**31.6**	**34.9**	**28.2**
	Cirrhosis of the liver	1.38	12.6	16.1	9.1
	Peptic ulcer disease	0.46	4.2	5.0	3.5
G	**Intentional injuries (suicide, murder, war, etc.)**	**2.84**	**26.0**	**37.0**	**14.9**
	Suicide	1.53	14.0	17.4	10.6
	Violence	0.98	9.0	14.2	3.7
	Maternal conditions	0.89	8.2	0.0	16.5
	Congenital abnormalities	0.86	7.9	8.1	7.7
	War	0.30	2.8	5.0	0.5
H	**Neuropsychiatric disorders**	**1.95**	**17.9**	**18.4**	**17.3**
	Diabetes mellitus	1.73	15.9	14.1	17.7
	Alzheimer's disease and other dementias	0.70	6.4	4.7	8.1
	Epilepsy	0.22	2.0	2.2	1.8
	Parkinson's disease	0.17	1.6	1.6	1.6
	Alcohol use disorders	0.16	1.5	2.5	0.4
	Drug use disorders	0.15	1.4	2.2	0.5
I	**Diseases of the genitourinary system**	**1.49**	**13.6**	**14.1**	**13.1**
	Nephritis/nephropathy	1.19	10.9	11.0	10.7
	Benign prostatic hyperplasia	0.06	0.5	1.0	0.0
J	**Nutritional deficiencies**	**0.85**	**7.8**	**6.9**	**8.7**
	Protein-energy malnutrition	0.46	4.2	4.2	4.2
	Endocrine/nutritional disorders	0.43	3.9	3.4	4.4
	Iron deficiency anemia	0.24	2.2	1.5	2.9

Source: World Health Organization, 2004

Figure 8.6 *Ten leading causes of death by sex*

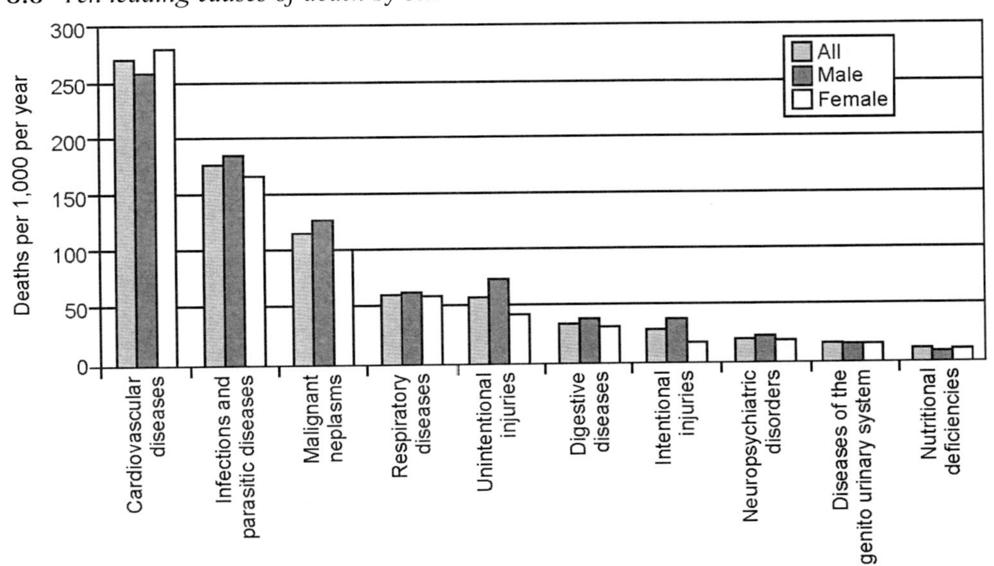

Females, more than males, succumb easily to cardiovascular and nutritional deficiency diseases. Male death largely outnumbers females in infectious and parasitic diseases, cancers in general and in unintentional and intentional injuries. Cancer deaths for females are mostly due to breast, cervical and ovarian cancer. Lung, stomach, colorectal and liver cancer are significantly high among males.

Worldwide, non-communicable conditions (cancer, cardiovascular diseases, ischemic heart, respiratory diseases, etc.) consumed 58.6 percent of lives; infectious and parasitic diseases killed one-third worldwide. HIV/AIDS remains one of the top causes of death in developing countries, especially in Africa. In 2001 it was the leading cause of death in non-industrialized regions, claiming 2.7 million lives. In sub-Saharan Africa alone, it claimed 1.9 million lives, and is significantly impacting the life expectancy in these countries. While HIV/AIDS is already an issue in the industrialized world, the number of deaths due to this is significantly less vis-à-vis developing countries. The leading cause of death in developing countries is *infectious and parasitic diseases* (43 percent). Infectious and parasitic diseases, including measles and malaria, are more frequent causes of death in sub-Saharan Africa than elsewhere. Respiratory infection disproportionately affects people living in South-East Asia and sub-Saharan Africa. These two regions are also particularly hit by maternal and perinatal conditions. Asia and the West Pacific region have a rate of non-communicable respiratory diseases, such as chronic bronchitis and emphysema, which is nearly 2.5 times higher than the rest of the world. The leading causes of death in developed countries are *atherosclerosis* (heart disease and stroke), *cancer*, and *other diseases related to obesity and aging*. Next to cardiovascular disease is cancer (over 29 percent of all deaths). Worldwide, cancers account for about 5.1 percent of the disease burden and 12.5 percent of all deaths. In India, cancers account for about 3.3 percent of the disease burden and about 9 percent of all deaths. Atherosclerosis and other diseases associated with age cause loss of homeostasis, leading to cardiac arrest, causing loss of oxygen and nutrient supply, leading to irreversible deterioration of the brain and other tissues. With improved medical competence, dying has become a state reaching which can be delayed considerably. Accidents and injuries are associated with 12 percent of disease burden and 9 percent of deaths across countries. Death in one's own residence, once normal, is now a rare event in the developed world. Proportion of deaths while under institutional care has been rising progressively in the developing countries as well.

According to National Vital Statistics report, USA, 2002, about 66 percent of all deaths in USA are for people aged 65 years and above. It is no wonder that 62 percent of all deaths in USA were due to cardiovascular diseases and malignant cancers and 80 percent of those occurred at ages 65 years and beyond. 6.5 percent deaths were due to accidents [4.5, i.e., 44 percent of this by motor vehicle accidents), suicide (1.3) and homicide (0.7)]. Among the leading causes of death among young people 15–24 years, the top three reasons are accidents (51.8 percent), homicide (21.3 percent) and suicide (16.3 percent). These figures clearly speak how causes of death change by age as also how a fast life for the younger generation could make life vulnerable in a developed country. Alzheimer's disease is also fast picking up in the developed countries. America has one of the finest health infrastructures in the world. Yet, 225,000 deaths (0.094 percent) out of a total of 2,403,351 deaths in USA in the year under reference were due to what are known as *iatrogenic causes* (mistakes caused by actions of health professionals). 19,000 deaths alone occurred due to faulty surgery and medication error.

Inferior sanitary conditions, lack of bacteria-free water for drinking, and lack of access to modern medical technology makes death in developing countries from infectious diseases more frequent than in developed countries. One such disease is tuberculosis, a bacterial disease which killed 1.7 million people in 2004. In an age when we believe that we have the knowledge and tools to conquer most diseases, the ancient scourge of tuberculosis still causes about 2 million deaths a year worldwide and several times more suffer from it – more than any other single infectious organism – reminding us that we still have a long way to go. Though equipped with drugs to treat TB effectively, we have not managed to eradicate this deadly infection. AIDS/HIV infection has made TB more lethal. Malaria caused about 400–900 million cases of fever and approximately one to three million deaths annually. Global warming may have a serious influence on spread of vector born diseases. AIDS/HIV death toll accounts for about 5 percent of all deaths in the world; in Africa alone it may reach 90–100 million by 2025.

According to Jean Ziegler, United Nations' special reporter on the Right to Food, mortality due to malnutrition/nutritional deficiency was behind 58 percent of all deaths in 2006. He said that while 62 million people died from all causes worldwide, more than 36 million died of hunger or diseases due to deficiencies in micronutrients. The WHO report warned that tobacco smoking killed 100 million people worldwide in the 20th century and could kill 1 billion around the world in the 21st century.

Many leading causes of death in the developed world can be postponed by diet and physical activity, but the accelerating incidence of disease with age still imposes limits on human longevity. The evolutionary cause of aging is, at best, only just beginning to be understood. It has been suggested that direct intervention in the aging process may now be the most effective intervention against major causes of death.

Every year, more than 20 million low birth weight (LBW) babies are born in the developing world. In some countries, India included, more than 30 percent of all children are born underweight. From the moment of birth, the scales are tipped against them. LBW babies face increased risk of dying in infancy, of stunted physical and cognitive growth during childhood, of reduced working capacity as adults and, if female, of giving birth to LBW babies themselves. Studies show that compared with normal babies, the risk of neonatal death is four times higher for infants who weigh less than 2.5 kilograms at birth and eighteen times higher for those who weigh less than 2.0 kilograms. LBW babies also suffer significantly higher rates of malnutrition and stunting later in childhood and as adults.

While birth weight has a significant role in childhood diseases and mortality, the body weight in the latter years can have impact on disability and death: *obesity* significantly increase mortality from cardiovascular disease (CVD), underweight increases mortality primarily from non-cancer, non-CVD causes, and overweight is seen to be associated with increased mortality from diabetes and kidney disease combined, but with reduced mortality from other non-cancer non-CVD causes of death. Overweight or underweight is calculated by *body mass index* (BMI). BMI is calculated as weight in kilograms divided by height in meters squared. A person is said to be underweight if his/her BMI is less than 18.5, overweight if 30<BMI >25. BMI for obesity is greater than 30.

Increased consumption of unhealthy foods compounded with increased prevalence of overweight is typically referred to as the "*Nutrition Transition*". It occurs in conjunction to the Epidemiological Transition and has serious implications in terms of public health outcomes, risk factors, economic growth and international nutrition policy. Nutrition transition is malnutrition ensuing not merely from a need for food, but the need for high-quality nourishment. Foods rich in vitamins, minerals, and micronutrients, found abundantly in fruits, vegetables, and whole grains have been substituted by fast-foods heavy in added sugar, saturated fat, and sodium. This trend, which began in industrialized countries, has now spread to developing countries. These developing countries, still stressed and struggling with hunger, are now dealing with health problems associated with obesity. Malnutrition once identified by emaciated bodies, is now also associated with obesity.

The causes described in Table 8.21, is a reflection of crude death rates cause-wise ascertained for the world population from the available statistics from different countries. But the crude death rate, which is applied to a whole population of people, can give a misleading impression. Number of deaths per 1,000 populations can even be higher for a country categorized as developed than in the less developed countries. This is because developed countries have relatively more older people, who are more likely to die in a given year (of course mostly by age-specific reasons), so that the overall mortality rate can be higher even if the mortality rate at any other lower age is lower. In fact, the differences in health status of any two countries (and between two segments of the same population) are best understood by death and morbidity rates in early infancy and childhood. A more realistic picture of mortality is given by a Life Table since it summarizes mortality experiences of the same cohort separately at each age. A Life Table therefore is necessary to give a good estimate of life expectancy.

There was a time, not long back, when infectious and parasitic diseases dominated the world's mortality scene. With decline in mortality as a consequence of gradual elimination of some of the dreaded diseases across the globe, life expectancy in the world population has increased greatly. This has become possible since infectious and parasitic diseases and diseases originating from nutritional deficiency have been put under considerable check even in the poorly developed countries. Improved health infrastructure and increased food intake are responsible for curtailing deaths due to these factors. The 'causes of death' pattern in today's developed countries was quite similar in 1930s to that in many of the developing countries as of today. Like demographic transition, all countries pass through mortality transitions, which in turn, bring in fertility transition and an increase in life expectancy. The dominance of cardiovascular diseases and various types of cancers and other non-communicable diseases in the developed countries is closely related to the ageing of the population, fast pace of life, as also because of food habit of the common people.

8.8 The Epidemiological Transition

Epidemiology (*epi*, upon; *demos*, people; *logos*, study) is the study of what "comes upon" groups of people. In demography and medical geography, epidemiological transition refers to a change in the disease pattern in a country away from *infectious and parasitic diseases* towards *degenerative diseases*. The epidemiological theory was originally proposed by Abdel R. Omran in 1971. In his words,

> Epidemiology is concerned with the distribution of disease and death, and with their determinants and consequences in population groups. Inasmuch as patterns of health and disease are integral components of population change, epidemiology's reservoir of knowledge about these patterns and their determinants in population groups serves not only as a basis for prediction of population change but also as a source of hypotheses that can be further tested to correct, refine and build population theory.

The theory of epidemiological transition focuses on the complex change in patterns of health and disease and on the interactions between these patterns and their demographic, economic and sociologic determinants and consequences. An epidemiological transition has paralleled the demographic and technological transitions in the now developed countries and is still happening in less-developed societies. From historical and contemporary data from various countries, which show some of the peculiar variations of the transition, Omran postulated three models of transition: **Classical or Western model**, **Accelerated Transition model**, depicted by Japan, and the **Contemporary or Delayed model** implied in the changes observed in many developing countries. Although the theory primarily is an attempt to describe and disentangle the determinants and consequences of changing disease patterns that have accompanied modernization in most western countries, Omran believes that the theory is good enough in shedding light on the tenacious population problems (fertility and migration) of lessdeveloped countries. Omran states,

> … [P]olicy makers tend to see high fertility as the intractable villain, creating acute population pressures and oppressive socioeconomic conditions in developing societies; consequently, programs to treat these onerous problems have been geared almost exclusively to birth control. One of the major practical implications stemming from historical studies of the epidemiologic transition in western countries is that disease control programs may be not only a prerequisite of fertility transition but an effective instrument of socioeconomic development as well.

In the formulation of his theory, Omran concentrates on five propositions:

Proposition one: Mortality and Population Dynamics:

Mortality is a fundamental factor in population dynamics.

Mortality's dominant role in population dynamics is implicit in theories of population cycles. The cyclical rises and falls in population size observed in animal and pre-modern human populations reflect sequential phases of population growth and decline; disregarding the possible selective influences of migration, these cyclic movements must ultimately be accounted for in terms of the range of variation in fertility and mortality.

Commenting on the fertility and mortality situations in pre-modern societies, Omran writes:

> … [T]he range for mortality was much greater as there was virtually no fixed upper limit to the death rate. Although 30 deaths per 1,000 population may be a reasonable approximation of mortality's lower asymptote, its upper asymptote in pre-modern societies could have been many times as high in epidemic and famine years… virtually no fixed upper limit to the death rate. Consequently, even if fertility approached its biologic maximum, depopulation could and did occur as a result of epidemics, wars and famines, which repeatedly pushed mortality levels to high peaks.

More than any other single factor, fluctuating but always high mortality offers the most likely explanation of the slow rate of world population growth until 1650 A.D. Even after this, with perennial epidemics, plagues, cholera, famines and wars acted unpredictably and virtually uncontrollably to produce recurring high peaks of mortality, uninterrupted population growth was not likely – even though fertility remained persistently high. The population started to grow as fluctuations in mortality became less severe and the peaks less frequent.

Proposition Two: Shifts in Mortality and Disease Patterns:

During the transition, a long-term shift occurs in mortality and disease patterns whereby pandemics of infection are gradually displaced by degenerative and man-made diseases as the chief form of morbidity and primary cause of death.

Typically, mortality patterns distinguish three major successive stages of the epidemiological transition:

1. *The Age of Pestilence and Famine* when mortality is high and fluctuating, thus preventing sustained population growth. Life expectancy at birth is low and variable, vacillating between 20 and 40 years.
2. *The Age of Receding Pandemics* when mortality declines progressively and the rate of decline accelerate as epidemic peaks become less frequent or disappear. Life expectancy at birth increases steadily from about 30 to about 50 years. Population growth is sustained and begins to describe an exponential curve.
3. *The Age of Degenerative and Man-Made Diseases* when mortality continues to decline and eventually approaches stability at a relatively low level. Life expectancy at birth rises gradually until it exceeds 50 years. It is at this stage that fertility becomes the crucial factor in population growth.

The *Age of Pestilence and Famine* can be taken as an extension of the pre-modern pattern of health and disease. Epidemics and famines tend to go hand in hand, since malnourished people are particularly susceptible to infectious diseases. The major determinants of death in this stage are the Malthusian "positive checks": epidemics, famines and wars.

In *the Age of Receding Pandemics*, death rates start to decline steadily and the proportion of deaths due to infectious diseases decreases as a result of improved nutrition and sanitation and the medical advances that accompany socioeconomic development. With extended life attained, the degenerative and non-communicable diseases starts becoming the principal taker-of-life.

Eventually, the third stage *the Age of Degenerative and Man-Made Diseases* arrives**.** Infectious and parasitic diseases come under great control so that chances of survival beyond childhood are greatly enhanced. Infant and child mortality almost come under total control and risk of death of women from pregnancy and childbirth related causes drastically decline. Infant mortality quickly comes down, often below 10 per 1,000 births. With communicable diseases coming under control, the age distribution of the population undergoes a major change. As a result, the degenerative and non-communicable diseases become the principal taker-of-life.

Proposition Three: Relative Risks of Mortality by Age and Sex:

During the epidemiologic transition the most profound changes in health and disease patterns obtain among children and young women.

Recession of pandemics is most beneficial to children of both sexes and to females in the adolescent and reproductive ages. Although all age groups benefit from the shift in disease patterns and the increase in life expectancy, the decline in childhood mortality is demonstrably the greatest, especially in the one to four year age group.

Proposition Four: Interacting Transition Variables:

The shifts in health and disease patterns that characterize the epidemiologic transition are closely associated with the demographic and socioeconomic transitions that constitute the modernization complex.

The determinants of the transition from infectious to degenerative disease predominance are by no means simple. We present below some of the major categories of disease determination.

The demographic changes: The decline in mortality that comes with the epidemiological transition widens the "demographic gap" and hence effects demographic change by boosting population growth. The lowered death rate indirectly impacts fertility, which in turn changes age composition of the population and increases the size of the working age group population.

As infectious diseases recede and larger segments of the population survive childhood, the dependency ratio becomes more balanced. Finally, during the *Age of Degenerative and Man-Made Diseases*, the tremendous improvements in survivorship registered among all age groups except the very old are reflected by a more uniform population distribution; at the same time the old age dependency ratio increases and the male to female ratio is typically less than unity within the older age groups. Non-communicable diseases tend to top the list of causes of disability and death.

Eco-biological determinants: There is a complex balance between disease agents, the level of hostility in the environment and the resistance of the host. It is well known that microorganisms constantly undergo changes that enable them to cope with an increasingly hostile environment. In fact, the development of mechanisms that permit survival of the most adaptable microorganisms is more rapid than the development of defense mechanisms that permit their hosts to combat microbial invaders. This adaptive process of microorganisms involves finding and exploiting weaknesses in the defenses of the host and can happen by means of several mechanisms: *alteration in antigenic identity, emergence of drug-resistant strains* and *dual infection*. However, even these determinants cannot be categorically specified. One outstanding example is the recession of plague in most of Europe and USA (Black Death ruled for long 300 years) toward the end of the seventeenth century. The reasons for this recession are not fully understood, although the mysterious disappearance of the *black rat* may have been a contributing factor. Nonetheless, it is relatively certain that with the possible exception of smallpox, the recession of plague and many other pandemics in Europe was in no way related to the progress of medical science.

A virus may reappear as more deadly by altering its *antigenic identity*. Virulent strains of influenza viruses, against which the population has no immunity, has time and again appeared and took heavy tolls of human lives, especially children and pregnant women. The appearance of a new strain of influenza virus can result in billions of cases of influenza and millions of deaths. These deaths are usually not recorded as due to influenza. They are registered under the terminal cause of death – mostly cardiac or chronic chest disease. This results in a misleading impression that the incidence of these latter conditions is increasing. Cholera presents a similar picture. When the *El Tor vibrio* became pathogenic in the early 1970s, it swept the world and practically took the place of the classical strain. In 1993, a new strain, O139, appeared and is replacing the *El Tor vibrio*. It did not spare any age group in areas where this strain spread.

Emergence of *drug-resistance strains* often baffles doctors and scientists. With the arrival of effective therapy for many infectious diseases, many scientists thought that these diseases would disappear. However, after several years of widespread use of certain antimicrobials, it became apparent that some strains of microorganisms could survive in the hostile environment of the drug. This has been observed more in diseases that require prolonged therapy with antimicrobials, such as tuberculosis. The limited resources that are available for treatment of patients suffering from such chronic diseases, especially in developing countries, result in interruption of therapy or use of inappropriate treatment regimens. The result is the appearance of resistant strains.

Dual infection has of late become a serious problem for medical treatment as also for clinical classification of diseases. With the appearance of HIV infection, which affects much the same population already infected with tuberculosis, there is a significant increase in the occurrence of clinical tuberculosis. This new combination has produced two phenomena: first, the risk of developing active tuberculosis as a result of HIV infection increases from 10 percent in a lifetime to 10 percent in the first year of infection; secondly, there is an increase in drug-resistant tuberculosis affecting HIV infected persons and spreading to others. WHO estimates that at least five million people are suffering both from HIV infection and tuberculosis.

Medical and public health determinants: These determinants are specific preventive and curative measures used to combat disease; they include improved public sanitation, immunization and the development of decisive therapies. Medical and public health factors came into play late in the western transition, but have an influence early in the accelerated and contemporary transitions. The reduction of mortality in Europe and other Western countries during the nineteenth century was determined primarily by eco-biologic and socioeconomic factors. The influence of medical factors had to wait until the twentieth century, by which time pandemics of infection had already receded significantly. The mortality decline in currently developing countries has been more recent and the effect of medical factors has been more direct and more prominent, as shown by the contemporary or delayed transition model. In the Afro-Asian countries in particular, the tremendous impact of imported medical technologies on mortality has been magnified by massive public health programs. Although it would be naive to attempt precise identification of the complex determinants in each case, it does seem apparent that the mortality transition in the now developed countries was predominantly socially determined, whereas the transition in the "third world countries" is being significantly influenced by medical technology.

Environmental factors: Discharge of wastes from industry, automobiles and other sources such as thermal power plant into the air, water and land as also the city wastes and agricultural run-off that contains insecticides, pesticides and chemical fertilizers often are behind the increase in some diseases such as cancer and chronic chest diseases, including asthma and bronchitis. Atomic bomb explosions at Hiroshima and Nagasaki and the explosion of the nuclear reactor at Chernobyl are responsible for thousands of deaths and very large numbers of cases of cancer. Radiation hazards are likely to increase further as more and more nuclear reactors come up for power generation or for other commercial use or for military purposes.

High density urban population, poor quality of sanitation, crowded public transport, etc. facilitate spread of infections, especially the diseases spread by droplets and those related to atmospheric pollution. With fast increase in urbanization, nurseries and daycare centers are mushrooming. Children attending daycare centers are known to be the transmitters of acute infections of the gastro-intestinal and respiratory tracts to their families.

In sudden *climatic change*, especially heat wave or cold spells, there is usually an excess of mortality rate in the population. It is mostly the older and sick people that succumb to such temperature change. Often health of these people was so compromised that they would have died in a short while even if there were no heat wave or cold spell. This temporal shift in the mortality rate is designated as *mortality displacement*. During the subsequent period of heat waves or cold spells a decrease in overall mortality rate is observed. This compensatory reduction in mortality suggests that the heat wave had affected especially those whose health unmistakably was poor.

Social, cultural and behavioral factors: The shift from an agricultural to an industrial society and its accompanying process of modernization produce changes that affect people's health, both physical and mental. Close community ties, which still persist among rural people, have become a rare social gift in urban life. A close community often acts as a shock-absorber by providing opportunities to share sorrow and happiness and to alleviate stress. An evident example of maladjustment due to urbanization is the traumatic encounter of rural youth with urban values. This frequently has a serious impact on mental health.

In rural communities where extended family life used to predominate, care of the elderly was essentially a family responsibility. This is no longer the case, particularly in urban areas. The elderly, who can afford the cost of living in an old-age home, are now looked after by professional people far away from their families. They no longer see their families growing and are deprived of the social environment required for a happy life.

The most potent change has happened in the lifestyle of people living/or working in urban areas. The fast pace of life has changed people's lifestyle. Lifestyle actually refers to the manner in which the social group translates situations into a pattern of behavior that produces what are called behavioral risks. Fast driving, eating junk food, drinking alcohol, weekend night life, etc. are responsible for different types of diseases, mostly non-communicable. The mass media, especially TV often have negative influences on health which comes from advertisement of commodities that really are not needed by the community, but the latter is made to believe that there is truth in what are advertised.

Urbanization and industrialization often are responsible for relegation of moral values. This has resulted in transmission of sexually transmitted diseases. One factor that has facilitated sexual promiscuity is the widespread availability and use of contraceptives.

The opening of trade routes between continents has helped the spread of infectious diseases. The Black Death in Europe in the 14th century and the cholera pandemics in the 19th and 20th centuries are well documented. The spread of syphilis in the 18th and 19th centuries has been related to wars and the movements of armies. More recently, the movement of a large number of troops by air from South-East Asia to the Pacific islands during World War II contributed to the introduction of dengue fever in the South-Pacific region. In the past two decades the spread of HIV/AIDS to many parts of the world has been directly related to *human mobility*. Many communicable diseases are introduced through human mobility for work, trade and through tourism.

Expansion of education and participation of women in the labor force: Urbanization and industrialization has been accompanied by two important cultural transformations: the expansion of education and the increased participation of women in the labor market. These have greatly changed the dynamics of families and communities, which have resulted in the use of contraceptives, reducing many of the problems related to reproduction by extending birth intervals and have contributed to greater maternal and neonatal survival by reducing exposure to high-risk pregnancies.

Proposition Five: Basic Models of the Epidemiologic Transition:

Peculiar variations in the pattern, the pace, the determinants and the consequences of population change differentiate three basic models of the epidemiologic transition: the classical or western model, the accelerated model and the contemporary or delayed model.

Through the description, analysis and comparison of mortality patterns in many societies and at different points in time, distinctive core patterns of the epidemiologic transition emerge. The fundamental purpose of delineating these models is to visualize the different matrices of determinants and consequences associated with mortality (and fertility) patterns and to elucidate some of the fundamental issues confronting population policy-makers. The models are briefly described below.

The **Classical (Western) Model of Transition** portrays a gradual shift in disease patterns. Characteristic of this model can be seen in the steady decline of infectious diseases and the moderate increase in cancer and cardiovascular diseases in the West till 1920. Since 1945 the increase in cardiovascular deaths is particularly striking with progressive transition from high mortality and high fertility (CDR>30, CBR>40) to low mortality and low fertility (CDR<10, CBR<20) that accompanied the process of modernization in most Western European societies. Slow unsteady rate of mortality decline of pre-modern and early modern periods gradually gave way to more steep declines around the turn of the twentieth century, by which time fertility had already turned downward.

Socioeconomic factors were the primary determinants of the classical transition: sanitary revolution in the late nineteenth century and medical and public health progress in the twentieth century. Exponential population growth and sustained economic development were major correlates of the secular downward trend of mortality. In the late phase of the classical transition, *degenerative and man-made diseases* gradually displaced infections as the leading causes of mortality and morbidity in the western countries. Explosive population growth could be contained since pandemics and famines receded slowly enough for economic growth to become sustained before low fertility determinants acted to narrow the demographic gap and temper spiraling population growth. Expectation of life at birth is over 76 years in most of the western countries.

The **Accelerated Epidemiological Transition** model describes the accelerated mortality transition that occurred most notably in Japan. A major distinction of the accelerated model is that the period taken for mortality to reach the 10 per 1,000 levels was much shorter than that in the classical model. Abortion played a major role in bringing down birth rate. This quick shift from Age of Receding Pandemics to Age of Degenerative and Man-Made Diseases was possible in Japan by improvement in survival of children under 15 and of women.

The **Contemporary Epidemiological Transition** model describes the transition in most of the developing countries. Though mortality started declining shortly after the turn of the century, it gathered momentum only since World War II. Public health initiatives and internationally sponsored health packages (immunization programs) as also better transportation and communication played a major role in a fast secular decline in mortality leaving fertility at substantially high levels. Population started to grow fast. Both national and international programs of "population control" designed to hasten fertility decline artificially are prominent features of this model in the developing countries. Despite unmistakable gains in the survival of women and children, infant and childhood mortality remains exceptionally high in most of these countries and in some, females of reproductive age continue to have higher mortality risks than males in the same age group.

The epidemiological transition theory and the epidemiological models, like the demographic transition theory, were built from the analysis of causes of death in the western developed countries, for the time period from the agricultural revolution until the late twentieth century. Prior to agricultural revolution, malnutrition (starving to death) must have been the more important killer than infectious diseases. Once agriculture was adopted as the primary mode of living, the denser settlement pattern of humans as well as closer proximity to animals and animal waste contributed to the spread of infectious diseases. Black Death (the plague) that hit hardest in the middle of the fourteenth century but which continued to reoccur for more than three centuries virtually disappeared from Europe as a result of changes in housing and sanitary practices that affected the way that rats, fleas, and humans interacted. The industrial revolution started in this benign environment. Other types of infectious diseases (cholera, influenza, smallpox, TB, pneumonia, etc.) remained vital killers, and were eventually conquered by improved nutrition, hygiene, and public health measures, and knowledge thereof. Medical advances played a small role, although the smallpox vaccine was important until well into the twentieth century. As we move into the twenty-first century, however, advances in bioterrorism may lead to increasing deaths from infectious diseases.

The objections raised against Demographic Transition Theory being regarded as a theory are equally applicable to the Epidemiological Transition Theory. The epidemiological transition model applies less well to the developing world. Western mortality decline, and the changing pattern of causes of death associated with it, was mostly a product of socioeconomic development. In contrast, there is a much less significant relationship between morality and development in developing countries. In the postwar decades, mortality declines in many of these countries were substantial. The West exported public health measures, death-reducing technologies and food grains to many developing countries. Deaths due to infectious diseases fell spectacularly even in the absence of much socio-economic development.

Epidemiological transition theory typifies gradual replacement of infectious and communicable diseases by degenerative and non-communicable diseases as expectation of life increases. This is where the biggest challenge comes: the emergence of new, and the reemergence of old, infectious diseases in the latter part of the twentieth century. It is apparent that this transition is more complex and dynamic: the health and disease patterns of a society evolve in diverse ways as a result of demographic, socioeconomic, technological, cultural, environmental and biological changes. It is rather a continuous transformation process – some diseases disappearing, others appearing or re-emerging. This also indicates that such a process is not unidirectional. In fact, a reversal of the trend sometimes occurs. There are some outstanding examples, such as the emergence of new infectious diseases like HIV/AIDS, and the increase in infections that were previously controlled, such as tuberculosis, dengue fever, malaria, even small pox and plague.

It is also important to note that several stages of transition may overlap in the same country. For example, the decline in infectious diseases may be slow or stagnant among some sections of the population while non-communicable diseases may be increasing rapidly in another sector of the same population. This is still happening in most of the developing countries where the less affluent sectors have a high incidence of infectious, communicable and nutrition deficiency diseases among children while the wealthier sectors show completely different patterns of illness.

Many obstacles to transition are not easily overcome by the partial interventions prevailing in many parts of the world. Socioeconomic transformation has not permeated to all social classes which resulted in vulnerability of some groups. The slowdown and reversal of the decline in mortality in many countries in the 1970s and 1980s was the result of austerity programs, which led to the erosion of the health infrastructure and elimination of intervention programs. Most of these are responses to international forces beyond the control of those countries. In the nineties, under-five mortality in many countries has increased by many folds.

Mortality data alone provide a very quick but inadequate picture of health condition prevailing in a country. The picture of epidemiological transition largely would remain incomplete if morbidity levels and causes of sickness are not taken into account. It is not easy to measure level of morbidity in a population, least to speak of statistics on cause-wise sickness. A large proportion of people recover from their sickness without health services intervention, so their cases go unrecorded. The knowledge of the level and extent of morbidity is central to assess its impact on socioeconomic output.

Also a distinction is necessary between "infection" and "disease". "Infection" implies that the causative agent has entered the body of the host and is multiplying, but not necessarily with the appearance of signs and symptoms. In contrast, the term "disease" refers to the occurrence of clinical manifestations. The latter causes the greater concern to health authorities. For example, hepatitis B and HIV infection may only result in an infected person becoming a carrier capable of transmitting the same to others without himself showing evidence of clinical manifestations, at least for some years and hence posing a covert threat to public health.

It is sometimes difficult to differentiate between communicable and non-communicable diseases. Researchers have identified that some common illnesses with poorly understood etiologies, once considered to be non-communicable diseases, may actually be at least partially the result of microbial infection. Examples are the relationship between *Helicobacter pylori* and peptic ulcer and the relation between human *papilloma virus* and cervical cancer. Also, rodent-borne *Hantaviruses* may play a role in hypertensive renal disease, and no doubt hepatitis B and C viruses are the main causes of primary hepatocellular carcinoma.

Probably the biggest challenge to epidemiological transition theory comes from the emergence of new HIV/AIDS, and the reemergence of old, infectious diseases (smallpox, malaria) in the latter part of the twentieth century. The reemergence of diseases that scientists believed had been conquered, and the evolution of antibiotic-resistant strains of bacteria has led to a reappraisal of the possible future role of microbes in mortality. It seems unlikely that infectious and parasitic diseases will overtake degenerative and chronic diseases as killers, but it is difficult to predict the relative importance of the two major categories of death causation in the future. This has led to a debate about epidemiological transition theory's end stage. Is the third stage the final one? A number of subsequent stages have been proposed by epidemiologists and demographers. The most popular is the Age of Delayed Degenerative Diseases, matching to declines in death rates due to cardiovascular disease observed in Western countries through the 1970s and 1980s. This stage corresponds with the "compression of morbidity" hypothesis proposed by James Fries, stating that the future holds quick deaths due to degenerative diseases at very old ages. In other words, the typical death will be from a sudden heart attack at around age 85. A radically different fifth stage is also proposed in light of increasing death rates due to viruses and bacteria. The anthropologist Ronald Barrett and his colleagues view the trend of increasing mortality due to infectious disease as characterizing a new epidemiological transition altogether. Others, such as Christopher Murray and Alan Lopez, taking both death and disability into account, argue that non-communicable diseases will take on increasing importance in the "global burden of disease".

8.9 Special Note on HIV/AIDS, TUBERCULOSIS and MALARIA

8.9.1 HIV/AIDS

In June 1981 the first report was published of a mysterious and fatal illness that initially appeared to affect only homosexual men. In the months that followed, however, the same illness was diagnosed in newborns, children, men, and women – a pattern strongly suggesting a blood-borne infection as the cause of the illness. The illness was initially identified by several terms (e.g., "gay bowel syndrome," "lymphadenopathy virus (LAV)," and AIDS-associated retrovirus (ARV). By 1982 this disease came to be known as "Acquired Immune Deficiency Syndrome" (AIDS) because of the impact of the infectious agent, "Human Immunodeficiency Virus" (HIV), on an infected person's immune system.

The cause of AIDS was identified in 1983 by the French researcher Luc Montagnier as a type of virus known as a "retrovirus". This newly identified retrovirus was in due course called Human Immunodeficiency Virus or HIV. Scientists have established HIV as the cause of AIDS. An

HIV-infected person who meets specific diagnostic criteria (i.e., has one or more of the twenty-five AIDS-defining conditions indicative of severe immunosuppression and/or a seriously compromised immune system) is said to have AIDS, the end stage of a continuous pathogenic process. Multiple factors influence the health and functioning of HIV-infected persons. For example, some persons who meet the diagnostic criteria for AIDS may feel well and function normally for years, while other HIV-infected persons who do not meet the diagnostic criteria for AIDS may not feel well and have reduced functioning in one or more areas of their lives.

An individual may be infected with HIV for ten years or even more without showing symptoms of infection. During this period the immune system of the untreated person gradually deteriorates, increasing his or her risk of acquiring "opportunistic" infections and developing certain malignancies. While HIV disease is still considered a fatal condition, the development of *antiretroviral drugs* in 1990s and other drugs to treat such infections led many infected individuals to believe that they can manage their disease for an extended period of time. Unfortunately, the view that HIV disease is a "chronic" and "manageable" condition may lead persons to engage in behaviors that place them at risk of infection.

Since HIV has spread to every country of the world, it is now considered a pandemic. By the end of 2001 an estimated 65 million persons worldwide had been infected with HIV and of these, 25 million had died. An estimated 14,000 persons worldwide are infected every day. 95 percent of the world's new AIDS cases are in underdeveloped countries, about 70 percent of them are from sub-Saharan Africa. In Botswana, for example, life expectancy dropped from about 63 years in the late 1980s to below 50 years in the late 1990s, and Zimbabwe has seen life expectancy fall from 57 to 44 years in the same period (UN 1999). The most alarming note is that globally 1 in every 100 people is infected with HIV. Millions of children in developing nations are infected and orphaned. The effects of HIV disease on the development in some countries have been devastating. By subjecting members of the most economically active and productive groups to a premature death, AIDS is imposing an enormous economic and social toll on the African continent. The economies in sub-Saharan and South Africa are in danger of collapse because of the epidemic.

How is HIV Spread? The major known ways by which HIV infection is spread are: (1) intimate sexual contact with an HIV-infected person; (2) exposure to contaminated blood or blood products either by direct inoculation, sharing of drug apparatus, transfusion, or other method; and (3) passage of the virus from an infected mother to her fetus or newborn in utero, during labor and delivery, or in the early newborn (including through breast-feeding). Some health care workers have become occupationally infected with HIV, but their numbers are small in light of the millions of contacts between health workers and persons with HIV infection.

HIV-infected blood, semen, vaginal fluid, breast milk, and other bodily fluids containing blood have the potential to transmit HIV. While HIV has been isolated from other cells and tissues, the importance of these bodily fluids in transmission is not quite clear. Health workers may come into contact with other bodily fluids that can potentially transmit HIV. There are no reports of HIV being transmitted by insects; by nonsexual bodily contact; through closed mouth or social kissing; or by contact with saliva, tears, or sweat. Transfusion of blood products can pose a risk of infection, but the risk is low in the developed countries, where all such products are carefully tested before use.

Several factors (called "cofactors") may play a role in the acquisition of HIV infection, influence its transmission, affect development of clinical signs and symptoms, and influence disease progression. Cofactors that have been mentioned in scientific literature include anal receptive sex resulting in repeated exposure to absorbed semen; coexistence of other infections (e.g., syphilis, hepatitis B); injection and recreational drug use; use of immunosuppressant drugs (e.g., cocaine, alcohol, or amyl/butyl nitrites); douching or enemas before sexual intercourse; malnutrition; stress; multiple sexual partners; and presence of genital ulcers.

Because of low immune system, HIV infected persons are easy pray of TB. One of the major reasons of current spread of tuberculosis, in spite the fact that this 'once dreaded disease' can be cured by systematic medication over a period of time, is the weak immune system in HIV infected persons.

The worst HIV-hit region is Africa, more specifically the sub-Saharan Africa. On average, life expectancy at birth for the entire globe has increased by 8 years (some regions, Arab states for example, increased by close to 15 years) between 1970–75 and 2000–05. Even the least developed countries maintained the world average level of life expectancy growth. Sub-Saharan region is the only exception to this. Life expectancy here increased only by 3.1 years, from 46.0 in 1970–75 to 49.1 years in 2000–05 since HIV/AIDS epidemic in some countries brought down life expectancies by 10 to 15 years. In the following table we present the HIV prevalence rate (5 percent or more in ages 15–49) of 17 countries, mostly from sub-Saharan Africa along with their life expectancies at two time periods and the prevalence rate of tuberculosis (per 100,000).

Table 8.22 *Prevalence rate of infection in seventeen most HIV infected countries, their life expectancies and prevalence rate of tuberculosis*

HDR Countrycode	*Country*	*HIVm Prevalence (% in 15–49)*	*Life expectancy*			*Tuberculosis per 100,000 population*
			1970–1975	*2000–2005*	*2005*	
141	Swaziland	33.4 [21.2–45.3)	49.6	43.9	40.9	1211
124	Botswana	24.1 [23.0–32.0]	56.0	46.6	48.4	556
138	Lesotho	23.2 [21.9–24.7]	49.8	44.6	42.6	588
151	Zimbabwe	20.1 [13.3–27.6]	55.6	40.0	40.9	631
125	Namibia	19.6 [6.6–31.7]	53.9	51.5	51.6	577
121	South Africa	16.6 [16.8–20.7]	53.7	53.4	50.8	511
165	Zambia	17.0 [15.9–18.1]	50.1	39.2	40.5	618
172	Mozambique	16.1 [12.5–20.0]	40.3	44.0	42.8	597
164	Malawi	14.1 [6.9–21.4]	41.8	45.0	46.3	518
171	Central African Republic	10.7 [4.5–17.2]	43.5	43.3	43.7	483
119	Gabon	7.9 [5.1–11.5]	48.7	56.8	56.2	385
166	Cote d'Ivorie	7.1 [4.3–9.7]	49.8	46.8	47.4	659
154	Uganda	6.7 [5.7–7.6]	51.0	47.8	49.7	559
159	Tanzania	6.5 [5.8–7.2]	47.6	49.7	51.0	496
148	Kenya	6.1 [5.2–7.0]	53.6	51.0	52.1	936
144	Cameron	5.4 [4.9–5.9]	47.0	49.9	49.8	206
168	Congo	5.3 [3.3–7.5]	46.0	45.0	54.0	541

Note: Data are point and range estimates based on new estimation models developed by UNAIDS. Range estimates are presented in brackets.

Source: UNDP: Human Development Report, 2007/2008

Fate of those suffering from HIV and many more who are likely to be infected in future appears to depend on how successful scientists and medical professionals will be in controlling HIV/AIDS, which is estimated to have taken anywhere between 1.9 million and 3.6 million lives worldwide in 1999 alone. Given the depression of the immune system that comes with AIDS, it is possible that even the high estimate is low; some persons with AIDS might be counted as dying from another infectious disease, tuberculosis for example, to which they are vulnerable.

Figure 8.7 *Change in life expectation in severely HIV infected countries*

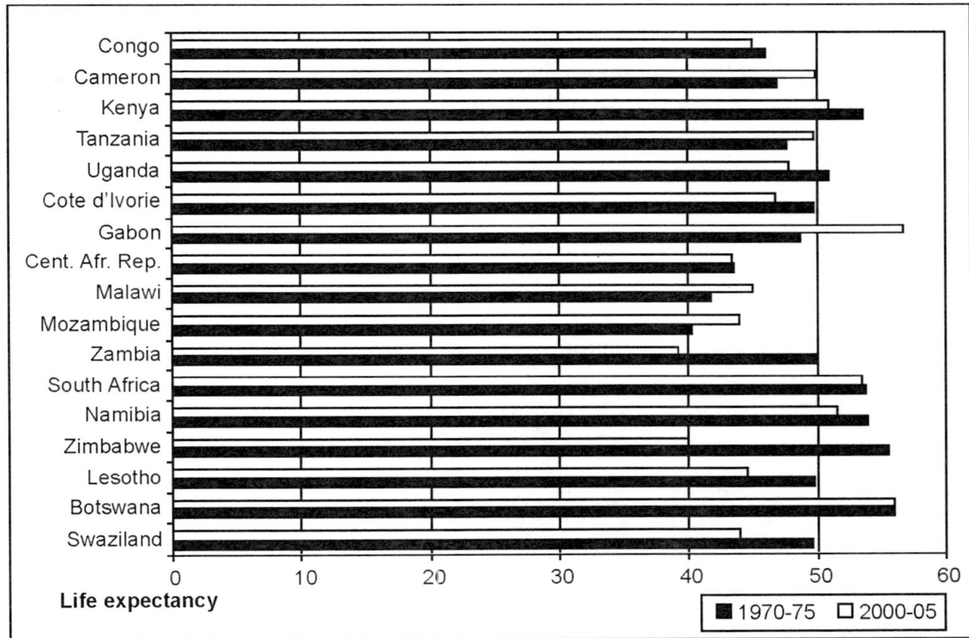

8.9.2 Tuberculosis

Tuberculosis, TB, is a common and often a deadly infectious disease caused by mycobacteria, mainly *Mycobacterium (or M) tuberculosis*. Tuberculosis usually attacks the lungs (as pulmonary TB) but can also affect the central nervous system, the lymphatic system, the circulatory system, the genitourinary system, the gastrointestinal system, bones, joints, and even the skin.

The typical symptoms of TB are a chronic cough with blood-tinged sputum, fever, night sweats and weight loss. The diagnosis relies on chest X-rays, a tuberculin skin test, blood tests, as well as microscopic examination and microbiological culture of bodily fluids. Tuberculosis treatment is difficult and requires long courses (8 to 12 months) of multiple antibiotics. Antibiotic resistance is a growing problem in multi-drug-resistant tuberculosis. Prevention relies on screening programs and vaccination, usually with BCG.

TB is spread through air when people who have the disease cough, sneeze or spit. One-third of the world's current population has been infected with *M. tuberculosis*, and new infections occur at a rate of one per second. About one in ten of these latent infections will eventually progress to active disease, which, if left untreated, kills more than half of its victims. In 2004, mortality and morbidity statistics included 14.6 million chronic active cases, 8.9 million new cases, and 1.6 million deaths, mostly in developing countries. In addition, a rising number of people in the developed world are contracting TB since their immune systems are compromised by immunosuppressive drugs substance abuse, or AIDS. In an age when we believe that we have the tools to conquer most diseases, the ancient scourge of tuberculosis still causes about 2 million deaths a year worldwide – more than any other single infectious organism – reminding us that we still have a long way to go. Even equipped with drugs to treat TB effectively, we have not managed to eradicate this deadly infection.

The distribution of tuberculosis is not uniform across the globe with about 80 percent of the population in Asian and African countries testing positive in tuberculin tests. New cases of TB are detected every year in the developed countries. This occurs most with the immigrants from countries where tuberculosis is endemic. In USA, the most desired destination for emigrants from all over the world, some 5–10 percent of the population tests positive. About 2 billion, roughly one-third of the world population, are infected with TB. TB is a frequent killer for people with AIDS because of compromised immune system. African states suffering from the HIV pandemic have experienced an annual 10 percent rise in TB cases.

Tuberculosis has co-evolved with humans for many thousands of years, and perhaps as much as several million years. During this evolution, *M. tuberculosis* has lost numerous coding and non-coding regions in its genome, losses that can be used to distinguish between strains of the bacteria. The implication is that *M. tuberculosis* strains differ geographically, so their genetic differences can be used to track the origins and movement of each strain.

People suffering from active pulmonary TB, expel infectious aerosol droplets 0.5 to 5 μm in diameter as they cough, sneeze or spit. A single sneeze can release up to 40,000 droplets. Each of these droplets may transmit the disease, since the infectious dose of tuberculosis is very low and the inhalation of just a single bacterium can cause a new infection.

Treatment for TB uses antibiotics to kill the bacteria. The two antibiotics most commonly used are rifampicin and isoniazid. However, instead of the short course of antibiotics typically used to cure other bacterial infections, TB requires much longer periods of treatment to entirely eliminate mycobacteria from the body.

8.9.3 Malaria

A disease that is transmitted to humans or other animals by an insect or other arthropod is called a *vector-borne disease*. The majority of vector-borne diseases survive in nature by utilizing animals as their vertebrate hosts. For malaria and dengue, humans are the major host, with no significant animal reservoirs. Widespread use of insecticides like DDT and improved sanitation almost eliminated Malaria from many countries. Evidence of the reemergence of malaria and dengue was first observed in the 1970s in Asia and the Americas. Sri Lanka and India are classic examples of the lack of sustainability of vertically structured prevention, control or elimination programs. Reasons for the emergence or resurgence of vector-borne diseases include the development of insecticide and drug resistance type; decreased resources for surveillance, prevention and control of vector-borne diseases; deterioration of the public health infrastructure required to deal with these diseases. Between 1 to 5 million people die from malaria every year. WHO puts the number of people affected annually at 300 millions. Malaria is most endemic in Africa. More than 1.1 million people died annually from malaria in the developing countries alone (WHO, 2002). Ninety per cent of these deaths are in Africa, home to the most deadly form of the virus. It kills an African child every 30 seconds. Malaria is responsible for 20 percent of Africa's under-five mortality and 10 percent of the continent's overall disease burden. Dengue fever, together with dengue haemorrhagic fever (DHF), is the world's fastest growing vector borne disease.

Global warming will increase malaria pandemic in developing countries, especially in South Asia and Africa. WHO has identified more than 30 new or resurgent diseases in the last three decades, the sort of explosion some experts say has not happened since the Industrial Revolution brought masses of people together in cities. Why? Global warming is fueling the spread of epidemics in areas unprepared for the diseases when mosquitoes, ticks, mice and other carriers are surviving warmer winters and expanding their range, bringing health threats with them. While WHO acknowledges that these outbreaks could also be connected with a decline in mosquito control programs, warmer temperatures mean malaria-carrying mosquitoes are able to live in northern climes, which could lead to a surge in malaria outside the tropics. Malaria is spreading in South America, South Africa, USA and even in Russia. It has already made a comeback in Korea and parts of Southern Europe. Scientists predict warmer temperatures will allow mosquitoes carrying Malaria and Dengue fever to travel outside the tropics. Since people in cooler climes lack immunity from previous exposure, that means transmission would be extensive.

9 Migration

9.1 Prehistoric Population Settlements

Throughout the history of human civilization people have moved from one place to another, sometime in small numbers, on occasions it has taken the form of mass exodus. We have very little knowledge about prehistoric migratory movement of man. It is an instinctive nature of all animals to move out for a better location whenever the life-support system in their erstwhile residential location got disturbed or destroyed for some natural or other reasons (food scarcity, encroachment by some other species, forest fire, avalanche and deluge). Man, the most intelligent of all biological species, have used this movement more judiciously for his individual welfare as also for the flock to which he belongs. The major difference between man and other biological species is that man can adjust to almost every type of environment. Man has the ability to convert a rather inhabitable and hostile region into a habitable one by his inventiveness and ability to muster strength through cooperation and collective work. The prehistoric population seems to have concentrated in only a few regions in varying proportions. Some 2,000 years back, Indian subcontinent was the home for half the population of the world (Table 1.1). The prehistoric distribution of population on the world canvas was largely determined by (a) the nature of physical environment, (b) the tools and techniques that were developed by the group to extract maximum from the resources offered by the particular physical environment, and (c) the social organization of the group. The latter two, broadly speaking, differentiated the cultures of different groups.

Population still continues to be sparse in Arctic and sub-Arctic regions, in sub-deserts and high altitude mountainous regions. The more hospitable regions – the costal plains and the river valleys, have grown much faster with higher population density because of conducive climate, the topography, the fertility of the soil and the bionetwork or the ecology of the environment. In prehistoric days these factors principally determined man's distribution over the earth. The situation has changed in the last 500 years and the deterministic equation between human settlements and ecological conditions has become somewhat weak.

The prehistoric population can be divided into two broad categories: (1) those depending mostly on hunting and fruit gathering from natural vegetation and the pastoral people dependent on their flocks lived in small clan or tribal groups and scattered over a large area. They would move out easily to a different location if the hunting facilities and natural vegetation would not support their mode of living. Since they were not tied to land, they could move out easily. Such peoples are believed to use force to take hold of neighboring lands or simply moved out to neighboring uninhabited places. (2) The other group was largely dependent on agriculture for their living. A deep bond between man and land started to build up as people began producing their own food through cultivation some 12,000 years back. Men started domesticating animals and with the help of some of these domesticated animals agricultural production went up which could support a much denser population than could be supported by fruit gathering and hunting alone. The settlements grew around river valleys in mild climates with reasonably good rainfall. Almost all great civilizations developed in river valleys.

With development of agriculture and improved food security, people had enough spare time to look for alternative choices beyond agriculture. The surplus of food grains could be moved to other locations that had shortage of food. The invention of wheel and the use of domestic animals in transportation helped develop trade and business with other human settlements, which gave a good base for cultural interaction. As the population density increased, more untilled land was converted into land for cultivation. The area of habitation was expanded and agricultural techniques gradually became more efficient. With time, the settlement area became inadequate to accommodate rising populations. River and road transportations were used extensively to transport some people from one location to another distant one and the new location in course of time became the new center for redistribution of a particular population group. Of course, whether the group would finally decide to settle in the new location depended upon if the migrants' techniques of living could adequately be applied or adapted to the requirements of the settled area.

Sea voyages played a major role in redistribution of population in different parts of the earth. Transportation through rivers like the Ganges and the Nile played a major role, perhaps a decisive role, not only in redistribution of population but also in cultural assimilation. Trade of grains and other agricultural commodities and natural products through rivers and its tributaries flourished bringing people from various walks of life with varied interests together. Population concentration in such places increased considerably; cities grew. Economic motive perhaps was most dominant in past migrations and it still continues to be the prime mover in modern migrations. As the population grew, it became necessary for many countries to disperse a segment of their population to some new locations. European countries were at the forefront in establishing colonies in America, Australia, Africa, India and others. European expansion in the last four or five centuries often were accentuated by political and military considerations. Economic factor however remained at the root. The search for better opportunities and improve one's position economically have remained the dominant motive in modern international and long distance migration. The attractiveness and economic opportunities of the receiving area or country were conveyed mostly from relative to relative or from friend to friend by letter or by word of mouth. The labor in tea-plantations in Assam have attracted people from the same locality of Chotonagpur of Bihar for generations; Gujarati community in USA has encouraged migration from Gujarat and even the community as a whole provided aids and protection to emigrants from Gujarat. Over the years, the Gujaratis have become a very powerful community in hotel and other business chains in USA. The United Kingdom deported some groups of people for their criminal or other tinted background to its colonial settlements. Many people often were forced to migrate abroad to escape persecution by authoritarian leadership (as in many African countries even today). The scale of migration and the freedom of movement the history witnessed in European countries are unlikely to happen again in any part of the world. Usually, such decisions to migrate were taken at individual or group level unaided by any public administrative decisions. At the same time some public policies operated behind some planned migration to other countries. For example, behind the establishment of British colonies in North America the government of the sending country had a positive interest. The colonial masters often encouraged emigration – promised them various aids, especially grant of large piece of land.

9.2 Meaning of Migration

It is not easy to give an exclusive definition of migration. Measurement of different types and intensity of migration is not possible without a precise definition of the term. The core element in the concept of migration is "change of usual place of residence with a view to permanently reside elsewhere". The problem arises with the phrase "usual place of residence". Most people have only one residence and therefore dealing migratory behavior of the majority of the population poses no real problem. But there are few others who have more than one "usual place of residence". They have houses at different places and often they would spend some time in all these houses. Or consider the students who stay in hostels or those who are resident members of some residential institutions although they have their own houses elsewhere. Such residential membership is observed with many other segments of a population – sales persons or persons whose occupation demands that they move from one place to another. This is equally true for persons in the armed forces.

Migration means movement of a person from one place to another with a view to reside there. What then do we mean by 'place of origin and destination'? Does it really refer to a house or a village or a district or some other province/state within or outside the country? Should we call a person migrant when he moves from one end of a village to the other or when he shifts from a rental house to one constructed by him in the same locality? A person may change his place of residence but comes back soon to the same house from where he moved out. Should this person be counted twice for purposes of migration? If we regard migration as movement of people from one place to another, then the person mentioned earlier should be registered twice in the list of migrants. But if the definition of migrants include the clause "with a view to permanently settling", then the person even moving out twice in the same year cannot be regarded as a migrant at all. A person may move to his 'summer residence' or to his 'ancestral home' for a month or so or to his son or daughter's house and stay there for a few months in the same year; yet his movement cannot be regarded as migration. In measurement of migration, the emphasis is on "with a view to permanently settle". If the period for which migration statistics is computed is 5 years or more, then the migration rate for the entire period would be considerably lower had the migration rate for the 5-year period been calculated by adding the yearly migration statistics.

From the issues discussed in the previous paragraph, it is fair to conclude that there is no universally accepted definition of migration – time, space and purpose of the movement are critical in understanding migration and migration related statistics. Two fundamental aspects of movement are: (1) desire to settle permanently (as when one moves from a rented house to his newly constructed house), and (2) staying for a limited period (as when one moves to his summer-house or stays with children's family for a while). With revolution in information technology and globalization of economy, a qualitative change in movement of people across the globe and also within the boundaries of a country is clearly emerging. Every country is relaxing immigration policy to benefit from the brainpower of the world. Visas are being granted in larger numbers to scientists, technologists and management specialists, especially the information and biotechnologists. They truly have become the citizens of the global village. There has occurred a silent revolution both in quality and quantity in internal and international migration. More and more people are joining modern occupations making people break the tie they so long had with their native place.

It becomes necessary that we differentiate *movements* from *migrations*. The social scientists generally have agreed on an operational definition of migration.

> A migrant is one who leaves his erstwhile residence and administrative area and moves to another residence under a new administrative area (police station, district, state or country) with a view to permanently settle there.

Movers, on the contrary, are those who leave their place of origin and settle at a new location, no matter if the destination place is in the same administrative area as his previous residence or a different one. That is, all migrants are movers, but only some movers are migrants

9.3 Certain Terms Associated with Migration

Place of Origin and Destination: The place the migrants leave is the 'place of origin' and the migrants become 'out-migrants' in respect to that place. The place where the migrants arrive and settle is the 'place of destination' and in respect to this place the migrants are 'in-migrants'. So migrants are simultaneously 'out-migrants' in respect to their place of origin and 'in-migrants' in respect to the place where they settle. In- and out-migrations generally refer to internal migration.

Immigration and Emigration: These terms are used in the context of international migration, that is, when the migration takes place between two countries. The migrants sent out from a country are called emigrants; they become immigrants to the receiving state. India receives a large number of immigrants from Bangladesh every year and sends a sizeable number of people to USA, other developed countries and Western Asia.

Gross and Net Migration: The 'gross migration' is the sum total of in-migration (as also immigration) and out-migration (including emigration) with reference to a particular area, smaller than the geographical area of the country. Mumbai, West Bengal and some other states in recent times have substantial net addition in its population through migration besides the natural increase due to excess of birth over death. The two most out-migrating states in India are Bihar and Uttar Pradesh. The net migration in most of the Southern states, especially Kerala, has been negative.

Migration Streams: This refers to movements of people from a common area of origin and to a common area of destination. Tea gardens in Assam received labor from Chotonagpur region over generations. In the South, the migration stream had for a long time remained from Karnataka and Kerala to Tamil Nadu. Of late, Bangalore in Karnataka has become the 'Silicon Valley" of India. Many global giants in IT have already opened their offices in Bangalore. It has become the destination for high profile IT and knowledge-based jobs for young persons from all over India.

9.4 Sources of Migration Data

Like birth and death, migration is a major variable that determines the size of a population in a particular place or region. If natural increase (birth – death) is one component of growth of a population, the other is migration. But unlike birth and death registration, most countries do not have any statutory body to record migration. Even in the developed countries where the administrative machinery is well tuned and efficient, information on internal migration is scanty and unreliable. Relatively reliable data on international migration – immigration and emigration – are available in most countries through visas issued by them. Often illegal migrants far outnumber those migrating legally. Much is discussed in international forums and survey studies on international migration are carried out; but very little attention has been paid to internal migration.

There are two major categories of establishments that keep records of migration. The first category is comprised of border road checkpoints, airports (air transit) and harbors (sea transit). The other establishment is the census organization, which collects information from all if they had resided at some other place prior to the date when they were counted at their present residence. Census statistics on migration can only be obtained every 10 years. Census schedules used by different countries have provisions for recording birth place and last place of residence of those counted. The population can easily be classified into two categories – those whose birthplace is the same as the place where they are counted and those whose birth place and counting place does not match. But this criterion of dividing population into migrants and non-migrants is often a non-starter for the simple reason that it really does not capture the nature of population movement for social and demographic analyses. With more and more births taking place under institutional care, most people would be recorded as migrants by this criterion in future. This criterion is good for locating those people who migrated from a different country.

The transit statistics from checkpoints give a correct picture of those migrants who used the route to get in or go out. The number of persons going out through the check-point A ($A \to B$) and those getting in through A ($B \to A$) give a good picture of total or gross migration through the point A ($A \to B + B \to A$) as also the net-migration (in-migration – out-migration) through the same point. Usually, summary reports of census give the net-migration figures for the states though no time frame is stated for the net-migration data. The census report does not include those cases that after in-migration die. Only those among the in-migrants who survive on the date of counting are counted for their migratory status. Of course the net-migrants between two time points can be worked out from the *survival ratio* of the migrants from the starting time point to the end of the time period. The procedures for computation of net-migrants between two time points (1971 and 1981) have been shown in Chapter 6, Table 6.8. Some sample surveys (NSS for example) report the nature and proportion of migrants in their samples.

Some other indexes of migration as *effectiveness of migration between two places* have also been discussed in the same place (equation 6.33). The indexes of migration discussed there can also be adapted to study age-sex specific migration as also for other factors as occupation, religion, education, etc.

9.5 Determinants of Migration

9.5.1 Push-Pull Dichotomy

Migration has popularly been discussed in the past in terms of *push-pull dichotomy*. The push factor is closely related to the place of origin and its surroundings. The pull or the attraction factor operates at the place of destination. That does neither mean that the forces emanating from the place of origin are all repulsive nor does it mean that everything of the place of destination is likable to the migrant. It is a balancing act between the negative valences of one's place of origin and the positive valences of the place of destination. The repulsive forces from the place of origin have roots in the following:

1. The natural increase of the population has put a serious pressure on the limited natural resources of the place and its neighborhood. The land-man ratio may have declined badly so that pursuing agriculture or similar such occupation appears non-remunerative to individuals. There is no viable alternative in the locality to absorb the surplus labor. They have to move out in search of earning their livelihood. One of the principal reasons for people moving out from villages to cities or towns is this fast declining land-man ratio whereby a large number of people are either rendered jobless or are made marginal farmers. This effect is largely felt on unskilled labor movement.

2. The depletion of natural resources (vegetative and mining), erosion of soil, frequent flood, earthquake, landslide and similar such natural disasters make living extremely difficult.
3. Unpredictable change in climate, drought and flood in successive years, tsunami like incidents, massive loss of life and property, household animals, etc. through earthquake or frequent cyclones make the living really hard.
4. Social, religious and political unrest (Nuxalite movement, attack on minority groups by religious fundamentalists, political vendetta and blood hunt) make life unsafe.
5. Lack of employment opportunity in the locality appropriate to one's ability and skill often is the major force that encourages young educated youths to look for employment elsewhere.
6. Acquisition of agricultural land for establishing industries, construction of roads and bridges, irrigation canals, dams, power plants, and the like force people out who are directly or indirectly dependent on the farm land. Millions have been uprooted from their ancestral homes and farm lands in China, especially since early 1980s when China plunged into large scale economic reform. The same is happening in India and many other developing countries as they endeavor to push the country's GDP growth rate through industrialization.

The attractive influences of the place of destination on the possible movers can be summarized as under:

1. Discovery of some important natural resource in the area. The gold deposits in Africa, Alaska and California attracted people from all over the globe.
2. Establishment of new industries and development of new technologies create opportunities for direct and indirect employment to many. The steel and other industries in Durgapur, the locomotive workshop at Chittaranjan, the IT hub in Bangalore and many other types of industrial activities attract unskilled, skilled and highly professional persons from far and near.
3. Peaceful political and industrial climate catch the attention of entrepreneurs and industrial giants to establish new factories and production units. Many industries were closed or were shifted to some new locations from West Bengal because of poor work-culture in the state, the militant attitude of the labor unions, political interference, frequent strikes, *gheraos* and suspension of work or lock-outs as a result. The party which is in power in the state for the last 32 years have realized that so long the combative attitude of the trade unions does not change, entrepreneurs would stay away from the state. With this change in attitude, the corporate houses are showing interest in West Bengal for many of their new projects. Soon West Bengal could become the destination of international and national IT giants and hi tech industries for the rich human resource of the state and other locational advantages. The environmental concern in the developed West has forced many of their polluting industries to be closed; many industrial giants as a result are moving out to developing countries where labor is cheap and the environmental laws are not very stringent. This is helping in creating employment opportunities for the people where the production units are established.
4. The pleasant climate and pollution-free environment often would attract people who are bothered by noise, pollution and fast pace of city life.

There are many other issues that act both as push and pull factors simultaneously. Whether these factors would be looked upon as repealing or attracting forces would depend largely upon the individual characteristics of the person, his demands and preferences.

1. The advanced technologies create new jobs for highly skilled and professional persons. Computer and information technology in recent years have generated a new kind of job opportunities that require extremely specialized and professional persons. But adoption of this advanced technology has also made many traditional jobs redundant. Computerization and single window customer service in banks, railways and air service have already reduced dependence on manpower and have brought down errors in checks and balances to a minimum. Tractors and power-tillers have made agricultural management more efficient, and in the process has rendered agricultural labor surplus. Small land holdings are increasingly becoming un-remunerative for farming.
2. Certain administrative decisions bring fortune to some and misfortune to others. The land ceiling policy of the government has forced many people to look for alternative sources of livelihood. The distribution of this vested land amongst landless labors encourages the landless labors to move out to the place where they are offered the land.
3. Improved lifestyle attracts many who can afford to spend more for their living. The relatively poor lot is forced to seek for a place where cost of living is appropriate to their earnings.
4. Many people would like to settle in places where many of his relations and friends already stay. Then there are others who would prefer to stay away from their close relations.

In the analysis of migration behavior *relative desirability or differential desirability or preference system* often is accepted as a better theoretical framework and more realistic than the push-pull dichotomy hypothesis. It is somewhat analogous to cost-benefit analysis of fertility or in the selection of a desired commodity. An individual makes a mental toss of attractive characteristics with the disagreeable ones of the place of destination and compares the same with his present residence and makes a final decision on the basis of checks and balances of either of the places. This *relative desirability hypothesis* suggests that migratory behavior of different persons cannot be understood in the same general terms. People have different likes and dislikes; the same set of references cannot be used to understand why some people move and others do not. Likes and dislikes of a person are unique. This uniqueness along with one's resource limitations decides one's migration strategy.

Simultaneously two or more places may encourage a person to leave his erstwhile place of residence. Each place will have some eye-catching features and some unattractive conditions too. The reasons for the family's eagerness to move out, the balance of the positive and negative affects associated with the destination places and a lot more things enter into this decision-making process. Decision-making involved in migration is a very complex process; some factors are so closely interdependent that their individual effect cannot be isolated from most others. It is for this reason that demographers study the phenomenon of migration from the migrants' angle rather than trying directly to fit a generalized cause-effect model. In this, we need answers to two issues:

1. What characteristics differentiate a migrant from a non-migrant and the degree of differences in these characteristics?
2. Not all migrants display similar type of movement. Some move out from villages, some from one town/city to another and some migrate to very long distant places. What commonalities and dissimilarities are observed among the various streams and levels of migration?

The answer to some of these questions can be had from the biological, social and personal characteristics of the migrants.

9.5.2 Biological Characteristics of Migrants

1. *Age:* The proportion of old-age people both in internal and international migration is low. The largest segment of the migrants comes from the age group 15–35 years. The younger people migrate often for better and higher education. Children and other dependents move out because their parents migrate for occupation or for some other reasons. Young but adult women move out of their parental home after marriage. Occupation or profession is the major reason for migration in the age group 20–30 years. People in the age group 25–35 years often would prefer a separate accommodation, close to their working place, after they are married. Young and unmarried people would not hesitate to migrate if that would help them to get a better start in life. Once married and children are born, movements get restricted because of the additional responsibilities reposed on them. With age, risk-taking mentality also evaporates. Even if willing to migrate, the greatly expanded family responsibility would prevent aged persons to seek a new place for living.
2. *Sex difference:* The proportion of females among the migrants diminishes with the distance of migration. Males also dominate in international migration. Occupation or profession is the principal reason behind all long distance migrations. Marriage is the dominant factor in migration of females. The housewife along with her children and other dependents has to accompany her husband as and when he migrates. Short distance migration is more common among women. However, not much difference is observed between sexes in short distance migration.
3. *Racial difference:* Whites more than the non-whites, migrate easily to distant places. The Europeans have settled in almost every part of the globe. The Keralites and Gujraties have migrated in large numbers to West Asia and USA. The Marwaries and the Punjabees can be seen at all the corners of the country.
4. *Difference in intellectual ability:* It is the more intelligent and professional persons who migrate easily to distant places. Because of their education and intelligence level they can easily adapt in a new environment. Language and culture of the place of destination pose no serious problem to them. Lowly educated and of lesser intelligent people are found to dominate the short distance migration, from one village to another or within the same police station or the same district.
5. *Physical strength:* Most migrants are found to be physically sound, agile, strong and of active habits. Sick and physically weak try to avoid the concomitant hazards for undertaking such movements.

9.5.3 Social Characteristics of Migrants

1. The principal reason for migration, especially among men, is the job or the employment opportunity in the destination place. It has been observed that increased income motivation is very strong both in internal and international migrations. Unemployed or marginally employed persons show greater willingness to migrate than those who are comfortably placed in their life.
2. The proportion of people with better intellectual disposition and professional training is high among the migrants, especially those making long distance movements. USA has attracted scientists and technologists and other professionals from all over the world. Brain drain is hotly debated in India. The most advanced laboratories, high quality of teaching in universities, plenty of opportunities for conducting research in variety of areas with necessary technical and

financial support from universities/foundations and many other facilities related to higher education have encouraged scientists and technologists from the developing countries migrate to many Western countries.

3. Rural to urban is the most popular stream of migration in all countries, developing or developed. The dominant motive for these migrants is to move away from farm to non-farm jobs.
4. Both community and religious press are found to operate when a large proportion of people from a geographical area found to move out to a common destination. Often some population groups are subjected to intense social, religious or political pressure for some reason or other. Under extreme provocation the whole of the population group may decide to move out to a place that they feel would provide necessary protection to them. Jews left Germany for Israel or other countries like USA where they could pursue their professions without any pressure from the administration and the local social, religious and political groups. The American Negroes moving out to southern region or repatriation of Hindus and Muslims to India and Pakistan after partition in 1947 or hundreds and thousands of Bengalese leaving Assam for West Bengal after intense agitation for 'drive away Bengalese from Assam' are examples of how political, religious or linguistic provocation may force whole of a minority community to look for an alternative destination.
5. Proportion of unmarried persons is more among those who migrate. Once married, a man or a woman is not free to take decisions all by him/her. The responsibility for children's and other member's wellbeing often acts as deterrent to migration.
6. The migrants are great movers as well. Once a decision is taken to leave the parental/ancestral home, the migrants will have less hesitation to move out again as and when the situation demands. That is, the resistance to changing the place of residence is greatly reduced once they have broken their long tie with their ancestral homes and the neighborhood.
7. Educated and professionals constitute a large proportion of the migrants.

9.5.4 Individual Characteristics of Migrants

1. The migrants are energetic and have high aspirations;
2. They are used to better life style, do not hesitate to say goodbye to traditions and are at ease to adjust to the demands of modern society;
3. They are passionate about fast life and have tall desire for the best things in life; and
4. A high proportion of the migrants suffer from numerous tensions. In consequence, problem of mental health is relatively high among migrants.

Even with lucrative offer for better placement and an assured high standard of living, many people, who have all the qualities for getting success through emigration, would hesitate to leave their habitual place of residence and country. Many would not like to be uprooted from their familiar social milieu, family members and friends even though communication and transport system have improved manifold in recent times. Internet and efficient telecommunications have made the world into a global village. But we know from our past experiences and observations that once out of sight the mental and physical link with the root family would become weak with the passage of time. Even the increasing ease of transportation and the speed of communication have failed to maintain the ties and bonds between the migrants and the homeland. For those who have migrated with an outstation assignment or those who emigrated with a definite plan to return at some future date, these issues do not have a lasting effect on them.

Our resistant to emigration would be considerably small if we would see that there will be enough familiar faces from our family and relations in the destination country and that the social environment in the receiving country/community would be nearly as conducive as that in the sending country. There is less resistance to short distance migration in all societies and in all countries. Short distance migration therefore constitutes the largest segment of all types of migration. But for a highly qualified and professional person, short distance migration often would not provide real scope for meeting his high aspirations and the desired life style. The intervening space between the place of destination and the place of origin often would fail to provide him with the type of job he wants for himself and the quality of accommodation, schools, doctors, clubs, etc., which he feels necessary for a person of his stature.

We have said earlier that migration is a highly complex process and is dependent mostly on personal qualities, drives and motivations. It is therefore not easy to offer a general causal model for migration. Further, data on migration, especially internal migration, vis-à-vis on birth and death, are too scanty for undertaking any rigorous analysis on migration behavior of a population or community.

9.6 Effects of Migration

Migration is basically a process of population redistribution, both at national and international level. The sending state loses some of its people to the receiving state. The parameter of the population of the sending state may change (the receiving state as well) if a particular segment of the population is found to migrate more than others – a particular age-sex group, a particular religious and caste group, professionals, skilled or unskilled labor, etc. If the scale of migration is very large, it may have lasting effect on the composition of the population both for sending and receiving states/regions. It is often observed that migrants prefer a particular area to others. This may have something to do with cultural similarity between the sending and the receiving area (already there could be a large number of migrants from the same area who have settled in that destination place, as between Assam tea gardens and Chotonagpur). After partition many Indian Muslims migrated to settle in Pakistan and many Hindus both from East and West Pakistan came and settled in bordering states. Punjab, West Bengal and Assam received such populations most. Movement of Hindus (Muslims as well) from Bangladesh (erstwhile East Pakistan) still continues and the villages on the international border are most affected by this illegae movement.

There was a time when the European countries sent people to different parts of the world and established their colonies. They were then sending nations. North America, Africa, Australia and New Zealand, India, etc. were on the receiving side. The direction of the flow has reversed in modern times, especially after the Second World War; people from the underdeveloped regions move to the developed countries for various reasons – education, jobs, better standard of living, seeking political asylum, etc. Most of these countries currently have stringent immigration policy to curb illegal migration trend.

The social demographers, however, are more interested to study the effect migration may have on the individuals moving out and also on the people where the migrants settle. No effect on biological characteristics of the migrants is observed (race, caste, religion, intellectual level, etc.). Whether there would be some effect on the physical capacity of the migrant will depend upon how easily one could adapt to the changing climatic conditions and the physical and social environment of the receiving state. The larger the difference between the sending and receiving areas, the greater would be the effort required to adapt to the changed environment. However, education, profession and social life of the migrants may change substantially depending upon the reasons for migration.

Demographers are really interested to know the possible effect migration may have on the two basic demographic variables – birth and death. They believe that when the migration between two areas continue for a long time and the volume of migration is large, both birth and death rate of the migrants may change producing significant effect on the composition of the population of the receiving state as also on their social institutions through cultural assimilation. The prime indicators for such changes are to be found in the answer to the following:

1. Would the settlers continue to follow their traditional beliefs and norms regarding birth and death, or would they try to adopt the norms about these of the receiving state?
2. Would the migrants continue to suffer from such diseases which were generally observed while they were in the sending state and would they display similar mortality rates as that in the place of their origin or would the occurrence of these events be dictated by the patterns observed in the receiving state or would they develop a middle course between these two?

No conclusive evidence for or against either of these things happening has been found as yet. The population scientists have assured us that some changes are bound to happen. But the scale of change would depend upon the individual and social characteristics of migrants. What is generally observed is that with the passage of time the migrants move a little away from their traditional beliefs and practices and accept some of the social and cultural traditions of the receiving population. That is, they continue to hold some of their own traditional values and at the same time they are not completely overwhelmed by the cultural and social traditions of the receiving society. In long distance permanent migration, the assimilation continues for generations and this could easily be observed when we compare the behavior patterns of two or more generations among migrants. In the first generation, this assimilation is slow; it gains momentum from the second generation and by third or fourth generation the assimilation is almost complete. It is the adaptability of the migrant population that would decide if some distinction was to be maintained between the indigenous population and the migrants. The assimilation would be far from perfect or the progress in adaptation would be slow if the two cultures were totally different. The adaptation, for this reason, is much faster in internal migration than in trans-boundary migration. Effectiveness of migration therefore would depend upon how soon the new social group can replace the migrants' erstwhile social group. Some of the diseases, little known in the receiving state, may surface there due to import of these diseases through the migrants.

The social consequences of migration, both in the sending and receiving regions, would depend largely on the following:

1. Magnitude of gross migration (in- and out-migration)
2. The areas of fundamental difference between the sending and receiving states or regions.
3. The magnitude of difference between personal and social characteristics between the movers and the non-movers.
4. The role played by the migrants in their new place of residence as also their nature of adjustment and integration into this new set up is extremely important both for the migrants and the sons of the soil. The adjustment process is greatly facilitated by the pre-selectivity of

migrants at the sending areas and by familiar contacts. Presence of friends and relatives at the place of destination is an important factor in destination selection and in matters of adjustment once the migrants have moved to their destination place.

5. How accommodating the receiving population is in respect to the social and cultural background of those trying to settle in.
6. Young persons dominate among the migrants (rural as well as urban). Some studies in India indicate that migrants tend to come from larger families and are often the younger sons of the family. When young working persons leave an area in large numbers, the ratio of dependents to workers rises.
7. When young, unmarried persons dominate among the migrants, especially among rural out-migrants, a serious imbalance in sex ratio may arise in rural areas and may often influence the proportion of persons able to find marriage partners.
8. Many social and economic equations may change drastically if the destination state attracts energetic and highly educated and skillful persons from other areas. Similarly, some states may lose out their talents to other states when it fails to provide adequate placement for their talented youths. The transfer of human capital may change the economic and social scenario both for the sending and destination areas.
9. Returning migrants often would spread new values and information about the outside world to people around him in his native place. He carries back many of the ideas from the new place. The more frequent he visits his native place, the greater impact he will have on the people he had left. He becomes an icon and a tool for cultural diffusion.
10. When unemployed youths migrate, especially from rural area, unemployment rates in the sending state may fall. However, when the migrants are students or are not in the labor force, there may not be observable change in unemployment levels. It is, therefore difficult to say the net effect of migration on employment and income of the sending area. Kerala is a major out-migrating state in South India. It sends out in large number skilled and semi-skilled labor to West Asia. They remit large sums back home. But it has been observed that this NRI remittance hardly has any impact on the state economy. The remittance is largely invested in real estates and therefore there is hardly any scope for investing this remittance in other sectors, especially the social sector.
11. In the days of labor-intensive growth of industries, the majority of the migrants were in low-income, low-profile jobs. The direct and immediate effect of such migration resulted in worsening of the over-all distribution in urban income and growth of slums. The modern capital-intensive enterprises have little room for unskilled labor. The entry of the migrants in modern industrial sectors ensures better income and improved standard of living.
12. The more the industrial and service sectors develop the more it escalates in-migration, necessitating expansion of the urban area and improvement of physical and social infrastructure. Since most cities in India (and many other developing countries) were planned for a fraction of their current population, severe shortage is experienced in all basic services. The transportation systems, water supply, drainage system, power distribution, that is, the very basic services offered by the cities suffer. The rising slum population encroaches upon whatever vacant land is available, lives almost without any public service, very little or no sanitary provision and stable drinking water facilities. In this intolerably insecure life, the poor people produce little wealth and receive little in return. Clearance of slums and hawkers taking full control of the

walkways in critical juncture of the cities and railway platforms has become an irksome problem for the government for the plain reason that the slum dwellers and hawkers mostly have patronage of various political parties (they are their solid vote banks) and the governments have no means to send them to alternative settlements or pay compensation for evicting them from the encroached lands, footpaths and railway platforms.

Although rural-urban migration, and for that matter in all types of migration, is primarily due to economic reasons, there is contradictory views and observations on the labor participation rate among the migrants. Those who view lower propensity of labor participation among migrants have cited certain reasons for that. When the migrants are 'target workers', that is, those who move to urban areas only for a specific time period with a specific intention of saving enough money to buy land or capital equipment back in their native villages, are likely to have less commitment at their work place than the indigenous population. It has also been observed that migration is mostly a calculated move by a person or a population group and therefore they prefer some areas to others for various physical, social and other reasons. The local politics (including work culture), social system and cultural traditions would in the long run influence the settlers in many different ways. Once they start marrying in the indigenous families, the cultural and social adaptations become quicker and easier. The migrants too have a considerable influence on the economic and social environment of the receiving state, especially if they are highly educated, intelligent and are engaged in high profile jobs. The sender state may suffer a loss in social and economic front by losing the cream of their society through migration. The sending population may temporarily suffer from an imbalance in age and sex structure in the population, especially when they lose a very significant segment of the active population. In fine, it can be said that migration has considerable effect on demographic, political, social and economic aspects of a population, be that a sending or a receiving one.

9.7 Types of Migration

Both internal and international migration is observed in all countries. The internal migration can be classified by *stream* and *distance* of migration.

9.7.1 Stream of Migration

1. Rural to urban, R-U
2. Rural to rural, R-R
3. Urban to rural, U-R
4. Urban to urban, U-U

The most important stream of internal migration is R-U. This is a universal phenomenon. Because of very large volume of migration from rural to urban areas, especially the large cities, urban population all over the world is growing very fast (the world average of urban population is close to 50 percent of the total population). And to accommodate this increased number, the city limits often have to be expanded by bringing the adjoining suburban areas under its jurisdiction. The growth of urban area and urban population is but a logical consequence of fast mode of industrialization in the developed countries. They needed extra labor to run their fast growing establishments. Industrialization simultaneously brought in changes in agricultural technology and management freeing a segment of labor from agriculture. In a sense, a strong urban ward movement in the developed countries can be looked upon as an index of industrial progress. The economically backward countries also experienced a movement of labor from rural areas for a different reason. The near population explosion situation in these countries put a tremendous pressure on agricultural land. With cultivable land per capita falling below a critical level, agriculture could not provide employment to its entire rural people. The labor made surplus by this falling land-man ratio, forced people to move out to seek alternative jobs for themselves. However, more of those in non-agricultural occupation, vis-à-vis landless agricultural labor, moved out in search of an alternative job. Therefore, the growth of urban population in the developing countries is much in excess in the context of their level of industrial and economic growth. Whereas the *pull factor* of the expanded job market created opportunity for alternative job opportunities for rural people in the developed countries, it is the *push factor* in developing countries that forced people to move out to urban areas in search of their livelihood.

Those who migrate to urban areas have different characteristics than those making R-R movement. Usually they are young, educated and have high aspiration level. For reasons of occupation or profession, males overwhelmingly dominate R-U stream. Often they are unmarried. Even if married, they would not take along their spouses, at least initially. It is for this reason that a smaller sex-ratio (F/M) in urban area is observed. Rural to urban migration in all developing countries is fast increasing; it is around 30 percent of all migrants in India.

Rural-rural migration is the strongest migration stream in most countries, especially in the developing ones, for a different reason altogether. Women, more than men, migrate in large proportion in almost all countries. The bride moves to bridegrooms place after marriage in most societies. In fact, close to 50 percent of female migrants move out for reasons of marriage. For cultural and other reasons, the married couples frequently come from nearby villages, often from within the same district.

Urban-urban migration is a very significant stream of migration in the developed countries. The people there do not hesitate to migrate from one city to another, often crossing the national boundaries, when a better job is found. Because of better communication and transportation facilities as also for better infrastructure, the address of most trade and commercial organizations is the city or its suburban areas. U-U migration is generally restricted between cities, especially metropolitan cities. Since only very highly professional persons constitute this migration stream, their share to total migrants is only about 10 percent in India.

Urban to rural migration is the weakest of the four streams of migration. This stream is mostly comprised of those migrants who moved out to urban areas (a) with a temporary mission after fulfilling of which they return back to their native place, and (b) the job seekers who after unsuccessful attempt at getting a reasonable livelihood in the destination place, go back to their places of origin. This is also referred to as *return migration.* Prof. Ashish Bose after analyzing the NSSO data came to the conclusion that for every 100 successful migrants from rural areas (success in the sense of security for their livelihood) encouraged another 254 people to migrate to cities. It is also observed that the proportion of unemployed among the migrants is less vis-à-vis the local residents.

9.7.2 Distance of Migration

1. *Short distance migration:* When people move out to areas under different police station but within the same district, the migration is referred to as short distance migration. Most of the R-R migrations refer to this category. This may happen with cities as well if the migrants move out to a different area of the same city but under different police station.

2. *Medium distance migration:* When the migrants settle in a district different from the earlier one but within the same state, the movement will be called medium distance migration. Actually distance in absolute term covered is not important. When a person moves from one village to an adjacent village but in a different district, the resulting migration would be reckoned as medium distance migration even though the distance traveled could be only a kilometer or even less.
3. *Long distance migration:* In long distance migration, the movement is between two states within the same country or between two different countries. Whereas (1) and (2) are exclusively related to internal migration, (3) refers to both internal and international migration. Many agricultural labors had migrated from Bihar and UP to Punjab – an agriculturally surplus state. Mumbai, Bangalore, Delhi, Chennai and some other cities receive labor and professionals from all over India; West Bengal receives people from various parts of the country as well as from Bangladesh. U-U migration generally is a long distance migration.

9.7.3 International Migration

There was a time when the populations in some of the countries were growing very fast encouraging emigration (most of the European countries were in this stage earlier). Because of stationary state in internal productions and resource utilizations, the economy of these countries could not meet the demands of their growing numbers. The discovery of America and the high quality of mining and other natural resources in Africa came as a boon for these countries. A large-scale emigration to both the Americas and Africa relieved these European countries from the pressure of population. Through population redistribution in the eighteenth and nineteenth century, the populous European countries could largely solve the problems arising out of huge population growth in these countries. The economic, social and political atmosphere was favorable for large-scale international migration. The intensity of mass exodus in that period could be gauged simply by studying the ratio of the white and non-white population (or racial difference) in the receiving countries.

Since World War II the international situation and the political and economic relations between countries curbed the international migration greatly. Every country took stringent legislative measures to prevent illegal immigration. Volume of international migration compared to the world population even today is small (191 million international migrants in a population over 6.5 billion). The proportion of people born in a different country but settled in India is less than 1 percent of total Indian population. Their share to total migrants (internal and international) is less than 3 percent. International migration is still observed between the African countries, mostly because of political volatility in some regions. In fact, most of them are refugees. In India and in many Asian countries refugees have the largest share among immigrants in these countries. Laos, Kampuchea and Vietnam experienced mass exodus to nearby Southeast Asian countries. Later, most of them migrated and settled in Europe and North America. The migrant labors have a decisive role in population redistribution in many West Asian countries. Because of political shakiness, population movement between countries in South America has also been observed. Presently, the target country for such population movement is North America and Europe.

Even at the beginning of the twentieth century many people from Europe moved out to distant places in search of better living. European countries too received migrants from different parts of the world. Since World War II such migrations have declined noticeably. The major target countries for emigration today are USA, Canada, Australia, UK, Germany and a few other countries in Europe and the oil-rich Arab countries.

International migration had never been a serious issue in India. It was only during partition in 1947 that India experienced a large scale international migration (about 7 million people from both sides moved to settle in the other part). Although India has open borders with Nepal and Bhutan, immigrants from these countries never were large.

Since the end of the cold war and the arrival of computer, IT, biotechnology and hi tech manufacturing industries, and also because of shortage of skilled and professional persons in the developed countries, the respective governments had to liberalize their immigration policy. WTO and other international agencies played an important role in liberalization of migration policy in most countries.

Since 1975 the volume of international migrants worldwide has more than doubled. At the beginning of the 21st century, one out of every 35 persons worldwide was an international migrant. In 2002, almost one in every 10 persons living in more developed regions was a migrant. Since 1960, the more developed regions of the world have experienced a gain in population through immigration from the less developed regions, and the net gain increased over this period. Between 1990 and 2000 the more developed countries were gaining about 2.6 million persons annually through net international migration and this migrated population accounted for two-thirds of the population growth in these regions.

Most of the world's 191 million international migrants are concentrated in a relatively small number of countries in North America, Europe, and the former Soviet Union. In 2005, the United States was home to more foreign-born residents than any other country – 38 million, or one of every five immigrants worldwide. The Russian Federation was second, with 12 million immigrants, and Germany third (10 million) (Population Bulletin, Sept. 2008). In recent years, globalization, uneven population growth, and economic differences across countries have increased the flow of people across national borders. In 1960, there were only 30 countries with half a million immigrants or more; by 2005, the number of countries with this distinction had more than doubled, 64.

Regional Patterns: Between 1990 and 2005, USA gained international migrants most (15 million), followed by Germany and Spain. Migrants from developing countries are drawn to the US and Europe by the higher wages and economic opportunities in these regions. This trend also has a strong demographic component. In 2005, there were 600 million workers in more developed countries, contrasted to 2.4 billion workers in the less developed countries. Many developed countries, particularly in Europe, are aging rapidly, TFRs far less than the replacement level and facing potential labor shortages in the coming decades. Just to maintain the sizes of their 1995 labor forces, France, Germany, Italy, and the UK had to quadruple current annual immigration levels, from 237,000 to 1.1 million. The largest flow of immigrants is from less developed to more developed countries (62 million in 2005), but there are almost as many (61 million) who move from one developing country to another. Many of these so called "south-south" migrants are moving for work opportunities (for example, Nepalese workers move to India for seasonal farm work). Others have moved to escape conflict or natural disasters. Refugee migration is most common in Africa. The continent has one-seventh of the world's current population but one-fourth of the world's 10 million refugees.

Africa has experienced large migration flows in recent decades, often in response to natural disasters, economic problems, or civil unrest. In 1994, Africa witnessed one of the world's largest exoduses in recent times – as many as 2 million Rwandans left their country, straining local infrastructures, contributing to the spread of infectious diseases and upsetting ethnic balances in neighboring countries.

Emigration does help relieve population pressures and reduce unemployment in sending countries. Migrant workers also send billions of dollars back home. These remittances are larger than the total of all official development assistance worldwide, and are among the fastest-growing international financial flows. Formal remittances to developing countries doubled between late 1980s and mid-1990s to almost $60 billion a year, doubled again by 2002, and doubled again to $240 billion in 2007 ($42 billion in recorded outward flows from the United States was by far the largest remittance in 2006). Most of the US money flows to Mexico, which received $25 billion in remittances in 2007. Mexico accounts for only 2 percent of the population living in developing countries but receives about 10 percent of remittances to developing countries.

Although migrant-sending countries benefit from remittances from those who left, they also lose some of their most industrious and brainy workers. In parts of the Caribbean, 70 percent of the highly educated work force has left to work in Canada, USA, or Europe. Some highly skilled workers do return to their home countries, but these return rates vary widely by country. Return rates have been relatively high in China and Korea, boosting economic development in these countries. India has had relatively low return rates, but this could change if USA continues to shift white-collar jobs overseas, creating new, local job opportunities for returning high-skilled workers.

The impact of migrants on receiving countries depends, in part, on the relative size of the foreign-born population. In the United States, foreign-born residents account for roughly 13 percent of the total population, but in some countries with high labor needs, the proportions are much higher. In the Persian Gulf states, which have long relied on migrant workers from South Asia to fill private sector jobs, more than 1 in 3 residents were foreign born in 2005. Many of the communicable diseases, not quite common in the developed countries, are spreading into developed countries through immigrants.

Immigrant population in USA: Immigration and higher fertility among minorities have put the United States on a path to become "majority-minority", when less than 50 percent of the population will be non-Hispanic white. Racial and ethnic minorities, which currently account for one-third of the US population, are projected to reach 50 percent by 2050. 2007 estimates from the US Census Bureau show that about 10 percent (302) of the country's 3,141 counties have already passed that mark. Another 218 counties have reached the "tipping point" toward becoming majority-minority in the next few years. Majority-minority counties come in all types – from large counties in major metropolitan areas (Bronx County in New York City) to small rural counties (Todd County in South Dakota). Such counties are highly concentrated in certain parts of the country – in particular, the South-East, the South-West (especially along the Mexican border), Central and Southern California, parts of the rural Great Plains, most of Alaska, and Hawai.

In most majority-minority counties, a single minority group makes up more than 50 percent of the county population. For example, most of majority-minority counties in the South-East are African American. Counties that are majority Hispanic are largely in the South-West as well as in Southern Florida and parts of California. And American Indians are the majority group in several counties in Alaska, the Great Plains, and the "four corners" area of Arizona, New Mexico, and Utah.

International migration is projected to remain high during the first half of the present century, although after 2010 net migration to the more developed regions of the world is expected to continue at a lower level, around 2.1 million a year instead of the high 2.6 million experienced in the

1990–2000 period. The more developed regions are expected to remain net receivers of international migrants, the major net receiving countries being USA (1.1 million), Germany (204,000), Canada (201,000), the UK (133,000), Italy (120,000) and Australia (100,000). The countries with the largest net annual emigration are projected to be China (–333,000), Mexico (–304,000), India (–245,000), the Philippines (–180,000), Pakistan (–173,000) and Indonesia (–168,000). Asian countries alone would have the lion's share in immigration in the developed countries. Between 2000 and 2050, a large increase in the percentage of immigrant population in these countries is expected, ranging from 6 to 25 per cent. If this migration trend continues unabated, immigrants ultimately may outnumber the original resident population. The larger size of the current and future immigrant populations in the developed countries may pose serious problems for the resident population. Since most of these immigrants would be highly qualified professionals, they will hold many important and key positions in universities, research establishments, knowledge-based and hi tech industries, bioengineering, medicine, corporate jobs and even in public offices (USA has Indian American governor, mayor and senators); they certainly would have significant say in matters relating to many policy issues. With larger numbers, the foreign origin populations may feel less need to adapt to local norms; they may become more confident in attempting to extend their own values, language and laws in the larger society.

9.8 Theories and Models of Migration

Several theories and models of migration have been suggested. They broadly can be distinguished into two types – "micro-analytic" and "macro-analytic". Individual's social, psychological and personal backgrounds as determinants of mobility are primarily discussed in the "micro models". Ecological determinants of population flow, like size and distance, receive greater emphasis in the "macro models". A judicious mix or amalgamation of different end-oriented models is necessary to understand the interacting influences of this background information in the context of social change and economic development.

The theoretical models on migration address largely to functional relations as are done in mathematics. Demographers talk of migration as a function of two places A and B, i.e., $M = F(A,B)$. Ravenstein, as early as 1880, spoke of three fundamental variables in explanation of migration:

1. The size of the populations in the place of origin and destination,
2. Population density in these two places, and
3. The distance between these two places.

The following summarizes the major points of Ravenstein's formulations:

(a) Migrants move from areas of low economic opportunity to those of high economic opportunity;
(b) Rural migrants move in stages. In the first instance, they select nearby towns, and then larger towns or cities that are at a considerable distance;
(c) Migration accelerates with improvement in the transport system as also with expansion of trade and industry;
(d) Each stream of rural-urban migration produces a counter-stream (urban-rural), mostly return-migration though. The former however dominates the latter; and
(e) Urban residents are less migratory than the rural. When they migrate, they migrate to a long distance;

Later, Adna Weber and others added a few other variables – demand for labor, financial and other sustaining resources – in the list submitted by Ravenstein.

In Everette Lee's theory of migration, decision to migrate and the process of migration is determined by *four* factors:

1. *Factors associated with the area of origin:* Each place of origin has certain compelling factors (political, social or economic) that trigger off movement to an outside area. These are negative factors.
2. *Factors associated with the area of destination:* More attractive forces operating at the destination increase migrant selectivity. Conversely, the stronger influence of repulsive forces at the destination reduces selectivity. Most attractive forces are found to operate in a nation's metropolitan cities. These areas therefore have the largest proportion of selectivity migrants.
3. *Intervening obstacles:* Migrant selectivity is raised through increased difficulty of the intervening obstacles.
4. *Personal factors:* Attention is drawn on individual's behavior and perception and decision-making process of the migrant. A "general scheme into which a variety of special movements can be placed" has been developed. Forces exerting influences on migrant's perception have been dichotomized into "pluses" and "minuses". Pluses refer to the "pull factors" of the destination areas, and minuses are the forces that "drive or push" them away. There could be "zeros" as well, in the event the competing forces are, more or less, evenly balanced.

Everette Lee has presented a set of hypothesis relating to *volume of migration, migration stream* and *migrants' personal characteristics.*

Hypothesis Related to Volume of Migration

(a) The volume of migration between regions will depend upon the *diversity of the areas or regions*;
(b) Volume of migration will depend upon *diversity of the people*;
(c) Volume of migration will depend upon the *effectiveness of intervening obstacle;*
(d) Volume of migration will depend upon *economic instability*;
(e) In absence of stringent laws against immigration and emigration, volume and rate of migration tend to increase with time; and
(f) The state of health of economy of a region or a country has decisive role on both volume and rate of migration.

Hypothesis Related to Stream and Counter-stream of Migration

(a) Migration generally takes place within the well-defined streams;
(b) A counter-stream develops for every important migration stream;
(c) Effectiveness of migration stream is enhanced when the incidents leading to migration originates from the negative factors associated with the place of origin;
(d) The similarity between the places of origin and destination will weaken the stream and counter-stream of migration;
(e) The more overriding the intervening obstacles are the more effective would be the stream of migration; and

(f) The effectiveness of a migration stream is closely related to economy of the sending and receiving regions. Migration streams are most effective in times of economic prosperity than when there is all-round economic depression.

Hypothesis Related to the Characteristics of Migrants

(a) Migration is person-centric;
(b) Those who migrate because of the positive valence associated with the receiving region, are positively selected migrants;
(c) Those who migrate because of the negative valence associated with the sending region, are negatively selected migrants. When the negative forces of the sending state is too strong, it is difficult to predict who would migrate and who would not;
(d) When all migrants are taken into consideration, the distribution of migrants would be bi-modal;
(e) The more distinctive the intervening obstacles are the more specific would be the migrants;
(f) Migration is more numerous at a certain stage of an individual's life. Migration therefore is organically linked to the population in that particular age group.

Demographic Graviation Model: Demographers have suggested various models for estimating the volume of migration between any two places. By taking cue from Newton's theory of gravitation, some demographers have talked of a *demographic gravitation model* to predict volume of migration. John Q. Stewart (1941) talked of a model, which relates in-migrants to the ratios of the size of population of the sending states to their distances from the receiving state. If the population size of the sending state (A, B, C...) is N and the physical distance between the sending and receiving state (X) is D, then the total in-migrants at X from A, B, C... would be

$$M = \frac{N_A}{D_A} + \frac{N_B}{D_B} + \frac{N_C}{D_C} + \ldots \qquad \ldots(9.1)$$

Stewart's equation is a modification of the equation suggested by W. G. Reilly in 1929. It reads

$$M = \frac{N}{D^2} \qquad \ldots(9.2)$$

A more appropriate use of Newton's gravitation theory is found in K. Zipf's formulation. According to Zipf, the population exchange between two places would be directly proportional to the product of the size of the populations in these two places and inversely proportional to the least distance connecting the two places. If P_A and P_B are the respective population sizes of places A and B, and D is the minimum distance between the two places, then

$$M(A \rightarrow B \text{ or } B \rightarrow A) = \frac{P_A \cdot P_B}{D} \qquad \ldots(9.3)$$

This formulation has been used quite extensively by many demographers to measure the extent of population exchange between two places. Obviously, M in this equation will depend upon the unit one chooses for D (km or mile). There is also a debate if the denominator should refer to a linear measure (D) or its square (D^2) as in the gravitation model. This model has been criticized mostly because it is symmetrical, suggesting equal probability of flow in both directions, which in reality is not.

Traver and Mcleod (1973) have spoken of a viable alternative. This is better known among demographers by *Peterson-Greenwood hypothesis*. This hypothesis has drawn heavily from the hypothesis on "accident-proneness" in industrial psychology. The psychologists have observed that the workers who did not have any record of involvement in any accident for a long period start getting involved in accidents once they happen to get associated in an accident. That is, every accident hastens the occurrence of subsequent accidents. To be precise, probability of an individual getting involved in an accident can be predicted from the previous records of accidents for the individual. A similar logic is applied to predict volume of population exchange between two places from the volume of migration registered between the two places in not too a distant past. Peterson-Greenwood hypothesis states that current or future migration rate at a place would be dependent upon the rate of migration experienced at the places in the previous generation. Some environmental pressures or desire to fulfilling one's personal aspirations led the earlier generations to move out. Whenever similar such situation develops, the succeeding generations would take cue from their predecessors. There are plentiful of instances that support this hypothesis. Inter-state migration streams in India have remained nearly unchanged for several decades. The destination countries for emigrants from most countries had remained unaltered. USA, UK, Canada and Australia still remain destinations for skilled and professional persons from other regions and countries.

Cornell Mobility Model (R. McGinnis, 1968) also makes similar statements about the movement of migrants along the dominant streams. A reflection of the Newton's laws of inertia is clearly observed in this model. The length of stay in the present residence, that is, how deep the roots are, play a decisive role in migration decisions of a person. The longer the period of stay, the greater would the person's solidarity with the neighborhood and its people. The person will have friends and relations in the vicinity. He may get deeply involved in the social and cultural activities so much so that a natural resistance to migrate may develop. Other things remaining unchanged (physical and social environment, opportunities available in the locality, etc.), the decision to migrate would be inversely related to the length of stay in the particular place of residence. The longer the period of stay, the greater will be the resistance to move out. Several studies conducted on migrant families suggest that the migrants usually do not stay at a place for very long time.

Samuel A. Stauffer (1960) has offered *Intervening Opportunities Hypothesis* (gravitational and economic demand model) for explaining migration behavior. According to this hypothesis, the size of the population moving out from A to B will be directly proportional to the potency of the opportunities offered by the receiving state or region (B) and inversely proportional to the opportunities and facilities available in the intermediate space between A and B. The major difficulty with this hypothesis comes from the key term 'opportunity', especially in the context of intermediate space. Stauffer has used the 'probability of getting a desirable accommodation' as the criterion for measuring opportunity-index. Other researchers have used other variables – demand of or supply of labor. Stauffer actually tried to bring together the gravitational and economic demand models under a single framework. In this attempt at unification, he substituted physical distance (mile or kilometer) by the 'nature of space in between the origin and destination'. That is, movement from A to B would be highly unlikely if the intermediate space between the origin and destination offers adequately those services and opportunities one may desire. Lack of opportunities and desired facilities in the intermediate space would strengthen one's resolve to migrate to the destination place. Those who are highly educated and have good professional training and experiences would have to undertake long distance migration since the space in between the place of origin and destination is unlikely to provide all his wants and requirements. For a semi-skilled and ordinary worker, long distance migration will not be needed since the space in between the origin and the probable destination would largely supply the basic necessities and opportunities demanded by him.

Mathematical models have extensively been used in analysis of various streams and distances of migration. All such mathematical models use 'distance' in some form or other, as an integral factor in the analysis. When the connectivity between two places was very poor or when alternative transportations were few, then a 100 miles distance was always less than 1,000 miles distance. It will take 24 hours or more to travel from Kolkata to Delhi – a distance a little over 900 miles. In the same time one can fly through half of the globe or more. Distance today often is measured by time, sometime even by money spent. The physical distance may be the same, but persons with different mentality would look at this distance quite differently. The nature of intervening obstacles is complex and people use different perspectives to assess them. Besides physical obstacles, many other impediments, such as language barrier, racial conflict, and economic, social and political hurdles may play significant role in migration decisions. For this and other reasons, the mathematical models of migration may appear to many as over-simplification of a highly complex decision-making process.

Michael P. Todaro's model employs perceived income and employment opportunities to explain migration. The major features of his model are:

1. Migration is stimulated primarily by rational economic considerations of relative benefits and costs, mostly financial, but some psychological as well.
2. Rural-urban migration depends on the probability that an urban labor can successfully find a modern-sector job as well as on the urban-rural income differential. Migration is then a response to the expected rather than actual earning experience.
3. Costs of moving reduces the probability of migration.
4. Migration rates in excess of urban job opportunity growth rates are not only possible but also rational and probable in the face of continued positive urban-rural expected income differentials. High rates of urban unemployment are therefore inevitable outcomes of the serious imbalances of economic opportunities between urban and rural areas of most underdeveloped countries.

Rural-urban migration in this model takes place in two stages. In the first step, the migrants arrive in an urban area, remain unemployed for a while or get engaged in some traditional job, often in an informal sector. In the second step, he probably succeeds in getting a job in the modern sector and the pay is much higher than what he used to earn before he migrated and also what he used to earn at the first step of migration. The earning in this phase has all the potential to neutralize the zero or low traditional sector earnings of the first step or even earlier. The migrants, even when not getting opportunity of employment in modern sector, would act rationally as long as the perceived value of the life span urban income exceeds the present value of the rural income plus the costs of relocation.

This model has been empirically tested in a number of countries, both with census aggregative and survey data, with mixed success. Some of the model's weaknesses are:

1. There is an implicit assumption in this model that the potential migrants have adequate information about the urban labor market and that they have equal access to urban jobs.
2. The model overlooks the fact that these migrants could acquire the skills necessary for getting employment in the modern sector.

3. Not much emphasis has been given to non-economic factors in the migrants' mobility decisions.
4. The assumption of homogeneity of skills and attitudes of the potential migrants is not a realistic one.

One of the most comprehensive models of economic development in the process of rural-urban labor transfer was developed by Lewis (1954) and later extended by Rains and Fei (1961). The model is popularly referred to as *L-F-R Model of Migration.*

The model believes that most of the underdeveloped countries have unlimited supply of labor, available at a subsistence rate, due to fast increasing size of their populations. This large reserve of labor force found in the "subsistence sector" (agriculture and other traditional sector) of the economy when transferred to the "capitalist sector", results in capital formation initiating economic development. Thus, this model is based on the concept of dual economy comprising a subsistence sector and a capitalist sector. With land-man ratio declining fast, subsistence sector cannot absorb all the rural aspirants for jobs. Unemployment and underemployment are closely associated with the subsistence sector. The capitalist or a modern sector is characterized by full employment. Labor in the capital sector vis-à-vis subsistence sector is literate, skilled and sophisticated. Productivity in the subsistence sector is low compared to capital sector. Average earning in subsistence sector is also very low. Productivity of the labor in the subsistence sector is close to zero. The average wage in the capitalist sector is consistently maintained at a higher level compared to wages in agriculture sector. Migration from the agriculture sector to the modern sector augments industrial production and increases margin of profit. The profit in the modern sector is ploughed back for further growth of the sector and the demand for more labor created in the modern sector encourages more people from the subsistence sector to move to the modern sector. This process comes to a halt only when the rate of expansion of demand for industrial labor far exceeds the population growth rate in rural areas. This model considers migration as an equilibrating mechanism that transfers surplus labor from subsistence sector to the labor-deficit modern sector.

Despite simplicity, the L-F-R model suffers from a number of limitations.

1. Though unemployment and underemployment in agriculture and other traditional sectors are largely behind rural-urban migration, the L-F-R model does not take a serious note of other social, political and physical factors that contribute in good measure to migration from villages to towns/cities.
2. A direct transfer of labor from the subsistence sector to the modern sector, as seen in this model, seems impracticable. The skill (or lack of it) and attitude of the migrants has an important function in the assimilation of migrant labors in modern industries, especially in hi techs.
3. The L-F-R model is over-optimistic in the power of the modern sector to absorb the surplus labor from subsistence sector. Industrialization in most developing countries has not created enough job opportunities from the surplus labor from the primary sector. Gunner Myrdal has shown that the whole idea of labor transfer is unrealistic in the underdeveloped countries. With the growth of hi tech modern industries, especially after the commencement of the globalization of economy, such labor transfer is hardly possible.
4. The assumption of near-zero marginal productivity in agriculture has not been confirmed empirically. Studies from several developing countries tend to indicate that under the given conditions of agricultural technology and agricultural management in the country, agricultural production is in consonance with the size of the labor in agriculture. Allocation of labor in

agriculture often appears optimal; any withdrawal of labor would bring in a fall in output unless yield-increasing innovations are simultaneously adopted.

9.9 Migration in India

Economic development, especially when this development is associated with a face-lift in technological adaptation, plays an important role in redistribution of population. This redistribution of population of course can happen due to various other reasons. From the earliest days of census in India, some information have always been collected on peoples' movement from within and outside the country. Prior to 1961 census, only information on birthplace were collected for each person enumerated. Since 1961 birthplace are being classified into urban and rural. The length of stay in the present residence was also collected for the first time in 1961. Since 1971, information on previous other residences are also been collected. In 1981, causes of migration were canvassed for the first time.

Prior to 1971 analysis on migration was based only on birthplace, which did not throw much light on the nature of migration, either internal or international. In Indian society even today a child is born at the place of maternal grandfather's family, especially in rural areas and in middle class families. Measurement of migration based on birthplace really does not throw much light on the social, political and economic effects, which may have on migration. Since independence, the geographical boundaries of various states have been redrawn, some bigger states have been split creating new states. Because of the change in the geographical boundaries in states, migration on the basis of birthplace alone would fail to capture very many issues related to migration. Such problems may also arise if migration were calculated on the basis of the last residence, but the magnitude of error is likely to be small since the time interval between changing place of residence is considerably small.

Many demographers and social scientists have conducted surveys on the different streams and causes of migration in India. Since 1950s quite a few surveys have been conducted on migration and urbanization at the instance of the Planning Commission of India. NSSO conducted many studies on migration and urbanization in its various rounds. Agro-Economic Research Center too has contributed much on this. Since these and other studies are sample surveys, they throw considerable light on social, economic and personal backgrounds of the migrants as also the causes for various types of migration. They throw considerable light on the characteristics of the migrants and the receiving and sending states on regional basis. However, a more general picture of the process of migration in India can be had every ten years only through census data. The more common observation from all the sample surveys indicates that the principal motive both in R-U and U-U migration is allurement for job or better job and not so much because of the civic amenities offered by the urban administration or cultural diversities of the urban population.

Sociologists and other social scientists look for changes in social stratification, social environment and the social institutions, more specifically the destabilization or pulling together the political institutions as the population density increases due to in-migration of people from various regions having diverse habits, beliefs and aspirations. Not much serious study has been conducted keeping these objectives in view. Most of the studies on migration address to such issues as inter-state exchange of population, the migration streams, relating volume of migration to distance of migration, and the effects migrations have on urbanization and industrial growth. Migration in many cases has remained only a constituent part of the survey project. There is hardly any fresh infusion of blood in these surveys; there is almost no originality in the theoretical orientations leading to these studies. The great treasure of ancient culture and cultural traditions of many developing countries like India and China have slowly changed by the aggressive influence of the Western culture. The traditional values are no longer as important as they had been even a few centuries back in the life of a common man. The pluralistic cosmopolitan culture have socially alienated people from one another; individual comfort and rat race for accumulation of greater wealth have created a greater imbalance in society, resulting in greater income inequality and increased social and political tension. The destabilizing forces are on the rise; the discordant voices have already become a potent source that challenges the unity of the country. How does migration fit into the scheme of things in this social scenario needs to be debated and discussed. (A more detailed discussion on migration in India is presented in Chapter 10 of *Changing Demographic Scenario in India* by the present author.)

10 Life Table

10.1 Why and What is a Life Table?

Death is the only demographic variable for which very precise and accurate measurements are available. Demographers have taken keen interest in analysis of death statistics of a population to understand many other population issues, especially composition and distribution of population and growth rate. The knowledge of the probability of dying, or conversely, the probability of surviving, to any particular age is of paramount importance in social and economic planning, and more specifically in insurance business for they need to know well in advance that an individual (or a group of individuals) would live to or die in a specified age. The calculation of the probability of dying (or surviving) at different ages is vitally related to the insurance premium that the company should charge for an individual of a particular age so that the insurance business can be sustained and profits made. If 1,000 individuals aged 25 years would together live 30,000 years up to the average age of 60 years, the insurance company can easily calculate the necessary premium the individuals must pay for every year on average for 35 years to make the insurance offer attractive to the person on whose life the sum is insured as also bring desired profit to the company. It is true that some people would die at various ages between 25 and 60. The revenue shortfall will be overcompensated by those who live beyond 60 years of age. It is a sort of gamble for the insurer and the probability that the insurer would win in this gamble would be dependent on how reliably and precisely one can calculate the probability of dying of a person at different ages. This probability of dying (or surviving) of a cohort at various ages is what we find from a Life Table.

John Graunt (1662), the father of modern demography, worked intently on the construction of Life Table. His contemporary Petty made important contribution to the evolution of Life Table. Edmund Halley made some modifications in Life Table to make it user-friendly especially for those in insurance business. Insurance business all over the world has become a booming business. It covers almost everything – health, fire, crop, flood, automobiles, accidents of various nature, other commodities and goods, transportation, and what not. In the last 300 years considerable effort has gone into making the Life Tables as precise and accurate as possible.

Leonard Euler (1760) brought in a radical change in the construction of Life Table. He stated clearly the fundamentals of a *Stable Population* (unchanging birth and death rates, fixed age and sex-specific population distribution). Following the leads given by Euler, the demographers and actuarists developed Life Tables that have close reference to both *Stable* and *Stationary Population*. In the beginning of the twentieth century a lot improvement was made in Life Tables through pioneering works of A.J. Lotka. The contribution of Lotka in demographic research is often compared to the contribution made by Newton in researches in physics.

Suppose a large number of persons are born at the same moment. Assume further that they are closed to migration. As days progress, some people who started their life together would die and the size of this cohort would constantly diminish. A day would come when all those who had started their life together would all die. The diminution of the size of the population due to reasons of death if continuously recorded in a tabular form would give a vivid picture of the changing size of the population over time for the group under study. This tabular picture of gradual decay of the cohort with time due to reasons of death is referred to as Life Table. Donald Bogue define it as "... [A] mathematical model that portrays mortality condition at a particular time among a population and provides a basis for measuring longevity. It is based on age specific mortality rates observed for a population for a particular year". Keyfitz defined it as "... [A] scheme for expressing the form of mortality in terms of probabilities. It is also a population model, covering the simplest case which is worth discussing; a cohort or group of people born at the same moment, closed to migration and followed through successive ages until they die". The Life Table depicts the history of gradual extinction of the cohort. It starts with the happy note of birth of all individuals and ends with a note of gloom that there are no survivals of those who started their career together several years back. Like many other demographic concepts, Life Table is a hypothetical construct and the portrayal of the distribution of the cohort over ages follow from certain assumptions:

1. The cohort is closed to migration, i.e., there is no out- and in-migration and change in its size take place only through mortality;
2. The mortality rates does not change over time, i.e., the given schedule of risks of life remains constant;
3. Except for the first few years, the incidences of mortality between two birthdays is evenly spread (number of deaths in the first six months is the same as that during the last six months of the year);
4. Life Tables are generally constructed separately for homogeneous groups – sexes, racial groups, occupational groups, different geographical locations, and etc. This is done because mortality rates differ from one group to another.

The cohort starts with an assumed number, usually 10,000 or 100,000. This is the *radix* or base year size of the population of a Life Table. This helps simplify the comparability of the survivors in the Life Table. Two or more Life Tables of the same or different time periods can also be compared. Suppose there are 65,459 survivors at age 29. Then survival rate at age 29 is 65,459/100,000 = 0.65459. The Life Table can be used to get ready answers to many questions. Some of these are:

- How many of those 100,000 babies who started their life together would celebrate their first, fifth, eighteenth, fifty-fifth or ninetieth birthday?
- What is the average expectation of life for those who started their life together?
- Those who are aged 5, or 25 or 59 today, how many more years on the average are they going to live?
- What is the probable death rate at different ages?
- How many person-years the cohort is likely to live between any two birthdays? and etc.

10.2 Types of Life Tables

Four types of Life Tables can be constructed:

1. Generation Life Table
2. Current Life Table
3. Complete Life Table, and
4. Abridged Life Table

Generation Life Table gives the real picture of life of a cohort. For example, let 100,000 babies (male or female) were born on January 1, 2001. The mortality of this group of persons is followed for all the years till the age when there are no more survivors. We get a collective mortality history of this select group from the Life Table. However, construction of such generation Life Table is beset with the stumbling block that one has to wait till the last member of the cohort dies. Theoretically, such Life Table can be constructed but its utility would be negligible. Over such a long period, the social and economic conditions of a country may have changed so much so that death rates mentioned in the table may have no relation with current mortality rates for various ages. It has some historical importance, but no practical utility.

Current Life Table is most commonly used. The cohort in such a Life Table is hypothetical and the various information contained in the table are synthetic. Based on current age specific death rates, the Life Table describes the life of members of the cohort. Current Life Table describes the current life events only or the average of the past three or five years of the same. For this reason, a true picture of the probability of survival of different segments, average expectation of life at different ages etc. is obtained from such Life Tables. If mortality rates in different segments remain unaltered for many years, the differences between Current Life Table and Generation Life Table vanishes largely. The countries where death rates have already reached a level, from which no further improvement can be expected, Life Tables for those countries can be used to forecast the chances of survival at various ages in the next 70–80 years provided there was no mass destruction of life due to natural disaster, war or some such unforeseeable factors.

Complete Life Table is constructed based on survival for each age. In such tables, even monthly or quarterly estimates of the first year of life may be given. However, construction of a Complete Life Table is not only strenuous, there are innumerable sources through which errors may enter into our computations. Information relating to age of persons is inaccurate when single year is used in the construction of Life Table. The error likely to be committed for a three or five-year period is far less than when information are analyzed for every single year.

Abridged Life Table often is preferred to a Complete Life Table for this reason. Abridged Life Table can be prepared in two ways. We first prepare a Complete Life Table and then convert this single year probabilities into five or ten-year age groups. In the second method, we calculate survival probabilities for each of the five or ten-year periods. There are several methods of deriving abridged Life Tables.

10.3 Structure of a Life Table

A Life Table consists of a number of columns representing various life events and as many number of rows as there are ages (or age groups) for which these events are estimated (Table 10.1).

Column 1, x: All the entries in the columns of a Life Table have reference to the first column x, which is the age of the cohort. In conventional statistical analysis x represents the class mark or mid-point of a class interval. If x is an integer, then the whole range of values starting from $x - 0.5$ to $x + 0.5$ is represented by a single quantity x. Thus, 14.5, 14.9, 15.1, 15.4… are all represented by the number 15. That is, if a person is 14 years and 9 months old and another is 15 years 5 months, both are represented by 15 years in statistical analysis. In Life Table analysis, however, age refers to the number of complete years that has elapsed between one's birth and the last birth day celebrated, that is, his age as on last birth day (*lbd*). In Life Table, age is therefore represented by whole numbers – 0, 1, 2…, 41, 42… Persons aged 25.1 or 25.3 or 25.95 years are all represented by the age 25. Some of the columns of the Life Table have reference to this completed or exact age (l_x, T_x and e_x^0, for example). There are other columns (d_x, q_x, p_x and L_x) that refer to age intermediate between x and x + 1 years.

Table 10.1 *Abridged Life Table of the general population, India 1976–80*

Age x	l_x	d_x	q_x	p_x	${}_nL_x$	T_x	e_x^0	${}_nm_x$	$q_x(est)\$$
1	2	3	4	5	6	7	8	9	10
<1	100,000	12,400	0.124	0.876	93800	5270408	52.704	0.1322	0.12400
1–5	87,600	6,884	0.07858	0.92142	336632	5176608	59.094	0.0818	0.07858
5–10	80,716	1,646	0.02039	0.97961	399465	4839976	59.963	0.0206	0.02039
10–15	79,070	748	0.00946	0.99054	393480	4440511	56.159	0.0095	0.00946
15–20	78,322	989	0.01263	0.98737	389138	4047031	51.672	0.01271	0.01263
20–25	77,333	1,274	0.01647	0.98353	383480	3657894	47.301	0.01661	0.01647
25–30	76,059	1,320	0.01735	0.98265	376995	3274414	43.051	0.01751	0.01736
30–35	74,739	1,467	0.01963	0.98037	370028	2897419	38.767	0.01982	0.01963
35–40	73,272	1,768	0.02413	0.97587	361940	2527391	34.493	0.02442	0.02413
40–45	71,504	2,407	0.03366	0.96634	351503	2165451	30.284	0.03424	0.03366
45–50	69,097	3,085	0.04465	0.95535	337773	1813949	26.252	0.04567	0.04465
50–55	66,012	4,678	0.07087	0.92913	318365	1476176	22.362	0.07347	0.07087
55–60	61,334	6,492	0.10585	0.89415	290440	1157811	18.877	0.11176	0.10585
60–65	54,842	9,034	0.16473	0.83527	251625	867371	15.816	0.17951	0.16473
65–70	45,808	10,214	0.22297	0.77703	203505	615746	13.442	0.25095	0.22297
70+	35,594	35,594	1	0	*412241	412241	11.582		

Source: Sample Registration Bulletin, Vol.XVIII, 1, 1984. Values for columns (6–9) have been calculated by the author. Last entry of col.6 (marked with *) refers to the value cited in SRS bulletin

$: $q_x = \dfrac{2m_x}{2+m_x}$

Column 2, l_x: This column shows the number of persons in the cohort l_0 who reached the exact age x (lbd) (or are likely to reach the exact age x). The entries in this column are always in whole numbers. As the value of x increases, the value of l_x monotonically decreases. The figures in this column indicate what part of the cohort has already reached or are likely to reach age x. When d_x is known, the value of l_{x+1} is calculated by subtracting d_x from the value of l_x in the previous row. The entries in this column therefore indicate the absolute number of persons who started their life together has survived till that age.

row 2 (1–5): 100,000 – 12,400 = 87,600

row 6 (20–25): 78,322 – 989 = 77,333

Column 3, d_x: d_x shows the number of persons dying or are likely to die between exact age x and the succeeding age x+1. This is the number obtained by subtracting l_{x+1} from l_x. Stated in a different manner, d_x is the number of persons reaching exact age x that would die before reaching exact age x+1, i.e., before the next birth day. d_x is always a whole number.

$$d_x = l_x - l_{x+1} \qquad \ldots(10.1)$$

$$d_{<1} = 100{,}000 - 87{,}600 = 12{,}400$$

$$d_{35-40} = 73{,}272 - 71{,}504 = 1{,}768$$

These numbers are the total number of deaths registered in the entire age intervals (0 – <1), (35–40) years… This column of the Life Table as also the next column q_x has strategic importance. If the entries in this column are known and the original cohort or base index is also known, the entire Life Table can be constructed.

Column 4, q_x: This column really is the most important aspect of a Life Table. Since Life Table is a historical record of death at various ages of the cohort, extreme care must be taken in computing the probability of dying between every age x and succeeding age $x+1$. q_x *is the probability that a person reaching exact age x will die before reaching the exact age x+1; or simply, it is the probability of dying between exact age x and x+1.* When we have an abridged Life Table, n will replace 1 in $x+1$ and we shall write ${}_nq_x$ for the probability of dying between exact age x and $x+n$. We have seen from equation (10.1) that d_x is the number of persons dying between exact age x and $x+1$. So, q_x is obtained by dividing d_x by l_x.

$$q_x = \frac{d_x}{l_x} = \frac{l_x - l_{x+1}}{l_x} = 1 - \frac{l_{x+1}}{l_x} \qquad \ldots(10.2)$$

$$q_{15-20} = d_{15-20}/l_{15-20} = 989/78{,}322 = 0.01263$$

or, $(l_{15-20} - l_{20-25})/l_{15-20} = (78{,}322 - 77{,}333)/78{,}322 = 0.01263$

A few other important relations can be deduced from equation 10.2.

$$l_x \times q_x = d_x \qquad \ldots(10.3)$$

$$l_{x+1} = l_x(1 - q_x) \qquad \ldots(10.4)$$

$$= l_x \times p_x \text{ (since } p_x + q_x = 1)$$

Column 5, p_x: Some Life Tables has this additional column. p_x indicates the probability of survival between exact age x and $x+1$. This relative can be obtained either by subtracting q_x from 1 or by dividing l_{x+1} by l_x.

$$p_x = \frac{l_{x+1}}{l_x} \; (l_{x+1} \le l_x)$$

$$= \frac{l_x - d_x}{l_x} = 1 - \frac{d_x}{l_x} = 1 - q_x \qquad \ldots(10.5)$$

or, $p_x + q_x = 1$

$$p_{20-25} = l_{25-30}/l_{20-25} = 76{,}059/77{,}333 = 0.98353$$

or, $= 1 - q_{20-25} = 1 - 0.01647 = 0.98353$

Column 6, L_x*: This column portrays the average number of survivals between exact ages x and x+1.* Suppose that there were 1,000 people at exact age x. Also assume that 200 people from these 1,000 people at age x die before reaching the succeeding age $x+1$. The remaining 800 attains the age $x+1$ and each of them have lived for 1 complete year between ages x and $x+1$. Of the 200 people dying between ages x and x+1, let us further assume that 30 died after 3 months, 100 after 6 months and 70 after 9 months. Then the 1,000 people who lived the whole year or part of the year collectively between x and x+1 year:

800 persons × 1 year	= 800.0 person-years
30 persons × 0.25 year	= 7.5 person-years
100 persons × 0.5 year	= 50.0 person-years, and
70 persons × 0.75 year	= 52.5 person-years
Together they have lived	= 910.0 person-years

That is, 1,000 persons together lived 910 years between exact age x and x+1. This is the same as saying that 910 persons lived for complete one year between ages x and x+1. That is to say, the average population between exact age x and x+1 is 910. Whereas l_x is always a whole number, L_x often would be a number involving fraction.

Entries in L_x column against each of the ages tell us how many years the cohort lived together between age x and x+1 (or $x+n$ in abridged Life Table). This is the number of persons in the Life Table stationary population belonging to the age group. The most important assumption involved in the construction of a Life Table is that people die every day; that is, death in a year is spread evenly over the entire period. This assumption, of course will not be valid in the initial years when mortality rate decreases with every passing day of the first month until it stabilizes around the end of the year. For deaths at higher ages, it is a reasonable assumption that deaths are equally spread between any two ages x and x+1. More specifically, the distribution of deaths between the time points x and x+1 will be rectangular. Let us divide the entire year into infinitesimally small units dt. The number of persons dying (d_x) in the tiny intervals dt would be the same. That is, if we add up these d_x's over the entire time period (1 year), we shall get d_x, the number of persons dying between exact age x and the succeeding age x+1. With the help of integral calculus we can easily calculate the number of years lived by the cohort between age x and x+1,

$$L_x = \int_0^1 l_{x+1}\,dt \qquad \ldots(10.6)$$

Since distribution of death is rectangular between any two time points, a close approximation of L_x is obtained by taking the average of l_x and l_{x+1}.

$$L_x = \frac{l_x + l_{x+1}}{2} \qquad \ldots(10.7)$$

$$= \frac{l_x + (l_x - d_x)}{2}$$

or, $$L_x = l_x - \frac{1}{2} d_x$$

Since the time period between x and x+1 is one year, we can take L_x as the average size of the cohort between x and x+1. In the abridged Life Table, the time gap (n) between any two tabulated ages is more than one year. The approximate size of L_x can be had from the following relations:

$${}_nL_x = (l_x + l_{x+n})\frac{n}{2} \qquad \ldots(10.8)$$

$${}_{20}L_{15} = (l_{15-20} + l_{20+25})(5/2) = (78{,}322 + 77{,}333)(5/2) = 38{,}9137.5$$

or, $T_{15-20} - T_{20-25} = 4{,}047{,}031 - 3{,}657{,}894 = 38{,}9137$

L_x can also be explained in a slightly different manner. Assume that every year l_x number of babies is born in the population. Age-specific death rates remain the same, that is, entries in q_x column remain unchanged. Obviously, the cohort is closed for migration. If such things continue to happen year after year, then a time would come in about 100 years or so when the age-sex composition of the population as also the size of the population are not changing; the average size of the population between age x and x+1 is equal to L_x. Such a population, which has unchanging age and sex composition, is known as *Stationary Population* in demographic parlance. L_x column of the Life Table describes the age distribution of such a stationary population.

Column 7, T_x: From the previous discussion we learnt that l_x number of people together live L_x number of years between exact age x and x+1. Similarly, L_{x+1} number of years between x+1 and x+2 years, L_{x+2} number of years between x+2 and x+3 years, etc. lived together by the cohort. That is, the cohort l_x, starting from exact age x till all of cohort die in the nth year (x and $x+n$) together live

$$L_x + L_{x+1} + L_{x+2} + \ldots + L_{x+n-1} \text{ years}$$

T_x column describes this.

$$T_x = \int_0^x l_{x+t}\,dt = L_x + L_{x+1} + L_{x+2} + \ldots + L_{x+n-1} \qquad \ldots(10.9)$$

T_x column therefore shows the number of surviving people at age x who still have some life left. T_x is the exact number of people in the cohort who are likely to reach exact age x. Stated in a slightly different manner, T_x is the future life taken together of the l_x number of people reaching exact age x. This also tells the number of people above exact age x in a Life Table stationary population. Following equation (10.9), we can write

$$T_{x+1} = L_{x+1} + L_{x+2} + L_{x+n-1} \qquad \ldots(10.10)$$

or, $T_x = L_x + T_{x+1}$

or, $L_x = T_x - T_{x+1}$

or, ${}_nL_x = T_x - T_{x+n}$

T_x is worked out by adding the values of the preceding from bottom to the top.

$$T_{<1} = L_{<1} + L_{1-5} + L_{5-10} + \ldots + L_{65-70} + L_{70+} = 93{,}800 + 336{,}632 + 399{,}465 + \ldots$$
$$+ 203{,}505 + 412{,}241 = 5{,}270{,}408$$

$$T_{1-5} = T_{<1} - L_{<1} = 5{,}270{,}408 - 93{,}800 = 51{,}76{,}608$$

$$T_{45-50} = T_{40-45} - L_{40-45} = 2{,}165{,}451 - 351{,}503 = 1{,}813{,}948$$

By the relation embodied in equation (10.10) we can easily calculate the exact number of people between any two ages x and $x+n$. One must distinguish between the two constructs ${}_nL_x$ and L_{x+n}. The first one refers to the 'size of the population between the exact ages x and $x+n$'. The second one, i.e., L_{x+n} refers to the 'average population size between exact ages $x+n$ and $x+n$+1'. In the first instance, the difference between two ages is n years, in the latter it is exactly 1 year.

Column 8, e_x^0: This function tells us the average expectation of life of those l_x persons who have reached the exact age x. This can also be interpreted as the number of years of life remaining for a person reaching the exact age *x*. e_x^0 is therefore a measure of average life expectancy of any person from the cohort reaching exact age *x*. Since T_x is the future life taken together of the l_x number of people reaching exact age *x*, dividing T_x by l_x gives the average expectation of life at age *x*.

$$e_x^0 = \frac{T_x}{l_x} \qquad \text{...(10.11)}$$

$$e_{<1}^0 = \frac{T_{<1}}{l_{<1}} = \frac{5,270,408}{100,000} = 52.70$$

$$e_{30-35}^0 = \frac{T_{30-35}}{l_{30-35}} = \frac{2,897,419}{74,739} = 38.77$$

Column 9, ${}_nm_x$: This additional column is sometimes found in some Life Table. *${}_nm_x$ actually refers to the ratio between the number of people dying between exact age x and x+n and the average population size between these two ages.* If ${}_nd_x$ is the number of people dying between age *x* and *x+n*, and ${}_nL_x$ is the average size of the population between these ages, then

$${}_nm_x = \frac{{}_nd_x}{{}_nL_x} = \frac{{}_nd_x}{T_x - T_{x+n}} = \frac{l_x - l_{x+n}}{T_x - T_{x+n}} \qquad \text{...(10.11)}$$

When *n* is equal to 1 year, that is age classification is by successive years, m_x, as defined above, is called the *central death rate* at age *x*. This actually is the *annual age specific death rate.* Putting *n*=1 in equation (10.11), we get

$$m_x = \frac{l_x - l_{x+1}}{T_x - T_{x+1}} = d_x\left(\frac{1}{L_x + L_{x+1} + \ldots + L_{x+n} - L_{x+1} - L_{x+2} - \ldots L_{x+n}}\right) \qquad \text{...(10.12)}$$

$$= \frac{d_x}{L_x}$$

ASDR uses the average size of the population for any age (mid-year population) in the denominator. L_x is the average size of the population between ages *x* and *x*+1. Had we used l_x instead of L_x, l_x being greater than L_x, m_x would be somewhat smaller than m_x computed using L_x.

We can also derive m_x's relationship with some other variables.

$$m_x = \frac{d_x}{L_x} = \frac{l_x - l_{x+1}}{\frac{l_x + l_{x+1}}{2}} = \frac{2(l_x - l_{x+1})}{l_x + l_{x+1}} \qquad \text{...10.13)}$$

$$= \left(\frac{2(l_x - l_{x+1})}{l_x}\right) \Big/ \left(1 + \frac{l_{x+1}}{l_x}\right) = 2\left(1 - \frac{l_{x+1}}{l_x}\right) \Big/ \left(1 + \frac{l_{x+1}}{l_x}\right) \qquad \text{...(10.14)}$$

(dividing numerator and denominator by l_x)

$$= \frac{2(1 - p_x)}{1 + p_x}$$

$$= \frac{2q_x}{1+(1-q_x)} \quad \text{...(10.15)}$$

$$= \frac{2q_x}{2-q_x}$$

This can further be simplified.

$$2q_x = 2m_x - m_x \cdot q_x \quad \text{...(10.16)}$$

or, $q_x = \dfrac{2m_x}{2+m_x}$

or, $\dfrac{1}{q_x} = \dfrac{2+m_x}{2m_x}$ ...(10.17)

or, $\dfrac{1}{q_x} = \dfrac{1}{m_x} + \dfrac{1}{2}$

or, $\dfrac{1}{q_x} - \dfrac{1}{m_x} = \dfrac{1}{2}$

When the age interval is more than 1 year (n = 3, 5, 10...), the following linear relationship is used.

$${}_nq_x = \frac{2n \times {}_nm_x}{2+n \times {}_nm_x} = \frac{n \times {}_nm_x}{1+\frac{1}{2}n \times {}_nm_x} \quad \text{...(10.18)}$$

A relation between m_x and p_x can likewise be established. We write $(1-p_x)$ for q_x in equation (10.16).

or, $(1-p_x) = \dfrac{2m_x}{2+m_x}$ ...(10.19)

or, $p_x = \dfrac{2-m_x}{2+m_x}$

It is clear then that the value of m_x is always higher than that of q_x and the difference between the two inverse ratios is a constant. This can be empirically verified. Take the two entries from row 1 ($x < 1$, Table 6.10.). The difference between the two inverse ratios is

$$\frac{1}{0.124} - \frac{1}{0.1322} = 8.0645 - 7.5643 = 0.5002$$

The interrelations between m_x and p_x or q_x give us an alternative to the construction of the Life Table when exact values of d_x are not known. Col. 10 of Table 10.1 shows the estimated values of q_x from m_x. The two sets of q_x's are almost the same since m_x was calculated from d_x and ${}_nL_x$.

Part of a hypothetical Life Table with most columns empty is presented below. We have discussed the relations between the Life Table variables. The blanks in Life Table are filled up easily from these stated relations.

Table 10.2 *Part of a hypothetical Life Table with most cells empty*

Age x	l_x	d_x	q_x	p_x	L_x	T_x	e_x^0	m_x
25	72,853					2,839,421		
26	71,365							

$$d_{25} = l_{25} - l_{26} = 72{,}853 - 71{,}365 = 1{,}488$$
$$q_x = d_{25} / l_{25} = 1{,}488/72{,}853 = 0.0204$$
$$p_{25} = l_{26} / l_{25} = 71{,}365/72{,}853 = 0.9796$$
$$(or, p_{25} = 1 - q_{25} = 1 - 0.0204 = 0.9796)$$
$$L_{25} = l_{25} - d_{25}/2 = 72{,}853 - 1{,}488/2 = 72109$$
$$L_{26} = T_{25} - L_{25} = 2{,}839{,}421 - 72{,}109 = 2{,}767{,}312$$
$$e_{25}^0 = T_{25} / l_{25} = 39\ yrs$$
$$e_{26}^0 T_{26} / l_{26} = 38.7\ yrs$$
$$m_{25} = d_{25} / L_{25} = 0.0206$$

Estimated value of the blanks in Table 10.2

Age x	l_x	d_x	q_x	p_x	L_x	T_x	e_x^0	m_x
25	72,853	1,488	0.0204	0.9796	72,109	2,839,421	39.0	0.0206
26	71,365					2,767,312	38.7	

Since d_x (q_x or p_x instead) for the age group 26 years is not known, most of the cells for row 26 remain empty. A few more illustrations:

Illustration (1) Complete the following part of the Life Table.

Table 10.3 *Part of a Life Table with missing entries*

x	l_x	d_x	q_x	p_x	L_x	T_x	e_x^0
38	71,187					2,987,312	
39	70,698						
40	69,526						
41	68,005						

Computations:

d_x

$d_x = l_x - l_{x+1}$

$d_{38} = 71{,}187 - 70{,}698 = 489$

$d_{39} = 70{,}698 - 69{,}526 = 1{,}172$

$d_{40} = 69{,}526 - 68{,}005 = 1{,}521$

q_x

$q_x = d_x / l_x$

$q_{38} = 489/71{,}187 = 0.0069$

$q_{39} = 1{,}172/70698 = 0.0166$

$q_{40} = 1{,}521/69{,}526 = 0.0219$

$\boldsymbol{p_x = 1 - q_x}$
$p_{38} = 1 - 0.0069 = 0.9931$
$p_{39} = 1 - 0.0166 = 0.9834$
$p_{40} = 1 - 0.0219 = 0.9781$

$\boldsymbol{L_x = l_x - d_x/2}$
$L_{38} = 71{,}187 - 489/2 = 70{,}942.5$
$L_{39} = 70{,}698 - 1{,}172/2 = 70{,}112$
$L_{40} = 69{,}526 - 1{,}521/2 = 68{,}765.5$

$\boldsymbol{T_x = T_{x-1} - L_{x-1}}$
$T_{38} = 2{,}987{,}312$
$T_{39} = 2{,}987{,}312 - 70{,}942.5 = 2{,}916{,}369.5$
$T_{40} = 2{,}916{,}369.5 - 70{,}112 = 2{,}846{,}257.5$
$T_{41} = 2{,}846{,}257.5 - 68{,}765.5 = 2{,}777{,}492$

$\boldsymbol{e_x^0 = T_x/l_x}$
$e_{38}^0 = 2{,}987{,}312/71{,}187 = 41.96$
$e_{39}^0 = 2{,}916{,}369.5/70{,}698 = 41.25$
$e_{40}^0 = 2{,}846{,}257.5/69{,}526 = 40.94$
$e_{41}^0 = 2{,}777{,}492/68{,}005 = 40.84$

Hence the complete Life Table would be as under:

Estimated values for missing data in Table 10.3

x	l_x	d_x	q_x	p_x	L_x	T_x	e_x^0
38	71,187	489	0.0069	0.9931	70,942.5	2,987,312	41.96
39	70,698	1,172	0.0166	0.9834	70,112	2,916,369.5	41.25
40	69,526	1,521	0.0219	0.9781	68,765.5	2,846,257.5	40.94
41	68,005					2,777,492	40.84

Illustration (2). Find the missing numbers from the extract of a Life Table.

Table 10.4 *Part of a Life Table with missing data*

x	l_x	d_x	q_x	p_x	L_x	T_x	e_x^0	m_x
23	75,167							
24	74,599							
25	73,656							
26	72,814							
27	71,729					2,497,386		

Computations:

$\boldsymbol{d_x = l_x - l_{x+1}}$
$d_{23} = 75{,}167 - 74{,}599 = 568$
$d_{24} = 74{,}599 - 73{,}656 = 743$
$d_{25} = 73{,}656 - 72{,}814 = 942$
$d_{26} = 72{,}814 - 71{,}729 = 1{,}085$
$d_{27} = 1{,}218$

$\boldsymbol{q_x = d_x/l_x}$
$q_{23} = 568/75{,}167 = 0.0076$
$d_{24} = 743/74599 = 0.0100$
$d_{25} = 942/73656 = 0.0128$
$d_{26} = 1{,}085/72{,}814 = 0.0149$
$d_{27} = 1.218/71{,}729 = 0.0170$

$\boldsymbol{p_x = 1 - q_x}$
$p_{23} = 1 - 0.0076 = 0.9924$
$p_{24} = 1 - 0.0100 = 0.9900$

$\boldsymbol{L_x = l_x - d_x/2}$
$L_{23} = 75{,}167 - 568/2 = 74{,}883$
$L_{24} = 74{,}599 - 743/2 = 74{,}227.5$

$p_{25} = 1 - 0.0128 = 0.9872$
$p_{26} = 1 - 0.0149 = 0.9851$
$p_{27} = 1 - 0.0170 = 0.9830$

$L_{25} = 73,656 - 942/2 = 73,185$
$L_{26} = 72,814 - 1,085/2 = 72,271.5$
$L_{27} = 71,729 - 1,218/2 = 71,120$

$\boldsymbol{T_{x-1} = T_x + L_{x-1}}$
$T_{23} = 2,789,341.5 + 74,883 = 2,864,224.5$
$T_{24} = 2,715,114 + 74,227.5 = 2,789,341.5$
$T_{25} = 2,569,657.5 + 73,185 = 2,715,114$
$T_{26} = 2,497,386 + 72,271.5 = 2,569,657.5$
$T_{27} = 2,497,386$

$\boldsymbol{e_x^0 = T_x / l_x}$
$e_{23}^0 = 2,864,224.5/75,167 = 38.10$
$e_{24}^0 = 2,789,341.5/74,599 = 37.39$
$e_{25}^0 = 2,715,114/73,656 = 36.06$
$e_{26}^0 = 2,569,657.5/72,814 = 35.29$
$e_{27}^0 = 2,497,386/71,729 = 34.82$

$$\boldsymbol{{}_n m_x = {}_n d_x / {}_n L_x}$$

$m_{23} = 568/74,883 = 0.0076$
$m_{24} = 743/74,227.5 = 0.0100$
$m_{25} = 942/73,185 = 0.0129$
$m_{26} = 1,085/72,271.5 = 0.0150$
$m_{27} = 1,218/71,120 = 0.0171$

The completed Life Table will now read

Estimated values for the missing data in Table 10.4

x	l_x	d_x	q_x	p_x	L_x	T_x	e_x^0	m_x
23	75,167	568	0.0076	0.9924	74,833	2,864,224.5	38.10	0.0076
24	74,599	743	0.0100	0.9900	74,227.5	2,789,341.5	37.39	0.0100
25	73,656	942	0.0128	0.9872	73,185	2,715,114	36.86	0.0129
26	72,814	1,085	0.0149	0.9851	72,271.5	2,569,657.5	35.60	0.0150
27	71,729	1,218	0.0170	0.9830	71,120	2,497,386	34.82	0.0171

Illustration (3). The following is an extract from Table 10.1. The entries of most of the columns are left out. We recalculate the missing values.

x	l_x	d_x	q_x	p_x	L_x	T_x	e_x^0
45–50	69,097					1,813,949	
50–55	66,012						
55–60	61,334						
60–65	54,842	9,034					

$\boldsymbol{d_x = l_x - l_{x+1}}$
${}_{50}d_{45} = 69,097 - 66,032 = 3,085$
${}_{55}d_{50} = 66,012 - 61,534 = 4,678$
${}_{60}d_{55} = 61,334 - 54842 = 6,492$
${}_{65}d_{60} = 9,034$

$\boldsymbol{q_x = d_x / l_x}$
${}_{50}q_{45} = 3,085/69,097 = 0.045$
${}_{55}q_{50} = 4,678/66,012 = 0.071$
${}_{60}q_{55} = 6,492/61,334 = 0.106$
${}_{65}q_{60} = 9,034/54,842 = 0.165$

$p_x - l_{x+n}.l_x$

${}_{50}p_{45} = 66{,}012/69{,}097 = 0.953$

${}_{55}p_{50} = 61{,}334/66{,}012 = 0.929$

${}_{60}p_{55} = 54{,}842/61{,}334 = 0.894$

${}_{65}p_{60} = 1 - 0.165 = 0.835$

$L_x = l_x - d_x/2$

${}_{50}L_{45} = (69{,}097 + 66{,}012).5/2 = 337{,}773$

${}_{55}L_{50} = (66{,}012 + 61.334).5/2 = 318{,}365$

${}_{60}L_{55} = (61{,}334 + 54{,}842).5/2 = 290{,}440$

${}_{65}L_{60} = (2 \times 54842 - 9{,}034).5/2 = 251625$

$T_{x-1} = T_x + L_{x-1}$

$T_{45-50} = 1{,}813{,}949$

$T_{50-55} = 1{,}813{,}949 - 333{,}775 = 1{,}476{,}176$

$T_{55-60} = 1{,}476{,}176 - 318{,}365 = 1{,}157{,}811$

$T_{60-65} = 1{,}157{,}811 - 290{,}440 = 867{,}371$

$e_x^0 = T_x/l_x$

$e_{45-50}^0 = 1{,}813{,}949/69{,}097 = 26.25$

$e_{50-55}^0 = 1{,}476{,}176/66{,}012 = 22.36$

$e_{55-60}^0 = 1{,}157{,}811/61{,}534 = 18.88$

$e_{60-65}^0 = 867{,}371/54{,}842 = 15.82$

The table with the missing data filled in is as under:

x	l_x	d_x	q_x	p_x	L_x	T_x	e_x^0
45–50	69,097	3,085	0.045	0.953	337,775	1,813,949	26.252
50–55	66,012	4,678	0.071	0.929	318,365	1,476,176	22.362
55–60	61,334	6,492	0.106	0.894	290,440	1,157,811	18.877
60–65	54,842	9,034	0.165	0.835	251,625	86,7371	15.816

10.4 Use of Age by Months for Measuring Infant Mortality

While calculating L_x, we assumed that distribution of deaths in the age interval x to x+1 was rectangular. It means that number of deaths registered every month or day of a year is almost the same. This is generally true at all higher ages, but such assumptions are very fallacious at earlier ages, in infancy. Death rates are at their highest soon after birth in all countries and in all times. In fact, deaths in the first week or month of birth are highly different from that in later weeks or months prior to first birthday. From second year onwards, death rates decline sharply and the variation in deaths by months become insignificant. To take cognizance of the huge differences in mortality between months of the first year of life, a specific strategy is undertaken to divide the birth year into months or quarters and death rate by month or quarter is presented in a complete Life Table. The column l_x for the first few rows is in months. Both d_x and q_x are calculated following the usual procedure. For calculating L_x in the first year of life, the unit shall be months.

$$L_x = \left(\frac{l_x + l_{x+1}}{2}\right)\frac{1}{12} \qquad \ldots(10.22)$$

When using quarterly aggregates, the multiplier 1/12 is to be replaced by 1/4 in the above equation. Such an exercise may prove futile if the birth and death registration system is not precise and accurate.

10.5 Mortality by Age Intervals Greater Than One Year

Abridged Life Tables are frequently used in place of Complete Life Table. Usually in such tables 5 or 10 year intervals are used instead of single year. Therefore some modifications in the usual notations are used. l_{x+n}, d_{x+n}, q_{x+n}, p_{x+n}, L_{x+n} are used in place of l_{x+1}, d_{x+1}, q_{x+1}, p_{x+1}, L_{x+1}. The width of the age interval has no effect on the relations between the variables. However, the straightforward relation we have assumed between L_x and l_x [$L_x = l_x - d_x/2$ or $(l_x + l_{x+1})/2$] suffers a little jolt. The greater the size of the age interval n the more biased the estimate $\left[{}_nL_x = (l_x + l_{x+n})\frac{n}{2} \right]$ would be. In estimating survival ratio we often use L_{x+n}/L_x in place of l_{x+n}/l_x. The biasing effect is not serious in such substitution. But the biasing effect could be serious when we estimate m_x and e_x^0 from the relation between L_x and l_x. For this reason, a little modification is made in the formula we use in estimation of ${}_nL_x$.

$$ {}_nL_x = \frac{n}{2}(l_x + l_{x+n}) + \frac{n}{24}({}_nd_{x+n} - {}_nd_x) \qquad \ldots(10.22) $$

This correction can be used only when the age interval between $x - n$ and x, n and $x+n$, and $x+n$ and $x+2n$ are the same. The value of ${}_nd_{x-n}$ is always somewhat greater than ${}_nd_{x+n}$. For this reason the value of ${}_nL_x$ from equation (10.22) is always a little smaller than the value obtained by using the relation (10.10).

10.6 Construction of Life Table

The most important component in a Life Table is q_x. If the radix (l_0) of the Life Table is known, the values of all other variables of the Life Table can be estimated. The age specific death rate of a population or a segment of the population can be found out either from death registration or from a large sample survey. To calculate the age specific death rate in a population we use

$$ m_x = \frac{D_x}{P_x}.\kappa \text{ (when the interval between two successive ages is 1)} $$

and $$ {}_nm_x = \frac{{}_nD_x}{{}_nP_x}.\kappa \text{ (when the interval between two successive ages is } n\text{)} $$

Here we make a difference in the notation used for referring age specific death rate in the Life Table (m_x) and the same obtained from the population (m_x^P) to which the Life Table refers. We change the notation of the equation (10.16) a little.

$$ q_x = \frac{2m_x^P}{2 + m_x^P} \qquad \ldots(10.23) $$

When the age intervals are more than 1, we use the equation noted below.

$$ {}_nq_x = \frac{2n \times {}_nm_x^P}{2 + n \times {}_nm_x^P} = \frac{n \times {}_nm_x^P}{1 + \frac{1}{2}n \times {}_nm_x^P} \qquad \ldots(10.24) $$

Although the relation between q_x and m_x^P is not totally free from error, it will give reasonably good estimates for other Life Table variables. The procedure used for computing probability of dying in other age groups cannot be used for computing probability of dying before the first birthday, q_o. We have discussed this issue earlier. Several methods have been suggested for computing q_o. We describe below the procedure suggested by Kuczynski.

One of the fundamental assumptions is that the cohort starts lives together, i.e., every one of the 100,000 (or 10,000) people are born on the same day, say, in 2001. In reality this never happens.

Even if they were born in the same year, some will be born in January, some in February and some in December on different dates. The primary stipulation in a Life Table is that those who were born in 2001 must remain alive for the rest of the days in 2001 and some days in 2002. If p' is the probability of survival for the remaining days of 2001 and p'' *for some days in 2002,* then the survival probability of those who were born in 2001 is

$$p_0 = p' \cdot p'' \qquad \text{...(10.25)}$$

For estimation of p' and p'', Kuczynski offered the following formulae:

$$p' = (B_0 - D''') / B_0 \qquad \text{...(10.26)}$$

and $$p'' = \frac{B^{-1} - D' - D''}{B^{-1} - D'} \qquad \text{...(10.27)}$$

where B^{-1} = the total number of babies born in the calendar year (2001);
B_0 = the total number of babies born in the current calendar year (2002);
D' = the number of babies born in 2001 and dying in the same calendar year, i.e., within 2001;
D'' = those who were born in the previous calendar year but died in the current year (2002) before their first birth day;
D''' = the number of babies dying in the current year (2002) from among those born in the current year (2002).

Then the survival probability p_o of those babies born in the last 365 days till their first birthday is given by

$$p_0 = \frac{(B_0 - D''')(B^{-1} - D' - D'')}{B_0(B^{-1} - D')} \qquad \text{...(10.28)}$$

We can calculate q_o easily from p_o. After calculating p_o and q_o from formulae (10.25) and (10.28), we can estimate the values of other columns representing other variables of Life Table. We take a hypothetical example to see how the equation (10.26) works and also the veracity of the equation (10.28).

Let $B^{-1} = 475$, $B_0 = 225$, $D' = 60$, $D'' = 20$, and $D''' = 30$. Then,

$$p' = (B_0 - D''') / B_0 = (225 - 30) / 225 = 0.867$$

$$p'' = \frac{B^{-1} - D' - D''}{B^{-1} - D'} = \frac{475 - 60 - 20}{475 - 60} = \frac{395}{415} = 0.952$$

Therefore, $p_0 = p' \cdot p'' = 0.867 \times 0.952 = 0.825$. The same by equation (10.28) is:

$$p_0 = \frac{B_0 - D'''(B^{-1} - D' - D'')}{B_0(B^{-1} - D')} = \frac{(226 - 30)(475 - 60 - 20)}{225(475 - 60)}$$

$$= \frac{77420}{93375} = 0.829$$

The results from equations (10.25) and (10.28) very closely agree, the difference is only about 4 in thousand. Had we assumed that all these (475 + 225) babies were born on the same date in a calendar year and out of these 700 babies born 110 died before their first birthday, p_0 calculated as 590/700 = 0.843 would have been more than 2 percent points higher than p_0 calculated by formula (10.25) or (10.28).

10.7 Uses of Life Table

Life Tables are put to various uses: from demographic projection of population to calculation of insurance premiums, annual depreciation of properties, growth of the size of the school-goers and labor force, life of biological species and to various other uses. It is used in the appraisal of accuracy in vital registration and census enumeration as well. Some of the major uses of Life Table are discussed below.

(a) *Expectation of life at birth.* Life Table is a useful tool for determination of average expectation of life based on current age specific mortality experiences in the population. It is used for comparisons at national and international levels. The survival ratio at different ages and Life Table stationary population can be obtained from it.

(b) *Population projections.* By using the present mortality rate and life expectation, we can project population for a future date. Such population projections are essential for economic and social planning. Both private and public sector organizations make use of Life Tables for estimating the cost for providing retirement benefits for their employees. Life insurance companies determine the premium for sums assured under different insurance plans. Medical sciences too can use this Table to estimate the life remaining for different types of critical illnesses.

The estimation of population distribution by age and sex at a future date is possible only through Life Table. Such projections become very realistic in countries where birth and death rates have stabilized at a lower level. Even if death rates change slightly, one can use the Life Table for good projection by making some adjustments here and there. The basic assumption in such projection is that age specific death rates observed in a Life Table are not significantly different from those observed in the current population. If there are P_x number of persons of aged x in the population and P_{x+n} number in $x+n$ age, then the following identity can be used to make the projection.

$$\frac{P_{x+n}}{P_x} = \frac{L_{x+n}}{L_n} \qquad \text{...(10.29)}$$

L_x and L_{x+n} here refer to person-years in the Life Table population in ages x and $x+n$. The equation can also be used to estimate population at an earlier date, not too distant of course.

$$\frac{P_{x-n}}{P_x} = \frac{L_{x-n}}{L_n}, \text{ or, } P_{x-n} = P_x\left(\frac{L_{x-n}}{L_x}\right) \qquad \text{...(10.30)}$$

(c) *Extension of Life Table concept to other areas.* Life Tables can be constructed for other living and non-living things. The life of an animal, a house, a radio/television/computer/car and other instruments (or their key components) can be estimated and annual depreciation rates determined.

(d) *Estimation of migration.* Life Table survival rates are used for estimation of net migration by age in a population. From the age distribution of a population for two different points (census data, for example) and the Life Table survival rates, one can easily estimate the survivors at a future data. The difference between this estimate and the actual enumerated population gives an idea about net migration between the two time points.

(e) *Survival rates by causes of death.* Death statistics may be reorganized to construct Life Tables by causes of death by age. Such a Life Table with two or more factors of decrement is called a *multiple decrement Life Table.* In a normal Life Table, all causes of death are clubbed together and treated as a single cause. We have separate columns (d_x) for major causes of death. All other columns with reference to deaths due to a particular cause are calculated. Even the state of maidenhood of a girl at a given age can be brought under Life Table and the causes of decrement of maidenhood at any age could be either due to marriage or death.

(f) *Mortality comparisons.* Life Tables for different regions/of the same region but for different time points can be compared for age structure since deaths alone can change the age structure of a Life Table population.

(g) *Change in marriage pattern.* Using 'age at marriage' information, Life Tables can help us show the changing marriage patterns or relatively steady marriage pattern over the years.

10.8 Stationary and Stable Population

The columns l_x, d_x and L_x of a Life Table respectively refer to the size of the cohort at exact age x years, the number of persons dying between ages x and $x + 1$ and the size of the population between ages x and $x + 1$. Further suppose that every year 100,000 babies are born (l_0) of which 20,000 die (d_x) every year. That is, 80,000 babies (l_1) celebrate their first birthday. 10,000 babies (d_1) of the 80,000 babies surviving their first birthday, die between the first and second birthday. Of the 70,000 children surviving at the end of the second birthday, another 5,000 die before their third birthday, and so on. This is repeated (with exact numbers for l_x, d_x and L_x) every year. That is, birth and age specific death rates and the age composition and the size of the population remain unaltered (l_x is closed to migration) for every year. Such a hypothetical construct is referred to as Stationary Population. The population with the stated characteristics can only be obtained from a Life Table. The sum total of the L_x column gives the mid-year size of the entire population. This is shown in the first entry (T_0) in the T_x column (Table 10.1). An estimate of CDR is obtained from the sum of the d_x column.

$$\text{CDR} = \frac{\sum_{0}^{w-1} d_x}{T_0} \cdot \kappa = \frac{l_0}{T_0} \cdot \kappa \qquad \ldots(10.31)$$

$$= \frac{1}{e_0^0} \cdot \kappa \text{ (since } \frac{T_0}{l_0} = e_0^0)$$

Since l_0 number of births generates a population of size T_0 in their life time, it can be said conversely that T_0 number of people gave birth to l_0 number of babies. Therefore,

$$\text{CBR} = \frac{l_0}{T_0} \cdot \kappa = \frac{1}{e_0^0} \cdot \kappa \qquad \ldots(10.32)$$

That makes it amply clear that in a stationary population CBR and CDR are equal. That is, neither the population increases nor it decreases. Year after year the size of the population and its age composition remain the same. Such an event can happen only in imagination. However, when the population of a country reaches nearly this hypothetical stage, the ASDRs in the population would be found to remain more or less at the same levels. Life Table stationary population actually gives the picture of an ideal condition as the birth and death rates come very close to each other.

Like stationary population, Stable Population is also a hypothetical construct. However, a stable population is considerably closer to reality than a stationary population. The basic assumptions for a stable population are the same as that of a stationary population:

1. Birth and death rates are the same (CBR = CDR)
2. The same number of babies is born every year
3. Age specific death rates are invariant
4. The population is closed to both in- and out-migration
5. The size of the population is also invariant

The distinguishing features of a stable population construct are:

1. Age specific birth rates are invariant, and
2. There is a natural increase in the size of population, but the growth rate is constant.

The population that follows closely all these assumptions would show the proportion of population in the age group to total population remains the same over the years ($p_x/\Sigma P_x$) although this proportion may vary from one age group to another. That is, shape of the population pyramid would remain the same although its area may show some change. When CDR and CBR are the same in a stable population, the size of the population over the years remains the same. That is, a stationary population is a special case of a stable population when there is exact replacement of deaths by new births.

When the same age specific birth and death rates are observed in a population over a long period of time, the resulting age and sex composition of the population follow closely a stable population. Although the concept of a stable population first appeared in the writings of Euler, it was left to Lotka to articulate its importance in demographic analysis. It was he who showed that a population subjected to constant fertility and mortality experiences for a sufficiently long time acquires an unchanging age distribution which is characteristic of the prevailing fertility and mortality rates, and which is independent of the initial age distribution. He called the end-product of such constant fertility and mortality conditions a *stable population*. Use of stable population in demographic analysis is on the rise in recent times, especially in preparing Model Life Tables for different countries or regions.

10.9 Growth in a Stable Population

Whether a country's population would be close to a stable population or not would depend by a long way upon the social, economic and political climate of the country as also upon such factors as war, massive earthquake and tsunami-like natural catastrophe, increase in the incidence of migration for some reason and loss of life in a specific segment of the population due to epidemic situation, etc. We have stated earlier that the stationary population is a special case of a stable population where birth rate annuls the effect of death rate in the population and the age composition of the population remains unchanged. Under that ideal condition, the size of the population is $\sum_{0}^{\omega-1} L_x$ and the population distribution is similar to that of L_x. Population growth rate is nil. But when the population is not stationary, complexities arise in the selection of the method to describe and analyze the distribution of the population. We need to develop special tools to measure birth and growth rate in the population. We need to develop a Stationary Life Table population in two stages.

We first write down the population distribution by age and sex assuming the population stationary. These numbers are then adjusted to the growth rate to yield a stable population. Birth and death rates in a stable population are calculated later since both the rates are dependent upon the age and sex composition of the population. How to get a stable population from a stationary Life Table population is described in Table 10.5.

Table 10.5 *Computation of a stable population from the abridged Life Table of males and females, India 1976–80*

							Stable population			
							Initial calculation		***Per 100,000 population***	
Age x	$x+\frac{n}{2}=a$	$r \cdot a$ *midpoint*	$e^{-r(col\,2)}$	${}_nL_x(M)$	${}_nL_x(M) \times 1.05$	${}_nL_x(F)$	*Male*	*Female*	*Male*	*Female*
1	*2*	*3*	*4*	*5*	*6*	*7*	*8*	*9*	*10*	*11*
0–5	2.5	0.05275	0.948617	434483	456207	424900	432766	403067	7652	7127
5–10	7.5	0.15825	0.853635	406370	426689	392997	364236	335476	6440	5932
10–15	12.5	0.26375	0.768164	400598	420628	386575	323111	296953	5713	5251
15–20	17.5	0.36925	0.691251	396606	416436	381756	287862	263889	5090	4666
20–25	22.5	0.47475	0.622039	391940	411537	375333	255992	233472	4526	4128
25–30	27.5	0.58025	0.559756	386514	405840	367663	227171	205802	4017	3639
30–35	32.5	0.68575	0.503710	380473	399497	359891	201231	181281	3558	3205
35–40	37.5	0.79125	0.453275	372328	390944	352011	177206	159558	3133	2821
40–45	42.5	0.89675	0.407891	360795	378835	342864	154523	139851	2732	2473
45–50	47.5	1.00225	0.367050	344699	361934	331697	132848	121749	2349	2153
50–55	52.5	1.10775	0.330299	321991	338091	316016	111671	104380	1974	1846
55–60	57.5	1.21325	0.297227	289932	304429	292958	90484	87075	1600	1540
60–65	62.5	1.31875	0.267467	246675	259009	258954	69276	69261	1225	1225
65–70	67.5	1.42425	0.240687	194925	204671	214106	49262	51532	871	911
70–100	85.0	1.79350	0.166375	321116	337172	412241	56097	68586	992	1213
Sum							**2933736**	**2721934**	**51872**	**48128**
Sum							**5655670**		**100,000**	

Steps in the computation of a Stable Population: Table 10.5

1. *Column* 1: It describes the age distribution.
2. *Column* 2: It gives the mid-point of the age distribution described in Col.1. The formula is $(x+n/2)$, where x is the starting age (age on lbd) of the age interval and n is the width of the interval. For example, the midpoint of the interval 0 – 4 is 0 + 5/2 = 2.5.
3. *Columns* 3 & 4: Between 1981 and 1990, the annual average growth rate r was 0.0211. This growth rate will have impact on each age segment of the Life Table population. Col.3 represents the values obtained by multiplying each of the midpoints by 0.0211. Thus, $a \times r = 2.5 \times$

0.211 = 0.05275; $a \times r$ = 42.5 × 0.0211 = 0.89675. Effect of the growth on the stationary population is expressed as e^{-ra} where e is the natural base of logarithm as against the common base 10. Logarithms to this base e are known as Napierian system (e = 2.7183…). Thus, for $x = 55 - 60,\ e^{-0.0211 \times 57.5} = 0.297227$. These values have been entered in col.4.

4. *Columns* 5, 6 & 7: The stationary populations presented in these columns, separately for men and women, are from the Life Table population data, India 1976–80. To preserve the male-female ratio in the population intact, ${}_5^mL_x$ has been multiplied by 1.05 (col. 6). For example, the ${}_5^mL_x$ entry against 20–25 was 391940, which after multiplication by 1.05 is 411537 (${}_5^mL_x \times 1.05 = 391940 \times 1.05 = 411537$) and has been entered in col. 6. Col.7 presents the Life Table population data for women.
5. *Columns* 8 & 9: Columns 3 & 4 gives us change in the median age for each age group. We have multiplied the entries in columns 5 and 7 by their corresponding changed median age (col.4) to obtain the initial size of the stable population for male and female in each age group (cols.6 & 7). For example,

   $${}_{30}^{m}L_{25} \times 0.559756 = 405{,}840 \times 0.559756 = 227{,}171$$

6. *Columns* 10 & 11: The sum total of each of the columns 8 and 9 (2933736+272193 = 5655670) divides each entry of columns 8 and 9 and they are adjusted for l_0 = 100,000. Thus,

   Age 0–5 (M): $(432{,}766/5{,}655{,}670) \times 100{,}000 = 7652$

   Age 35–40 (F): $(159{,}558\ /\ 5{,}655{,}670) \times 100{,}000 = 2821$

The adjusted stable population shows that there were 51872 males and 48128 females in a total population of 100,000.

Table 10.6 *Birth, death and population growth rate in a stable population*

$x - x + 5$	$x + 2.5$	${}_5i_x$	${}_5^fi_x = {}_5i_x \times .4878$	${}_5^fL_x$	${}_5^fL_x / {}^fl_0$	*Col.6 ×Col.4*	*a′ = Col.2 ×Col.7*	*r′(x+2.5)*	$e^{-r'(x+2.5)}$	*1+E (Col. 10 × Col.7)*
1	*2*	*3*	*4*	*5*	*6*	*7*	*8*	*9*	*10*	*11*
15–20	17.5	0.055	0.026829	381756	3.81756	0.102421	1.792373	0.149835	0.860849	0.08817
20–25	22.5	0.187	0.091219	375335	3.75335	0.342375	7.703445	0.192645	0.8247747	0.28238
25–30	27.5	0.186	0.090731	367663	3.67663	0.333584	9.173548	0.235455	0.7902112	0.2636
30–35	32.5	0.137	0.066829	359891	3.59891	0.24051	7.816579	0.278265	0.7570962	0.18209
35–40	37.5	0.088	0.042926	352011	3.52011	0.151106	5.666462	0.321075	0.7253688	0.10961
40–45	42.5	0.046	0.022439	342864	3.42864	0.076935	3.269719	0.363885	0.6949711	0.05347
45–50	47.5	0.021	0.010244	331697	3.31697	0.033978	1.613973	0.406695	0.6658472	0.02262
Sum		0.72	0.351216	2511217		1.280909	37.0361			1.00194

1. *Column* 3: Age specific fertility for Indian women as on 1981 has been copied in this column.
2. *Column* 4: Estimates of age specific female birth rate has been shown in this column. This is calculated by multiplying age specific birth rate ${}_5i_x$ by the sex ratio in the population [F/(F+M), i.e.,100/(100+105) = 0.4878].

$${}_{20}^{f}i_{15} = {}_{20}i_{15} \times 0.4878 = 0.055 \times 0.4878 = 0.026829$$

3. *Column* 5: It states the average size of the cohort in a particular age group (${}^{f}_{5}L_x$). This has been copied from the female Life Table (1976–80), the same as given in col.7 of 10.5.
4. *Column* 6: The average number of years a woman is likely to remain in a particular age group is shown in this column. This is obtained by dividing the entries in column 5 by 100,000. Average stay in age 35–40 years:

   $${}_{40}^{f}L_{35} / l_0 = 352{,}011 / 100{,}000 = 3.52011 \text{ years.}$$

5. *Column* 7: The average number of female children likely to be born in a particular age group to every woman in that age group (considering the average length of stay in the age group) is shown in this column. This is calculated by multiplying col.4 by col.6 entries. For example, the average number of female children born to every woman in age group 30–35 years is $col.4 \times col.6 = {}_{35}^{f}i_{30} \times ({}_{35}^{f}L_{30} / l_0) = 0.066629 \times 3.59891 = 0.24051$. The sum total of this column gives the possible number of female births (1.280909) by a woman in her reproductive period. This is the replacement level (female babies replacing their mothers – F_2/F_1).
6. *Column* 8: The probable age difference of the mother and the child in the age groups in a stable population is shown in col.8 (a'). This is obtained by multiplying col.2 by col.7.
   Age group 20–25: 22.5 × 0.342375 =7.703445
   The average age difference between a child and her mother, which is calculated as the most likely age of the mother at the time she gave birth to her last female baby divided by the average number of female babies:

   $$\bar{a}' = \frac{\sum col \cdot 8}{\sum col \cdot 7} = \frac{37.0361}{1.280909} = 28.91392$$

   A first approximation of the population growth (r') in the stable population is calculated from $\bar{a}'$ and *col.7 total* by the following relation.

   $$r' = \left(\frac{1}{\bar{a}'}\right)\log_e{}^{F_2/F_1} = \left(\frac{1}{\bar{a}'}\right)\log_e 1.280909 = \frac{0.24757}{28.91392} = 0.008562$$

7. *Column* 9: Compute $r'(x+2.5)$ for entries in col.2 and post them in col.9.
8. *Column* 10: Population growth in every age group in the stable population is calculated by $e^{-r'(x+2.5)}$ and entered in col.10. Thus,
   for age group 15–20: $e^{-r'(15+2.5)} = 2.7183^{-0.00856 \times 17.5} = 0.86084914$
9. *Column* 11: Col.7 is multiplied by col.10 and entered in col.11. Had there been no error the estimated value of the growth rate, sum total of col.11 should be equal to 1.00. When the sum of col.11 is greater than or less than 1.00, it is taken for granted that some growth of the population was under or over estimated. Hence the column head 1 + E.

   1+E = 1.00194, giving E = 0.00194

   Corrected average annual growth rate in the stable population is calculated by the formula

   $$r = r' + \frac{E}{\bar{a}' + \frac{E}{r'}} = 0.008562 + \frac{0.00194}{28.91392 + \frac{0.00194}{0.008562}} = 0.008628$$

That is, the average annual growth rate is 0.8 percent per annum.

Birth and death rates in a stable population are related to cols. 6 & 7 of the Life Table population (Table 10.5). Calculation of intrinsic birth rate, separately for females, males and persons in the stable population has been shown below.

$$\text{Intrinsic birth rate of females} = \frac{{}^{f}l_0}{\Sigma\,{}_5^{f}L_x} = \frac{100{,}000}{2721934} = 0.036739$$

or, 36.7 per thousand.

$$\text{Intrinsic birth rate of males} = \frac{{}^{m}l_0}{\Sigma\,{}_5^{m}L_x} = \frac{100{,}000}{2933736} = 0.034086$$

or, 34.1 per thousand.

$$\text{Intrinsic total birth rate} = \frac{l_0 \times 2.05}{\Sigma\,{}_5^{m}L_x + \Sigma\,{}_5^{f}L_x} = \frac{100{,}000 \times 2.05}{2933736 + 2721934} = 0.036247$$

or, 36.2 per thousand. $\Sigma\,{}_5^{m}L_x$ and $\Sigma\,{}_5^{f}L_x$ are obtained from Table 10.5.

When age specific birth and death rates in a population are maintained at fixed levels for a great many years, the growth rate in the population is also maintained at a fixed level. When this is observed, the birth and death rates in the stable population are referred to as *intrinsic birth and death rates*. The intrinsic rates of course are hypothetical.

We have discussed the problems that one encounters when trying to compare two or more populations for their birth and death rates. Intrinsic rates can ease such problems considerably. In the stationary population it was assumed that total number of births and total number of deaths in a year is the same and therefore the population size does not change with year. But in a stable population the population resulting from the birth of 100,000 babies in the first year shall decide the number of babies that would be born in the later years.

10.10 Model Life Tables

The one and only purpose of construction of *Model Life Tables* is not for study of age patterns of mortality or disease processes. They are primarily an aid to the estimation of demographic parameters, especially for countries with limited data and for preparation of population projections. Many of the most useful methods for estimating birth and death rates in countries with poor data quality rely on knowledge of, or assumptions about the age pattern of mortality. Population projections call for knowledge of base-year age-specific mortality rates as well as assumptions of how mortality might change by age and sex over the years. Models provide examples of typical age patterns of mortality change.

Demographic models attempt to represent demographic processes in the form of a mathematical function or set of functions relating to two or more demographic variables. The purpose of demographic modeling is simplification and to reduce a confusing mass of numbers to a manageable few – intelligible basic parameters. Two different types of modeling are done. One group of models addresses specifically to the observed data; the other type of models are associated with a set of simple assumptions or postulates. Stable population model is a clear example of the latter where the fundamental assumptions are that both fertility and mortality in the population have maintained at some constant levels for a sufficiently long time. Yet, a model of this type is regarded as a good approximation of a demographic phenomenon to the extent it reflects the actual process. Model Life Tables are examples of the first kind since they are derived from actual data. This synthetic Model Life Tables take close look at the age specific mortality rates and the relation that exists between mortality in various segments of the population. Most demographic models are compromises between these two – purely empirical and purely theoretical.

Construction of Life Table has become a routine feature in almost all countries. Demographers have observed that although the birth and death rates and their distributions differ widely from one country to another or even one population segment from another in the same country, there is considerable similarity when Life Tables are constructed on the rates of these vital events and their distribution in the population. Demography experts have long been working on constructing a few Model Life Tables based on similarity in mortality and expectation of life so that population and population related issues can be discussed and analyzed with reference to these few Model Life Tables. We used standard mortality rate (based on some standard population) to compare mortality situations in different countries or populations. Model Life Table can be looked upon as a standard against which mortality and expectation of life of different countries or populations are compared. Modeling is welcome in demography since it shows how amalgamation of a mathematical theory with reality is made possible. Of course, this blend is more successful in some areas (nuptiality, for example) than many others.

10.10.1 Coale-Demeny Model

Coale and Demeny suggestions of *Regional Model Life Tables and Stable Populations* (1966) have drawn attention of many. We present here some general aspects of these models without going through the nitty-gritty's of their construction. In their analysis of empirical life tables recorded in developed societies over the past 150 years, the authors selected 192 Life Tables (out of original set of 326) by sex for actual population. The Life Tables covered several time periods and heavily biased with Western experiences. Only 16 tables were from Africa and Asia; the remaining 176 Life Tables were from Europe, North America, Australia and New Zealand. All these tables were derived from registration data and from complete enumerations. Most tables were prepared on their national canvas. After examining all these tables, a "standard pattern" (the pattern exhibited by the majority of the tables) was decided upon.

Ansley Coale and Paul Demeny identified four distinct patterns of mortality corresponding to geographical areas of Europe: one pattern corresponding to Northern European countries, a second to Southern European countries, a third to Eastern European countries, and a fourth, more heterogeneous, group consisting mainly of Western European countries and overseas populations of Western European stock. They observed four different mortality patterns in these tables. These patterns were identified as "North", "South", "East" and "West". The nomenclature is because of predominance of European countries belonging to various regions in these categories. It is for this reason that these four groups of tables are referred to as regional models. Samuel Preston later demonstrated that these four patterns of mortality are associated with different patterns of causes of death within each geographical region and identified a fifth "non-Western" pattern, consisting almost entirely of Latin American countries, with a different cause of death structure and resultant age pattern of mortality.

East Model. Life Tables of countries like Austria, Germany (before 1900), East Germany (after the World War II), northern and central Italy, Czechoslovakia and Poland formed the basis of this model. When the pattern of mortality rates in these tables were compared against the "standard", their deviations from the standard follow a U-shaped distribution – higher death rates in infancy and at higher ages (over 50 years). Life expectancy in these tables ranged from a low of 36.6 to a high of 72.3 years. A total of 31 tables were included in the East Model.

North Model. The model was derived from 9 tables from countries like Iceland, Norway, and Sweden. Low infant mortality coupled with relatively high child mortality and mortality rates above age 50 that fall increasingly below those of the standard population. Tuberculosis is endemic in many regions and it is believed that it has significant effect on mortality in middle age range, 10 to 40. In fact, death rates in this age range have positive deviations from the standard pattern. Life expectancy in the North Model stable population ranged between 44.4 years and 74.7 years. The populations of the countries where tuberculosis still is a major concern are likely to be represented by the North Model.

South Model. This model has been generated from 22 Life Tables of Spain, Portugal, Italy, especially the southern part, and the region of Sicily. High mortality is noticed in children below 5 years, comparatively lower mortality between ages 40 and 60 and high mortality above age 65 in relation to the standard. Life expectancy ranges from a low of 35.7 years to a high of 68.8 years.

West Model. This model is derived from the residual tables. The mortality pattern in this model does not deviate systematically from the standard pattern. However, the pulled data from these tables display death rates at various ages more close to the standard pattern than those from which other models are derived. Since this model is based on largest number of Life Tables from different regions, West Model represent the most general pattern of mortality and age distribution. For this reason, the West Model becomes the first choice for the countries where death related statistics are insufficient. Life expectancy for countries under this model ranges from 38.6 to 75.2 years. The model published by United Nations in 1950 has close similarity in age distribution with the West Model.

Which of the models is most suitable for a particular country? There is no easy answer to this question. The countries where reliable data related to mortality are easily available, the choice is much easier. But there are many countries for which available population data are not only meager, most such data probably could not be cleared by for any advanced demographic analysis. Where the data are scanty and deficient, only a few broad guidelines can be prescribed for selecting a particular model.

1. It has been observed that in populations where breast feeding is the principal source for nutrition and such feeding continues for a year or more, child mortality (${}_4q_1$) is high relative to infant mortality (${}_1q_0$). The incidences of death from infective, parasitic and malnutrition are comparatively small among infants provided of course they get enough non-infected breast milk. Since infant and child mortality in these populations closely resemble such parameters in the North model, it would be worth trying this.
2. Breast feeding is increasingly becoming rare in many countries. Where the physical environment is not conducive to child care, the alternatives to breast milk could become a major source of infection, contamination and malnutrition, resulting in high infant mortality. The South model may suit such populations.
3. High infant mortality and lack of breast feeding are not always causally linked. Mothers themselves suffer from extreme malnutrition in the poor countries. Although breast feeding is quite common in such countries, their babies suffer from acute malnutrition. Either the South or the North model is likely to be more relevant for these countries than other models.

4. In many countries neonatal mortality due to tetanus and some other infection is often high compared to incidences of child mortality. The age-specific death rates in these countries are likely to match with that in the East model.
5. The countries that are very poor in information relating to various aspects of population may look clues from some other countries that are known to have similar cultural traditions as their own and have similar level of economic progress. The model life table for these countries are likely to suit them as well
6. The West model, in a sense, is a versatile model. Therefore, whenever in doubt (for poor data quality in country and lack of information on many other issues), it would be worth trying the West Life Table Model.

10.10.2 UN Model Life Table for Developing Countries

The pioneering effort in the development of model life tables goes to the United Nations some fifty years ago and resulted in the publication of Age and Sex Patterns of Mortality: Model Life Tables for Under-developed Countries (1956). A decade later, in 1966, Ansley Coale and Paul Demeny at Princeton University published a new set of model life tables based mainly on historical European experience, which we discussed briefly in the previous section. Those tables became the most commonly used set of model life tables within the demographic community. Recent evidences however suggest that age patterns of mortality in many developing countries differ systematically from those of historical European experience, and the Coale-Demeny tables are therefore not fully appropriate to demographic research in developing countries. Since 1970 demographic surveys in developing countries have increased and there is noticeable improvement in vital registration systems. Besides, new techniques have been developed for estimating childhood mortality and for evaluating the completeness of registration of adult deaths by age and sex, usually in conjunction with census age distributions and/or rates of population growth (see United Nations (1983): Manual X: Indirect Techniques for Demographic Estimation). Based on current age and sex-specific mortality data from many developing countries, United Nations published *Model Life Tables for Developing Countries* in 1982. The models are founded on new sets of age-sex patterns of mortality which are based on reliably documented data from developing countries and believed to be more applicable to demographic analysis within the developing regions. 72 input life tables (36 male and 36 female) were constructed for 22 less developed countries. The set of life tables consists of 16 male-female pairs from 10 Latin American countries, 19 pairs from 11 Asian countries, and only 1 pair from the African continent.

Age-sex distributions and age-specific sex ratios were analyzed both graphically and by calculation of usual indices for all countries. Data exhibiting high levels of error were excluded. Age patterns of death rates were also graphed. In all known reliable age patterns, mortality declines from a high level during the first days of life to a trough somewhere during the later childhood years and rises again monotonically thereafter. All mortality curves that did not follow this essential pattern were excluded, as were curves in which the age-specific rates were very erratic. These checks and balances resulted in the acceptance of 36 male-female Life Tables from 22 less developed countries for inclusion in the refined data base.

Age-sex patterns of mortality, which comprised the refined input data set, were stratified into clusters by one graphical and two statistical procedures, each cluster having a distinct average age pattern of mortality. The graphical procedure was very simple. For each input life table (male or female), the ratios $R(x) = {}_n q_x / {}_n q_x^{\omega}$ were calculated, where ${}_n q_x$ is the mortality rate at age x for the given life table and ${}_n q_x^{\omega}$ is the mortality rate at age x in the Coale-Demeny West region model life table with the same life expectancy at age 10. The R(x) values were then plotted against age for each life table and the plots were arranged according to similarity of patterns. All three methods, graphical and statistical, produced essentially the same clusters. There were four clear pattern groups and a few others that did not fit together well or into any other groups. The four pattern groups or clusters were as follows:

First Cluster: Colombia, Costa Rica, El Salvador, Guatemala, Honduras, Mexico and Peru and some non-American countries as Philippines, Sri Lanka and Thailand.

Second Cluster: Chile

Third Cluster: India, Iran, Bangladesh and Tunisia.

Fourth Cluster: Guyana, Hong Kong, the Republic of Korea, Singapore and Trinidad and Tobago among the male populations, and Guyana, Singapore and Trinidad and Tobago among the female populations.

The four patterns, so distinguished, have been labeled *the Latin American pattern, the Chilean pattern, the South Asian pattern, and the Far Eastern pattern,* respectively, according to the geographical region which is predominant within each cluster. Life Tables from Israel and Kuwait as also those for the female populations of Hong Kong and the Republic of Korea did not cohere into any of these clusters; they were therefore included only in construction of the *general pattern of mortality* (the fifth pattern).

The above-mentioned patterns account for many of the variations of mortality in the less developed countries of Latin America, Asia and possibly Northern Africa. Age patterns of mortality in sub-Saharan Africa remain unknown due to the extreme unreliability of the limited data available. Along with the model life tables, the UN has produced models of sex differences in life expectancy, single-year mortality, and stable populations. A manual of computer programs to facilitate use of these models has also been prepared.

The following is the reproduction of UN Population Division's Life Table for India.

Table 10.7 *UN Life Table for India, 1971–76*

Age	${}_n m_x$	${}_n q_x$	l_x	${}_n d_x$	${}_n L_x$	${}_n S_x$	T_x	e_x	n
				(a) Male					
0	.14201	.12967	100000	12967	91312	.83650 a	4879199	48.792	0.330
1	.02448	.09196	87033	8003	326938	.93331 b	4787887	55.012	1.352
5	.00491	.02425	79029	1917	390355	.98191	4460949	56.447	2.500
10	.00237	.01178	77113	908	383292	.98775	4070594	52.788	2.500
15	.00260	.01292	76204	984	378597	.98640	3687302	48.387	2.537
20	.00291	.01445	75220	1087	373448	.98403	3308704	43.987	2.560
25	.00357	.01770	74133	1312	367485	.98062	2935256	39.594	2.575
30	.00433	.02143	72821	1560	360362	.97480	2567771	35.261	2.600
35	.00603	.02972	71261	2118	351280	.96483	2207409	30.976	2.628

Cont'd...

Cont'd...

Age	$_nm_x$	$_nq_x$	l_x	$_nd_x$	$_nL_x$	$_nS_x$	T_x	e_x	n
40	.00850	.04167	69143	2881	338927	.94819	1856129	26.845	2.644
45	.01313	.06368	66262	4220	321367	.92300	1517202	22.897	2.644
50	.01934	.09246	62042	5737	296622	.88567	1195834	19.275	2.631
55	.02991	.13955	56306	7858	262709	.83417	899212	15.970	2.605
60	.04317	.19527	48448	9460	219143	.77268	636503	13.138	2.559
65	.06102	.26502	38988	10332	169328	.59429 c	417360	10.705	2.521
70	.11553		28655	28655	248032	248032		8.656	8.656
				(b) Female					
0	.15044	.13704	100000	13704	91092	.82426 a	4738203	47.382	0.350
1	.02850	.10603	86296	9150	321038	.92225 b	4647110	53.851	1.361
5	.00594	.02927	77146	2258	380088	.97850	4326072	56.076	2.500
10•	.00272	.01351	74889	1012	371915	.98451	3945984	52.691	2.500
15	.00368	.01824	73877	1347	366154	.97949	3574069	48.379	2.602
20	.00460	.02275	72530	1650	358646	.97500	3207915	44.229	2.574
25	.00549	.02708	70880	1920	349680	.97176	2849269	40.199	2.541
30	.00593	.02922	68960	2015	339805	.96967	2499590	36.247	2.521
35	.00644	.03170	66945	2122	329501	.96594	2159784	32.262	2.538
40	.00758	.03722	64823	2413	318279	.95716	1830283	28.235	2.581
45	01023	.04994	62411	3117	304644	.93970	1512005	24.227	2.623
50	.01513	.07305	59294	4331	286274	.90844	1207361	20.362	2.646
55	.02396	.11337	54963	6231	260064	.86167	921087	16.758	2.633
60	.03637	.16724	48732	8150	224088	.79766	661024	13.565	2.599
65	.05538	.24393	40582	9899	178746	.59091 c	436936	10.767	2.559
70	11884		30683	30683	258189	258189		8.415	8.415

a Value given is for survivorship of 5 cohorts of birth to age group 0–4 = L(0,5)/500,000

b Value given is for $_5S_0 * {_5L_5}/{_5L_0}$

c Value given is $_{5+}S_{65+} * T_{70}/T_{65}$.

11 Population Projection

11.1 Introduction

Population scientists have remained busy in developing devices, which would enable them to forecast population size, its composition and other related population components at a future date. For several obvious reasons such anticipation is necessary. Various categories of people are interested in such predictions for their own specific reasons. Among them are agricultural scientists, economists, social planners, administrators and many others including those in manufacturing, trade and commerce who ought to have a clear picture of the social scenario likely to develop from the growth of population and its composition at a future date. A scientific comparison between the recent past and the present of the changing demands for various commodities and services can only help build up strategies to meet the demands of the future. Population scientists warned long back that the scientists need urgently to develop alternative sources of energy (non-conventional) to cope with its fast mounting demands due to energy-intensive modern technology and rapid increase in the size of world population. They predicted that world reserve of natural gas, petroleum and coal (all non-renewable) would be seriously impacted even before the beginning of this millennium. How accurate they were is proven by the fact that crude oil, which was sold in the international market at around $20 a barrel a few years back, soared up to $75 a barrel in mid-2005 and then to $147 in July 2008, nearly double just in three years. Demand on additional land is fast increasing to set up new industries, housing complexes, entertainment parks, ports, highways and for other non-agricultural uses. Cultivable land is shrinking fast as a result. For future food security we need to bring additional lands under cultivation; the vast stretch of land till now regarded as barren or unsuitable for farming, need to be converted into farm land through major irrigation projects and better scientific agricultural management. Soon we shall need to explore the sea as well for our food, minerals and supply of many other basic necessities.

Changes in population related events have a decided role in national planning exercises; it has a far-reaching impact on international understanding and in trade relations as well. Often some of the major developments in population related issues in the developing and under-developed countries become an important matter for other countries' planning programs. For example, 75 percent of the shortfall in food grains in the under developed countries, especially in Africa, are met through import from the developed countries, mainly USA, Canada and Australia. The OPEC countries regulate oil production keeping an eye on the oil prices in the international market. Many countries produce things and equipments, including defense materials, mostly for exports. Many countries escalate their defense expenditure because of threat perception resulting from some political developments or instability in some population characteristics, e.g., oppression on certain section of the population forcing them to migrate to the neighboring countries.

Population projections[1] differ widely in their geographic coverage, time horizon, types of output, and use. Spatial dimensions can range from local areas (like counties or cities) to the entire world. Local-area projections tend to use shorter time horizons, often less than 10 years, whereas national and global projections can extend to decades and centuries into the future. These longer term projections, however, produce a more limited number of output variables, primarily population broken down by age and sex and some times net immigration or net emigration. In contrast, projections for smaller regions often would include other characteristics as well – educational and labor force composition, urban-rural divide, land use, household type, energy need, resource depletion, etc.

Commercial organizations often use projections for marketing research and generally want a single most likely forecast. They typically want population classified by socioeconomic categories such as income and consumption habits in addition to age and sex, and division by place of residence. Government planners will be more concerned with population aging and its potential social and economic consequences. They may therefore desire longer-term projections, and want to know more about the health status and living arrangements of the elderly. The social advocacy groups often would look at the most likely scenario in not too distant a future resulting from different policy prescriptions. Environmentalists would be concerned with the impact the population growth would have on the environment. As such, their interest would be to understand how the policy prescriptions bring changes in GHG emissions, conservation of natural resources and biodiversity, water management, and the like. Global change researchers often use projections as exogenous inputs to studies on topics such as energy consumption, food supply, and global warming. These studies usually require projections with long time horizons (a century or more) and a range of scenarios rather than a single most likely projection.

Planning at the state/national or international level takes cue from the probable growth of population and changes in the structure of the population in near or distant future. The country develops its social security plan (pension, health insurance, etc.) keeping an eye on the probable size of the old-age population as also the likely changes in birth, death and marriage rates, usually no more than thirty or forty years hereafter. The transient changes in a population often can be tackled through budgetary provisions. But for a more comprehensive planning we need to have a clear idea about the probable size of the numbers as also the likely changes in the population composition and their characteristics. Therefore, population projection is not a mere intellectual exercise; economists, politicians, social planners and business enterprises are keen to use this advance knowledge of future growth and changes in population parameters to their mutual advantage. Population projection and anticipations in changes in birth, death, migration, marriage rate, etc. and distribution of consumption-expenditure remains the basic ingredients for all social, economic and business planning. Projections describe possible trends in human resources, the changing needs of a population, and provide a sound basis for judging if actions need be initiated to alter demographic trends.

---

1 The terms *population estimate, population projection,* and *population forecast* are often confused. A population estimate may be made for any point in time. A population projection, on the other hand, is a conditional statement based on the outcome of a particular set of assumptions regarding the components of future population trends and therefore such projections are to be regarded as prediction. When an element of judgment is added to the projections, it becomes a forecast. A population forecast is a projection; but here an analyst believes his projected picture is the most likely one of the future population. Whereas projections are nonjudgmental, forecasts are explicitly judgmental. Since projections by definition are illustrative and not predictive, they cannot be proven right or wrong by future events.

Population projection is a mathematical exercise to peep into the past or future population scenario of a country or a region, of course with certain assumptions, using accumulated knowledge and data relating to the past available at the point of time the projection is attempted. These assumptions regarding the course of movement of birth and death rate (as also migration when projecting population of a state or a region) are closely linked to medical and health interventions, food security and its equitable distribution, climatic variability, social and cultural setting, the growth path of economy and a host other factors that have the potency to influence the population dynamics. Credibility of a population projection obviously depends upon how precise and accurate the measures relating to birth, death and migration are and how the cultural, social and economic factors are integrated into this canvas while making the projection.

The earliest systematic global population projection dates to Notestein (1945), although many national level projection efforts began over half a century earlier. Since the 1950s, the United Nations has taken a lead role in the production of projections and dissemination of their results. Later efforts, most of which continue to date, have been undertaken by some other institutions such as the United States Census Bureau, the World Bank, and the International Institute for Applied Systems Analysis (IIASA). Global long-run population projections usually are not undertaken by individual researchers. Individual researchers tend to create projections at the national or sub-national level and at this level they have made significant contributions to varying methodologies.

11.2 Baseline Data

Accurate baseline data on population size, age structure, fertility, mortality, and net migration rates are critical to producing accurate population projections. So are quality data on past trends in population dynamics and vital rates, which play important role in predicting future trends.

National periodic population censuses remain the primary source of demographic data in most countries. In countries where census data are nonexistent or considered inaccurate, data from sample surveys are often used. The United Nations Population Division produces the most widely used compilation of current and past estimates of population size, age structure, and vital rates based on these and other sources (Sample Registration Scheme, for example). In the more developed countries (MDC), detailed statistics on fertility and mortality are usually available along with dependable periodic census counts. These can be combined to produce a relatively consistent picture of historical population change in these areas. However, even in MDC data on international migration is very inadequate. As a result, net international migration is assigned to the residual estimate – the difference between the population change and the vital event counts – birth and death.

Estimations for less developed countries (LDC) are more difficult due to scarce/unreliable data. Therefore, often indirect estimation techniques have to be used, occasionally by inferring rates and levels from other countries in the same region with similar socio-economic characteristics. Even after this, projection of fertility and mortality trends is difficult, especially because of unreliability of the census data (benchmark data for projection) for many of these LDC. Many international and national bodies make projections based on the same base line and census data. Since they often use different projection techniques and their assumptions regarding trends in vital and other rates are different, the resulting projected populations differ. However, such differences often are no more than 0.1 percent for world (or regional) population. However, country-level projection may show as much as 10 percent or more discrepancies.

11.3 Types and Methods of Population Projection

A wide variety of methods are available for projection: *simple extrapolation, complex extrapolation, simple ratio, complex ratios, cohort survival and cohort component.* Choice of projection method depends upon the needs of the user. The *ratio method* of population projection is a reliable method at the sub-national level (state or district or block). Suppose we want a district level projection from the state population. Let D_{t_1} is the population size of a district at time point t_1 and S_{t_1} is that for the state population at the same time point of which D_{t_1} is a part. The ratio of the two is calculated as

$$R_{t_1} = \frac{D_{t_1}}{S_{t_1}}$$

Now assumptions are made on the future value of the ratio [the district may have gained (or lost) population from the exodus from (or to) neighboring districts (assuming rate of natural increase remaining unchanged). It is assumed that the new ratio is R_{t_2}. If the state population at time t_2 is S_{t_2}, then population of the district at t_2 can be obtained from the following:

$$R_{t_2} = \frac{D_{t_2}}{S_{t_2}} \quad or, \quad D_{t_2} = R_{t_2} \times S_{t_2} \qquad \text{...(11.1)}$$

Such projections of course are possible only when state level population size S_{t_2} is available. This would give a reasonably good projection for districts.

Projection is necessarily a "multi-criteria decision making process" (MCDM) since it gives sensible answer to most of our given problem. There are a number of MCDM methods for making decisions: identify the criteria of interest, rank the criteria in order of importance, and weight the criteria. Predictive efficiency is indeed the most important criteria for choosing a method. More complex methods do not necessarily produce more accurate predictions, and no single method is consistently more accurate than others.

Prediction accuracy increases with size of population. It is generally better for areas with slow but steady positive growth rate, less so in areas with fast population increase or decrease. Prediction accuracy generally declines as the projection horizon increases. The length of the base period should generally correspond to the projection horizon. But evidences suggest that too long base period (more than 10 years) for the input data (birth, death, migrations, etc.) may increase error.

It is generally recommended that a number of projections on the same population base be made, either changing assumptions or opting for a different method. Every projection has errors. By combining them, the errors across these projections may be canceled out, at least partially.

Two types of projections are most frequently carried out, especially for larger populations.

1. Mathematical Method of Curve Fitting and
2. Cohort-Component Method.

11.3.1 Mathematical Method of Curve Fitting

Mathematical methods use formulae and equations to forecast future population. Interpolation and extrapolation of the population are done to obtain the estimate for the desired year(s).

Since complete census is conducted only periodically, usually every ten years, *Simple Interpolation* usually finds out the population size (and some of the population characteristics) in between the two time points. That is, statistics for the intermediate points are computed from the values of two time points, which are known from census enumerations. The likely size of the population in 1992 or 1997 could be estimated from the known population sizes in 1991and 2001. But most frequently our interest is to know in advance what the size of the population would be, say, after a gap of 5, 10 or 15 years since the last census. Unlike interpolation where population values for two fixed time points are known, the latter deals with open-ended interval, only the population value is known from the latest census results. This method of estimation is done by *Extrapolation.* From the 2001 census in India we can estimate what the population size was on 1st March 2005 or what the population size is very likely in the next census in 2011 or beyond. A similar exercise could be undertaken for constituent states for population, birth and death rates or some other social and economic indicators. This type of peep into the future is generally referred to as *Population Projection*.

Interpolation: Two methods of interpolation – *arithmetic and geometric* – are employed and the latter method gives a better approximation. There is a restriction for using either of the methods of interpolation: the two anchor points must not be too far away. The closer the two end points, the better would be the estimation for any intermediate point by either of the methods.

In arithmetic method of interpolation it is assumed that the absolute yearly (or monthly/quarterly/half-yearly) change in the values of the population (or some other characteristics) remains the same. For example, to estimate the population sizes for the years 1972, 1973..., we first find out the absolute growth of population between the two census points 1971 and 1981 (the two census populations were 548,159,652 and 685,184,692 respectively in India) and the absolute increase in the decade works out at 137,025,040. The average annual absolute growth of population is 13,702,504. With this information, the population in India on 1st March 1975 was likely to be (548,159,652 + 4 × 13,702,504 = 602,969,668). The formula for *linear interpolation* is

$$P_e = P_1 + \frac{n}{N}(P_2 - P_1) \qquad \ldots(11.2)$$

where P_e = Projected population for any intermediate year

P_1 and P_2 = Size of population in the two succeeding census years

N = Total number of years between the two census counts

n = Number of years between the projection year and the preceding census.

Table 11.1 gives the estimated values of the population of India between the years 1971 and 1981, both by arithmetic and geometric method of interpolation.

Table 11.1 *Estimates of population in India for various years between 1971 and 1981*

Year	Method of estimation	
	Arithmetic method	Geometric method (r = 0.023)
1971*	548,159,652	548,159,652
1972	561,862,156	560,767,322
1973	575,564,660	573,664,962
1974	589,267,164	586,859,252
1975	602,969,668	600,357,012
1976	616,672,172	614,165,222
1977	630,374,676	628,291,022
1978	644,077,180	642,741,712
1979	657,779,684	657,524,762
1980	671,482,188	672,647,822
1981*	685,184,692	685,184,692

* *Census India data*

The assumption of equal absolute increase every year leads to the admission that growth rate has been declining every year. Between 1971 and 1972 the calculated growth rate is 100 × (13,702,504/548,159,652) or 2.50 percent and that between 1980 and 1981 is 100 × (13,702,504/671,482,188) or 2.04 percent, which is 18.4 percent smaller than the growth rate in the first year. Even in the decades when population growth rates were increasing monotonically, 1950's and 1960's for example, the end years of the decades would show slower rates compared to those at the beginning of the decades when arithmetic method is used for projection.

Extrapolation assumes that yearly growth rates may remain constant or vary. Even if the yearly growth rates vary, they do not vary widely and these varying growth rates can be represented by a lone figure – the geometric average of the annual growth rates. If P_1 is the population at the last census year and P_2 is that for the year for which prediction is made, then the relation between P_1 and P_2 can be established by the *compound interest law*.

$$P_2 = P_1(1+r)^n \qquad \ldots(11.3)$$

where, r is the average population growth rate and n the number of years between the two time points, so that $(1+r)^n = P_2/P_1$. More commonly, *exponential growth rate* is used in such calculations. The equation is

$$P_2/P_1 = e^{rn} \qquad \ldots(11.4)$$

e being the Naperian base of logarithm (approximately 2.7183). Thus, the decadal growth rate between 1951 and 1961 in India was

$$\frac{439m}{361m} = 2.7183^{10r}$$

or, $\log 439 - \log 361 = r \times 10 \log 2.7183$

or, $r \times 10 \times 0.4343 = 2.5575 - 2.5024$

or, $r = \dfrac{0.0551}{4.343} = 0.01269$, i.e., 1.269 per cent.

With r calculated at 2.3 percent, the estimated populations for the years (1971–1981) are shown in the second column in Table 11.1.

When we have reliable data for birth, death and migration for the census year, post-censal prediction can reasonably be done through extrapolation. However, whether we are using interpolation or extrapolation the estimated values are likely to contain good amount of error the more the years for which predictions are made are away from the base year from which the estimates are obtained. When birth, death and migration rates remain more or less unchanged in the entire period, projection through interpolation or extrapolation can produce good estimates.

Instead of *Compound Interest Law* we can use *Geometric Mean*

1. when the population sizes of two census years are available, and
2. when population estimate of any mid-census year is desired.

$$P_m \sqrt{P_1 \times P_2} \qquad \ldots(11.5)$$

where P_1 and P_2 are census figures for population in two succeeding census years (say 1991 and 2001) from which the projection is to be obtained, and P_m is the estimate of the population at the middle year of the two censuses. 1991 census returned 843.93 million people in India, which in the next census in 2001 rose to 1027.02 million. An estimate of the size of the population of India in 1996 would be

$$P_{1996} = \sqrt{P_{1991} \times P_{2001}} = \sqrt{843.93 \times 1027.02} = 930.98 \text{ million}$$

11.3.2 Cohort-Component Method

Various methods are available for projection of population. Most of them are equally competent and there is hardly any major difference between the techniques employed by them. Accuracy of predictions by all these methods depends largely on the clarity and trustworthiness of the various component measures that are used in projections. In the last 50 years the quality of demographic data collected by various agencies largely follow the prescribed procedures by statisticians. The statistical information on birth, death, marriage, migration and life expectancy at birth – the important components in population projection – is more reliable today in most countries than they were a few decades back. For example, Sample Registration Scheme (SRS) data, which are obtained from a sample that covers only around 0.7 percent of the entire Indian population, have proven to be highly reliable. Mathematical models are useful only when censuses are carried out in succession and the registration system is so efficient that data on birth, death, migration, etc. can be used freely for making any meaningful population projections. Mathematical models can at best give an estimate about the size of the total population at a future data, but will not provide any information about age and sex distribution in the future population unless segment-specific projections are made. When mathematical models are used, success in forecasting will depend upon the type of curve one chooses. A population increasing by a constant rate and another by varying rates cannot be described by the same curve.

Cohort-Component of Growth or simply *Component Method* is widely used for projection of populations. The statistical information on variables that directly influence the growth of population (components of growth) are taken into account in this method. The component method actually projects the population on the assumption that the growth components would change in certain specific manner. A schedule is prepared accordingly. P.K. Whelpton used the component method as early as 1936. The prediction equation is no different from the one that is used to measure natural increase in population resulting from birth, death and migration.

$$P_{(t+a)} = P_t + B_{(t+a)} - D_{(t+a)} + I_{(t+a)} - O_{(t+a)} \quad \ldots(11.6)$$

where P_t = Population size at a time t

a = Time interval between t and the year for which projection is made

$B_{(t+a)}$ = Number of births during the time interval

$D_{(t+a)}$ = Number of deaths during the time interval

$I_{(t+a)}$ = Number of immigrants during the time interval, and

$O_{(t+a)}$ = Number of out-migrants during the time interval.

The following information, precise and accurate, is a must for making projections by component method.

1. Single year age-sex distribution
2. Size of population by sex and age for the year based on which population projection is to be made

3. Age and sex specific death rates (to be used in the form of survival ratios)
4. Age specific birth rates for women for ages 15 to 49
5. Age specific migration rates
6. Precise statistics for any other variable, which we may decide to use in the projection.

Usually, more than one projection is made for a population. Since all predictions are statements of probabilities and also since birth, death and migration rates of the population is likely to experience some change between the base year and the year for which the projection is made are all in terms of defined ranges. Usually three sets of projections are made for the same population – *high, medium and low* depending upon which values from the defined ranges are used in the projection. Thus, a CBR of 18 may be considered achievable by 2016, but CBR 20 is a sure shot. It would be unfortunate if we end up with CBR 22. The government must plan to achieve CBR 18, which would result in a considerable smaller size compared to CBR 20. High projection (CBR 22) must be avoided at all costs in the interest of the growth of wellbeing of the population.

Given the initial size of the population and the survival factors, the projection can proceed according to the plan laid down in Table 11.2.

Table 11.2 *Schedule for population projection by component method*

Age x	*Starting population (year 0)* ^0P_x	*Survival factor for one year* p_x	*Population in year 1 after base year* ^1P_x	*Population in year 2 after base year* ^2P_x	*Population in year 3 after base year* ^3P_x
1	*2*	*3*	*4*	*5*	*6*
—					
—					
10	$^0P_{10}$	p_{10}			
11	$^0P_{11}$	p_{11}	$^0P_{10}\cdot p_{10} = {}^1P_{11}$		
12	$^0P_{12}$	p_{12}	$^0P_{11}\cdot p_{11} = {}^1P_{12}$	$^1P_{11}\cdot p_{11} = {}^2P_{12}$	
13	$^0P_{13}$	p_{13}	$^0P_{12}\cdot p_{12} = {}^1P_{13}$	$^1P_{12}\cdot p_{12} = {}^2P_{13}$	$^2P_{12}\cdot p_{12} = {}^3P_{13}$
14	$^0P_{14}$	p_{14}	$^0P_{13}\cdot p_{13} = {}^1P_{14}$	$^1P_{13}\cdot p_{13} = {}^2P_{14}$	$^2P_{13}\cdot p_{13} = {}^3P_{14}$
15	$^0P_{15}$	p_{15}	$^0P_{14}\cdot p_{14} = {}^1P_{15}$	$^1P_{14}\cdot p_{14} = {}^2P_{15}$	$^2P_{14}\cdot p_{14} = {}^3P_{15}$
16		p_{16}	$^0P_{15}\cdot p_{15} = {}^1P_{16}$	$^1P_{15}\cdot p_{15} = {}^2P_{16}$	$^2P_{15}\cdot p_{15} = {}^3P_{16}$
17		p_{17}		$^1P_{16}\cdot p_{16} = {}^2P_{17}$	$^2P_{16}\cdot p_{16} = {}^3P_{17}$
18					$^2P_{17}\cdot p_{17} = {}^3P_{18}$
—					
	$\sum_0^\infty {}^0P_x$		$\sum_1^\infty {}^1P_x$	$\sum_2^\infty {}^2P_x$	$\sum_3^\infty {}^3P_x$

The steps in the component method of projection are:

1. Select the base year for projection. This is our '0' year in the projection exercise. Usually, the year of the last census is taken as the base year.

2. The first column (x) starts with 0 and goes up to the age beyond which no survival is reported. Usually, 1-year age gap is employed. An interval of 5 years is also used occasionally (0–4, 5–9, …).
3. The second column (${}^0P_x$) details the base year population totals for each age as have been found out from the census.
4. From the Life Table of the census population, the probability of dying ($q_x = d_x/l_x$)) for each age group is found out. $1 - q_{x-½} = p_x$ gives the survival ratio for each age. Column three then gives the probability of surviving to the next birthday of those whose *last birth day* (*lbd*) was x.
5. The fourth column actually determines the actual size of the age-specific populations one year after the base year. The base year population (${}^0P_x$) multiplied by the survival ratio (p_x) for the year gives the size of the population in age $x + 1$, first year after the base year. The column is designated as ${}^1P_x$.

$${}^0P_x . p_x = {}^1P_x \qquad \text{...(11.7)}$$

In Table 11.2 the size of population in age 14 is obtained by ${}^0P_{13} \cdot p_{13} = {}^1P_{14}$. This is entered against age 14 under column 4. This way we find the reduced population size for every age group one year after the base year.

It is to be noted that the products are entered at one age higher (one step down the column) to the right, and thus the computations proceed diagonally downwards. The same procedure is employed to calculate the surviving numbers for every age in the second, third, fourth… year after the base year. The survival factors need not remain unchanged, as in the table. When the CBR of a population is decreasing very slowly, the age specific death rates too are likely to follow the same decreasing trend with some exception at lower and higher ages. When the incremental change is very small, the values of p_x for successive years can be assumed to remain at certain constant levels if the year for which projection is made is not far away from the base year. When distant forecasting is necessary, a new set of values for p_x can be obtained through extrapolation and the population size for every age can be computed from this new set of survival factor values. ${}^n\text{p}_{14}$ would mean the survival ratio in the nth year for age 14.

For the '0' age group (0–1 year), the population size generally is not taken from the census data. Let us assume 2001 as our base year (N). We would multiply the population in year 2000 (year N–1) at each age (or age group) by the appropriate age specific fertility factor. The sum of all these products would give an estimate of the number of birth in the period of 12 months between the year $N - 1$ and N. Multiplying this by an appropriate survival factor (L_0/l_0), the expected number of infants at age 0 *lbd* in year n then is obtained. For every year after the base year (N+1, N+2…) infant population has to be re-estimated. This has to be entered in the diagram and then successively 'survived' down a diagonal. By comparing the entries in the second column with that of fourth, fifth,… (${}^nP_x - {}^0P_x$) we obtain the absolute change of the size of the population in every age group. We can also calculate the relative change of the population by $({}^nP_x - {}^0P_x)/{}^0P_x$.

The basic projection formula, taking into account all the three factors birth, death and migration can be written as

$${}^nP_x = {}^{n-1}P_{x-1}(1 - {}^{n-1}q_{x-\frac{1}{2}}) \pm {}^nM_x \qquad \text{...(11.8)}$$

where ${}^nP_x$ = number of persons in midyear n aged x last birthday,

${}^{n}M_x$ = net number of migrants in period midyear $n - 1$ to midyear n who were aged x last birthday at midyear n,

${}^{n-1}q_{x-1/2}$ = probability of dying within a year for a person age $x - 1$ last birthday at midyear $n - 1$.

Number of net migrants usually is small. The mortality of migrants between the date of migration and midyear n is small and therefore is ignored. At age '0' the formula used is

$$ {}^{n}P_0 = {}^{n}B(1 - {}^{n-1}{}_{\frac{1}{2}}q_0) \pm {}^{n}M_0 \qquad \ldots(11.9)$$

where ${}^{n}B$ = number of live births in period mid-year $n - 1$ to mid year n.

${}^{n-1}{}_{\frac{1}{2}}q_0$ = probability that a baby born between midyear $n - 1$ to midyear n will die before the end of that period,

${}^{n}M_0$ = net number of infant migrants in the discussed period.

While computing population size in age '0', we need to decide if the age-specific rates are computed from the entire population or only on the female population. It really does not matter if we are using the general or female population for computing the size in '0' age if the available statistics is sufficiently reliable. Logically, however, it is better to use female age specific birth rate since fertility is usually confined between the ages 15 and 49 years. It is to remind the reader that the social and economic factors have larger impact on birth than on death. Computation scheme for the number of babies in age '0' is shown in the Table 11.4 . We need to have a parallel scheme for projection of female population, which would be used for estimating population size in '0' age.

Table 11.3 *Scheme for projection of female population by component method*

Age x	*Starting population (year 0)* ${}^{0}P_x$	*Survival factor for one year* p_x	*Population in year 1 after base year* ${}^{1}P_x$	*Population in year 2 after base year* ${}^{2}P_x$	*Population in year 3 after base year* ${}^{3}P_x$
1	*2*	*3*	*4*	*5*	*6*
—					
10	${}^{f}_{0}P_{10}$	${}^{f}p_{10}$			
11	${}^{f}_{0}P_{11}$	${}^{f}p_{11}$	${}^{f}{}_{0}P_{10}\cdot p_{10} = {}^{f}_{1}P_{11}$		
12	${}^{f}_{0}P_{12}$	${}^{f}p_{12}$	${}^{f}{}_{0}P_{11}\cdot p_{11} = {}^{f}_{1}P_{12}$	${}^{f}_{1}P_{11}\cdot p_{11} = {}^{f}_{2}P_{12}$	
13	${}^{f}_{0}P_{13}$	${}^{f}p_{13}$	${}^{f}{}_{0}P_{12}\cdot p_{12} = {}^{f}_{1}P_{13}$	${}^{f}_{1}P_{12}\cdot p_{12} = {}^{f}_{2}P_{13}$	${}^{f}_{2}P_{12}\cdot p_{12} = {}^{f}_{3}P_{13}$
14	${}^{f}_{0}P_{14}$	${}^{f}p_{14}$	${}^{f}{}_{0}P_{13}\cdot p_{13} = {}^{f}_{1}P_{14}$	${}^{f}_{1}P_{13}\cdot p_{13} = {}^{f}_{2}P_{14}$	${}^{f}_{2}P_{13}\cdot p_{13} = {}^{f}_{3}P_{14}$
15	${}^{f}_{0}P_{15}$	${}^{f}p_{15}$	${}^{f}{}_{0}P_{14}\cdot p_{14} = {}^{f}_{1}P_{15}$	${}^{f}_{1}P_{14}\cdot p_{14} = {}^{f}_{2}P_{15}$	${}^{f}_{2}P_{14}\cdot p_{14} = {}^{f}_{3}P_{15}$
16		${}^{f}p_{16}$	${}^{f}{}_{0}P_{15}\cdot p_{15} = {}^{f}_{1}P_{16}$	${}^{f}_{1}P_{15}\cdot p_{15} = {}^{f}_{2}P_{16}$	${}^{f}_{2}P_{15}\cdot p_{15} = {}^{f}_{3}P_{16}$
17		${}^{f}p_{17}$		${}^{f}_{1}P_{16}\cdot p_{16} = {}^{f}_{2}P_{17}$	${}^{f}_{2}P_{16}\cdot p_{16} = {}^{f}_{3}P_{17}$
18					${}^{f}_{2}P_{17}\cdot p_{17} = {}^{f}_{3}P_{18}$
—					
	$\sum_{0}^{\infty}{}^{f}_{0}P_x$		$\sum_{1}^{\infty}{}^{f}_{1}P_x$	$\sum_{2}^{\infty}{}^{f}_{2}P_x$	$\sum_{3}^{\infty}{}^{f}_{3}P_x$

Table 11.4 *Number of babies estimated to be born and how many of them are likely to survive*

Age x	*Age specific fertility i_x**	*Female population in one year before the base year ${}^{f}_{-1}P_x$ ***	*Female population in the base year ${}^{f}_{0}P_x$ ***	*Number of babies in the base year $i_x \cdot {}^{f}_{-1}p_x$*	*Number of babies in the first year $i_x \cdot {}^{f}_{0}p_x$*	*Female population in the second year ${}^{f}_{1}P_x$*	*Number of babies in the second year $i_x \cdot {}^{f}_{1}P_x$*
1	*2*	*3*	*4*	*5*	*6*	*7*	*8*
15	i_{15}	${}^{f}_{-1}P_{15}$	${}^{f}_{0}P_{15}$	$i_{15} \cdot {}^{f}_{-1}P_{15}$	$i_{15} \cdot {}^{f}_{0}P_{15}$	${}^{f}_{1}P_{15}$	$i_{15} \cdot {}^{f}_{1}P_{15}$
16	i_{16}	${}^{f}_{-1}P_{16}$	${}^{f}_{0}P_{16}$	$i_{16} \cdot {}^{f}_{-1}P_{16}$	$i_{16} \cdot {}^{f}_{0}P_{16}$	${}^{f}_{1}P_{16}$	$i_{16} \cdot {}^{f}_{1}P_{16}$
17	i_{17}	${}^{f}_{-1}P_{17}$	${}^{f}_{0}P_{17}$	$i_{17} \cdot {}^{f}_{-1}P_{17}$	$i_{17} \cdot {}^{f}_{0}P_{17}$	${}^{f}_{1}P_{17}$	$i_{17} \cdot {}^{f}_{1}P_{17}$
—							
49	i_{49}	${}^{f}_{-1}P_{49}$	${}^{f}_{0}P_{49}$	$i_{17} \cdot {}^{f}_{-1}P_{49}$	$i_{17} \cdot {}^{f}_{0}P_{49}$	${}^{f}_{1}P_{49}$	$i_{17} \cdot {}^{f}_{1}P_{49}$

* Age specific fertility is obtained from the latest census data or a recently conducted large sample survey.
** Size of female population for each age for the base period, the preceding year and subsequent years are obtained from Table 11.3.

Instead of single year age distribution, a 5-year age distribution is generally used for women population. Those who are aged 10–14 years today would enter into reproductive age group five years hence. Those in 45–49 years all of them would leave the reproductive period even if all of them were alive. The size of the female population, more specifically those in the reproductive age group, would become available from Table 11.3. On the basis of the data from this table, how many children at every age of women in reproductive age group would be born is calculated (Table 11.4).

From Table 11.4 we get the following information:

(a) Number of newly born babies in the base year: $\sum i_x \cdot {}^{f}_{-1}p_x$ (col. 5)

(b) Number of babies in the first year after the base year: $\sum i_x \cdot {}^{f}_{0}p_x$ (col.6)

(c) Number of babies from age '0' to the beginning of age '1':

$$\frac{1}{2}\left(\sum i_x \cdot {}^{f}_{-1}P_x + \sum i_x \cdot {}^{f}_{0}P_x\right) = A(say) \quad \text{...(11.10)}$$

(d) Number of female babies among the babies calculated in (c) is:

$$A \times \left(\frac{F}{F+M}\right) = G(say) \quad \text{...(11.11)}$$

(e) Number of male babies born among the number of babies calculated in (c) is

$$A \times \left(\frac{M}{F+M}\right) = A - G = B(say) \quad \text{...(11.12)}$$

(f) The female babies those are likely to survive till their first birthday is $G \cdot {}^{f}L_0/{}^{f}l_0$. The same for male babies is $B \cdot {}^{m}L_0/{}^{m}l_0$.

(g) Therefore, the total number of babies who are aged less than one year is

$$G \cdot {}^{f}L_0/{}^{f}l_0 + B \cdot {}^{m}L_0/{}^{m}l_0 \qquad \ldots(11.13)$$

The values of ${}^{f}L_0/{}^{f}l_0$ and ${}^{m}L_0/{}^{m}l_0$ can be found out from the female and male Life Tables respectively. Following the same procedure, persons aged '0' in the first, second, ... year after the base year can be found out.

(h) The population of net migrants for each year can be found out by extrapolation and added to the base populations to forecast the population at a future date.

This is to remind the readers that for a large gap between the projection year and the base year a correction in survival and fertility rates would be necessary. The same statistics cannot be used over and over again. Through extrapolation (trend analysis) these rates must be re-estimated for every five years forward movement from the base year. That we have used different survival and fertility rates must be indicated in the computation as well. If p_x and i_x symbolize base year statistics, then ${}^{N}p_x$, ${}^{N+5}p_x$, ${}^{N+10}p_x$..., ${}^{N}i_x$, ${}^{N+5}i_x$, ${}^{N+10}i_x$...symbolize the same statistics for *N*th, *N*+5, *N*+10 ... years after base year respectively. Generally, population projection by Component Method for any age initially is for 14 years. The survivors of the female babies who are aged '0' years today would enter the reproductive age group 14 years hence. *Flow chart* has been devised to enable uninterrupted

Figure. 11.1 *Flow-chart for population projection by component method*

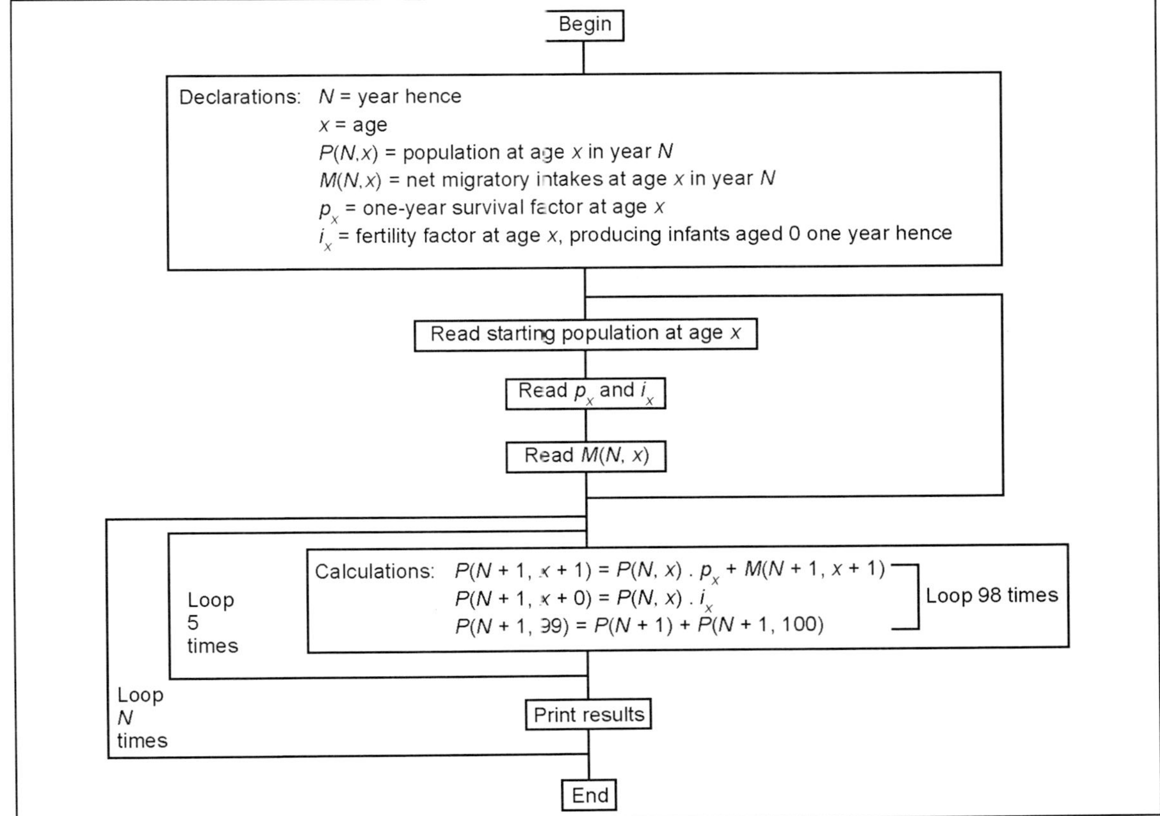

(Reproduced from Peter Cox: *Demography*. Indian reprint 1990)

continuous computation making use of the information fed to the computer. An illustration of such a flow-chart is given in Figure 11.1.

No two projections for the same population would yield identical results simply because of the fact that no two projections go by the same assumptions. There was a time, in the 1950s and earlier, when mortality in the population received greater importance since death rates in all countries were declining fast, birth rate remained relatively unchanged or changing only very slowly. Since 1980s the situation has changed considerably; death rates in most of the developing countries, except in Africa, have reached a stage when further decline in the general mortality rate would be almost totally dependent upon infant and child mortality. In the next 15–20 years if they can bring down IMR and child mortality to 30 or 40 percent of their current levels, the general death rate in their population may even go below the level of CDR presently observed in the developed countries. The developed countries are likely to show an upward movement of the death rate because of a fast rise in the old age population and a further drop in the proportion of the young age group.

For mortality assumptions, varied indicators are used. Though expectation of life is most commonly used in projections, CDR and IMR are also used. For fertility assumptions, a very wide range of indicators have been used – CBR, TFR, CWR, marriage rate, couple protection rate and annual population growth rate. Most projections however do not take migration as one of the major components in the estimation. But there are many countries in Africa, Central America and in some other regions that experience considerable international migration from time to time. The spread of preventive and curative medicines as also spread of health services are also taken into consideration in the estimation of future mortality rates. The most common procedure followed in making various estimates for components is to develop trend curves based on recent past experiences.

All projections specify assumptions about birth, death and some other rates (migration, marriage rate, life expectancy, etc.). However, how these rates – most vital for projections – are arrived at often is not clearly stated. Historical analysis of these events often followed by time series analysis with supporting evidences from demographic theory and most frequently a very detailed discussion with the experts in the field, form the basis of these assumptions. Most often three variants of projections for the same country or region or global population are documented – high, medium and low. The purpose of these three projections is to advice the planners to come out with policy prescriptions that will ensure that the population does not follow the high growth model. Emphasis of national policies would be to direct all socioeconomic activities that would concur as much as possible with the fundamentals of the low growth model.

11.4 United Nations Projection for World Population

Every two years the United Nations Department of Economic and Social Affairs' Population Division prepares the official estimates and projections of world, regional and national population size and growth, and demographic indicators. The Population Division has adopted two major innovations for a new set of long-range population projections based on the 2002 Revision. For the first time, the long-range projections are made at the national level for each of the 228 countries. Besides, the time horizon for the projections has been extended to 2300, so as to allow for the eventual stabilization of the population in at least one scenario.

In these projections (medium), world population peaks at 9.22 billion in 2075. Population therefore grows slightly beyond the level of 8.92 billion projected for 2050 in the 2002 Revision, on which these projections are based. However, after reaching its maximum, World population declines slightly and then resumes the upward course, slowly, to reach a level of 8.97 billion by 2300, not much different from the projected 2050 figure. In the high scenario, world population will go from 10.63 billion in 2050 to 36.44 billion in 2300. In the low scenario, over the same span, world population will be cut by one-fourth, and over the entire period to 2300, by two-thirds, from 7.41 billion in 2050 to 2.31 billion in 2300.

Figure 11.2 *Estimated world population, 1950–2000 and 2000– 2050*

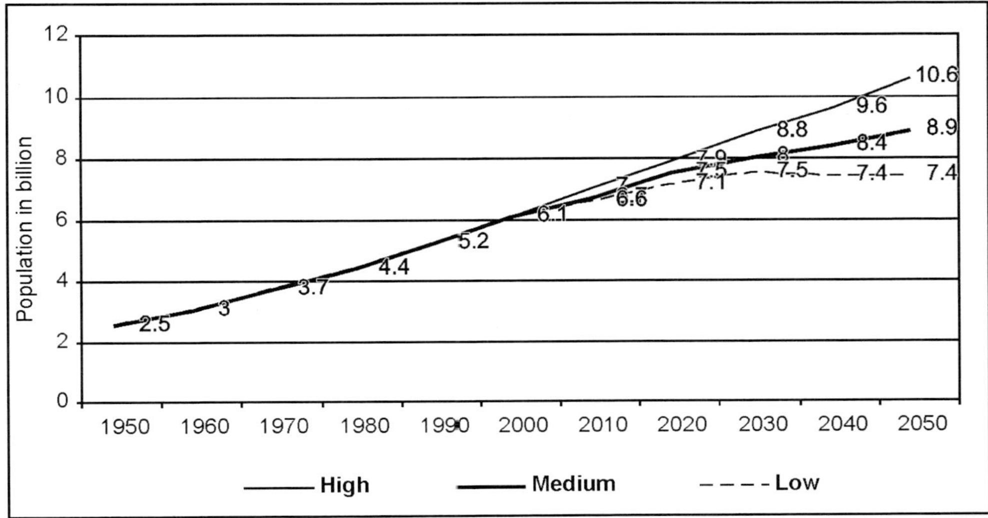

Figure 11.3 *Estimated world population—1950–2000 and projections 2000–2300*

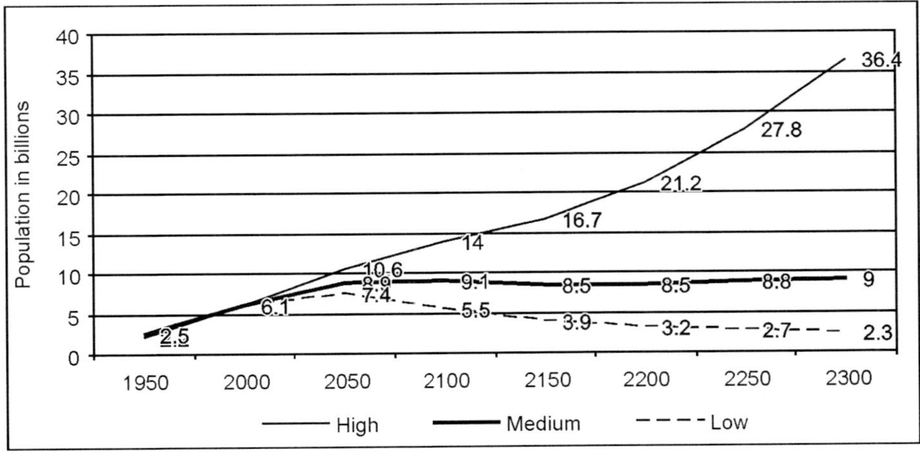

This pattern (medium variant) "rise – decline – rise" results from assumptions about future trends in vital rates: that, country by country, fertility will fall below replacement level – though in some cases not for decades – and eventually return to replacement level; and that, country by country, life expectancy will eventually follow a path of uninterrupted but slowing increase. With alternative assumptions about fertility, long-range trends could be quite different. With long-range total fertility 0.3 children above replacement, the projected world population in 2300 is four times as large as the main projection (medium); with total fertility 0.2 children below replacement, world population in 2300 is about one-quarter of the main projection.

Population growth in Asia looks strikingly large, at 1.5 billion over 50 years. However, Asia's share of world population would actually dip slightly, from 61 per cent in 2000 to 59 per cent in 2050. Growth will be much faster in Africa, which will add 1.0 billion in 50 years and its population share to the world population would almost double the current level. Average annual rates of population change show that Africa has experienced considerably faster growth than any other major area, for most of the 1950–2000 periods. Growth rates reached a higher peak in Africa (2.86 percent) than anywhere else – in the early 1980s, at least 15 years after growth had begun to decline in every other major area. Though the decline started late, Africa is expected to follow a downward growth path similar to that observed in other major areas. Europe is at the other end of the spectrum, with growth rates having just turned negative and continuing to fall up to 2050.

Though growth rates are at different levels, their decline is projected to be similar across major areas. The MDC show slightly slower decline in growth rates than the LDC, mainly because of international migration. If net migration were set to zero, the lines would be more nearly parallel. International migration is particularly important for Northern America accounting for 0.5 percentage points of growth rate for 2000–2050. The same in Europe would be 0.1–0.2 points. Though the gap between total fertility in Africa and that in every other major area still is large, by 2050 levels are expected to converge in a narrow band between 1.84 and 1.92 children per woman. Europe will take the longest to enter this band, and will do so through rising fertility, in contrast to falling fertility in other major areas.

Similar demographic paths in the long run are expected for all regions and countries, given similar assumptions for different countries about long range vital rate trends. However, since initial assumptions differ, and because this gives rise to some variations in trends, countries and regions will not be exactly alike even by 2300. The more developed and less developed regions of today will still be demographically distinguishable, at least, in respect to life expectancies and proportions in old ages. Regions and countries will go through similar critical stages of growth – zero growth, sub-replacement fertility, a return to positive growth – of course at different points in the future, giving rise to a global demographic map with areas that shrink and stretch at different times in the next three centuries.

Europe and Africa will be particularly out of phase. Europe will hit its low point in growth in 2050, Africa not till 80 years later, well after all other major areas. From 2000 to 2100, Europe's share to world population will be cut to half, 12.0 to 5.9 percent, while Africa's almost doubles, from 13.1 to 24.9 percent. While shares of world population for major areas will rise and fall over the following two centuries, the distribution by 2300 most likely will resemble that in 2100.

Divergent patterns of growth expected to be observed are summarized below.

- Three African regions – Eastern Africa, Middle Africa, and Western Africa – will grow unusually fast in comparison to every other region through 2100, even though total fertility will be close to replacement by 2050.
- Southern Africa is experiencing a decline in life expectancy to a lower level than anywhere else, but life expectancy will rebound, rise quite rapidly, and overtake other African regions.
- Asian regions will grow fastest to the west, slowest to the east, but in every case with growth rates, at least up to 2100, below Eastern, Middle and Western Africa. By 2100, Asia, instead of being four-and-a half times as populous as Africa, will be only 2.2 times as numerous.

- Latin America and the Caribbean is the most homogenous major area, with most of its regions following relatively parallel fertility and life expectancy paths.
- Northern America is the only region that will not experience negative growth, mainly due to projected migration up to 2050. (No migration is incorporated in projections beyond that date.)
- Europe, like Asia, will experience higher growth to the west, lower growth to the east. Eastern Europe stands out with low life expectancy, and even in the long run does not catch up with other regions.

Projection Assumptions

Fertility at the world level is projected to decline from 2.8 children per woman in 1995–2000 to about 2 children in 2045–2050. Over the long run, total fertility is projected to settle at 1.85 children per woman in each country. Because of uncertainty about this long-range level, the high scenario has total fertility levels gradually diverging, eventually reaching a level 0.5 points higher than that in the medium scenario (2.35 vs. 1.85). The low scenario has total fertility settling at 0.5 points below that in the medium scenario, for an eventual level of 1.35, well below replacement level. The spread of 0.5 children above or below the medium variant was to reach by 2050 at the latest, but not the ultimate levels. Fertility in developed countries, which is already relatively close to the long-range levels, is assumed to reach them (whether medium, high, or low) by the period 2045–2050. Fertility in developing countries also moves toward these levels, but since in some cases it is still well above them, it does not necessarily reach them by 2050. All countries are projected to have reached replacement fertility by 2175, but past fertility trends continue to affect population trends for another 50 years.

Mortality is projected by assuming that life expectancy rises according to one of three schedules, reflecting fast, medium, or slow improvements in existing mortality data for the specific country (United Nations, 2004). Each schedule provides for slower gains at higher levels. In the medium schedule, the annual gain in life expectancy is likely to be 0.4 years for males and 0.5 years for females from an initial combined life expectancy level of 60 years (typical of LDC). But the gain shrinks to 0.1 years for males and 0.2 years for females from an initial life expectancy level of 75 years (typical of MDC). Depending on their mortality experience, countries may stay on the chosen schedule of life expectancy improvement until 2050 or move to the medium schedule by 2025. However, the impact of the HIV/AIDS epidemic is explicitly accounted for in 53 "highly" affected countries where HIV/AIDS prevalence level is at least 1.9 per cent. In these cases, non-AIDS mortality is projected to decline – but in most cases with slower improvements. The further assumption is added that HIV transmission gradually declines beginning in 2010. The result is a slower rise in life expectancy in these countries compared to others, or an actual decline. Overall, at the world level, life expectancy at birth within the 2002 Revision was projected to increase from 64.6 years in 1995–2000 to 74.3 years in 2045–2050. By 2045–2050, life expectancy in Africa is projected to be 11 years shorter than in the next lowest case. The other major areas will be bunched, though not too tightly, between 76 and 82 years of life expectancy, with Asia and Latin America and the Caribbean behind the more developed regions. By 2100, life expectancy is expected to vary across countries from 66 to 97 years, and by 2300 from 87 to 106 years.

Whereas the world median age in 2000 was 26 years, it will be 44 and 48 years respectively by 2100 and 2300. Before they reach the point where those over 40 years are half the population, countries go through a period labeled the *demographic window*[2], when the proportion of children under 15 years falls much below 30 per cent (in 2005 it was 28.3 percent) and the proportion of people 65 years and older is still below 8 per cent (5.5 percent only in developing countries). For some years, the proportion of the population in between 15 and 65 years, the working age, will be particularly prominent in the population. Europe entered the *demographic window* before 1950 and is now leaving it and entering a third age when older people are particularly noteworthy in the age distribution. Between 2100 and 2300, the proportion of world population of 65 years and older will increase by one-third (from 24 to 32 percent) and the proportion for 80 years and older will double (from 8.5 to 17 percent). Much of Africa however will not enter the *demographic window* until 2045. Old age burden on society will be raised manifold.

Mortality exerts some additional influence on the growth rate. Across major areas, its effect on growth largely counteracts that of fertility, since where fertility is higher, mortality also tends to be higher. Over time, life expectancy is expected to rise fairly smoothly. Africa again stands out, not only because of the much lower level of life expectancy but also because it is the only major area where projections show decline in life expectancy for any period.

Assumptions are also made about international migration, based on past migration estimates and on public policy toward migrants. Migration assumptions are specified country by country. The United States, which receives the largest number of immigrants, is estimated as having 6.3 million net migrants in 1995–2000 and is projected to have only slightly fewer – 5.5 million – in 2045–2050. China and Mexico lose the largest net number of net migrants in 1995–2000 and also in 2045–2050. Migration assumptions have no effect on world projections but do affect country and regional results.

Additional Assumptions for Projections after 2050

To extend the projections to 2300, additional assumptions about the period after 2050 are needed. If fertility levels were projected to continue indefinitely at 1.85 children per woman, as the 50-year projections assume, long-range population decline would be inevitable. However, fertility is projected to stay below replacement level continuously for no more than 100 years per country over the period from 1950 forward, and to return to replacement level after 100 years, or by the year 2175, whichever comes first. Replacement level, given the low mortality rates expected in the next century, would be around 2.05 children per woman. With this assumption, countries that now have below-replacement fertility return to replacement earlier than countries with fertility well above replacement, which first progress downward to a level of 1.85 in accordance with the models used for 50-year projections, and then take 100 years to return to replacement level.

The high growth scenario in the 50-year projections assumes that total fertility stays 0.5 children above the level in the medium scenario. Beyond 2050, this gap is initially narrowed to 0.25 children and then increased to approximately 0.3 children once fertility in the medium scenario returns to replacement. The long-range gap is approximate since fertility in the high scenario is

2 *Demographic Window* is defined to be that period of time in a nation's demographic evolution when the proportion of population in working age group is particularly prominent. The UN Population Department has defined it as a period when the proportion of children under 15 years falls below 30 per cent and the proportion of people 65 years and older is still below 15 per cent. Typically, the demographic window of opportunity lasts for 30–40 years depending upon the country. Because of the mechanical link between fertility levels and age structures, the timing and duration of this period is closely associated to those of fertility decline.

Table 11.5 *Population and average annual rate of change of the world and development groups: estimates and three scenarios – 1950–2300*

Year (period)	World			More developed regions			Less developed regions		
	Medium	High	Low	Medium	High	Low	Medium	High	Low
1950	2 519	—	—	813	—	—	1 706	—	—
1975	4 068	—	—	1 047	—	—	3 021	—	—
2000	6 071	6 071	6 071	1 194	1 194	1 194	4 877	4 877	4 877
2025	7 851	8 365	7 334	1 241	1 282	1 199	6 610	7 082	6 135
2050	8 919	10 633	7 409	1 220	1 370	1 084	7 699	9 263	6 325
2075	9 221	12 494	6 601	1 153	1 467	904	8 068	11 027	5 696
2100	9 064	14 018	5 491	1 131	1 651	766	7 933	12 367	4 726
2125	8 734	15 296	4 556	1 137	1 885	679	7 597	13 411	3 877
2150	8 494	16 722	3 921	1 161	2 152	633	7 333	14 571	3 288
2175	8 434	18 696	3 481	1 185	2 454	593	7 249	16 242	2 889
2200	8 499	21 236	3 165	1 207	2 795	554	7 291	18 441	2 612
2225	8 622	24 301	2 920	1 228	3 179	517	7 395	21 122	2 403
2250	8 752	27 842	2 704	1 246	3 612	482	7 506	24 230	2 223
2275	8 868	31 868	2 501	1 263	4 100	448	7 605	27 768	2 053
2300	8 972	36 444	2 310	1 278	4 650	416	7 694	31 793	1 894
				Average annual rate of change (per cent)					
1950–75	1.92	—	—	1.01	—	—	2.29	—	—
1975–00	1.60	—	—	0.52	—	—	1.92	—	—
2000–25	1.03	1.28	0.76	0.16	0.29	0.02	1.22	1.49	0.92
2025–50	0.51	0.96	0.04	–0.07	0.26	–0.41	0.61	1.07	0.12
2050–75	0.13	0.64	–0.46	–0.23	0.27	–0.72	0.19	0.70	–0.42
2075–00	–0.07	0.46	–0.74	–0.08	0.47	–0.67	–0.07	0.46	–0.75
2100–25	–0.15	0.35	–0.75	0.02	0.53	0.48	0.17	0.32	–0.79
2125–50	–0.11	0.36	–0.60	0.08	0.53	–0.28	–0.14	0.33	–0.66
2150–75	–0.03	0.45	–0.48	0.08	0.53	–0.27	–0.05	0.43	–0.52
2175–00	0.03	0.51	–0.38	0.07	0.52	–0.27	0.02	0.51	–0.40
2200–25	0.06	0.54	–0.32	0.07	0.52	–0.28	0.06	0.54	–0.33
2225–50	0.06	0.54	–0.31	0.06	0.51	–0.28	0.06	0.55	–0.31
2050–75	0.05	0.54	–0.31	0.05	0.51	–0.29	0.05	0.55	–0.32
2075–00	0.05	0.54	–0.32	0.05	0.50	–0.29	0.05	0.54	–0.32

Source: UN Population Division (2004): World Population to 2300

Figure 11.4 *Average annual rate of change (medium, high and low)—World*

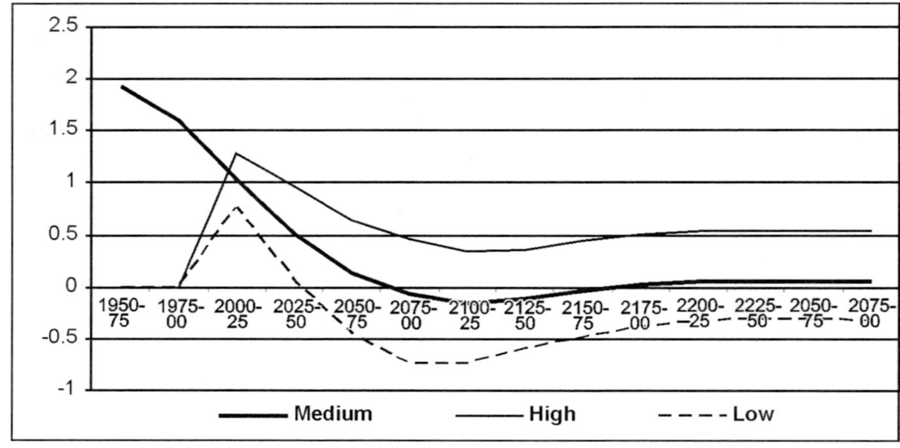

Figure 11.5 *Average annual rate of change (medium, high and low)—MDC*

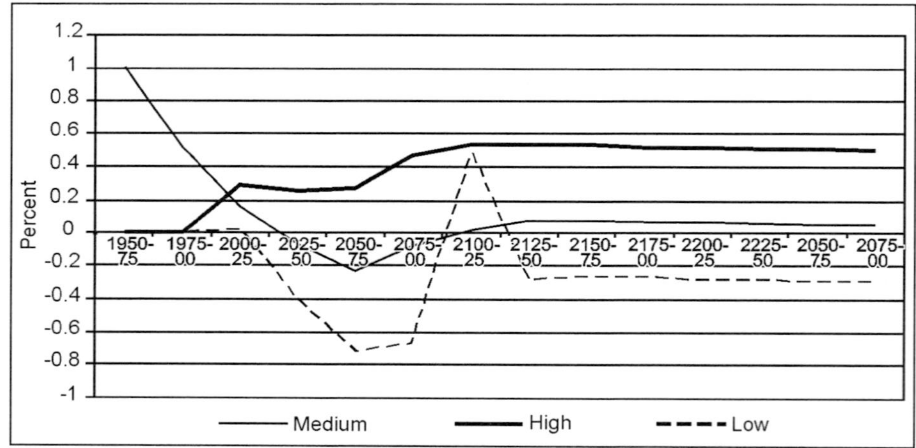

Figure 11.6 *Average annual rate of change (medium, high and low)—LDC*

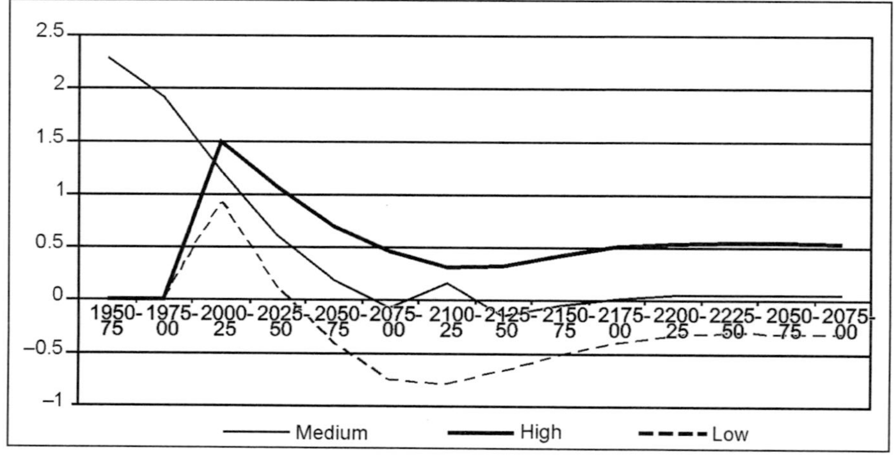

fixed, eventually, at 2.35 children, whereas replacement-level fertility in the medium scenario varies well across countries. The low scenario in the 50-year projections assumes that total fertility stays 0.5 children below the level in the medium scenario. This gap then narrows to 0.25 children after 2050, and narrows further, once replacement level is reached in the medium scenario, to approximately 0.2 children.

The mortality effect can never be eliminated under the assumption of continuously rising life expectancy. This will continue to affect the age structure, but one can eliminate effects of changing fertility on the age structure. The zero-growth scenario can be accomplished only by pushing births equal to deaths beginning 50 years after replacement fertility is reached in a given country. Under this scenario, projected population growth is essentially zero in every one of 192 countries, which have current populations 100,000 or more, beginning in 2225. Beyond 2150, therefore, number of births apparently makes no direct contribution to population growth, and population change beyond that point – and in earlier periods too in some but not all countries – can be interpreted as due to mortality change or the age structure.

12 Human Development

12.1 Introduction

Pattern of global partnership for development, unemployment rate and poverty level in a country are very closely interlinked. A high GDP growth is no guarantee of proportional poverty reduction. The UN report "World Economic Situation and Prospects 2007" clearly indicates that the momentum of past few years' high economic growth is likely to keep the growth in developing countries robust in 2007 and beyond. UN report also indicates that while economic growth has been strong worldwide in the past few years, it has failed in reduction in unemployment rates. Employment growth has remained disappointing, more so in the developing countries and economies in transition, despite exceptionally strong output growth in the region of 7 percent. This is because the hi tech growth path followed in most of these countries create fewer jobs for every per capita rise in GDP and the surplus labors from agriculture and other traditional sectors do not have the necessary skill for placement in the few jobs that are created. The developing countries suffer from the predicament that they have huge surplus labor, yet they are groping how the labor shortage in hi tech industries, especially in IT sector, could be sorted out. Unemployment and pseudo-employment are likely to remain a major headache for these states quite for sometime.

There is no consensus even among the economists as to what development really stands for. Development no doubt implies change and describes the process of economic and social transformation within countries. It is generally true that if the economy is growing sufficiently rapidly, the general socio-economic wellbeing of the whole population improves, not of course by the same degree. This naturally suggests that if we have to choose a single indicator of development, there can be no two opinions as to the utility of using per capita national income or output for the same. But what is true of a developed economy is not necessarily true of a developing economy. Even the developing countries that registered significant gains in GNP (China and India), show highly skewed income distribution. In many developing countries distributive and social justice does not accompany faster growth of economy and capital accumulation. Many economists today are arguing that economic policy of a country be directed to attack the causes of poverty so that a decent living for all can be assured even if that means a temporary slowing down the economic growth. An integrated approach to development has been accepted which embraces the major economic and social objectives paying due emphasis on the values which societies strive for.

Human development in a sense is about building human capabilities – the range of things that people can do, and what they can be. Individuals' freedom and rights matter a great deal; but they have little freedom to choose between what are offered when they are poor, sick or unwell, illiterate, discriminated against, threatened by violent conflict or denied a political voice. The most basic capabilities for human development are a long life with decent living and education. Other capabilities include participatory role in social and political decision-making process. To capture some of these capabilities of an individual and the country as a whole, United Nations Development Program

(UNDP) has been working on four indexes, namely Human Development Index (HDI), Human Poverty Index (HPI), Gender-related Development Index (GDI) and Gender Empowerment Index (GEM).

12.2 The Fate of Millennium Development Goals

At the start of the new millennium, 189 countries of the world jointly made a solemn pledge that under the aegis of United Nations they would try "to free our fellow men, women and children from the abject and dehumanizing conditions of extreme poverty". The declaration, in a shared commitment to universal human rights and social justice, made a few time-bound targets – the Millennium Development Goals (MDG). They include the following:

Box 1 *Millennium development goals*

Goal 1: Eradicate extreme hunger and poverty. Halving the proportion of people living on less than $1 a day and halving malnutrition.

Goal 2: Achieve universal primary education. Ensuring that all children are able to complete primary education.

Goal 3: Promote gender equality and empower women. Eliminating gender disparity in primary and secondary schooling, preferably by 2005 and no later than 2015.

Goal 4: Reduce child mortality. Cutting the under-five death rate by two-thirds.

Goal 5: Improve maternal health. Reducing the maternal mortality rate by three-quarters.

Goal 6: Combat HIV/AIDS, malaria and other diseases. Halting and beginning to reverse HIV/AIDS and other killer diseases.

Goal 7: Ensure environmental stability. Cutting by half the proportion of people without sustainable access to safe drinking water and sanitation.

Goal 8: Develop a global partnership for development. Reforming aid and trade with special treatment for the poorest countries.

The deadline for delivery is 2015. The MDGs are the most comprehensive and most detailed set of human development goals.

UNDP has carried out trend analysis using 1990–2003 data and have made projection for 2015 on key MDGs assuming the present trend continues. The analysts admit that good quality data are not available for many countries. There are many other factors not given due consideration while drawing plans for projection. For example, *tsunami*-like incidences, global warming and ecological pressure on food chain, scientists all over the world believe, may adversely affect programs for reduction of malnutrition. If the widely predicted outbreak of bird flue were to materialize, it may have devastating impact on public health across countries. There is already a large gap between MDG target and outcome on current trends.

The industrial economies (G–8) in 2005 made some declaration for aids and debt relief to the poorest countries. Except that the report card on progress in other areas does not appear flattering. Most countries are off track for most of MDGs. They are faltering in many key areas.

From the trend data available for different countries, it is believed that of the countries under the scanner only 60 would be able to reduce child mortality by two-thirds by 2015 and 107 only by 2035. Less than 20 percent of the developing world's populations are on track to meet the MDG target. Unfortunately, neither India nor China is in this list. This means there would be 4.4 million additional child deaths (sub-Saharan Africa alone would be responsible for 3 million child deaths) over and above the figure projected in MDG and there would be a cumulative additional 41 million child deaths between 2005 and 2015. If the present trend continues, the sub-Saharan African countries could reach the target only in 2115. More than 45 percent of child deaths occur in 52 countries that are going backwards or making little progress in reducing child mortality (India is one of them). Largest share of child deaths is among the poorer segment of populations in most countries. Though child death rates are falling in almost all countries, it is doing so very slowly among the poor. Cross-country data show that fall in child mortality among the poorest 20 percent is only half the average rate of decline. It clearly indicates that the gap in child mortality between the poor and the rich is widening. Maternal mortality trends cannot be traced with any degree of certainty for want of reliable information from most countries.

The trend analysis suggests that the target of halving the number of people without sustainable access to safe water would be missed by about 210 million people. Another 2 billion people would also lack access to improved sanitation in 2015. The bulk of the deficit would be in sub-Saharan Africa.

As regards poverty alleviation and reduction of malnutrition, the global target for 2015 would be largely met if the present pattern of economic growth rate and distribution continues. China and India are likely to contribute most in reaching this global target. The incidence of global $1 a day poverty is likely to fall from 21 percent to 14 percent by 2015. However, poverty in sub-Saharan Africa is likely to escalate – from about 24 percent today to 41 percent in 2015.

Prospects for reaching the target on malnutrition are even less promising. The incidence of malnutrition has fallen since 1990, from 20 percent to 17 percent. However, population growth has left the number of malnourished people unchanged. The pace of progress will have to double to reach the 2015 target. On the current trajectory there would still be around 670 million people suffering from malnutrition in 2015, 230 million more than if the target were achieved. Sub-Saharan Africa would again account for almost 60 percent of the deficit.

The target of achieving universal primary education by 2015 is likely to be missed by at least a decade. 46 countries are unlikely to achieve universal primary education before 2040 if the present trends do not improve. There would be 47 million children out of schools by 2015, 19 million would be from sub-Saharan Africa. Gender parity in school enrolment would also be missed. If the present trend is not altered significantly, there is little hope that gender disparity in primary education would be eliminated before 2040.

Gender empowerment remains a far cry even in most democracies. Politics still remain the overwhelming domain of men. Globally, only 15 percent of legislative seats are held by women. There are countries where women have no representation (Saudi Arabia and UAE, for example). Women even are debarred by law from voting or holding public office in some countries.

There is a belief that Islam remains an obstacle to women empowerment. Malaysia, a Muslim country, has Gender Empowerment Measure (GEM) higher than that of Korean Republic, Hungary and Greece. There is also a popular belief that gender disparity automatically diminishes at higher levels of income. Japan and Italy, two top industrialized countries, with per capita GDP over $27,000, have GEM 0.534 and 0.589 respectively. They even rank lower in GEM compared to Costa Rica and Argentina. Japan and Netherlands are democracies with almost similar HDI, yet Netherlands' GEM score is more than 140 percent of the GEM of Japan.

Table 12.1 *Shortfall in reaching the millennium development goals – the human cost*

Countries in the regions	Child mortality – cumulative cost of the missed target			No access to safe water – the human cost			Income poverty – the human cost			Children not enrolled in schools – the human cost			Girls not enrolled in schools – the human cost		
	2003	2015	Cumulative shortfall	2003	2015	Short fall	2003	2015	Shortfall	2003	2015	Shortfall	2003	2015	Shortfall
1	2	3	4	5	6	7	8	9	10	11	12	13	14	15	16
Sub-Saharan Africa	4.8	5.1	28.1	278.2	198.8	80.1	313.0	352.7	218.7	45.5	18.7	18.7	23.8	9.6	3.8
Arab States	0.6	0.5	3.0	46.7	19.0	6.7	7.0	9.5	7.5	8.8	5.7	5.7	6.0	3.5	0.5
East Asia & the Pacific	1.2	0.7	2.9	419.0	190.7	14.6	271.0	17.2	7.5	10.0	15.8	11.3	4.9	7.1	0.7
South Asia	3.5	2.2	7.2	232.8	108.9	103.8	431.0	395.0	101.4	42.3	4.0	4.0	23.6	9.6	0.0
Latin America & the Caribbean	0.4	0.1	0.2	55.0	8.1	4.9	50.0	51.0	44.4	3.3	0.9	0.9	1.5	1.1	1.1
All developing countries	10.5	8.6	41.4	1036.6	525.2	209.9	1,072.0	826.7	379.9	109.9	46.7	46.7	58.8	30.9	6.0

Figures in millions
Source: Human Development Report 2005

We now concentrate our discussion on the various measures of development indices developed by UNDP and see how things have changed in the last 15 years.

12.3 Human Development Index

The Rationale, Assumptions and Technology Involved for Developing Various Indices.

Since 1990 UNDP has been publishing Human Development Report (HDR) – an excellent discourse on contemporary development across the globe – the high-income and developing countries. UNDP gratefully acknowledges debt to Prof. Amartya Sen, whose work has shaped the evolution of the *Human Development Report* over the years. Prof. Sen is very much conscious of the crudeness of Human Development Index HDI[1] and tried to direct attention of interested persons to the rich collection of information on a variety of social, economic, health and political features that comes out with every HDR. He felt that HDI, though crude, could serve as an alternative measure of human development, supplementing GNP, especially for comparative analysis. Purchasing power of an individual alone does not automatically capture an individual's attainment in many other areas of wellbeing – one's health, education, freedom to shape one's life and to enlarge his choice domain. 'Right to live' and 'development' are not synonymous. Prof Sen remembers what Mahbub ul Haq, the originator of Human Development Report (1990), said about the crudeness of the HDI measure. He demanded that "We need a measure of the same level of vulgarity as GNP – just one number – but a measure that is not as blind to social aspects of human lives as GNP is".

HDI has three component indicators – longevity, education and per capita income. Longevity is measured by *expectation of life at birth*; educational attainment is measured by a combination of *adult* (*15 years+*) *literacy* (*two-thirds weight*) *and the combined gross primary, secondary and tertiary enrolment ratio* (*one-third weight*); and standard of living as measured by *real GDP per capita*. Performance in each dimension is expressed as a value between 0 and 1 by applying the following general formula:

$$\text{Dimension index} = \frac{\text{actual}\, x_i \text{ value} - \text{minimum}\, x_i \text{ value}}{\text{maximum}\, x_i \text{ value} - \text{minimum}\, x_i \text{ value}} \quad \ldots(12.1)$$

HDI is then calculated as a simple average of the *dimension indices*. Box 2 illustrates the goalposts for calculation of HDI.

Box 2 *Goalposts for calculating the HDI*

Indicator	***Maximum value***	***Minimum value***
Life expectancy at birth (years)	85	25
Adult literacy rate (%)	100	0
Combined gross enrolment ratio (%)	100	0
GDP per capita (PPP US $)	40,000	100

Although income enters into all the dimensions of human development (in healthy life and in knowledge), its independent inclusion in computing human development index was sought as a

1 …I did not initially see much merit in the HDI itself, which, as it happened, I was privileged to help devise. I had… considerable skepticism… about trying to catch in one simple number a complex reality about human development and deprivation. In, Amartya Sen, Assessing Human Development, Human Development Report 1999, UNDP.

proxy for a decent standard of living. The authors of HDR felt that income needs to be included in computing the composite index for the simple reason that achieving a respectable level of development one cannot deny the importance of income, at the same time one does not require unlimited income for respectable level human development. Constructing an income index therefore must discount incomes beyond the threshold level.

Prior to 1999 Human Development Report, a more complicated procedure was followed in computation of income index.

$$W(y) = y^* \text{ for } 0 < y < y^*$$

$$= y^* + 2[(y - y^*)^{1/2}] \text{ for } y^* < y < 2y^* \quad \ldots(12.2)$$

$$= y^* + 2(y^{*1/2}) + 3(y - 2y^*)^{1/3} \text{ for } 2y^* < y < 3y^*$$

The problem with (12.2) is that it discounts income above the threshold level (world average) very heavily. The new formula adopted for computing income index since 1999 reads

$$W(y) = \frac{\log y - \log y_{min}}{\log y_{max} - \log y_{min}} \quad \ldots(12.3)$$

This formula does not discount income as severely as the formula used earlier (12.2). This is clearly reflected in the following graph.

Figure 12.1 *Income discounting under the old and new formulas*

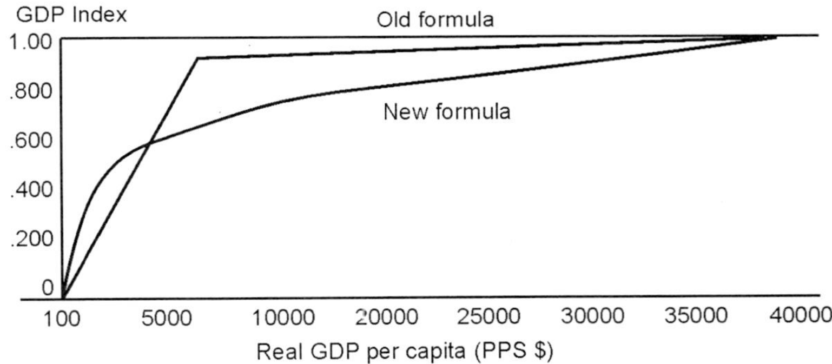

Illustration of computation of HDI using 2003 data for India:

$$\text{Life expectancy index} = \frac{63.3 - 25}{85 - 25} = 0.638$$

Education index is calculated in two stages – adult literacy index and gross enrolment index.

$$\text{Adult literacy index} = \frac{61.0 - 0}{100 - 0} = 0.61$$

$$\text{Gross enrolment index} = \frac{60 - 0}{100 - 0} 0.60$$

Education index = (2/3) adult literacy index +

(1/3) Gross enrolment index = (2/3)×0.61 + (1/3)×0.60 = 0.607 ...(12.4)

For calculation of GDP index, GDP per capita of the country and GDP per capita maximum and GDP per capita minimum are expressed in logarithmic values.

$$\text{Income (GDP) index} = \frac{\log(2{,}892) - \log(100)}{\log(40{,}000) - \log(100)} = 0.562$$

Therefore, HDI = (1/3)[Life expectancy index + Education index + GDP index]

= (1/3)[0.638 + 0.607 + 0.562] = **0.602** ...(12.5)

A few other indexes are also reported in the Human Development Report.

The Human Poverty Index – HPI–1 and HPI–2

The Human Poverty Index for developing countries (HPI–1) concentrates on deprivations to three essential dimensions of wellbeing already reflected in HDI.

- Deprivation relating to longevity, that is, vulnerability to death at an early age.
- Deprivation relating to knowledge – being excluded from the world of reading and communication.
- Economic deprivation – lack of adequate economic provisioning for a decent living.

In computation of HPI–1, the deprivation in longevity is represented by the percentage of people not expected to survive to age 40 (P_1); deprivation in knowledge by the percentage of adults (15 years and older) who are illiterate (P_2); and deprivation of a decent living is a composite (P_3) of three variables – percentage of people without access to safe drinking water (P_{31}), percentage of people without access to health services (P_{32}) and the percentage of moderately and severely underweight children under five (P_{33}). The composite variable P_3 is calculated by taking a simple average of the three deprivations P_{31}, P_{32} and P_{33}. Thus

$$P_3 = (1/3)(P_{31} + P_{32} + P_{33}) \qquad \text{...(12.6)}$$

The formula for computing HPI–1 is given by

$$\text{HPI}-1 = [1/3(P_1^\alpha + P_2^\alpha + P_3^\alpha)]^{1/\alpha}$$

$$\text{With } \alpha = 3,\ \text{HPI}-1 = [1/3(P_1^3 + P_2^3 + P_3^3)]^{1/3} \qquad \text{...(12.7)}$$

The percentage of people deprived of access to health services (P_{32}) has been dropped since reliable data on access to health services for recent years are not available for many countries. P_3 is currently computed from the unweighted average of two remaining variables.

P_3 = (1/2) (population without sustainable access to an improved water source)

+ (1/2) (children underweight for age) ...(12.8)

Illustration with data for India, 2003:

P_1 = Probability at birth not surviving to age 40 = 16.6%

P_2 = Adult illiteracy rate = 39.0%

P_{31} = Percentage of people without sustainable access to safe water = 14%

P_{32} = Percentage of children underweight for age = 47%

P_3 = Unweighted average of P_{31} and P_{32} = 30.5%

$\alpha = 3$

HPI–1 for India $= (1/3)(16.6^3 + 39.0^3 + 30.5^3)^{1/3} = 31.3$ per cent

Human Poverty Index for selected OECD countries (Organization for Economic Cooperation and Development): HPI–2 measures the same deprivations as HPI–1 and also captures social isolation. Some modifications of course had to be made considering the situations prevailing in the industrially developed countries. Therefore HPI–1 and HPI–2 are not comparable by any logic. The four dimensions included in HPI–2 are:

- A long and healthy life – vulnerability to death at a relatively early age, as measured by the probability at birth of not surviving to age 60 (P_1)
- Knowledge – exclusion from the world of reading and communications, as measured by the percentage of adults (aged 15–65) lacking functional literacy skills (P_2)
- A decent standard of living – as measured by the percentage of people living below the income poverty line (50 percent of the median adjusted household disposable income) (P_3)
- Social exclusion – as measured by the rate of long-term unemployment (12 months or more) (P_4).

The formula for calculating the HPI–2 is as follows:

$$\text{HPI}-2 = \left[\frac{1}{4}(P_1^{\alpha} + P_2^{\alpha} + P_3^{\alpha} + P_4^{\alpha})\right]^{1/\alpha} \qquad \text{...(12.10)}$$

An example: USA in 2003

$P_1 = 11.8\%$

$P_2 = 20.0\%$

$P_3 = 17.0\%$

$P_4 = 0.7\%$

$\alpha = 3$

$\text{HPI}-2 = [1/4(11.8^3 + 20.0^3 + 17.0^3 + 0.7^3)]^{1/3} = 15.4$ percent

Note: Value of α has an important impact on HPI. Had α been taken as 1, HPI would be an unweighted simple average of the deprivations. Raising the power gives an opportunity to give greater weight to the dimension in which most deprivation is noticed. Raising the power to infinity, the index would be totally determined by the dimension on which the deprivation is most.

Two other indexes, Gender-related Development Index, GDI, and Gender Empowerment Measure, GEM, are also reported in Human Development Reports. These two indexes are not as yet sound for international comparisons since the related data are not easily available for many countries. Whereas GDI tries to capture the inequality between men and women after adjusting achievement of each country in longevity, educational attainment and income in accordance with the disparity in achievement between men and women, GEM measures *relative empowerment* of men and women in political and economic spheres of activity. Focusing on women's *opportunities* rather than their capabilities, GEM captures gender inequality in three key areas:

1. Political participation and decision-making power,
2. Economic participation and decision-making power,
3. Power over economic resources,

HDI, HPI–1, HPI–2 and GDI use the same basic components, but make different measurements. This is stated in the following Box.

Box 3 *Basic components of HDI, HPI and GDI*

Index	*Longevity*	*Knowledge*	*Decent standard of living*	*Participation or exclusion*
HDI	Life expectancy at birth	1. Adult literacy 2. Combined enrolment ratio	GDP per capita (PPP US $)	
HPI–1	Probability at birth of not surviving to age 40	Adult literacy rate	Deprivation in economic provisioning, measured by 1. Percentage of people deprived of safe water sources 2. Percentage of children under-five who are underweight	
HPI–2	Probability at birth of not surviving to age 60.	Percentage of adults lacking functional literacy skills	Percentage of people living below the income poverty line (50 percent of median disposable household income)	Long-term unemployment (12 months or more)
GDI	Female and male life expectancy at birth	1. Female and adult literacy rates 2. Female and male combined primary secondary and tertiary enrolment ratio	Estimated female and male earned income, reflecting women's and men's command over resources	

12.4 What Does HDI Reveal?

On the basis of HDI, countries are put into three categories: 0.800 and above (High Human Development), 0.500 to 0.800 (Medium Human Development) and below 0.500 (Low Human Development). Although Human Development Report and HDI for the countries were first published in 1990, UNDP estimated HDI of the countries for 1975, 1980 and 1985 utilizing relevant information from various sources. Over the years HDI for most countries have risen steadily except a few reversals in the 1990s. Trend of HDI over the years is presented in the adjoining figure and the table below.

Figure 12.1(a) *HDI Trend, 1975–2001*

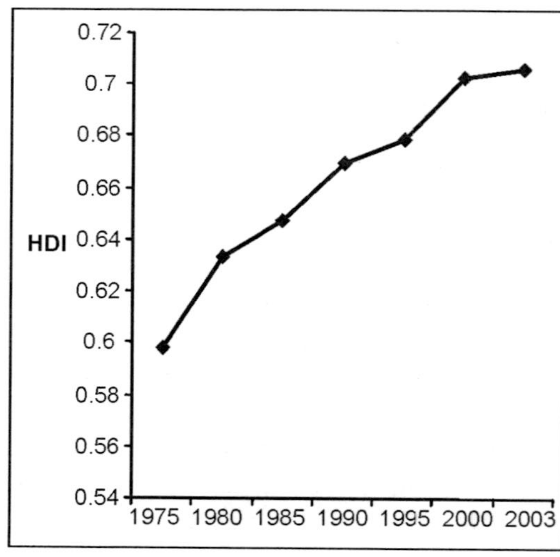

Table 12.2 *Distribution of countries by HDI Values, 1975–2003*

HDI range	*1975*	*1980*	*1985*	*1990*	*1995*	*2000*	*2003*
<.249	2 (1.96)	0	1 (0.83)	1 (0.74)	0	0	0
0.250–0.349	15 (14.70)	10 (8.85)	7 (5.79)	7 (5.15)	9 (6.21)	3 (2.56)	6 (3.38)
0.350–0.499	17 (16.67)	22 (19.47)	24 (19.83)	21 (15.44)	23 (15.86)	19 (16.24)	26 (14.69)
0.500–0.649	24 (23.52)	25 (22.12)	22 (18.18)	23 (16.91)	20 (13.79)	18 (15.38)	23 (12.99)
0.650–0.799	22 (21 57)	29 (25.66)	36 (29.75)	43 (31.62)	51 (35.17)	35 (29.91)	65 (36.72)
0.800–0.899	22 (21.57)	27 (23.89)	29 (23.97)	32 (23.52)	22 (15.17)	21 (17.95)	29 (16.38)
>0.900	0	0	2 (1.65)	9 (6.62)	20 (13.79)	21 (17.95)	28 (15.81)
Number of Countries	102 (100)	113 (100)	121 (100)	136 (100)	145 (100)	117 (100)	177 (100)

Note: Figures in parentheses are percentages to total number of countries.
Computed from UNDP: Human Development Report 2005

Table 12.3 *Mean HDI and CV over the years*

		1975	*1980*	*1985*	*1990*	*1995*	*2000*	*2003*
All countries	N	102	113	121	136	145	117	177
	AV	0.598	0.633	0.647	0.670	0.679	0.703	0.706
	SD	0.197	0.188	0.185	0.182	0.183	0.188	0.178
	CV	32.90	29.76	28.66	27.18	26.89	26.71	25.18

Computed from Human Development Report 2005 (UNDP).

Figure 12.2 *HDI trend, 1975–2003*

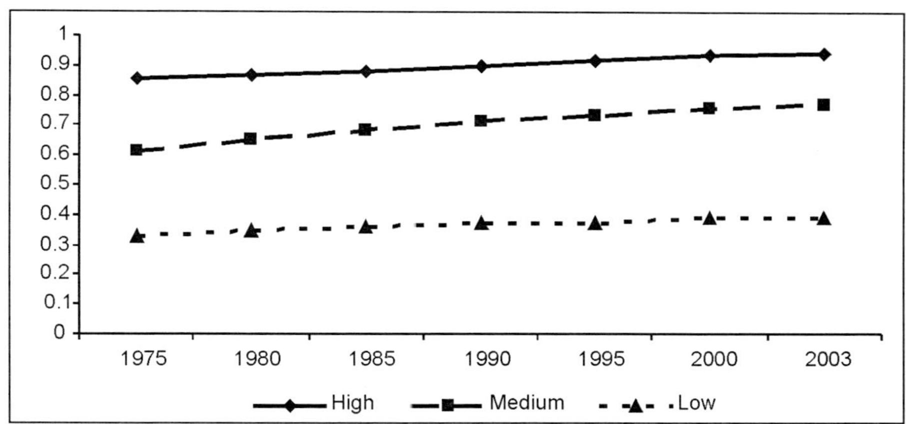

The mean HDI for the countries have gone up at a regular pace till 2000 but in the years between 2000 and 2003 it has advanced only marginally. Whereas the average HDI has improved by 18 percent during the period under review, variations in HDI values among the countries continue to be high. From one-third of the countries in Low HDI category in 1975, the percentage has dropped to 18 percent in 2003 (Table 12.2). The proportion of countries in High HDI category increased steadily till 2000 and then registered a slight drop in 2003. The share of Medium HDI countries all these years continued just below 50 percent level till 1995; their share dropped by 4 percent in 2000 (the number of countries for which HDI values are available dropped very sharply; the number made a quantum jump again in 2003), but regaining the lost share in 2003. A remarkable change has occurred among High HDI countries in HDI range 0.900 and above (Super HDI). Whereas there were not a single country in that range till 1980, in 2003 there were as many as 28 countries, about 50 percent of all the countries in High HDI category. Most spectacular improvement is observed for 5 countries that were in the Medium HDI category in 1975 moved to the Super HDI category in 2003: Hong Kong from 0.761 in 1975 moved to 0.916 in 2003, Israel from 0.795 to 0.915, Singapore from 0.725 to 0.907, Portugal from 0.787 to 0.904 and Rep. of Korea from 0.707 to 0.901. Ireland too recorded a very impressive improvement, from 0.811 in 1975 to 0.946 in 2003.

Figure 12.3 *Spectacular improvement in HDI of five countries*

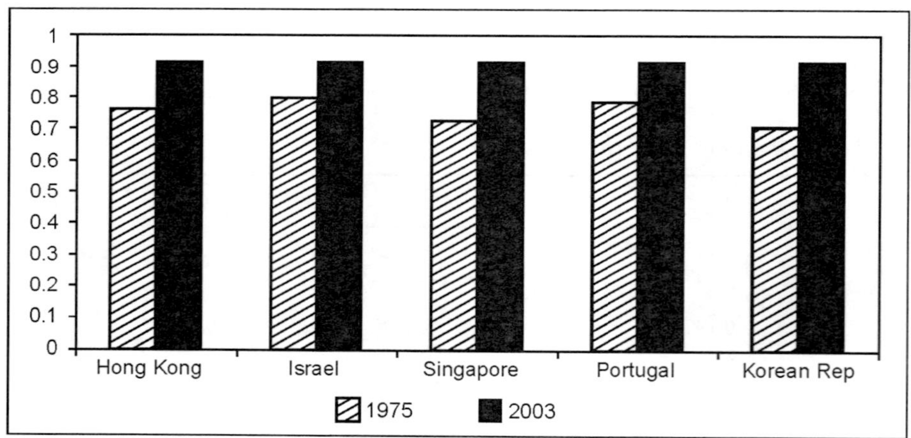

For the past few decades human capabilities as measured by HDI has been converging in the sense that CVs for HDI distribution for different country groups are dipping. The developing countries are fast catching up with the developed countries in respect to life expectancy, child mortality and literacy in the non-normative scale. For a large number of countries, mostly in sub-Saharan Africa, the divergence has increased of late. HIV/AIDS has become an epidemic in many of these countries. This has not only brought down life expectancy, productivity in most of these countries has fallen so much so that it has affected the functioning of every social, economic and welfare institutions. Right to live and right to get a good education and a decent standard of living, it appears has become linked to which country a person is born.

HDI reversals: Amid overall progress in HDI, a number of countries suffered *reversals*. Eighteen developing countries with a combined population of 460 million recorded lower HDI scores in 2003 compared to those in 1990. These 18 countries are from two regions – 12 are from sub-Saharan Africa and the other 6 are from the former Soviet Union. Three high human development countries, namely Australia, Belgium and UK also slid backwards between 2000 and 2003. Many countries suffered in their relative ranks among the countries. South Africa experienced the steepest fall, 35 places. Zimbabwe went down by 23 places and Botswana by 21 places. Whereas the free fall in HDI and relative position of some of the countries in sub-Saharan Africa is due to economic stagnation primarily due to spread of HIV/AIDS, the reversals in countries of the erstwhile Soviet Union is primarily due to economic disturbance that followed the disintegration of the former Soviet Union. Tajikistan's HDI ranking fell by 21 places, Ukraine by 17 places and Russian Federation by 15 places. Russia's fall, however, has substantially been due to the country's 48 place drop in life expectancy ranking between 1990 and 2003. Human Development Report 2003 shows life expectancy among Russian men is a meager 59 years (it was 70 years in mid-eighties), even below the life expectancy of men in India, and for women 72 years, showing one of the largest gender gap in life expectancy in the world – with a combined average of 65 years. In fact, Russia's life expectancy is the lowest among all the industrially developed countries.

Table 12. 4 *Countries experiencing HDI reversals*

1980–90	*1990–2003*
Congo, Dem. Rep. of the Guyana, Haiti, Niger, Rwanda, Zambia	Botswana, Cameroon, Central African Republic Congo, Dem. Rep. of the Côte d'Ivoire, Kazakhstan, Kenya, Lesotho Moldova, Rep. of Russian Federation, South Africa, Swaziland, Tajikistan, Tanzania, U. Rep. of Ukraine, Zambia, Zimbabwe

If HDI is believed to capture, at least approximately, the status of social and economic developments of peoples in a country, it must be admitted that some real progress has been made in this direction since 1975. It is a fact that expectation of life at birth has been increasing (except for reversals in some sub-Saharan African countries due to rapid spread of HIV/AIDS) indicating health situation in developing countries is far better than what it was a few decades back. Between 1970 and 1999, the world aggregate life expectancy at birth has gone up from around 59 years to 66.7 years (in the least developed countries from 43.4 years to 51.7 years, in sub-Saharan Africa from 44.1 years to 48.8 years). If we go back to 1960, life expectancy in developing and developed countries increased by 16 and 6 years respectively over the years. But between 1980 and 2003, the gap between the two groups has closed only by 2 years. If we advance the base period to 1990, the gap in life expectancy has been reduced by a meager 3 months between the developed and developing countries. That is, the convergence has come almost to a halt. If somebody is born in Sierra Leon, he is expected to live 42 years less than someone born in Japan. The large health inequalities between countries draw our attention to what has been described as the "law of inverse care" – the availability of medical care is inversely related to need. Health financing inequalities are central to this hypothesis. Per capita spending

Figure 12.3(a) *Under five mortality (Reproduced from HDR 2005)*

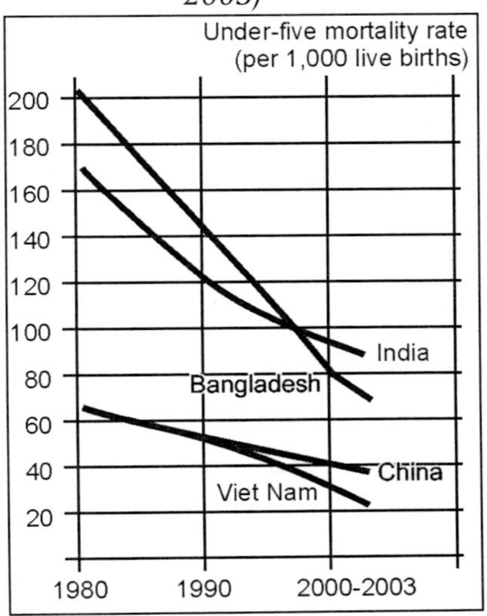

on health in high income OECD countries with the lowest health risk is an average of more than \$3,000 a year (much more than the per capita annual income in many underdeveloped countries); it is \$78, even much less, in low-income countries that have the highest health risks. The increase in life expectancy is partly due to falling child mortality. Child and maternal healthcare in a country are the barometers for the state of public health, nutrition and women empowerment among others.

Today there are 2 million fewer child deaths than what it was in 1990 and that the chance of survival to age 5 years has increased by 15 percent. There are more than 150 million children under age 5 who are underweight and over 10 million children dying annually from preventable causes. Every two minutes, of the four people dying from malaria three are children. For every child who dies, many more will fall sick and miss school, trapped in a vicious circle that links poor health in childhood to poverty in adulthood. Sub-Saharan Africa's share to child mortality has been rising. This region accounts for 20 percent of all births and 44 percent of all child deaths. UN data show that child mortality in the world has declined from 2.3 percent in 1980s to 1.9 percent of total number of deaths in 2000–03.

HDI of India and Bangladesh in 1999 respectively were 0.571 and 0.470. In 2003, HDI of India stood at 0.602 and that for Bangladesh advanced to 0.520. Whereas India's improvement in HDI was mostly due to improvement in Education and GDP index (by 0.05 and 0.04 respectively), the improvement in HDI in Bangladesh came from improvement in Life Expectancy index (from 0.57 to 0.63) and Education index (from 0.39 to 0.45). Bangladesh has done remarkably well in reducing under-five and infant mortality rates. From 239 under-five mortality rates in 1970, Bangladesh has brought it down to 69 and IMR from 143 to 46. In the same period India brought down child mortality from 202 to 87 and IMR from 127 to 63. China and Vietnam had almost the same under-five child mortality rate in 1980. But Vietnam has done exceedingly well in reducing child mortality in the last two decades.

The improved general health situation in developing countries can be attributed to better access to safe source of drinking water and sanitation – a fact that is supported by reduced mortality through *communicable* and *infectious diseases* the worldover. Over 1.2 million additional people have gained access to safe drinking water in the last decade. Global immunization program, it appears, has averted about half a million untimely deaths. Maternal mortality is still alarming in the poorer countries; 98 percent of about half a million women dying every year due to causes related to pregnancy are from poor countries. The risk of dying from pregnancy-related causes ranges from 1 in 18 in Nigeria to 1 in 8,700 in Canada. In sub-Saharan Africa maternal mortality is as high as 920 per 100,000 live births and that in South Asia are 540 per 100,000 live births. The incidence of malnutrition has fallen since 1990, from 20 percent to 17 percent. On the current trajectory, there would be around 670 million people in 2015 suffering from malnutrition. Sub-Saharan Africa would be the major contributor to the population of malnourished (HDR 2005).

Figure 12.4 *Children out of schools (million), in 2001 (HDR 2005)*

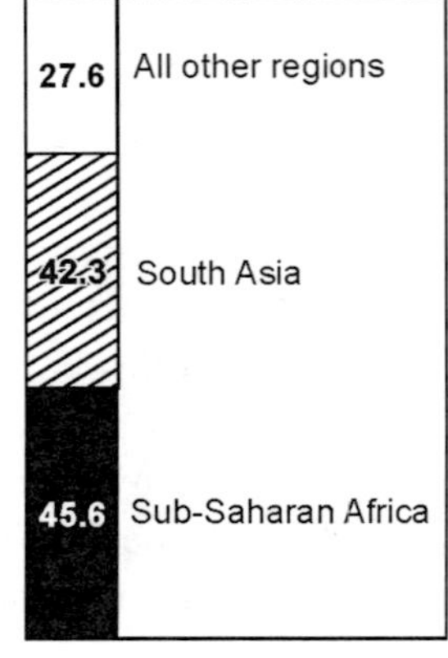

Education is a critical component of human development and a key to progress in most other areas. In spite of impressive advances in educational attainments (a gain of 6

percent over 70 percent literacy in the developing countries a decade back), over 800 million adult people of the world have no basic literacy skills. In today's increasing knowledge-based market economy, about 115 million children are denied even primary education. Women unfortunately have two-thirds shares of the illiterate adults. In spite that the literacy gap between men and women is narrowing. If the present trend is not altered, achieving universal primary education by 2015 would be missed at least by a decade.

Unfortunately, more than 300 million children (about 175 million are girls) are out of school at the primary and secondary levels. Most of the children who are not enrolled in the school system are mostly from sub-Saharan Africa and South Asia. Gender parity in primary and secondary enrolment is unlikely to be met by 2015. India and Pakistan and the sub-Saharan African countries would remain responsible for this shortfall. The intensity of education has advanced by half a year in the past decade. The average 'year of schooling' in South Asia (less than 4 years) is less than half the level in high-income countries. While the gap in average primary level enrolment is declining between the rich and the poor countries (rich countries already have near 100 percent enrolment), the difference in 'average year of schooling' between the poor and the rich countries is widening. Access to higher education remains a privilege of the rich countries in general and the richer segment of the population in the poorer countries in particular.

Clear evidences are there that income poverty intensity has been falling. *Head count* remains the most popular method in estimating people lying below poverty line. Countries have different benchmark for drawing poverty lines (even different poverty lines for different states or regions within the same country) and therefore no comparable estimate of intensity of poverty from that information is available. UNDP uses $1 per day per capita (presently it is revised to $1.25) as the poverty line (there are legitimate criticisms against this being used as the poverty line) to chart cross-country poverty trends. Such a static indicator often would fail to grasp the dynamic nature of poverty. Whatever criticism is raised against using $1 a day as the poverty line, poverty reduction trends can be established even by this static point. Whereas 28 percent of people of the world were below this line in 1990, the same declined to 21 percent in 2003. In absolute number, it is seen that there are 130 million fewer people below the poverty line today. Even then, over 1.2 billion people live on less than $1 a day (1993 PPP US $) and another 1.5 billion people between $1 and $2 a day. About 40 percent of the world population constitutes a global underclass. It is estimated that over 850 million people including children suffer from malnutrition. Malnutrition weakens the immune system. It is therefore no wonder that malaria, tuberculosis, measles and other infectious and parasitic diseases cause death and disability to millions, especially children, in the poorer countries.

Poverty reduction can be achieved only by economic growth and its equitable distribution among people. In the 1990s, the average annual economic growth rate in the developing countries was 1.5 percent. Since 2000, the growth rate has increased to 3.4 percent per annum (over 6 percent since 2004) – double the average growth rate in the high-income countries. Of course there are wide variations between regions and countries in economic growth rate – countries in East Asia and the Pacific, which share 31 percent of world population, had grown at or around 6 percent between 1975–99; South Asian countries (23 percent of world total) grew by only around 2.3 percent (in spite India achieving average growth rate over 6 percent); Latin American and the Caribbean countries (share 8 percent of world population) by 0.8 percent, Arab States (4 percent of world population) by 0.25 percent and sub-Saharan African countries (10 percent of world population) by (–)1.0 percent. Sub-Saharan African countries have posted a 1.2 percent per capita GDP growth between 2000 and

2003 after more than two decades of declining average income. Even then, the average income in sub-Saharan Africa is lower today (2001) than what it was in 1990. Sub-Saharan Africa had almost 100 million people living on less than $1 a day in 2001. Central, Eastern Europe and the CIS registered a dramatic rise in poverty – number of people living with less than $2 a day rose from 23 million in 1990 to 93 million in 2001 in this region.

Table 12.5 *Decline in income poverty, 1981–2001*

Region	*1981*	*1984*	*1987*	*1990*	*1993*	*1996*	*1999*	*2001*
East Asia & the Pacific	56.7	38.8	28.0	29.5	24.9	15.9	15.3	14.3
Europe & Central Asia	0.8	0.6	0.4	0.5	3.7	4.4	6.3	3.5
Latin America & the Caribbean	10.1	12.2	11.3	11.6	11.8	9.4	10.5	9.9
Middle East & North Africa	5.1	3.8	3.2	2.3	1.6	2.0	2.7	2.4
South Asia	51.5	46.8	45.0	41.3	40.1	36.7	32.8	31.9
Sub-Saharan Africa	41.6	46.3	46.9	44.5	44.1	46.1	45.7	46.4
World	40.4	33.0	28.5	27.9	26.3	22.3	21.5	20.7

Source: World Bank 2005

Bangladesh and China are two fastest climbers in HDI. Since 1990 Bangladesh gained 14 places in HDI ranking with GDP ranking increasing only by 10 places. China, on the other hand, improved its GDP ranking by 32 places but HDI ranking climbed only by 20 places. As far as HDI is concerned, China's economic advances far outpaced social advances. The drivers of social change are different for different countries. Take the example of three countries, China, Bangladesh and Uganda who all have increased their HDI by over 20 percent since 1990. Undoubtedly, for China the principal driver in this change is their exceptional achievement in economic front. For Uganda, the upward HDI push comes principally from education, especially from school enrolment. The push also comes, on a small measure though, from economy. Bangladesh achieved a more balanced achievement in all the three fronts than what China and Uganda did.

For the policy makers, decomposed HDI is more important than HDI alone. Decomposition gives insight into the forthcoming challenges the countries must address for resource allocation for the greatest wellbeing of their people, more so for those who are lagging much behind others. Wealth generation is no guarantee to sustainable human development. Instances are there where a country has very high average income but the country's HDI appears not quite at par with the per capita GDP of the country.

Figure 12.5 *Different income similar HDI (adapted from HDR 2005)*

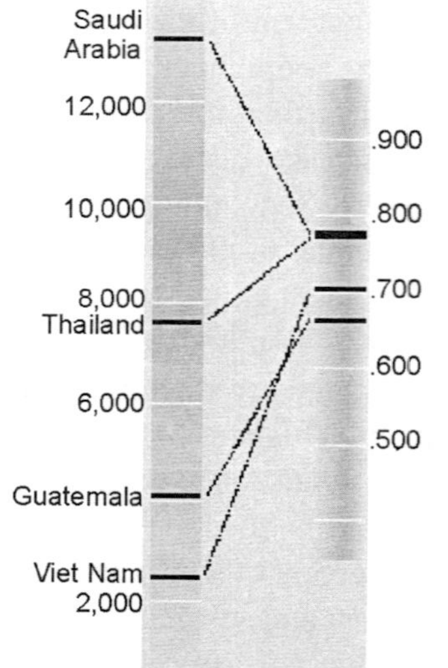

Saudi Arabia in 1999 had GDP per capita at $10,815 and HDI 0.754. Thailand had the same HDI as Saudi Arabia, but its per capita GDP, was only $6,132. Thailand's education index was 0.84 compared to Saudi Arab's 0.71. Mexico and Venezuela both had the same life expectancy and education index, but Mexico was ahead in HDI (0.790) compared to Venezuela's HDI of 0.765. Large gaps seen between GDP and HDI rankings (GDPI–HDI) is taken as an indicator of structural inequalities that block the transmission from wealth creation to human development.

On the average, people born in a developing country today can expect being wealthier, healthier and better educated than their earlier generations. They also are more likely to live in a multi-party democracy and less likely to be affected by conflict. Since 1990, the world has witnessed the disintegration of the Soviet Union, violent conflict in Eastern Europe, West Asia, and genocide in wars in Afghanistan and Iraq and in many other parts of the world. Despite the challenges posed for human development by violent conflict, there are some positive signs. Although the last 15 years have seen many civil wars, the number of conflicts has fallen since 1990 through negotiation under UN auspices.

Many perceive democracy as a fundamental aspect of human development when it is conceived as 'freedom to choose and participate in social, economic and political decision-making processes'. Democracy by itself therefore is a human development indicator and a means towards wider human development goals. Multi-party elections – now the world's preferred form of governance – are one such condition.

Most democracies admit independent judiciary, put constraints on executive power, give freedom to the press and respect human rights. Such admissions give substance to the form of electoral choice.[2] The multi-party democracy has risen from 39 percent to 56 percent since 1990. That is, 1.4 billion more people are living under multi-party democracies today. Even two-thirds of people in violence-stricken Africa now live under multi-party democratic governance. But it must not be forgotten that multi-party elections can often provide a smokescreen that obscures overbearing executive power, limitations on press freedom and human rights abuses that strip democracy of its meaning. Even elections are rigged; violent deaths result as a result of serious conflict between political parties. There are corruption at various levels; taking decisions on most issues often take a very long time for reasons of achieving consensus; policy decisions on volatile issues like labor and economic reforms, abolition of subsidies, taxation policy, foreign direct investment in key sectors and many other internal and external issues, especially when a combine of different political parties are in the treasury bench. Of the world's two most populous countries, India is a thriving democracy, but in China political reforms have lagged behind economic reforms. China has gone ahead with its economic reform agenda unhindered by any open opposition. India had to struggle even to open up its economy by stages. Manmohan Singh nearly sacrificed his UPA government to get the Indo-US nuclear agreement through.

Gender parity and empowerment cut a sorry figure across countries, especially in the poorer ones. Gender inequality is a major barrier to poverty reduction and progress in health and educational attainments. India, the largest democracy in the world, still has a poor track record in elimination of gender bias. Mortality among girls aged 1–5 is 50 percent higher than that for boys. The higher mortality rates among girls and women from birth to about age 30 years upsets the normal demographic balance, pointing to structural inequalities in nutrition, healthcare and status.

2 A conflict is brewing up between judiciary and legislators in India over many issues as accountability of legislators, criminal proceedings against elected members, caste-based reservation in higher studies and employment, ban on certain trade union activities that disrupt civic life, and etc.

This probably is the plausible explanation of "missing women" in South Asia in general and India and China in particular.

Gender equality is generally poor in Muslim countries, but that does not mean that Islam necessarily is an obstacle to female empowerment. Malaysia has GEM above Greece, Hungary or Uruguay and not far behind Poland, Mexico, and Japan. There is also no evidence that female empowerment improves with higher levels of income. Japan, Italy and Singapore have per capita GDP income above US $ 20,000, yet their performances in GEM are poor. Sri Lanka, Columbia, Ukraine, Russian Federation and Belize have female legislators, senior officials and managers as percentage of total in excess of 35 percent, yet GEM in most of these countries are far less than 0.500.

Female empowerment is a much more complex social issue than HDI, HPI or GDI. Religion, social norms, political culture and public attitudes matter as much as democratic governance, economic wealth and overall human development in defining opportunities for women. A bill intending to ensure women's representation in parliament and assemblies has been lying with the Indian parliament for years since no political consensus could be reached.

12.5 Inequality and Human Development

MDGs and HDI do not directly address to inequality since they both are 'distribution neutral'. Any change in these is measured by aggregating and averaging at the national level. Targets in child and infant mortality reduction, school enrolment ratio, gender equality, access to safe water and sanitation, access to electricity, life expectancy growth and income growth, etc. could be achieved at the national level by improvement of these parameters in selected population groups – urban population, high income groups, male population, organized workforce, etc. even though the poorer and deprived section of the population – the rural poor, backward communities and women – could show only marginal or no improvement in these areas. That is, rate of improvement in one small segment of the population in education, health care and income could grossly compensate the deficits among peoples in other sectors. India still has a poor 4 years of intensity of schooling, yet the size of scientific and technical manpower (in absolute number) is envy to many developed countries.

The country level data may show a good convergence in human development indices. The Table 12.6 and the Figure 12.6 show that there is considerable convergence between Medium and High HDI categories but there is hardly any convergence in the two other differences – High-Low and Medium-Low. This is in spite the fact that in some critical areas the inequalities across nations have declined. The Low HDI countries have improved adult literacy and combined enrolment ratio in schools, but have faltered both in life expectancy and GDP per capita. They lost about 6.6 years in life expectancy and per capita income by $154 during 2000–03.

Table 12.6 *Divergence and convergence of the countries in different HDI categories*

HDI categories	*1975*	*1980*	*1985*	*1990*	*1995*	*2000*	*2003*
High-Low	0.458	0.444	0.446	0.451	0.457	0.469	0.468
High-Medium	0.265	0.244	0.233	0.207	0.206	0.218	0.196
Medium-Low	0.193	0.200	0.213	0.244	0.251	0.251	0.272

Computed from Human Development Report 2005.

Figure 12.6 *Divergence/convergence in HDI over the years*

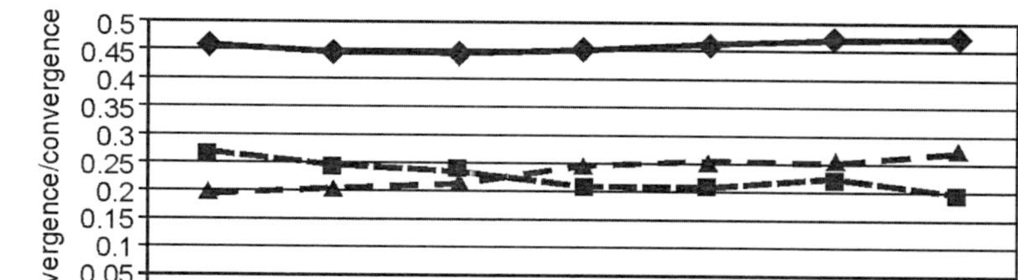

Whereas life expectancy and literacy gaps between countries of the world are converging, income growth has varied considerably among countries. It is both converging and diverging – with some regions closing the gap and others drifting away. In 1960, per capita income in East Asia and the Pacific, South Asia, sub-Saharan Africa and the least developed countries together had around 1/10 of the per capita income of the high income OECD countries. Latin America and the Caribbean did better in economic front – they had from 1/3 to 1/2 of the per capita income of the OECD countries. In 40 years since 1960, the bunching was broken. East Asia and the Pacific registered an impressive income growth. The ratio of its income to that of OECD countries currently stands at around 1/5. South Asia faltered badly in the 1970s and then made up in the 1980s and 1990s. But the GDP ratio still remains at 1/10 of the OECD countries. Sub-Saharan Africa performed very badly since 1960 and its GDP ratio to OECD income deteriorated from 1/9 in 1960 to about 1/18 in 1998. Latin America and the Caribbean's maintained their standard relative to that of OECD. The fastest growing region is East Asia and the Pacific followed by South Asia.

If the world were a country, it would have had an average purchasing power parity income of $5,533 and a median income of $1,700 in 2000. The difference between the average and the median indicates concentration of income at the higher end. 80 percent of the world population lives below the average income. The average income of the top 20 percent is 50 times that of the poorest 20 percent. One in every two persons in sub-Saharan Africa are located among the poorest 20 percent of the world population compared to one in every five in East Asia and the Pacific and one in every four in South Asia. The richest countries overwhelmingly dominate the top 20 percent with nine of every ten of their citizens finding a place in that celebrity category. Latin America and the Caribbean shows very high inequality in income distribution – 25 percent of the region's population are in the top 20 percent income category and more than 8 percent are in the poorest 20 percent of the global income distribution. The global income inequality continued to increase till about early 1990s. Incomes in China and India (over 2.4 billion peoples between them) in specific and the income surge in East Asia and the Pacific in general have succeeded in the reversal of the trend. Income growth rates in China and India are at a much higher level (over 8 percent) than are found in the developed economies. If we compare incomes of the poorest 10 percent with that of the richest 10 percent of the world population, the inequality appears more glaring, 1:103. The global wealth is so much concentrated in the hands of a few wealthy countries that a small transfer of this wealth either directly in the form of aids and debt relief or by transfer of technology on easy terms and abolition/substantial reduction of subsidies to food and other export goods, could generate very large increases in incomes of the poor. UNDP calculation shows that to bring 1 billion people above the now below $1 poverty line (2000 purchasing power parity) would require $300 billion to be transferred to the poorest countries. This is equivalent to less than 2 percent of the income of the richest 10 percent of the world's population, or less than the subsidies they give to their farmers to maintain their dominance in the world food market.

The developments in the last decade for most of the poorer countries have been disheartening – the poverty level in these countries has not been reduced much and some even have fallen further behind the rich countries; even their per capita income has declined. About two-thirds of global income inequality is accounted for by inequality between the countries and rest by inequalities within the countries.

Table 12.7 *Cross country study of per capita GDP (PPP US $) distribution*

Income range (US $)	*Number of countries*	*Percentage to total number of countries*
<2,000	42	24.71
2,000–4,000	24	14.12
4,000–7,000	36	21.18
7,000–12,000	22	12.94
12,000–20,000	21	12.35
20,000–30,000	16	9.41
>30,000	9	5.29
Total	170	100

Computed from HDR 2005.

There are about 25 percent of the countries (42 countries) where a common man has to live with per capita GDP income of less than $2,000. As many as 14 countries (13 from sub-Saharan Africa and one country Yemen from Arab States) reported per capita GDP income less than $1,000 (Sierra Leon had per capita GDP at $548). On the other extreme are over 27 percent countries (46 numbers) where per capita GDP is in excess of $20,000 (9 countries have per capita income over $30,000, Luxembourg has a sky high income of $62,299 per capita).

Regional composition of the poorest people has been changing. Around 1980, one half of the poorest 20 percent of the world population lived in South Asia. It is one-third today. It is likely to decline to 20 percent or even less by 2015.

Sub-Saharan Africa has been witnessing decline in average income since 1980. From around 15 percent share of the poorest 20 percent of the world population in 1980,

Figure 12.7 *Shifting share of the world's poorest (HDR 2005)*

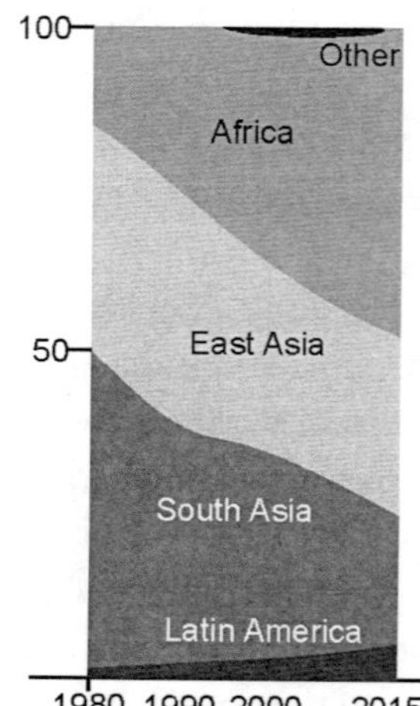

sub-Saharan Africa has more than doubled (36 percent) its share in the last two decades. By 2015 more than 45 percent of the poor of the world would be from sub-Saharan Africa. Every second person in this region would belong to the club of the poorest 20 percent of the world. One in every five persons in East Asia and the Pacific still are among the poorest 20 percent of the world.

It is widely accepted that income inequality between countries and between individuals is an inevitable outcome when market forces dominate the world economies. We looked at income inequality between the poor and rich countries. We turn our attention to inequalities within the countries. It is a fact that households with low income are also frequently denied adequate health care, have poor access to safe sources of drinking water, sanitation and electricity. The following Table gives a glimpse at how income inequality within the country leads to discrimination in many vital areas. Extreme inequalities in opportunity and life-chance have a direct bearing on what people can be and what they can do – that is, on human capabilities. People who are poor-share the larger share of deprivation than people who are not. Accelerated progress among the poor is probably the most effective route for faster national progress.

Table 12.8 *Statistical indicators of rich-poor gap in a few selected countries*

Country	*Share of GDP (%)*		*Births attended by skilled hands (%)*		*One-year-olds fully immunized (%)*		*Infant mortality rate*		*Under five mortality rate*	
	Poorest	*Richest*	*Poorest*	*Richest*	*Poorest*	*Richest*	*Poorest*	*Richest*	*Poorest*	*Richest*
Brazil	2.4	63.2	71.6	98.6	56.6	73.8	83.2	28.6	98.9	33.3
Niger	2.8	53.3	4.2	62.8	4.6	50.9	131.1	85.8	281.8	183.7
Peru	2.9	53.2	13.0	87.5	57.9	81.1	63.5	13.9	92.6	17.6
Zambia	3.3	56.6	19.7	91.1	63.9	80.0	115.2	56.7	191.7	92.4
Bolivia	4.0	49.1	19.8	97.9	21.8	30.6	106.5	3.9	146.5	25.5
India	8.9	43.3	16.4	84.4	21.3	63.8	96.5	38.1	141.3	45.5

Compiled from HDR 2005.

Chances of staying alive are often limited when somebody is born in a poor household. Most probably the child would be born unattended by a doctor or a paramedical staff. The chance of the child's survival till his/her first birthday is far less if he/she is not born in a rich household. The chance of survival of the child in a poor household beyond age 5 is really bleak. There are countries where IMR and child mortality in the 20 percent poorest households are four to five times higher than that of the children born in the 20 percent richest households. Instances are plentiful that show that maternal mortality among women in the poorest 20 percent is several times higher than that among women in the richest 20 percent. Women who die during pregnancy or birth related causes would most likely be without much formal education and very many of them would not have sufficient nutritious food during the period of pregnancy, or access to safe sources of drinking water and sanitation. They are less likely to have received any prenatal healthcare. Even if their children survive, they are unlikely to be immunized against many of the avoidable diseases.

Poverty creates a vicious cycle. The children born in a poor household are less likely to survive or get some meaningful education. Children who even do not complete school education are

Figure 12.8 *Share of GDP by the poorest and richest 20% of the population*

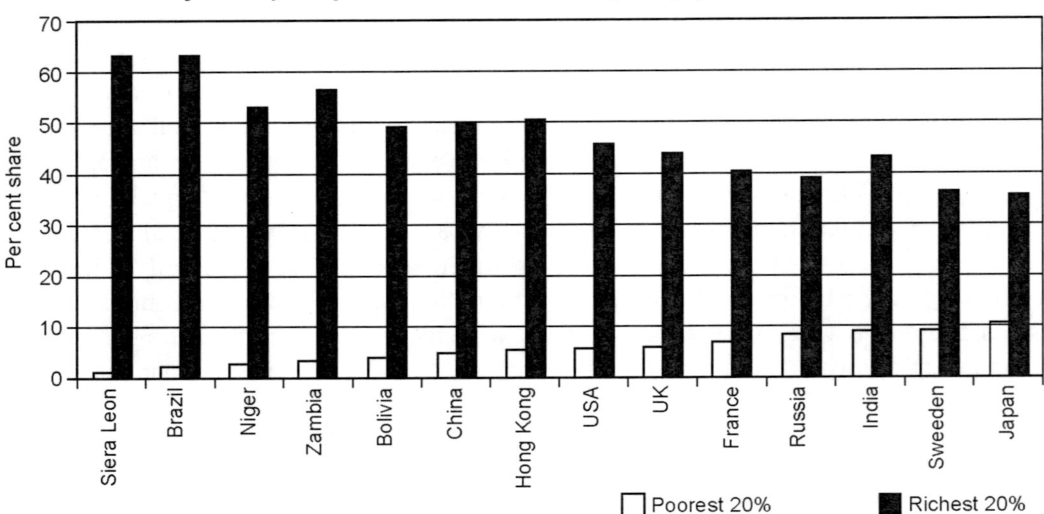

unlikely to develop skills necessary for a good job and respectable income. When they themselves become parents, they would fail to provide basic necessities to their children. The cycle of deprivation is transmitted through generations. The poor in the rich countries too have unequal basic life chances. A poor person from a developed country may have better basic life chances compared to a poor born in a poor country. Yet large inequalities are observed almost in every aspect of social, economic and political life in the developed countries. A person in the poorest 5 percent in USA will have 25 percent truncated life expectancy compared to those in the richest 5 percent. While there are other social and economic barriers, financial matters remain the most important contributor to inequality in health, education and consumption.

The poor are most deprived in the poorest of the poor countries. The differences in the share of country's GDP between the richest 20 percent and poorest 20 percent in the poorer countries often are more than twice than that in the rich countries. The extent to which the distribution of income/consumption within a country deviates from a balanced distribution is measured by Gini index. A value of 0 is indicative of perfect equality, a value of 100 perfect inequality. A value in excess of 50 is usually reckoned as high degree of inequality.

Income inequality varies widely across regions. South Asia has the lowest Gini index, 33.4 (Figure 12.9), even smaller than that in high-income OECD countries. All the other regions, including East Asia and the Pacific, display high degree of income inequality. Sub-Saharan Africa as a region displays the highest degree of income inequality (over 72).

The more balanced an income distribution, the less is income inequality. Brazil's average income is three

Figure 12.9 *Gini coefficient (income distribution HDR 2005)*

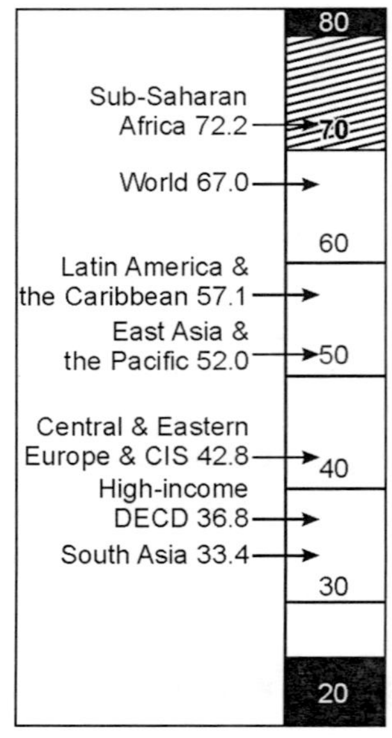

times higher than the average income in Vietnam. But the poorest 20 percent in Brazil have an average income far smaller than that among the poorest 20 percent in Vietnam. Similar examples are plentiful across countries. This tends to suggest that per capita GDP/average income often obscures the distribution pattern of real welfare. Ranking of many countries in HDI would go down had GDP indexes been computed on the average income of the poorest 20 percent instead of the usual average income in the population. Brazil, for example, would have gone down in ranking by 52 places had the country's GDP been revised on the income average of the poorest 20 percent, life and education indices remaining the same. Even Sweden, where inequality between the rich and the poor is relatively small, would go down in HDI ranking from 6 to 25 had the calculations been based on the poorest 20 percent.

Table 12.9 *Difference in HDI ranks based on national average and the poorest 20 percent for a selected few countries*

Country	*HDI rank*		
	Whole population	*Poorest 20%*	*Difference*
Mexico	53	108	55
Brazil	63	115	52
Chile	36	85	49
Argentina	34	78	44
Thailand	72	108	36
Russian Federation	62	95	33
Belarus	66	98	32
China	85	115	30
United States	10	31	21
Sweden	6	25	19

Source: Human Development Report, 2005

Table 12.10 *Inequalities within selected few countries (HDR 2005)*

Country	*Gini coefficient*	*Country*	*Gini coefficient*	*Country*	*Gini coefficient*
Namibia	70.7	Philippines	46.1	Sri Lanka	33.2
Brazil	59.3	China	44.7	France	32.7
South Africa	57.8	Thailand	43.2	India	32.5
Chile	57.1	Kenya	42.5	Russian Fed.	31.0
Zimbabwe	56.8	United States	40.9	Ethiopia	30.0
Mexico	54.6	Viet Nam	37.0	Albania	28.2
Zambia	52.6	United Kingdom	36.0	Hungary	26.9
Argentina	52.2	Egypt	34.4	Sweden	25.0
Malaysia	49.2	Poland	34.1	Japan	24.9

There are other layers of inequality in all countries, rich and poor. There is discrimination by race and ethnicity, by location (urban-rural), by occupation, by gender, by wealth along with other pointers for disadvantage. They interact to create reinforcing cycles of disadvantages that continue to perpetuate through generations.

The incidence of poverty and other deprivation is widespread among backward castes and indigenous groups in India. One good thing about Indian economy is that income inequality (Gini coefficient 32.5) is not as strong as are observed in many developed and developing countries (Table

12.10). The inequality in per capita consumption expenditure (1999–2000) is less strong in rural areas (Gini coefficient 25.8, ranging from 14.9 in Meghalaya to 27.9 in Tamil Nadu among the states) than in urban areas (Gini coefficient 34.1, from a low of 20.5 in Meghalaya to 39.8 in Tamil Nadu).

China moved 14 places up in HDI ranking during 1990s. This the country achieved primarily due to extremely fast GDP growth with per capita income rising three-folds at constant purchasing power terms. But indications are plenty that progress in many social sectors is starting to lag behind the economic growth performance. The gaps between the rich and poor provinces are widening. Child mortality is increasing by 0.5 percent for girls while it is declining by 2.3 percent a year for boys. With market reforms, the onus of healthcare financing has been shifted to households. Although China spends 5 percent of GDP on healthcare, over 60 percent of health financing has been privatized. Over 70 percent of rural population has no health insurance cover.

Most democratically elected governments accept in principle that extra attention needs to be given to improvement of wellbeing of the poor and the disadvantaged. The policy makers are trying to work out a growth model that would insure faster GDP growth and enough domestic savings for investment and at the same time see that the resulting income growth reaches reasonably well to the poor and the disadvantaged. That is, performance of the state in the economic front is to be judged by the degree by which the generated income relates to poverty reduction. Most democratic governments have realized that a concession or subsidy or an increase in the minimum wage rate to ease the life of the poor would pay back to the nation in the long run than if a similar package were offered to the wealthier section of the population. The redistribution mechanics suffer a jolt when the inequality is very sharp and the numbers of the poor and the disadvantaged are huge.

Any sum spent on child healthcare and extending access to education is welcome for the simple reason that it would help the poor and the disadvantaged to equip themselves to participate and contribute meaningfully to national growth. With the fast changes observed in technology up-gradation in today's market-driven economy, there would be increased demand for educated and skilled workers across countries. The democratic governments would find space to concentrate on developing the social infrastructure if the financial sector is left to the market, of course with an efficient regulatory mechanism put in place.

Income inequality analysis of the data available for different countries makes it amply clear that so long income inequality remains strong the possibility of achieving equality in other areas of human wellbeing and enlarging peoples' choice would remain a far cry. The income inequality would come down as the poor people start to contribute significantly to the growth process. This they can do when they are assured of good health and have access to quality education. Increased output and rising productivity are key to their greater share to the increments to growth than they do now.

12.6 Gender Disparities

Human Development Index is a versatile index that captures performance of countries as providers of basic necessities to their populations. However, since HDI is a measure of average achievement, it masks the differences in human development between men and women. GDI makes amend to that.

HDR 2005 has detailed information for computing HDI for as many as 177 countries. GDI is computed for 140 countries for which required information are available. Related information for GDI are lacking for many of the high and medium human development countries. For about 21 percent of the countries' GDI rankings are lower than their HDI; more than one-third of them are from High HDI countries. The rank differences in a few instances are as high as 5. Only Trinidad and Tobago among High HDI countries had GDI less than 0.800. None of the Low HDI countries had GDI in excess of 0.500. None of the Medium HDI countries had GDI in excess of 0.800, but 3 of them displayed GDI short of 0.500. Average GDI (0.697) for these countries was very close to the average HDI (0.706) for all countries. Considerable drop in GDI ranking compared to HDI ranking was observed for Ireland (–3), Japan (–3) and Chili (–3) among the high HDI countries. Finland moved up by 3 spots in GDI ranking over its HDI rank. Oman, Saudi Arabia, Peru, Lebanon, Paraguay, Belize, and Pakistan – all from Medium HDI group had GDI ranks smaller than their HDI ranks, by 4 or 5 steps. Yemen is the only country in Low HDI whose GDI ranking was 4 points behind its HDI ranking. India had the same rank both in HDI and GDI. These observations seem to indicate that gender equality is not very closely related to the country's income level or the stage of human development the country is in. The results also seem to indicate that gender equality can be achieved across cultures.

HDR 2005 reports GEM for 80 countries (High HDI 46, Medium HDI 31 and Low HDI 3). Top three countries in GEM are Norway (0.928), Denmark (0.860) and Sweden (0.852). The lowest GEM recorded is 0.123 (Yemen). Average GEM for High HDI countries is 0.667, the same for Medium HDI countries is 0.432. As many as 10 countries have GEM in excess of 0.800. In 1997, only Norway had GEM more than 0.800. Only 33 countries achieved a GEM of more than 0.500 in 1997. In 2003, 52 countries (65 percent of the countries for which GEM is available) achieved GEM larger than 0.500. Included in this list is Tanzania, which has better GEM (0.538) than it's HDI (0.418). Four countries in High HDI category that achieved GEM of less than 0.500 are Bahrain (0.393), Chile (0.475), Korean Republic (0.479) and Malta (0.486). GEM data confirms that by strengthening the capabilities of women more and more opportunities are created asking them to participate in economic and political life.

Even though Bangladesh has done remarkably well in improving the country's HDI in the last 15 years, the country's GEM score has declined from 0.304 in 1997 to 0.218 in 2003. This is in spite the fact that both the posts of the Prime Minister and the Leader of the Opposition have been held by women in Bangladesh in the last 15 years. Females' share is only 2 percent in the parliament; female senior officials and managers constitute about 8 percent and the estimated ratio of female to male earned income is 0.54. With almost similar HDI as Bangladesh, GEM of Pakistan is 0.379. In spite of better representation in the parliament (20.6 per cent), female representation as legislators and senior officials is a meager 2 percent in Pakistan and the ratio of female to male earned income is a poor 0.34.

Some developing countries like Rwanda, Costa Rica, Grenada, South Africa, Mozambique and a few others have outperformed Japan, Italy, France, UK, USA and a few other developed countries in gender equality in political and professional activities. The distribution of GEM and its components carry a significant message: high income is not a prerequisite to creating opportunities for women in public life.

12.7 Poverty and Deprivation

HDR 2005 puts 57 countries in High Human Development, 88 in Medium Human Development and 32 in Low Human Development category. HPI includes 22 countries from High HDI, 85 from

Medium HDI and all the 32 countries from Low HDI. HPI–1 is however calculated for a total of 103 countries (all considered developing) from among 139 countries in the list. The HPI–1 data reveals the following:

- The human poverty ranges from a low of 3.8 percent in Uruguay to a high of 64.4 percent in Niger. All the 10 countries in High HDI category included in this series had HPI less than 10 percent.
- HPI–1 score for medium HDI group ranged from 8.5 percent in occupied Palestinian Territories to 48.4 percent in Botswana. There were as many as 20 countries in this group that displayed HPI–1 over 30 percent.
- The lowest HPI–1 score among Low HDI countries is 35.3 percent. There are 7 countries in this cluster that registered more than 50 percent HPI–1.
- A comparison of HDI and HPI–1 values shows that the countries can have similar HDI but different HPI–1 values (Qatar and Chile, Ethiopia and Burundi, for example).
- Correlation between the HDI and HPI–1 ranks for the countries is almost perfect, indicating high HPI–1 among low HDI and low HPI among high HDI countries.

The disaggregated HPI–1 data show strong disparities in poverty between the states in India. Human deprivation is highest in Bihar (HPI 52 percent) and least in Kerala (20 percent). The disaggregated data also document a better progress in human development and less deprivation for people in urban areas than those in rural areas (HPI in urban area 22 percent, that in rural area 45 percent in 1991).

18 industrialized countries have been included in HPI–2 in HDR 2005. Sweden has the lowest human poverty with HPI–2 at 6.5 percent followed by Norway (7 percent), Netherlands and Finland (both at 8.2 percent). Highest HPI–2 is recorded in Italy, with 29.9 percent. UK, USA and Ireland have HPI–2 around 15 percent. Luxembourg has the highest per capita GDP ($62,298), yet its human poverty level is considerably high, 11.1 percent. All the 18 countries included in HPI–2 list have HDI in excess of 0.928 and per capita income not less than $26,000. Achieving high human development does not necessarily eliminate human deprivation. Netherlands and UK have almost the same HDI, yet HPI–2 of UK is close double that in the former. Italy, with education index 0.95, still has 47 percent of population in 16–65 age groups lacking functional literacy. In UK and USA 21.8 and 20 percent respectively of the adults have no functional literacy (they mostly include the immigrant and non-white population). Long-term unemployment as percentage to total workforce in France and Italy is as high as 4.2 and 5.1 percent respectively. 17 percent of the population in USA (mostly non-White) were below 50 percent of country's median income in 1999–2000. The same in Australia and Canada were 14.3 and 12.8 percent respectively.

Figure 12.10 *Same HDI but different HPI*

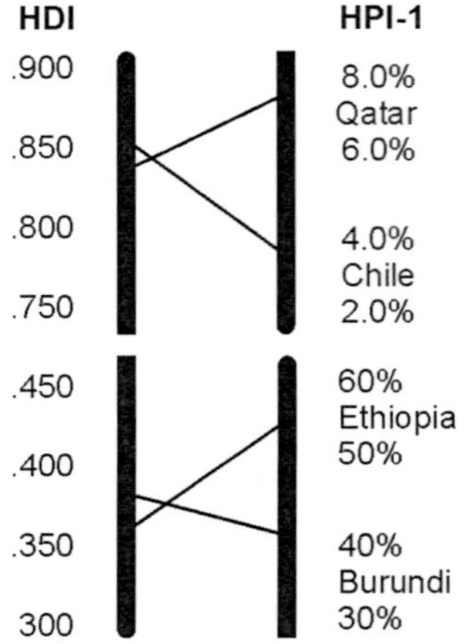

13 Population and Development

13.1 Introduction

There are very distinct signals that the human civilization may face a most devastating crisis in the twenty-first century and the root cause behind this would be the phenomenal rise in numbers, which already has reached a point of explosion. Vulnerability syndromes of modern-technology-based civilization are the 4 Ps – population, poverty, pollution and proliferation (of nuclear weapons). Population is precursor to the other three.

From a low of 1,600 million around 1900 AD, the estimated world population was around 6,514 million in 2005. We are taking around 12 years to add 1,000 million to our existing totals. The world average annual growth rate (1.6 percent between 1975–2005.) is likely to come down to around 1.1 percent between 2005 and 2015 and the size of the world population would be around 7,296 million in 2015 (HDR, 2007/08). Although the developing countries are likely to contribute most (126 million) in overshooting the population target, OECD countries also are likely to contribute 24 million for this missed target. Arab States (53 million), South Asia (39 million) and Latin America and the Caribbean (16 million) are likely to contribute most to this addition over the MDG goal. Even with increased mortality due to high prevalence of HIV/AIDS, sub-Saharan Africa would overshoot the region's MDG target by 11 million. If India fails to achieve the average growth rate of 1.3 percent between 2003 and 2015, it alone could have over 1,300 million to world population of 7,296 million in 2015. If the world population continues to grow at or around the present level, an individual may have less than 1 square meter of land space to stand upon in less than 600 years.

At the start of the new millennium, the world's governments gathered at the United Nations and made a solemn promise to eradicate victims of global poverty. They signed the Millennium Declaration – a pledge "to free our fellow men, women and children from the abject and dehumanizing conditions of extreme poverty". The declaration (see Chapter 12) provides a bold vision rooted in a shared commitment to universal human rights and social justice and a commitment to meet time-bound targets – the Millennium Development Goals (MDGs). These include halving extreme poverty, cutting child deaths, providing education for all children, rolling back infectious and parasitic diseases and diseases due to nutritional deficiency and forging a new global partnership to deliver results. The deadline for delivery is 2015.

After five years the countries met again to review the report card. The report card is more than depressing. Most countries, especially the poorer countries, are off track for most of the MDGs. Uncontrolled growths of population always accompany many other troubles that really disturbs and distorts all development efforts. The poor and the disadvantaged countries are falling behind the developed ones. The little bit of growth in economic activities that are achieved are likely to be mopped up just in providing the basic minimums to the growing mouths.

There are several areas that have already been hit hard by rapid growth of population. We select only a few major areas where developments cannot be understood without reference to growth of population.

13.2 Economic Development

The world today is distinctly divided between two levels of economy – economy of the affluent and that of the backward ones. In the developed economies are the countries like USA, Japan, Canada, Australia and most of the European countries; Third World countries (most of Asian, African and Latin American countries) constitute the less developed block. With the breaking away of Soviet Union and East European countries, the Second World countries have almost vanished. The world has become uni-polar.

Between 1950 and 1970, the average annual growth rate of GDP was around 5 percent in the low-income countries contrasted to 2–4 percent in the high-income nations. If per capita GDP is computed, which is more meaningful than GDP, the average economic growth in low-income country works out at 2.2 percent per annum against 3.4 percent or higher in the high-income countries. Whereas the low-income countries' population grew on an average by 2.4 percent annually in 1970s and 1980s, the annual population growth rate in the same period in high-income countries was 1 percent or smaller. Presently, most developed countries have population growth rates close to zero; some even have negative growth rates. Even with higher growth rate of GDP, the low-income countries have failed to improve the general standard of living of their people. United Nations has estimated that the less developed countries require 1–5 percent increase in savings simply to provide the necessary capital to maintain the living standard at a constant level. The population in India between 1971 and 1984 grew by about 2.25 percent annually. The GDP in the same period grew by 3.36 percent (at 1970–71 price level) and the per capita income grew only by a meager 1.21 percent. That is, the quantum of increase in income of an average Indian fell short of the required increase even for maintaining the same standard of living. In the nineties GDP growth rate in India hovered over 6 percent and population growth rate around 1.9 percent per annum. Per capita income grew by twice or more as much as the growth between 1971 and 1984.

Economists till recently believed that if an economy can grow sufficiently rapidly (5 percent or more), the general wellbeing of the whole population will improve or at least its capacity for improvement will be enhanced. A number of studies have shown that despite high income growth in the low-income world, the actual economic welfare achieved for the common man is only marginal because of highly skewed income distribution.

Myrdal has shown that inequalities are increasing more rapidly with economic growth in India. More and more economists today also feel that economic growth does not automatically assure prosperity to common man. As long the causes of poverty and unemployment are not seriously addressed, they argue, income inequality would shoot up with every increase in GDP. Alleviation of poverty, generation of employment and reduction in inequality among others are looked into as milestones for a developed economy.

Today 5,215 million people (2005) belong to the Third World countries out of an estimated 6,514 million over the entire globe. About 1,200 million people would be below the poverty line, all from the Third World countries. The tide of poverty that engulfed the world previously has started to take a turn. The proportion of population below the poverty line (below US $ 1 per head per day) has come down considerably; the decline has slowed down since 1996. Sub-Saharan Africa is to take the major blame for that. Nearly 100 million more people in this region are living on less than US $ 1 a day than what it was in 1990. Average incomes in sub-Saharan Africa are even smaller than what that was in 1990. There is a large variation between countries and between regions. The most remarkable change has occurred in the countries in East Asia and the Pacific; in just twenty years poverty ratio in the region has come down from 56.7 to 14.3. The poverty ratio saw a dramatic decline in the 1990s. This has been possible mostly due to China emerging as a major economic power. Performance of South Asian region in controlling poverty is also noteworthy (from 51.5 percent in 1981 to 31.9 percent in 2001). India has contributed very significantly in reduction of poverty in this region. Global poverty reduction has been driven largely by these two regions, more specifically by two countries China and India. Latin America and the Middle East showed no signs of progress. The Central and Eastern Europe and the CIS registered an increase in poverty.

Since the middle of 1990s the poverty level is declining at one-fifth of the 1980–86 rates. This is despite the fact that average per capita growth rate in the developing countries in 1990s was more than double the same in the previous decade. Between 1990 and 2001 the incidence of $1 a day poverty declined by 50 percent. That is, 130 million fewer people are lying below the international poverty line today. 90 percent of this decline took place between 1980 and 1996.

Table 13.1 *Decline in income poverty[1], 1981–2001*

Region	*1981*	*1984*	*1987*	*1990*	*1993*	*1996*	*1999*	*2001*
East Asia & the Pacific	56.7	38.8	28.0	29.5	24.9	15.9	15.3	14.3
Europe & Central Asia	0.8	0.6	0.4	0.5	3.7	4.4	6.3	3.5
Latin America & the Caribbean	10.1	12.2	11.3	11.6	11.6	9.4	10.5	9.9
Middle East & North Africa	5.1	3.8	3.2	2.3	1.8	2.0	2.7	2.4
South Asia	51.5	46.8	45.0	41.3	40.1	36.7	32.8	31.9
Sub-Saharan Africa	41.6	46.3	46.9	44.5	44.1	46.1	45.7	46.4
World	40.4	33.0	28.5	27.9	26.3	22.3	21.5	20.7

Source: UNDP, HDR 2005
1. Population below US $ 1 per capita per day.

The progress of decline in income poverty has two economic components: economic growth and the share of this growth realized by the poor. Poverty reduction is not possible in a stagnating economy. Poverty reduction in East Asia is clearly associated with high income growth rate. Had India continued with 1 percent per capita annual income growth rate experienced during the two decades prior to 1980, it would have taken India 66 years to double the per capita income. Since 1980, average annual per capita income in India is growing by over 4 percent. With this per capita growth, incomes double in 17 years. Per capita growth of income is less encouraging in other regions. China reduced $1 per day poverty by 50 percent between 1990 and 2001, 90 percent of this came between 1990 and 1996. The average per capita income in sub-Saharan Africa is even lower today than it was in 1990. Recovery in recent years (1.2 percent growth rate) however has been noticed. Sub-Saharan Africa is likely to regain 1990 income levels by 2012. Central and Eastern Europe and the CIS experienced a dramatic turn around in population below $2 a day, from 23 million in 1990 to 93 million in 2001, that is, from 5 percent to 20 percent in the population. Middle East and Latin America did not show significant change in per capita income.

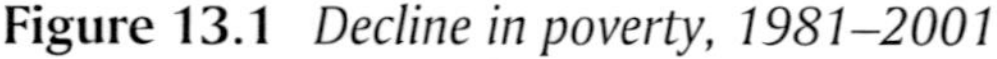
Figure 13.1 *Decline in poverty, 1981–2001*

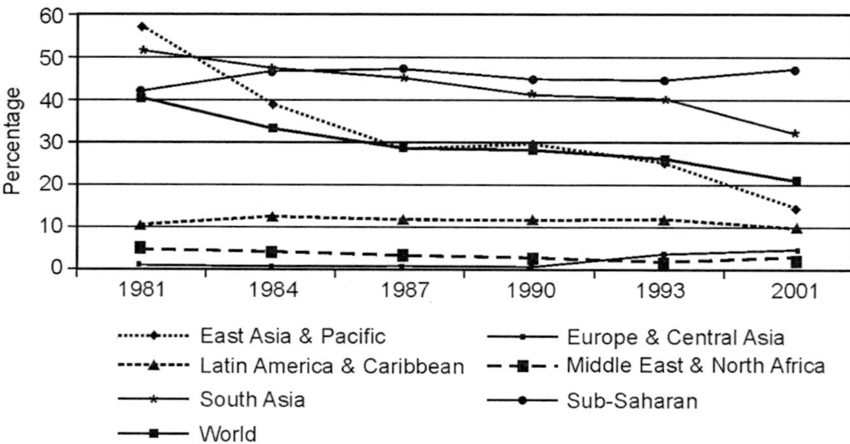

Estimates show that the economy of the developing countries have to grow between 1–2 percent per capita if poverty was to be halved within a span of 25 years. More than 1 billion people were living in countries that have annual per capita income growth rate below this level. 69 countries posted growth rates below 1 percent per capita. Under the globalization regime, volatility linked to capital markets marked the collapse of economies in many East Asian and Latin American countries in mid-1990s. Poverty in Argentina increased three-folds between 2000 and 2003. 30 million people were forced below international poverty line in Russia in the 1998 financial crisis.

Table 13.2 *Annual GDP per capita growth rate 1990–2003*

Region	***Countries/ populations[1]***	***Per capita growth rate***			
		Negative	***0%–1%***	***1%–2%***	***> 2%***
Arab States	Countries	5	4	2	5
	Population	34	70	19	139
East Asia & the Pacific	Countries	4	1	3	13
	Population	3	6	81	1,814
Latin America & the Caribbean	Countries	4	8	9	12
	Population	43	74	345	79
South Asia	Countries	0	0	1	7
	Population	0	0	152	1,324
Sub-Saharan Africa	Countries	18	8	8	11
	Population	319	108	171	76
Central & Eastern Europe & CIS	Countries	10	5	1	11
	Population	253	58	10	85
High income OECD	Countries	0	2	6	15
	Population	0	135	224	510
World	Countries	41	28	32	76
	Population	653	450	1,081	4,030

Source: UNDP, HDR 2005

1. In million

Health situation in the third world countries is generally poor by all standards. Nearly 70 percent of babies born in these countries would be without the necessary health care. One out of every third child would suffer from malnutrition. In absolute terms, this is likely to be 200 million. Some 3 million children would die every year because even the minimum of preventive care is unlikely to be provided to them. One million mothers would die every year from birth-related causes. Over 1 billion people would remain without sustainable access to safe drinking water and 2.6 billion without access to improved sanitation. Diseases transmitted through water and human waste are the second leading cause of death among children worldwide, after respiratory tract infection. Nearly 4,000 children die everyday, many of which could have been prevented through immunization, supply of safe drinking water and improved sanitation.

Controlling child mortality is the greatest challenge facing the international community today. The slowdown in progress since 1990 has set the world on a course of failure in meeting MDG. On current trends, the reduction of child mortality by 2/3 visualized in MDG could be achieved only in 2045, that is, we would be behind the schedule by 30 years. About 1/3 of the populations living in developing countries are likely to achieve the MDG target set for 2015, but none from countries in sub-Saharan Africa with large populations. Even this will remain unmet both in China and India. This would result in additional 4.4 million child deaths over and above the MDG target for the year 2015; almost all of them happening in the developing countries, especially in sub-Saharan Africa. On the current trends, the sub-Saharan Africa would take more than 100 years to achieve the child mortality level targeted for 2015.

Child death rates have an important bearing upon the availability of safe drinking water. According to HDR 2005, 1,037 million people in the developing countries are denied access to safe drinking water. Trend analysis suggests that the target of halving the number of people without sustainable access to safe water sources would be missed by about 210 million people. Another 2 billion people would also lack access to improved sanitation.

The principal reason for child death is income poverty. UNDP data suggest that halving the global poverty level would largely be achieved by 2015 if the present growth pattern in the poor countries continues and if a bigger share in increment in growth is captured by the poor. China and India are likely to contribute most in global poverty reduction. But most other developing countries are likely to miss the target.

In spite of very high economic growth rates achieved in China and India, investment in social sector, especially in health and education, has not improved much. Public expenditure on health as percentage of GDP in China has remained stationary at 2 percent between 1990 and 2002; the same in India remained at 1.3. Private expenditure on health

Figure 13.2 *Under-five child mortality gap between rich and poor (HDR 2005)*

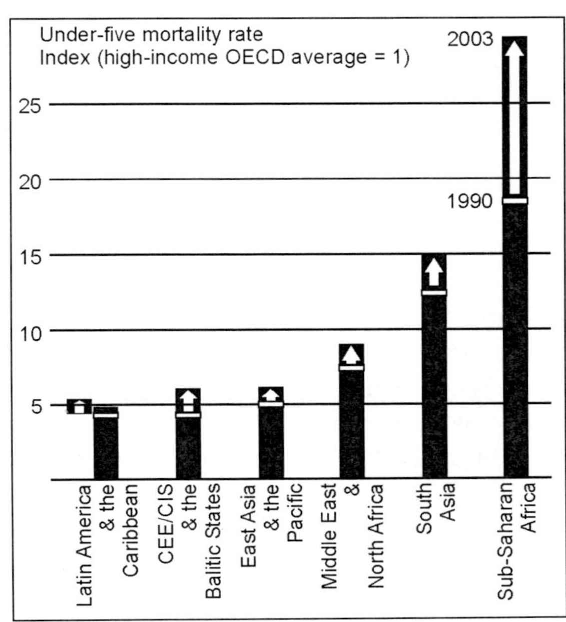

in India in 2003 was 4.8 percent of GDP and the same in China was 3.8 percent. This is in spite the fact that the two economies were growing at a robust pace. 14 and 23 percent of the respective populations in India and China are still without sustainable access to safe water. Expenditure pattern in social sector in most other developing countries is similar to that in China and India or even worse

In today's market driven economy, the national governments are forced to mobilize the limited resources at their disposal for infrastructure development (rail, road, port, communication, housing, etc.) to augment domestic and foreign direct investment in industrial sector. The domestic savings are just not sufficient to pay ample attention to the social sector after meeting commitments on infrastructure development. The GDP growth rate both in India and China is largely due to pouring of money from private sources in manufacturing, infrastructure and service sector. The impact of GDP growth is yet to be felt in the social sector.

There is no doubt that the living standards, absolute or relative, in all countries, developed and developing, are rising. The poorer countries have immense potential to increase their per capita income. Relative differences will narrow as long as the per capita income growth rate of the developing countries exceeds that of the developed countries. This excess growth is absolutely necessary if the absolute differences were to be narrowed down and eliminated in the long run. Narrowing of relative differences may even widen the absolute difference when the gap is very wide to start with. An average Indian, for example, lives on an equivalent of $564 (PPP US $ 2,892) compared with an average American living on $27,648 (PPP US $ 37,562) per annum. Suppose the Indian's income rises by 30 percent and the American's registers only a 5 percent increase in the same time. An Indian is now better off relative to his previous income, but is not he worse off compared to an average American? The American's command over goods and services far exceeds that of an Indian.

Although the GDP per capita has substantially gone up during the period of economic liberalization, income inequality between countries as also between the different segments of a population has not declined. Turning to the consideration of the distribution of world income in relation to the population, we find that the developing countries have to bear the burden of 79 percent of the world population and yet its share to world GDP is less than 20 percent. The least developed countries' share to world GDP is only 0.6 percent when its share of world total is over 11 percent. There is no evidence that the distribution of world income is narrowing.

In 1960, the richest 20 percent of the world population had income 30 times greater than that of the poorest 20 percent. In 1990, the ratio was 60 times greater. It is 103 in 2003. For most of the world's poorest countries the past decade has shown a disheartening trend – not only have they failed to reduce poverty, they are falling further behind rich countries.

It is easily forgotten that the rich-poor divide of nations is relatively a recent phenomenon. All countries were at subsistence level, and as recently as 200 years back at the time of industrial revolution, absolute differences in living standards between the countries on the average were not great. Whereas the high income OECD countries have per capita income well over $29,000, the average per capita income in the developing countries today is around $1,939 per annum, which is about the real per capita income measured at current prices in Western Europe around 150 years ago. It is true that living standards in the developing countries have been rising faster since the World War II. The same is true of the developed countries as well, but the gap between the rich and the poor countries is getting wider. Although development consists of more than a rise in per capita income, income inequalities between the countries are the essence of the so-called development gap.

Figure 13.3 *Growth convergence and absolute income convergence (reproduced from HDR 2005)*

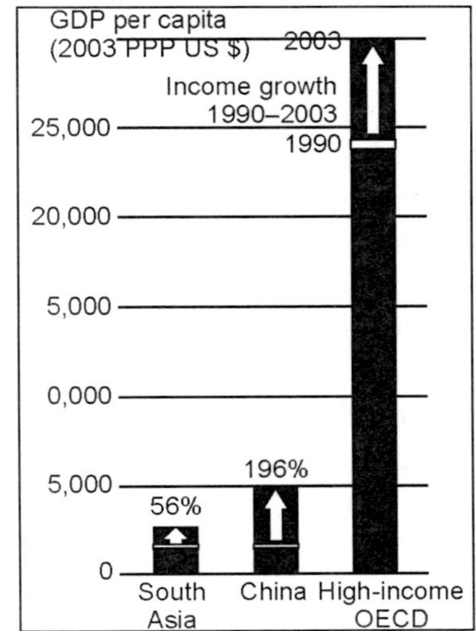

The richest 20 percent of the world population consume about 84 percent of world GDP, 82 percent of energy, 90 percent of fuel oil and 85 percent of forest product. World Bank report (1992) tells us that 24 top nations share about 15.5 percent of world population and 82 percent of world GDP. 43 low-income countries' share of world GDP is a meager 4 percent although their share to world population is over 58 percent. India, for example, accommodates about 17 percent of world population in a land area that is about 2.4 percent of the world landmass. However, 1070 millions' share to world GDP is only 2 percent (which was less than 1.2 percent in mid-nineties). The developed countries practically regulate 85 percent of world trade, commerce and investment. The income growths in China and India (over 2.4 billion people together) have put some check on the income inequality between the rich and the poor at the world canvas. The income generated in these two largest countries if taken out of the income totals of the developing countries, the income inequality between the rich and the poor countries would be seen to have widened further in the last decade. High GDP growth rates in China and India has reversed the trend towards increased income inequality that started in and around 1820 and continued until 1992. Even with the growth trends observed during 2000–2005, it would take India another 100 years to catch up with high income countries. Even if the high-income countries stop growing today and Latin America and sub-Saharan Africa continue on their current growth trajectories, it would take Latin America until 2177 and Africa until 2236 to catch up with the developed economies. Most developing regions are falling behind; catching up with the high income countries is becoming extremely remote because of so high initial income gaps. A simple arithmetic shows that if both sub-Saharan Africa and high income OECD were to grow by 3 percent, the sub-Saharan African countries would add an extra $51 in per capita income and the OECD countries would add $854 per capita.

It is a fact that no country, developed and developing, can entirely depend upon domestic resources for many of their major developmental activities. FDI and loans from international agencies (World Bank, IMF, etc.) play a very important role in this track. Let us examine the issue of official financial flows – at lending and repayments. In 2000, many low and medium developed countries received a total of US $ 53.6 billion from the global multilateral banks and bilateral aid agencies. These countries in the same year paid to their lenders a total sum of US $ 77.6 billion in repayment and interest on earlier loans. That is, they had to ask for loan to repay their earlier loans with interest and in the process the net outflow from these countries was US $ 24 billion. This definitely does not confirm that the rich are helping the poor countries to come out of their woes. This in fact tells us that the rich are being supported by the increasing tax burden on poorer countries. Peru, for example, ends up with paying as much as 25 percent of country's tax revenue in repayments and interest on loans. FDI does not help the poorer countries either since 86 percent of

FDI transaction is within the OECD countries. The whole of Africa received US $ 7.5 billion in FDI in 2000, less than 0.5 percent of the world's total FDI.

An intellectual exercise by A.P. Thirlwal for the future comparative position of the poor countries is cited here to show the magnitude of development task needed for attaining an equitable world living standard. Four questions have been put to mathematical treatment.

1. Given the recent growth experience of the poor countries, how long would it take them to reach the current average level of per capita income in the industrialized countries?
2. Given the recent growth experience of the poor countries relative to the industrialized countries, how many years would it take for the per capita income gap to be eliminated?
3. Given the rate of growth of the industrialized countries from now until the year 2010 (say), how fast would the poor countries have to grow for per capita incomes to be equalized by that date?
4. Given the rate of growth of the industrialized countries, how fast would the poor countries have to grow merely to prevent the absolute per capita income gap between rich and poor countries from being any wider in the year 2010 than now?

The Answers:

1. At a per capita income growth rate of 2 percent, it would take the average poor country (assuming per capita income $1,200) **95** years to reach the current level of living in the industrialized countries.
2. Elimination of per capita income gap between rich and poor countries seems improbable. In all probability, the gap would widen further. For a country starting with an average per capita income $1,000 and growing at 4 percent, it would take 309 years to eliminate the gap. Even a country like Korea (per capita income $5,000), growing at 7 percent will take 36 years to catch up the industrialized countries growing at 3 percent.
3. The solution to the third problem appears trickier than the first two propositions. To attain the estimated per capita income in the industrialized countries in the year 2010, poor countries would have to grow over 18 percent per annum. The magnitude of the development task is colossal. Most of the poorer countries would require six-fold or more increase in per capita income to attain the living levels of the people of the industrialized countries. This would necessitate a ratio of investment to national income of 50 percent or more.
4. The growth rate that needs to be achieved to prevent the present development gap from widening further is about 14 percent. This is also not feasible. The obvious implication is that the gap between the rich and poorer countries will almost certainly be wider in the coming years, given the assumed 3 percent growth rate in the industrialized countries.

The prediction work undertaken was on the assumption that the developed countries would continue to grow at 3 percent per annum, which is the historical average for the period 1950–90. With lower growth rate in the developed countries and reasonably higher growth rate in the developing countries, the gap can certainly be reduced but cannot be eliminated. Income equality is an impracticable ideal. The primary concern therefore is to ensure a 'tolerable' standard of living in all countries through equitable distribution of the average level of real income. There will be debate about the per capita income level that should be regarded as the target for achieving the 'tolerable' living standards. Certainly the current average per capita income level of the developed countries cannot be a pragmatic target for the poorer countries to achieve. It may take a century or more to achieve that even if every thing goes smoothly in this long term global planning.

Problems of developing countries are not confined to low levels of per capita income. Developing countries generally experience very high levels of unemployment – visible and disguised. Their income distributions tend to be much more inegalitarian, and the levels of health, nutrition and education are often abysmally low. Increasingly, policy in the developing countries is becoming concerned with these other dimensions of the development gap.

We have noted the limitations on the part of the developing countries to undertake massive programs to consolidate their position at a much higher level of development. But they can hasten their transition from their present 'low' to 'tolerable' living standards if they can cut down sizably the time needed for demographic transition. The developed countries took some 300 years to walk up the different stages of transition. They were beset with the fact that scientific, technological and industrial revolution came at a time when they already had passed through the critical stages of transition. These revolutionary changes in science, technology and industry, in transportation and communication, especially in the information sector have come as a boon to the developing countries to try them effectively and efficiently to take up programs for converting starving, illiterate and ignorant billions into assets in their march for progress.

Political celebrities, economists and international bodies speak of a 'global village' and 'global community'. From Stockholm to Rio, all participating nations equivocally opined that the grave injustice done by mankind to nature has made the earth less hospitable for sustaining human civilization. If 'consumer culture' of the West is responsible for the present level of pollution of the earth, 'poverty' may still become the greatest pollutant to unsettle the ecological balance that still exists. Whereas the developed countries are culprits for over utilization of natural resources, the poorer countries are wasting resources through inefficient technology and production management. A large share of burden for keeping the environment clean and healthy and maintaining the bio-diversity so urgently needed to maintain ecological balance of the earth has fallen on the shoulders of the developing countries. The folly of the developed countries in the past few hundred years has to be remedied substantially by the developing countries. The developed countries have to come forward with their technology and scientific innovations to help alleviate the poverty of the poorer countries, help them generate enough employment to absorb the new entrants to the job market and assist and encourage creating a social and political atmosphere that will convert human conglomerations into human capitals. The image of 'donor countries' need to be substituted by the one 'aggrieved for its past mistakes'. Human civilization cannot progress and prosper if one part of it remains starved, illiterate, ill nurtured, subjugated and without any choice.

13.3 Rural Development

Development of the developing countries actually refers to the development of the teeming millions – the rural mass, which constitute about 70–80 percent of their populations. A growth in the economic front soon changes the lifestyle of the middle and the upper-middle class people who largely dominate the power-equations in cities and towns. The ripple resulting from economic growth often is not perceptible in the rural sector. They are the worst sufferers when things go wrong with our economy. For example, the Great Bengal Famine did not upset the people of cities and towns, the upper and the middle class people as much as it did to those low in social hierarchy and living in rural Bengal. Between two and three million people, mostly belonging to rural area and backward castes and communities died in that food crisis. Therefore, development of a developing country should largely be discussed on matters related to rural development.

Rural development primarily implies

1. increase in labor productivity resulting in growing income;
2. increase in rural employment opportunities sufficient to absorb the new entrants into the labor force; and
3. adoption of corrective mechanisms that would weaken rural-urban migration and encourage reverse migration.

On all these counts the developing countries lag far behind the developed ones. This is primarily due to factors such as:

(a) high growth of rural population;
(b) lack of land reforms;
(c) fast diminishing land-man ratio;
(d) fragmentation of agricultural land resulting in uneconomic land holding;
(e) low productivity because of failure to adopt modern methods of cultivation on a wider scale and lack of scientific agro-management;
(f) with increased liberalization on imports, even food grains, the poor domestic cultivators are unable to compete with the price of the highly subsidized imported farm products;
(g) surplus farm labors (especially when land-use pattern is changing fast as a result of industrialization and growth of urban areas), which lack education and skill, cannot be absorbed in modern capital-intensive hi tech industries;
(h) failure to establish agro-based rural industries;
(i) failure to undertake planning from the grass-root level;
(j) infrastructural deficiency – illiteracy, lack of health care facilities, lack of transportation facilities, social and economic barrier to economic development, etc.

Economic progress of most of the developing countries has been low, especially if we compare it with the spectacular performances of East Asian and South-East Asian countries. Most developing countries, either by their own realization or by the pressure from IMF, World Bank and other funding agencies, have adopted market-oriented economic policy. The open-door policy though has geared up economic growth in spite of profound political instability, has also, it is feared, increased economic inequality. The growth rate in GNP in India has been maintained over 8 percent in the last few years. It is estimated that about 1 percent growth of population in a developing country may require as much as 4–5 percent of GNP to maintain the standard of living at the current level. India's current population growth rate is estimated at around 1.5 percent per annum and it would require about 7 percent of GNP to create new schools, hospitals, houses, food, roads, etc. just for maintaining the present standard of living. Most of the Third World countries have population growth rate around 2 percent. It is therefore no wonder that income inequalities are increasing in these countries and large segment of their populations, mostly rural, has to live at subsistence level. Unless growth of population is checked, health conditions get better, functional literacy improves and additional employments generated, these countries cannot generate sufficient surplus that can be used for improving the living standard of their people. The developed countries in spite of their lower GNP growth rate have real savings in GNP because of low population growth rate. This enables their governments to spend more on improving the quality of human capital by extending and improving educational facilities and health care, transportation and communication network, etc.

The industrial revolution in the eighteenth and nineteenth century became possible because of surplus labor from agriculture and surplus agricultural production. Labor-intensive industrial production prospered since there was no dearth of labor; competition among labors kept the overhead expenditure of the products low and the products in the domestic and international market competitive. Skill component of the labor was not as important as it is today.

Agriculture, which had a lion's share in a country's GDP even in the early twentieth century, has lost a good deal of its weight in current GDP composition; a country's GDP is now dominated by the service and industrial sectors. Food production in most of these traditionally agriculture-dependent countries has to be improved fast to cope with the growth of population for the simple reason that they do not have any surplus foreign exchange to import food grains. Unless agricultural productivity is improved, the domestic producers cannot remain competitive in this free trade regime, especially since USA, EU and other countries spend a very huge proportion of their GDP as subsidies to their farmers who constitute only 2–5 percent of their workforce contrasted to over 60 percent in most of the developing countries. The developing countries need to adopt modern agricultural technology and management to keep the prices of farm produces down. But that would mean extensive use of tractors and other agricultural implements, and bring as much land as possible under irrigation. The result: more displacement of labor from traditional agriculture. Many of the developed and high developing countries import food grains since they do not have the natural resources, enough farm land and water for irrigation. Most of these countries are either highly industrially developed or have huge petroleum reserves. Foreign exchange is no problem for these countries.

13.4 Technological Advancement

Malthus was harshly criticized, probably rightly so, for his lack of vision about the progress of the material world as a result of progress of science and technology. Marx and Engel were hopeful of a bright future for mankind as they had enormous faith in the unlimited growth and power of science and technology. Their argument was that the capital, labor and science together would thwart the possibility of famine and other disasters since these three together would assure unlimited productivity of land and create new other resources to bear the burden of enlarged population.

The industrial revolution showed how technology could be used to exploit nature. Between the industrial revolution in 1830 and the beginning of the 21st century, some 5,000 million people have been added. Although a large majority of this 6,500+ million people of today are deprived of a decent living, in fact 20 percent or more of them are still lying below the international poverty line, consumption in absolute terms have increased manifold. Increased supply of food and other consumption materials and energy has been possible through extensive exploitation of natural resources, though often to a point of extinction of some of these assets.

Technology has provided the means to bear the burden of increased population. It has remained at the heart of human progress since earliest times. At the same time, it must also be admitted that technology has largely been responsible for the irreparable damage to all the four components of earth as a living place – air, water, soil and bio-diversity. Lifting of underground water is rising by 7–8 percent every year. Fertile agricultural land has to be sacrificed for industries, construction of more houses and roads. An estimate showed that by 2000 AD only about 50 percent of the agricultural land would be available for cultivation compared to the land area available in 1975. Consumption of petroleum products is increasing by 8–10 percent every year and by the first quarter of the 21st century the sources of petroleum will have largely dried up. The whooping rise in crude oil prices (reaching peak US $ 147 in July, 2008) in the world market confirms this fear.

A sweeping shift from agriculture to industry was necessary to give stability to our economy and widen the employment market. Agriculture alone could not bear the weight of such a huge number. Science and technology so far have foiled Malthusian prediction. Famine and natural calamity have taken no decisive role in checking population growth. War still continues, but there has been a shift of emphasis – from destruction of human lives to destabilization of economic backbone and political stability of a country. Science and technology have given us a greater lease of life; the expectation of life for an average man has increased beyond expectation. In the developed countries the absolute number of their senior citizens has already created many social problems. An average man on this globe can now expect to live beyond 67 years. In the more developed countries it is over 75 years. Proportion of old age people in the population could be close to one-fifth of the population before long. Death rates in all countries have fallen sharply in the last 50 years, more so in the developing countries. Famine and epidemic are no more heard of because of large and vastly improved transportation and communication network, expanded public distribution system and invention of preventive and curative medicines. The famines that occurred sporadically in different parts of the world in the last century (Great Bengal Famine, 1943–44, famine in Ethiopia in 1983–84) cannot be related to population pressure. Whereas the War Policy of the British along with some natural calamities and stoppage of import of rice from Burma caused Bengal Famine in the main, the famine in Ethiopia was largely due to faulty policy of the government. India braced a near famine situation in the sixties due to repeated crop failures, but it successfully overcame it through large scale import of wheat and rice from USA and other countries. Science and technology have given us the confidence in our capability which we lacked in the pre-industrial era.

Our quest for truth (science) in the past 400 years has enhanced our knowledge about nature. But the mechanistic approach of physical sciences has left us with the habit of observing natural events and natural processes in their isolation. We often have ignored, knowingly or unknowingly, the interconnections that exist among different objects and things. We have discovered many a fundamental laws of this universe, applied them successfully to improve our technology. The 'development model' that has been followed in most countries in the post-industrial revolution, is primarily the one followed and masterminded in the developed West. Economic progress has been equated to development in this model. That is, a linear relation exists between economic progress and 'development'. Production and more production, cost efficiency and creating a global market for the products are the principal features of this model. Success of the production-oriented development model lies in its spread of consumer culture. The technological revolution has accelerated the faster exploitation of some of the finite natural resources.

Unlike the labor-intensive pre-industrial economy, modern economy is capital-intensive and energy driven. Use of hi tech requires extensive use of power, which is usually obtained from fossil fuels. Indiscriminate drilling and excavation for oil, minerals and coals have spoiled the ecological balance in many countries. The price-tag linked with this technological revolution has to be paid heavily by our future generations. The technology thrust of the market economy, many feel, may ultimately destroy the balance in nature.

The modern technology for increasing agricultural production has a very high environmental cost. The green revolution technology with its high dependence on chemical inputs (fertilizers and pesticides), water supply and selected varieties of seeds, has spectacularly increased output in the short term; but over time led to falling water tables due to intense use of ground water, decline in soil fertility with excessive fertilizer use, pollution of water by pesticides from agricultural run-off, the loss of genetic diversity with monoculture cultivation and the marginalization of indigenous knowledge.

A singular feature of modern technology is to drastically reduce the importance of human and animal labor and increase the capital input in the form of energy and computer-designed machines. Instead of human slaves we now have energy slaves. An average person in developed countries often use 200 times more energy compared to consumption by a person in the third world country. Average per capita annual consumption of electricity in USA in 2002 stood at 10,458 kWh compared to 1,484 kWh in China and 569 kWh in India. Consumer culture in the developed West is considered as the principal reason for polluting the global environment. For example, USA alone releases six thousand metric tons of CO_2 in atmosphere every year (24.4 percent share of world total emission in 2000) as against one thousand metric ton of the same by India (4.7 percent of world total emission). On per capita basis, an average American releases 17 times more CO_2 than does an average Indian. Social cost of environmental degradation in Europe is estimated at 4 percent of its GDP. The same in USA is between 2 and 12 percent. An estimate of environmental degradation in India in 1992 was equivalent to 10,000 million dollar, which was about 4.5 percent of the country's GDP.

Throughout the human civilization it has been observed that only a small fraction of the total population enjoy the fruits of hard labor of many, depriving those who produce them. By the signing of the GATT and formation of WTO and opening up the economy, it is felt that the inequality between the rich and the poor countries will increase further for the simple reason that the local entrepreneurs will find it hard to sell their produces at competitive rates because of their inability to modernize their production system and improve production efficiency. The technologically advanced industrial giants are fast capturing even the domestic markets of the developing countries. The multinational giants while establishing their factories in the developing countries are taking the advantage of cheap labor and resources of these countries and soft environmental laws. They are targeting the ever expanding upper and middle class of these countries, the potential buyers of their hi tech products. The Seattle conference of trade officials of 135 countries, two-third of which was from technologically backward countries, were busy discussing trade and tariff rules that would help expand the market of the MNC's under the cover of opening up world trade market for every nation on a competitive footing. USA in this session tried in vain to include labor standard in the WTO agenda. American labors are anxious about loosing their jobs to third world imports. That remains the principal reason for the stirrings in their heart for poor third-world workers. The inclusion of labor standards in WTO, though a matter of discretion of ILO, has been fought bitterly by the representatives of developing countries and has succeeded, at least temporarily, in thwarting the misadventure of the developed block of nations. America's concern for the quality of life of the third-world labor is not matched by its policy on immigration. They are not even willing to discuss this issue in WTO saying that the question of free market of immigration is a matter to be discussed as a policy matter by the countries' immigration departments.

Many of the MNCs have established production units in the developing countries and exporting their products to the developed countries thus avoiding the restriction imposed on such productions in their home soil. Not only the developed countries are utilizing the natural resources of the Third World countries for their own consumption, they are exposing the local people to long and short-term health and environmental hazards because of relentless spread of toxic industrial wastes. Bhopal tragedy at the instance of Union Carbide is still a nightmare for thousands of families that were victims of the greed of technology and recklessness of the management.

No one questions the need for technological innovation for human progress. Recent digital, genetic and molecular breakthroughs have given us a chance to use these technologies for poverty eradication. The history tells us that the technology diffusion, both among and within countries, remains uneven. The technological innovations contribute directly to enhance human capabilities – improves people's health, nutrition, living standards, knowledge and ability to participate aggressively in social, economic and political issues of the community and the nation. A recent study by World Bank showed that technical progress alone accounted for 40–50 percent of mortality reduction between 1960 and 1990. Technological innovation has now become precursor to human development because of its impact on economic growth through increased productivity and product diversification as also in providing better health care. Medical breakthroughs such as immunizations and antibiotics resulted in faster gains in mortality reduction in the developing countries in the 20th century, which Europe had to achieve through better nutrition, sanitation and mass education, spanned over 300 years. Technology increases crop yields, industrial productivity, opens up opportunities for educated and skilled persons in research and development and in the service sector. Educated farmers and factory workers can learn, muster and use new technologies with ease and more efficiently.

Technological advancement has successfully combated the pressure of population so far. It has at the same time opened up a new gate for acute concern. The technology we have over the years developed has not always been environment friendly. Ecological balance all over the world has been seriously disturbed. Pollution of air, waters and land has become challenging issues before mankind. Input ratio in energy-intensive production technology is very high; it is widening the gap between the rich and the poor countries. Free market economy has forced the governments of poorer countries in investing a high proportion of their national income on import of technology to bridge the gap in their trade balance with other countries, often in neglect of their basic sectors like health, education and agriculture. This has created a self-perpetuating-chain-of-poverty.

Converting technology into an instrument for human development requires huge investment, especially in the knowledge sector, and efforts to create and diffuse innovations among the masses. Marketing of innovative products is not easy in a developing country where most of the poor people of the world live. When incomes of the majority are very low, the private investors are unlikely to buy the technical know-how or engage in developing technologies for innovative products for which the domestic market is too small.

HDR 2001 for the first time tried to develop a measure to compare Technological Achievement Index (TAI) for different countries. TAI is based on four dimensions: technology creation (number of patents granted per capita), diffusion of recent innovations (number of internet hosts per capita and technology exports), diffusion of old innovations (land line and mobiles per capita and electricity consumption per capita), and human skill (mean years of schooling and gross tertiary science enrolment ratio).

Most of the developing countries track record in technology innovation is very low.

13.5 Food Security, Population Growth and Sustainable Development

The French revolution in late 18th century created a sense of belief that such revolutions would usher in an age of reform in traditional social system and structure and will improve the quality of life of the common man. A bright future awaits us, so thought Rousseau, Condorcet and others since they believed that science and human motivation could create a world of plenty and a social system in which man could live happily and peacefully. Malthus could not accept this optimism of the contemporary social philosophers and intellectuals. Malthus saw that population itself was inescapable a barrier to the achievement of these dreams. He predicted that scarcity of food and other basic necessities resulting from excessive growth of population will itself put a brake on the growth of population.

The critics of Malthus were convinced that population growth cannot exceed the growth of food production. Science and technology will take care of food production and supply of other basic necessities. Growth and advancement of science and technology will at least be at par with the growth of population. Even a capitalistic economist like Julian Simon said that there was nothing to worry about the growth of population. Demand of a commodity will increase as the population increases. This increased demand will be met by *increased productivity through better technology*.

It is true that in spite high growth of world population, food availability for per capita consumption has increased, not diminished. Famine even in the so-called backward regions has become a remote possibility. It is a fact that some of the African countries often face near-famine situations. Experts, however, attribute the shortage of food supply to the faulty economic policy of governments. Price control, subsidy and emphasis on cooperative farming were against the market economy and this was reflected in drop in productivity in countries where such controls were in operation. Between 1970 and 1985, population in the developed countries increased by only 14 percent but their food production rose by 51 percent. In the developing countries the respective figures were 42 and 46 percent. A snap shot of per capita cereal consumption and calorie supply between 1965 and 1995 is presented below.

Table 13.3 *Population, per capita calorie supply and total cereal consumption*

Year	*Population*		*Per capita calorie supply*		*Total cereal consumption*	
	Total (million)	*Annual growth (%)*	*Total kcal*	*Annual growth (%)*	*Total Mmt*	*Annual growth (%)*
1965	3,337		2,356		942	
1975	4,075	2.0	2,428	0.3	1,234	2.7
1985	4,837	1.8	2,642	0.9	1,605	2.7
1995	5,666	1.6	2,733	0.3	1,811	1.2
Growth: 1965–95		1.8		0.5		2.2

Source: FAO, 1998

The world's average per capita calorie supply from cereal and other products has increased by 16 percent; from 2,356 kcal in 1965 to 2,733 kcal in 1995. With a 70 percent increase in population between 1965 and 1995, the world's total cereal consumption over this period has almost doubled; from 942 million metric ton (Mmt) in 1965 to 1811 Mmt in 1995. Except for the decade ending 1995, a period that witnessed turmoil in former Soviet Union, East Europe and some parts of West Asia, growth of cereal consumption exceeded the average annual population growth rate. Although calorie supply has increased substantially, around 60 percent of this still come from cereal products,

Figure 13.4 *Population and cereal consumption growth rate*

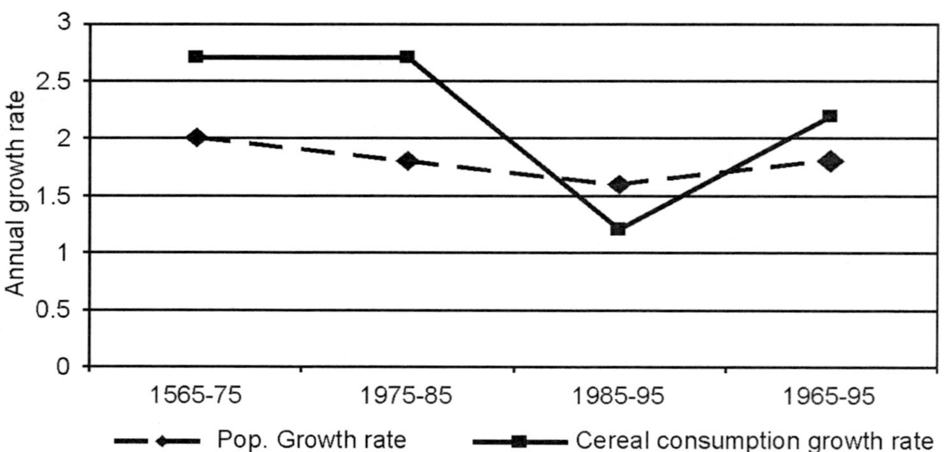

a little over one-third from other crop products (vegetables, fruits, tubers, etc.) and rest from animal products (meat, milk and milk products) and beverages. It must not be forgotten that a sizeable proportion of the cereals goes as animal feed to get better quality meat and also for industrial purposes. Industry share of cereals and other crops is likely to increase to produce bio-diesels and ethanol – a partial substitute for petroleum products.

World's total crop production has increased by 1.9 percent annually on average between 1965 and 1995. This is in spite the fact that the total crop area has increased only by 0.33 percent per annum in the same period. It is clear that the productivity growth has been the major driving force in providing food security despite very high population growth. Several factors have contributed to increase in productivity. Foremost among them are bringing more crop land under irrigation (1.9 percent growth in irrigation per annum), high-yielding variety (HYV) of seeds and agronomic practices. Although it is difficult to ascertain the exact contribution of these factors individually to growth of productivity, expansion of irrigation facilities definitely has played a major role. Net

Figure 13.5 *Irrigated cereal area and production*

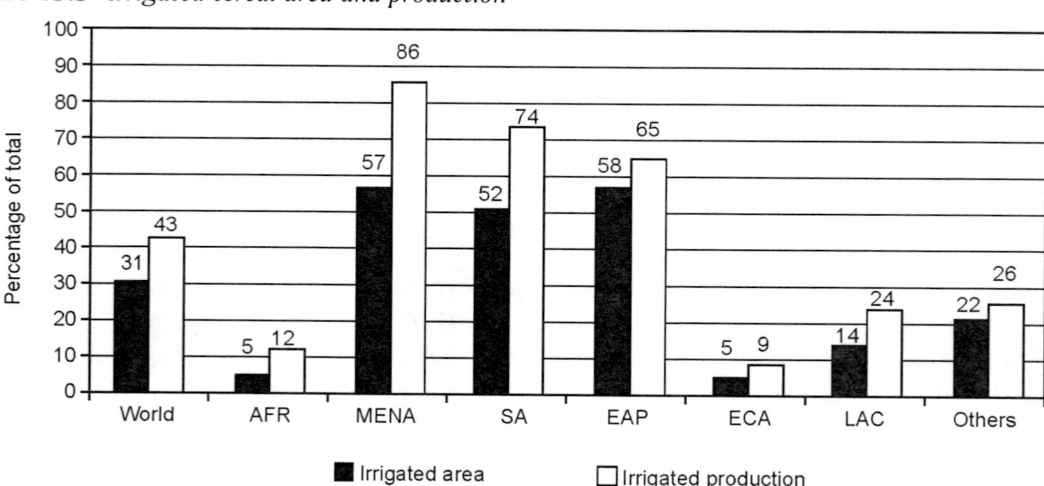

(Adapted from IWMI: Water for Rural Development)

irrigated area according FAO report (1998) has increased by 73 percent, from 150 million hectare acre (mha) in 1965 to 260 mha in 1995. Though world's total irrigated area is about 31 percent of the total harvested area, it accounts for 43 percent of total crop production.

According to World Development Report 2003, about 2 mha of land worldwide (23 percent of all cropland, pasture, forest, and woodland) have been degraded since 1950. 16 percent of these lands are so badly degraded that their recovery would be too costly. The problem of feeding a fast growing urban population calls for a better management of interaction with nature, more specifically with land and water (intensification rather than extensification of agriculture). A successful rural-urban transition requires elimination of poverty for those who stay in the countryside and better preparation (education and skill) for those who opt to move to cities. Intensification of agriculture and increased productivity of land are key to minimize pressure on biodiversity.

About one-fourth of the population (1.3 billion) in the developing countries survives on fragile lands – vulnerable to degradation, erosion, floods, and landslides. They account for most of the people living below the international poverty line (US $ 1 per head per day). But they have a modest portfolio of assets – land, traditional social capital, human capital and indigenous knowledge and know-how. The potentials of these assets have neither been fully utilized by the persons themselves nor by the local and national institutions.

About 55 percent of the world's total population in 1995 was estimated to be rural. In 1995, 45 percent of the total population (more than 2.5 billion people) was estimated to depend directly or indirectly on agriculture for their livelihood. Half of this population was the economically active labor force, and 43 percent of it constituted the female labor force. About 70 percent of people surviving on less than $1 a day live in rural areas and wholly or substantially earn their livelihood through small-scale agriculture. Men are moving fast to non-farm employment. Women make up an increasingly large proportion of the agricultural labor force in the developing countries.

Despite growth in other exports, agriculture still accounts for more than one-third of export earnings in half of all developing countries. Although many developing countries have comparative advantage in agriculture due to low labor costs, long growing seasons and favorable climates, they are not gaining their share in international agricultural trade. Their share in international agricultural market stood at 43 percent in 1999, the rest dominated by the OECD countries, despite the fact that agricultural exports (including processed agricultural products) constituted only 7 percent of total export earnings of OECD countries.

Let us take a close look at how cereal production changed in different regions between 1965 and 1995.

Figure 13.6 *Agriculture in terms of GDP, employment and exports for rich and poor countries*

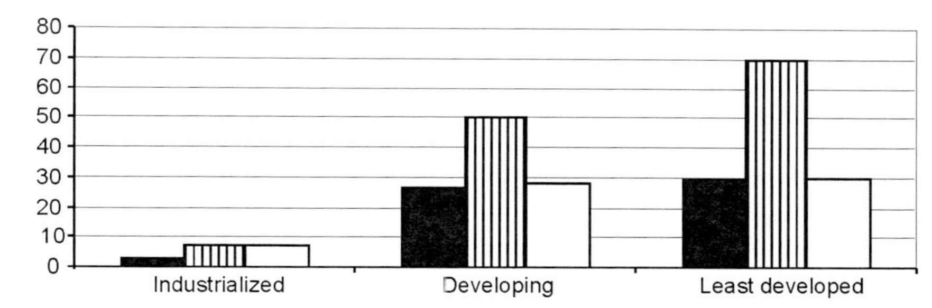

South Asia (SA): Total cereal production in SA has gone up from 106 Mmt in 1965 to 231 Mmt in 1995, a 218 percent rise. The region was in surplus mode between 1965 and 1985. Since 1985 the region has gone to deficit mode. The calories consumption in the region increased from 2,020 kcal to 2,369 kcal during this period. Animal product still has a very small share of a common man's dish although in the 30 years under review its share has gone up by 48 percent (from 5.9 in 1965 to 7.5 percent in 1995).

East Asia and the Pacific (EAP): Average per capita calories supply in EAP region has increased by 37 percent, from 1,950 in 1965 to 2,735 kcal in 1995. Contribution of animal protein in the daily calories supply has increased by 227 percent (from 115 kcal to 389 kcal). Total cereal consumption has increased from 186 Mmt in 1965 to 507 Mmt in 1995, a large proportion of which is imported from other countries. Total cereal production in the 30 years has gone up from 183 Mmt to 476 Mmt in 1995. The region continues to be in deficit mode since 1975. The industrial and service sectors in some of the countries in this region have grown fast in 1980s and 1990s (Malaysia, Indonesia, Philippines, for example). These countries are net importers of cereals. Animal products in per capita calories supply have gone up from 5.9 percent to 14 percent in these 30 years. The total cereal production in the period increased at an annual rate of 0.2 percent. The growth of food production in this region has been by productivity growth.

Europe and Central Asia (ECA): Per capita calories supply in ECA has increased by a whooping 168 percent, from 1,995 kcal in 1965 to 3,349 kcal in 1995. A clear change in the diet chart of a common man is noticed – a shift from non-vegetarian diet to vegetarian diet, a 46 percent shift. Contribution of cereal products in daily calories supply has increased by 13 percent. Contribution of other crop products in the daily calories supply has increased by 55 percent. The crop production has declined since 1985 as a result of decrease in land area under crop production since 1975 even though productivity has increased by 45 percent. Total cereal consumption has slumped as a result. This region has to import large quantities of food grain from other regions. Rural population in ECA is one of the lowest in the world.

Africa: Africa experienced an average annual population growth rate of 2.8 percent between 1965 and 1995, which is higher than the growth rates in most other regions. However, the per capita daily calorie supply has increased by 0.2 percent per annum, from 2,144 kcal in 1965 to 2,298 kcal in 1995. Supply of calorie from cereals has remained stagnated around 45–46 percent. A sizeable proportion of calories in daily diet chart come from roots and tuber products. The contribution of animal products in the daily chart has declined from 13 percent in 1965 to 11 percent in 1995 in terms of calorie supply. Even though cereal production in the region has increased by around 2.8 percent per annum mostly by bringing more land under agriculture, this is insufficient in view of the increasing demand resulting from high population growth. Productivity growth in the region has been quite low in view of the fact that the crop area under irrigation is less than 8 percent of the total crop area. The region continues to import large quantity of cereals.

Middle East and North Africa (MENA): Population growth in this region is highest among all other regions. The annual average growth rate of population in this region has been 2.9 percent between 1965 and 1995. Per capita calories supply has increased by 140 percent, from 2,102 to 2,951 (4.3 percent annually). Growth of food production in the region could never match the growth of population. The deficit in cereal production has increased over time and stood around 40 percent in 1995. Cereals in daily diet had declined over time with corresponding increase in other crops in the common man's dish. Proportion of agricultural population has declined from around 59 percent in 1965 to 30 percent in 1995.

Figure 13.7 *Cereal production and production surplus/deficit in Africa region*

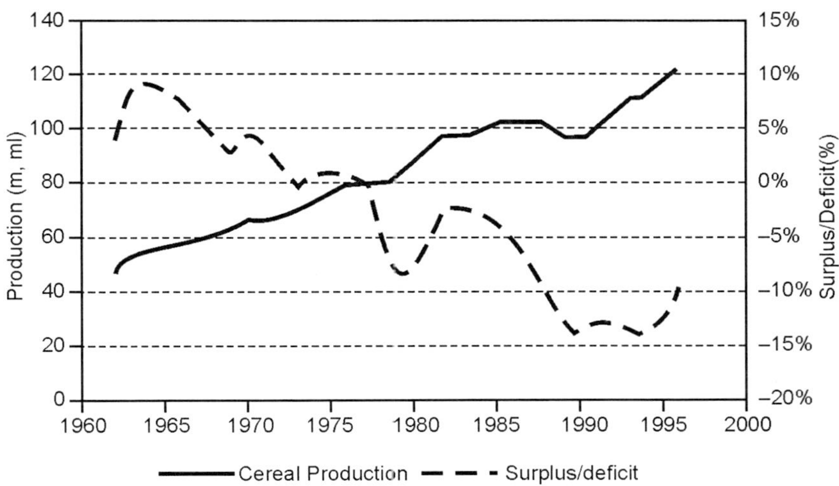

(Reproduced from IWMI: Water for Rural Development)

Latin America and the Caribbean (LAC): The population in the region has increased by over 90 percent between 1965 and 1995. Growth of fcod cereals consumption is marginal (9 percent), but increase in consumption of animal products by 36 percent have resulted in total consumption by 162 percent. That is, a large proportion of the cereals are used as animal feed to get better quality of meat. Share of animal products in daily calories supply has increased from 15.7 percent to 18 percent. Per capita calories supply has increased by 15 percent, from 2,394 kcal in 1965 to 2,774 kcal in 1995. Although cereal production has increased substantially over time, the region remains dependent on import of food grains to meet their growing demands.

Figure 13.8 *Cereal production and production surplus/deficit in MENA region*

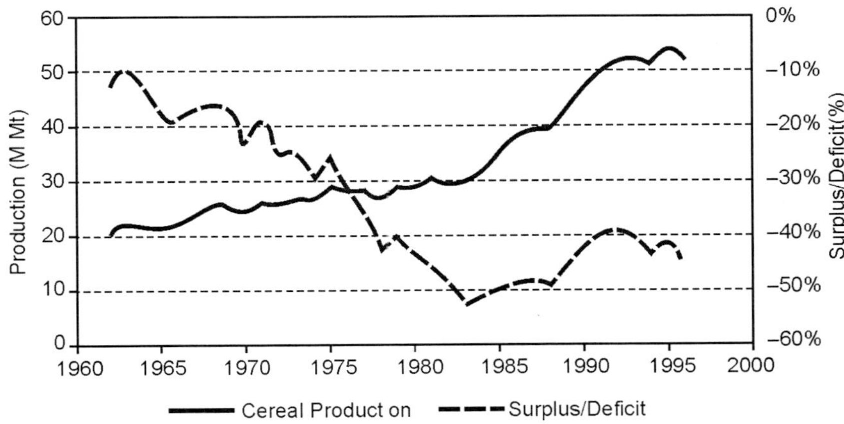

(Reproduced from IWMI: Water for Rural Development)

Cereal productions in the developing countries, except probably in ECA, are likely to gain considerable momentum in the next few years to reduce production deficits with respect to consumption and restrict import of food grains from other countries. International Water

Management Institute (IWMI) projection shows that production deficit in the developing countries is likely to go up from 109 Mmt in 1995 to 119 Mmt in 2025. The production deficit in respect to consumption in developing countries however is likely to drop from 9 percent in 1995 to 7 percent in 2025. African region's production deficit is likely to increase from 9 percent in 1995 to 15 percent in 2025. Water scarcity may force increase in cereal import in MENA region. Although the developed countries will continue to increase their production at a slower pace, their production surplus will come down from 22 percent in 1995 to 18 percent in 2025.

Figure 13.9 *Cereal production and production surplus/deficit in LAC region*

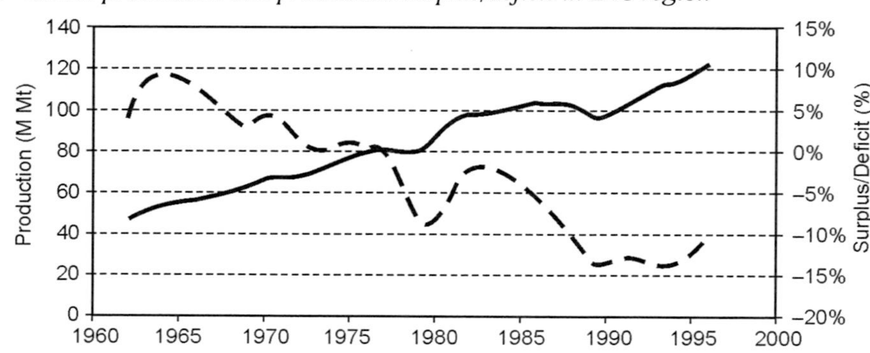

Calorie supplies (composition of daily diet)**.** The following graphs show how composition of per capita daily calories supply from cereals and animal products has changed in the major regions during 1965–1995.

More than 65 percent of the daily calories need is provided by cereals, both directly through cereal products and indirectly through animal products. The daily food chart of a common man varies from one region to another and within the same region and the country. The poorer regions like Africa and South Asia still depend on cereals for calories supply; rich countries spend more for every unit of calories intake since they still prefer non-vegetarian dishes and spend plentifully on beverages. The production of 1 kg good meat requires several kg of equivalent crop product to feed the animals. The decision to go vegetarian or non-vegetarian has a large bearing upon crop availability for human consumption alone. As the income goes up, there is a general tendency even in the poorer countries to reduce direct consumption of cereals and increase the indirect cereal consumption through animal products in their daily dishes. This 'food to feed use' of cereals

Figure 13.10 *Percentage share of cereals in per capita per day calorie supply*

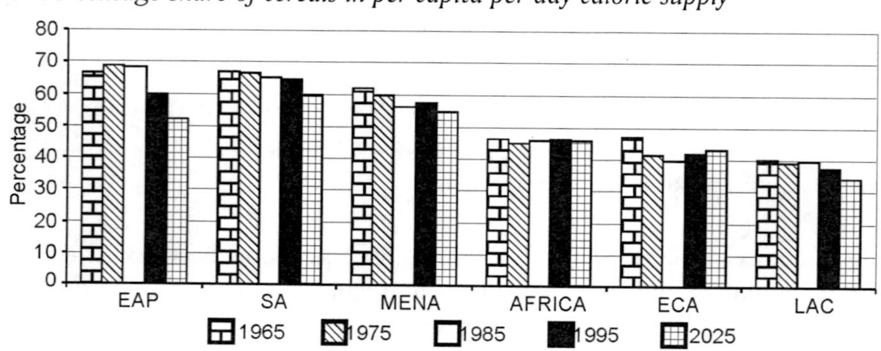

Figure 13.11 *Percentage share of animal proteins in per capita per day calorie supply*

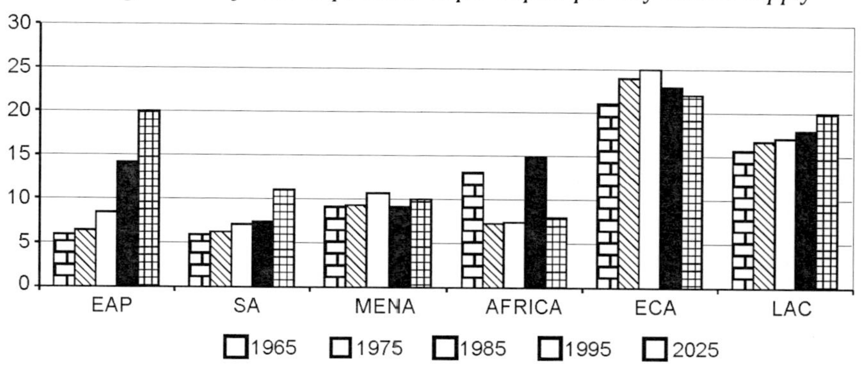

resulted in an increased demand for cereal production. Even though the LAC countries' cereal production grew by an average of 2.5 percent per annum between 1965 and 1995 and the population grew by an average of 2.2 percent in the same period, these countries had to import huge quantity of cereals because of their increased emphasis on animal products in their daily diet, especially in more developed countries. Of late, there is a shift form red meat to white meat in high calories consuming nations and also increase in the share of vegetables, pulses and fruits in their daily diet. These shifts, along with significant improvement in efficiency of converting feed into animal products, can be expected to free up some feed cereals. It is projected that the share of cereals used as food in per day per capita calories supply will decline steadily across the regions between 1995 and 2025. Share of animal product in the calories supply is likely to go up in regions EAP, SA and LAC; only marginal increase/decrease of animal products is expected in MENA, Africa and ECA regions. The developed countries' share of both cereal and animal products in per capita calories supply is likely to decline marginally and each will have a share of around 26 percent in the per capita per day calories supply.

Presently, 50 percent of the cereals produced in the world are used as 'food' cereals and 36 percent as 'feed' cereals (mostly in the developed countries) and the rest for industrial and other uses. By 2025, food cereals would constitute around 48 percent of total cereals produced and the share of feed cereals is likely to go up to about 39 percent. 60 percent of the cereals produced in the developed countries are currently used as feed to animals, and only 22 percent as food. The respective shares in the developing countries are 25.6 and 62 percent. The pattern of use of cereals is likely to remain unaltered in the developed countries in 2025, but in the developing countries the feed use of cereals could go up to about 32 percent and food use of cereals down to 57 percent by 2025. Food cereal consumption in developing countries is likely to increase by 1.1 percent annually and feed cereal consumption is expected to increase by 2.1 percent.

Nutrition and Health: Low absolute levels of income can have serious consequences for nutrition and health of individuals. FAO has estimated that there are at least one billion people suffering from various degrees of malnutrition, which includes two-thirds of world's one billion children. Malnutrition is a major cause of low birth weight and infant mortality, which in the developing countries is more than twice as high as in the developed countries. Malnutrition stunts growth and development. The two-way relation between poverty and malnutrition is – low income is a cause of malnutrition and malnutrition in turn is a cause of low income by impairing work efficiency and productivity.

Table 13.4 *Food, feed and total cereals consumption*

Region	Food cereals (Mmt)			Feed cereals (Mmt)			Total cereals (Mmt)		
	1995	2025	Growth (%)	1995	2025	Growth (%)	1995	2025	Growth (%)
All countries	865	1172	1.0	615	938	1.4	1718	2419	1.1
Developed countries	113	132	0.5	304	363	0.6	505	600	0.6
Developing countries	752	1040	1.1	311	575	2.1	1213	1819	1.4
AFRICA	66	134	2.4	8	16	2.4	87	178	2.4
MENA	59	91	1.5	25	55	2.6	93	161	1.8
SA	201	309	1.4	4	11	3.6	227	356	1.5
EAP	326	385	0.6	130	297	2.8	511	755	1.3
ECA	66	69	0.1	106	118	0.4	220	236	0.2
LAC	58	85	1.3	55	109	2.3	124	210	1.8
Other Countries	89	99	0.3	288	334	0.5	455	523	0.5

Source: IWMI: Water for Rural Development

The average daily calories supply per capita from food is a good indicator of nutritional consumption. Nutritional poverty can be checked only by providing sufficient calories supply per capita through a balanced supply of cereals, animal products, vegetables, fruits, etc. that are also rich in proteins, minerals and vitamins. It has been estimated that a minimum of 2,200 kcal supply per day per capita is essential for preventing nutritional poverty.

Per capita daily calories supply in 1995 for all regions was more than 2,200 kcal. The calories requirement is not the same for all categories of individuals. Nature of physical labor undertaken by an individual determines his/her calories needs. Rural people, especially those engaged in agriculture or in unskilled wage jobs, generally would require higher calories compared to that of an average person living in urban area. Due to income and occupational reasons there exists variation in per capita calories supply between regions, as also between and within countries in the same region. To make sure that no one receives less than 2,200 kcal per day, the national average must be high enough, somewhere between 2,700 and 3,000 kcal per person per day. Accesses to minimum quantity of food by the poorest of the poor can be assured if the national average is considerably high.

There is considerable doubt if a minimum of 2,200 kcal per head per day supply could be assured for a great many people in South Asia and Africa even as late as 2025. That is, food-poverty-nutritional-deficiency would continue in these regions in spite of the estimated faster growth of per capita calories supply between 1995 and 2025. This is because these two regions had a lower base of calories supply in 1995.

Poverty and Entitlements: Malnutrition is caused by lack of access to food, but this does not depend only on the availability of food; it also depends on people's *entitlement to food.* Vast sections of population may go short of food, and experience famine-like conditions, not because food has become scarce, but because their entitlement to food has been impaired. This is the powerful thesis put forward by Prof. Amartya Sen, who argues that to understand poverty and starvation, or

Table 13.5 *Population and per capita daily calories supply*

Region	Population (million)			Per capita calories supply (kcal)		
	1995	2025	Growth (%)	1995	2025	Growth (%)
AFRICA	533	989	2.1	2197	2413	0.3
MENA	271	443	1.7	2954	3035	0.1
SA	1233	1762	1.2	2360	2741	0.5
EAP	1759	2158	0.7	2740	3034	0.3
ECA	386	401	0.1	2995	3075	0.1
LAC	461	644	1.1	2791	3196	0.5
Others[1]	779	818	0.2	3356	3649	0.3
Developed countries	893	984	0.3	3342	3579	0.2
Developing countries	4529	6232	1.1	2599	2867	0.3
All countries	5422	7217	1.0	2722	2964	0.3

Source: IWMI: Water for Rural Development

1. North America, European Union, Australia, New Zealand and Japan are in this category

malnutrition associated with it, it is necessary to understand both ownership patterns and exchange entitlements, which requires in turn an understanding of modes of production and the class structure. Entitlement to food depends on the ability of individuals to exchange productive resources and goods for food. Exchange entitlements may deteriorate independently of a general decline in the supply of food, which raises its price and worsens the terms of trade for other goods. Job opportunities may diminish, real wages or productivity may fall, and other people may become better off and demand more food. Prof. Sen has shown that in 1943 Bengal Famine starvation occurred because food entitlements shrunk first as a result of a rise in the price of food due to military procurement, second, because the price of other commodities fell as more monetary demand was switched to food, and third, because of a fall in the output of other goods. China did not experience famine not because food production increased, but because of the result of a shift in the entitlement system through guaranteed employment and social security provisions.

Poverty Alleviation Programs: Various international agencies are assisting in poverty alleviation programs of the developing countries.

Figure 13.12 *Rising share of exports in GDP (%) (Reproduced from HDR 2005)*

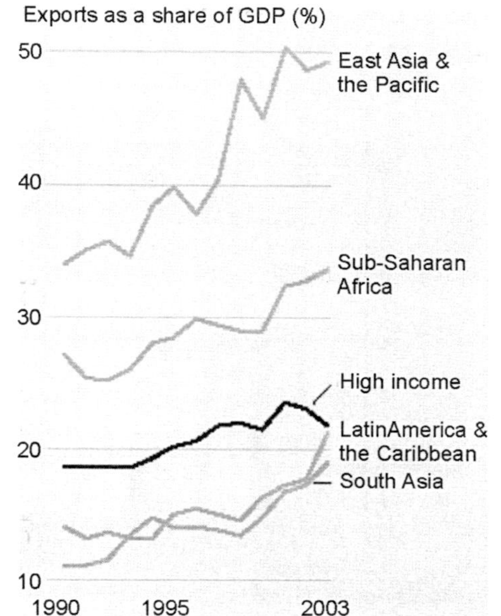

World Bank lending on this rose from $500 million in 1970 to $3,300 million in 1989, that is, from 8 percent to 20 percent of the total lending program. Of the total in 1989, a sum of $1,800 million was spent on basic needs including education, health and drinking water supply compared to only $340 million in 1970. The rest was spent on rural development and small-scale industrial projects.

The prosperity generated by globalization has given us an opportunity to convert this prosperity to eradicate poverty of millions in the developing and least developed countries. Multilateral trade has now become a reality and a powerful engine driving global integration. World trade in the last decade almost has doubled to US $ 9 trillion in 2003. Global production has increased slowly and the share of export to world GDP as also in the incomes of most countries has been increasing. In fact, more than one-third of income in sub-Saharan Africa comes from export of various types of raw materials. The developing countries collectively have expanded their share of manufactured exports, and currently account for about one-fourth of global manufactured exports. Export growth in developing countries has outstripped growth in industrially developed countries across all technology sectors – but most spectacularly in high tech. However, the developing countries have been hit most in trade transaction in agriculture, which is their forte, when the developed countries resorted to protectionism (farm subsidy) for the fear of losing market share. Rural population in the developing countries would be adversely affected by possible increase in free food trade. Many of the developing countries will have little fund left for rural developmental activities after paying the import bill for food with the little foreign exchange they earn from other sectors. More than 50 percent of the total population in SA, EAP and Africa would still live in rural areas by 2025, and a majority of them would be in agriculture to earn their livelihood.

Transnational pricing and subsidies: The farmers from the developing countries suffer a huge loss for their cash crops. Transnational corporations (TNCs) control prices in a way that farmers get less for their produces. For example, coffee exporting countries (Costa Rica, Brazil and others) earned around US $ 10–12 billion while retail sales were worth US $ 30 billion in 1990. By 2002, retail sales went up to US $ 70 billion, but earnings of coffee producing countries were cut by half to about US $ 5.5 billion. In Southern India, the auction prices for tea fell by 33 percent – from Rs.69 per kg in 1998 to Rs.46 in 2004. This price was really below the cost of production, estimated at

Figure 13.13 *Global export share for different regions*

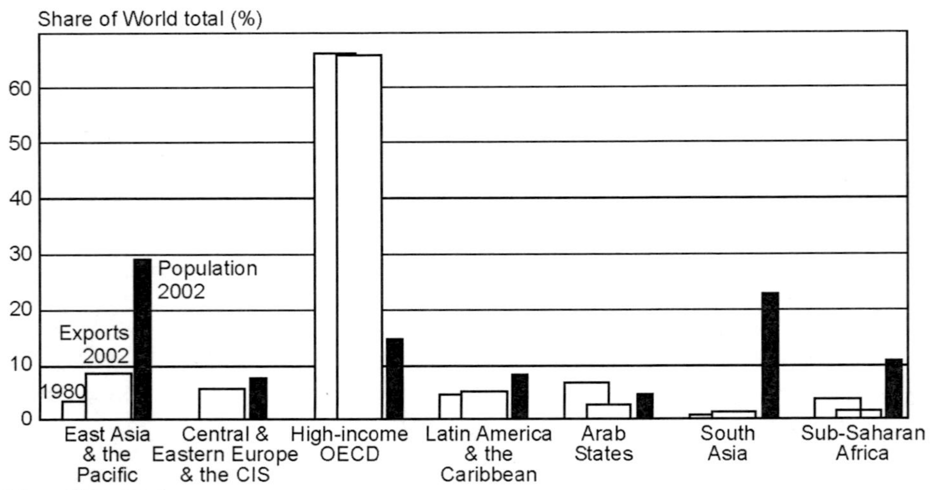

(Reproduced from HDR 2005)

Rs.75 per kg in 2004. But the shareholders of Hindustan Lever Ltd, which has a 34 percent share of the Indian packaged tea market, are getting four times the dividend they received in 1996.

After two decades of rapid trade growth, the relative positions of various regions in world trade have not changed much. The high-income countries, with a world population share of only 15 percent still have two-thirds share of world exports, almost the same position they held in 1980. There is hardly any indication of convergence in terms of their current market share.

World Trade Organization (WTO) provides the necessary platform to evolve, modify and change the rules of the game. In the declaration of Doha round of WTO, the rich countries promised "to reduce or as appropriate eliminate tariffs as well as non-tariff barriers on products of export interest to developing countries". The governments of the rich countries found it difficult to convert promises into actions because of vehement opposition from their giant traders. The conclave of the developed countries still remains rigid on granting space to other countries that may in the long run go against the interest of their big traders. Trade barriers remain intact, agricultural subsidies have been increased, and rich countries have aggressively pursued rules on investment, services and intellectual property that threaten to reinforce global inequalities.

The low-income countries exporting to high-income countries face tariffs three to four times higher than the barriers applied in trade between high-income countries. Developing countries' share to imports by developed countries is less than one-third, but they contribute about two-thirds of the tariff (import tax) collected in these countries, For example, Vietnam pays $470 million in taxes for exports to USA worth only $4.7 billion, while UK pays approximately the same amount by way of taxes for exports worth $50 billion. The Figure 13.14 illustrates the perverse taxation policy pursued by USA for import from the developed and developing countries. The developed countries often would put restriction on country-specific products for import from the developing countries. Agriculture remains the flashpoint for international tensions since the Doha round of WTO.

Subsidies. There is a great deal of debate and world-wide protests against the manner in which the rich countries, especially European Union (EU) and USA, dictate food trade in the world market. The farmers in the developed countries receive huge subsidy from their respective governments in food cereal and other crop production as also in exports of food. The agenda of 'development', taking into account the interest of both the North and the South, was discussed for the first time in Doha round of WTO meet in 2001. The final draft on time-frame on abolition of farm-subsidies in the ministerial meet in WTO in 2005 asks all the countries to phase out their agricultural export subsidies by 2013. But export subsidies constitute only 3.5 percent of EU's total farm subsidies. The US and the EU insist that the developing countries, especially India and Brazil, reduce import tariffs and open their markets. But the developing countries maintain that all kinds of subsidies, especially on farm products, must be withdrawn before they can consider opening up markets. The developed countries took 50

Figure 13.14 *Discriminatory import tax rates in USA (HDR 2005)*

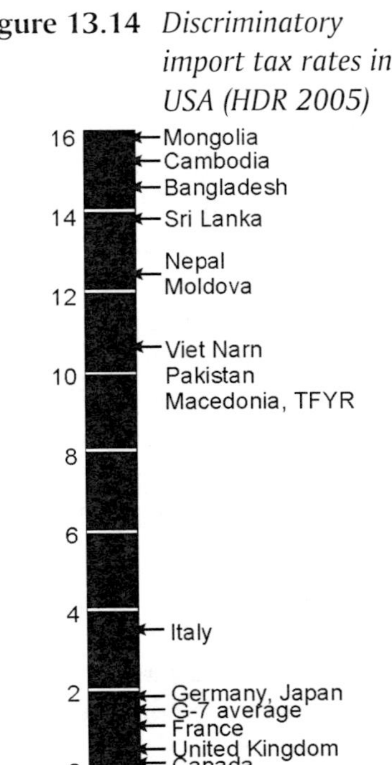

years to open up their manufacturing markets. Yet they are asking the developing countries, which till now largely depends on agriculture, to open up their markets at a lightning pace.

Figure 13.15 *Rich country support to agriculture (US $ billion)*

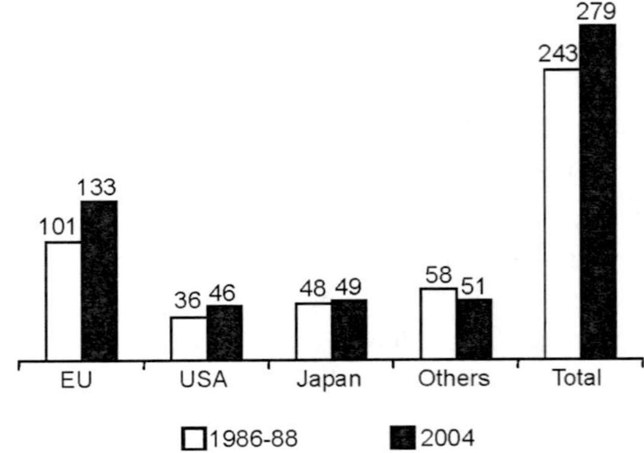

The EU's Common Agricultural Policy (CAP) generously allocates subsidies to farmers, a meager 2 percent of total employment, worth more than 40 percent of the EU total budget. A modest estimate suggests that the developing countries lose about $24 billion a year in agricultural income due to agricultural protectionism and subsidy policies in the developed countries. The issue of subsidies, the main sticking point, had been shelved and the door kept open for an increase in subsidies in the name of rural development. USA rice policies harm domestic producers in many developing countries. In 2002–03, USA produced rice at $415 a ton but exported the same at $274 a ton, a price that can not be matched by the developing countries. Because of import of rice from USA many rice farmers have even been pushed out from their domestic markets, killing the rural economy.

Market competitiveness has worsened for some of the LDCs that rely heavily on exporting agricultural raw material (cotton, for example) placing the livelihood of their massive rural poor into uncertainty. EU and the USA are the world's farm subsidy superpowers. The developed country support to agricultural production amounts to $350 billion a year. Every country gives some subsidy to agricultural producers (in fertilizer, power, irrigation, etc.). Even this small subsidy to the farmers costs many of these countries so much so that their governments cannot allocate sufficient fund for the social sectors like education and health (the agriculture sector consumes about one-third of total electricity produced in India, but contributes less than 5 percent to revenue earned by State Electricity Boards). Price distortions caused by subsidies by the rich countries affect the small stakeholders in the developing countries, especially in LDCs where millions are engaged in farming in small landholdings. High levels of government subsidies insulate big farmers in rich countries against any destabilization in the world market. The poorer countries are not in a position to provide more support to their farmers to remain competitive in the world market. Most of the developing countries are historically in debt trap to many international funding agencies. They have to earn dollars by all means for paying interest on borrowings as also to improve the balance of payment (BOP) situation because of import of technology, machinery and even raw materials from the developed countries.

Existing OECD agricultural subsidies need to be suitably curtailed since they promote overproduction, environmentally damaging production systems, and encourage the farmers to export at prices below the costs of production. Subsidies are administered measures that help keep prices above market levels for producers or below market levels for consumers. By definition, subsidies are policy measures designed to have market effects that are beneficial to the economy as a whole. While subsidies can have positive effects and may be introduced with the best of intentions, they can equally have hidden or long-term social or environmental costs. Subsidies become perverse when their long-term social costs outweigh any benefits.

Subsidies come in all shapes and sizes (direct/indirect, implicit/explicit, and broad/narrow) and can be implemented through a range of policy instruments (direct support, tax incentives, food credits, targeted provision of infrastructure, and so on). Subsidies are considered perverse either when they have not been phased-out according to changing circumstances or because they are implemented without accurate account of their hidden effects, or externalities. Among the common characteristics that all subsidies share are their inherently contentious political nature and, they are much easier to put in place than to phase-out (All political parties in India oppose withdrawal of subsidies on petroleum products, fertilizers or power in domestic and agriculture sector to protect their political constituency). The decision to phase out is most likely to be contested by those who benefit from the subsidy even when continuation of the subsidy is proven to be harmful to the national economy or when its social and environmental costs far exceed the benefits accruing to the producers/consumers.

Since export restrictions of most items have largely been lifted under WTO agreement, agricultural products from the OECD countries at much below the domestic market prices are entering into developing countries; the poor marginal farmers of these countries, without much access to subsidy from their own governments, have been put into abysmal and unfair competition. They often have to sell their produces at cost prices, at times below it. Farming in their own land has become so unproductive that they are forced to sell their land and work as agricultural labor on the same land. Incidences of suicide among small farmers are rising in many developing countries. Millions of small farmers who earn less than US $ 400 a year have to compete with US and EU farmers who receive on average subsidy worth US $ 21,000 and US $ 16,000 per annum respectively. A modest estimate puts rich countries' subsidies to their farmers at US $ 350 billions; about five times the aid that flows from these countries and exceeds the total income of 1.2 billion people living in extreme poverty. USA's 'emergency farm payments' even exceeds the UN's entire humanitarian aids budget. The most malicious aspect of agricultural subsidization in rich countries for developing country producers is the practice of 'export dumping'. Goods are said to be 'dumped' onto world markets when they are sold at prices much below the cost of their production. The US and EU together contribute about half of all wheat exports, and their export prices are 46 per cent and 34 per cent below costs of production respectively. EU is the world's largest exporter of skimmed-milk powder, which it exports at prices around half the cost of production. EU is the largest sugar exporter and sells it at a quarter of production costs.

Figure 13.16 *Subsidy to farmers of USA and EU*

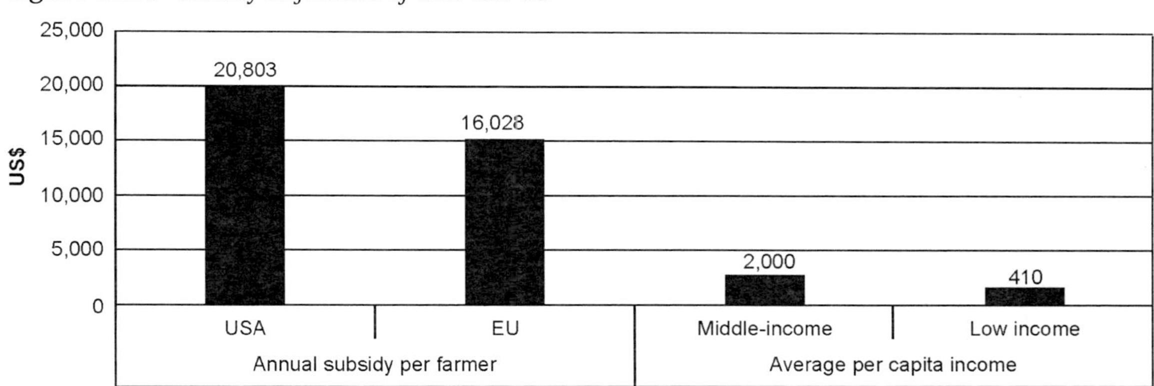

As the developing countries liberalize imports, they have to evolve strategy to develop export growth to balance the trade. They increasingly had to concentrate on environmentally harmful inputs (chemical fertilizers, pesticides, more water) for agricultural intensification. The developing countries need gradually to bring down whatever subsidies they provide to producers/consumers in various sectors including agriculture. Elimination of subsidy can be an important source for allocating more funds on social infrastructure and poverty eradication. The global subsidy is estimated at over US $ 1 trillion. Subsidy reduction would liberate financial resources both in developed and developing countries to pay for sustainable developmental needs and transfers.

Food Production: At the global level the problem of nutrition essentially is a problem of distribution. The world is physically capable of producing enough food to feed its inhabitants adequately. Since World War II global food production has generally kept pace with population growth, and the world is probably capable of producing food ten times or so of the present level. The total world crop production between 1965 and 1995 has nearly doubled. However, the worrying factor is that most of the increases in world food production in recent years have occurred in the developed West, more specifically in North America. The developing countries' crop production barely kept pace with population growth and often there has been no margin of safety. The dangers of dependence on North America became crystal clear in 1972 when world food production since the World War II fell for the first time. Stocks of wheat amounted to only four weeks of global consumption. A crop failure in just one major producing area could have spelt disaster. Even by the end of the twentieth century, millions of people have their lives threatened by the vagaries of weather, or sudden political upheavals which impair their ability to import food. This precarious situation has arisen because of neglect of agriculture. Both the international agencies and national governments of the developing countries, many believe, erroneously saw industrialization as the road to development and starved agriculture of adequate resources. International agencies supported industrialization liberally but rarely lent money for agricultural projects.

IWMI predicts that cereal production between 1995 and 2025 is projected to grow by about 1.1 percent per annum, just matching the average annual population growth rate during these years. But with the increasing feed use of cereals, there could be serious deficit in cereal consumption in the regions – AFRICA, MENA and LAC. SA, EAP and ECA will have either a small shortage of cereals produced for consumption or a small surplus. The small deficit of about 3 percent in SA will be due to inability of Pakistan to meet its projected demand for cereal production in 2025. It is only in 'others' category countries that there would be a huge surplus (26 percent) of cereal production as percentage of total cereal consumption. Many in the cereal deficit countries are either planning or already have resorted to allocate more land on high value crops and place more emphasis for the development of other sectors to earn high returns in the international market so that they can generate enough resources to import food grains from the world market.

If the past trend is any indication, agricultural expansions in most countries, except in Africa, have almost

Table 13.6 *Annual growth of crop production and other related statistics*

Period	Annual growth (%)			
	Crop production	Crop area	Crop yield	Irrigated area
1965–75	2.4	0.3	2.0	2.3
1975–85	2.6	0.5	2.2	1.8
1985–95	1.8	0.2	1.6	1.5
1965–95	2.3	0.3	1.9	1.9

Source: FAO 1998.

reached their possible limits. With very little scope for expansion in land frontiers, future increase in food production in most regions has to come from productivity increases and arranging supplementary irrigation to marginal rain-fed lands. For the African and some other countries that rely heavily on rain-fed cultivation, the ongoing climatic change has become a matter of deep concern because of unreliable rainfall patterns. The potentially water deficit MENA countries will need to transfer water to high value sectors, and in agriculture they will need to shift to high value crops and import more food grains. Irrigated cereal areas both in ECA and LAC regions are small (5 and 14 percent respectively) and no major shift from rain-fed farming is expected in future.

It has been projected that consumption of water for industrial use would double and even may quadruple in some developing regions by 2025. The countries will need to allocate more water for the environmental sector to flush out salt and other pollutants, to prevent siltation in rivers and other water bodies, and to maintain the ecosystems. Judicial use of water in various sectors shall remain the king pin for sustainable agricultural development. There is no other alternative than crop productivity enhancement to address to rural poverty reduction and rural development.

Food grain production in India since independence has gone up by about 400 percent and population in the same period by about 275 percent. From around 400 grams of food grains per head per day, it has risen to about 500 grams per head per day. In the first 25 years after independence, growth of food production was almost the same as the growth of population. This primarily was due to less attention paid to agriculture sector as a result of increased emphasis on heavy industries in the first three Five-Year Plans. But during the last 30 years, the growth of food production has considerably exceeded the growth of population as a result of adoption of modern farm practices. An impressive feature of agricultural management in post-independent India is the increase in productivity per unit area of land through intensive cultivation. The present emphasis on capital-intensive management is paying rich dividend. Today, this agricultural management policy is followed more or less in all the developing countries. A FAO survey observed that between 1948–71 food productions in the developing countries increased by 40 percent although the total area of cultivable land increased by 50 percent in the same period. The developing countries increased their food production by bringing more land under cultivation rather than by intensive agriculture. In the same period food production in the developed countries went up by 90 percent although only 9 percent new land was added to the cultivable land available in 1948. The developed countries made better use of the potential of their land by applying better agricultural technology.

Population in the developed countries, less than 20 percent of the world total, consumes about 75 percent of food grains that are consumed in the rest of the world. This very high consumption in the developed countries is because they use 67 percent of their food grains as animal feed. This they do because they still today are very high consumers of animal protein. An average American consumes a little less than twice his body weight of animal protein a year. An average Indian today can afford to have only 4–5 kg of animal protein a year (it was only 1 kg two decades back). For getting good quality meat, animals have to be fed high quality food grains along with good fodder. It is estimated that 2 kg of food grains are required for 1 kg of quality chicken meat; some 7 kg food grains are to be fed for getting 1 kg of beef. That is, to procure 1 calorie equivalent of food, 10 calories energy must be used as input. Even a century back, it required a fraction of calories to procure 1 calorie equivalent of food. Conversion of energy into equivalent food has become less efficient in the present age compared to conversion rates of the earlier days when science and technology were just developing. This additional energy comes from massive use of natural resources, which could have been preserved for better use by our future generations. We are using nature as our liquid capital without realizing that the source for the ready capital is getting dried up everyday.

Keeping in mind that the population is still growing fast in the developing countries and that average calories intake per day per individual in the world has to be raised to around 2,700 kcal from today's 2,200 kcal and that a very large proportion of this calories supply shall have to come from cereals, increase in cereal production would remain a top priority. This can be achieved mainly through productivity improvements with some growth in crop area. The growth in productivity would depend considerably upon availability of water to bring more land under multiple crops and other necessary inputs and agro-economic management.

We also need to look at the international food market-subsidy equation from another perspective. Suppose, that OECD countries (who have a world food trade share over 60 percent) decide to substantially cut down subsidies given to their farmers. The food price in the world market would rise steeply. The farmers of the developing countries would get a better price for their produces and the increased market price probably would encourage them to add more inputs to increase productivity from unit agricultural land. In the long run this would bring disaster to the wage earning poor people. Most of these wage labors are poorly literate and unskilled, and their *real wage* is not increasing visibly. With this change in scenario, these poor people will have to spend a very large share of their earned income on food alone leaving almost nothing to spend on simple industry-produced items as clothes, sugar, cooking oil and the like. Increased mechanized agriculture ultimately would force the small and marginal farmers to sell their land to big farmers. That would displace a sizeable labor from agriculture and the employment situation in many countries would worsen. Food production at the national level would increase; the government would be able to cut down a substantial amount of subsidies granted on fertilizers, electricity and irrigation. The poor countries that have to import huge amount of food grains would be worst hit if the agricultural prices in the international market rise.

The moment India and China decide to import food, the prices in the world market rise rapidly. Because of fall in wheat production in the major wheat producing states like Punjab, Haryana and Uttar Pradesh, the government of India decided to import 5 million tons of wheat between May and December 2007. The price of wheat in the world market was about US $ 263 per ton including the cost of transport. The announcement of import of such a large quantity of wheat within a short span of time pushed the wheat price up to US $ 320 per ton, a 20 percent increase.

The general rise in price of food grains in the world market has something to do with the unpredictable climate changes resulting in widespread drought in USA, Ukraine and Russia. Added to this is the increased demand for 'bio-fuel' (ethanol and bio-diesel). World Food Organization already has forecast that food prices may go up by 20 to 50 percent in the next few years. They have cited two major reasons for this: demand increase for food grains in India and China, and the sudden increase in the demand for bio-fuel. The agricultural subsidy in EU and USA kept the prices in the world food market at a reasonably lower level. But the increased demand for bio-fuel is changing the whole scenario appreciably. Area of cultivation of maize, the principal source for bio-fuel, has increased by 19 percent. Crop area for cotton has decreased by 28 percent and that for soybean by 15 percent in USA alone, which has resulted in increase in price of maize by 60 percent, wheat by 53 percent and soybean by 40 percent in the world market. This certainly has a telling effect on the price of milk products and animal proteins since the major components of animal feed are maize, wheat and soybean. Historically, consumer price index (CPI) in developing countries is very sensitive to change in food prices. Increase in food prices in the developed countries has only a marginal effect on inflation and CPI.

Modern Agro-management: Modern agro-management is concerned with increase in production per unit area of land. Scientists have developed special high-yielding variety (HYV) seeds. HYVs have almost replaced our traditional varieties. Not very long ago, some 42,000 varieties of rice were available in India alone. At present, only about 10 HYV seeds are used in about 75 percent of land where rice is cultivated. These seeds are imported at a very high cost. The local varieties were much adapted to local climatic conditions. Instead of using these seeds for developing indigenous HYVs, we are importing HYV seeds from Philippines, Japan, USA, and others that are not best suited to our climatic and other environmental conditions.

Scientists have found that with such genetic specialization, these HYV seeds are easy prey to pests and many diseases. Pest control throughout the world has become a tough problem. The excessive use of pesticides and insecticides are harmful to birds, helpful insects and even to animals. The residues of these pesticides are carried to ponds and rivers by rain affecting the aqua life.

Extensive use of these HYV seeds has improved the food granaries all over the world. It has brought in *green revolution* in many countries including India. India, in fact, is aspiring for a second *green revolution* and expects the technical know-how from USA would become available in this regard. Erstwhile US President George Bush's visit to India culminated in a joint declaration, which included USA's agreement to supply nuclear fuels to support India's growing need for green power and for other civilian uses. The declaration also included collaboration between the two largest democracies in agricultural research and management besides collaboration in many other areas.

Modern agricultural management has frustrated Malthusian prediction. But improved agro-technology has created a few problems as well. Excessive use of chemical fertilizer over the years increases acidity and salinity of the soil. Multiple crops from the same piece of land make the soil infertile within a few years. To counteract this, chemical fertilizers as input are required in larger doses to obtain the desired yield. The prescription is that the nature and quantum of chemical fertilizers to be used for a piece of land be decided after proper soil testing. This often is ignored in the developing countries. Because of high input cost, the poor and marginal farmers are unable to reap harvest from these improved agricultural practices.

In our eagerness to use industrialization as the road to development, enough attention has not been paid to agriculture. International development agencies need to take into cognizance the immense possibility of improving agricultural production in the developing countries on a very big scale. Their agriculture must not be allowed to be starved of resources. Land reform among others is urgently needed. Insurance cover should be given against crop failure due to weather condition and natural calamity.

Hydrological Problems: HYV requires plenty of water and additional fertilizer. The input cost therefore is heavy and often beyond the reach of small and marginal farmers who constitute the majority of farmers in the third world countries. Till the advent of HYV, farming was dependent mostly on rainwater. Cultivation of HYV requires plenty of water because of use of chemical fertilizers in large doses. The direct and indirect cost of irrigation is enormous. Continuous lifting of ground water through deep tube-wells (canal or river water is available to only a small proportion of cultivable land) and shallows has affected the water level forcing the farmers to go further deep in search of a good ground water reserve. It has affected us in many ways. Supply of drinking water, especially in areas away from rivers, has already become a serious issue in many countries. To put a check on indiscriminate use of precious water, the international funding agencies are pressing hard to levy high rates of tax for water consumption. The polluted river waters are also not safe for drinking even after very expensive treatments. The agricultural scientists are promoting a new definition of 'efficiency' – *agricultural production for every drop of water used.*

In 1995, 69 percent of total cereal area was under rain fed cultivation. By 2025, total cereal area is likely to go up by 7 percent from the 1995 level (11 percent in developing regions and a reduction by 7 percent in the developed regions).

Down under the water table is the water reservoir, the rocky bed which contains a mineral called *arsenopyrite*. Although arsenic is deadly poisonous, arsenopyrite is harmless since it is insoluble in water. It is for this reason that arsenic poisoning through drinking water was not heard of even a few decades back. Of late, many tube-wells are lifting water, which is heavily laden with arsenic. Although death due to arsenic poisoning is still insignificant, a large segment of population of West Bengal and Bangladesh is in the grip of this dreaded toxic chemical. Hydrologists are of the opinion that since most of the deep tube-wells use pipes of diameter 30–40 cm, a powerful pump can draw 5 to 100 million liter of water in 24 hours. The *cone of depression* may cover an area of some 800 square kilometer on the surface. The surface water will be dragged down causing the earth surface to sink gradually. This problem has been observed in many countries where deep tube-wells are extensively used for agricultural irrigation. About 3,500 sq km of land in California has sunk by about 10 meters; 50 sq km of Houston city has sunk by 2 meters causing extensive damage to house and airport. The same thing has happened in Mexico City where land surface has sunk by about 7 meters.

Some hydrologists consider arsenic poisoning of drinking water may have something to do with the *draw-down effect* of the water tables. When a powerful pump is run continuously for hours, there would be so much drawn down of the water table that the aerated zone containing highly active oxygen may extend even to the arsenopyrite bed. Oxygen rich water may react with arsenopyrite yielding a variety of arsenic oxides and arsenus acid, which are considerably soluble in water. Through the underground *flow line* this arsenic-rich water may travel to distant places poisoning the ground water. This could be the reason for certain outburst of arsenic poisoning in many districts of West Bengal in India.

Some restrictions have been imposed or are being imposed on deep tube-wells because of lowering of the water table and other consequences stated above. Use of underground water for irrigation and industrial purposes (the Cola companies for example) has created another serious problem of slightly different nature. There were about 900 tube-wells in peninsular region of Gujarat in India in the early sixties. In the nineties, the number swelled up to about half a million. This installation of tube-wells was largely to help irrigation for production of more food grains. Water table in the region has gone down so much so that saline water from the sea has already spoiled over 1.2 million hectors of cultivable land.

Earlier, our cropping was dependent on rainfall besides irrigation from ponds and canals. Such cropping practice helped maintain some balance in the ecology of the region. Nature has met with very harsh treatment for our demand for more food grains and other cash crops. Salinity and acidity of soils have increased. Initial gains from HYV cultivation is nearly over. A solution to this problem is to bring more and more lands under rainwater cultivation and concentrate on small irrigation projects by reclaiming water-sheds, ponds, canals where rainwater and run-offs can be stored.

Productivity of our land is fast declining. For the same amount of production we now have to use fertilizers and other inputs at a much higher dose. Production of food grains in the developing countries would continue to increase for a considerable time since modern method of cultivation is still followed only in a small proportion of cultivable land. Use of chemical fertilizers and pesticides has affected the whole food-chain. Unscientific use of pesticides has created these pests resistant to many sprays. Pesticide residues have contaminated river water, ponds and even the ground water. Although use of DDT in pest control was banned in USA long back, DDT residues are still found in their ground water. Presence of chemicals and pesticides in large doses is found in vegetables, fruits, meat and fish and in drinking water. Unless we put a heavy check on the growth of our population, this rat-race for more food will ultimately prove Malthusian Doctrine true. West, which initiated the use of chemical fertilizers and pesticides and is still making a huge business by exporting fertilizers and pesticides to the developing countries, now wants for themselves food grains, vegetables and fruits that are grown using bio-fertilizers.

Discussion of on environment pollution, schools of thought and movements to curb environmental pollution are presented in Chapter 14.

13.6 Energy Consumption

Accelerating economic growth and achieving a better standard of living demand availability of adequate clean energy at an affordable price. Unlike other commodities electricity cannot be stored in the conventional sense for future use, cannot be substituted by something else, and generation and consumption of electricity have to be simultaneous and instantaneous. To remain competitive in domestic and international market, the production process of any commodity must be delinked from conventional human or animal energy and entrusted to a system that can precisely and accurately carry out a set of programmed operations to deliver the designed quality product independent of direct human interference or participation. Growth of population in the last hundred years has forced us to adopt energy-intensive (and therefore capital-intensive) production processes to increase food production, build more houses for residential and other uses, opt for a faster mode of transportation and communication, diversify and intensify industrial productions to cater to the growing demands and changing aspirations of people and generate employment opportunities for varied types of job aspirants. The stage of economic development a country is in can be fairly measured by its per capita consumption of power. The principal bulk consumers of power are industries, residential units, transport and communication, and of course agriculture.

The world total energy consumption (TEC) in 1990 was 363 EJ (exa Joule) or 3.63×10^{11} Giga Watt (1GW = 10^9 Watt, Watt W = voltage V × electric current A, and A = Joules J/second) of which 178.9 EJ (49.56 percent of TEC) was consumed by North America, Western Europe, Japan, Australia and New Zealand. India's share was a meager 2.9 percent and China's share was 8.29 percent. Fossil fuels accounted for 81 percent of TEC (coal 25 percent, oil 36 percent and natural gas 20 percent); alternative sources (nuclear, wind, hydro, geothermal, bio-mass, etc.) shared 13 percent and traditional (timber fuel) 6 percent. Per capita consumption in the world was about 68.7 GJ per annum (12.6 GJ in India) compared to 348 GJ in North America and 26.4GJ in China.

Consumption of electricity per capita varies widely by regions and countries. Per capita consumption of electricity in the high income OECD countries is about four times that of a common man around the globe. It is no wonder that the percentage share of the developed countries in the release of GHG in atmosphere is about 50 percent of total emissions by all countries. Per capita electricity consumption of a common man has increased by 156 percent between 1980 and 2002; in the same period per capita consumption in high income countries increased by 118 percent. In the low income countries, the per capita consumption of electricity was a meager 339 KWh a year even in 2002. India was even behind the South Asian average with a per capita consumption standing at 576 KWh/year.

Whereas OECD countries consumed energy about twice the amount consumed in non-OECD region in 1970, total electricity consumption in the non-OECD countries is likely to be 15 percent more than what the OECD countries would consume by 2015. Electrification rate in the developing countries in 1990 was less than 50 percent (world average of 60 percent). The world average of electrification was a little less than 75 percent in 2000; the developing countries were 10 points behind this. Sub-Saharan Africa would continue to remain starved in electricity generation by the world standard for many more years to come. The situation appears quite gloomy in South Asia too. A faster improvement in the region as a whole is expected, and India would contribute the most. East Asia, North Africa, Middle East and Latin America are likely to achieve cent percent electrification before 2015. Transmission and distribution (T&D) losses remain a major concern in the developing countries. T&D losses in India, are as high as 25 percent.

Table 13.7 *Electricity consumption per capita, 1980–2002 (Kilowatt-hours)*

Regions/countries	**1980[a]**	**1998[b]**	**2002[a]**
WORLD	1573	2074	2465
Arab States	626	1312	1946
East Asia and the Pacific	329	818	1439
Latin America and the Caribbean	1019	1464	1927
South Asia	171	387	576
Sub-Saharan Africa	434	480	536
Central & Eastern Europe and the CIS	3294	2893	3329
Developing countries	388	757	1155
Least developed countries	83	76	106
OECD	5761	6969	8815
High income	8616	8406	10198
Medium income	623	1370	1653
Low income	174	362	399
INDIA	173	384	569

a: HDR 2005, b: HDR 2001

Note: Energy consumption data cited in HDR 2001 and 2005 for 1980 differ considerably

Source: HDR 2001, 2005

Table 13.8 *World energy consumption by region and fuel (in 10^{15} BTU)*

Region & Energy source	***1970***	***1993***	***2010***	***2015***	***Annual % change***	
					1970–93	***1993–2015***
1	*2*	*3*	*4*	*5*	*6*	*7*
OECD	135.1	190.7	239.8	251.4	1.5	1.3
Oil	70.6	82.1	97.2	100.0	0.7	0.9
Natural gas	27.1	38.9	58.1	65.0	1.6	2.4
Coal	27.7	34.7	40.8	42.1	1.0	0.9
Nuclear	0.8	18.1	18.9	16.7	14.5	–0.4
Renewable	8.8	16.8	24.8	27.6	2.9	2.3
Non-OECD	71.7	158.3	255.3	291.0	3.5	2.8
Oil	27.2	54.1	90.5	102.8	3.0	3.0
Natural gas	9.1	36.2	59.9	68.7	6.2	3.0
Coal	32.0	52.9	81.0	92.5	2.2	2.6
Nuclear	0.1	4.0	5.4	4.9	17.4	1.0
Renewable	3.3	11.2	18.6	22.0	5.5	3.1

Source: IEA 1995, 1996

Figure 13.17 *Electrification rates by region*

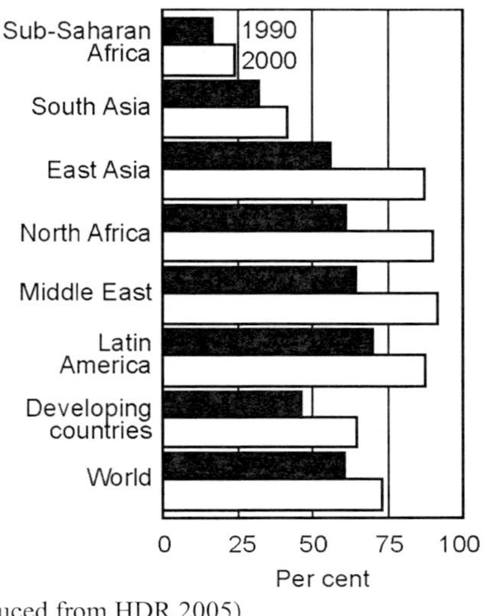

(Reproduced from HDR 2005)

Figure 13.18 *Electricity losses, selected countries*

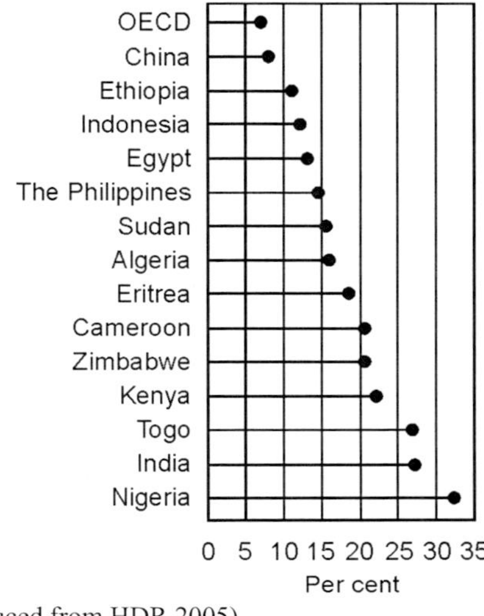

(Reproduced from HDR 2005)

Though the world still has vast coal reserve, the experts agree that natural gas needs to be used more aggressively for power generation for several reasons: though non-renewable, gas reserve is plenty, energy from it is cleaner than by burning of coal, and unlike crude oil the price of natural gas in the world market is likely to remain low and stable. Pressure is on the developing countries to produce as much cleaner energy as possible. China and India, who would be dominating the world scenario in electricity generation in the coming decades, have to find out alternative sources for power generation. India has been planning to bring natural gas from Iran and Myanmar through pipelines via Pakistan and Bangladesh respectively. India is also looking for procuring nuclear fuels, reactors and technology from other countries to set up additional nuclear plants as also for a secured supply of nuclear fuels for its existing plants engaged in generation of electricity. Many would like to see the recently concluded US-India nuclear deal from this perspective.

The International Energy Agency (IEA) in 2004 estimated that the new worldwide energy capacity required by rising economic growth, especially in the developing countries, would derive 1,400 GW from burning coal (half of it in India and China), 470 GW from burning oil, 439 GW from hydro, and about 400 GW from renewable sources (mostly from solar and wind power). By 2030, IEA estimate shows that additional energy required worldwide would be around 4,700 GW of which only 150 GW could come from nuclear plants. Government of India's Planning Commission's expert committee on integrated energy policy forecasts that to sustain a yearly GDP growth rate of 8–9 percent, the country needs by 2031 a power generation capacity of 778,095 MW and increased primary energy supply by three to four times to meet the electricity consumption that is likely to be five to seven times the current consumption level. Although India has 214 billion tons of hard coal reserve (about 7 percent of world's total reserve), only 84 billion tons are recoverable reserves of anthracite and bituminous coal. With 5 percent annual increase in production, the coal reserves are likely to last for about 40–50 years. We need therefore to look for alternative sources of energy fast.

Nuclear energy: Commercial nuclear plants are definitely one such viable option. The Expert Committee, Government of India admits that the nuclear energy theoretically offers the most potent means to long-term energy security. However, it has been argued by many, especially those opposing setting up new nuclear energy plants, that construction of gas-based power plants would be economical than construction of new nuclear plants by borrowing technology and buying equipments and fuels at enormous costs from other countries.

There is no doubt that fission of an atom in nuclear reactor produces several million times the energy produced by conventional burning of one atom of carbon from fossil fuels. Even if there is an abundance of natural gas for generating electricity for generations to come, the potential for cheap energy from nuclear fuel, many strategic analysts assert, seems unlimited. Nearly all nuclear reactors all over the world use uranium as the fuel; and the uranium reserves are practically unlimited. The sea water has so much of uranium that the same when extracted and purified can alone give us all the electricity we need for millions of years. We need not use this uranium for its enormous cost of extraction and purification. Even if the nuclear energy production dramatically increases, the world still will have conventional reserves in ores for production of electricity for over 100 years. With design improvements, the new reactors can give us 100 times as much energy from a kg of uranium as the existing reactors do. India has only a modest reserve of uranium, 95,000 tons (1 percent of world's reserve) from which 61,000 tons may be obtained for power generation. The nuclear reactors require enriched uranium. Natural uranium contains 99.3 percent of U-238 non-fissionable isotope and only 0.7 percent of fissionable radioactive U-235 isotope. Nuclear reactors require enriched uranium or 'yellow cake' in which proportion of U-235 has been increased at least to 4–5 percent. Most modern reactors need 15–20 percent enriched uranium. The separation and enrichment process is really expensive (nuclear bombs require more than 90 percent of U-235 or Pu-239). The developed West has been trying hard to develop fast breeder reactor (FBR) for generation of electricity since the FBR reactor can actually produce more fissionable fuel than they use.[1] India has a very limited reserve of uranium but has about 360,000 tons of monazite deposits along its sea coast (Kerala in particular) which when mined may yield 225,000 tons of thorium metal (Th-232). India is trying to develop Fast Breeder Reactor (FBR) intending to use her vast thorium reserve. It is said that this FBR reactor would produce as much or more fuel as bye product as the quantity it needs to generate electricity from this reactor. India's first 40 MW Fast Breeder Test Reactor (FBTR) attained criticality on 18th October 1985. India has developed the technology to produce plutonium rich U-Pu mixed carbide fuel. This can be used in the Fast Breeder Reactor. Another FBR – the 500MW prototype fast breeder reactor (PFBR) – is expected to be commissioned at Kalpakkam near Chennai by 2010. The thorium-based reactor, which India is trying to develop for commercial electricity generation, as is claimed by Indian scientists, would yield much fissionable material Pu-239 and U-233 than it burns only in a period of two and half years. That is

1 Under appropriate conditions, the neutrons given off by *fission* reactions can breed more fuel from otherwise non-fissionable isotopes like U-238. The non-fissionable U-238 is 140 times more abundantly available than fissionable U-235. Bombardment of U-238 with neutrons released from U-235 leads to the production of fissionable plutonium Pu-239. The fissionable fuel is highly enriched U-235. The reactor fuel is surrounded by a 'blanket' of non-fissionable U-238 and the reactor does not use any moderator. The fast neutrons are efficient in transmuting U-238 to Pu-239. India is developing FBR that will use Th-232 as fertile material and Pu-239 as fissionable material. Liquid sodium, instead of water, would be used as a coolant and would act as a very efficient heat transfer medium. The range of operating temperature of liquid sodium is very high since solid sodium melts at 98°C and it does not boil till 892°C. Its larger specific heat enables it as an efficient heat-transfer fluid.

the 'seed' for firing a second reactor (Pu-239) can be obtained from the nuclear chain reaction of the first reactor. The proposed FTBR would use Pu-239 as the 'fission' material and Thorium-232 as the 'fertile' material.

Renewable sources of energy: The choice between energy sources depends on abundance of various resources in the country, technologies available, and on the costs determined by history and geography. France's civilian nuclear reactors (59 out of 444 reactors worldover) produce about 78 percent of the country's electricity requirements, the rest comes from hydro-electricity. Only 20 percent of total electricity demand in USA is met by its 104 nuclear reactors (USA did not add any new reactor since 1978), and Japan has 34 percent of electricity from 54 reactors. Nuclear reactors contribute about 4 percent to India's total electricity demand.

Subsidies given to fossil fuels are probably the single most important impediment against renewable energy. UNDP assessment report states that governments gave subsidies worth US $ 250–300 billion to fossil fuels in 1990s. A non-governmental agency report (Green Scissors Campaign) assessed that US government spent US $ 111.5 billion on energy research and developmental plan between 1948 and 1998. As much as 60 percent of this amount was spent on nuclear energy research and another 20 percent on fossil fuel research. In fact, in all OECD countries, 80 percent of public money for energy research was spent on nuclear energy alone in the last 50 years although only about 17 percent of the world total energy comes from nuclear sources. The European Union gave more than US $ 72 billion to coal mining industries between 1994 and 2001. IEA estimates that some US $ 16 trillion will be invested worldwide in energy infrastructure during 2001–2030. About 60 percent of this will go to power generation and distribution. Half of this investment would be in the developing countries.

Very soon environmental and health costs for using different types of fuels for electricity generation and for other purposes will have to be taken into cognizance. This 'external cost', researches show, would double the cost of producing electricity from coal or oil and cost of electricity generated from gas would increase by 30 percent. In EU, this external cost for electricity generation from fossil fuels would be 1–2 percent of EU GDP, not including the cost of global warming. These costs ultimately will have to be paid by the consumers. If the aggregate external cost of road transport is added to this, it would be somewhere in the range 3–4 percent of GDP. The current average cost of generation of electricity from coal in EU is £ 4 cent/KWh (US cent 4.8/KWh). The additional external cost would take it to £13c/kwh (US $ 15.6c/KWh). This would be about 2.5 times higher than the current cost of generation of electricity from wind and half of that from solar photo-voltaic (PV) systems. Once the environmental costs are taken into account and subsidies on fossil fuels removed, renewable technologies can compete with fossil fuel technologies.

According to IEA fact-sheet, renewable energy in 2000 accounted for 13.8 percent of world's total primary energy supply. Combustible renewables and wastes comprised 80 percent of renewables, followed by hydropower (16.5 percent).

For electricity generation (global total), renewable sources share was 19 percent, next only to 39 percent for coal and well ahead of nuclear (17 percent), natural gas (17 percent) and oil (8 percent). Most of the electricity generated from renewables comes from hydro power plant (92 percent) followed by combustible wastes (5 percent). Geothermal, solar and wind together accounted for less than 3 percent in 2000. Whereas biomass among the renewables is most popular

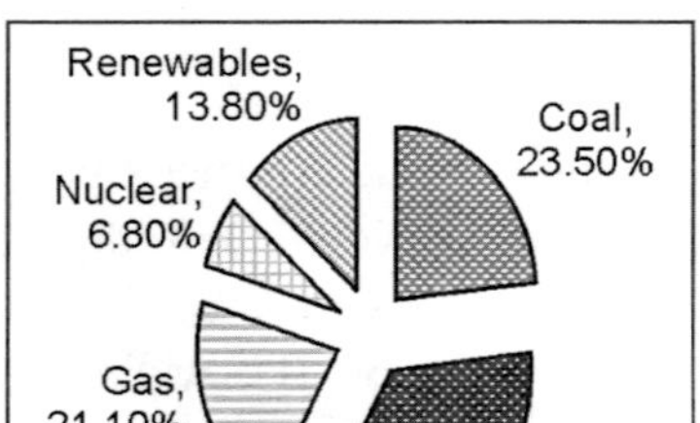

Figure 13.21 *Global energy supply sources*

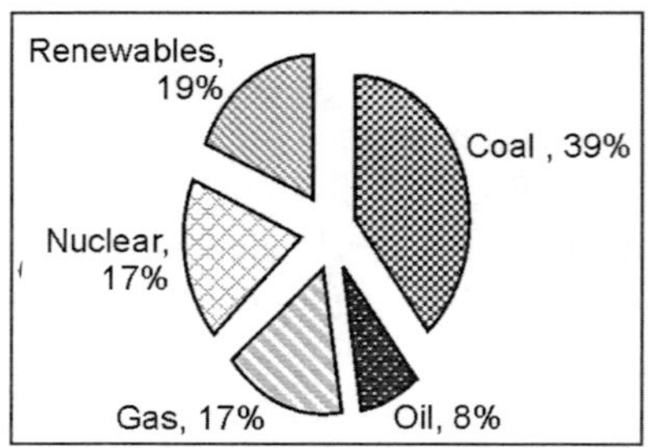

Figure 13.22 *Global electricity supply sources*

in regions like Asia, Latin America and Africa, solar and wind energy are most popular in OECD countries.

The fact that renewable energy can help in fighting climate change is indisputable. There are no two opinions that the primary responsibility for the climate change worldover lies with industrialized North. They must cut emissions. The projection of world energy consumption (Table 13.7 & 13.8) indicates that energy consumption in non-OECD countries would grow much faster vis-à-vis OECD countries and by 2010, the total energy consumption in non-OECD countries will exceed the same in OECD countries. Share of renewable energy in the total energy consumption in OECD countries in 1993 was 8.8 percent; in 2010, it would go up by 1.5 percent. In the non-OECD countries, its share in 2010 is likely to remain almost at the same level as it had been in 1993, 7.01 percent. Since the developing countries' energy consumption in 2010 is likely to increase by 161 percent compared to consumptions in 1993, the developing countries need to be provided with funds and necessary technologies to invest more in non-carbon based energy trajectory. The World Bank group in 2003 recommended the Bank to invest its funds in renewable energy development, emission-reducing projects and other efforts that delink energy use from GHG emissions.

13.7 Waste Disposal

Consumerism of the rich countries has left the third world countries in a precarious condition. The developed countries spare no opportunity to increasing their trade with the third world countries, even with their industrial wastes. They are aware that the industrial wastes can harm a country and her people more than the benefits it can obtain from the industrial production processes. The health conscious West has resorted to indiscriminate dumping of industrial wastes or destroying them through fire or other means. Third World countries have been selected for dumping their non-biodegradable wastes. In 1993, USA transported 4,500 tons of waste plastic bottles to India alone. They were sent for recycling purposes with the recycled product sent back to USA. Only about 60–70 percent of such plastic bottles are recyclable and the rest have to be dumped in India. UN statistics show that in 1990 alone 400 Mmt of wastes were produced by industries all over the world, 98 percent of which came from 24 OECD countries.

The Third World countries import industrial and other wastes from the developed countries purely for economic reasons. India is potentially short in plastic, lead, zinc and many other highly toxic materials. The developed countries are too eager to get rid of these toxic wastes and in the process they still make lot of money from this waste transfer. Large quantities of used batteries, zinc, copper and aluminum wastes are imported in India every year from USA, Canada, Australia, UK, and others. In 1994, a high level committee from Australia came to India to settle a deal for importing industrial wastes from that country. Earlier, African countries were the unrivaled dumping grounds of such wastes. The Organization of African Unity, comprised of 69 African nations, signed a declaration preventing import-export of all types of wastes. Since then the Indian sub-continent has become the target land for exporting the waste products. Most of the multi-national giants even are exploring the possibility of shifting many of their industries producing toxic wastes to the third world countries. Although a memorandum of understanding banning export-import of any type of wastes after 1998 has been signed by all nations, we still have to wait and see if this lucrative waste-trade can be stopped altogether. India (Gujarat, in particular) has remained the destination for ship-breaking for many countries. The Supreme Court of India had to intervene when a ship from France was sent to India for breaking which contained several tons of asbestos and other highly carcinogenic toxic substances.

Production in industries and powerhouses will have to be increased rapidly to cope with the mounting demands and growing numbers. Most nations have laws for controlling pollution of earth, water and air. However, their implementation is difficult in a fast growing country. Waste management often is more costly than production management. The developed countries realized this and decided to find places in the third world countries to shift waste-intensive industries. The problem of the developed nations will reach a climax once waste management laws are implemented internationally. Already a dialogue is on if the outer space, more specifically moon, can be used as a dumping ground for highly toxic electronic and radioactive wastes. Disposal of radioactive wastes from nuclear houses and demolition of such powerhouses once they have lived their full life are serious issues before the scientists and politicians. Chernobyl disaster is still fresh in our memory.

14 Environmental Concern

Road to Rio

14.1 Environmental Pollution

Times magazine described prevention and control of pollution of the environment as the greatest challenge of the 21st century. Environmentalists like Eugene Leden went as far as to say that the future of mankind has been leased out to this ever-degrading environment. Technological progress has solved many of our problems, but indiscriminate use of natural resources and dumping of various types of poisonous wastes in atmosphere, soil and water bodies have created a condition which is not at all conducive to various life forms on this earth. Fertilizers and pesticide run-offs have polluted most of our natural water bodies, making them unfit for aquatic life and human use. The traditional view that air, water and light are free ingredients for all our productive exercises has long been abandoned. Cleaner environment requires judicious use of these ingredients in our every day life.

Social cost of environmental pollution in Europe is estimated at over 4 percent of GDP. This cost in USA is between 2 and 12 percent. In 1992, the cost of pollution of environment in India was estimated at about US $ 10 billions, which was about 4.5 percent of the country's GDP. Water pollution alone accounted for about US $ 5.7 billion. Soil erosion costs 4–6 percent of agricultural income. Deforestation costs about 214 million dollars every year. The campaign for Cleaner Production has helped the industries in New Zealand to bring down their costs by 50–100 percent. A survey in Czeck Republic shows that cleaner production has helped reduce industrial wastes by about 22 thousand tons a year, which is equivalent to saving of 240 million dollars. In Ho Chi Min City of Vietnam, over 10,000 women are busy making consumer goods by recycling household wastes. Brazil is making ethanol from sugarcane juice and using this as substitute for petrol.

It was only from the sixties of the last century that environment has become a principal component in our development planning. Department of Environment has been set up in most countries and has become a key ministry in the final approval of any project – industrial, irrigation, power generation, town planning and what not. The Apex Court in India has taken keen interest in pollution control. From time to time it has intervened on its own or in response to some public interest litigation (PIL) in matters of pollution – industrial, emission from automobiles and power generation plants, industries in densely populated residential areas, etc.

The environmental scientists all over the world are anxious about the possible effect of unrestricted growth of population on environment, natural resources and bio-diversity. They fear that population growth along with sharp rise in consumption level in the name of improving the standard of living of the masses will exploit nature so much so that it will damage our environment and ecosystem beyond repair. The imbalance in the ecosystem ultimately will be a great hindrance to maintaining the normal food chain, which will affect the entire biological world.

Size of population is definitely related to the nature of ecological disturbance in a country. But the number speaks only a part of the truth. India is three and half times more populour than USA although the later has three times more land area. An average American exploits nature several hundred times more than does an average Indian. From the World Resources Institute published report in 1987 we see that USA released CFC (chloro-fluro-carbon, which directly attacks ozone layer in atmosphere) 500 times more than did India. Ozone hole, which already has drawn a serious attention of scientists, permits ultraviolate and other dangerous cosmic rays to freely enter into our atmosphere; they could ultimately become a potential source of destroying life on earth. An average person in the developed countries vis-à-vis the developing ones extract more from their lands to keep their intake of high quality food at a very high level. This is true of other consumption items – power, water, forest product (wood blocks and compressed wood are used for construction of a very large proportion of residential houses in USA) and the like. It is not a fact that the problem of numbers is a problem of the Third World countries alone. The developed countries too suffer from their numbers primarily due to their reckless consumption of earth resources and blind search for more and more comfort in living.

14.2 Land Resource

Farm land: Fertile soil and water are the two most vital natural resources for sustainable development. Although soil is a 'renewable resource' (good farming practice and pasture management help maintain its structure and fertility), the world's stock of good soil is declining because of soil erosion, salinization, deforestation, desertification, pollution and growth of urban centers and industrial and other uses. Soil degradation is a risk to poverty and livelihoods for many in the developing countries.

A modest estimate show that an area equal to the entire cultivated area of India today, about 140 million hectares (mha) will be lost to the world in about 25 years if soil erosion continues unabated. Between 5 and 7 mha of agricultural land are being eroded every year all over the world.

The future of India and all other developing countries depends largely on the health of their farm land. India today has over 1 billion people. To feed them the annual production of food grain has to be around 250 million tons. Bringing much more land under cultivation is out of question. Our passion for rapid industrial growth and developing the necessary infrastructure to attract more funds from the private and international investors, thousands of acres of fertile agricultural land are lost every year. Crop area is unlikely to increase much even if we try to bring more fallow land for cultivation. Therefore, it is through intensive farming and crop rotation that such targets can be reached. Can we achieve it with our existing infrastructure and input resources? 'Save the soil and water' should have been the slogan of the era; 'save the oil' remains the more important slogan for politicians worldover.

India has plenty of unharnessed water resources. According to FAO estimate, the irrigated area in the developing countries is expected to expand from 105 mha in 1980 to around 148 mha in 2000, with three-quarters of this expansion taking place in the Far East, and three-quarters of that in India alone. With the resources available, India has the potential of reaching 300 million metric tones of food grain (US out-put around 260 Mmt). Certain calculations put agricultural potential in India at 3.5 times its present level.

Soil Degradation and Erosion: Such dreams may never be realized primarily due to mismanagement of our soil. Nearly 53 percent of total land area in India is susceptible to serious environmental degradation. Of the cultivated landmass in India, 60 percent of it requires immediate soil conservation measures. 40–100 tones of topsoil per ha of the Deccan black soil is lost every year. The loss of soil in India was estimated at 6,000 mt in 1972, which in terms of loss in soil nutrients (nitrogen, phosphorous, potassium and other micronutrients) amounted to Rs.7,000 million in that year. The scientists say that India is losing as large quantity of inorganic fertilizer every year through soil erosion as it is injecting them artificially. This is true for most other countries as well.

Urbanization is also taking heavy toll of our precious agricultural land. The concrete jungle, tar road and brickfields are consuming large area of our good cropping land. But such soil loss is to be considered small compared to the annual loss we incur due to soil erosion alone. The National Commission on Flood in India estimated a total area of 20 mha was affected by flood in 1971. In 10 years it rose to 40 mha. This is despite the flood protection measures taken by the government at a considerable cost.

Silting of the riverbeds and artificial reservoirs often is the cause of flood. It is estimated that due to siltation alone India continues to lose about 60,000 ha every year. The choking of the estuaries and harbors are other adverse instances of the impact of eroded soil carried to the sea. A land mass about the size 24 km × 11 km is coming up (Purbasha) in Bay of Bengal as a result of accumulation of silt.

Soil Salinity: Over US $ 2,000 million has been spent in India alone in developing surface and ground water irrigation system in 30 years after independence. A similar amount is in the pipeline since the sixth plan for developing the irrigation system. It is estimated that about 50 mha of agricultural land will be brought under irrigation system. The irrigation canals bring the farmers the most important input for agricultural production, but they have become potential sources for water-logging and salinity of soils. Increase in salinity has something to do with the rising ground water table. Ground irrigation projects in coastal regions (Gujarat peninsula, for example) have forced sea-water to invade the agricultural lands.

14.3 Water

World Water Conference held in Argentina in 1972 revealed that if a half-gallon bottle represented all the worlds' water, the quantity of fresh water would be about half a teaspoonful. Only a little over 2.5 percent of world's total water resources can provide us with fresh water. 70 percent of the fresh water resources are in the form of ice caps. Another 29 percent is attributable to soil moisture and water stored in deep aquifers not accessible for humans. Only 0.03 percent of the world's total water resource (less than 1 percent of fresh water), internally renewable, comes from rivers, lakes, streams and ponds. This on an average is around 43,000 km^3. Between 1965 and 1995, availability of water from renewable resources has declined by 40 percent (IIWM, 2001).

Not all *internally renewable water resources* (IRWR) can be controlled by humans. Even with best of technology, the *potentially utilizable water resource* (PUWR) is 33 percent of IRWR. This amounts to 2,370 km^3; 14 percent of this are developed and diverted as *Primary Water Supply* (PWS). A part of it is evaporated. Of the total water thus available for human use, 74 percent goes in irrigation, 18 percent for industrial use and only 8 percent for domestic consumption. The developing countries use 85 percent of PWS for irrigation compared to only 42 percent in the developed countries. The developed countries use 44 percent of PWS for industrial use compared to only 9 percent in the developing countries. South Asia use 96 percent of PWS in agriculture and a meager 2 percent in industries. Fresh water is becoming a scarce commodity every day as individuals, industries and farmers pour their wastes and filths into the nearest sink.

Figure 14.1 *World's water supply*

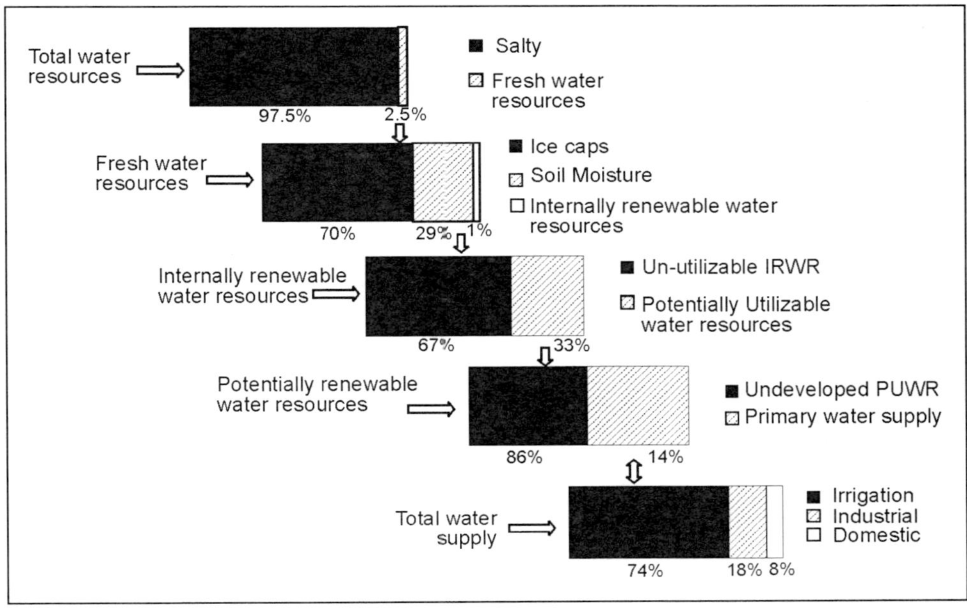

(Reproduced from 'Water for Rural Development', IIWM, 2001)

Water availability for various types of uses is not uniformly distributed over regions and countries. International Institute of Water Management (IIWM) has broadly categorized regions into three broad groups depending upon their water needs.

(I) Water-Scarce Areas
(II) High Potential Areas
(III) High Need Areas

Countries in the Middle East and North Africa, large parts of South Asia, China, Europe and Central Asia are *water-scarce areas* in the sense that additional water cannot be tapped in the said regions for more development. These countries have to face the challenge of reallocating available

Figure 14.2 *World's population and per capita availability of IRWR*

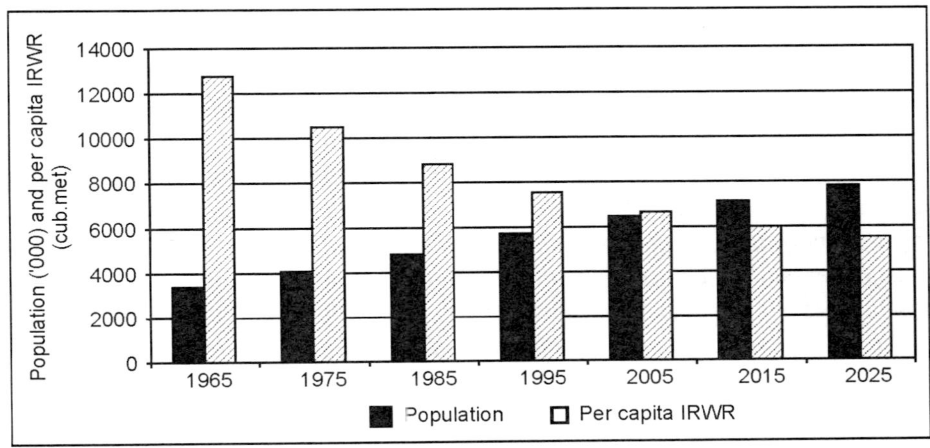

water from lower-value use, as in traditional agriculture, to higher value use, as in industries, cities, and high-value agriculture.

High-potential areas, as per IIWM water scarcity map, are South Asia (SA), East Asia and the Pacific (EAP) and Latin America and the Caribbean (LAC). In the Ganges basin, home to 500 million people, many of them are amongst the poorest of the world there is a huge scope for increasing water production for meeting the various needs for industries, cities and agriculture. There is plenty of water in the monsoon months, regularly flooding the adjoining areas; but during most of the remaining months, availability of water is reduced drastically.

The figure below shows the regional variation in availability of IRWR. The EAP region with more than one-third of world's population has only 19 percent of the IRWR. LAC countries with only 8 percent of world's population share are endowed with 34 percent of world's IRWR. North American (NAME) region has 16 percent of world's IRWR and only 5 percent of world's total population. SA with over one-fifth of world population has only 5 percent of the renewable water resources. Four regions, namely, Europe and Central Asia (ECA), LAC, Australia and New Zealand (AUNZ) and North America (NAME) enjoy greater share of world IRWR compared to their share in the world population.

Figure 14.3 *Distribution of population and IRWR*

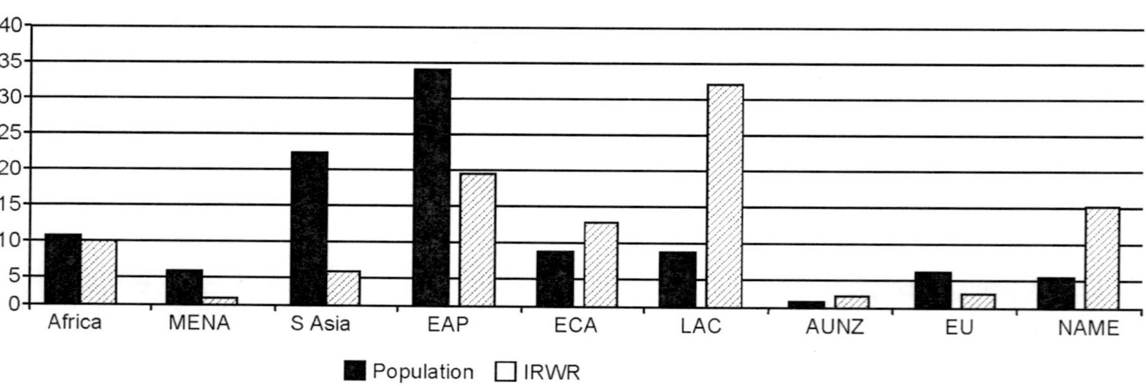

There are considerable variations in regional water endowments. For example, the Amazon basin in Brazil generates almost half of IRWR for LAC and its share to LAC population is only one-third. The Central African countries, with only 12 percent of the total population, generate more than 40 percent of the IRWR of the African region. The Southern African countries, with 15 percent of the total African population, generate only 8 percent of the IRWR. Water scarcity is an every day reality in sub-Saharan Africa. There are many pockets in the region that are economically water scarce although they have plenty of utilizable resources. These countries are too poor to invest in using good technology to tap this water resource.

With rising income, urbanization and industrialization, allocation of water for various uses is fast changing. Water is a basic need in the domestic sector and is a very important component in the growth of industries. Water use in these two sectors receives the tallest attention of planners; agriculture, the most prolific user of water, is pushed to the third spot in their eyes. The growth of irrigation in a country or region therefore has to be seen in the context of leftover from domestic and industrial requirements.

The MENA region is already withdrawing substantially high percentage (79 percent) of their potentially utilizable water. Most of the countries in the region are already water scarce, a reason why they have to import huge quantity of food. Some countries like Saudi Arabia and Kuwait are investing a lot on desalinization plants. This cannot be a plausible alternative to most other countries that are in short supply of IRWR. The SA region follows next with 43 percent. By 2025, the SA region will have to develop 52 percent of their PUWR to meet future demand. India, which is not water scarce at present, is likely to run into trouble with its IRWR by 2025. The situation may worsen if global warming and the Asian Brown Cloud (ABC) blanket cover continue to hasten melting of ice in the snow caps and thousands of glaciers in the Himalayas. China, situated in EAP region, too is likely to cross the threshold of physical scarcity in 2025. The African region has sufficient water resources but Southern Africa will be in the same situation as China in 2025. Compared to MENA and SA, other regions' primary water supplies are relatively small portions of their PUWR.

IIWM forecasts that the developing countries would have substantial cereal deficit (419 Mmt, equivalent to 17 percent of their consumption) by 2025. This could happen since no significant growth in rain-fed and irrigated crop area. Such impact will be most in SA and EAP regions.

The total available water for use in India is about 1,900 billion cubic meters per annum. Rivers, lakes and ponds contribute about 86 percent of this. In India, most of the annual rainfall happens within 100 hours spanning over a few months. It is estimated that only 38 percent of the IRWR can potentially be controlled for human use. Most of the rains in China are received in the monsoon months, mainly in the Yangtze River basin in the south. A large part of it cannot be stored or controlled; it flows to the sea without being used for productive purposes. The Congo basin in the African region and the Amazon basin in Brazil in the LAC region have almost the same fate as the Yangtze River in China.

A staggering 70 percent of available water in India is polluted. Community wastes from human settlements account for four times as much waste as industrial effluents. Most of the waste waters are released into watercourses without treatment. It is estimated that over 8 million workdays are lost every year due to water-related diseases.

Water pollution severely affects aqua life. Industrial pollutants in the untreated water discharge and run-off from the farm lands have the primary responsibility for this. The industrial pollutants affect the industries most. The rise of pollution in the Damodar River in India is affecting the power units of DPL. The latter's demineralizing plants get exhausted in four hours instead of the rated eight hours.

Bottled water: When potable water already has become a precious commodity, bottled water and soft drinks are heavily taxing our ecosystem. A study published by Earth Policy Institute, Washington shows that bottled water consumption has globally doubled between 1999 and 2004. In India, demand for bottled water tripled between 1999 and 2004. Sample studies show that bottled water is no healthier than tap water even in the industrially developed countries, but is 10,000 times more expensive. One liter of bottled water is sometimes even costlier than one liter of petrol in some countries. Making plastic bottles to meet just the US demand for bottled water, more than 1.5 billion barrels of oil are required annually. USA alone consumed about 26 billion liters of bottled water in 2004.

Nature of Water Pollution: Our earth is an oxygen-water planet. Water is required for a variety of reasons – drinking, cleaning, bathing, irrigating, and cooling and in industrial production of almost everything. Nature is our only source for this invaluable commodity. Water evaporated from sea, river and lake comes back as rain. A river 'inhales' oxygen with every swirl of the water and this oxygen maintain the aqua life. The green aquatic plants release through photosynthesis oxygen into water. Indiscriminate discharge of effluent and industrial wastes directly into the rivers has greatly reduced the natural process of oxygenation of water. The aerobes are the natural purifier of water carrying wastes. The suspended and dissolved particles are consumed by the aerobes and in doing so they consume heavily the oxygen in water. Algae present in water absorb the inorganic and mineral matters produced by the aerobes and convert it back into useful organic matters. In this, they release oxygen through photosynthesis.

The wastes discharged into water often contain host of disease germs. Rivers have a variety of protozoa that destroy many of these germs. The survival of these aquatic protozoa depends upon the oxygen content of the water. Unless the algae supply the needed oxygen, the aquatic protozoa cannot survive. With the supply of oxygen diminishing, the presence of aerobes and aquatic protozoa diminishes.

Scientists have devised various parameters for measuring pollution and purity of water. Waste discharges into rivers are quantified as total solids (TS), absorbed or dissolved solids (DS) and suspended solids (SS). The principal bacteria that accompany these solids are *E coli.* These are measured in terms of the most probable number (MPN).

For consuming and destroying these solids and bacteria, oxygen is required by the aerobes and protozoa. The amount of oxygen required to sustain these organisms is called the *biological oxygen demand* (BOD). The *chemical oxygen demand* (COD) refers to oxygen used up in converting organic wastes into inorganic materials. When BOD and COD begin to overtake dissolved oxygen (DO) level, rivers are said to *die.* Other parameters used for measuring pollution and purity of water are temperature, pH, free ammonia, chloride, nitrite, etc., conductivity, hardness and trace metals. For each of these parameters scientists have prescribed a range of 'acceptable' values for different types of water use. For instance, MPN value for potable water ideally is zero per 100 ml of water. But different countries follow different norms. Japan, for example, recommends less than 50 per 100 ml for class I water. The Indian standard for inland surface water recommends no more than 5,000 MPN per 100 ml. Before Yamuna enters Delhi, 100 ml of water contains about 7,500 coliform organisms. Further down as Yamuna receives the waste discharge from Delhi, the MPN skyrockets to 24,000,000 per 100 ml. One can imagine the value of MPN at points further down as the Ganges cover the cities like Kanpur and Kolkata.

Pure clean water should have a BOD less than 5 parts per million (ppm) or 3 mg per liter. The municipal and industrial wastes regularly exceed this number, even after intensive treatment. Large scale pollution of the Damodar River near Asansol in West Bengal results in BOD values as high as 270 mg/liter and suspended particles are well in excess of 100,000 mg/liter.

The challenge facing the planners all over the world, especially those who already are deficient in fresh water reserve, is to ensure that the poorest have ready access to clean water in sufficient quantities for their domestic and other uses for a sustainable livelihood. Freshwater ecosystem resources probably are of greatest importance in semi-arid regions in terms of food security and better health.

14.4 Forests

The ever-increasing number in the thickly populated developing countries forced destruction of much of their forests to increase area for habitation, construction of dams, roads and industries, land for cultivation and to obtain timber and fuel for household and other uses. It is estimated that over 13 million hectare acres (mha) from tropical forests is lost every year. This deforestation trend has worrying ecological consequences. The fast increase in green house gases (GHG) and the climatic change all over the world in recent years, make it imperative that we restore some of the lost forest cover. Pressure has been mounting through international forums for preservation of forest in the developing countries in the interest of stability of global atmosphere. In fact, loans and aids from international agencies often are tagged to population control and forest preservation and bio-diversity programs. How this pressure is mounting is easily seen if we look at the dependence of these countries on foreign aids. Between 1970 and 1992, the foreign debt of these countries increased from $100,000 million to about $1,500,000 million. In 1992, the developing countries had to pay over $160,000 million by way of interest and part payment of principal. Roughly one-fourth of annual budget in India covers provision for loan repayment (internal and external, with interest).

Some 100 years back, India had about three times as much forest area as it has today. Whereas the prescribed minimum of forest land for a country is one-third of its total area, the forest department statistics claims approximately 23 percent of the country's total area under forest cover, that is, about 75 mha. However, this figure is disputed even by other official agencies. National Committee of Environmental Planning (NCEP) is of the opinion that no more than 12 percent of the country's total land surface is under adequate tree cover. International Union for the Conservation of Nature (IUCN) estimated a loss of 2.5 mha of mangrove forests in the first 80 years of the last century. Forests can resist extreme environmental hazards – water-logging, salinity, infertility, high winds and absorption of CO_2 and release of O_2 in the atmosphere.

Excessive *deforestation* has increased floods, soil erosion and siltation in dams and rivers and changed the microclimate. The ecological bank has been drained so much so that we are approaching towards bankruptcy. Flood damages alone cost India well over Rs.10,000 million every year besides loss of lives, domestic animals and houses. Increasingly forest products like firewood and timber are being denied to a large section of our population. Shortfall of firewood alone was estimated at over 180 million cubic meters by the beginning of this millennium.

India has 15 percent of world's cattle and 45 percent of buffaloes. Grazing intensity is high in most of the forest areas. In addition to depletion of forest cover, trampling by cattle hardens soil preventing vegetative regeneration. Extension of irrigation facilities and supply of drinking water (large dams like Sardar Sarovar Dam on river Narmada) to bring more land under cultivation has led to submerge of forests, habitats, and decrease in the land available for grazing and cultivation. As a result, graziers are forced to rely more on forests. The wisdom of our politicians to allow *forest villages* to grow added to the problem. Even after independence, the government in its effort to provide settlement to the refugees, large forest area was converted into human settlements (Dandakaranya, for example).

Social Forestry: A new consciousness about the importance of forest in our everyday life is on the rise even among the commoners. Government and NGOs are encouraging forestry aimed at meeting the requirements of fuel, fodder, fruit and timber. Afforestation has picked up some momentum in recent times in India. New social forestry projects with the assistance from international financial institutions have been started in various states with encouraging results. Even the mercantile giants have come out with lucrative tree *plantation programs* to attract investment from the public. Such plantation program seems to concentrate on monoculture, that is, plantation of those trees that grow fast or have high timber value. Such monoculture does not help maintain bio-diversity in nature.

Share of Forest Area: FAO Production Year Book 1985 showed that share of Forest and Wood land on this earth stood at 31 percent of the land area. In fact, its share dropped by about 1 percent between 1975 and 1983. Africa and Asia together are the home of 70 percent of world population. Yet their combined share of total forest area to world's total is only 31 percent. Latin America has the highest share, 23 percent. More than 50 percent of its land area is under forest cover. Considering the size of population, North America has a very high share of total forest area. Per capita forest and woodland is highest in Latin America (2.95 ha) followed by North America (2.90 ha). The developed countries still have better per capita share of forest and wood land (1.65 ha) than that in the developing countries (0.75 ha).

The world has been loosing about 2 percent of forest cover every year. Due to deforestation alone Sahara desert had increased its area by over 70,000 sq km in the last 70 years. During the last 100 years vast stretches of forest area has been converted into pastureland to feed the developed countries with high quality meat. In course of time, a large proportion of this land has totally become unproductive even as pasture land, and has become desert. 95 percent of dry and arid region have become deserts. The loss of forest cover and improper use of land have created another problem. The *topsoil* washed out by rains is deposited as silt in rivers, barrages and lakes. A large quantity of this soil is carried to sea. Floods have become a regular feature in many countries owing to rise of riverbed as a result of silt deposit. Every year 25,000 million tons of topsoil is lost; India alone accounts for nearly one-fourth of this. Further, urbanization and expansion of the cities often would be at the expense of ponds and marshy lands.

Global Forest Resources Assessment – 2005 by FAO admits that the rate of net loss of earth's forest area is slowing down. Between 1990 and 2000 the forest area decreased at the rate of 8.9 mha per year. The same came down to 7.3 mha per year during 2000–2005. South America (4.3 mha) and Africa (4 mha) continued to register the largest net loss of forests followed by Oceania, North and Central America (each with 350,000 ha annually); Asia, which had a net loss of 800,000 ha per year in the 1990s, reported a net gain of 1 mha per year from 2000 to 2005. This primarily is due to large-scale plantations. Of the 10 countries in the world with largest plantation areas, 6 are in Asia – China, India, Indonesia, Japan, Thailand and Vietnam. India posted an increase in forest area by about 290,000 ha per annum during 2000–2005 because of increase in plantations.

36 percent of global forest area is accounted for by primary or natural forests. Between 2000 and 2005 more than 1 mha of natural forest was lost per year to agriculture and large plantations. It is estimated that in the period 2001–03, 2.6 mha per annum of natural forest was lost in India, while that under plantation forestry increased by 2.9 mha, giving a net increase in forest cover by 300,000 ha per year. Productive plantations all over the globe, initiated primarily for wood and fiber production, account for 78 percent of all plantation forests, while protective plantations (established for conservation of soil and water) account for only 22 percent.

Biodiversity: Biodiversity sustains life and livelihoods. It is estimated that 40 percent of global economy is based on biological products and processes. The volume and the highest range of diversity are to be found in the tropics. For example, there is more biodiversity in one tiny island off the coast of Panama than there is in all of Great Britain; meager 7 percent of the Earth's surface holds between half and three quarters of the world's biodiversity. These biodiversity rich countries are being used by industrially advanced countries as reservoirs of biological and genetic resources to develop new products such as crop varieties, drugs, bio-pesticides, oils and as sources of other 'goods and services', such as timber and clean air.

Deforestation, large-scale encroachment upon pastureland, reclamation of marshy land is telling upon the bio-diversity in nature. *Before man appeared on this earth, the background extinction rate in nature was one species of mammals every 100 years and one species of plant every 200 years. Currently, one species is lost every hour. Since the year 1500, 245 species from four taxonomic groups – mammals, birds, reptiles and amphibians – have become extinct. Scientists fear that by 2025 AD, 25,000 species of plant, 359 species of bird and 200 species of mammals are likely to be eliminated.* While extinction is a natural process, the current human-caused rate of species loss is estimated at 100–1,000 times more than the natural rates. The problem with many species facing extinction is that many of them are located in single locations or sites. Unfortunately, many of these sites lack any legal protection. Highest concentration of these sites is found in Andes of South America, Brazil's Atlantic forests, and throughout the Caribbean and Madagascar. A vast majority of these sites are located in developing countries. Obviously, for many of these sites providing necessary fund for efficient management is the major problem.

Scientists could identify only a small fraction of innumerable life form on this earth. The genetic diversity is a precious gift of nature. Genetic diversity is responsible for maintaining this ecosystem. Scientists have observed that the ecosystem has changed rapidly in the last 100 years. Indiscriminate destruction of forest and marshy land, massive use of insecticides and pesticides, use of chemical fertilizers and massive discharge of industrial wastes and city effluents have shattered the genetic diversity in nature.

14.5 Atmospheric Pollution and Global Warming

At the start of our discussion on environmental pollution we stated how our atmosphere was getting polluted everyday as a result of free discharge of toxic gases like CO_2, CO, oxides of sulfur and nitrogen, ozone, CFC and other hydrocarbons and particulate matters from our industries, power-houses, automobiles and domestic burning of fuels. The Greenhouse Gases (GHG), both natural and anthropogenic, absorbs and emits radiation at specific wavelengths within the spectrum of thermal infrared radiation emitted by the Earth's surface, the atmosphere itself, and by clouds. GHG are essential to maintaining the temperature of the Earth. However, an excess of GHG can raise the temperature of the planet to lethal levels. Industrial processes, power houses, automobile emissions and fossil fuel processing and distribution together contribute about 63 percent of total GHG emissions. Till very recently, USA was at the top of the list in total GHG emissions. China has overtaken the lead since 2006. USA, of course, is miles ahead of China in per capita GHG emissions.

For the past several centuries, human activities have been increasingly polluting air and water and land, eroding the soil, altering Earth's climate thereby fragmenting and eliminating the habitat of many plants and animals, and depleting the natural reserve of non–renewable resources. The capacity of natural ecosystems to regenerate or maintain renewable resources and ecosystem services, such as the provision of clean air and water, the control of flooding, the maintenance of a tolerable climate, the conservation and regeneration of fertile soil, and the preservation of genetic and other forms of biological diversity has been damaged; the possibility of a repair in the near future appears bleak.

The combustion of fossil fuel causes acidification of the lower atmosphere with resultant acid rain, which harms or destroys plant and animal life in lakes. Increased combustion of fossil fuels though is closely related to the increased affluence of parts of the human population, the massive increase in the population in the developing countries, especially in the context of open-door economy, is adding fire to the fuel.

The three components of *environmental impact* (I) are: *population* (P), per capita *affluence* level (A) and impact from the *technologies* (T) used to achieve that level of per capita affluence. The stage is set by the impact equation, $I = P \times A \times T$. The vital reason for this non-linear relationship is the *synergic effect*.[1] Climate warming is one of the causes of deforestation, both being related to human population growth and stress biodiversity in forested areas of the world. Deforestation reduces the size of the area available to plant and animal species and since many species occupy relatively small total geographical areas, this leads to species loss in forest ecosystems.

As GHG build up in the atmosphere, the earth's surface temperature rises and the area of the earth covered by ice and snow shrinks. Ice and snow reflect much more light and heat than does the darker bare ground or the ocean. As the former decreases, the latter increases in consequence. With reduced snow and ice cover, more sunlight is absorbed by the earth's surface, resulting in additional warming of the planet and further melt-down of snow cap. The greater the global warming, the more would be the use of air-conditioning, which will lead to more use of electricity. A third of CO_2 released by human activity is absorbed in the 'carbon sinks' – the ocean and the forests. But the rate of removal of CO_2 is a declining function of the amount that has already been removed, and so, in effect, is a declining function of population size at a fixed per capita *affluence level* and fixed *technology*.

One very significant feedback to global warming is the increase in population size, one that is associated with agriculture. CO_2 and other gases are produced by decomposition of organic matters in soil. Warm climate accelerates decomposition of organic substances. It is the change in the size of population (P) that directly influences technology (T) use even for maintaining a fixed per capita affluence level (A).

Air pollution is not confined to industrialized countries or cities. The air pollution effect spreads soon to adjoining areas, the small towns and villages and then crosses the boundary of the nation and the continent. Problem arising out of discharge of CFC, used extensively in cooling and refrigeration, in the atmosphere is likely to be sorted out soon since the international community has decided a ban on the use of CFC in refrigeration and cooling machines. Most countries have taken steps to implement this international agreement. The alternatives suggested would be more environment-friendly but would cost more and we have to wait and see how well the developing countries absorb the cost of technology transfer in this regard. The cross-over to new technology has become easier because of lifting of import restrictions on variety of items under the WTO regime. The domestic producers have been forced to adopt alternatives to CFC to remain competitive in the market.

On the global scale the steady increase of CO_2 content in atmosphere holds out a threat of catastrophic climatic change. CO_2 concentration in atmosphere was 280 parts per million (ppm) some 300 years ago. It was 316 ppm in 1959 and 367 in 1998. Presently it is 387 ppm by volume. The effect is visible in most parts of the world. Scientists have already observed the 'greenhouse gas effect' due to heavy concentration of CO_2 and other gases and particulate matters in atmosphere. The average temperatures have gone up more during the last century than at any other period in the past 1,200 years, claimed by researches carried out in UK. Between 1969–71 and 1996–98, the average global temperature had gone up from 13.99°C to 14.43°C. Because of rise in the average temperature of the earth in the last 100 years, the glaciers in the mountains are receding; ice in the

1 *Synergic effect* is the phenomenon in which the combined effect of two or more things is greater than the sum of the effects of the causes acting in isolation.

poles is melting; sea level is rising inundating many coastal regions. NASA in a recent press release confirmed that 14 percent of the Arctic Ice, of the size of Pakistan/Turkey has disappeared between 2004 and 2006 as a result of global warming, especially the ocean waters. The ice in the Arctic sea which was 8–10 meters thick is only 2 meters thick today. The growing CO_2 concentration is likely to create shield that will prevent sunrays to reach the earth. If things continue for long, Ice Age is likely to appear again on the earth.

Climate change due to warming up of atmosphere is forcing plants and animals to disperse and migrate. When there is a physical barrier to movement to suitable places, the species could die out. Climate change has hit insects (like butterflies) and birds the hardest. Migratory birds are finding hard with this global climate change. The breeding period of these birds usually synchronizes with a time when food is available in plenty. The climate change has thrown the chain out of gear. Even the North Bering Sea, which is frozen for most of the year, the seasonal melt is starting much earlier. This is forcing the gray whales to move farther north for cold water, while animals like walrus and sea birds are facing food shortage.

The United States, the principal polluter of atmosphere, has perpetually been in denial about global warming, especially after the Earth Summit held in Rio De Janeiro in 1992. USA, the only global superpower, did not sign the 1997 Kyoto Protocol on global warming. US were and still are reluctant to agree that global climate change is largely induced by human action. The US Climate Change Science Program (CCSP) report (2006) clearly indicates that there is a strong link between rising temperatures of earth's surface and the higher atmosphere and human induced GHG. Even energy experts warned that this substantial increase in temperature will lead to a scenario, which they called the "roasted world". In the past it has been alleged that the US government manipulated reports submitted by various agencies and scientific communities on global warming (references to global warming was deleted from such reports in news releases). It was only in 2005 the US Senate adopted a 'non-binding resolution' acknowledging the scientific consensus on the relationship between rising CO_2 emissions and increasing global temperature. Incidences like Hurricane Katrina probably had forced USA to take decisive action on climate change. California is the first state in the US that decided to set limits on statewide GHG emissions and expects to bring down GHG emissions by 25 percent by 2020.

In a recent simulation study (*Nature*, 2005), conducted by several British scientists from different universities and the Hadley Center for Climate Prediction and Research, using spare power of 95,000 PCs of people from 140 countries (8,000 years of computing time for 60,000 simulations) has shown global warming could be worse than believed – global temperature could rise by 2–11°C by 2050. Previous studies predicted that doubling the pre-industrial levels of CO_2 emission could raise the temperature by 2–5°C.

A blanket of haze, about three-kilometer thick, hangs over Indian Ocean. This is the Atmospheric Brown Cloud (ABC, earlier it was called Asian Brown Cloud). Brown haze, unlike the GHG, contains a cocktail of aerosols (sulfates, soot, carbon and mineral dusts about millionth of a centimeter in size. The composition of ABC is still not fully known); it reduces sunlight and lowers the temperature. During the northeast monsoons, ABC moves thousands of miles to the Indian Ocean and cool it. This reduces evaporation and decreases the amount of rainfall. Scientists fear that this atmospheric development could change the monsoon cycle. It is observed that the monsoon clouds are migrating south of India, raining more on the sea than on the landmass. The costal areas are flooded and the main land receives less rain. In southeast of China, this haze has been reducing sunlight by two percent every 10 years since 1950. There have been severe storms and floods in southern China and drought in the north in recent years. The haze may reduce precipitation over northwest India, Pakistan, Afghanistan, western China, and the western central Asian region by 20–40 percent. Scientists predict that winter harvests of rice in India may drop by 10 percent. Since ABC can travel half the globe in three weeks time, it could change the rainfall patterns across the Americas and beyond. Similar brown clouds were found over Europe. Therefore, ABC is no more Asia-specific.

Scientists from California University, NASA and Scripps Institution of Oceanography recently carried out complex measurements of temperature, humidity, floating particulate matter, etc. in ABC with the help of unmanned planes. It recorded 50 percent higher atmospheric temperature around the cloud. The scientists came to the conclusion that the temperature in the Himalayan region was fast rising because of the blanket cover by this cloud. Ice in the mountain caps and all the Himalayan glaciers are melting fast releasing huge quantity of water into the river systems in China, India and other South Asian countries that originate from the Himalayan Mountains. Floods are now becoming a regular feature in these countries. Fast melting of glaciers during the hotter months invariably would result in drought in the later months. Both GHG and the Brown Cloud together are responsible for the rise in atmospheric temperature in the Himalayan region.

Whereas GHG is the major cause of warming of the Indian Ocean, Brown clouds, in contrast, obstructs entry of sunlight. In a sense they mask global warming. If the causes of Brown cloud are curbed, the Indian Ocean will be much hotter. More evaporation will produce more rainfall, but that may cause floods in regions that generally receive heavy rainfall. Scientists have found that aerosols have a short span of life, and therefore their spread can be checked by using cleaner fuels with efficient burning mechanisms.

Climatic aberration has hit hardest the least polluting countries. Scientists apprehend that the poorest countries may see a dramatic rise in deaths from vector borne infectious diseases and malnutrition as a consequence of climate change caused by more polluting developed countries. The sea level is estimated to have risen by about 40 centimeters before the end of the last millennium. The risk of flooding caused by costal storms will put millions of people at a great risk. Already people from some islands have to be relocated because of rising seas and storm surges. Climatic variations and extreme weather events have a significant effect on diseases as influenza, diarrhea, cholera, malaria, meningitis, dengue, encephalitis, and other bacterial and viral infections. WHO estimates that warming and precipitation trends due to anthropogenic climate change have been claiming 150,000 lives annually in the last 30 years. Malaria epidemic in Indian subcontinent, Colombia, Venezuela and Uganda have been associated with climate variability due to *El Nino*. Regions at highest risk of adverse health effects from climate change include coastlines along the Pacific and Indian Ocean and sub-Saharan Africa. Africa and Indian subcontinent have some of the lowest carbon dioxide emissions (below one ton per capita per annum). Yet, some of these regions face very grave risk from warming-related diseases. The biggest emitters of CO_2 (6 tons per capita a year), USA and Australia have the least risk from global warming-related diseases.

Most countries have passed laws to curb environmental pollution. India has passed Acts against water pollution (1974), air pollution (1981) and environmental pollution (1986). But implementation of the laws is not easy. Road traffic in India is rising fast to keep pace with its numbers. Consumption of fossil fuel is fast rising. Prior purification of emitted gases and suspended particles from powerhouses and vehicles are a costly affair. Restricting the life of a public vehicle will only complicate our transportation network and adversely affect our already bleak employment situation.

Level of SO_2 and particulate matter is increasing fast in areas having high concentration of chemical industries. Chembur in Maharashtra has now become 'Gas Chamber'. Surveys conducted by WHO show that most of the Indian cities already have exceeded the permissible limits of the toxic gases and suspended particles in atmosphere. Capital Delhi had the highest atmospheric pollution before CNG conversion of public vehicles. The environmentalists fear that emissions from the gigantic refinery at Mathura will slowly destroy the precious Taj. The growth of petro-chemical complexes around our refineries will further increase air pollution. 'Acid rains' have already caused acute problems in North America and Europe. Crops and forests have badly been damaged by acid rains. Fish in the lakes of southern Norway have virtually been eliminated by acid rain.

Kolkata, a mega-city in India, emits around 1,500 tons of pollutants a day of which suspended particulate matters and carbon monoxide's share is nearly 80 percent. It is no wonder therefore that most of the Kolkata's population suffer from respiratory diseases. The problem becomes acute in winter months. The city remains under the cover of 'smog' from evening to late in the morning. This is despite the fact that coal as a fuel for cooking has been replaced by LPG in most families except those in slums.

Global warming has six tenets: 1. Global warming is happening; 2. It is happening because of our fault; 3. It will continue unless we mend our ways; 4. If it continues, we are in grave danger; 5. We know how to slow down or even reverse the warming process; and 6. The benefits from doing that will far exceed the costs.

The first tenet is clearly true – earth has become warmer beyond doubt. Scientists have confirmed that global warming has been a factor for the unpredictable climate change observed in various parts of the globe.

As regards the second, we do not know how much human activity is really responsible for this temperature rise. The activities obviously include economic growth and wealth creation – action that makes possible improved wellbeing (better nutrition, medicine, education, etc.). The question is: Are we willing to accept slowing down of economic activity in order to regulate the planet's climate?

We do not know how much we must change our economic activity to produce a particular reduction of warming. We still have some doubts if warming is necessarily dangerous. Was life better when thick ice covered our habitats? Was it better or worse when people could farm in Greenland? Are we sure if the climate in the eighties of the last century was exactly right, and that we should go back to that stage no matter what the costs are?

It could cost tens of trillions in expenditure and foregone economic activity to try fine-tuning the planet's atmospheric temperature. We do not know if these trillions would purchase benefits commensurate with the benefits that would have come from social wealth that was not produced.

Nothing the developed countries can do to reduce GHG emissions while 129 other developing countries spout black air in their attempt to develop their economy.

The new fuel, ethanol, produces just a little more energy than it takes to manufacturing it. Price of corn has doubled in a year. Forests will be felled to clear land for growing more corn or sugarcane.

14.6 Environmental Concern and Road to Rio

The biophysical environment serves many essential functions for human populations as also for other species. Of these, three most fundamental functions can be singled out.

First, the environment is the repository of all the resources for sustenance of life form on this earth – air, water and land are essential for production of food, timber and firewood, building shelters, roads, industries and a vast range of economic goods that have become a part of our daily life. Environment is regarded as the "sustenance base" for human civilization, a "supply depot" for most of our basic necessities. Some of these resources are potentially renewable, such as forests, air and water, while others like fossil fuels and minerals, are nonrenewable and therefore finite. But when we use our resources faster than the rate at which the nature can renew some of them or clean them, a scarcity of resources results.

Second, human beings and all other living creatures produce "wastes" while using these resources. Humans produce a far greater variety and quantity of wastes than do any other species. The nature acts as a "sink" or "waste repository" for these wastes. Nature gives our resources back by recycling the wastes into useful/harmless substances (trees absorb CO_2 and returns O_2, bio-degradable wastes are converted into fertilizers). But with rising population and increased variety of wastes in great quantities have created conditions where wastes are much in excess of what the environment can process or clean up. Consequence – various forms of "pollution".

Third, the planet earth provides home, a living space or a "habitat" for every biological species. If the density of population of a species in the specified habitat exceeds a naturally driven limit, catastrophe results – extinction of some species or movement to some other locations resulting in conflict between the inhabitants and the migrants and a great loss of biodiversity. Unlike other biological species, human population has survived and will survive much longer since it has the skill and intelligence to recreate some of its used resources and even invent alternative sources or use the same quantity of resource for multipurpose uses at the same time.

Human overuse of natural resources has put the nature in the doc for its inability to perform the three basic functions. In consequence, environmental pollution, resource scarcity and space crunch are the outcome. Environment has multifaceted functions. Often one function of the environment becomes an obstacle to some other function. A land is used both as a living space and a site for waste disposal. But a space used for waste dumping becomes unsuitable for living. Converting a farmland or a forest area into a housing complex or an industrial hub can no longer be used for food production or as a habitat for wildlife. The living-space function came into limelight in the late 1970s when it was discovered that the neighborhood in Niagara Falls, New York, was built on the abandoned chemical site leaking toxic materials.

Human beings have realized that even with intelligent manipulation, environmental problems in the form of pollution and resource depletion cannot be overlooked any more. It was in the 1960s and 1970s when problems relating to environmental issues became a pressing topic in international forums. The major attention has been on atmospheric (GHG concentration and ozone holes) and water pollution. The energy crisis in the mid-seventies highlighted the dependence of industries on fossil fuels whose supply was fast diminishing. The heat trap produced by the GHG gases was raising the earth's atmospheric temperature. "Biodiversity" and "Climate change" came to be discussed very frequently in the scientific community, among environmental activists and in international forums. "Global warming" is a reality today and already its impact has been felt in the climate change in almost all the parts of the earth.

Fallout of enviromental pollution: The fallout of environmental pollution gave rise to two parallel movements – the measurement of the extent of damage already done to environment, more specifically to the eco-system and its impact on bio-diversity, on human health and the projected impact on the health of the mother earth. Natural and biological scientists are continuously thrashing out these aspects. The other form of the movement is to organize people around the globe to discuss and debate environment and related issues to develop public opinion on the preservation of our environment and eco-system, to press upon governments to adopt policies to put a check on the degeneration of the environment from indiscriminate and inefficient use of natural resources, to encourage the use of cleaner and more efficient technology, to adopt policies for conservation of biodiversity and prevent further degradation of air, water, forest cover and soil. This aspect of the issue is very closely linked with public opinion, peoples' awareness and active participation. It is in this context that the social and behavioral scientists can play a key role.

Environmental pollution has brought together scientists from all disciplines on to a common platform. Whereas the disciplines like physics, chemistry, bio-physics and bio-chemistry, etc. are busy in identifying pollutants and their individual and combined effect on atmosphere, water bodies, ground water, vegetative growth and change in soil character, biology and medical science are coming out with fresh observations every day how this polluted environment is leaving a deep impact on human health and all other living organisms leading to increase in extinction rates of various species and squeezing the rich biodiversity of our nature. Environmental economists are making efforts to measure the environmental costs vis-à-vis benefits derived from the fast changing energy-intensive production system. Of late, environmental activism and conservation movement has added a very important social dimension to the entire issue of ecological balance and preservation of environment.

In the industrially developed countries public opinion is very strong against polluting industries, but not against products making of which pollute the environment. The multinational companies (MNCs) have been forced to shift polluting industries to the less developed countries where public opinion against pollution is not strong as yet, anti-pollution laws are not followed stringently and people, because of their acute poverty and unemployment, would welcome any move that will help generate employment and give them two square meals a day. Bhopal tragedy is a nightmare to thousands of families that were directly hit by the highly toxic gas leak. Yet, the public opinion is still not against setting up of similar such industries so long they give them jobs and do not blow up frequently. Every year thousands of human lives, domestic animals, precious farmland and shelters are lost due to man-made floods followed by droughts. Billions of dollars are spent every year in the name of disaster management; yet the same tragedy happens every year. The poor has no choice – either he is a victim of a Bhopal like tragedy or a victim of inept management borne out of the nexus between bureaucrats, politicians and business magnets.

A developing country like India has environmental problems having roots in:

- *Lack of development*: The poor people have no substitute for firewood. Deforestation therefore continues unabated. Soil erosion and water pollution increase everyday. Such problems have root in slow pace of development.
- *Lack of environmental safeguards:* This results from deficiencies in policy formulation and implementation – no effective safeguards for air and water pollution from discharges from industries, pesticides and chemical fertilizers run-off into streams, hazardous waste disposal, etc.
- *Global environmental crisis*: Ozone depletion, marine pollution, automobile emission, global warming, etc. affect all, rich and poor.

The first of the environmental problems is linked to lack of development and the second to the impact of development projects. We do not have enough capital to manage all these classes of problems. We care for our development projects but we need to address issues that are linked to faster economic development. We cannot afford to have low development and less pollution in view of hungry mouths of teeming millions. Similarly, we cannot allow high economic growth at the cost of environment.

From a very modest beginning with a very general approach, increasing attention is being paid to specific issues. As a result, environmental studies have come of age and social and behavioral scientists today are concentrating hard on improving the measurement scales to make cross-cultural and longitudinal comparisons possible. Van Liere and Dunlap and many others have done yeoman's service for providing tools and techniques to the young scientists to carry forward researches on 'environment' with a better theoretical foundation and more sensitive and trustworthy tools of measurement. It is felt that the social scientists can help bring into the fore what the public opinion is about environmental pollution and concomitant issues, inter-sectoral differences in the perception of the problem, etc. Social surveys not only capture the current mood of the surveyed sample on a particular issue in a time frame, it also helps the respondents to think about the issue with greater depth and much wider perspective. The survey questions posed often would trigger a new chain of thought among many of those interviewed, which till then were below the surface level of their conscious deliberations. The surveys themselves introduce a process of dialogue and help expand one's range of information and re-evaluate one's position in respect to the problems posed.

What is true in a developed economy may not hold exactly in a developing economy like India. The consumption habits of the people have a significant role in their attitude and opinion about a particular issue. The greatest polluter of earth's atmosphere is the burning of coal and use of fossil fuels in automobiles besides the untreated discharges of city wastes as also discharges from industrial plants. The restriction imposed on the use of fossil fuels could bring down the level of air pollution greatly. But the people in the affluent countries are not yet willing to cut down their consumption habit and adopt an alternative to the use of private automobiles for transportation purposes. They would swallow gallons of Coke and Pepsi but would not allow the bottles to be recycled in their country. They would encourage recycling so long the recycling does not affect their health. The paradox of the 'clean air' movement lies there.

The governments in developing countries have recently taken a few regulatory and economic instruments for improving environmental quality. In India, many industries have installed costly pollution control equipments in compliance with certain laws; but they often do not use them since the cost of compliance is often much higher than non-compliance. Often we have good laws with clearly stated objectives, but the economic basis of regulations often is weak. The "polluter pay" principle has achieved better compliance of pollution control regulations in many countries (Malaysia, for example), but the same could not be applied in many others for fear that the industries instead of controlling pollution through increased efficiency would pass on the entire cost of "polluter pay" to the consumers. It is time the social scientists take up the instrument of public opinion for enforcing the potential polluters adopt such technology that would pollute our air, water and soil least.

In the 1960s, waves of protest by environmentalists and social activists against environmental management swept across the developed countries and later in the developing countries. Environmental pressure groups like the Friends of the Earth, Sierra Club, World Wildlife Fund, and Greenpeace amongst others and Save Narmada and Chipko movement in India have become successful in getting widespread media coverage. They have done creditable job to arouse environment-awareness among people and press governments to enact laws and take appropriate measures to curb environment population. United Nations also have declared Environment Day (June 5) asking "Governments of the world undertake worldwide activities reaffirming their concern for the preservation and enhancement of the human environment, with a view to deepening environmental awareness" among masses.

To begin with, these environmental activists were mostly localized and against issues that were at most regional. Globalization of environmental problems was generated from these local protests against toxic and chemical pollution, acid rain, dumping of pollutants and pollution of the aqua environment. Although talks about protection of environment were heard even before the First World War, especially for protection of some species of migratory birds, the real attempt to make pollution a global issue began with the publication of 'Limits to Growth" thesis by Club of Rome and then the Stockholm Conference (UN Conference on Human Environment, Stockholm, 1972). 113 countries and about 400 intergovernmental and NGOs participated in the Conference. Environment has since become an international political issue. The Conference made Action Plan covering 109 recommendations putting emphasis on global assessment program, environmental management activities and supporting measures through education and training. The relationship between economic development and environmental pollution was also formally recognized. The United Nations Conference on Environment and Development, also known as the Rio Summit (Earth Summit), the second major conference on environment was held in Rio de Janeiro from June 3 to June 14, 1992.

Before we take up the deliberations of the Stockholm and Rio Conference, we briefly glance through how different schools of thought and activity groups have viewed various issues relating to environmental degradation.

14.7 Schools of Thought

Neo-Classical Approach

It is based on the Malthusian doctrine that all worldly unhappiness is primarily due to unrestricted growth of population. Environmental pollution, especially in the underdeveloped economies, is primarily due to increase in population pressure on the limited resources. Adequate funds are not readily available for housing, basic health and education. The state as a welfare agency fails even to provide the basic utility services.

Pigouvian and Paretian approach to the problem of pollution, the most popular of the neoclassical documentations, assert that those who pollute the environment do so to 'reduce their costs of production'. Pollution thus increases social costs. The solution is to reduce the divergence between two costs, that is making the polluting farms and industries pay for their folly. The farms as a result will have to pay more attention to reduce pollution (technology upgradation) lest they have to pay heavy penalties for their offences.

The scale and complexity of the environmental problem are not exactly reflected in this approach. Air pollution, ozone holes, spread of desert, sub-soil and river water pollution, oil slick in seas, nuclear explosion, etc. are problems of global nature and cannot be tackled locally by any nation through legislative and punitive measures. Illness and death from radiation or cancer from ultraviolate radiation due to depletion of ozone layer are hazards for which no compensation can be asked.

GNP Approach

Implicit in the economic model that relates GNP for alleviation of poverty is the assertion that pollution-free environment is possible only at the cost of industrial development, which alone can increase GNP of a nation. If economic growth is brought to a close, poverty and unemployment will result. The emphasis on production, productivity and hi tech will bring problems of pollution and shortage of natural resources under control.

It tantamount to accepting the fact that no development program is possible that will not pollute our environment in some way or the other. Pollution cannot be eliminated but can be kept under some control by using appropriate technology and restricting our demand for some commodities/utilities that are seen to harm the environment most. Standard of living cannot be improved and employment generated unless we consume more of our resources, especially energy. We cannot emphasize on pollution at the cost of billions remaining hungry, ill nourished and unemployed. No doubt attention has to be paid to pollution, argues these economists, but the pessimism of Malthusian doctrine need not worry us so much. The earth has sustained the growth of population because scientists have devised methods that enabled us in discovering new deposits of minerals, fuel oil and gas, scientific method of farming, alternate sources of renewable and non-renewable energy – nuclear, solar, wind, geothermal, etc. We have not as yet made use of vast potential of the sea bed. The underwater source of minerals is so vast that even if our mining rate is 400 million metric tons a year, the sea bed would virtually supply us all our minerals for an unlimited period of time. The sea can provide us all the uranium that we may require if we have to go nuclear for energy production. It is further argued that with increase in the standard of living, people will automatically put a check on the growth of population. The decadal growth of world population already has reached its plateau in the eighties and there is a definite sign that death rates even in the developing countries will have reached a level soon from where further improvements will occur only very slowly. The decline in birth rate already has overtaken the decline in death rate in many countries.

Ecological Approach

Environmental activists are not to be confused with ecologists. There is a fundamental difference between the two. The techno-centric environmental activists look at problems of environment as 'external' to the development process; that is, they admit that some damage to environment is inevitable. They therefore argue for adoption of more efficient technology to produce fewer waste products and keep the environment free from pollution as much as possible. Wellbeing of human beings occupies the center stage of environmental activism. The domain of ecology is much broader – human being, sub-human beings and the entire biological kingdom cannot be looked in isolation. They are integral parts of a larger and more enduring system.

Ecology (Greek 'oikos', meaning habitat) is presently defined to include all living systems in the environment – plant, animal, human being, marine and all micro-biological systems. It is a branch of biology dealing with the relations between organisms and their environment. Ecological disturbance or disequilibrium is a major concern of increasing pollution as well as large scale migration within the country or crossing the border.

Ecologists are strongly opposed to GNP thesis on pollution. The depletion of scarce resources and fast extinction of biological species as a result of deforestation, air and marine pollution are primarily responsible for reduction of genetic diversity in the living systems. They strongly urge to stop the mad race for development. Countries should go slow on development. If the developing nations also try to achieve the same standard of living as are enjoyed in the developed countries, earth's natural resources would soon be exhausted and the pollution level of the earth will escalate to such a height that the in-built system of purification in nature will fail to cope up with the pollution levels. They neither advocate a status quo in the environment nor they ask us to opt for a living as part of nature, as was with our primitive predecessors. The sickness, starvation and uncertainty that have been the name of life for centuries have to be avoided by all means. The eco scientists, also referred to as *Structuralists*, believe that the race for development will aggravate the disparity between rich and poor; inflation, unemployment and social chaos will result; and the manner in which pollution is gaining momentum will make the earth unfit for living (for most life-forms). Perspectives of development have to be understood in relation to the impact it is likely to have on the nature that nurtures us.

Ecologists themselves are divided on their ideological stands. The extremist group (often referred as 'deep ecologist') does not want to analyze the environment from the standpoint of modern industry-related development. They believe that environmental degradation is deeply rooted in industrial activity. They are opposed to machine-induced developmental processes; they ask for development through the path of agricultural revolution that seeks no inputs from chemical and related technology. The moderate ecologists, on the other hand, are not opposed to industrial development. They argue that machine and technology alone cannot bring solution to all our earthly problems. We need to carefully delineate what our basic requirements are and pursue industrial development without tampering the ecological balance.

The Club of Rome Approach (Limits to Growth)

The Club of Rome (formed in 1968), a group passionately campaigning for preservation of environment, foresees that our over emphasis on industrial activity will ruin the industrial society itself. In its second report, the opening paragraph starts with a serious warning: *The world has cancer, and the cancer is man.*

In 1972, in the book *The Limits to Growth* (Donella H. Meadows, Dennis l. Meadows, Jorgen Randers, William W. Behrens III), first report of the Club of Rome was published. The book was an instantaneous best-seller. It emphasized on the predicament of mankind. Based on a technique known as *Systems Dynamics,* developed by Prof. J. Forrester at MIT, a large-scale computer model was constructed to simulate likely future outcomes of the world economy. The most prominent feature of systems dynamics is the use of feedback loops to explain behavior. The *feedback loop* is a closed path that connects an action to its effect on the surrounding conditions which, in turn, can influence further action.

The World Model, as it was called, was built specifically to investigate five major trends of global concern – accelerating industrialization, rapid population growth, widespread malnutrition, depletion of nonrenewable resources, and a deteriorating environment. The basis of the method is the recognition that the structure of any system – the many circular, interlocking, sometimes time-delayed relationships among its components – is often just as important in determining its behavior as the individual components themselves. All these elements are increasing exponentially.

One key idea that the book *The Limits to Growth* discusses is that the rate of resource use is increasing by a constant growth rate annually. Current known reserve (775 million tons of chromium reserve, for instance) divided current yearly absolute use (1.85 million tons), gives the static index of 418 years. But the rate of chromium consumption was growing at 2.6 percent annually. With a constant rate of annual growth of 2.6 percent, the resource will last only for $\ln[\ln(1+0.026)*(418+1)/\ln(1+0.026)=93$ years. The formula for calculating the amount of time left for a resource with constant consumption growth is

$$y = \frac{\log\left[1-(1-g)^{*}\frac{R}{C}\right]}{\log(g)} - 1\text{, where}$$

y = years left

g = 1.026 (2.6 percent annual consumption growth)

R = reserve

C = consumption (annually)

The equation stated above clearly states that y is finite even if new resources (R) are discovered. The calculations are more complex than what are suggested. When as many as five different quantities are growing simultaneously in a system, and when all the quantities are interrelated in a complex way, analysis of the causes of growth and of the future behavior of the system become very difficult indeed. The conclusions reached from the computer simulation are:

1. If the present growth trends of the five major variables continue unchanged, the limits to growth on this planet will be reached sometime within the next one hundred years. There would be a rather sudden and uncontrollable decline in both population and industrial capacity.
2. It is possible to alter these growth trends and to establish a condition of ecological and economic stability that is *sustainable* far into the future. A state of global equilibrium could be designed so that the basic material needs of each person on earth are satisfied and each person has an equal opportunity to realize his individual human potential.

The thesis reasoned that people would strive for the second outcome rather than the first. The sooner they begin working to attain it, the greater will be their chances of success.

The remedy to rising pollution, they advocate, is 'Zero Growth' policy and adoption of a life style that will not encourage consumerism and use fossil fuel for purposes of automobiles, synthetic fibers, air-conditioning, etc.

A section of critics call The Limit to Growth a pro-Malthusian thesis. The Club of Rome approach has been opposed by many on the ground that nature has immense power for self-purification and science and technology can do miracles. They say that we never are in dearth of energy even if the conventional non-renewable resources are dried up. Solar energy is unlimited, so is wind, nuclear and biodegradable products. We can tap other non-conventional sources for our energy requirements. Poverty cannot be the destiny of man. We have ample evidence of mankind's ingenuity and social flexibility. There are, of course, many likely changes in the system, some are already taking place. The Green Revolution raised agricultural yields in non-industrialized countries. Knowledge about modern methods of birth control is spreading fast.

Although the history of human effort contains numerous incidents of mankind's failure to live within physical limits, it is success in overcoming limits that forms the cultural tradition of many dominant people in today's world. Over the past three hundred years, mankind has compiled an impressive record of pushing back the apparent limits to population and economic growth by a series of spectacular technological advances. Since the recent history of a large part of human society has been so continuously successful, it is quite natural that many people expect technological breakthrough to go on raising physical ceilings indefinitely. Man's living standard has to improve even if that means polluting our environment. The cry for pollution control is the strategy of the rich to keep the poor poor. The rich man is spoiling the environment and asking the poor to bear the burden.

United Nations Environment Program (UNEP), formed in December 1972, observed that an average citizen of a poor country consumes energy and material resources in his life time which is equivalent to only six months consumption of an average man in a developed country. They oppose the 'zero growth' thesis on the ground that it is a ploy to perpetuate the difference between the rich and the poor nations for the current level of distribution of resources and their consumption clearly favors the rich.

It is indeed an accepted policy of most of the developing nations to allow certain degree of environmental degradation as a price for gcing industrial to solve their problems of poverty and unemployment.

The Founex Consensus

The 1972 Stockholm Declaration secured its place in the history as 'the first global action plan for the environment'. The primary thrust behind the Conference 'came from the developed world and the initial focus was on environmental problems of industrialization'. The plight of the developing world was not the motivating factor behind the conference. Since its initial focus was on First World environmental problems, United Nations soon realized that the slated conference did not receive much support from the developing countries. If majority of the developing countries did not support the conference then the Stockholm Conference slated for 1972 could not be called truly global. To alleviate the fears of the developing world and to forge consensus on the issues to be discussed, a preparatory conference of 'experts' was arranged in Founex, Switzerland. The report of the Founex Committee was crucial since it ensured the success of Stockholm as also because it was in the Committee report that the crucial link between environmental protection and developmental concerns was forged.

The group of experts on the invitation of UN Conference on Human Environment recognized the 'current concern with environmental issues have emerged out of the problems experienced by the industrially developed countries' and also recognized that the developing countries faced a different set of environmental changes. The Committee opined that the third world countries cannot neglect the problem of growth and should also take lessons from the experience of the developed countries so that pollution problem can be taken care of early. The Conference, in fact, regarded *poverty itself a type of pollution. Poverty is both a cause of and an effect of environmental degradation.* Poverty drives people to undertake such actions that have unfavorable consequences on environment (clearing of forests for agriculture and housing, wood for fire, repeated use of the same land for multiple cropping thereby making soil infertile and erosion prone, etc.). Poverty also will result/aggravate by environmental degradation. The poor vis-à-vis the rich are the worst sufferers from environmental degradation due to their economic and nutritional status.

Income inequality also is related to environmental degradation. While the rich remains extravagant on use of energy for their luxurious living, poor are forced to degrade nature by use of firewood and coal for energy for their domestic use. While the rich landowners have the option for rotating crops and putting some land under rest to allow them to regain normal fertility, the poor over utilize their land, often without crop rotation, causing soil infertility and soil erosion.

14.8 Stockholm Conference (1972)

The text that came out from the Stockholm Conference was a document of political compromise as can be seen from the wide ranging issues covered by the 26 principles of declaration. The importance of the Declaration in the context of an evolution of the concept of *sustainable development* was the emphasis it placed on the link between development and environmental protection. More fundamentally, the Declaration clearly pointed out that development and environmental protection are not, of necessity, in conflict. Stockholm Conference took the view that pollution is due to *consumption explosion* than population explosion although the latter causes the former to rise further. USA uses as much energy for its air-conditioning as the whole of China uses for all purposes. Indira Gandhi while speaking at the Conference, said, "Countries with but a small fraction of the world population consume the bulk of world's production of minerals, fossil fuels and so on …the increase of one inhabitant in a effluent country, at his level of living, is equivalent to an increase of many Asians, Africans or Latin Americans at their current material level of living."

The Stockholm Conference had quite a few important outcomes:

1. Development of national environmental policies and creation of separate ministry in many countries, which in latter years would play a crucial role in sanction of economic projects;
2. Many countries, especially the developed ones, made extensive legislations to prevent pollution;
3. UN Environmental Program (UNEP) became a catalyst in promoting awareness and action concerning environmental issues;
4. The Stockholm declaration established a number of principles among which sovereign right to exploit national resources combined with responsibility for trans-boundary pollution was of high significance.

The positive synergy between development and environmental protection is illustrated at various places in the Declaration. Principle 1, for example links 'adequate conditions of life' with 'an environment of quality that permits a life of dignity'; Principle 9 recognizes that environmental deficiencies 'can best be remedied by accelerated development'; Principle 8 links development to 'favorable living conditions' and 'working environment'; Principle 5 urges that development process must not over-exploit non-renewable resources to the point of exhaustion. Two very important principles of sustainable development was struck in the Declaration – the principle of inter-generational equity, i.e., environment must be safeguarded for the present and future generations, and safeguard natural resources of the earth for the benefit of the present and future generations. Principle 12 urges that resources 'should be made available to preserve and improve environment and particular requirement of the developing countries'. Similarly, Principle 5 requires that benefits from exploitation of the natural resources should be 'shared by all mankind'.

United Nations Environment Program (UNEP)

UNEP, formed in line with the recommendations of Stockholm Conference, with its headquarters in Kenya, has played a key role in promoting measures for preventing environmental degradation and developing concepts in relation to environment-development interactions. It has tried to push forward the view that the choice is never between development and pollution, but between different combinations of the two, subject to two over-riding constraints: an 'outer limit' beyond which development cannot be pushed without putting survival of human race at risk, and an 'inner limit' defined by poverty level and basic human needs for survival, below which concern for environment need not be pushed.

Although approaches of environmentalists and others differ, they all agree on one point that prevention of environmental pollution be given top priority in any planning for development. Our environment is to be regarded as the pooled resource of land, air and water, which constitute the physical, social and psychological living space of every living species. Increase in population obviously puts a pressure on our environment because of increased use of land, water and air resources and discharge of toxic wastes into the environment. Feeding the vast population and providing them with shelter and employment for ensuring a reasonably decent living are primary concerns for all governments. Making these provisions readily available to masses is possible only through greater exploitation of nature. According to law of conservation of mass, everything we use as food, consumer goods and even air and water will sooner or later be returned to the nature as waste. Disposal of some of these wastes away from living area often is a problem of vast magnitude, more so if they are not biodegradable. The wastes (end or by-products) generated by our economic production system become an input to our eco-system. Some of these inputs may benefit some of the living species; others may be harmed or even destroyed altogether. Although the nature has an amazing purification system of its own, the residuals of our economic system often are so large, diverse and fast accumulating that there is often not sufficient time for endogenous species to make genetic and phenotype adjustments. It is a proven fact that even a small biological imbalance may cause invasion of *flora and fauna* from other regions that may cause further ecological disruption.

Whether we admit it or not, the environment increasingly gets more polluted as we try to make the living of billions better and still better. The developed countries did all the damage to nature, unknowingly though. The heavy price for this damage is to be paid by the developing countries in the name of preservation of global environment. Population explosion in the developing countries of course has a share in environmental degradation, but it is very small compared to the slowly growing population in the developed countries where individuals are extravagant in the use of energy and all other resources. The third world countries will hasten the disaster if they try to achieve the living standard of even the lowly placed countries among the developed West. It is rightly said, "Consumer explosion vis-à-vis population explosion is responsible for all that has happened to our environment". An addition of a single member to the population in a developed country is equivalent to addition of a few hundreds in underdeveloped countries taken together. If the developed countries do not drastically cut their consumption habits of vital economic goods and services, people in the developing countries cannot make headway in their poverty alleviation program because of the prices of the fundamental resource-components in the international market and the costly hi tech required for cost-efficient productivity. In spite of several conferences held (Stockholm and Rio Conference, for instance) to discuss and develop plan and strategies to combat pollution, the rich countries did not show eagerness to change their consumption habit or slow down their pace of development. The earth is like a space station with a very finite resource. The resources of this space station are to be used judiciously and wastes recycled to keep it operating for a longer duration.

The multinational giants have taken a large stride to pollute the environment of the less developed and less polluted countries. The developed countries have very strict and effective pollution control laws. The developing countries too have anti-pollution laws, but their implementation is not as strict as is in the West. They are therefore agreeable to absorb certain degree of environmental degradation as a price for their effort to eradicating poverty and unemployment from their soil. With the opening up of economy in most countries, the global industrial giants are grabbing the opportunity thus created to start industries/shift the existing ones, which either were to be closed down in their own country or were prevented from further expansion due to strong anti-pollution laws.

Several initiatives on international environment and development issues kept the diplomats and environmentalists busy in the 1970s and 1980s. London Dumping Convention, Vienna Convention on Ozone Layer, Mediterranean Action Plan, etc. dealt with trans-boundary pollution. A number of North-South agreements were reached. Ten years after Stockholm Conference, UNEP reviewed the progress. It was decided that a much greater long term integrated environmental planning was needed since the environmental problem grew visibly from local to regional and then to global level.

The World Commission on Environment and Development (WCED), formed by the United Nations General Assembly in September 1983 under Norwegian Prime Minister Harlem Brundtland, analyzed economic and environmental issues and the interactions between them. The Brundtland Report (1987) emphasized that human activities be directed towards a pathway of 'sustainable development' with environment seen not as an obstacle to growth but rather as an aspect which needed to be reflected in all the policies if growth was to be sustained. Sustainable development ensures that the maximum rate of resource consumption and waste discharge for a selected development portfolio would be sustained indefinitely, in a defined planning region, without progressively impairing its bio-productivity and ecological integrity. UNEP's 'Environmental Perspectives to the Year 2000 and Beyond' gave the framework for national and international action to translate Brundtland Report into reality. UN in 1989 decided to convene the United Nations Conference on Environment and Development (UNCED). Brazilian government offered to host the Conference in Rio de Janeiro on the 20th anniversary of the Stockholm Conference and UNCED became dubbed "the Earth Summit".

14.9 Brundtland Commission Report

Between the Stockholm and the Rio Conference, perhaps the most influential event towards the mainstreaming of sustainable development was the Brundtland Commission Report. The Commission was chaired by Norwegian Prime Minister Gro Harlem Brundtland. The report is perhaps best known for the definition it offered to *sustainable development.* The Commission defined it as *"the development that meets the needs of the present generation without compromising the ability of future generations to meet their own needs"*. The two striking elements in this definition is: (i) essential needs of the world's poor must be given priority, and (ii) the idea of limitations imposed by the state of technology and social organization on the environment's ability to meet the present and future needs.

The Commission identified the major problem areas and the causes of the problems. The Commission focused on population, food security, species and the ecosystems, energy, industry, and the human urban settlements. It is this integrated approach to environment and socioeconomic issues that makes the report so outstanding. The Report recognizes that environment and development are interwoven *'into a seamless net of causes and effects'*. The Commission is all bent for measures that help in poverty alleviation through the integrated approach.

The Commission made several proposals:

1. International communities at all levels (global, regional, and national) to integrate environmental concerns with development activities;
2. The need to strengthen agencies charged with protection of environment such as UNEP;

3. Increase in cooperation between non-governmental organizations, scientific bodies and other members of the international community that would lead to an increased capacity to identify and assess environmental hazards;
4. Need to include NGOs, scientific bodies and industries in the decision-making and implementation process;
5. Prepare a UN declaration on environment and sustainable development;
6. Involvement of multilateral financial institutions in the process towards sustainable development.

This Report provided a lot of input to the UN Conference on Environment and Development held in Rio in 1992.

14.10 The Rio Declaration

The United Nations' Conference on Environment and Development (UNCED) in Rio de Janeiro, June 1992, popularly known as "Rio Earth Summit" was unique in that 178 governments participated in it. In addition to intergovernmental conference, over 500 groups with special concerns and expertise on environment and development issue participated around the central theme. The Rio Summit received unprecedented publicity. Yet, it is not clear if the summit can be claimed as an outstanding success or a failure.

The preparation of the Earth Summit started in right earnest. Several working groups were set up. The First Preparatory Committee (PrepCom I) in August 1990 (Nairobi) discussed and identified the subjects the governments really wanted to see addressed. It was stressed that most developing countries wanted that their priority of national development become the prime theme on the environmental agenda. PrepCom I also defined the terms for broad participation of NGOs. PrepCom II, Geneva (March 1991), reviewed the background documentation provided by the secretariat. PrepCom III, Geneva (August 1991), discussed how to approach and coordinate the variety of issues for Agenda 21, which latter became a massive document consisting of 40 chapters outlining an 'action plan' for sustainable development. PrepCom IV met in New York in March 1992 and the Rio Declaration took its final shape, and 85 percent of the text of Agenda 21 was agreed. The rest, the more controversial issues, were left for final negotiations at the Conference in Rio. The PrepCom meetings saw participation of NGOs as observers. They were also allowed to speak and submit written proposals. Governments were invited to submit their national report on environment and development as a part of preparation for UNCED.

The Rio Conference saw signing of two legally binding agreements and other three non-legally binding agreements by nearly all participating countries. Non-binding instruments are Rio Declaration, Agenda 21 and the Forest Principles. Binding instruments are the United Nations Framework Convention on Climate Change and the Convention on Biodiversity.

Several key principles enunciated in the Stockholm Declaration are repeated in the Rio Declaration. The most important example is the notion that states have the sovereign right to exploit their natural resources, subject to the provision that such rights to exercise in a manner that causes no harm in territories beyond the state's jurisdiction. In Stockholm Declaration, the states have the 'right to exploit their own resources pursuant to their own environmental policies', while in the Rio Declaration 'environmental policies' is replaced by 'developmental and environmental policies'. The inclusion of 'developmental' has important consequences for balancing the three values of sustainable development. Similar such differences are to be found in some other 'Principle' too.

The Rio Declaration has the effect of pushing 'sustainable development' into the mainstream international law. Regardless of whether sustainable development is accepted as a principle of international law or just a concept used in international law, it became difficult after Rio for international lawyers to ignore sustainable development. Ten years after Rio another World Summit on Sustainable Development (WSSD) was held in Johannesburg. The summit was yet another step in the normative development of the principle of sustainable development.

Convention on Climate Change (CCC)

This first treaty took long 15 months to complete just before the deadline of the Rio Conference. It was a treaty designed to combat 'Global Warming'. Measurements since 1957 showed that atmospheric concentration of CO_2 was rising due to human activities, particularly due to burning of fossil fuel and deforestation. Subsequent studies show that concentration of other 'Greenhouse Gases' (GHG) is also rising. These gases absorb infrared radiation and warm the earth's surface, changing climates in various ways. By 1987 a broad consensus was arrived at on the nature and potential seriousness of the problem. Although convinced about the seriousness of the problem (GHG effect and ozone hole in particular), it became a difficult task to bind many countries, developed and developing, to commitments to limit the release of GHG. The developing countries feared that the issue was a conspiracy by northern countries to prevent/slowdown their development. In fact, it became and still is a complex international political issue.

The ultimate objective of the convention was to achieve stabilization of GHG concentration at a level that would prevent dangerous anthropogenic interference with the climate system. However it was recognized that some climatic change is inevitable, but stabilization of the GHG concentration was to be achieved within a time frame to allow the ecosystem to adapt naturally. It was accepted that the developed countries shall take the lead and would provide necessary funds for the measures the developing countries would have to undertake to control emission of GHG. 153 countries plus the EC signed the document at Rio.

In Kyoto in 1997, nations around the world agreed that the Clean Development Mechanism (CDM) was a competent way to combat climate change. The Kyoto Protocol asked for mandatory reductions in emissions of carbon dioxide, methane, nitrous oxide and other GHG to 1990 level by 2000, with an overall target of a 5 percent reduction from 1990 levels in the first commitment period, 2008–2012. But countries differ in their ability or willingness to forego carbon emissions in favor of global benefits, especially since 70 percent of all carbon emissions are from USA, EU and the former USSR. Moreover, each country has its own priorities; for example, China has plentiful coal deposits that it wishes to use for electricity generation, while USA is not as enthusiastic as Europe about pricing gasoline so as to restrict its consumption.

A recent United Nations report (Intergovernmental Panel for Climate Change, IPCC, Bangkok, 2007) underlines the impending threat to life of all forms on the only living planet known to man. The Panel of scientists has emphatically said that the key to the control mechanism lies with man alone. It is the market, which accentuated the climate problem, can be asked to take the initiative. This would be based on the principle of 'polluter pay' or more specifically, tax the industries that spout CO_2. For example, for every unit of CO_2 emission the industrial unit may be asked to pay, say US $ 100, and this will help maintain a control over atmospheric pollution to a large extent. These scientists have estimated that with such penalty provisions, the industries would be forced to cut down their GHG emissions through adoption of more efficient technology and switching over to alternative sources of cleaner energy. The money thus earned could be used for developing world-wide mechanisms to bring the current rate of increase in atmospheric temperature under considerable control by 2025 although a total control over global warming would not be feasible. Obviously, such taxation would hit hard the petroleum industry most, consumption of fuel oil by public and industries would come down. To keep the global warming under a check is often referred to as *migration strategy*. The gradual increase in atmospheric temperature and change in climatic conditions are but natural phenomena. The thing has aggravated in the last one hundred year due to heavy human interference. A total check on the rise in atmospheric temperature is a remote possibility since that would require about US $ 37 trillion (1 followed by 18 zeros) to be spent in the next 20 years.

The admission that global warming cannot be put under complete check, we need to develop another strategy to see that even this gradual rise in atmospheric temperature does not jeopardize our living with starved economy, especially in the agriculture sector. This would be our *adaptation strategy*. On both counts (migration and adaptation strategy) we need huge allotment for R & D.

The IPCC recommended carbon dioxide emission taxation policy would push the price of petroleum products up, a step that would bring down its consumption and generate fund for cleaning the environment. Another policy prescription is *carbon trading* (or emission trading). This has emanated from 1997 Kyoto protocol. The regulatory authority would fix up an emission norm for every industry. The industry has to bring down its emissions to the certified level. There are more polluting industries, there are less polluting industries and therefore the certified emission limits would be different for different industries. For the industry which is comparatively low polluting (though in excess of the permissible emission level), it would be considerably difficult and costly to curb emission by a unit than an industry that has high pollution level. The carbon-trading principle adopted in Kyoto protocol directs that such permits can be sold to another establishment. The gain from such carbon trading is multifaceted. First, this ensures the total emission limits from these two industries together conform to prescribed norms. Second, this trading is economically beneficial for both. Third, the same amount of expenditure brings down pollution by a larger amount than contemplated in the certified emission limits. An example will clarify how this trading can bring down more emission than contemplated. Suppose each of these industries is asked to bring down emission by 10 units. Also suppose that the less polluting industry needs to spend $1,000 for every 10 unit reduction of emission, and the second industry can achieve the same reduction at a cost of only $500. That is, a total of 20 unit reduction in emission will be achieved by a total expenditure of $1,500. If the first industry buys the permit from the second industry at a cost of $750 so that the former does not need to reduce the emission level at all, it saves $250 through the deal. The second industry now has $1,250 for emission reduction and this sum can effect 25 unit reduction of carbon emission. This carbon trading is most effective when the deal is struck between two industries, one located in developed and the other in the third world country. The hi tech industries have less emission but any further emission control would be very expensive. Though emission is very high in third world countries, controlling the same is cheaper, especially when a large sum comes from the industrialized countries. That is, the industrialized countries do not bring down their own emissions but help bring down the world's total emission level by this trade agreement with the third world countries.

There is another way by which GHG emissions can be put under check. This policy has two component parts – one part deals with increasing 'energy efficiency', that is, develop a technology that requires less energy without compromising on quantity and quality of production. The less the consumption of energy the less would be pollution. The second part of the policy is to use 'clean technology'. In this the energy used produces less pollution. Solar energy, wind energy, bio fuels etc. are 'clean fuels'.

A change in lifestyle, especially among the richer section of society can put some check on pollution. If people start to use public transports like local trains, trams, metros and buses instead of using personal cars, pollution from automobile discharge can be reduced appreciably. If people show reluctance to using public transports, the state or the local administration can restrict entry of personal vehicles in 'central business districts' and force commuters to travel in public transports while in the business district. Alternatively, the administration can impose heavy entry and parking fees for all privately owned vehicles. A large increase in sales tax on cars can also bring down the number of private cars plying on the road.

Another important method of containing environmental pollution is to plant more trees and increase the earth's green cover. More mangroves plantation in coastal regions also would give better soil bondage preventing erosion.

One very important aspect of the fallout of global warming has not received much attention from environmental activists. This is how to adapt to this inevitable global increase in temperature – the 'adaptation strategy'. Even if GHG emissions are put under some check, GHG gases in atmosphere would continue to increase as the populations increase. An increase in atmospheric temperature would change the climate so much so that agricultural production, which still is widely dependent on rainwater, may suffer badly. We need to look for alternative sources of water for agricultural and domestic uses as monsoons become erratic, unpredictable. Global warming would increase sea level inundating coastal regions and small islands. For all these eventualities we have to develop 'adaptation strategies'.

The IPCC report has urged every nation, especially the industrially developed countries, to come out with executable plans to cut down GHG emissions to arrest the rise in atmospheric temperature as quickly as possible. The developed countries need to bring down their energy intensive consumption habit and the developing countries like China, India and others need to adopt cleaner and more efficient technology to restrict their GHG emissions. The energy need to sustain the growth path followed both in the developing and developed countries need to concentrate more on renewable sources of energy. To attain this, countries need to change their practice of giving huge subsidies to fossil fuels and transfer this subsidy amount to R & D in the renewable energy sector.

Even if the countries fully agree with the deliberations of the Kyoto Protocol, the implementation of the policies would require about US $ 150 billion every year. It is a big sum but not so big if we compare the amount the developed countries spend on subsidies to energy and agricultural sector as also in other disguised subsidies to their products to remain in control in the world market. An estimate shows that investment of an amount equivalent to US $ 70/80 billion per annum is necessary to bring health, education, supply of drinking water, electricity and improvement and laying of new sewerage lines in the third world countries to an acceptable standard. In the interest of the future global health of our environment, this investment in the social sector of the third world countries is absolutely necessary.

It is not easy to accord priority to one and starving the other. The results from the investment in the environmental sector would become fully visible only after 50 years. On the other hand, the improvements envisaged in spending on social sector of the third world countries would make their average citizen twice wealthier as they are today in the same time frame. There is always a political compulsion for every democratically elected government to push forward their economic agenda: development through industrialization and modernization of the agricultural and other traditional sectors to eradicate poverty and improve the standard of living of their citizens. Such a growth policy cannot always remain environment friendly.

Then there is the age old debate on who are to be held responsible for the current health of the world environment. Industrialization in the developed countries took place at the expense of the environment. But now they are demanding that the developing countries, especially India and China (currently at 3rd and 1st spot in total GHG emission respectively), must tune their economic activity ensuring the protection of the global environment. The developed North is trying to roll the ball back into the third world countries' court asking them to go slow on industrialization and adopt appropriate technology to bring down emission. Then there is also the question about what various countries should do to prevent atmospheric temperature from rising. When USA demands China and India strictly adhere to emission norms for their electricity generation and other industrial units, they express their unwillingness to cut down their fuel consumption. They argue that such action will slow down their growth potential, which eventually would have far reaching effect on the growth and stability of the world market. USA is advocating adoption of 'clean technology' to the world to bring down emission. They have the technology which they can share with others, of course with a cost.

Just after the World Environment Day 5th June, 2008, G–8+5 countries met in Germany. Global warming was discussed and debated in this summit of global leaders. The outcome appears to be a little positive. The participating countries agreed that in view of the global warming up phenomenon the carbon emissions must be cut down by 50 percent by 2050. Although USA was stridently resisting the mandatory cuts proposed by EU, it became a signatory to this document indicating that USA did not reject the target outright and showed willingness to give some serious thought to this global issue. Critics of the US policy are skeptic if this signing can be taken as an indication of a real change in heart of the most polluting country that had consistently remained insensitive to the looming danger that may assume devastating proportions sooner rather than later. By far the most positive statement on global warming came from China, rated as the largest emitter of CO_2 and particulate matters. The country set out a model for arresting emission that can be emulated by others as well. It emphasized that measure to thwart warming to be integrated with development, without sacrificing economic growth of the country. Cleaner technology, improved energy efficiency, streamlined agriculture and forest expansion are intended to restructure its economy. On the eve of this summit, Australia indicated its willingness to redefine its strategy on environmental pollution when it annulled the use of incandescent bulbs in the country whose conversion efficiency was only 10 percent compared to 80 percent energy conversion efficiency of compact fluorescent lamps (CFL).

The latest climate report released at the Bally climate meet put India, Pakistan and Bangladesh among the potential hot spots where climate change could aggravate tensions. Himalayan glacier retreat will threaten water supply, monsoon changes could harm crop production, rising sea level may submerge vast stretches of coastal land and cyclones could threaten densely populated towns in South Asia. The report has also identified North Africa, Southern Africa, Central Asia, China, and the Gulf of the Mexico region as other potential hot spots for climate-change induced violence.

Convention on Biodiversity (CBD)

The convention seeks to conserve biodiversity of the planet through protection of species and ecosystems. Governments are asked to develop 'national strategies', plans and programs for protecting biodiversity. The developed countries, it was contemplated, shall meet the 'agreed full incremental costs' of developing countries for undertaking such measures under the convention. It is estimated that 40 percent of the global economy is based on biological products and the volume and the highest range of biodiversity are found in the developing countries, especially in tropics. A mere 7 percent of the Earth's surface holds between half and three-quarters of the world's biodiversity. Industrially advanced countries are using these reservoirs of biological and genetic resources in the developing countries to develop new products. The economically advanced world is asking the poorer countries to conserve this biodiversity so that the MNCs can remain in total control of the benefits of this genetic pool.

UNEP estimates that there are about 30 million species on Earth of which only about 1.5 million have ever been described. UNEP also estimates that one-quarter of earth's species risk extinction within the next 300 years. It is the developing countries that have greater diversity of species. The developed countries wanted exchange of biological resources in return for access to technologies. The developing countries however insisted on sovereign rights over their genetic resources within their territories as also easy access to benefits resulting from the use of such resources in the shape of biotechnology. These demands were unacceptable to many countries that wanted to view biodiversity as a common heritage of human kinds and biotechnology to be the concern of industry.

The final draft completed in May 1992 in Nairobi reflects compromise by both sides. UNEP convention acknowledged 'sovereign rights' of states over their national resources, i.e., genetic resources cannot be viewed as a common reserve. However, the convention also urged that the states must be obligated to protect domestic genetic pool, use them sustainably, and facilitate their use by others. 155 countries signed the Convention in Rio.

Negotiation of a Bio-safety Protocol in 2000 recommended that the UN keep an eye on rules for imports of genetically modified (GM) foods. The Protocol also recommended that governments will be within their rights to ban imports of GM seeds and crops if they believe these may threaten the environment or people's health. Bio-safety and TRIPs (trade-related aspects of intellectual property rights) are also issues on which the global movement towards free trade has clashed with groups expressing concerns on environmental, health and labor standards during the WTO conference in 1999 (Seattle). However, the Bio-safety Protocol does not ask for restrictions on experimentation with GM crops. Such experimentations are taking place on a wider scale even in developing countries. The environmentalists and activists are debating all over the world on CBD, especially bio-prospecting, GM crops, and TRIPs. They speak loudly against transnational corporations (TNCs) for their intention to seek full access and monopoly over the genetic and biological wealth of the developing countries.

Rio Declaration. Rio Declaration on Environment and Development presents 27 principles of environment and development intended to build upon the Stockholm Conference. In order to achieve sustainable development, environmental protection shall form an integral part of the development process. Compared to Stockholm Declaration, Rio Declaration has more to do with action plan and implementation. Some of the more important principles are as under.

1. Human beings are at the center of concerns for sustainable development.
2. States have the sovereign right to exploit their own resources pursuant to their own environmental and developmental policies provided that their activities do not cause damage to the environment of other states.
3. The right to development must be fulfilled keeping an eye on the needs of the present and future generations.
4. In order to achieve sustainable development, environmental protection shall constitute an integral part of the development program.
5. Eradication of poverty is an indispensable requirement for sustainable development.
6. The developing and poor countries and those most environmentally vulnerable shall be given special priority.
7. The developed countries have a special responsibility in the international pursuit of sustainable development with special reference to health and integrity of Earth's ecosystem.
8. States should reduce and eliminate unsustainable patterns of production and consumption and promote appropriate demographic policies.
9. States shall enact effective environmental legislation covering compensation for victims of pollution and other environmental damage.
10. States should prevent relocation and transfer to other states of any activities and substances that cause severe environmental degradation or are found to be harmful to human health.
11. The polluter should in principle bear the cost of pollution.
12. States shall immediately notify other states of any natural disaster or other emergencies that are likely to produce sudden harmful effects on the environment of other states (keeping the Chernobyl disaster in mind)
13. Women have a vital role in environmental management.
14. The environment and natural resources of people under oppression, domination and occupation shall be protected.
15. Warfare is inherently destructive to sustainable development.

The official product of UNCED resides a few agreements, all of which were finally approved at the Earth Summit. We have briefly outlined the conventions on Climate Change, on Biodiversity and Rio declaration. The fourth one is Agenda 21, a document comprised of 40 chapters outlining 'action plans' for sustainable development in 21st century. It is not a legal document; governments have the option of accepting/rejecting the recommendations. Agenda 21 covers several topics including those covered by UNCED conventions or other existing conventions. Agenda 21 have 4 broad sections, which address the major areas of political action.

(I) Social and Economic development
(II) Natural Resources, fragile ecosystem and related human captivities
(III) Strengthening the Role of Major Groups
(IV) Means of Implementation

Section I has a number of subsections: international cooperation to accelerate sustainable development in developing countries and related domestic policies; combating poverty; changing consumption patterns (this specially refers to industrialized countries); demographic dynamics and sustainability (synergistic relationship between demographic trends and social, economic and environmental issues); protection and promotion of human health (in the context of environmental and socio-economic development); promoting sustainable human settlement development; integration of environment and development decision-making.

Section II deals with protection of atmosphere – efficiency in energy and transport sector, emission restriction from industries, steps to check depletion of atmospheric ozone layer and transboundary air pollution; sustainable human settlement; integration of environment and development decision-making; planning and management of land resources; combating deforestation, desertification and drought; conservation of biodiversity; environmentally sound bio-technology; protection of seas and oceans; protection of fresh water supply resources; management of toxic chemicals; management of hazardous wastes and sewage related issues; management of radio-active wastes.

In Section III there are 10 chapters with considerable overlap in their themes. This section stresses the need for participation of children and youth in the decision-making process, role of indigenous people and their communities in their relationship with land. The vital role of NGOs in participatory democracy is highlighted. Decentralization of power to local bodies and involvement of the workers and trade unions in sustainable development activities are stressed. Business and industry, scientific and technological community and all those other communities that count should be made to contribute liberally to the decision-making process concerning environment and sustainable development.

The financial resource to be tapped for implementation of Agenda 21 is covered in section IV. 7 chapters have been devoted on this. The Operational Development Assistance (ODA) statements reflect acceptance of UN target of 0.7 percent of World GNP to be spent for protection of environment. Several donor countries reaffirmed their commitments in this regard. USA and a few others wanted to look at the matter carefully. Poorer developing countries considered financial resources as the key issue for the implementation of Agenda 21. G-77 countries demanded that 2000AD reach UN goal of ODA 0.7 percent of GNP from developed countries. However many developed countries (USA, UK and Germany, for example) were opposed to such a timetable. Besides financial measures, this section deals with topics such as transfer of environmentally sound technology; national mechanism and international cooperation; international institutional arrangement – Commission on Sustainable Development (CSD) which was to operate as the main follow-up institution; international instruments on environmental development; and information for decision-making..

The success for implementing each UNCED program area requires constant flow of finance. The poorer countries need the financial and technical assistance most. It is estimated that for full implementation of Agenda 21 a sum of $600 billion per year would be required of which $125 billion per year is to be spent in aid or in soft loans to developing countries. However, available intergovernmental finance remains more or less constant at about half the target level.

Agenda 21 presents a masterpiece of action for sustainable development throughout the world. Although it is not legally binding on every nation, Agenda 21 finds its importance in that it is a negotiated document agreed among more than 150 governments. It serves as an extensive guidebook to sustainable development ever prepared. It will remain as a reference book of ideas, principles and approaches for many years to come.

15 World Population Policies and Programs

15.1 Primitive People and Pre-Historic Growth

From time immemorial survival has been the primary urge for all living creatures. This 'urge for survival' must not be confused or equated to some 'population policy', though they may trigger formulation of a social policy for the betterment of a population group. Nature has given us discernible faculties that lend us to develop and think out mechanisms that are most likely to insure our survival and progress. Both biological and social adaptations remain key to survival. But these adaptations alone do not determine population policies. All policies are much more than what we call the basic instincts of biological beings. Policies are deliberate; they are socially engineered and addresses to a whole group of individuals within a geographically and politically defined space. Man in this biological world is privileged by the distinctive faculty – intelligence – which enables him to look back into the past, evaluate his relations with the biological world and the surrounding events to foresee what awaits him in the future. This gives him an opportunity to organize his life, develop adequate means of survival and also how to live better.

Man as an individual can acquire some of these through personal efforts, but much of it remains beyond his personal endeavor. He has learnt from the history, from his personal and collective experience, and from traditions and customs that all his goals can be reached only through collective effort of the population group to which he belongs. *This deliberate intent to ensure survival and improved standard of living for all, even for the future generations, can be termed as the population policy of an aggregative population.* What are desirable in the context of a specific population group may not stand tall for other groups. Different population groups have different requirements, diverse social and cultural backgrounds, necessitating special population policies. In the broader context, we can include any policy and action plan that have explicit objective of influencing the size and composition of a population as a population policy. *Population programs* are action plans for implementation of the policy, often in stages and spread over time and space, and review the program impact, make necessary amends to make the program more effective. The medium-term objective of Government of India (NPP 2000) is to bring the TFR down to replacement level by 2010, through vigorous implementation of inter-sectoral operational strategies. The programs adopted for reaching the policy objectives show that broadly a three-part program has been worked out. The programs include the following:

- A range of voluntary family planning services and information, so that people can learn about family planning and avoid unwanted pregnancy;
- Basic health care for all; and
- Education, social and economic opportunity and empowerment, especially for women.

In the distant past, life was very brief since man had to live on the bounties and mercy of nature. Birth rate had to be maintained almost at the biological limit to compensate huge losses of lives from natural crisis, diseases, lack of nutrition, and in constant fight against predators and invasion by other groups. The major concern of this pre-historic people was to insure that there were enough adult females in their reproductive age to compensate early deaths, and adult males to fight invaders and predators and for collection of food and other necessities of life. New types of crisis often would demand a different type of personal and group behavior. Such social policies often had an important effect on the demographic parameters of the group, but such social policy cannot strictly be labeled as a population policy in the sense the term is used today. But unlike other policies concerning health, or education, or agriculture, the objectives of a population policy are not only less precise, they often are related to many other issues that often are not intrinsically related to demographic parameters. When we speak of health policy we know it seeks to provide best possible health related services to the greatest number of persons.

Some of the practices of the primitive people are often very suggestive for their concern about the size and composition of their group. Since they often had to travel from one hunting ground to another, crippled and weak babies and very old persons were regarded as serious burdens for the group. No wonder that they had to die even though they could have lived longer had the group members looked at them a little kindly. The exposure of the crippled and the weak babies was a general practice. This often was deliberate since the intention was to develop strong and hardy people. We do not know if such a policy was ever a deliberate population policy or arose simply as a process of adaptation to the press of the circumstance. Though deliberate, one cannot be sure if such policy can be equated to a population policy.

Polyandry (one woman having more than one husband) at that point of time probably was the logical option because of shortage of adult females. Prolonged breast feeding (even till the mid-childhood stage and beyond) was a necessity for the children to survive because of lack of provision of child-consumable food. This prolonged breast feeding may have given the women time to recover their health before the next conception. The average number of children actually borne by these women must have been far below the potential fertility (fecundity) of the average female in those populations. These and other traditional social practices definitely helped in maintaining an age-sex structure in the group. Often it was the demand of the circumstances that necessitated the primitive people to make adjustment and modification of their behavior.

Many rulers in the world history have encouraged higher rate of reproduction among their subjects. This they did to draft able bodied persons to increase their military strength. They often believed that the power of the throne would be exhibited by the numbers that were governed by it. The strength derived from numbers has even fascinated many of the recent dictators – Hitler, Mussolini, and Stalin. Large families still are praised in many societies. Even the tax payers in many countries today are granted monetary benefits for their children. But such social attitudes regarding growth of population do not necessarily refer to a defined population policy in the sense this term is used worldwide.

15.2 Population Policy in the Present Context

Population policy today is an integral part of national planning for economic and social development, especially in most of the developing countries. The social scientists and politicians still need to answer a fundamental question: How justified the state is in forcing a population policy on its citizens? It is a historical truth that the basic objective of the state is to ensure the maximum wellbeing of its citizens. In the discharge of this responsibility the state formulates policies and action plans that would promote economic and social development of the country. Such policies and action plans for economic and social development of the country cannot be worked out unless the state knows the number and the composition of the population for whom the policy would address, as also the specific requirements of the diverse population groups. The state's concern in the demographic domain appears to follow directly from the responsibility reposed on it for maximizing the wellbeing of its citizens. The critics argue that it does not necessarily justify state intervention in every aspect of population parameters. Most states do not interfere in one's religious faith, personal preferences and choices, freedom to hold opinions and express them and take decisions on personal matters so long such decisions are not contrary to the laws framed by the state for all citizens to abide by, or do not infringe upon others' rights and privileges as free citizens of the country. The Universal Declaration of Human Rights by the United Nations in 1948 pronounced that all men and women at birth and throughout their lives are free and are entitled to the basic human rights to life, liberty, and prosperity. The state must respect these basic tenets and show the same in its own actions, and avoid anything that would tantamount to preventing citizens from exercising their rights. To exercise the right to prosperity, the citizens must have access to education and the state must take adequate steps to develop a national educational policy that would guarantee basic education to every citizen without discrimination. The state would be within its right to make education compulsory to ensure that every citizen receives a minimum of education to develop their skills commensurate with their intellectual level. Right to life also means right to good health. Right to good health asks the state to develop the necessary health infrastructure, supply of potable water, sanitation, environmental cleanliness, etc. Out of liberty arise certain obligations for every citizen. For instance, the right to health demands that every citizen is obliged to look into the interests of others. Compulsory vaccination is one such social obligation. "The right to good health" empowers the state to adopt concrete, even restrictive measures to ensure good health and prosperity not only of the current generation but of the future generations as well.

When the state formulates plans and programs for education or health, there is no confusion among the citizens as to what the real objectives are. Education ensures skill development, cultural integration and professionalism in the citizens' pursuit to occupational career. Attention of the state to health sector is most welcome by everyone since good health is a prerequisite to success in all spheres – occupation, family life and in the discharge of all the duties and responsibilities the society expects of every citizen. People understand what important role the state can play in developing a platform which the citizens can use in the pursuit of their personal and collective goals – decent standard of living. However, our understanding of the relationship between personal and social wellbeing, economic and social development on the one hand, and the demographic parameters on the other, is still not very clear.

State interventions often are welcome when some demographic parameters are seen to threaten the poise of civic life by derailing economic and social progress. This incompatible situation is seen to appear when demographic parameters move in directions that appear unwholesome to the country's collective existence and wellbeing in the long run. Indications of a serious imbalance in areas such as age-sex composition and distribution of the population, fast growth or decrease in population, all or some of which have the potential to destabilize citizens' personal and collective interests, calls for a state intervention. Such interventions by the state are well documented in the history of modern civilization. A case in example is the "family code" enacted in France in 1939 to correct the declining growth of population consequential to the huge loss of lives in the World War I and the severe economic crisis in the 1930s. 'Birth strike' had to be revoked in Russia because of extensive loss of lives in the two World Wars and the civil war, famine and epidemics that followed the 1917 revolution. Japan promulgated Eugenic Protection Law in 1948 to facilitate induced abortion to bring the population growth rate under control to revitalize country's economy which received a serious jolt by Japan's defeat in World War II and large scale repatriation of Japanese from the countries that were under Japan's control before the World War II. Since World War II, many countries around the world experienced very high population growth. They needed a time space to chart their course of economic and social development in the post-war developments; the fast growing populations were great hindrance even to plan their social and economic development courses; a fast declining population growth rate in countries like France and many other Western European countries appeared to derail their economic growth path.

'Right to raise family' remains the most fundamental right in all societies. Even in many Constitutions family is accepted as the basic unit of society, and this was emphatically acknowledged in the World Population Plan of Action adopted in Bucharest in 1974. It gives absolute freedom to citizens to take decision about conception and carry pregnancy to its ultimate effect. Issuing 'birth card' (as was imposed in China) or forcing people to undergo sterilization or abortion (as was carried out in India during Emergency) would be a clear violation of Human Rights. In this context, the *financial incentives* given to acceptors of sterilization or some other methods of birth prevention (not as compensation for expenses) would tantamount to state's encroachment on citizens 'freedom to choose'. Special aid and assistance during motherhood and childhood who have their first child at mother's age beyond 19 (1976 Act for Prevention of Child Marriage in India lays down the minimum age at marriage of a girl at 18 years) without discrimination cannot be regarded as state's infringement on the 'right to raise family'. Admitting privacy in adult sexuality and reproduction, states role in birth planning cannot be ignored altogether. The responsibility for the consequences of reproduction, that is, health care of mother and child, and the education of the child are increasingly being socialized. The couples have the autonomy 'to have or not have a child'; but many 'rights of the child' (to good health, to education, to culture, etc.) are responsibilities of the state. The couples may on their own decide or be willing to have fewer babies and the state needs to provide help and assistance to support them in reaching the desired number of children.

In this dilemma of state's intervention and acknowledgement of 'human right' of every citizen, it must be admitted that the state's role in the wellbeing of its citizens, not only the present but the future generations as well, is becoming key to achieving pride and prosperity of the nation. State takes decisions for the collective humanity; individual's decisions are primarily related to his/her family. The fundamental human rights given to citizens demands that the citizens too acknowledge that they have certain obligation to the state as well. The collective institutions that take up responsibilities for education, health, social security, communication and transportation, justice, and the like have rather weakened the role of family, which for centuries were considered theirs. No one would argue about the state's authority to change or modify the rules for admission in higher education, change the bank rates and credit policies, or withdraw subsidies in a phased manner, and amend land reform policy to accelerate the process of industrialization and economic growth under the press of circumstances.

Most economic and social policies have both short and long term components. But demographic changes practically have no short term component. Decision to make vaccination against small pox in early 1950s in India made complete elimination of the dreaded disease from the Indian soil some 23 years later. The effect of a drastic drop in birth rate would be felt in the labor market 20 years thereafter. The effect of 'baby boom' in Europe and America in 1940s was felt in the early 1960s when a huge excess of youths entered the employment market. Any event under the domain of demography requires observation over a long period of time to assess their periodic fluctuations, persistent and sporadic causes behind them, analyze the sequence of concomitant factors to understand the nature of changes in the offing. It is through a detailed study of the events in the past and present that a policy decision can be worked out for modification of the demographic parameters. Even with extreme coercion adopted for birth control (birth-in-turn mandate), China could not bring down population growth down to less than 1 percent (Hua told the Chinese Parliament in 1978 that this target must be met within 3 years) before the mid-1990s.

The legitimacy of a population policy becomes evident since all the developmental efforts of the state are intricately linked to the population numbers and their composition. The state is in a far better position than an individual for achieving the collective interest of the nation, both for present and future generations. The time horizon involved in population change is exceptionally too long in comparison to what the politicians and the man on the street visualize. A very detailed long term policy is needed for achieving desired changes in the demographic structures.

The state functions like a modern corporate house. Like the corporate house, the state's objectivity is in improving productivity in all spheres so that the fruits of social and economic development are absorbed for the welfare of the common man. Improvement in productivity is functionally related to the technology adopted and the skill quality of the labor. The capital-intensive production (market economy demands it) requires fewer highly skilled and professional persons and the best of the technology. To keep the production efficiency high, the management needs to be given some legitimate power to hire or fire the labor. When the population growth is very high, the state needs to develop mechanisms to bring down the growth rate so that skill maximization of growth becomes attainable. Similarly, when the population growth is very low or negative, the state needs to activate all its apparatus to see that because of shortage of skilled manpower, national economy and wellbeing of its citizen do not suffer. Some educational institutions, hospitals, industries and other social and economic agencies may have to be closed for the simple reason that they cannot be manned by professionals and skilled labors and there are few takers of the services rendered by these institutions. Reproduction definitely is a private domain of couples. But the state needs to remind them that the couples must keep in mind the consequences of frequent births to the health of the mother and child and also that the state has to mobilize additional resources to discharge its responsibility for the care of health and education of the children born as also to prevent maternity adversities. The state therefore has a legitimate right to ask couples to choose from among the viable options – better health of mother and child, better facilities for education for developing skills and possibility of obtaining a better standard of living not only for them, but also for generations to come on the one hand, and inefficient health care and educational facilities leading to greater inequality in health attainment, skill development and purchasing power. The state can activate its machinery to make people understand how the welfare of the state could be impacted by demographic parameters. The common man needs to be reminded of his/her dual responsibility – responsibility to the family raised by him/her and to the nation.

15.3 Population Growth in Modern Demographic Era

The modern demographic era has been taken to have started from 1650. It is around this time that the population of the world was believed to have reached 500 million (some estimates put it at 600 million). Many of the important changes in population growth pattern, especially in the West, are seen to have occurred since about this time. By 1820, the world population doubled. Since then, the doubling of population has taken progressively fewer years (vide Table 1.1). Today we are adding 1,000 million or around to the existing population every 12 years. Between 1975 and 2003, the world population has grown by 155 percent (annual average growth rate 1.6 percent), from 4073.7 to

6313.8 million. By 2015, the world average annual growth rate is likely to come down to 1.1–1.2 percent. Even then, because of the large population base, the estimated population in 2015 is likely to reach a staggering 7219.4 million (HDR, 2005).

Although we acknowledge that some kind of a census was in operation in some parts of the world even before the Christian era began, it must be admitted that there is hardly any recorded evidence about birth and death rates before 1650. But it is almost certain that the average females did not give births full to their fertility potential even if it is assumed that they remained sexually active during their entire reproductive period. Scientists have no doubt whatsoever that there are no differences in fecundity between nations, races, and population classes within any society. This they believe is a historical truth. Evidences suggest that there is (in the past as well) considerable variation in fertility between women in all societies and in all social groups. Evidences also suggest that in all fertility description and analysis, fecundity, which at best determines the possible upper limit, is to be considered a constant factor. But the same cannot be said about fertility, which is largely culturally determined as also by the general health status of the people. There could be some variation in birth rates between peoples (mostly tribal) who largely depended on hunting, fruit gathering, and fishing and on herds and flocks for their sustenance, and those who were better settled.

The knowledge of prevalent death rates and causes of death in pre-industrial society is as hazy as are the birth rates. Natural increase in pre-industrial society, and, in fact, in all societies, is primarily determined by death rates. Hunger, famine, epidemic, natural disaster like tsunami, tornado, earthquake, etc. and war can cause a colossal loss of lives instantaneously as these death haunting causes appear on the scene. These *positive checks* were the principal causes for slow growth of population in pre-historic and pre-industrial era. Historical evidences suggest that death rates varied greatly even in the same society between two time points. But such dramatic change in birth rate is rarely seen in the history. It takes long time to adjust birth rates to the need of the situation. The *preventive checks* primarily operate on birth rates by reducing fertility level of females in different age groups.

The period 1650–1820 AD can be regarded as the beginning of a new era of population growth. Unlike pre-1650, we have some idea about how social and economic changes were taking place at least in some parts of the world (West) that had a direct bearing on the growth of population. Around 500 million people have been estimated to have been added between 1650 and 1820 with an estimated average growth rate of 0.3–0.4 percent per annum.

From the middle of the seventeenth century, population related statistics became more and more reliable since counting of people (some specific groups or in some specific regions), though not on a periodical basis always, were undertaken in some countries. The available data from various sources and intelligent guesses clearly indicate that world population growth gained considerable momentum between 1820 and 1930. Some 1,000 million people were added in these 110 years. This trend of population growth was noticeable much earlier. Malthusian doctrine has been the result of a very careful analysis of the population trends in many countries as also their economic progresses and agricultural production.

15.4 Population Growth Changed by Two World Wars

The two World Wars in the first half of the twentieth century are landmark events to demographers not for heavy loss of populations, especially among the young adults in the countries where the two wars were mostly fought, but because the two wars saw discoveries of a few life saving drugs and preventive medicines and vast improvement in the transport and communication network. The scientific discoveries and technological innovations quickly changed the social scenario altogether – agricultural and industrial production went up sharply, health facilities even in the poor countries improved considerably, and growth of industries led to faster urbanization.

The wars in pre-industrial days were clashes between two nations or two cultures. The demographic effects were unidirectional – loss of lives, loss of property and wealth of the vanquished. But that really did not have a very significant lasting effect on growth of population and population composition. Famine, epidemic and natural catastrophe had more far reaching effect on the demographic parameters than these wars. The two World Wars have seen how science and technology can be used very effectively in mass destruction. The two Wars also saw large mobilization of military forces, which effected separation of great numbers of husbands from their wives for long periods and also preventing many marriages which normally would have taken place had there been no massive mobilization of forces. The mass mobilization saw export and import of diseases from various parts of the world. Deaths both in the armed forces and in the civilian population were in much excess of deaths normally expected had there been no war. To this was added the birth deficit.

In the first quarter of the twentieth century there were indications that a significant change in the pattern of world population was in the offing. Jenner's discovery in 1798 of effective inoculation against small pox had a revolutionary impact on developing preventive vaccines against many infectious diseases. However, the discovery did not make much headway for a long period even in Europe. Since the beginning of the twentieth century immunization against several frightful diseases became possible. Since 1930, more specifically during World War II, most countries, even in the underdeveloped world, had access to many of these preventive medicines. Most countries involved in World War II required their military personnel to undertake inoculations against typhoid, cholera, yellow fever, small pox and plague. Vaccines against tuberculosis also became available by then. The children in the developed countries were inoculated particularly against diseases to which they were most prone (whooping cough, diphtheria, scarlet fever and the like). The fruits of these innovations soon spread from the industrially developed countries to the less developed countries. Since there was no evidence whatever, the birth rates in the non-European countries had by the time started to decline significantly, the first effect of this increasing control of death rate among all these people was to push up the population growth rate. The technological and scientific revolutions helped increase food production fast enough to take care of the fast growing numbers.

The military losses in World War I were because of involvement of vast size of armed forces as also, at least partly, due to the kind of weapons used and the trench warfare. Many of these wounded people died from infected wounds. The use of antiseptics, the discovery of penicillin and the miracle curative drug sulfa and later antibiotics brought down the death rates since 1930. The populations involved in World War I did not have the advantage of these drugs and antiseptics. The countries involved in World War II were successful in controlling one of man's greatest curses – malaria. To keep the disability rate of the armed forces that moved to areas where malaria was widespread, the new found insecticide DDT was used very effectively.

The civilian deaths in World War I, though high, was smaller than what was experienced during World War II. The types of civilian death in World War II had no parallel in the history of warfare, not even in World War I. Aerial bombing, both by Germans and the Allied Powers caused extensive damages to civilian populations and their properties. UK suffered very heavily both early in the war and again near its close. After the initial setback, Allied Powers hit back at Germans. But the greatest tragedy happened in the German concentration camps where Jews, the anti-Nazis and all the conquered people engaged in putting up resistance, were exterminated to terrorize the world.

The worst sufferer in the two World Wars was Russia. Direct military losses were very heavy. Besides the losses of lives in World War I, the revolution in 1917 in USSR and the famine in 1918–1922 and the epidemics that followed caused enormous loss of lives. The war and the revolution prevented Russia from taking suitable measures to contain the famine and the epidemics that accompanied it. The net effect of the war, revolution, famine and the epidemics was that the population in Russia grew from an estimated 140 million in 1914 to only about 147 million in 1926. Had there been no war or revolution or famine or epidemic, the population of Russia could have been around 175 million by 1926. USSR added only 7 million in 12 years between 1914 and 1926, whereas expected increase should have been 35 million under normal circumstance. Of the 28 million deficits, according to an estimate by Lorimer, 2 million were from military losses, 10 million from birth deficits and an excess of 16 million civilian deaths resulting from civil war following the revolution in 1917, to the famines of 1918–1922 and the epidemic accompanying the famine. Lorimer suggested that about one-third of this total deficit of about 28 million (1914–1926) occurred during the war but before 1917 revolution.

War losses in World War II in USSR were very large, much higher than the losses during World War I. One estimate (Timasheff) puts it at 37.5 million – military deaths 7 million, birth deficit 10.9 million, civilian deaths 18.5 million and emigration 1.3 million. That there was a great shortage of adult males in USSR is evident from 1959 census. The deficit of males was estimated at 20.8 million. The estimated deficits of males in 1939 and 1926 were 7.8 and 5.1 million respectively. This clearly shows the terrific loss of civilian males as well as military personnel during World War II. With such an accumulated decline in sex ratio, the birth rate in USSR declined so much so that it took many postwar years to attain some semblance of balance in sex ratio in the population. The estimated war losses in Europe and in the countries settled from Europe, military and civilians put together in the two World Wars, were 50 million or more. Outside Europe, Japan suffered the greatest loss of civilian population in World War II due to dropping of atom bombs by USA in Hiroshima and Nagasaki towards the very end of the war in 1945.

Direct military losses in Germany in World War II was estimated at over 3 million, about one-half greater than such losses in World War I. Ledermann has estimated that about 400,000 civilians may have been killed in the aerial bombing of Germany and that an excess of deaths in the civilian population of similar magnitude due to military causes, while birth deficits accounted for 1 million. He puts the total war losses in Germany in World War II at around 5 million. The total war losses in 1914–1919 was over 5.4 million of which birth deficit alone was over 3.2 million and military losses about 2 million. Of course these estimates do not include the excess civilian deaths due to killing in concentration camps.

The war losses in Europe west of Germany in World War II were generally less than the losses experienced in World War I. Military losses in France in World War II were about one-tenth of the losses in World War I. About 600,000 deaths in France were directly related to war (military, civilian, war prisoners and men deported to Germany for forced labor). Birth rates in France did not decline as much as it did in World War I, especially in respect to their population growth. France, in fact, suffered far less from World War II than that from World War I. UK had similar such experiences as in France but the direct war losses in UK was much more than that in France. Population growth in Western Europe as a whole was not quite upset by World War II. The story was quite different in Eastern and Southern Europe and in Germany.

If we compare the birth rates, pre-war, during war, and post-war period, they dropped very significantly in most European countries during World War I. This was the likely effect of mobilization of large military forces for a long period and the massacre of war prisoners by Germans. But things were quite different in World War II. In most of the West European countries the birth rates in World War II did not decline as much as it did in World War I. The following table gives an idea about how this vital component of population growth responded to the two war situations.

Table 15.1 *Birth rates as affected by the two world wars*

Country	*World War I*			*World War II*		
	Pre-war 1910–14	*War 1914–19*	*Post-war 1920–24*	*Pre-war 1937–39*	*War 1940–44*	*Post-war 1947–49*
1	*2*	*3*	*4*	*5*	*6*	*7*
England & Wales	24.2	19.4	21.4	14.9	15.5	18.3
France	18.8	11.3	19.8	14.9	14.9	21.1
Germany	28.2	16.8	23.1	19.6	17.3	16.9
Austria	29.6	15.8	22.6	15.8	19.1	17.4
Netherlands	28.2	25.5	26.5	20.3	21.8	25.6
Norway	25.6	24.2	23.4	15.4	17.7	20.5
Denmark	26.4	23.8	23.1	18.0	20.3	20.4

Source: Reproduced from Thomson & Lewis: *Population Problems*, Fifth Edition

Birth rates for most countries in Europe showed almost an upward trend between 1937 and 1949. The experiences from the World War I probably made them wiser. Many had opportunity to take shelter in some other countries that were less targeted by the Germans. The loss of lives in Europe and countries settled from Europe was almost similar in the two Wars – 50 million or so.

15.5 Population Growth Since World War II

At the beginning of the twentieth century, the world population was around 1,600 million. In the previous 80 years world population grew by 800 million. In spite of massive loss of lives due to World War I, famines and epidemics in many parts of the world, 400 million people were added to 1900 population in 1930. In the 20 years after 1930, which saw the great devastation of World War II, 540 million people were added, i.e., on an average 27 million people added every year. This is in spite the fact that in excess of 50 million people were obliterated from Europe alone during 1941–45. Though natural death rates in Europe and other industrially developed countries came down fast as a result of the discovery of many preventive and curative medicines, death rates in rest of the world, though declining fast, still were high. This is because only very modest health services were available in most countries outside Europe and North America. The World War II was a boon in the sense that the new 'miracle drugs' (sulfa and later the antibiotics and DDT) brought the new era of death control, especially in the underdeveloped countries. It is estimated that death rates among soldiers from infected wounds during the World War II was brought to one-half or less of what it was in World War I by the application of sulfa drugs and the newly discovered antibiotics. The less developed countries, which were also very poor, had very inefficient health infrastructure and therefore only the wealthier and influential persons could take the full advantage of these discoveries. But the situation changed overnight during the Second World War.

The more developed countries brought down their death rates over a long period of time primarily through better sanitation, health awareness, improved nutrition, education, and better health infrastructure even without having the advantages of these 'miracle' drugs and vaccines. The backward countries, on the other hand, could bring down deaths very quickly from infectious and many other killer diseases even when they were lacking proper sanitation, health awareness, education and had inefficient health care establishments. Even cultural barriers, ignorance and lack of education did not seriously interfere in accepting these curative and preventive medicines and sprays when they observed their amazing effects on people who volunteered to try them for remedial or prevention of diseases. The health services in many of the underdeveloped countries, including India, became better organized and mass oriented after World War II. The effect of this improved health care in these countries became clearly visible when within a short span of time their population started to grow very fast. There can be no doubt that the faster increase in the growth of population was due to fast decline in the death rate. Sri Lanka's death rate remained around 22 between 1939 and 1945; but by 1959 it came down to only 9. But these underdeveloped countries did not show clear signs of decline in birth rate concurrent to their falling death rate. Populations in many underdeveloped countries were growing at over 2.5 per cent a year. Some of the Latin American countries had even higher growth rates (2.8 per cent) because they had even higher birth rates (CBR 42, CDR 19). In the 10 years since 1950 some 520 million people were added to the world population. Asian countries alone added about 300 million (average CBR 41 and CDR 22, growth rate 1.9 per cent) and Europe adding only 32 million in these 10 years (average CBR 19 and CDR 11 and average annual growth rate 0.7 per cent). In the next 20 years net addition to the world population was 1,420 million, a little less than the total addition in 130 years since 1820.

World population continued to grow at around 2 percent per annum till about 1980. The high growth rates in the developing and very backward regions were to an extent compensated by fast decline in growth rate in the developed regions (from 1.3 in 1950–55 to 0.6 around 1980). Growth rates in Asia and Latin America reached their peaks around 1970. Growth rate in Africa started to show signs of decline around 1985. Because of wide variation in growth rates between regions, the world has witnessed considerable change in the population distribution. The population of the high income industrially developed countries stood at 19.2 per cent in 1975. By 2003, their share to the world population came down to only 15 per cent. The average annual growth rate in low income countries was 2.1 percent for the period 1975–2003 as against 0.7 in the high income and 1.4 in the middle income countries (the annual average TFR of 6.0, 4.5 and 2.2 respectively in low, middle and high income countries). Even after considerable improvement in vital rates across the globe, the Earth is still gaining 78 million people annually, roughly the equivalent of adding a new United Kingdom and Australia combined each year, or a city the size of Philadelphia every week. In 1800, London was the world's largest city with about 1 million people. Today, 326 metropolitan areas have more than 1 million people each and 16 cities have more than 10 million people. By 2025, some 650 cities are likely to have populations of more than 1 million each. USA is the industrially developed country that still has fertility very close to the replacement level TFR of 2.06. The average number of children born per woman in USA still is 2.03. The average fertility in all European countries is 1.4. Even some of the developing nations like Taiwan and South Korea have average fertility below 1.6 per woman.

Since the beginning of the nineteenth century the easy availability of dependable primary data on population from various parts of the world encouraged the demographers to build up appropriate methodologies and develop analytical tools for analysis of numerous issues related to population. The statisticians contributed very significantly by providing supporting statistical theories and tools in drawing conclusions from the analysis of these vital population data. Analysis of age and sex-specific death rates obtained greater significance in all demographic analysis. The idea of Standardized and Expected death rates enabled us with tools to compare death rates of one population with others and of the same population but at different points of time. Incidences of death remained at the focus of our attention because until in recent times all our efforts remained confined to prevention of untimely deaths, that is, survival.

The discovery of preventive and curative medicines and insecticides in the form of sprays, health awareness, improved health infrastructure, improved transport and communication network and rapid progress of medical science brought down death rates for all ages rapidly and average longevity increased as a result. Famines and epidemics could be largely prevented or brought under control through quick dispatch of food, medicine and doctors and supporting health workers to the affected areas. Growth of population gained a momentum as a result. Our attention now shifted, at least partly, to birth rates in various segments of the population. *Fertility and fertility differentials* have outclassed conventional demographic analysis. The relations that exist between birth rate, death rate and the population structure have given us a very complex *analytical theory of population*. The concept of *stable population* is at the center of this analytical theory. As early as 1760, Leonard Euler demonstrated that if birth and death rates in a population remain unchanged for a long time, and if the population is insulated from in- and out-migration, the population distribution by age and sex and the sex ratio at all ages remain constant no matter how fast the population is growing. Many studies have been carried out since the concept of *stable population* was developed by Euler in the analysis of population data (R. Bockh, 1879 and R. R. Kiczynski, 1928 for example). But the most outstanding research on stable population was carried out by A. J. Lotka. He clearly established the relevance of analytical theory in experimental and exploratory studies in demographic research. Lotka "developed a complete general theory of the interrelations of the primary biological processes, including the age and sex structures and other functions of the stable populations and the relations of generational to instantaneous changes in closed mammalian population under constant conditions" (Lorimer).

The attention to birth rate and population growth rate gained prominence after World War II. In spite of heavy war losses of lives in the two World Wars, the death rate in all countries continued to decline fast. The population projections undertaken by United Nations in early 1950s failed miserably to predict the future population growth as report of censuses taken around 1960 in various countries started to come in. The projections failed because the assumptions made regarding birth and death rate and expectation of life at birth did not match with what had happened in reality.

UN Survey: Concerns relating to size and faster growth of population were expressed in international forums. The United Nations conducted a survey in 1963 to appraise a state's attitude towards growth of population and the need for birth planning. The survey also tried to relate economic progress of the country to such attitudes and opinions. More than fifty countries sent their comments and opinions on the issues raised in the inquiry. On the basis of their expressed opinions, these countries could be divided into three broad groups.

(I) Growth of population hinders economic growth and wellbeing of a country;
(II) Growth of population facilitates economic growth; and
(III) There is no close relation between growth of population and economic advancement.

Asian, African and Latin American countries generally agreed that population growth in their countries was a major cause for depressing or halting their economic growth. Most of the developed countries did not agree that population growth hinders economic growth. Many of these countries even went on to express that population growth plays an encouraging and supporting role in the economic progress of a country. Those countries that believed in Marxian school of thought did not consider that population and economic growth were essentially related. Growth of population and growth of economy needed to be evaluated independent of each other. They neither would say that population growth favored economic growth nor would say that population growth was an obstacle to economic progress.

One thing became clear from this limited survey that large size of the population was considered impediment to economic development in the economically poorer countries. These were the countries where the national economy was almost totally dependent on traditional agriculture; there was either no industrial activity or industrialization had just began; proportion of literates in the population was very low; transport and communication network were very inadequate; people were superstitious and still had an unflinching faith in traditions, and birth rates were very high. Their people were accustomed for generations and centuries to give a large number of births. Children still were considered securities to parents in their old age.

The United Nations conducted a second survey soon after. The observations from the survey are summarized as under:

1. The economic growth is slow in the countries with large population.
2. Even though the agricultural production in these countries has increased, per capita food production has not increased much due to high population growth.
3. Agriculture alone is incapable of absorbing the growing number of job seekers. The problem of unemployment is fast mounting causing serious social problems.
4. Housing problems are intensifying.
5. A very large proportion of GDP was needed to be spent on health, education and rearing of the new born babies. Even after spending large sums on these, still there is no sign of improvement in the quality of these welfare activities.
6. Often there are no forecasts about possible attainments in standard of living in the national policy formulations. Even if there was any, the gap between achievement and target framed was too large.

The increased population pressure of the world has created a situation leading to mass extinction of species unequaled since the disappearance of the dinosaurs 65 million years ago. A survey report published in 1996 by the World Conservation Union estimated that one-fourth of all mammals and amphibians, one-fifth of all reptiles, more than one-third of all fish and 11 percent of birds are in danger of extinction.

Besides greenhouse gas (GHG) concentration in the atmosphere with its concomitant consequences, the most important development in the last century is shortage of water for irrigation, domestic, and industrial uses. Life-threatening water shortages are very likely in many parts of the world. In India, which is likely to add 17 million people a year, water tables are dropping 3.3 feet to 9.9 feet a year. The result could be less water for irrigation, cutting India's grain harvest by one-fourth and increasing hunger and malnutrition.

The efforts to empower women and to increase access to contraception – which reduces fertility rates and the spread of AIDS as well – continue to meet resistance from Islamic nations and the Catholic Church. Ironically, some of the lowest birth rates in the world today are in predominantly Catholic countries like Italy and Spain (1.2), Portugal (1.5), and Ireland (1.9).

Most of the opposition to family planning comes from groups opposed to abortion, but the argument extends well beyond the abortion issue. Some family planning opponents cite below-replacement fertility rates in Europe and the United States and the increasingly aging populations of those countries, as reason to encourage families to have more children, not less. There are people and organizations that believe "overpopulation is a myth". Some of them believe that technology will take care of the population, whatever its size. Others argue that either the decline in birth rate in the Third World countries will be accelerated through increased family planning exercises or death rates will escalate as a result of water scarcity, starvation or diseases like HIV/AIDS, as has already begun to happen in Africa. Some of the developed countries seem to have gone back on their commitments to provide funds and supports for population control. United States, for example, has cut the grants to half for international family planning organizations.

15.6 Can there be a World Population Policy?

The traditional practices that encouraged high birth rate for the survival of the community and the mankind can hardly be called a population policy. The policy decision arises only when contradictory effects appear on the social scene. Repeated births definitely weaken the health of the mother (in consequence the health of the child) and her active participation in the household chores and wider social activities including direct participation in the family's economic wellbeing. Nearly the entire period of existence on this earth, the primary concern of mankind has been to fight against all adversaries. They were miles behind in their preparedness than what we are today.

But as man learned to cultivate rice, wheat and other food grains, vegetables and fruits and learned to preserve them for future use and also as the food production increased through better agricultural management, man gained considerable immunity to many diseases. Shelter and improved nutritional level, his intelligence and ability to organize life assured man of survival and to live better in this world. The real turn around in population thought came around the industrial revolution and subsequent developments in preventive and curative medicines.

At some point of time it is highly probable that the average fertility level of mankind might have gone up as a consequence of removal of a few social restrictions on marital relations – the purification time after child birth shortened, duration of breast feeding brought down, restrictions on widow remarriage removed, early marriage encouraged by social and economic demands, abortion discouraged, etc. The improvement in agriculture through irrigation and multiple crops and extending acreage encouraged population growth to sustain the surge in food production. Improvement in housing and the use of minerals also contributed a lot to support a larger population.

The almost incredible achievement in public health services since the World War II, all countries of the world came to realize that there was a need to give careful attention to increasing population growth since death rates in all ages is dipping fast, especially in the third world countries. We now realize that many of our natural resources are fast depleting due to their over exploitation to provide better living facilities to people. In our endeavor to achieving better standard of living, we have resorted to energy-intensive productions ignoring the impact it could have on our environment, the eco-system and even on the expanding labor force. Our land, water and atmosphere are seriously polluted today. As a result of worldwide climate change, deluge has descended upon regions known to be drought prone for the last 100 years or more. The unemployment rate, especially in the developed and fast growing developing economy, is one of the highest today for a variety of reasons.

The death rates in many developed countries are currently so low that further improvement in this regard is very unlikely. The age composition in these countries indicates that their death rates may go up considerably because the proportion of the aged (65 years and older) in the population would escalate considerably. This proportion was round 15 percent in 2000. It is quite likely that these countries will have every fifth person in the old-age category. Theoretically, birth rate can be brought down to zero; but that can never happen to death rates. People in the developed countries marry late, prefer a child or two, and that too in their late years. As a result, many developed countries would experience negative population growth rate (already there are quite a few). In spite of additional incentives given for each birth with full baby care protection, these countries have not succeeded in increasing their birth rates. These countries may need to change their immigration policies lest they are forced to shutting down many of their schools, colleges, hospitals and some industrial and other establishments.

A very efficient public health system in the developing countries is an essential prerequisite if we ever could agree on a world population policy – harmonious adjustment between population growth and increase in supplies and services necessary for a decent living. Although some population policy exists, at least on paper (often international aids and soft loans have a clause relating to population and environmental policy) in most developing countries, many of them admit that the stated policies could not be implemented as effectively as they would have liked. Unless people voluntarily adopts birth control measures, no democratically elected government can assure cooperation with other countries in a world population policy – adjusting to a number to one's ability to support them well.

In spite of remarkable achievements in containing world population growth rate in the last few decades, the situation still remains bleak in Africa, Middle East and South Asia. African women still have six children on an average, Niger leading the world with 7.5 children per woman. Despite control of fertility in most countries, the world population would continue to grow rapidly due to what the population scientists call the "demographic momentum". There are about 1 billion people between the ages 15 and 24 and another 2 billion below 15 years in the world population.

There are numerous obstacles to agreeing on a world population policy – nationalism, racism, religious diversity, ethnicity and conflict of ideologies, to name a few major hurdles. Citizens of every single country are more concerned with the welfare of their own people than with people from other countries. People in a country like India compared to those in most other countries speak in innumerable languages, follow almost all the major religious faiths observed in the world, and are divided into innumerable caste groups. China too resembles India in many respects. It is very difficult to develop a least common minimum ground that would be acceptable to all the diverse communities without much ado. Western countries did not have to face such formidable cultural diversity while developing a social and political consensus on issues that relate to the interest of the country as a whole.

It is indeed very difficult to find a common platform from which the world leaders can seriously discuss the problem of population pressure and evolve a plan of action giving due importance to voices of every nation. Whether it is the United Nations or the World Trade Organization or the World Bank, IMF or some other international funding agency, the developed countries work as a block and try to impose their decisions on the rest of the countries that are dependent on them for technology and also for aids for various economic and welfare projects in their own countries. The underdeveloped countries understand very well this ploy by the developed countries. But they do not find a way out of this hopeless situation. They need FDI in plenty to repay their debts with World Bank and IMF. They need huge investment in infrastructure and industries to create jobs for their unemployed youth and reduce the poverty level.

Economic liberalization has intensified the North-South divide. In almost all international forums, two issues invariably are discussed: atmospheric pollution (GHG and climate change) and population growth in the developing countries. Even after admitting that they played and they still have a major role in environmental degradation, the developed countries are unwilling to compromise with their consumption habits and energy-intensive productions; they are trying to push through the responsibility for cleaning up atmospheric pollution on to the developing countries. This means that the developing countries need to put a brake on GHG emissions and conserve all their forest covers for preserving biodiversity. That is, the developing countries must cut down their population growth rate fast so that a near zero growth rate of world population is achieved as early possible. Since the environmental laws in the developed countries are very stringent and their peoples are very scary about all types of pollutions, the developed countries are shifting their more polluting production units to the developing countries that are rich in natural resources, where the environmental laws still are almost non-existent, and the standard of living of the common man is awfully low. By luring these countries with FDI, the developed countries are trying to consolidate their economic empire at the cost of resources of the developing countries and keep their own citizens happy not having to ask them for a compromise with their lifestyle. Through IMF and World Bank they are forcing the developing countries to stop subsidies on fertilizers, food grains and many other commodities and basic services; yet these countries would not heed to the demand that they withdraw huge subsidies given to oil companies and their farmers, the latter incidentally constitute only about 2–5 percent of the total labor force in these countries. The highly subsidized farming in these countries is not providing a level playing field to the farmers in the developing countries to become competitive in the world food grain market. India told in the Bucharest Conference in 1974 that population growth in the developing countries is definitely a very worrying issue and that must be tackled on a war footing. But the real distress signal comes from the consumer-culture of the developed West. A single birth in Europe or in USA nullifies the effect of prevention of 300 births in India or elsewhere. The consumption demand of the developed West would soon force them to look towards the underdeveloped countries for their rich natural resources and biodiversity. Their fast increasing consumption expenditure would only bring the ‘dooms day’ for the humanity closer.

From demographic point of view, the twentieth century world was characterized by a sharp decline in mortality all over the world. Further decline in general mortality would be quite slow except in a few selected pockets (mostly in Africa). The twenty-first century would remain in the demographic history of the world as the period of consolidation of birth rate all over the world at a level consistent with the demands of economic health of the countries. Whereas the increasing pressure of population has rendered the social and economic fabric of the developing countries like India extremely vulnerable, most countries in Europe, America and East Asia also have serious problems but for an altogether different reason – the sluggish or declining population growth. There are about seventy countries in the world today (Italy, Spain, Ireland, Germany, France, Russia, Canada, Japan and number of countries in the Pacific and other regions) where birth rates are far below the level of sustainable growth in most socio-economic parameters. The social scientists are also worried for the fast declining birth rate in these countries. They believe that complexity of modern fast life has become an impediment to child bearing.

There could be very many reasons for the reverse turn of population growth curve in these countries. The social scientists believe that the great increase in cost of rearing children, time constraints of parents, frequent travel to long distances, the fear of losing figure resulting from child bearing and unwillingness of women to get involved in household chores are some of the reasons behind decline in formal marriage and birth rates. The immigration policies of most of these countries even in this age of economic globalization have acted against the growth of population. This has created many multifaceted social and economic predicaments. Governments have to take care of a huge number of pensioners; sometimes their numbers far overwhelm the actual labor force. Health expenditure is mounting fast. The increased economic liberalization has led to revision of tax structures in most countries. In consequence, the governments are facing difficulties in financing welfare schemes for the senior citizens. The fast decline in the young age population has seriously affected the labor force, especially in hi tech and in scientific research. To increase birth rate, many countries have introduced promotional programs including economic incentives and tax concessions. Germany, for example, has decided to grant 'parent money' (US $ 13,000) to each family for every birth registered in 2007 and beyond. Such promotional policies are observed in France, Italy, Sweden and other countries. Russia and Japan too are not far behind these countries in promoting additional births. The slogan in the developed and high developing countries seems 'the more… the merrier'.

South Korea is facing a very peculiar problem. The apprentice doctors are not finding enough number of 'delivery cases' to get a first hand knowledge relating to pregnancy and birth of a baby. It is reported that they are importing from USA hi-tech models that would deliver artificial babies to enable these young apprentices to study various aspects of birth of baby.

An ideal population policy looks at the size and desired population composition on a long term perspective (stable population) – 30 or more years into the future. To achieve the desired goals in the time frame, the country may take short term action plans – universal immunization of children and pregnant women, prenatal and postnatal health care, health insurance and the like. After a few years a fresh look at the existing situations are taken and, if necessary, revised plan of action are worked out for achieving the goals set in policy prescriptions. That is why every population projection has three variants – high (to be avoided by all means), low (which is the most desirable scenario for the country) and the medium variant, which is a compromised position between the two extremes. There are only a few countries which have national population policies (India is one amongst these few). Most of the poorly developed countries have adopted population programs, often at the instance of the donor countries or IMF and World Bank. Therefore, they take up mostly those programs for which international aids or soft loans are available. Of course they are alarmed by their high population growth. Even the developed countries that have very low TFR, are taking up measures to boost up marriage and birth rate and liberalizing immigration policy lest they have to shut down schools, colleges and production units. Both pro- and anti-natalist countries adopt corrective measures for creating conditions favorable for maintaining population at an optimum level.

A world population policy in the real sense of the term, if ever becomes feasible, must address not only the demographic issues, but also work for a fool-proof mechanism to bring environmental pollution under control, especially atmospheric pollution which is the cause of global warming, optimum and efficient use of natural resources, use of chemical fertilizers and pesticides, over exploitation of ground water, and bring down the inequality between the rich and the poor. With so many preconditions, it is highly improbable that a world population policy can ever materialize that would bind the humanity together and ask every country to work as equal partner for attaining a common collective goal.

15.7 Population Policies/Programs in Selected Regions/Countries

Western Europe

Almost all the countries in Western Europe, in fact, in all the industrially developed countries, have very efficient public health services, good education system and efficient economy. These countries document very low birth and death rates, especially among infants and children, and very high expectation of life. Populations in these countries have been growing slowly compared to most countries in other regions. These countries generally did not have to face the consequences of a faster growth of population than could be absorbed by the expansion of their economy. During much of the nineteenth century, the most commonly accepted view was that unrestricted population growth could be more than compensated by increased productivity and venturing upon new resources, from within or abroad. Although a real increase in living standard resulting from the agricultural and industrial revolutions did not allow these countries to feel the pressure of a rising population, it must be pointed out that until about 1900, the Western European farmers did move out in large numbers to different parts of the world in search of a better living, since in spite of industrial revolution, their wages did not increase much in 100 years.

Three major factors have been identified that contributed to the pro-natalist/*laissez-fair* attitude towards growth of population that generally prevailed in the Western world: great improvement in agricultural production, improvement in all manner of mechanical technologies, and easy access to new land and other resources. Out-migration to their settled colonies often came as a respite whenever the population growth rate threatened their economy in the past. The stress had always been on improving the efficiency of the national economy, which assured better living even for the poorer section of the population. Even the poorer families in the Western Europe, especially in the Scandinavian countries, were often much above the average in standard of living compared to those in most other countries.

The poorer families in these countries were found to have above average family size and often needed some state support to achieving a reasonably decent standard of living. It became a matter of public policy that these families should have access to information and means to control their family size. When such information were suitably transmitted and the general level of living was reasonably good, there was no need to insist on restricting the family size. In matters of health and education of children the governments exhibited a very liberal attitude. However, the public policy in these countries has been to discourage, even to prevent marriage of mentally subnormal persons or prevent subnormal couples from having babies. There was no direct campaign either for smaller or for larger families. At some critical times when depopulation was on the card, the state declared financial incentive in the form of child allowance for every child born to a couple.

France

A special mention must be made about the population policy or programs in France. The decline of birth rate in France due to voluntary birth control became very large after the Franco-Prussian war in 1870–1871. The population growth dipped considerably in France compared to that in the neighboring countries. At the beginning of the twentieth century, there was even no natural increase for a few years. Compounded to this, the country lost over 2 million lives in World War I. The government came out with a family assistance program hoping that that would encourage more couples to become parents of more babies and induce a steady growth of the population. This policy paid dividend and at the beginning of World War II a small population growth rate of 6 per 1,000 per annum was attained. However, whether this small increase in growth rate is due to increase in birth rate or decrease in death rate is not clearly known. The financial incentives offered could have only a marginal role in the growth of population since France's economy recovered soon after World War II. Military losses in World War II were of smaller magnitude compared to those in World War I. The two World Wars and the persistent encouragement by the policy makers for population growth might have created a condition favorable for small increases in average family size. The welfare services like education and public health were of highest quality in France. The French policy makers did not need to pay additional attention on these services for further improvement.

Generally the policy makers in the developed West displayed a *laissez-fair* or *hands-off* policy in birth planning. The second industrial revolution – automation – that followed World War II led to considerable shrinkage in the employment market. This had a direct impact on natural increase in population – marriages were delayed or postponed, if married, child birth was avoided. The baby boom during and immediately after World War II brought a huge number of young aspirants in the labor market which was going through a period of turmoil because of introduction of automation in industries as also because of the momentum the economy gained in the two World Wars to boost production were lost. The great transition from conventional labor-intensive production to automation and then to computer hi-techs and IT revolution since the eighties did not favor high population growth. Annual population growth rate in France in 2002 was 0.5 percent with CBR 13 and CDR 9 and TFR 1.9. 76 percent of France's population lives in urban areas.

Japan

The Japanese leaders wanted a rapidly growing population in the years before World War II for they believed that this was necessary to enlarge the Japanese population so that there could be enough settlers in their conquered territories. Propaganda for birth control was forbidden; quite a few people were put behind the bar who openly advocated against this policy. Japan could amass large resources from the acquired territories in the wars with China and Russia. Korea, Formosa and Manchuria were brought within the Japanese Empire with little costs in lives and money. Japan wanted to become the most dominant power in Asia and challenge the other great powers in Europe and America. Japan's acquired lands and resources, it felt, would support a rapidly growing population.

Japan lost World War II and lost the support of the growing middle class for Japan's imperialist policy. Repatriation of over 6 million Japanese nationals within a year of the end of the war added greatly to Japanese economic hardship in postwar days. Some of the repatriates were military personnel, mostly young and those still unmarried married soon. The death rate in Japan also started to decline fast. Japan's death rate before the war was 17 per 1,000 per annum which reached a staggering high of 29 per 1,000 in the concluding years of World War II. The average death rate experienced in the next 15 years came down to 8 or 9 per 1,000 population per year. The sudden increase in birth rate and enormous drop in death rate saw Japan's highest ever increase in population growth rate.

Japanese people are one of the highest educated and better skilled people in the world and are known for their innovative ideas. The growing population problem after the war became the consistent theme in radio broadcasts and news papers. Japanese people speak in one language contrasted to China and India, and they are culturally very united too. A very large proportion of the Japanese lived in cities and worked in industries, which are one of the finest by any standard. Japan has one of the most skillful medical and paramedical staff to undertake sterilization and abortion with greatest safety. Legal restrictions were removed for performing abortion and sterilization. Japanese people regard their Emperor with great reverence. Restriction on the size of the family met his approval.

In 1948, abortion, though not formally approved for termination of pregnancy, became the principal arsenal through legislation (Eugenic Protection Act, 1948) for bringing down the Japanese birth rate. In a period of only 8 years, the birth rate came down from 34 to 18 per 1,000. It is believed that one and a half million abortions alone were carried out in 1952 while the number of live births in the year was 2 million. Japanese showed to the world that abortion, though dangerous on many counts, was the only practical immediate solution for achieving a big fall in fertility. Subsequently, abortions for personal, social and economic reasons were legalized. Importance of abortion in birth control has come down considerably since the use of contraceptives gained popularity in all parts of the world.

Even in USSR at certain point of time abortion was the dominant method of birth control. 10 million abortions were reported in USSR in 1970. 1.23 million abortions were reported from USA in 1980. Both IMR and child mortality in Japan came down from around 14 in 1970 to around 5 in 1999. The average annual population growth rate in Japan was 0.5 percent during 1975–99. In 2002, the population growth rate was down to 0.1 percent per annum with CBR 9 and CDR 8. TFR in Japan has come down from 2.1 in 1975–80 to 1.4 in 1995–2000 and to 1.3 in 2002. Nearly 80 percent of Japanese live in urban areas. Percentage of the population below 15 years is less than 14, and more than one-fourth of Japan's population is 65 years or older. Japan has the highest life expectancy, around 82 years. By 2015, Japan's population would be in declining mode, – 0.1 percent per annum. Japan spends about 7.8 percent of GDP on health care (state's share 6.3 percent of GDP).

USSR

The Great Soviet Encyclopedia (1955) says "There cannot be any surplus population under a socialist regime, in spite of rapid demographic growth". In 1947, Rabichko, the Soviet delegate to UN Population Commission, said:

> We consider any proposition formulated by this commission in favor of limiting marriages or births in wedlock as barbarous. Over population is only a fruit of capitalism; an adequate social regime can meet any increase of population. It is the economy which should be adapted to the population, and not vice versa.

Contradictions often are clearly visible in what they say when upholding the tenets of Marxian philosophy and what actions they take at the ground level. At the time of Revolution in USSR (1917), numerous evidences suggest that the birth rate in USSR was 40 per 1,000 or even more. Before the Revolution, Lenin opposed "birth strike". But the same great leader after the Revolution encouraged the use contraceptives and abortions 'purely on humanitarian grounds'. In the early stages of development of socialism, especially in the years after World War I, young age dependency in USSR came down, which helped immensely the post-war recovery of economy of the country. At the beginning of the World War II, USSR had 10 million fewer children had the birth rates prevailing during the World War I still continued. The birth restrictions, which was imposed after World War I, was withdrawn at the end of World War II to make a quick recovery from the great many losses of lives in USSR in the two wars. A quick replacement for war losses was urgently needed to build Russian economy in the post-war cold-war days. Abortion, which was legalized in 1920, was declared illegal in 1936. It was declared legal again in 1950. Most East European countries promoted induced abortions as one of the principal methods of birth control. According to the UN Demographic Yearbook, birth rate in USSR might have come down to 25 or so around 1960 and to 17 around 1980. The momentum for birth control gained through the years continued unhindered even though USSR was going through serious political, social and economic upheavals in the 1980s, as a result of which USSR disintegrated in 1991 and the socialist regime came to a sudden halt. But that did not alter the fast declining trend in birth rates in most of the countries resulting from this disintegration of the Soviet Union. UN Population Division Report (2003) shows CBR at 9, CDR at 15, and the average annual population growth rate at –0.6 for Russian Federation. The population was growing at over 1.8 percent per annum at around 1960. Between 1960 and 1970 the average growth rate came down to 1 percent. Between 1980 and 1985 the average growth rate in Soviet Union was 0.8 percent with birth rate around 18 and death rate 10. Currently, CDR in Russian Federation has taken a U-turn while birth rate maintained the course of decline. The current TFR is 1.1, and annual growth rate (–) 0.5 percent per annum. Ukraine also demonstrated very similar demographic changes.

The leaders of USSR do not appear to have supported any one population program (policy?) consistently. While prizing mothers with many children with economic and other incentives, the state made abortions safe and cheap, organized nurseries for day-care of children for women working in factories and offices, and granted long maternity leaves and free medical services. The state encouraged compulsory education of children and made appropriate provisions for higher education for those who showed promise. Even when the state was making every arrangement for safe abortion, it saw that supply of contraceptives was adequately available to all. The state encouraged women in taking regular jobs in industries, offices and in other professions. Russia followed the same path which the Western world pursued to encourage women to take greater economic and social roles outside the limits of their families. All over the world it has been witnessed that women in labor force prefer small families. Housing always has remained a critical problem in USSR, especially in cities. Some surveys have indicated that women did not want more children mostly because of living space, more so in urban areas.

Even as early as 1975, more than 65 percent of Russian people lived in urban areas; the proportion has increased to 73 percent in 2003. Even though the socialist regime has fallen in 1991, peoples' attitude toward birth control remains strong. It is debated if the programs, which actually have arrested the population growth rate in USSR, were deliberately planned as a definite population policy. The national planners seem to have been preoccupied with the desire to increase the speed of industrialization with special emphasis on defense, nuclear and space research not paying much attention to the effects this economic growth policy would have on agriculture and population growth. USSR is incredibly rich in natural resources to support any natural increase in the population. Yet, USSR was never quite self-sufficient in agriculture. The Soviet system of collective and state-farming failed to motivate people to remain on land to produce food grains more efficiently. The Socialist regime had forbidden private initiative in the settlement of new lands.

It is very strange that life expectancy at birth in Russian Federation is among the lowest for industrialized countries. It was 64.8 years in 2000–05 against the average of 79 years in Western Europe. It was 69 years in 1970–75. Since 1990, male mortality in Russian Federation has increased. The incidences of male mortality and economic uncertainty since the break-up of USSR in 1991 have brought down Russian Federation's Human Development Index. HDI of Russia in 1990 was 0.815; it came down to 0.771 in 1995 and gradually regained to 0.902 in 2005. The number of additional deaths during 1992–2001 is estimated at 2.5–3 million. In absence of war, famine or health epidemics there is no historical precedence for this scale of loss of human lives. With normal mortality, it is estimated that Russian Federation would have 7 million more people today. Life expectancy at birth of males in 2003 was 59 years and of females 72 years – the highest gender gap in life expectancy in the world. On analysis of the causes for death, it appears that people in Russian Federation suffers in large proportion from cardiovascular diseases reflecting dietary and life style factors. Infectious diseases like tuberculosis (150 per 100,000 population) and HIV/AIDS (1.1 percent of persons aged 15–49) are at threatening levels. Overconsumption of alcohol increased incidences of homicide and suicide in the country.

China

The People's Republic of China (PRC) was established on October 1, 1949. After the inception of Socialist regime in 1949, the first most important legislation passed in China was *Marriage Law* in 1950 fixing minimum age at marriage – 21 for men and 18 for women. The law also wanted to put an end to traditional arranged marriages, which witnessed dowry and other transactions, concubine, bigamy, and child marriage. It served two purposes – reduce women's dependence on husbands and improve their status and urging them to join the labor force. This was a very important step for women moving towards equality with men. After the changeover of guards, the first census taken in China in 1953 showed the total population at 600 million including the overseas Chinese and the population of Formosa.

Mao Zedong's first political campaigns after founding the People's Republic were land reform and suppression of counter-revolutionaries, which centered on mass executions – often before organized crowds. In the first four years of communist regime, China accomplished a complete redistribution of land holdings, liquidated the 'landlord class', vested the land in the state and redistributed the acquired land to peasants. This precipitated violence and social tension in the early years; local famines were recurrent. Mao himself claimed a total of 700,000 people killed during these early years 1949–53. However, since there was a policy to select "at least one landlord, and usually several, in virtually every village for public execution", 1 million deaths seems to be an absolute minimum, and many authors agree on a figure somewhere between 2 and 5 million dead. A byproduct of this land reform agenda was the development of an administrative apparatus to reach every village in every political subdivision. These administrative units became the most important source for obtaining information about various aspects of the Chinese population for purposes of planning national, social and economic development as also for planning community development of all sorts. The Communist leaders got panicked by the fact that the census figures were far in excess of what they had expected. In the first Five-Year Plan (1953–58), new industrial plants assisted by USSR, were built and the industry began to produce enough capital and China no longer needed the USSR's support. In 1954 soon after the census results were known, a *birth control campaign* was launched and was pressed quite vigorously for four years. The reasons cited for birth control were improvement of health of mother and child, provision of better facilities for education of children and youth and to release more female for the national labor force. The campaigns were concentrated on postponement of marriage by several years beyond the minimum age at marriage enacted by the Marriage Law and, if already married, use of contraception both for preventing large families and for larger spacing of births as well. Officially, the political leaders and administrators did not openly say that the population was too large for the Chinese economy. The Chinese leaders felt that birth control was needed at that critical juncture to give the Communist regime a time to amend the ills of the previous regimes and take measures to improve substantially the living standard of the common man. Here is a typical propaganda statement that clearly tells the nature of brain storming sessions the Chinese leadership had to go through before inventing the strange reasoning to justify their campaign for birth control:

> In order to lessen the difficulties currently facing us, to protect the health of maternity womanhood and finally to ensure that the next generation may be brought up better, we are not opposed at all to birth control. At the same time publicity given by certain newspapers and magazines to the methods of birth control is necessary as well as proper. This has no point in common with Malthus' theory at all.

It may not be a matter of coincidence that China legalized abortion in 1957, the year when Mao Zedong called for a zero-growth population for China. He is supposed to have spoken, "Steps be taken to keep our population for a long time at a stable level, say, of 600,000,000." In 1972, the government decided to bear the cost of all abortions.

Contradictions galore in China's views on population control expressed at different points of time. The first birth control campaign came to a sudden halt in 1958 even though the Chairman of the Communist party just a year back called for a zero growth in population and that abortions were legalized. The reason for desertion of much canvassed birth control program for four years was the Great Leap Forward movement launched in 1958 (second Five-Year Plan). Programs pursued during this time include the *Hundred Flowers Campaign*, in which Mao indicated his supposed willingness to consider different opinions about how China should be governed. Initially the policy was seen as a way of weakening those within his party who opposed him, but Mao was surprised by the extent of criticism and the fact that it began to be directed at his own leadership. It was only then that he used this for identifying and subsequently persecuting those critical of his government. The Hundred Flowers movement, many believed, led to the condemnation, silencing, and death of many citizens, linked to Mao's Anti-Rightist Movement, with death tolls possibly in the millions.

The much publicized bumper food production in 1957, which later showed to be non-existent, might have induced the leaders to believe that agricultural production was on the right track and therefore the economy was in a position to support any increase in the population. Official promotional program was called off in 1958. Individuals however were given free hand to practice contraception or otherwise. This *Great Leap Forward* led to the *commune movement*: organizing the entire Chinese population into thousands of people's communes, each having 25,000–40,000 members, and involuntary relocations of various segments of population. Each commune was to be developed as self-sufficient economic and social unit. Communes would perform many functions and render services generally regarded as responsibilities of family members. This arrangement would free a vast number of females for labor force for national and community economic development projects. Care of children would be taken up by the commune or the school when the mothers are away at their work places. These units would provide all the health and educational facilities at a much lower cost compared to what the traditional families had to spend on these counts earlier. The function of these communes, many observers felt, was aimed at destroying the root of traditional family fabric. The military-like communes would also help in segregation of sexes. Some observers believed that the leaders were under the impression that organization of communes could more than compensate the effects likely to have been achieved through birth control campaign started in 1954. All private food production was banned; livestock and farm implements were brought under collective ownership. Food production went down sharply both in 1959 and 1960. There was no recovery in 1961.

The years 1959–61 saw great disaster in agriculture in China. This necessitated stoppage of building of further communes. Millions of people who migrated to cities and towns to work in massive infrastructure projects and small-scale industries were sent back to villages to their families to work on farms as underemployed workers. In an effort to win favor with their superiors and avoid being purged, each layer in the party hierarchy exaggerated the amount of grain produced under them. Based on the fabricated success, party cadres were ordered to requisition a high amount of the true harvest for state use primarily in the cities and urban areas but also for export. The net result, compounded in some areas by drought and in others by floods, was that the rural peasants were not left enough to eat and many millions starved to death in what is thought to be the most devastating famine (Great Famine) in human history.[1] This famine was a direct cause of death of tens of millions of Chinese peasants between 1959 and 1962. Many children who became emaciated and malnourished during years of hardship and struggle for survival, died shortly after the Great Leap Forward came to an end in 1962. The economic disaster that followed crop failures in consecutive years frightened the leaders. Economic progress came to a dead halt. Mao lost esteem among many of the top party cadres and was eventually forced to abandon the policy in 1962. At the Party conference in Beijing in January 1962, overwhelming majority of the members present including state President Liu Shaoqi (Mao remained the Chairman) denounced the *Great Leap Forward* as responsible for widespread famine.

The *second birth control campaign* (1962–66) had to be started only four years after the first campaign was dropped. The difference between the new and the earlier campaign is not quite clear except that postponement of marriage was more emphasized in the second campaign. Chou En Lai in 1964 said:

> We believe in planned parenthood, but it is not easy to introduce all at once in China and it is more difficult to achieve in rural areas, where most of our people live...The first thing is to encourage late marriage.

Men were advised to marry not earlier than 28 and women not before 25. Those who in spite of the advice marry early and have large families were called 'unpatriots'. The new campaign also emphasized people to adopt two-child norm with three to five years spacing between children. The campaign was organized around the theme that service to the state, i.e., furthering the state

---

1 American demographer Dr Judith Banister made an attempt to estimate the number of famine deaths from 1953, 1964 and 1982 census data. The results were published in 1984. Keeping in mind the lengthy gaps between the censuses and doubts over the reliability of the data, Banister concluded that the official data implied that around 15 million excess deaths were incurred in China during 1958–61. Based on her modelling of Chinese demographics during the period and taking account of the assumed underreporting during the famine years, she was willing to put the figure at around 30 million. Various other sources have put the figure between 20 and 72 million.

economic program and military power was more important than raising a family. That the cost of *vasectomy* after 2–3 children would be borne by the state was emphasized in the campaign.

Facing the prospect of losing his place on the political stage, Mao launched the *Cultural Revolution* in 1966. The Revolution led to the destruction of much of China's cultural heritage and imprisonment of a huge number of Chinese citizens, as well as creating general economic and social chaos in the country. Mao declared the Cultural Revolution to be over in 1969. By that time Mao realized that he no longer enjoyed the same hold over the party that he had a few years back. Lin Biao, named successor to Mao, alleged to have been planning to overthrow Mao, died in a plane crash when trying to flee China, probably anticipating his arrest.

The *third birth control campaign* began somewhat tentatively in 1968. Since the print media and the radio were strictly under state control, often objective and neutral assessment of the impacts of various policies on economic and population issues became the casualty. The local administrative units were given certain tasks and targets. To keep their achievement records clean, often data were furnished that had little bearing on the ground situation. Even the reported birth rates in many rural areas were startlingly low. Whereas a few of such brigades reported CBR as high as 38 in 1972, scores of other brigades reported average CBR in 20's and even around 10. The central authorities themselves seemed doubtful of such success stories from local units.

The rein of the campaign after Mao's death in 1976 was taken up by Chairman Hua Kuo-feng, who reportedly was the leader of the birth control advocates in the State Council. The third campaign started rather tentatively with appeals to young people not to be swept away by the "wave of getting married now". By 1970, there were clear indications that a broader birth control campaign was being activated and that birth control by then had become a permanent feature of China's domestic policy. An intense drive for birth control was launched in 1972–73.

Economic reforms were started in China in 1978. Hua, while presenting the National Plan at the Fifth National People's Congress (China's parliament) said that planned population growth is needed for the planned economic growth of China. He asserted that the annual rate of growth of population must be brought to 1 percent within 3 years. Some of the administrative measures taken for achieving the goal are: late marriage – 25 and 23 years for rural and 27 and 25 years for urban men and women respectively; no couple should have more than two children and a reasonable interval for the birth of the second child.

Hua presented to the nation only four other specific targets – rates of growth of industry and agriculture, total food grain and steel output. This declaration makes it very clear that China was all prepared to launch a long drawn program that would see the country on a high economic growth path and for achieving the stated goals it would not hesitate to make compromises on some ideological issues. The government was determined to launch upon family planning campaign on a national scale with the same zeal with which it decided to pursue a grain harvest of 400 million by 1985. The economic growth path that China chalked out for the country was implemented with right earnest since the beginning of 1980s. Private ownership of land was given back to farmers in 1982. The incentive to grow more food that was lacking in *collective farming* came back as farmers were allowed to sell their produces in the open market. The economic reform that followed is now a very important chapter in China's history; China has now become the principal destination of FDIs. The average annual GDP growth rate in China since the middle of 1990s has been around 8–10 percent. This has become possible because of huge investment in infrastructure growth and growth in hi tech industrial, manufacturing and service sector. Only a few decades back 70 percent of China's GDP came from agriculture; it has dropped to only 6 percent in 2005. This is comparable to the relative shares of agriculture in most of the industrially developed countries.

The Constitution of China prescribes that "citizens must support the leadership of communist party and that "it is the lofty duty of every citizen to defend the motherland." But both Hua and the Constitution were rather silent about the universality of the birth control. A subsequent explanation by official release shows that the "less than 1 percent growth rate is an average that will not apply to the entire country without exception:

> Family planning is encouraged only in areas of dense population. In sparsely populated national minority areas and certain other areas, population growth is encouraged.... In the case of members of minority nationalities with a big family who have the wish for family planning, proper advice and facilities are provided."

In 1979, when China embraced economic reform, the government presented new guidelines for criminal proceedings which did not include abortion. From 1979 one-child norm was canvassed. The government emphasized on four birth control methods – abortion, vasectomy, tubectomy and IUD. The planned birth program became an integral part of Chinese life. The transition to this mode began with the reorientation of the Chinese health system. The emphasis was on rural health with the "barefoot doctors" at the lowest level, up through a referral system of clinics and mobile medical units to hospitals at the apex. The full integration of this system came about in post-1965 era. Public health campaign was conducted not only against major communicable diseases, but against flies and other insects carrying diseases as well. A very effective system of medical services was created in the 1960s. Every revolutionary committee had a sub-committee for birth control. In 1971–72, the returning visitors described how the local units decided on who were to have babies in the coming year. "Birth-in-turn" planning became a very important addition in China's birth control program. The presence of party members in these local committees made these coercive birth planning operations easier. (P.C.Chen's *report on the birth planning in China has been discussed in some detail while we presented Marx's views on population growth: Chapter 4.7*).

Most communist countries even today maintain some secrecy on matters relating to their populations. The information that are given out by the state controlled media often do not match with the experiences of foreign visitors and those emigrated from China. The economic liberalizations have opened the door for foreign nationals to visit, even settle and participate in China's daily life. Credibility of information trickling out from China has improved greatly today. The financial institutions like World Bank, IMF and other agencies sponsored by UN and some Foundations have been allowed to conduct surveys on some limited issues. The organizations preparing the feasibility report for domestic or multinational companies in India have done the same for many companies in China.

The Chinese style of socialism, since the beginning of economic globalization, has taken a somewhat different path leaving aside the much acclaimed proletariat brotherhood and economic equality. As the central bureaucratic planning failed, they turned their attention somewhat away from the development of the domestic market for the poor.

External trade and FDI have played an important role in China's economic performance. Trade as a share of GDP rose from 13 percent in 1980 to 50 percent in 2002; FDI inflow was more than $50 bn in 2002 (4 percent of GDP); accumulated net FDI inflows since 1980 were $440 billion. China remains the most preferred destination for FDI followed by India. Domestic demand has also been strong, and the investment ratio has been very high.

But this fast growing economy in China is not without blemishes. There is growing inequality and marginalization of a significant section of the population despite this rapid economic growth. In consequence, China is increasingly relying on the authority of the party in power than on participatory democracy to keep the political scene stable while propelling market-led growth. In the post-liberalization scenario, the richest 20 percent's share of national income in 1998 stood at 46.6 percent and that for the poorest 20 percent a meager 5.9 percent in China. By 2001, the share of the richest 20 percent went up to 50 percent and the poorest 20 percent's share down to 4.7 percent. Inequality as measured by the ratio of the richest 20 percent's share of national income to that of the poorest 20 percent has gone up from 8.0 to 10.7 between 1998 and 2001. The Gini index, which measures inequality, has gone up from 40.3 in 1998 to 44.7 in 2001, also indicating that inequality in China is growing fast.

In the past two decades, China's per capita expenditure at constant purchasing power terms has risen by three-fold. But there is the disturbing report that the social progress is starting to lag far behind economic progress. There is considerable slowing down in the rate of reduction in child death. Children living in poorer provinces and in rural China have the highest death rate. Household healthcare expenditure is mounting fast. Children in the poorest provinces face an alarmingly high child death rate. Child death rate in urban areas on average is about one-third of that in rural areas. Current studies show that child mortality among girls is increasing by 0.5 percent a year while the same is falling by 2.3 percent a year for boys. A recent survey shows that there are 117 males for every 100 females in China. That is, sex ratio (F/M) in the population in China is much worse compared even to that in India. One-child norm has also kept young men and women away from marriage. Parents are really worried to see their children married.

Until 1980, health of the rural poor was covered by cooperative medical system. With market reforms, that system has been dismantled. This has shifted the burden of financing health care costs from public providers to household transfers. Most people now have to buy health insurance, meet costs as they arise or go without healthcare. Some 70–80 percent of rural people have no health insurance cover today. The average per capita health spending in urban China is 3.5 times the level in rural China. No doubt that the economic reform has generated important gains in many areas, but market principles seemed to have been extended too far in the health sector.

Although China still spends over 5 percent of GDP on healthcare, public spending on health is less than 2 percent of GDP. In effect, health financing has been privatized. Fiscal decentralization has reinforced the transfer to market based services. Poorer provinces and districts are unable to raise enough revenues to continue with the most basic services. This includes even immunization. Immunization coverage (DPT) dropped from 97 percent in 1990 to 90 percent in 2002. High healthcare costs are causes of household poverty and a deterrent to using available health services. The inequality rooted in privatized healthcare financing may even defer the attainment of health goals in China. The Chinese government is now under pressure to review its health policy, especially with the rural poor.

Despite the economic liberalization being controlled by the state through its party apparatus, some discontent has surfaced of late. Access to basics – health and education – has worsened in many areas, especially for those without regular public sector jobs. The dissent voices are not still loud because the absolute control of the administration is at the hand of communist party and that the party dictates the term of all economic liberalization within the narrow boundaries of political dissent. Workers in China and other socialist countries have as yet no right to strike, especially in units involving foreign investment.

Earlier, the government acquired agricultural lands for the sake of industries, roads, irrigation projects, etc. Those who were displaced from their land were helped to find alternative occupations. The responsibility of finding these alternatives for the displaced persons lay with the organization acquiring the land. These displaced persons were given due certificates for their land acquisition and the holders of such certificates were entitled to receive many social services like health insurance, pension and other benefits after their retirement. Their children were given free education and health care and food at a nominal cost. This scheme became very popular among the Chinese farmers. The security that was granted earlier to the people who were displaced from their land is not comparable to the one-time financial compensation that followed as the economic liberalization started. People today are displaced from their land and homes in much larger numbers for the purpose of large irrigation projects, construction of high ways, housing complexes, special economic zones and industries. The government acquires the land, develops it and gives them to industries and others. Persons displaced in the process have no political right to represent their cases. The ease with which such acquisitions of land and other property are possible in China or Vietnam cannot be thought of in a democratic country. People in China do not have any mechanism to register their voices against unilateral withdrawal of much of the state financed basic health and educational services that were granted in the earlier phase of socialist regime.

In 1999, China backtracked a little and passed a law regulating the acquisition of agricultural land. The new law assured that acquisition of farm land shall in no way affect the lives of the farmer and their profession. A compensation scheme for the land to be acquired was worked out: 3 to 6 times the average income generated from the agricultural land in the last 3 years to be paid as economic compensation. In addition, they are to be given a sum which is twice the average price of agricultural produces for rehabilitation. These two modes of compensations together however shall not exceed the amount which is twenty times the value of the calculated average agricultural income. This reform in the land acquisition policy clearly indicates that the farmers were given some space for bargain.

The momentum gained in birth control movement has remained operational even though the government has withdrawn many of the facilities granted to people earlier. The movement could be sustained as a great many people moved to urban areas where living is costly and there is huge scarcity of accommodation.

UN data, 2002 indicate China's population growth rate at the beginning of this millennium was 0.7 percent per annum, CBR 15, CDR 7 and TFR 1.8. Only about 1 percent of total births are recorded for women who are under age 20. 39 percent of the population lives in urban areas. Mortality under age 5 is 43 per 1,000. Proportion of the population under age 15 is 23 and that for age 60 years and older is 10.

India

Population growth in India between the censuses taken in 1872 and 1921 is a good example of how *positive checks* like intense food shortage and violence of epidemics have a direct bearing on the growth of a population. In traditional agriculture, food grains production was almost totally dependent on rainfall. Weak monsoons in successive years brought down the availability of food grains so much so that the poor people could not procure them from the market. In absence of any public distribution system (PDS) at that time, mass hunger was inevitable whenever there was a repeated crop failure. Famines are inevitably associated in the visitation of diseases, often resulting in epidemics. Population in India either rose marginally or did not rise whenever famines and epidemics became rampant in major parts of the country. A good monsoon not only saw bumper food production, the incidences of epidemics came down sharply as well. A fairly large increase in population was experienced compared to periods when famines and epidemics were rampant.

The beginning of 1921–31 saw a substantial decline of the influence of these positive checks as a result of improvement of transport system and better disaster management program. Some improvement in the agricultural practices contributed in a significant way in food supply. Better quarantine regulations in port cities, attention to public and household sanitation and expanded health services, especially the availability of miracle drugs and more effective insecticides played a major role in curtailing many of the avoidable deaths and diseases. In consequence, the population started to grow and its momentum greatly increased after World War II.

Indian scholars have keenly observed how population growth curve moved along with the intensity of food supply and epidemics long before World War I. With the fast growth of population after World War I, they felt, India would be facing the Malthusian Dilemma that her population growth would overtake improvements in the welfare of the great masses of people.

The economic crisis of 1929 did not distress India as much as it did to many other countries, rich and poor. The civil disobedience movement in the early 1930s, also rapid consolidation in the informal household sector and strident movement of agrarian reforms kept India's economy at a comfortable level. India's economy and public health got a tremendous push through in the World War II and a near 100 percent employment situation prevailed. All these boosted population growth.

The Census Commissioner in 1931 advised the Government of India to adopt programs for birth control. The first family planning clinic in India probably was opened by Prof. R. D. Carve in 1925 in Bombay (now Mumbai). But the first public advocacy for limiting family size was strongly presented by P. K. Wattal in 1916 in his book *The Population Problem in India.* He advocated family limitations both from health and socio-economic conditions of Indian population. Since 1930, family planning clinics were opened in some states at the initiative of the government and private agencies. Indian National Congress and a few other associations came forward openly in favor of adoption of birth control measures to keep the rise in population under some control. The resolution by the Planning Commission set up by the Indian National Congress in 1935 came out with a few historic resolutions:

1. Gradually increase the age at marriage of both the sexes;
2. Mentally handicapped and similar other disabled persons (epileptics) are to be prevented from entering into marriage lock and those already married must undergo sterilization to prevent transmissible diseases of serious nature;
3. Polygamy has to be stopped altogether; and
4. Family planning centers to be opened throughout the country to provide help and advice to people on family planning issues at a minimum cost.

The Bhor Committee (1946) appointed by the Central government also recommended strongly on deliberate limitation of family size.

India after independence became the historic first to officially adopt a family planning policy in 1952 with the expressed desire for a lower rate of population growth and stabilize the population at a level consistent with the requirements of the national economy. The National Family Planning Commission admitted that birth planning was a very sensitive issue and therefore it should not be imposed on people. The Commission acknowledged that individuals should have the freedom to accept or reject it. However, the state will make necessary arrangements for propagating the message that Indians need to control birth in the larger interest of nation building as also for the healthcare of mother and child. The government started using extensively all types of media to educate people on the benefits of adopting a 'small family norm'. It started opening family planning clinics, family planning units in hospitals and health centers all through out the country. These clinics were to advice and help select the method of birth control methods free of cost.

The family planning program in first two plans, which really was an experience gathering exercise, is popularly called *Clinical Approach*. At the end of the second plan period 4,165 family planning centers were established to cater assistance and advice to those who visit them. These clinics were equipped to provide available birth control measures. A review of the performance in the first two plan periods made it clear that opening family planning centers alone would be of little help for promoting family planning among the masses. Extensive campaign was needed to improve awareness of the people. It was felt that the message of family planning has to be taken to the illiterate, superstitious and poverty-stricken masses. The campaign for birth control must be taken to these people through those who they are familiar with and are respected in their own community. Mass education and mass contact are to be achieved through these 'extension workers' who are selected from the operation areas and are given an extensive exposure on the design of the plan and how persons adopting family planning are likely to be benefitted from it. The dependability of a communication depends on what actually are communicated, the source of communication, and the guiles of the communicator. This is the *Extension Approach* in family planning initiated in 1962–63 from the feedback obtained from the earlier experiences. The extension workers were the persons on the spot to dispel with all the misconceptions and superstitions about family planning among the poorly educated rural masses. They were the facilitators, the 'catalysts' in the campaign for family planning. The UN Evaluation Mission in 1965 recommended that family planning needed to be incorporated in the general social welfare and health care policy. The Mission also stressed on the stringent application of the law regulating the minimum age at marriage, make abortion legal under certain conditions and review some of the advantages given to families on account of births in the family (tax concessions), etc.

In 1962, a target was set to bring down birth rate to 25 per 1,000 by 1973. The target was based on observations that (1) fertility was already low among couples in upper classes, (2) momentum was gaining for acceptance of family planning in rural areas, and (3) surveys showed that a high proportion of couples still in their reproductive age did not wish additional children. Calculations showed that CBR 25 would be possible only if 40 percent of eligible couples were protected by contraception. In 1969, the Planning Commission revised the target to CBR 32 by 1974. On the advice of the second UN Mission in 1969, the government decided to make the family planning centers fully equipped to provide assistance on a wide range of birth control methods. As in a cafeteria the customers have a preference of buying things of their choice, the family planning clinics needed to be equipped to provide assistance in a wide range of birth control methods and the couples would be free to chose any one for their liking. Hence the program came to be known as *Cafeteria Approach.*

In 1971, India passed the Medical Terminancy of Pregnancy Act (MTP Act). By 1969, sterilization has become the principal method for effective birth control. 'Camps for mass sterilization' were organized in various parts of the country. Soon public opinion went against this mass sterilization for various reasons. The government had but no other alternative than to go slow on it. Sterilization came down to about 700,000 in 1973–74 from 3,122,000 in 1972–73. Then came the declaration of Emergency. On June 26, 1975, "internal emergency" was declared in the country as a fall-out of Allahabad High Court's judgment invalidating the election of the Prime Minister, Mrs Indira Gandhi. The government came out with a 20-point program immediately after promulgation of emergency. But this did not include any statement regarding family planning. On April 16, 1976 the National Population Policy Statement was released by the government. It was placed in the Parliament but was never discussed or adopted. The government took a U-turn on its commitment to leave birth control entirely to personal decisions of couples. The opening paragraph of the Statement argued that

- reducing the rate of population increase "will have to be treated as top national priority and commitment",
- "to wait for education and economic development to bring about a drop in fertility is not a practical solution", and
- population control must play a crucial role in the movement toward economic independence and social transformation

CBR in India stood at 34 in 1974. The government was determined to bring it down to 25 by 1984 at the latest. Ever since family planning program was launched, the emphasis generally has been on sterilization. The 1976 Statement went as far as to declare that "public opinion was ready to accept more stringent measures for family planning than before". The Policy Statement even gave legislation power to states to pass laws by which sterilization could be made compulsory after a couple had three children. Increased monitory compensation for such package was also promised. The nine months of the engine of oppression saw 8 million sterilization (6 million vasectomies), which was about 50 percent of all sterilizations done in the whole world in that year. What India could achieve in family planning in the 20 years after its inception was more than matched in the 19-month period of emergency. Corruption and fraud were rampant in such a massive operation. 'Operation sterilization' became a major issue in the 1977 Parliamentary election in which the ruling Congress party under Indira Gandhi's leadership lost very badly. Indira Gandhi herself lost the election and was sent to jail. In the very first year of Janata government headed by Morarji Desai, the number of sterilization came down to a meager 600,000, that is, on an average about 50,000 sterilizations a month compared to about 1 million sterilizations every month during the last nine months of Congress rule.

There were apprehensions that the Janata government would dismantle the family planning program. But that really did not happen although the family planning program did not receive as much attention as it should have in view of the very high population growth rate the country was passing through. 'Family Planning' since the days Janata government came to be known as 'Family Welfare'. Janata government also tabled a population policy in Parliament in 1977. That too had the same fate as the 1976 Statement. By 1978, the government received danger signals from various quarters including its bureaucratic apparatus about the poor performance of the family planning program. The Prime Minister Morarji Desai (who took over the charge of the Department of Health and Family Welfare after Raj Narain was removed from the office), Sanjeeva Reddy, then the President of India and Jai Prakash Narain, the chief architect for combining the opposition parties under the banner of Janata Party in his crusade against Indira Gandhi-led Congress party, were also worried by the slowing down of the family planning program with the change of the government. A Working Group on Population Policy was constituted in late 1978, which in its interim report recommended that the mortality decline should receive equal attention as birth control. The interim report asked for a 50 percent reduction in IMR (the prevailing rate was 120 per 1,000) by 1996. The report asked for a time-bound fertility and mortality goals for the country for achieving replacement level fertility before the end of the millennium. The Working Group divided the states into three groups on the basis of contraception performance and set different dates for achieving their targets. By 2001, all states were expected to achieve NRR 1. Extensive coverage in newspaper, radio and television became a regular feature for birth control campaign. The government also emphasized on selecting one part-time worker (Community Health Volunteers, CHVs) from each of about 600,000 villages in India, give them intensive training for three months to enable them to provide rudimentary curative services and to encouraging and promoting public health and family planning.

Janata Party disintegrated in 1979 and Mrs Indira Gandhi came back to power with a thumping majority in the Parliament in the midterm election held in January 1980. Indira Gandhi was fully aware that high population growth would be a serious road block to alleviation of poverty and achievement of national development objectives. For her government, however, it would have been risky to take a very dynamic stand on family planning program remembering the fact that the people of India overthrew her government in 1977, and one of the major deciding factor in the change of mood of the common man was the excesses committed in the name of family planning during the period of Emergency. Sterilization coverage gradually regained even during the Janata government rule at the center and by the time of assassination of Indira Gandhi in 1984, number of sterilizations in 1983–84 rose to 4.53 million (15 percent vasectomy and 85 percent tubectomy). Over 2 million IUD were also inserted in the same year. In 2000–01, the number of sterilizations recorded was 4.74 million, 97.7 percent of this was by women acceptors. The National Health Policy of 1983 emphasized the need for "securing the small family norm, through voluntary efforts and moving towards the goal of population stabilization". While adopting the Health Policy, Parliament emphasized the need for a separate National Population Policy.

The National Development Council appointed a Committee on Population in 1991 with Karunakaran as Chairman. The Committee proposed the formulation of a National Population Policy to take a "a long term holistic view of development, population growth and environmental protection" and to "suggest policies and guidelines (for) formulation of programs" and "a monitoring mechanism with short, medium and long term perspectives and goals". Dr. M. S. Swaminathan was entrusted with the task of framing a draft of National Population Policy. The cabinet Group of Ministers prepared the final draft for the approval of the Cabinet.

The National Population Policy, 2000 (NPP 2000) affirms the commitment of government towards voluntary and informed choice and consent of citizens while availing of reproductive health care services, and continuation of the *target free* approach in administering family planning services. The NPP 2000 especially emphasized on improved family planning services in demographically weak 8 States viz., Uttar Pradesh, Bihar, Madhya Pradesh, Rajasthan, Orissa, Jharkhand, Chattisgarh and Uttaranchal. The NPP 2000 provides a policy framework for advancing goals and prioritizing strategies during the next decade, to meet the reproductive and child health needs of the people of India, and to achieve replacement levels (TFR 2.1) by 2010. It is based upon the need to simultaneously address issues of child survival, maternal health, and contraception, while increasing outreach and coverage of a comprehensive package of reproductive and child heath services by government, industry and the voluntary non-government sector, working in partnership.

Some of the promotional and motivational measures recommended in NPP 2000 are:

(i) Panchayats and Zila Parishads will be rewarded and honored for exemplary performance in universalizing the small family norm, achieving reductions in infant mortality and birth rates, and promoting literacy with completion of primary schooling.
(ii) The Balika Samridhi Yojana would be instituted to promote survival and care of the girl child. A cash incentive of Rs.500 will be awarded at the birth of the girl child of birth order 1 or 2.
(iii) Maternity Benefit Scheme would continue. A cash incentive of Rs.500 would be awarded to mothers who have their first child after 19 years of age (birth of the first or second child only). The cash award in future would be linked to compliance with ante-natal check-up, institutional delivery by trained birth attendant, registration of birth and BCG immunization.
(iv) A Family Welfare-linked Health Insurance Plan would be established. Couples below the poverty line, who undergo sterilization with not more than two living children, would become eligible (along with children) for health insurance (for hospitalization) not exceeding Rs.5,000, and a personal accident insurance cover for the spouse undergoing sterilization.
(v) Couples below the poverty line, who marry after the legal age of marriage, register their marriage, have their first child after the mother reaches the age of 21, accept the small family norm, and adopt a terminal method after the birth of the second child, would be rewarded.
(vi) To facilitate and promote participation of women in paid employment, crèches and child care centers would be opened in rural areas and urban slums.
(vii) A wider, affordable choice of contraceptives will be made accessible at diverse delivery points with counseling services to enable acceptors to exercise voluntary and informed consent.
(viii) Facilities for safe abortion will be strengthened and expanded.
(ix) Strict enforcement of Child Marriage Restraint Act, 1976.
(x) Strict enforcement of the Pre-Natal Diagnostic Techniques Act, 1994.
(xi) Soft loans to ensure mobility of the ANMs will be increased.
(xii) The 42nd Constitutional Amendment freezed the number of representatives in the Parliament on the basis of population at 1971 Census until 2001. This freeze would be extended until 2026.

Registered MTP cases have nearly doubled between 1981 and 2001, from 388,405 to 723,142. About quarter of the MTP cases were followed by sterilization and another 15 percent were given IUDs. Since the days of Janata Party rule, highest number of sterilization in a single year was recorded in 1985–86 (4.9 million, which was 25.9 percent of all acceptors by all methods). Although the absolute number of sterilizations remained much above 4 million marks in most years since 1983–84, the share of sterilization to total acceptors by all methods has gone down sharply and since 1996–97 it is hovering between 12.1 and 12.9 percent. IUD has gained considerable popularity after introduction of Copper-T in 1980–81. Since then proportion of IUD users has remained around 17 percent. Use of oral pills has increased considerably in recent years, about 20 percent of all acceptors. More than two-thirds of sterilization acceptors are rural people. IUD insertion is also most popular in rural areas. Couples effectively protected due to all methods in 2000–01 stood at 51.2 percent. Between 1981–82 and 1999–2000, estimated 257.4 million births, due to all methods, have been averted. In 2002, the estimated CDR, CBR, IMR and TFR were 8.1, 23, 50 and 2.6 respectively. The annual population growth rate in 2006 is estimated at 1.5.

Achievements of the family planning program are summarized Table 15.2.

Table 15.2 *Family welfare program achievements at a glance in India*

Parameters	***Previous level***	***Current level***
CBR	40.8 (1951)	25.8 (2000)
CDR	25.1 (1951)	8.5 (2000)
TFR	6.0 (1951)	2.9 (NFHS II)
Age of wife at the time of acceptance of sterilization:		
Vasectomy	31.6 (1980–91)	29.1 (1999–00)
Tubectomy	30.5 (1980–81)	28.3 (1999–00)
Surviving children at the time of:		
Vasectomy	3.5 (1980–81)	2.5 (1999–00)
Tubectomy	3.7 (1960–81)	2.9 (1999–00)
IUD	2.6 (1980–81)	2.1 (1999–00)
IMR	146 (1951– 61)	68 (2000)
Neo-natal mortality rate	70 (1981)	44 (2000)
Post-natal mortality rate	41 (1981)	23 (2000)
Child mortality rate (0–4 yrs)	57.3 (1972)	20.4 (1999)
Maternal mortality rate	437 (1992–93)	407 (1998)
Married couples by age of wife (15–49)	15.0% (1961)	9% (1991)
Couple protection rate (CPR)	10.4% (1971)	51.2% (2000)

For a more detailed discussion on Population Policy in India, please refer to "Family Planning Program in India", *Changing Demographic Scenario in India*, Chapter 13 by the present author.

Appendices

Appendix 1 *WORLD POPULATION 2002 (United Nations Population Division Department of Economic and Social Affairs)*

Country or area	Mid-year population (thousands)			Density (pop/ km^2)	% urban	Annual population growth rate (%)	CBR	CDR	TFR	% of all births to women under age 20	Life expected at birth (years)	Mortality under age 5 (per 1,000)	% of population	
													Under age 15	60 or older
1	2	3	4	6	6	7	8	9	10	11	12	13	14	15
	2003	2025	2050	Mid-2003		2000-2005							Mid-2003	
WORLD	6301463	7851455	8918724	46	48	1.2	21	9	2.7	11	65	81	29	10
More developed regions	1203296	1241377	1219662	23	76	0.2	11	10	1.6	8	76	10	17	20
Less developed regions	5098167	6610079	7699061	62	42	1.5	24	9	2.9	11	63	89	32	8
Least developed countries	718080	1148840	1674521	35	27	2.4	39	15	5.1	17	50	161	43	5
AFRICA	850558	1292085	1803298	28	39	2.2	37	15	4.9	16	49	148	42	5
Eastern Africa	270317	423117	614457	43	26	2.2	41	19	5.6	16	43	163	45	4
Burundi	6825	12328	19459	245	10	3.1	44	21	6.8	7	41	188	46	4
Comoros	768	1266	1816	344	35	2.8	37	8	4.9	9	61	92	42	4
Djibouti	703	992	1395	30	85	1.6	40	18	5.7	8	46	177	43	5
Eritrea	4141	7261	10539	35	20	3.7	40	12	5.4	16	53	106	45	4
Ethiopia	70678	116006	170987	64	17	2.5	43	18	6.1	13	45	173	46	5
Kenya	31987	39917	43984	55	36	1.5	33	17	4.0	15	45	118	41	4
Madagascar	17404	30249	46292	30	31	2.8	42	13	5.7	17	54	147	45	5
Malawi	12105	18245	25949	102	16	2.0	45	24	6.1	19	38	186	46	5
Mauritius	1221	1415	1461	599	42	1.0	16	7	1.9	8	72	18	25	9
Mozambique	18863	25350	31275	24	36	1.8	41	23	5.6	14	38	215	44	5

1	*2*	*3*	*4*	*6*	*6*	*7*	*8*	*9*	*10*	*11*	*12*	*13*	*14*	*15*
Réunion	756	932	1014	301	73	1.4	19	5	2.3	8	75	10	27	10
Rwanda	8387	12509	16973	318	7	2.2	44	22	5.7	7	39	179	45	4
Seychelles	81	93	97	178	66	0.9	—	—	—	—	—	—	—	—
Somalia	9890	20978	39669	16	29	4.2	52	18	7.3	22	48	195	48	4
Uganda	25827	54883	103248	109	15	3.2	51	17	7.1	23	46	147	50	4
U. R. of Tanzania	36977	53435	69112	39	35	1.9	39	18	5.1	18	43	162	45	4
Zambia	10812	14401	18528	14	40	1.2	42	28	5.6	20	32	185	47	5
Zimbabwe	12891	12857	12658	33	37	0.5	32	27	3.9	19	33	114	43	5
Middle Africa	100583	172134	266301	15	37	2.7	47	20	6.3	23	43	207	46	5
Angola	13625	25162	43131	11	36	3.2	52	24	7.2	23	40	247	48	4
Cameroon	16018	20831	24948	34	51	1.8	35	17	4.6	19	46	148	42	6
Central African Republic	3865	5193	6563	6	43	1.3	38	22	4.9	19	40	173	43	6
Chad	8598	15770	25359	7	25	3.0	48	20	6.7	21	45	201	47	5
Congo	3724	6750	10643	11	67	2.6	44	15	6.3	18	48	125	47	5
Dem. R. of the Congo	52771	95448	151644	23	32	2.9	50	21	6.7	25	42	219	47	4
Equatorial Guinea	494	812	1177	18	51	2.6	43	17	5.9	23	49	173	44	6
Gabon	1329	1915	2488	5	84	1.8	32	11	4.0	19	57	92	41	6
Sao Tome and Principe	161	254	349	167	49	2.5	33	6	4.0	13	70	41	41	6
Northern Africa	183598	254150	306046	22	50	1.9	26	7	3.2	7	66	66	34	7
Algeria	31800	42429	48667	13	59	1.7	23	5	2.8	4	70	48	33	6
Egypt	71931	103165	127407	72	43	2.0	27	6	3.3	10	69	48	35	7

1	2	3	4	6	6	7	8	9	10	11	12	13	14	15
Libyan Arab Jamahiriya	5551	7785	9248	3	89	1.9	23	4	3.0	2	73	23	31	6
Morocco	30566	40721	47064	68	57	1.6	23	6	2.7	6	69	52	31	7
Sudan	33610	47536	60133	13	39	2.2	33	12	4.4	9	56	127	39	6
Tunisia	9832	12037	12887	60	67	1.1	17	5	2.0	2	73	26	28	8
Western Sahara	308	478	641	1	96	2.6	28	8	3.9	11	64	71	35	6
Southern Africa	51678	49576	46602	19	56	0.6	24	18	2.8	15	46	88	34	6
Botswana	1785	1614	1380	3	50	0.9	31	21	3.7	18	40	104	40	5
Lesotho	1802	1608	1377	59	30	0.1	31	26	3.8	11	35	152	40	7
Namibia	1987	2350	2654	2	32	1.4	33	18	4.6	12	44	107	43	6
South Africa	45026	42962	40243	37	59	0.6	23	17	2.6	16	48	80	33	6
Swaziland	1077	1042	948	62	27	0.8	34	25	4.5	8	34	147	43	5
Western Africa	244381	393108	569891	40	41	2.6	41	15	5.6	16	50	151	45	5
Benin	6736	11120	15602	60	45	2.6	42	14	5.7	15	51	156	45	4
Burkina Faso	13002	24527	42373	47	18	3.0	48	17	6.7	16	46	160	49	4
Cape Verde	463	666	812	115	66	2.0	28	5	3.3	18	70	36	39	6
Côte d'Ivoire	16631	22140	27572	52	45	1.6	35	20	4.7	20	41	173	41	5
Gambia	1426	2177	2905	126	33	2.7	36	13	4.7	18	54	134	41	6
Ghana	20922	30618	39548	88	37	2.2	32	10	4.1	14	58	93	40	5
Guinea	8480	13704	19591	34	29	1.6	43	16	5.8	20	49	176	44	5
Guinea-Bissau	1493	2774	4719	41	34	2.9	50	20	7.1	20	45	210	47	5
Liberia	3367	6081	9821	30	47	4.0	50	22	6.8	25	41	229	47	4
Mali	13007	25679	45998	10	32	3.0	50	16	7.0	21	49	181	49	4
Mauritania	2893	4973	7497	3	62	3.0	42	14	5.8	13	52	156	43	5
Niger	11972	25722	53037	9	22	3.6	55	19	8.0	22	46	210	50	3

1	*2*	*3*	*4*	*6*	*6*	*7*	*8*	*9*	*10*	*11*	*12*	*13*	*14*	*15*
Nigeria	12009	192115	258478	134	47	2.5	39	14	5.4	14	51	133	44	5
Saint Helena	5	5	5	41	74	0.0	—	—	—	—	—	—	—	—
Senegal	10095	15663	21589	51	50	2.4	37	12	5.0	13	53	112	43	4
Sierra Leone	4971	7593	10339	69	39	3.8	50	29	6.5	22	34	307	44	5
Togo	4909	7551	10005	86	35	2.3	38	15	5.3	12	50	136	44	5
ASIA	3823390	4742232	5222058	120	39	1.3	21	8	2.5	8	67	71	29	9
Eastern Asia	1512321	1655784	1590070	129	44	0.7	14	7	1.8	1	72	40	22	12
China	1304196	1445100	1395182	136	39	0.7	15	7	1.8	1	71	43	23	10
China, Hong Kong SAR	7049	8492	9431	6746	100	1.1	9	6	1.0	2	80	5	15	15
China, Macao SAR	464	549	578	25775	99	0.9	10	5	1.1	3	79	10	19	10
People's Rep. of Korea	22664	24665	24966	188	61	0.5	16	11	2.0	0	63	58	26	11
Japan	127654	123444	109722	338	79	0.1	9	8	1.3	1	82	4	14	25
Mongolia	2594	3368	3773	2	57	1.3	22	7	2.4	14	64	85	32	6
Republic of Korea	47700	50165	46418	482	84	0.6	12	6	1.4	1	75	7	20	12
South-central Asia	1 563173	2 097128	2463916	145	31	1.7	26	9	3.2	10	63	93	34	7
Afghanistan	23897	44940	69517	37	23	3.9	47	21	6.8	12	43	280	43	5
Bangladesh	146736	208268	254599	1019	27	2.0	29	8	3.5	21	61	87	38	5
Bhutan	2257	3701	5288	48	8	3.0	35	9	5.0	9	63	80	41	7
India	1065462	1369284	1531438	324	28	1.5	24	8	3.0	9	64	84	33	8
Iran	68920	90927	105485	42	66	1.2	20	5	2.3	11	70	39	32	6
Kazakhstan	15433	15388	13941	6	56	-0.4	16	9	2.0	14	66	58	25	11
Kyrgyzstan	5138	6484	7235	26	34	1.4	22	7	2.6	8	69	46	32	8

1	2	3	4	6	6	7	8	9	10	11	12	13	14	15
Maldives	318	559	819	1068	29	3.0	36	6	5.3	8	67	49	42	5
Nepal	25164	37831	50810	179	13	2.2	33	10	4.3	18	60	98	40	6
Pakistan	153578	249766	348700	193	34	2.4	36	10	5.1	7	61	128	41	6
Sri Lanka	19065	21464	21172	291	24	0.8	16	7	2.0	6	73	23	25	10
Tajikistan	6245	8193	9552	44	28	0.9	24	6	3.1	6	69	73	36	7
Turkmenistan	4 867	6549	7541	10	45	1.5	22	6	2.7	4	67	68	34	6
Uzbekistan	26 093	33774	37818	58	37	1.5	22	6	2.4	14	70	52	34	7
South-Eastern Asia	543193	687621	767250	121	40	1.4	22	7	2.5	10	67	55	31	7
Brunei Darussalam	358	527	685	62	74	2.3	23	3	2.5	5	76	7	30	5
Cambodia	14144	21899	29567	78	19	2.4	34	10	4.8	11	57	107	41	5
Dem. Republic of Timor-Leste	778	1197	1433	52	8	4.0	24	13	3.8	7	50	183	36	5
Indonesia	219883	270113	293797	115	44	1.3	21	7	2.4	13	67	52	30	8
Lao People's Dem. Rep.	5657	8635	11448	24	21	2.3	36	13	4.8	14	54	141	42	5
Malaysia	24425	33479	39551	74	59	1.9	23	5	2.9	4	73	13	33	7
Myanmar	49485	59760	64493	73	29	1.3	24	11	2.9	5	57	128	32	7
Philippines	79999	108589	126965	267	61	1.8	25	5	3.2	8	70	35	36	6
Singapore	4253	4905	4538	6882	100	1.7	10	5	1.4	2	78	4	21	11
Thailand	62833	73869	77079	122	20	1.0	17	7	1.9	13	69	25	25	9
Viet Nam	81377	104649	117693	245	25	1.3	20	6	2.3	5	69	45	31	7
Western Asia	204703	301699	400822	43	65	2.1	27	6	3.4	9	69	57	35	7
Armenia	3061	2866	2334	103	67	-0.5	10	8	1.2	17	72	20	20	13
Azerbaijan	8370	10222	10942	97	52	0.9	18	6	2.1	10	72	40	29	9

1	*2*	*3*	*4*	*6*	*6*	*7*	*8*	*9*	*10*	*11*	*12*	*13*	*14*	*15*
Bahrain	724	1034	1270	1068	93	2.2	20	3	2.7	4	74	18	29	4
Cyprus	802	892	892	87	71	0.8	13	8	1.9	3	78	8	22	16
Georgia	5126	4429	3472	74	57	-0.9	10	10	1.4	13	74	22	19	19
Iraq	25175	41707	57932	57	67	2.7	35	9	4.8	6	61	108	41	5
Israel	6433	8598	9989	291	92	2.0	20	6	2.7	4	79	9	28	13
Jordan	5473	8116	10154	61	79	2.7	28	4	3.6	5	71	27	38	5
Kuwait	2521	3930	4926	142	96	3.5	20	2	2.7	5	77	13	26	3
Lebanon	3653	4554	4946	351	91	1.6	19	5	2.2	6	74	20	29	9
Palestinian Territory	3557	6903	11114	573	68	3.6	39	4	5.6	12	72	24	46	5
Oman	2851	4785	6812	13	78	2.9	32	3	5.0	10	72	23	37	4
Qatar	610	790	874	55	93	1.5	17	4	3.2	4	72	15	26	3
Saudi Arabia	24217	39751	54738	11	88	2.9	32	4	4.5	6	72	24	39	4
Syrian Arab Republic	17800	26979	34174	96	52	2.4	28	4	3.3	7	72	26	37	5
Turkey	71325	88995	97759	92	67	1.4	21	6	2.4	10	71	49	30	8
United Arab Emirates	2995	3944	4112	36	88	1.9	17	2	2.8	11	75	15	25	3
Yemen	20010	43204	84385	38	26	3.5	45	9	7.0	14	60	98	49	4
EUROPE	726338	696036	631938	32	74	-0.1	10	11	1.4	7	74	11	16	21
Eastern Europe	300264	267070	221736	16	68	-0.5	9	13	1.2	13	69	19	16	18
Belarus	9895	8950	7539	48	70	-0.5	9	13	1.2	12	70	15	16	19
Bulgaria	7897	6609	5255	71	67	-0.8	8	15	1.1	17	71	19	14	22
Czech Republic	10236	9806	8553	130	75	-0.1	9	11	1.2	6	75	6	15	19
Hungary	9877	8865	7589	106	65	-0.5	9	14	1.2	8	72	11	16	20
Poland	38587	37337	33004	119	63	-0.1	10	10	1.3	7	74	11	17	17

1	2	3	4	6	6	7	8	9	10	11	12	13	14	15
Republic of Moldova	4267	4096	3580	127	42	-0.1	11	11	1.4	18	69	24	20	14
Romania	22334	20806	18063	94	56	-0.2	10	12	1.3	13	71	25	17	19
Russian Federation	143246	124428	101456	8	73	-0.6	9	15	1.1	14	67	22	16	18
Slovakia	5402	5397	4948	110	58	0.1	10	10	1.3	9	74	10	18	16
Ukraine	48523	40775	31749	80	68	-0.8	8	14	1.2	17	70	18	16	21
Northern Europe	94816	99134	100072	54	83	0.2	11	10	1.6	5	78	7	18	21
Channel Islands	145	141	126	743	29	0.1	11	10	1.5	4	78	7	17	20
Denmark	5364	5469	5273	125	85	0.2	12	11	1.8	2	77	6	19	21
Estonia	1323	1017	657	29	69	-1.1	9	14	1.2	12	72	11	16	22
Faeroe Islands	47	52	53	33	39	0.7	—	—	—	—	—	—	—	—
Finland	5207	5289	4941	15	59	0.2	11	10	1.7	2	78	5	18	21
Iceland	290	325	330	3	93	0.8	14	7	2.0	5	80	4	23	15
Ireland	3956	4668	4996	56	60	1.1	14	8	1.9	4	77	7	21	15
Isle of Man	75	80	78	127	77	0.5	—	—	—	—	—	—	—	—
Latvia	2307	1857	1331	36	60	-0.9	8	14	1.1	12	71	18	16	22
Lithuania	3444	3035	2526	53	69	-0.6	9	12	1.3	11	73	11	19	20
Norway	4533	4859	4895	14	76	0.4	12	10	1.8	3	79	6	20	20
Sweden	8876	9055	8700	20	83	0.1	10	11	1.6	2	80	4	18	23
United Kingdom	59251	63287	66166	243	90	0.3	11	10	1.6	6	78	7	18	21
Southern Europe	146365	140630	125596	111	67	0.1	10	10	1.3	3	78	9	15	22
Albania	3166	3629	3670	110	44	0.7	18	5	2.3	4	74	34	28	10
Andorra	71	115	165	157	92	2.6	—	—	—	—	—	—	—	—
Bosnia and Herzegovina	4161	4183	3564	81	44	1.1	10	8	1.3	9	74	16	17	15

1	*2*	*3*	*4*	*6*	*6*	7	*8*	*9*	*10*	*11*	*12*	*13*	*14*	*15*
Croatia	4428	4088	3587	78	59	-0.2	11	12	1.7	5	74	9	17	22
Gibraltar	27	27	24	4542	100	0.1	—	—	—	—	—	—	—	—
Greece	10976	10707	9814	83	61	0.1	9	10	1.3	3	78	8	15	24
Holy See	1	1	1	1784	100	0.0	—	—	—	—	—	—	—	—
Italy	57423	52939	44875	191	67	-0.1	9	11	1.2	2	79	7	14	25
Malta	394	418	402	1248	92	0.4	12	8	1.8	4	78	8	19	18
Portugal	10062	9834	9027	109	68	0.1	11	11	1.5	5	76	8	17	21
San Marino	28	32	34	452	91	1.0	—	—	—	—	—	—	—	—
Serbia and Montenegro	10527	10230	9371	103	52	-0.1	12	11	1.7	8	73	15	19	18
Slovenia	1984	1859	1569	98	49	-0.1	8	10	1.1	3	76	7	15	20
Spain	41060	40369	37336	81	78	0.2	9	9	1.2	2	79	7	14	22
TFYR Macedonia	2056	2199	2156	80	59	0.5	14	8	1.9	9	74	18	22	15
Western Europe	184893	189201	184534	167	83	0.2	10	10	1.6	3	79	6	17	22
Austria	8116	7 979	7376	97	68	0.0	9	10	1.3	4	79	6	16	22
Belgium	10318	10516	10221	338	98	0.2	11	10	1.7	2	79	6	17	22
France	60144	64165	64230	109	76	0.5	13	9	1.9	2	79	6	19	20
Germany	82476	81959	79145	231	88	0.1	9	11	1.4	4	78	6	15	24
Liechtenstein	34	38	40	210	22	0.8	—	—	—	—	—	—	—	—
Luxembourg	453	580	716	175	93	1.3	13	8	1.7	2	78	7	19	18
Monaco	34	40	42	23090	100	0.9	—	—	—	—	—	—	—	—
Netherlands	16149	17123	16954	395	90	0.5	12	9	1.7	1	78	6	18	19
Switzerland	7169	6801	5810	174	67	0.0	9	10	1.4	2	79	6	16	23

1	*2*	*3*	*4*	*6*	*6*	*7*	*8*	*9*	*10*	*11*	*12*	*13*	*14*	*15*
LATIN AMERICA AND THE CARIBBEAN	543246	686857	767685	26	77	1.4	22	6	2.5	16	70	41	31	8
Caribbean	38692	44586	45814	165	64	0.9	20	9	2.4	17	67	58	28	11
Anguilla	12	16	19	123	100	1.7	—	—	—	—	—	—	—	—
Antigua and Barbuda	73	78	77	166	38	0.5	—	—	—	—	—	—	—	—
Aruba	100	143	184	516	51	2.0	—	—	—	—	—	—	—	—
Bahamas	314	374	395	23	89	1.1	19	8	2.3	14	67	24	29	9
Barbados	270	283	258	629	52	0.4	12	8	1.5	13	77	12	19	13
British Virgin Islands	21	29	36	137	64	1.8	—	—	—	—	—	—	—	—
Cayman Islands	40	67	89	156	100	3.0	—	—	—	—	—	—	—	—
Cuba	11300	11479	10074	102	76	0.3	12	7	1.6	20	77	10	20	15
Dominica	79	80	76	105	72	0.3	—	—	—	—	—	—	—	—
Dominican Republic	8745	10955	11876	179	67	1.5	23	7	2.7	21	67	53	32	7
Grenada	80	74	63	233	39	-0.3	—	—	—	—	—	—	—	—
Guadeloupe	440	485	467	258	100	0.8	16	6	2.1	5	78	10	25	13
Haiti	8326	10670	12429	300	38	1.3	30	15	4.0	13	50	112	38	6
Jamaica	2651	3263	3669	241	58	0.9	20	6	2.4	20	76	25	30	10
Martinique	393	424	413	356	96	0.6	14	7	1.9	8	79	9	23	16
Montserrat	4	4	4	34	13	0.3	—	—	—	—	—	—	—	—
Netherlands Antilles	221	250	249	276	70	0.8	15	6	2.1	12	76	14	24	13
Puerto Rico	3879	4073	3723	436	76	0.5	14	8	1.9	17	76	12	23	16

1	2	3	4	6	6	7	8	9	10	11	12	13	14	15
Saint Kitts and Nevis	42	38	32	160	35	-0.3	—	—	—	—	—	—	—	—
Saint Lucia	149	167	163	240	38	0.8	20	6	2.3	16	73	19	30	8
Saint Vincent and the Grenadines	120	130	129	309	58	0.6	20	6	2.2	19	74	18	30	9
Trinidad and Tobago	1303	1340	1221	254	75	0.3	14	7	1.6	14	71	19	22	10
Turks and Caicos Islands	21	35	38	48	46	3.5	—	—	—	—	—	—	—	—
United States Virgin Is.	111	129	133	321	47	0.9	14	6	2.1	13	78	11	25	15
Central America	142275	186441	211758	57	69	1.7	24	5	2.8	16	72	38	34	7
Belize	256	356	421	11	48	2.1	27	5	3.2	17	71	42	38	6
Costa Rica	4173	5621	6512	82	61	1.9	19	4	2.3	20	78	12	30	8
El Salvador	6515	8418	9793	310	64	1.6	25	6	2.9	17	71	35	35	8
Guatemala	12347	19456	26166	113	41	2.6	34	7	4.4	18	66	54	43	5
Honduras	6941	10115	12630	62	56	2.3	30	6	3.7	19	69	48	40	5
Mexico	103457	129866	140228	53	75	1.5	22	5	2.5	15	73	34	32	7
Nicaragua	5466	8318	10868	42	57	2.4	32	5	3.7	24	70	45	42	5
Panama	3120	4290	5140	41	57	1.8	23	5	2.7	18	75	27	31	8
South America	362278	455829	510113	20	81	1.4	21	7	2.5	16	70	40	30	9
Argentina	38428	47043	52805	14	89	1.2	19	8	2.4	14	74	23	27	14
Bolivia	8808	12495	15748	8	64	1.9	29	8	3.8	14	64	72	39	7
Brazil	178470	216372	233140	21	83	1.2	20	7	2.2	18	68	46	28	8
Chile	15805	19651	21805	21	87	1.2	18	6	2.4	10	76	14	27	11
Colombia	44222	58157	67491	39	77	1.6	22	5	2.6	17	72	33	32	7

1	*2*	*3*	*4*	*6*	*6*	*7*	*8*	*9*	*10*	*11*	*12*	*13*	*14*	*15*
Ecuador	13003	16704	18724	46	64	1.5	23	6	2.8	15	71	55	33	7
Falkland Is. (Malvinas)	3	3	3	0	82	0.5	—	—	—	—	—	—	—	—
French Guiana	178	273	354	2	75	2.5	24	4	3.3	16	75	16	35	6
Guyana	765	724	507	4	38	0.2	22	9	2.3	15	63	70	30	7
Paraguay	5878	9173	12111	14	58	2.4	30	5	3.8	14	71	45	38	6
Peru	27167	35622	41105	21	74	1.5	23	6	2.9	12	70	52	33	7
Suriname	436	486	459	3	76	0.8	22	6	2.5	10	71	29	31	8
Uruguay	3415	3875	4128	19	93	0.7	17	9	2.3	15	75	15	24	17
Venezuela	25699	35252	41733	28	88	1.9	23	5	2.7	21	74	22	33	7
NORTH AMERICA	325698	394312	447931	15	78	1.0	14	8	2.1	12	77	8	21	16
Bermuda	82	90	92	1539	100	0.7	—	—	—	—	—	—	—	—
Canada	31510	36128	39085	3	79	0.8	10	8	1.5	5	79	6	18	17
Greenland	57	58	54	0	83	0.3	—	—	—	—	—	—	—	—
Saint-Pierre-et-Miquelon	6	6	6	26	92	0.1	—	—	—	—	—	—	—	—
United States of America	294043	358030	408695	31	78	1.0	14	8	2.1	13	77	8	21	16
OCEANIA	32234	39933	45815	4	75	1.2	17	8	2.3	7	74	35	25	14
Australia/New Zealand	23606	27584	30072	3	91	0.9	13	7	1.7	5	79	7	20	17
Australia	19731	23205	25560	3	92	1.0	12	7	1.7	4	79	7	20	17
New Zealand	3875	4379	4512	14	86	0.8	14	8	2.0	7	78	7	22	16
Melanesia	7468	10833	13968	14	25	2.1	30	8	3.9	10	60	72	40	4
Fiji	839	965	969	46	52	1.0	24	5	2.9	11	70	22	32	6
New Caledonia	228	315	382	12	80	1.9	19	5	2.5	7	75	10	29	9

1	*2*	*3*	*4*	*6*	*6*	*7*	*8*	*9*	*10*	*11*	*12*	*13*	*14*	*15*
Papua New Guinea	5711	8443	11110	12	18	2.2	32	9	4.1	10	58	85	41	4
Solomon Islands	477	783	1071	17	21	2.9	33	5	4.4	8	69	30	42	4
Vanuatu	212	327	435	17	23	2.4	30	5	4.1	9	69	35	41	5
Micronesia	526	709	863	170	44	1.7	25	5	3.4	10	72	26	35	7
Guam	163	215	248	301	40	1.5	20	5	2.9	14	75	11	31	9
Kiribati	88	112	129	121	39	1.4	—	—	—	—	—	—	—	—
Marshall Islands	53	65	72	293	66	1.2	—	—	—	—	—	—	—	—
Fed. States of Micronesia	109	122	158	156	29	0.8	28	6	3.8	7	69	42	39	5
Nauru	13	20	27	622	100	2.3	—	—	—	—	—	—	—	—
Northern Mariana Is.	79	145	191	171	53	4.0	—	—	—	—	—	—	—	—
Palau	20	30	39	45	69	2.1	—	—	—	—	—	—	—	—
Polynesia	635	807	912	75	41	1.3	24	6	3.2	8	71	26	34	7
American Samoa	62	95	131	311	54	2.4	—	—	—	—	—	—	—	—
Cook Islands	18	18	17	78	59	0.2	—	—	—	—	—	—	—	—
French Polynesia	244	316	355	61	53	1.5	20	5	2.4	11	73	11	29	7
Niue	2	1	1	7	34	-1.2	—	—	—	—	—	—	—	—
Pitcairn	0	0	0	13	0	0.0	—	—	—	—	—	—	—	—
Samoa	178	224	254	63	23	1.0	29	5	4.1	8	70	32	40	6
Tokelau	2	1	1	127	0	-0.1	—	—	—	—	—	—	—	—
Tonga	104	121	122	139	33	1.0	27	7	3.7	3	69	42	37	8
Tuvalu	11	13	15	408	55	1.2	—	—	—	—	—	—	—	—
Wallis and Futuna Is.	15	16	16	74	0	0.6	—	—	—	—	—	—	—	—

Appendix 2 *International Statistical Classification of Diseases and Related Health Problems 10th Revision (Version for 2007)*

Chapter List

Chapter I Certain Infectious and Parasitic Diseases (A00-B99)

A00-A09	Intestinal infectious diseases
A15-A19	Tuberculosis
A20-A28	Certain zoonotic bacterial diseases
A30-A49	Other bacterial diseases
A50-A64	Infections with a predominantly sexual mode of transmission
A65-A69	Other spirochaetal diseases
A70-A74	Other diseases caused by chlamydiae
A75-A79	Rickettsioses
A80-A89	Viral infections of the central nervous system
A90-A99	Arthropod-borne viral fevers and viral haemorrhagic fevers
B00-B09	Viral infections characterized by skin and mucous membrane lesions
B15-B19	Viral hepatitis
B20-B24	Human immunodeficiency virus [HIV] disease
B25-B34	Other viral diseases
B35-B49	Mycoses
B50-B64	Protozoal diseases
B65-B83	Helminthiases
B85-B89	Pediculosis, acariasis and other infestations
B90-B94	Sequelae of infectious and parasitic diseases
B95-B97	Bacterial, viral and other infectious agents
B99	Other infectious diseases

Chapter II Neoplasms (C00-D48)

C00-C97	Malignant neoplasms		
	C00-C75	Malignant neoplasms, stated or presumed to be primary, of specified sites, except of lymphoid, haematopoietic and related tissue	
		C00-C14	Lip, oral cavity and pharynx
		C15-C26	Digestive organs
		C30-C39	Respiratory and intrathoracic organs
		C40-C41	Bone and articular cartilage
		C43-C44	Skin
		C45-C49	Mesothelial and soft tissue
		C50	Breast
		C51-C58	Female genital organs

		C60-C63	Male genital organs
		C64-C68	Urinary tract
		C69-C72	Eye, brain and other parts of central nervous system
		C73-C75	Thyroid and other endocrine glands
	C76-C80	Malignant neoplasms of ill-defined, secondary and unspecified sites	
	C81-C96	Malignant neoplasms, stated or presumed to be primary, of lymphoid, haematopoietic and related tissue	
	C97	Malignant neoplasms of independent (primary) multiple sites	
D00-D09	In situ neoplasms		
D10-D36	Benign neoplasms		
D37-D48	Neoplasms of uncertain or unknown behavior		

Chapter III Diseases of The Blood and Blood-forming Organs and Certain Disorders Involving the Immune Mechanism (D50-D89)

D50-D53	Nutritional anemia
D55-D59	Haemolytic anemia
D60-D64	Aplastic and other anemia
D65-D69	Coagulation defects, purpura and other hemorrhagic conditions
D70-D77	Other diseases of blood and blood-forming organs
D80-D89	Certain disorders involving the immune mechanism

Chapter IV Endocrine, Nutritional and Metabolic Diseases (E00-E90)

E00-E07	Disorders of thyroid gland
E10-E14	Diabetes mellitus
E15-E16	Other disorders of glucose regulation and pancreatic internal secretion
E20-E35	Disorders of other endocrine glands
E40-E46	Malnutrition
E50-E64	Other nutritional deficiencies
E65-E68	Obesity and other hyperalimentation
E70-E90	Metabolic disorders

Chapter V Mental and Behavioural Disorders (F00-F99)

F00-F09	Organic, including symptomatic, mental disorders
F10-F19	Mental and behavioural disorders due to psychoactive substance use
F20-F29	Schizophrenia, schizotypal and delusional disorders

F30-F39	Mood [affective] disorders
F40-F48	Neurotic, stress-related and somatoform disorders
F50-F59	Behavioural syndromes associated with physiological disturbances and physical factors
F60-F69	Disorders of adult personality and behaviour
F70-F79	Mental retardation
F80-F89	Disorders of psychological development
F90-F98	Behavioural and emotional disorders with onset usually occurring in childhood and adolescence
F99	Unspecified mental disorder

Chapter VI Diseases of the Nervous System (G00-G99)

G00-G09	Inflammatory diseases of the central nervous system
G10-G13	Systemic atrophies primarily affecting the central nervous system
G20-G26	Extrapyramidal and movement disorders
G30-G32	Other degenerative diseases of the nervous system
G35-G37	Demyelinating diseases of the central nervous system
G40-G47	Episodic and paroxysmal disorders
G50-G59	Nerve, nerve root and plexus disorders
G60-G64	Polyneuropathies and other disorders of the peripheral nervous system
G70-G73	Diseases of myoneural junction and muscle
G80-G83	Cerebral palsy and other paralytic syndromes
G90-G99	Other disorders of the nervous system

Chapter VII Diseases of the Eye and Adnexa (H00-H59)

H00-H06	Disorders of eyelid, lacrimal system and orbit
H10-H13	Disorders of conjunctiva
H15-H22	Disorders of sclera, cornea, iris and ciliary body
H25-H28	Disorders of lens
H30-H36	Disorders of choroids and retina
H40-H42	Glaucoma
H43-H45	Disorders of vitreous body and globe
H46-H48	Disorders of optic nerve and visual pathways
H49-H52	Disorders of ocular muscles, binocular movement, accommodation and refraction
H53-H54	Visual disturbances and blindness
H55-H59	Other disorders of eye and adnexa

Chapter VIII Diseases of the Ear and Mastoid Process (H60-H95)

H60-H62	Diseases of external ear
H65-H75	Diseases of middle ear and mastoid
H80-H83	Diseases of inner ear
H90-H95	Other disorders of ear

Chapter IX Diseases of the Circulatory System (I00-I99)

I00-I02	Acute rheumatic fever
I05-I09	Chronic rheumatic heart diseases
I10-I15	Hypertensive diseases
I20-I25	Ischemic heart diseases
I26-I28	Pulmonary heart disease and diseases of pulmonary circulation
I30-I52	Other forms of heart disease
I60-I69	Cerebrovascular diseases
I70-I79	Diseases of arteries, arterioles and capillaries
I80-I89	Diseases of veins, lymphatic vessels and lymph nodes, not elsewhere classified
I95-I99	Other and unspecified disorders of the circulatory system

Chapter X Diseases of the Respiratory System (J00-J99)

J00-J06	Acute upper respiratory infections
J09-J18	Influenza and pneumonia
J20-J22	Other acute lower respiratory infections
J30-J39	Other diseases of upper respiratory tract
J40-J47	Chronic lower respiratory diseases
J60-J70	Lung diseases due to external agents
J80-J84	Other respiratory diseases principally affecting the interstitium
J85-J86	Suppurative and necrotic conditions of lower respiratory tract
J90-J94	Other diseases of pleura
J95-J99	Other diseases of the respiratory system

Chapter XI Diseases of the Digestive System (K00-K93)

K00-K14	Diseases of oral cavity, salivary glands and jaws
K20-K31	Diseases of esophagus, stomach and duodenum
K35-K38	Diseases of appendix
K40-K46	Hernia
K50-K52	Non-infective enteritis and colitis
K55-K63	Other diseases of intestines
K65-K67	Diseases of peritoneum
K70-K77	Diseases of liver
K80-K87	Disorders of gallbladder, biliary tract and pancreas
K90-K93	Other diseases of the digestive system

Chapter XII Diseases of the Skin and Subcutaneous Tissue (L00-L99)

L00-L08	Infections of the skin and subcutaneous tissue
L10-L14	Bullous disorders
L20-L30	Dermatitis and eczema
L40-L45	Papulosquamous disorders
L50-L54	Urticaria and erythema
L55-L59	Radiation-related disorders of the skin and subcutaneous tissue
L60-L75	Disorders of skin appendages
L80-L99	Other disorders of the skin and subcutaneous tissue

Chapter XIII Diseases of the Musculoskeletal System and Connective Tissue (M00-M99)

M00-M25	Arthropathies	
	M00-M03	Infectious arthropathies
	M05-M14	Inflammatory polyarthropathies
	M15-M19	Arthrosis
	M20-M25	Other joint disorders
M30-M36	Systemic connective tissue disorders	
M40-M54	Dorsopathies	
	M40-M43	Deforming dorsopathies
	M45-M49	Spondylopathies
	M50-M54	Other dorsopathies
M60-M79	Soft tissue disorders	
	M60-M63	Disorders of muscles
	M65-M68	Disorders of synovium and tendon
	M70-M79	Other soft tissue disorders
M80-M94	Osteopathies and chondropathies	
	M80-M85	Disorders of bone density and structure
	M86-M90	Other osteopathies
	M91-M94	Chondropathies
M95-M99	Other disorders of the musculoskeletal system and connective tissue	

Chapter XIV Diseases of the Genitourinary System (N00-N99)

N00-N08	Glomerular diseases
N10-N16	Renal tubulo-interstitial diseases
N17-N19	Renal failure
N20-N23	Urolithiasis
N25-N29	Other disorders of kidney and ureter
N30-N39	Other diseases of urinary system
N40-N51	Diseases of male genital organs
N60-N64	Disorders of breast

N70-N77	Inflammatory diseases of female pelvic organs
N80-N98	Non-inflammatory disorders of female genital tract
N99	Other disorders of genitourinary tract

Chapter XV Pregnancy, Childbirth and the Puerperium (O00-O99)

O00-O08	Pregnancy with abortive outcome
O10-O16	Oedema, proteinuria and hypertensive disorders in pregnancy, childbirth and the puerperium
O20-O29	Other maternal disorders predominantly related to pregnancy
O30-O48	Maternal care related to the fetus and amniotic cavity and possible delivery problems
O60-O75	Complications of labor and delivery
O80-O84	Delivery
O85-O92	Complications predominantly related to the puerperium
O94-O99	Other obstetric conditions, not elsewhere classified

Chapter XVI Certain Conditions Originating in the Perinatal Period (P00-P96)

P00-P04	Fetus and newborn affected by maternal factors and by complications of pregnancy, labour and delivery
P05-P08	Disorders related to length of gestation and fetal growth
P10-P15	Birth trauma
P20-P29	Respiratory and cardiovascular disorders specific to the perinatal period
P35-P39	Infections specific to the perinatal period
P50-P61	Haemorrhagic and haematological disorders of fetus and newborn
P70-P74	Transitory endocrine and metabolic disorders specific to fetus and newborn
P75-P78	Digestive system disorders of fetus and newborn
P80-P83	Conditions involving the integument and temperature regulation of fetus and newborn
P90-P96	Other disorders originating in the perinatal period

Chapter XVII Congenital Malformations, Deformations and Chromosomal Abnormalities (Q00-Q99)

Q00-Q07	Congenital malformations of the nervous system
Q10-Q18	Congenital malformations of eye, ear, face and neck
Q20-Q28	Congenital malformations of the circulatory system
Q30-Q34	Congenital malformations of the respiratory system
Q35-Q37	Cleft lip and cleft palate
Q38-Q45	Other congenital malformations of the digestive system
Q50-Q56	Congenital malformations of genital organs
Q60-Q64	Congenital malformations of the urinary system
Q65-Q79	Congenital malformations and deformations of the musculoskeletal system
Q80-Q89	Other congenital malformations
Q90-Q99	Chromosomal abnormalities, not elsewhere classified

Chapter XVIII Symptoms, Signs and Abnormal Clinical and Laboratory Findings, not elsewhere classified (R00-R99)

R00-R09	Symptoms and signs involving the circulatory and respiratory systems
R10-R19	Symptoms and signs involving the digestive system and abdomen
R20-R23	Symptoms and signs involving the skin and subcutaneous tissue
R25-R29	Symptoms and signs involving the nervous and musculoskeletal systems
R30-R39	Symptoms and signs involving the urinary system
R40-R46	Symptoms and signs involving cognition, perception, emotional state and behaviour
R47-R49	Symptoms and signs involving speech and voice
R50-R69	General symptoms and signs
R70-R79	Abnormal findings on examination of blood, without diagnosis
R80-R82	Abnormal findings on examination of urine, without diagnosis
R83-R89	Abnormal findings on examination of other body fluids, substances and tissues, without diagnosis
R90-R94	Abnormal findings on diagnostic imaging and in function studies, without diagnosis
R95-R99	Ill-defined and unknown causes of mortality

Chapter XIX Injury, Poisoning and Certain other Consequences of External Causes (S00-T98)

S00-S09	Injuries to the head	
S10-S19	Injuries to the neck	
S20-S29	Injuries to the thorax	
S30-S39	Injuries to the abdomen, lower back, lumbar spine and pelvis	
S40-S49	Injuries to the shoulder and upper arm	
S50-S59	Injuries to the elbow and forearm	
S60-S69	Injuries to the wrist and hand	
S70-S79	Injuries to the hip and thigh	
S80-S89	Injuries to the knee and lower leg	
S90-S99	Injuries to the ankle and foot	
T00-T07	Injuries involving multiple body regions	
T08-T14	Injuries to unspecified part of trunk, limb or body region	
T15-T19	Effects of foreign body entering through natural orifice	
T20-T32	Burns and corrosions	
	T20-T25	Burns and corrosions of external body surface, specified by site
	T26-T28	Burns and corrosions confined to eye and internal organs
	T29-T32	Burns and corrosions of multiple and unspecified body regions
T33-T35	Frostbite	
T36-T50	Poisoning by drugs, medicaments and biological substances	
T51-T65	Toxic effects of substances chiefly nonmedicinal as to source	
T66-T78	Other and unspecified effects of external causes	

T79	Certain early complications of trauma
T80-T88	Complications of surgical and medical care, not elsewhere classified
T90-T98	Sequelae of injuries, of poisoning and of other consequences of external causes

Chapter XX External Causes of Morbidity and Mortality (V01-Y98)

V01-X59	Accidents		
	V01-V99	Transport accidents	
		V01-V09	Pedestrian injured in transport accident
		V10-V19	Pedal cyclist injured in transport accident
		V20-V29	Motorcycle rider injured in transport accident
		V30-V39	Occupant of three-wheeled motor vehicle injured in transport accident
		V40-V49	Car occupant injured in transport accident
		V50-V59	Occupant of pick-up truck or van injured in transport accident
		V60-V69	Occupant of heavy transport vehicle injured in transport accident
		V70-V79	Bus occupant injured in transport accident
		V80-V89	Other land transport accidents
		V90-V94	Water transport accidents
		V95-V97	Air and space transport accidents
		V98-V99	Other and unspecified transport accidents
	W00-X59	Other external causes of accidental injury	
		W00-W19	Falls
		W20-W49	Exposure to inanimate mechanical forces
		W50-W64	Exposure to animate mechanical forces
		W65-W74	Accidental drowning and submersion
		W75-W84	Other accidental threats to breathing
		W85-W99	Exposure to electric current, radiation and extreme ambient air temperature and pressure
		X00-X09	Exposure to smoke, fire and flames
		X10-X19	Contact with heat and hot substances
		X20-X29	Contact with venomous animals and plants
		X30-X39	Exposure to forces of nature
		X40-X49	Accidental poisoning by and exposure to noxious substances
		X50-X57	Overexertion, travel and privation
		X58-X59	Accidental exposure to other and unspecified factors
X60-X84			Intentional self-harm
X85-Y09			Assault
Y10-Y34			Event of undetermined intent
Y35-Y36			Legal intervention and operations of war
Y40-Y84			Complications of medical and surgical care

	Y40-Y59	Drugs, medicaments and biological substances causing adverse effects in therapeutic use
	Y60-Y69	Misadventures to patients during surgical and medical care
	Y70-Y82	Medical devices associated with adverse incidents in diagnostic and therapeutic use
	Y83-Y84	Surgical and other medical procedures as the cause of abnormal reaction of the patient, or of later complication, without mention of misadventure at the time of the procedure
Y85-Y89		Sequelae of external causes of morbidity and mortality
Y90-Y98		Supplementary factors related to causes of morbidity and mortality classified elsewhere

Chapter XXI Factors Influencing Health Status and Contact with Health Services (Z00-Z99)

Z00-Z13	Persons encountering health services for examination and investigation
Z20-Z29	Persons with potential health hazards related to communicable diseases
Z30-Z39	Persons encountering health services in circumstances related to reproduction
Z40-Z54	Persons encountering health services for specific procedures and health care
Z55-Z65	Persons with potential health hazards related to socioeconomic and psychosocial circumstances
Z70-Z76	Persons encountering health services in other circumstances
Z80-Z99	Persons with potential health hazards related to family and personal history and certain conditions influencing health status

Chapter XXII Codes for Special Purposes (U00-U99)

U00-U49	Provisional assignment of new diseases of uncertain etiology
U80-U89	Bacterial agents resistant to antibiotics

Source: World Health Organization

Selected Readings

Agarwala, S.N. (1962): *Age at Marriage in India*. Allahabad: Kitab Mahal.

Ambannavar, J.P. (1975): *Second India Studies*. New Delhi: McMillan.

Barclay, G.W. (1958): *Techniques of Population Analysis*. New York: John Wiley.

Becker, G.S. (1960): "An Economic Analysis of Fertility", in *Demographic and Economic Change in Developed Countries*, Conference Series II, Princeton: Princeton University Press.

— and H.G. Lewis (1973): "On the Interaction Between the Quality and Quantity of Children", *J. Pol. Econ.*, 81(2).

Behrman, S.J., L. Corsa and R. Fredman (1969): *Fertility and Family Planning: A World View*. Ann Arbor: University of Michigan Press.

Benedict, B. (1975): " Social Regulation of Fertility", in G.A. Harrison and Boyce (ed): The Structure of Human Population. Oxford: Clarendon Press.

Bhende, A.A. and T. Kanitkar (2000): *Principles of Population Studies*. New Delhi: Himalaya Publishing House.

Billings, John S. (1893): "The Diminished Birth-rate in the United States," as reproduced in "An 1893 View of the American Fertility Decline." *Population and Development Review*, 1976 2(2).

Bongaarts, J. (1978): "Framework for Analyzing Proximate Determinants of Fertility". *Population and Development Review*. 4(1).

— (1982): "The Fertility-inhibiting Effects of the Intermediate Fertility Variables". *Studies in Family Planning*. 13(6+7).

Boserup, E. (1965): *The Conditions of Agricultural Growth*. New York, Aldine.

— (1981): *Population and Technological Change: A Study of Long-term Trends*. Chicago: University of Chicago Press.

Bogue, D.J. (1969): *Principles of Demography*. New York: John Wiley.

Caldwell J.C. (1976): "Towards a Restatement of Demographic Transition Theory", *Population Development Review*, 2(3+4).

— (1982): *Theory of Fertility Decline*. London: Academic Press.

— (1986): "Routes to Low Mortality in Poor Countries", *Population Development Review*, 2(2).

— (1997): "The Global Fertility Transition: The Need for a Unifying Theory". *Population and Development Review* 23(4).

Cassen, R.H. (1982): *India, Population, Economy, Society*. London: Macmillan.

Chandrasekhar, S. (1972): *Infant Mortality, Population Growth and Family Planning*. London: Allen & Unwin.

Chen, P.C. (1982): "Evolution of China's Birth Planning Policy" World Population and Fertility Planning Technologies.

Coale, A.J. and E.M. Hoover (1958): *Population Growth and Economic Development in Low Income Countries: A Case Study of India's Population*. Princeton: Princeton University Press.

— E.M. Hoover and P. Demeny (1966): *Regional Model Life Tables and Stable Populations*. Princeton, N. J., Princeton University Press.

— and C.Y. Tye (1961): "The Significance of Age Pattern of Fertility in High Fertility Population". *Milbank Memorial Fund Qtly., XXXIX (4).*

Cohen, J.E. (1995): *How Many People Can the Earth Support?* New York: Norton.

Coleman, D.A. (2006): "Immigration and Ethnic Change in Low-fertility Countries: A Third Demographic Transition". *Population and Development Review* 32(3).

Cox, P.R. (1970): *Demography*. Cambridge: Cambridge University Press.

Davis, K. (1950): *Human Society*. New York: McMillan.

—, Mikhail S. Bernstam, and Rita Ricardo-Cambell (1986): "Below- Replacement Fertility in Industrial Societies." *Population and Development Review*, Supplement to Volume 12.

DeJong, G.F. (1975): "Pattern of Human Fertility", in G.A. Harrison and A.J. Boyce (ed): *The Structure of Human Population*. Oxford: Clarendon Press.

Desai, P.B. (1975): *A Survey of Research in Demography*. Bombay: Popular Prakashan.

Drake, M. (1975): "Perspective of Historical Demography", in, G.A. Harrison and A.J. Boyce (ed): *The Structure of Human Population*. Oxford: Clarendon Press.

Dreze, J. and Amartya Sen (1995): *India: Economic Development and Social Opportunity*. New Delhi: Oxford University Press.

Driver, E.D. (1963): *Differential Fertility in Central India*, Princeton: Princeton University Press.

Easterlin, R.A. (1969): 'Towards a Socioeconomic Theory of Fertility: A Survey of Recent Research on Economic Factors in American Fertility' In, S.J. Behrman, L. Corsa and R. Freedman (eds): *Fertility and Family Planning: A World View*. Ann Arbor: Univ. Michigan Press.

— (1978): "The Economics and Sociology of Fertility: A Synthesis," in Charles Tilly (ed.) *Historical Studies of Changing Fertility*. Princeton, NJ: Princeton University Press.

FAO (Food and Agricultural Organization) (2004): *The State of Food Security in the World 2004*. Rome.

— (2005): FAO Statistical Data Base. Rome.

Frejka, T. (1987): *The Future of Population Growth: Alternative Path to Population*. New York: John Wiley.

Freedman D., R.A. Easterlin, Harvey Libenstein, V.K. Oppenheimer, R.D. Lee and W.C. Sanderson (1976): "Fertility, Aspirations and Resources: A Symposium on Easterlin Hypothesis." *Population and Development Review* 2(3+4).

Goon, A.M., M.K. Gupta and B. Dasgupta (1968): *Fundamentals of Statistics,* Vol II, Calcutta: The World Press.

Harrison, G.A. and A.J. Boyce (eds) (1975): *The Structure of Human Population*. Oxford: Clarendon Press.

Harte, J. (2007): "Human Population as a Dynamic Factor in Environmental Degradation". *Population and Environment*, 28.

Hoffman, L.W. and M.L.Hoffman (1973): 'The Value of Children to Parents'. In, J.T. Fawcett (Ed): *Psychological Perspectives on Population*. New York: Basic Books.

Houser, P.M. and O.D. Duncan (eds) (1959): *The Study of Population: An Inventory and Appraisal*. Chicago: University Chicago Press.

IEA (International Energy Agency) (2000): *World Energy Outlook 2000*.

ILO (International Labor Organization) (2001); *World Employment Report 2001*. Geneva.

International Planned Parenthood Federation (1973): *Family Planning in Five Continents*. London: IPPI.

Kaplan, H. (1994): "Evolutionary and Wealth Flows Theories of Fertility: Empirical Tests and New Models". *Population and Development Review*, 20.

Kuznets, S. (1979): *Growth, Population and Income Distribution: Selected Essays*. New York: Norton.

Lee, R.D. (1986): 'Malthus and Boserup: A Dynamic Synthesis' in D Coleman and R Schofield (eds.) *The State of Population Theory: Forward From Malthus*. London: Basil Blackwell.

Libenstein, H. (1976): 'Economics, Politics and the Population Problems', in *Population Development Review*, 3(3).

Lorimer, Frank (1959): 'The Development of Demography', in, P.M. Houser and O.D. Duncan (ed.) (1959): *The Study of Population: An Inventory and Appraisal*. Chicago: University of Chicago Press.

Macunovich, Diane J. (1996): 'Relative Income and Price of Time: Exploring their Effects on U.S. Fertility and Female Labor Force Participation', in Fertility in the United States: New Patterns, New Theories, *Population and Development Review*, supplement to Volume 22: 223–257.

Maslow, A. (1954): *Motivation and Personality*. New York: Harper.

Myrdal, G. (1968): *Asian Drama: An Inquiry into the Poverty of Nations*. Knopf Publishing Group.

Nag, Moni (1962): *Factors Affecting Human Fertility*. New Haven: Yale University Publication.

Notestein, F.W. (1945): 'Population: The Long View', in, T.W. Schultz (ed): *Food for the World*. Chicago: Chicago University Press.

Omran, A.R. (1971): "The Epidemiologic Transition: A Theory of the Epidemiology of Population Change", *Milbank Memorial Fund Quarterly*, 49.

Population Reference Bureau (2001): *World Population Data Sheet*. Washington, DC.

Preston, S.H. (1976): *Mortaliry Patterns in National Populations*. New York: Academic Press.

Sauvy, A. (1969): *General Theory of Population*. London: Weldenfeld & Nicholson.

Sen, Amartya (1992): *Inequality Re-Examined*. Oxford: Clarendon Press.

— (1999): *Development as Freedom*. Oxford: Oxford University Press.

Smith, T.L. (1960): *Fundamentals of Population Study*. New York: Lippincott.

Srivastava, O.S. (1983): *A Text Book of Demography*. New Delhi: Vikas.

Thomlinson, R. (1975): *Population Dynamics: Causes and Consequences in World Demographic Change*. NY: Random House.

Thomson, W.S. and D.T. Lewis (1965): *Population Problems*. New York: McGraw-Hill.

United Nations (1953): *The Determinants and Consequences of Population Trends*. New York: UN.

— (1983): Manual X: Indirect Techniques for Demographic Estimation. New York: UN.

— (2000): "Millennium Declaration." A/RES/55/2, 18 September, New York.

— (2005): *World Population Prospects 1950 –2050: The 2004 Revision*. New York: Population Division.

— and Government of India (1961): *The Mysore Population Study*. New York: Population Division, UN.

UN Millennium Project (2005): *Combating AIDS in the Developing World: HIV/AIDS, Malaria, TB, and Access to Essential Medicines*. Working Group on HIV/AIDS. London: Earthscan.

UNDP (United Nations Development Program): *Human Development Report*, various years, New York: Oxford Univ. Press.

— (1990): *Human Development Report 1990: Concept and Measurement of Human Development*. New York: Oxford University Press.

UNESCO (United Nations Educational, Scientific and Cultural Organization) (1999): *Statistical Yearbook 1999*. Paris.

UNICEF (United Nation's Children's Educational Fund) (2001): *The State of the World Children 2001: Early Childhood*. New York: Oxford University Press.

Willis, R.J. (1982): "The Direction of Intergenerational Transfers and Demographic Transition: The Caldwell Hypothesis Reexamined". *Population and Development Review*, 8.

World Bank: *World Development Report*, various issues, Washington.

WHO (World Health Organization (2000): *World Health Report – Health Systems: Improving Performance*. Geneva.

Young, L.B. (1960): *Population in Perspective*. New York: Oxford University Press.

Yunus, Muhammad (2004): "Grameen Bank, Microcredit and Millennium Development Goals", *Economic Political Weekly*, 39(36).

Index

I

K

L

M

N

O

OK